Africa's International Investment Law Regimes

Africa's International Investment Law Regimes

WON L. KIDANE

OXFORD
UNIVERSITY PRESS

OXFORD
UNIVERSITY PRESS

Oxford University Press is a department of the University of Oxford. It furthers the University's objective of excellence in research, scholarship, and education by publishing worldwide. Oxford is a registered trade mark of Oxford University Press in the UK and certain other countries.

Published in the United States of America by Oxford University Press
198 Madison Avenue, New York, NY 10016, United States of America.

Library of Congress Cataloging-in-Publication Data
Names: Kidane, Won L., author.
Title: Africa's international investment law regimes / Won L. Kidane.
Description: New York : Oxford University Press, 2023. |
Includes bibliographical references and index. |
Identifiers: LCCN 2023033302 | ISBN 9780197745571 (hardback) |
ISBN 9780197745595 (epub) | ISBN 9780197745588 (updf) |
ISBN 9780197745601 (online)
Subjects: LCSH: Investments, Foreign—Law and legislation—Africa. |
Investments—Law and legislation—Africa.
Classification: LCC KQC747.K53 2023 | DDC 346/.092096—dc23/eng/20230919
LC record available at https://lccn.loc.gov/2023033302

DOI: 10.1093/oso/9780197745571.001.0001

Printed by Integrated Books International, United States of America

Note to Readers

This publication is designed to provide accurate and authoritative information in regard to the subject matter covered. It is based upon sources believed to be accurate and reliable and is intended to be current as of the time it was written. It is sold with the understanding that the publisher is not engaged in rendering legal, accounting, or other professional services. If legal advice or other expert assistance is required, the services of a competent professional person should be sought. Also, to confirm that the information has not been affected or changed by recent developments, traditional legal research techniques should be used, including checking primary sources where appropriate.

(Based on the Declaration of Principles jointly adopted by a Committee of the American Bar Association and a Committee of Publishers and Associations.)

CONTENTS

PART I
HISTORICAL AND CONCEPTUAL BACKGROUND

Decolonization restored African states' sovereign independence. The postcolonial period was, however, characterized by major economic disruptions that resulted in chronically weakened economies. The newly independent African states faced a profound dilemma between economic liberalization and openness on the one hand, and the maintenance of regulatory autonomy on the other. Confronted with unrelenting poverty and inadequate infrastructure, African states needed direct foreign investment to boost their economies. However, most foreign investors were cautious about investing in African countries due to the perceived lack of clear and predictable legal regimes necessary to protect foreign investments from expropriation and other forms of harm.

This necessitated the development of Africa's international investment law regimes at the global, regional, and bilateral levels. Historically, Africa has contributed more to the development of the rules and institutions pertaining to international investment law than any other area of international law.

Part I, divided into Chapters 1 through 3, provides a general historical and conceptual framework to the discussions of the various sources of law and their evolution in subsequent parts. Chapter 1 discusses the four elements Salacuse has identified a given regime must constitute: (1) principles, (2) norms, (3) rules, and (4) decision-making processes. Chapter 2 distinguishes customary international law as a source of international investment law and identifies the difficulties of applying customary international law in investment disputes. Chapter 3 describes the influence of the African states on the International Centre for Settlement of Investment Disputes (ICSID) and defines the role they have played in making ICSID an important mechanism for investment disputes.

PART I

1
Historical and Conceptual Background, Analytical Framework, Scope of Coverage, and Sequence

Historical Context

During the nineteenth and twentieth centuries, colonial powers protected their investments in Africa, as they did in their other colonies, by colonial and quasi-colonial legal regimes of coercion and extraterritoriality that exempted nationals and capitals of the colonial powers from local jurisdiction.[1] Decolonization has in large measure restored African states' sovereign autonomy to negotiate the terms of their economic engagement and "gradually legalized" their relationships.[2] Such autonomy, however, came with severe disabilities associated with chronic underdevelopment. Because the rules and institutions of international economic law have their roots in the world of hierarchy and patronage, their adaptation to Africa's postcolonial circumstances proved difficult.

The dilemma between economic liberalization and openness and the maintenance of regulatory autonomy is not a uniquely African dilemma, but has more serious implications for Africa because of the experiences of history and its existing position within the global economic hierarchy.

During the initial few decades following the end of colonial rule, Africa preoccupied itself with the excruciating task of digging itself out of the vestiges of centuries of foreign domination and entrenched poverty. This included the establishment of the Organization of African Unity (OAU),[3] membership in the United Nations (UN)[4] and the General Agreement on Tariffs and Trade

[1] *See* Muthucumaraswamy Sornarajah, The International Law On Foreign Investment 19 (3rd ed. 2010). Extraterritorial jurisdiction was operationalized through unequal treaties of capitulation. These regimes existed in Africa (Egypt, Morocco), Asia (China, Japan, Thailand), and the Middle East (Turkey). *See* Charles Lipson, Standing Guard: Protecting Foreign Capital In The Nineteenth And Twentieth Centuries 11–12 (1985).

[2] *See* Yves Dezalay & Bryant G. Garth, Dealing In Virtue: International Commercial Arbitration And The Construction Of A Transnational Legal Order 64 (1996) (characterizing the postcolonial period of ordering economic relations as "gradual legalization" of North–South relations).

[3] The most important postcolonial legal event for Africa was the establishment of the Organization of African Unity (OAU) described in the following terms: "In May 1963, 32 Heads of independent African States met in Addis Ababa Ethiopia to sign the Charter creating Africa's first post-independence continental institution, The Organisation of African Unity (OAU). The OAU was the manifestation of the pan-African vision for an Africa that was united, free and in control of its own destiny and this was solemnised in the OAU." *About the African Union*, African Union, https://au.int/en/overview (last visited Dec. 27, 2022).

[4] Information about dates of United Nations membership is available at *Growth in United Nations Membership*, United Nations, https://www.un.org/en/about-us/growth-in-un-membership (last visited

Africa's International Investment Law Regimes. Won L. Kidane, Oxford University Press. © Oxford University Press 2023.
DOI: 10.1093/oso/9780197745571.003.0001

(GATT),[5] and the adoption of the Convention on the Settlement of Investment Disputes between States and Nationals of Other States (ICSID),[6] and the signing of other treaties in the international economic field.[7]

Historically, Africa has contributed more to the development of the rules and institutions pertaining to international investment law than it has to any other area of international law. Ironically, however, that is entirely due to its subordinate position within the global economic hierarchy as a suspect recipient of foreign capital. The suspicion was a function both of measures of expropriation that some African governments took in the immediate postcolonial period[8] and the perception that Africa's postcolonial domestic legal regimes were inadequate to offer the required levels of protection to foreign investment without moderating external substantive standards and international dispute settlement mechanisms.[9]

Dec. 27, 2022). Original members included Egypt, Ethiopia, and Liberia. Most African states joined between 1960 and 1970 with the largest number in 1960.

[5] South Africa and Zimbabwe (then South Rhodesia) were original members of GATT for obvious reasons, but many others joined GATT no sooner than they won their independence (Benin, Sep. 12, 1963; Burkina Faso, May 3, 1963; Burundi, May 3, 1965; Cameroon, May 3, 1963; Central African Republic, May 3, 1963; Congo, Republic of, May 3, 1963; Gabon, May 3, 1963; Malawi, Aug. 28, 1964; Niger, Dec. 31, 1963; Nigeria, Nov. 18, 1960; Senegal, Sep. 27, 1963; Tanzania, Dec. 9, 1961.) *The 128 Countries That Had Signed GATT by 1994*, World Trade Organization, https://www.wto.org/english/thewto_e/gattemm_e.htm (last visited Dec. 27, 2022).

[6] Convention *on the Settlement of Investment Disputes Between States and Nationals of Other States*, 17 U.S.T. 1270, 575 U.N.T.S. 159 (Oct. 14, 1966), https://icsid.worldbank.org/en [hereinafter ICSID Convention]. African membership is as follows: Algeria, Mar. 22, 1996; Benin, Oct. 14, 1966; Botswana, Feb. 14, 1970; Burkina Faso, Oct. 14, 1966, Burundi, Dec. 5, 1969; Cabo Verde, Jan. 26, 2011; Cameroon, Feb. 2, 1967; Central African Republic, Oct. 14, 1966; Chad, Oct. 14, 1966; Congo, Democratic Republic, May 29, 1970; Congo, Republic, Oct. 14, 1966; Côte d'Ivoire, Oct. 14, 1966; Egypt, Arab Republic, June 2, 1972; Gabon, Oct. 14, 1966; Gambia, The, Jan. 26, 1975; Ghana, Oct. 14, 1966; Guinea, Dec. 4, 1968; Kenya, Feb. 2, 1967; Lesotho, Aug. 7, 1969; Liberia, July 16, 1970; Madagascar, Oct. 14, 1966; Malawi, Oct. 14, 1966; Mali, Feb. 2, 1978; Mauritania, Oct. 14, 1966; Mauritius, July 02, 1969; Morocco, June 10, 1967; Mozambique, July 07, 1995; Niger, Dec. 14, 1966, Nigeria, Oct. 14, 1966; Rwanda, Oct. 14, 1979; Senegal, May 21, 1967; Seychelles, Apr. 19, 1978; Sierra Leone, Oct. 14, 1966; Somalia, Mar. 30, 1968; South Sudan, May 09, 2012; Sudan, May 09, 1973; Tanzania, June 17, 1992; Togo, Sep. 10, 1967; Tunisia, Oct. 14, 1966; Uganda, Oct. 14, 1966; Zambia, July 17, 1970; Zimbabwe, July 19, 1994. *Database of ICSID Member States*, ICSID, https://icsid.worldbank.org/en/Pages/about/Database-of-Member-States.aspx (last visited Dec. 27, 2022).

[7] Most notable among these is The Convention on the Recognition and Enforcement of Foreign Arbitral Awards (The New York Convention). United Nations Commission on International Trade Law, *Convention on the Recognition and Enforcement of Foreign Arbitral Awards* (New York), June 10, 1958, 330 U.N.T.S., 21 U.S.T. 2517, 7 I.L.M. 1046, https://uncitral.un.org/sites/uncitral.un.org/files/media-documents/uncitral/en/new-york-convention-e.pdf.

[8] A notable example is Libya's expropriation of Western oil interests that led to the famous oil and gas cases. For a discussion of the circumstances that led to these cases and the cases themselves *see generally* Robert Von Mehren & Nicholas P. Kourides, *International Arbitration between States and Private Parties: The Libyan Nationalization Cases*, 75 Am. J. Int'l L. 476 (1981). These cases are recognized as the "'founding acts' for the international arbitration community." Dezalay & Garth, Dealing In Virtue: International Commercial Arbitration And The Construction Of A Transnational Legal Order, at 64–65.

[9] *See* Jeswald W. Salacuse, *The Emerging Global Regime for Investment*, 51 Harv. Int'l L. J. 427, 436–37 (2010) ("The existing international law at the end of World War II—what one might call the 'ancient régime'—failed to adequately protect the foreign investments of their [capital-exporting] nationals from injurious actions by host country governments. The need for such protection was heightened by the prospect of postwar economic expansion and the decolonization of territories that had previously been under the control of capital-exporting states"). *See also* Andreas F. Lowenfeld, International Economic Law 536–37 (2d ed. 2008) ("By the early 1960s, following the wave of decolonization in Africa and parts of Asia,

A combination of such perception and a dose of objective reality propelled the development of robust regimes of international investment law relating to Africa at the global, regional, and bilateral levels. These investment law regimes are, however, accompanied by profound uncertainties that were left to linger through Africa's own participation.

By the twentieth century, Western liberal democracies considered compensation for expropriation an established norm of international law.[10] Although this understanding never stood unopposed,[11] the expropriation that took place after the 1917 Russian Revolution lent the opposing view a powerful ideological, political, and economic power, which essentially lasted until the collapse of the Soviet Union and the Eastern Bloc in 1991.[12] The most notable development that occurred during that time, to which the newly independent African states had contributed, is the

and a wave of take-overs of foreign investments throughout the Third World, it had become apparent that it would be very difficult to achieve consensus on the obligations of host countries toward alien investment (read multinational corporations). The leading international aid institution, the World Bank, began to consider how, on the one hand, it could avoid becoming embroiled in controversies between home and host states concerning expropriation, and on the other hand, how it could assist the resolution of such controversies").

[10] *See* Elihu Root, *The Basis of Protection to Citizens Residing Abroad*, 4 AJIL 517, 528 (1910) ("There is a standard of justice, very simple, very fundamental, and of such general acceptance by all civilized counties as to form a part of the international law of the world. The condition upon which any country is entitled to measure the justice due from it to an alien by the justice which it accords to its own citizens is that its system of law and administration shall confirm to this standard. If any country's system of law and administration does not conform to that standard, although the people of the country may be content or compelled to live under it, no other country can be compelled to accept it as furnishing a satisfactory measure of treatment to its citizens").

[11] The 1938 exchange of letters between US Secretary of State Cordell Hull and the Mexican Foreign Ministry is often cited as evidence of the differing understanding of the state of the law of the time. Hull wrote:

> The taking of property without compensation is not expropriation. It is confiscation. .... We cannot question the right of a foreign government to treat its own nationals in this fashion if it so desires. This is a matter of domestic concern. But we cannot admit that a foreign government may take the property of American nationals in disregard of the rule of compensation under international law. Nor can we admit that any government unilaterally and through its municipal legislation can, as in this instant case, nullify this universally accepted principle of international law, based as it is on reason, equity and justice..... The right of prompt and just compensation for expropriated property is a part of this [international legal] structure.

Letter from Cordell Hull, US Secretary of State, to Francisco Castillo Nájera, Mex. Ambassador to the US (July 21, 1938), *as reprinted in* Lowenfeld, Jeswald W. Salacuse, *The Emerging Global Regime for Investment*, 51 Harv. Int'l L. J. 427, 436–37 (2010) at 476. The Mexican Minster of Foreign Affairs wrote:

> My Government maintains ... [that] there does not exist in international law any principle universally accepted by countries, nor by the writers of treatises on this subject, that would render obligatory the giving of adequate compensation for expropriations of a general and impersonal character. Nevertheless, Mexico admits, in obedience to her own laws, that she is indeed under obligation to indemnify in an adequate manner; but the doctrine which she maintains on the subject, which is based on the most authoritative opinions of writers of treatises on international law, is that the time and manner of such payment must be determined by her own laws.

Letter from Mex. Minister of Foreign Affairs to US Ambassador at Mexico City (Aug. 3, 1938), *as reprinted in* Lowenfeld, Jeswald W. Salacuse, *The Emerging Global Regime for Investment*, 51 Harv. Int'l L. J. 427, 436–37 (2010), at 477.

[12] See Rudolf Dolzer & Christoph Schreuer, Principles of International Investment Law 5 (2d ed. 2012).

New International Economic Order (NIEO). The essence of this effort is articulated in the United Nations General Assembly Resolution of 1974 on the question of expropriation:

> Each state has the right: ... (c) To nationalize, expropriate or transfer ownership of foreign property, in which case appropriate compensation should be paid by the State adopting such measure, taking into account its relevant laws and regulations and all circumstances that the State considers pertinent. In any case where the question of compensation gives rise to a controversy, it shall be settled under the domestic law of the nationalizing State and by its tribunals, unless it is freely and mutually agreed by all States concerned that other peaceful means be sought on the basis of the sovereign equality of States and in accordance with the principle of free choice of means.[13]

This resolution was passed by a vote of 115 in favor, 6 against, and 10 abstentions. All participating African countries voted in favor of this Resolution. The opposing votes came from Belgium, Denmark, Federal Republic of Germany, Luxembourg, the United Kingdom, and the United States. The abstaining countries were Austria, Canada, France, Israel, Italy, Japan, the Netherlands, Norway, and Spain.[14] As Dolzer and Schreuer put it, "together with the end of the Soviet Union, the Socialist view of property had collapsed and that the call for economic independence had brought a major economic crisis, rather than more welfare," and Latin American countries began concluding investment treaties containing principles contrary to the *Calvo doctrine*.[15]

Africa's story is slightly more complicated. Having overwhelmingly supported the ICSID Convention in 1965 contrary to the Latin American *Calvo doctrine*-based opposition, African countries had by 1982 signed no less than 110 BITs with non-African countries, mainly with the developed world.[16] African treaties signed after NIEO GA Resolution on the Charter of Economic Rights and Duties of States and before the collapse of the Soviet Union contained principles significantly different from those contained in NIEO Resolution. For example, the 1989 Bilateral Investment Treaty between the United States and the Democratic Republic of Congo (DRC) contains the following classic Hull formulation on expropriation and compensation:

[13] UN G.A. Res. 3281 (Dec. 12, 1974) (Charter of Economic Rights and Duties of States). Full text is available at https://documents-dds-ny.un.org/doc/RESOLUTION/GEN/NR0/738/83/IMG/NR073883.pdf?OpenElement.

[14] *See* 14 I.L.M. 265 (1975).

[15] Dolzer & Schreuer, Principles of International Investment Law 5 at 5. For a good description of the origin and essence of the doctrine, *see* Santiago Montt, State Liability in Investment Treaty Arbitration: Global Constitutional and Administrative Law in the BIT Generation 38–45 (2009). The core of the *Calvo doctrine* is that "the responsibility of governments towards foreigners cannot be greater than the responsibility of governments towards their own citizens" at 39 (quoting Carlos Calvo, 3 Le Droit International Théorique et Pratique; Précédé d'un Exposé Historique Des Progrés de la Science du Droit des Gens (5th ed. Arthur Rousseau, Paris 1896) 138, §1276). Dolzer and Schreuer say "Calvo's view would have left room for all the vagaries of domestic law, allowing both strong guarantees, but also a complete lack of protection." Dolzer & Schreuer, Principles of International Investment Law, at 2–3.

[16] *See* United Nations Economic Commission for Africa, *Investment Policies and Bilateral Investment Treaties in Africa: Implications for Regional Integration*, Feb. 2016, https://archive.uneca.org/sites/default/files/PublicationFiles/eng_investment_landscaping_study.pdf.

> No investment or any part of an investment of a national or a company of either Party shall be expropriated or nationalized by the other Party or subjected to any other measure or series of measures, direct or indirect, tantamount to expropriation, unless the expropriation: (a) is done for a public purpose; (b) is accomplished under due process of law; (c) is not discriminatory; (d) does not violate any specific provision on contractual stability or expropriation contained in an investment agreement between the national or company concerned and the Party making the expropriation; and (e) is accompanied by prompt, adequate and effectively realizable compensation.[17]

Over the years that followed, the DRC was called upon to answer charges of expropriation and violations of other principles at least eight times before ICSID tribunals, which made it the second most frequent respondent state.[18] Many of the disputes were arbitrated under principles contained in the BITs rather than domestic law norms as provided in the NIEO Resolution on expropriation. The NIEO Resolution never acquired the force of law despite its full support by the developing world.

These differences of opinion on the fundamentals of the governing principles are believed to have contributed to the lack of progress in the direction of a multilateral treaty.[19] As Dolzer and Schreuer put it:

> In 1961, two years after the era of bilateral treaties had begun, the World Bank took the lead to address the emerging international legal framework of foreign investment, pointing to this mandate and to the link between economic development, international cooperation, and the role of private international investment. The debates then underway in the OECD in preparation of the 1962 Draft Convention on the Protection of Foreign Property and also in the United Nations regarding customary law was deeply divided and that the prospect of reaching a global consensus on the substance of investment rules was minimal.[20]

In view of this lack of consensus on substantive principles, the World Bank, through the then General Counsel, Aaron Broches, focused on the creation of procedural infrastructure for the resolution of disputes, resulting in the adoption of the ICSID Convention with significant African support.[21]

Even after the creation of ICSID, the OECD had attempted one more time to table a draft Multilateral Treaty in 1998. The draft was never supported by the United States because "the level of protection for foreign investment appeared unsatisfactory due to a number of compromises."[22] In reality, the bilateral negotiations remained more acceptable to the more developed economies.[23] Although the jurisprudential

[17] Treaty Concerning the Reciprocal Encouragement and Protection of Investment, with Protocol, Aug. 3, 1984, United States-Zaire, S. Treaty Doc. No. 99-17, 99th Cong., 2d Sess. (1986).

[18] *Investment Policies and Bilateral Investment Treaties in Africa: Implications for Regional Integration*, Feb. 2016, at ix.

[19] *See* Dolzer & Schreuer, Principles of International Investment Law at 8.

[20] *Id.* at 9.

[21] For a fuller discussion of Africa's participation, see Chapter 3.

[22] *See* Dolzer & Schreuer, Principles of International Investment Law at 10.

[23] *See* Salacuse, *The Emerging Global Regime for Investment*, at 464.

uncertainty that necessarily accompanied the fragmentation of norms appeared acceptable to the developed economies in the several decades that followed the adoption of the ICSID Convention, the use of the same corpus of rules of law in disputes among developed economies in more recent times reinvigorated the debate about the propriety of some of the substantive rules and the soundness of the mechanisms of dispute settlement.[24]

Conceptual Background and Analytical Framework

Africa has once again, by happenstance of history, found itself in the middle of this debate. The United Nations Commission on International Trade Law (UNCITRAL) set up working Group III for the reform of investor state arbitration.[25] The European Commission has also rather vigorously embarked on reform ideas focusing on Multilateral Investment Court (MIC),[26] which has already been included in the EU-Canada[27] and EU-Vietnam Treaties.[28] Although the UNCITRAL endeavor is limited to seeking a solution to the real and perceived deficiencies of the investor state arbitration mechanism, the newly signed EU treaties contain reformulated substantive principles.

At this moment in history, Africa is reckoning with its postcolonial choices and charting its future course of action. The newly adopted African Continental Free Trade Area (CAFTA)[29] is an embodiment of its contemporary outlook. As of this writing, its member states are negotiating a protocol on investment. Whether African states succeed in agreeing on a continent-wide investment protocol or not, Africa currently finds itself at a stage where it needs to critically appraise its existing investment law regimes and evaluate the choices that it has made. This book aims at critically evaluating past choices and providing analytical tools for the formulation and execution of future directions.

The international investment law regimes routinely interact with the domestic investment regimes of each country in a wide variety of ways. Most African countries have (in addition to membership to multilateral, regional, and bilateral international investment agreements and other arrangements) also adopted domestic investment laws and policies with implications on the international investment law regimes that they are a part of. These domestic laws often contain some of the same legal principles

[24] Some of the most notable cases that attracted political and academic attention include the NAFTA case Methanex Corp. v. United States, Final Award of the Tribunal on Jurisdiction and Merits (Aug. 3, 2005), 44 I.L.M. 1345 (2005), and the conflicting awards in CME Czech Republic B.V. v. Czech Republic, UNCITRAL, Partial Award (Sep. 13, 2001), 9 ICSID Rep. 121 (2006), and Lauder v. Czech Republic, UNCITRAL, Final Award (Sep. 3, 2001), 9 ICSID Rep. 66 (2006).

[25] Comprehensive information on the workings of UNCITRAL Working Group III is available at https://uncitral.un.org/en/working_groups/3/investor-state.

[26] Comprehensive information on the EU's Multilateral Investment Court Project is available at http://trade.ec.europa.eu/doclib/press/index.cfm?id=1608.

[27] The text and additional information on the EU-Canada Comprehensive Economic and Trade Agreement (CETA) is available at https://ec.europa.eu/trade/policy/in-focus/ceta/.

[28] The text and additional information on the EU-Vietnam Investment Protection Agreement is available at https://ec.europa.eu/trade/policy/in-focus/eu-vietnam-agreement/.

[29] The text and additional information on CAFTA is available at https://au.int/en/cfta.

enshrined in investment treaties and often provide for mechanisms of dispute settlement akin to investment treaties. Not infrequently, the investors and the states' rights and obligations are determined on the basis of the international and domestic regimes cumulatively. This book treats all of these sources of law as constituting Africa's international investment regimes and provides a detailed description and critical appraisal of each set of sources of law and mechanisms of dispute settlement in keeping with Africa's growing economic interactions with the rest of the world.

As a preliminary definitional matter, the use of the term "regime" or "regimes" in Africa's international investment law regimes avoids the controversy surrounding whether or not there is an international investment law system anchored around ICSID[30] and instead deals with its intricacies that invite the controversy without seeking to resolve the issue. If the final analysis leans toward the existence or nonexistence of a "system," it would do so without particular design.

Regime theory also lends the analytical tool for the evaluation of the fragmented sources of African international investment law norms and processes. In his profound book *The Law of Investment Treaties*,[31] Jeswald Salacuse applies regime theory to investment treaties arguing that they constitute a regime. This book extends regime theory to customary international law as a tool of treaty interpretation, case law creating de facto precedent,[32] and other sources of

[30] David Caron aptly summarizes the essence of the debate on whether or not it is a system or merely a framework in the following terms:

> ICSID can be schizophrenic in this way—on the one hand, imagining ICSID as a framework calls for a concentrated focus on the particular dispute, while at the same time, imagining ICSID as a system represents an attempt to rearrange all of the free standing arbitrations as though they were part of a court system. This situation can lead to great surprise and frustration when the realization hits home that patterns sometimes present are more coincidental than planned. The question of whether there is a system present depends on whether the questions shared by the various tribunals are identical, or perhaps nearly so. Certainly ICSID tribunals share the procedural and jurisdictional limitations of the ICSID convention, but they do not necessarily address the same identical substantive questions since usually different concessions or BITs are involved. However, in the case of NAFTA Chapter 11 arbitration, for example, the tribunals are all part of a de facto system in that they all share the substantive text.

David D. Caron, *Investor State Arbitration: Strategic and Tactical Perspectives on Legitimacy*, 32 SUFFOLK TRANSNAT'L L. REV. 513, 516 (2009). The preponderance of the theoretical debate pertains to international commercial arbitration. For a fuller treatment of the theories of international arbitration, *see generally* JAN PAULSSON, DENIAL OF JUSTICE IN INTERNATIONAL LAW (2005); EMMANUEL GAILLARD, LEGAL THEORY OF INTERNATIONAL ARBITRATION (2010); and a collection of essays in THE BACKLASH AGAINST INVESTMENT ARBITRATION: PERCEPTIONS AND REALITY (Michael Waibel et al. eds., 2010).

[31] JESWALD SALACUSE, THE LAW OF INVESTMENT TREATIES (2010).

[32] There is no agreement as to whether international investment law is distinct and mature and common enough to lend itself to restatement along the lines of the American Law Institute's (ALI) Restatement of Common Law. *See, e.g.*, *Can International Investment Law Be Restated? Or is Jurisprudence Constante the El Dorado of Investment Treaty Lawyers?*, BIICL Investment Treaty Forum Keynote Speech Sep. 2014, in 2014–2015 YEARBOOK ON INTERNATIONAL INVESTMENT LAW AND POLICY 101–10 (Andrea K. Bjorklund ed., OUP 2016). "Given the unsettled state of several areas of investment jurisprudence, restating the law of international investment would be extremely difficult, and might be too ambitious. This does not mean that I am abandoning my belief in the eventual emergence of a *jurisprudence constante*. In practice, however, I suspect we might hope to achieve not one single *jurisprudence constante* but rather agreement about uniform interpretations of particularly phrased provisions, thereby creating harmonious lines and introducing an element of predictability, but all the while paying due attention to differences in treaty language, thereby honoring the decisions states made in negotiating their treaties" (102).

soft law[33] that collectively constitute the broader area of international investment law.

In international relations theory, as Salacuse notes, a regime is defined as "principles, norms rules and decision-making procedures around which actors' expectations converge in a given area of international relations."[34] Relying on prior international relations theory works, he continues to point out that regimes essentially "constrain and regularize the behavior of participants, affect which issues among protagonists are on and off the agenda, determine which activities are legitimatized or condemned, and influenced where, and how conflicts are resolved."[35]

Building on these definitions, Salacuse identifies four elements that a given regime must constitute: (1) principles, (2) norms, (3) rules, and (4) decision-making processes.[36] Principles are defined as "beliefs of fact, causation, and rectitude,"[37] which are akin to the objectives that the regime seeks to accomplish. These principles are often the types of declarations that investment treaties make in their preamble such as the promotion and protection of investment for mutual development.[38] Additional features of principles include predictability or "calculability of transactions."[39]

Norms are defined in simple terms as "standards of behavior defined in terms of rights and obligations."[40] Although Salacuse limits his analysis to treaties, these norms may be contained in a wide variety of sources of law including customary international law and even arguably some soft law that come from "arbitral precedent."[41] An example of a norm for Salacuse is the "fair and equitable treatment" standard.[42] Regime rules are narrower and less indeterminate than norms. They are "specific prescriptions and proscriptions for actions."[43] An example of this is the rule on the payment of compensation for expropriation.[44] In the international investment field, regime decision-making is more easily describable as it essentially pertains to international investment arbitration, primarily investor–state arbitration, although it could theoretically include state-to-state arbitration.[45]

[33] Black's Law Dictionary defines soft law as: "collectively, rules that are neither strictly binding nor completely lacking in legal significance." *Soft Law*, BLACK'S LAW DICTIONARY (11th ed. 2019).

[34] Salacuse, The Law of Investment Treaties at 6 (quoting STEPHEN D. KRASNER, *Structural Causes and Regimes Consequences: Regimes as Intervening Variables, in* INTERNATIONAL REGIMES 2 (1983)).

[35] *Id.* at 6 (quoting D. J. Puchala & R. F. Hopkins, *International Regimes: Lessons for Intervening Variables, in* INTERNATIONAL REGIMES 2 (SD Kramer ed., 1983)).

[36] *Id.* (citing ANDREAS HASENCLEVER ET AL, THEORIES OF INTERNATIONAL REGIMES 9 (1997).

[37] *Id.* at 7 (quoting Krasner, *Structural Causes*, SALACUSE, THE LAW OF INVESTMENT TREATIES, at 2).

[38] *Id.* at 7.

[39] *Id.* at 7–8 (citing Richard Swedberg, *Max Weber's Contribution to the Economic Sociology of Law*, ANNU. REV. L. SOC. SCI. 61, 61–81 (2006)).

[40] *Id.* at 9.

[41] Salacuse does not address soft law but addresses customary law in the context only of its invocation as a competing rule rather than as a source of law for interpretation of treaties, which this book emphasizes.

[42] Salacuse, The Law of Investment Treaties, at 9.

[43] *Id.*

[44] *Id.* at 10. The question of quantum is less specific and may not be classified as a rule given the uncertainty in treaty as well as customary international law.

[45] *Id.* at 10–11. Salacuse includes nonbinding mechanisms of dispute resolution in his analysis.

Scope of Coverage and Sequence

Applying regime theory as defined above, this book critically appraises Africa's international law regimes comprised of international treaties, international customary law, arbitral and judicial decisions, and other soft law sources and evaluates how a better understanding of the existing regime informs the contemporary reform efforts. It accomplishes these objectives organized in six parts and 29 chapters.

Part I (Chapters 1–3) provides a general historical and conceptual framework to the discussions of the various sources of law and their evolution in subsequent parts.

Part II (Chapters 4–11) begins the appraisal of more than 60 years of arbitral jurisprudence focusing on the procedural principles, norms, and rules that have emerged out of a subset of the more 144 African ICSID cases[46] interpreting large numbers of investment treaties. It provides this analysis in a systematic and critical manner centering on the development of the procedures of dispute settlement.

Part III (Chapters 12–19) delves into the development of substantive norms, focusing on some of the most contentious substantive principles that reform efforts revolve around.

Part IV (Chapters 20–23) focuses on Africa's Regional investment treaties. It identifies the most important regional investment treaties and offers a detailed commentary on the choices that the various Regional Economic Communities (RECs) have made in light of their contribution to the contemporary reform process.

Part V (Chapters 24–26) surveys Africa's bilateral investment treaties and provides a detailed analysis of their substantive rules and mechanisms of dispute settlement and their interactions with one another, forming a significant part of Africa's international investment law regime. The discussion follows a geographic and temporal organizational model.

Part VI (Chapters 27–29) provides a critique of what is considered the embodiment of the most contemporary African direction on international investment law, the Pan African Investment Code (PAIC).

[46] A list of all concluded ICSID cases (as of Jan. 2023) is available at https://icsid.worldbank.org/cases/concluded.

2
Africa and the Normative Development of International Investment Law

The African Origin of the Multilateral International Investment Regime

What began with the World Bank's innocuous mid-December 1963 African legal consultative meeting in Addis Ababa eventually led to the establishment of ICSID and its administration of more than 180 African cases over the decades that followed, of which 36 are pending.[1] Whether the Bank's then General Counsel, Mr. Aron Broches, who is credited for conceiving the idea of ICISD and who personally chaired the African consultations (and his African colleagues who supported the idea, such as T. O. Elias, who later became the president of the ICJ), would have imagined the level of prominence that the institution that they were debating in 1963 would attain is anyone's speculation, but the institution that they created has performed exactly as what they intended it to perform, although along the way it has also accumulated a measure of acrimonious criticism.[2]

Influenced by the *Calvo Doctrine*,[3] the Latin American countries had overwhelmingly rejected the idea of a World Bank affiliated dispute settlement mechanism.[4] As

[1] The record of proceedings of this African consultative meeting are documented in ICSID, 2–1 History of the Convention: Documents Concerning the Origin and Formulation of the Convention 236, 236–98 (1968) [hereinafter History of ICSID].

[2] *See, e.g.*, Waibel et al., David D. Caron, *Investor State Arbitration: Strategic and Tactical Perspectives on Legitimacy*, 32 Suffolk Transnat'l L. Rev. 513, 516 (2009). Louis Wells identifies what he calls the three reasons for the backlash: "The inconsistency of the decisions rendered by arbitral panels … the very rigid view of contracts that panels have tended to take...the seeming insensitivity of arbitration panels to signals that corruption or incompetency might have involved in the original negotiations or subsequent renegotiations of the agreements that gave rise to the disputes." Louis T. Wells, *Backlash to Investment Arbitration: Three Causes*, *in* Waibel et al., at 341–52.

[3] For the doctrine, see Rudolf Dolzer & Christoph Schreuer, Principles of International Investment Law 5 (2d ed. 2012), at 5. For a good description of the origin and essence of the doctrine, *see* Santiago Montt, State Liability in Investment Treaty Arbitration: Global Constitutional and Administrative Law in the BIT Generation 38–45 (2009), at 38–45.

[4] During the Bank's Latin American consultation, Mr. Ribeiro of Brazil said: "Despite the optional character of the draft Convention, foreign investors would be granted a legally privileged position, in violation of the principle of full equality before the law." History of ICSID at 306. Bolivian representative, Mr. Escobar also said: "The sovereignty of States could not be subordinated to the authority of an international institution without being seriously impaired … those responsible for preparing the draft had failed to appreciate its adverse effects. Thus the Bank itself seemed to be displaying a lack of confidence in the institutions of the countries wishing to attract foreign capital." *Id.* at 308. The idea of ICSID was totally rejected in 1964 in the Tokyo meeting. *See id.* at 540 ("*El No de Tokyo*"). For commentary *see, e.g.*, Paul C. Szasz, *The Investment Disputes Convention and Latin America*, 11 Va. J. Int'l L. 256, 259–61 (1971) ("that the Convention, which of course can be used only in relation to an alien investor, offends against the rule that foreigners must be treated equally with citizens") (citing José R. Chiriboga, *International Arbitration*, 4 Int'l L. 801, 804 (1970)).

Africa's International Investment Law Regimes. Won L. Kidane, Oxford University Press. © Oxford University Press 2023.
DOI: 10.1093/oso/9780197745571.003.0002

a result, it is not unreasonable to conclude that ICSID would not have come into existence, at least at the time that it did, had it not been for African support. The foundation of the most influential international investment law regime was thus laid in Africa. This, as a matter of fact, goes beyond the political support that Africa provided. Remarkably, the first 15 nations (out of 22 required) to ratify the ICSID Convention were African states.[5] Moreover, unsurprisingly, the first respondent state in ICSID arbitration was an African state.[6] With more than 180 (with 36 pending) cases that followed over the decades constituting close to a quarter of the total caseload, Africa was essentially the testing ground for all of the contentious substantive principles and jurisdictional intricacies of international investment law.[7]

The existence of a body of law called "international investment law" that permits a systematic and coherent appraisal is currently not in doubt, but it is surrounded by profound doubts. Lowenfeld aptly states that "if there is not yet worldwide consensus, and no widely accepted treaty comparable to the GATT/WTO system, there is nevertheless a network of institutions, treaties, and decisions that together may be said to constitute the state of international law on transnational private investment as of mid-year 2007."[8] However, influential writings on international investment law do not necessarily coincide in their characterization of its origin and evolution much less on its substantive content and structural characteristics.

The Three Schools of Thought on the Character of International Investment Law

There are at least three not necessarily competing narratives that attempt to explicate the evolution, existing content, and character of international investment law. For purposes of this book, they are called the *ideological school, the hierarchical school,* and the *doctrinal school.*

The first and more dominant view is the view of the Global North that traces the development and characterizes its content from a predominantly ideological standpoint. The second viewpoint employs a counterhegemonic prism in attempting to understand the conditions and the position of the Global South in the world's historical economic hierarchy. The third characterizes the development of the law in the area as a pure function of the resolution of recurring doctrinal dilemmas. While most writings account for all three perspectives, no coherent set of scholarly work has yet

[5] *Database of ICSID Member States,* Convention *on the Settlement of Investment Disputes Between States and Nationals of Other States,* 17 U.S.T. 1270, 575 U.N.T.S. 159 (Oct. 14, 1966) (providing list of contracting states and other signatories).

[6] *See* Holiday Inns S.A. & Others v. Morocco, ICSID Case No. ARB/72/1 (1972).

[7] A list of all concluded ICSID cases (as of Jan. 2023) is available at https://icsid.worldbank.org/cases/concluded. A list of all pending cases is available at https://icsid.worldbank.org/cases/pending.

[8] Andreas F. Lowenfeld, International Economic Law 536–37 (2d ed. 2008), at 468. As random as it might seem, mid-year 2007 appears to be the time he finished writing the manuscript of the second edition published in 2008.

persuasively linked the structural deficiencies and incoherence in the jurisprudence to particular defects in its origin. There are, however, attempts that could be classified into the categories indicated above.

In explaining the evolution and current state of international investment law, the ideological school focuses on economic theories on the private ownership of property and the means of production. The counterhegemonic hierarchical school, on the other hand, focuses on history. The first, by default, regards Africa as a marginal player, limiting its role to only supplying fact patterns in investor–state arbitration cases. The second brings Africa to the fore as it regards international investment law as an instrument invented to correct irregularities associated with uncontained underdevelopment for the benefit of investors from the capital exporting world. Neither viewpoint disregards the other, and hence the classification rather appears one of degree of focus. The third school focuses on technical legal doctrine that attempts to find a balance between the state's right to regulate and the investor's legitimate interest of protection of investment regardless of the North–South status of the home or host state.

Lowenfeld and Muchliniski are among those that emphasize the ideological underpinnings. Andreas Lowenfeld begins the section on international investment law in his leading treatise on International Economic Law with Justice Harlan's famous statement in the 1964 US Supreme Court case *Banco Nacional de Cuba v. Sabbatino*, that "there are few if any issues in international law today, on which opinion seems to be so divided as the limitations on a state's power to expropriate the property of aliens."[9] He adds that this decision "upset a great many people in the international investment community, in the United States and elsewhere."[10] The Supreme Court did indeed question the universality of an assumption of those that wanted it to pronounce a rule of decision on the issue of expropriation of alien property by saying that "it rests upon the sanguine presupposition that the decisions of the courts of the world's major capital exporting country and principal proponent of the free enterprise system would be accepted as disinterested expressions of sound legal principle by those adhering to widely different ideologies."[11]

Lowenfeld further notes that "in the mid-1960s the Supreme Court's characterization of the law of international investment was essentially accurate."[12] That is principally because

[9] Lowenfeld, International Economic Law, at 467 (quoting Banco Nacional de Cuba v. Sabbatino, 376 U.S. 398, 428 (1964)).

[10] *Id.* He reproduces a segment of Justice White's vigorous dissent to show the opposing view. It reads: "I am dismayed that the Court has, with one broad stroke, declared the ascertainment and application of international law beyond the competence of the courts of the United States in a large and important category of cases. . . . Of course, there are many unsettled areas of international law, as there are of domestic law, and these areas present sensitive problems of accommodating the interests of nations that subscribe to divergent economic and political systems. It may be that certain nationalizations of property for a public purpose fall within this area . . . But none of these considerations relieve a court of the obligation to make an inquiry into the validity of the foreign act, none of them warrant a flat rule of no inquiry at all." LOWENFELD, International Economic Law at 458–59.

[11] *Id.* at 434.

[12] *Id.* at 467.

> large sections of the world regarded the Hull rule [prompt, adequate and effective compensation] and its analogues as law made in other times by and for the imperialist powers ... In large parts of what came to be known as the "Third World" and among a few Western scholars, other values, such as the 'social function of property' and redistribution of wealth competed with the traditional Western conceptions of private property and protection of aliens.[13]

He cites the collapse of the Soviet Union and the economic disadvantages that came to be associated with the state ownership of the means of production. Beginning in the 1980s, this was taken as offering evidence of the advantages of the ideology of private ownership and stronger legal protection of private ownership of property.[14] He concludes:

> In short, the assumptions of the 1960s and 1970s that informed much of the world's attitude towards direct foreign investment, and therefore to the law governing such investment, proved to be erroneous. That realization, not universal and not arrived at everywhere at the same time, in turn led to a changed understanding of the applicable law—in part to a return to older principles, in part to creation of new devices, such as bilateral investment treaties, investment guarantees, various facilities for dispute settlement, and a new set of common criteria for the treatment of foreign investment.[15]

Peter Muchliniski's view is similar. He notes that

> the regulation of relations between states and foreign investors may be said to have begun with the development, by the major powers, of international norms relating to the treatment of aliens and their property, including expropriation, in the first half of the 20th century. In addition, it should be noted that there have always been challenges to such norms, in particular, from socialist states, which opposed norms based on notions of private property, and newly independent post-colonial states, especially during the period of African and Asian de-colonization after World War II.[16]

Dolzer and Schreuer's view significantly coincides with Lowenfeld's and Muchlinski's ideological view. Their analysis is almost identical although they begin at an earlier period in history, namely 1796, the year John Adams negotiated the first Treaty on Friendship, Commerce and Navigation with France on behalf of the United States. He said: "There is no principle of the law of nations more firmly established than which entities the property of strangers within the jurisdiction of another country in friendship with their own to the protection of its sovereign by all efforts in his power."[17] For the proponents of the ideological school, this understanding

[13] *Id.* at 467–68.
[14] *Id.* at 468.
[15] *Id.*
[16] Peter Muchlinski, *Policy Issues*, *in* THE OXFORD HANDBOOK OF INTERNATIONAL INVESTMENT LAW 4 (2008).
[17] Dolzer & Schreuer, Principles of International Investment Law, at 2. In 1910, Elihu Root famously repeated what John Adams had said in 1796 in more elaborate terms as follows: "There is a standard of justice, very simple, very fundamental, and of such general acceptance by all civilized countries as to form a part of

came to be questioned in 1917 due to the triumph of the communist ideology of the Communist Revolution in Russia.[18] Although the Soviet Union justified the expropriation of alien property under the principle of national treatment akin to the *Calvo doctrine*, the Lena Goldfields arbitration of 1930 offered compensation to expropriated foreign interests on the basis of unlawful enrichment,[19] effectively avoiding the most important ideological question. The idea of the treatment of foreign capital better than domestic capital did not fade away into the chronicles of history. As recently as 1986, the European Court of Human Rights has declared that

> especially as regards a taking of property effected in the context of a social reform, there may well be good grounds for drawing a distinction between nationals and non-nationals as far as compensation is concerned. To begin with, non-nationals are more vulnerable to domestic legislation: unlike nationals, they will generally have played no part in the election or designation of its authors nor have been consulted on its adoption. Secondly, although a taking of property must always be effected in the public interest, different considerations may apply to nationals and non-nationals and there may well be legitimate reason for requiring nationals to bear a greater burden in the public interest than non-nationals.[20]

While the ideological school attempts to explain the origins and evolution of international investment law in these terms, for the hierarchical school, international investment law is a means of moderating the transition from a coercive hierarchical economic relationship to an egalitarian equilibrium. For this school, the law is still in a state of transition. Kate Miles, partly relying on Charles Lipson's extensive historical account in *Standing Guard*,[21] observes that what had begun as a normative milieu for the ordering of transnational economic affairs among European states horizontally[22] transitioned from "a base of reciprocity, to one of imposition" during colonialism.[23] For her, as for Lipson, international investment law orders a series of vertical relationships.

the international law of the world. The condition upon which any country is entitled to measure the justice due from it to an alien by the justice that it accords to its own citizens is that its system of law and administration shall conform to this general standard. If any country's system of law and administration does not conform to that standard, although the people of the country may be content or compelled to live under it, no other country can be compelled to accept it as furnishing a satisfactory measure of treatment to its citizens." Id. (quoting E. Root, *The Basis of Protection to Citizens Residing Abroad*, 4 AJIL 517, 528 (1910))

[18] *See* Dolzer & Schreuer, Principles of International Investment Law, at 2.

[19] *See id.* and sources cited therein.

[20] *Id.* at 3 (quoting ECtHR, James & Others v. UK, Judgment, Feb. 21, 1986, at ¶ 63); *see also* Lemire v. Ukraine, ICSID Case No. ARB/06/18, Award (Mar. 28, 2011) at ¶ 57.

[21] Charles Lipson, Standing Guard: Protecting Foreign Capital in The Nineteenth and Twentieth Centuries (1985).

[22] Kate Miles, The Origins of International Investment Law: Empire, Environment and The Safeguards of Capital 21 (2013); *see, e.g.*, Lipson, Standing Guard: Protecting Foreign Capital in The Nineteenth and Twentieth Centuries, at 11–12; H. Neufeld, The International Protection of Private Creditors From The Treaties of Westphalia To The Congress of Vienna (1648–1815) 6 (1971); Frank G. Dawson & Ivan L. Head, International Law, National Tribunals and The Rights of Aliens 5 (1971).

[23] Miles, The Origins of International Investment Law: Empire, Environment and The Safeguards of Capital, at 21.

M. Sornarajah offers a fuller account of what could be considered as the essence of the hierarchical school.[24] The core of his observation is contained in the following passage:

> In the eighteenth and nineteenth centuries, investment was a largely made in the context of colonial expansion. Such investment did not need protection as the colonial legal systems were integrated with those of the imperial powers and the imperial system gave sufficient protection for the investment, which went into colonies. In this context, the need for international law on foreign investment was minimal.[25]

Sir Elihu Lauterpacht appears to view the matter from a doctrinal perspective. In prefacing Schreuer's commentary of the ICSID Convention, he observes that

> the idea for the International Convention for the Settlement of Disputes ... was first conceived in 1961 by Aron Broches, then the General Counsel of the World Bank. This initiative carried forward a more general one for the protection of international investment that had begun in the Organization for European Economic Co-operation (now the Organization for Economic Co-operation and Development) in the late 1950s and that ended in the production in 1962 of the OECD Draft Convention on the Protection of Foreign Property.[26]

According to him, the OCED failed to secure a multilateral agreement because of a disagreement on the state of the law on "the appropriate level of compensation payable upon nationalization or expropriation of foreign investments"[27]—a difficulty that has since recurred in other efforts to produce multilateral agreement on the subject. To avoid confronting the problem of defining the substantive norms, "the then divided state of opinion"[28] chose to focus on "effective procedures for the impartial settlement of disputes rather than by constantly seeking multilateral agreement on the establishment of general substantive standards."[29] The relegation of the definition of substantive standards to mostly bilateral treaties has

[24] MUTHUCUMARASWAMY SORNARAJAH, THE INTERNATIONAL LAW ON FOREIGN INVESTMENT 19 (3d ed. 2010), at 19.

[25] *Id.* at 24–25. The rest of the relevant paragraphs read: "Power was the final arbitrator of foreign investment disputes in this early period. The use of force to settle investment disputes outside the colonial context was a frequent occurrence. The use of overt or covert force to coerce the settlement of disputes continued even after the Second World War and into the post-colonial period. There were spectacular instances of such uses of force. But doctrine had to be constructed to justify the use of force. Capital-exporting countries, which operated outside the colonial context, were keen to devise some legal justification for pursuing the claims of their nationals and for the use of force if such use becomes necessary." *Id.* Others agree that international investment law is essentially a postcolonial normative replacement. *See, e.g.*, G. VAN HARTEN, INVESTMENT TREATY ARBITRATION AND PUBLIC LAW 14 (2007)("An international regime for investor protection is thus an integral aspect of the post-colonial era").

[26] Elihu Lauterpacht, *Preface*, *in* THE ICSID CONVENTION: A COMMENTARY (Christoph H. Schreuer ed., 2001), at xi.

[27] *Id.*

[28] *Id.*

[29] *Id.*

recognizably remained a significant source of the uncertainties of international investment law.

Relatedly, Jeswald Salacuse suggests that bilateralism is not necessarily a course of action that the more powerful economies disliked. In his own words: "Given the asymmetric nature of bilateral negotiations between a strong, developed country, and a usually much weaker developing country, the bilateral setting allows the developed country to use its power more effectively than does a multilateral setting, where the power may be much diluted."[30]

A similar fusion of ideology, hierarchy and doctrine is also discernable from Jean d'Aspremont's writing. He says in particular that

> international investment law constitutes the stage of the pitted confrontation between liberal and communitarian approaches to the world economy. The former, usually embraced—albeit not necessarily—by capital-exporting States favoring a market-based system where investment, property rights and the rule of law are respected come into view with the latter traditionally spearheaded—but not automatically—by capital-importing States geared towards economic decolonization and the preservation of societal self-determination.[31]

A closer look at his writing suggests that he regards international investment law as more of "an umbrella under which the ideological battle for the regulation of the global flux of capital is very much truistic."[32]

For Joost Pauwelyn, the evolution of international investment law is more of an accident than a any particular design a at any particular time for anyone's particular benefit.[33] He does not deny, however, that it has in large measure been influenced by historical events.[34] Pauwelyn emphasizes the incrementality and pragmatism of the growth. It grew out of

> centuries old rules on diplomatic protection and treatment of aliens, treaties on friendship, commerce and navigation (FCN treaties) and evolving generations of BITs and FTAs, UN resolutions, ILC reports and draft articles, World Bank, OECD and IBA guidelines and codes of practice, rulings and awards by the PCIJ, ICJ, Iran-US, mixed claims, ICSID and UNCITRAL tribunals, studies and critiques by academics, NGOs, and influential organizations like UNCTAD.[35]

[30] Jeswald W. Salacuse, *The Emerging Global Regime for Investment*, 51 HARV. INT'L L. J. 427, 436–37 (2010), at 464.

[31] Jean d'Aspremont, *International Customary Investment Law: Story of a Paradox*, *in* INTERNATIONAL INVESTMENT LAW: THE SOURCES OF RIGHTS AND OBLIGATIONS, (Tracisio Gazzini & Eric De Brabandere eds., 2012) at 7, 1–47.

[32] *Id.*

[33] *See* Joost Pauwelyn, *Rational Design or Accidental Evolution? The Emergence of International Investment Law*, *in* THE FOUNDATIONS OF INTERNATIONAL INVESTMENT LAW: BRINGING THEORY INTO PRACTICE 15 (Zachary Douglas, Joost Pauwelyn & Jorge E. Vinuales eds. 2014).

[34] That it was "heavily influenced by historical events and happenstance: colonization and protection of foreign investors through gunboat diplomacy up to the early twentieth century; decolonization and a general aversion against investment by developing countries in the 1950s to 1970s." *Id.* at 15.

[35] *Id.*

Pauwleyn's assessment suggests that these schools of thought are not entirely irreconcilable although he assigns the role of economic and power hierarchy less weight than the proponents of the hierarchical school.

In seeking a pragmatic solution to existing dilemmas of legal doctrine and process, the doctrinal school assigns the historical evolution of the law as marginal a role as textualists would assign to legislative history in statutory interpretation and focus on legal theories and principles. In so doing, it acknowledges the limitations of history in resolving existing legal problems and confronts the difficulties from the standpoint of legal theory and principles.

The most contemporary, dominant, and mainstream debate is thus essentially doctrinal in nature. It seeks to resolve an old dilemma between the state's right to regulating its affairs within its territories on the one hand and providing foreign investors security and protection that the investors would consider sufficient enough for them to commit their resources on the other.

Arbitral tribunals in each investor state arbitration case struggle to determine their jurisdiction and ascertain the applicable rules of law for the settlement of disputes before them. International organizations, academic fora, business interests, nonprofit organizations, and lawyers and academics that David Schneiderman calls "Investment law's *Alibis*"[36] likewise attempt to influence the debate in different directions. International investment law is currently in a state of unprecedented scrutiny and reckoning.[37] Africa is also attempting to understand its position within the global trading system and reconsidering the terms of its economic interactions both vertically and horizontally. In doing so, the understanding of the laws and jurisprudence that it helped shape is critical in fashioning its future positions on the principles of law that govern its economic relations within itself and with the rest of the world.

Africa's concerns about the existing state of international investment law and the mechanisms of its enforcement have similarities and differences with the overall global concerns that are now being debated. The framing of the issues surrounding international investment law and its enforcement is essential in understanding the state and progression of Africa's international investment law regimes. The next section thus frames the important issues under consideration at the global level.

[36] David Schneiderman, Investment Law's Alibis 5–6 (Cambridge 2022) ("What is of interest is how powerful actors have justified and managed politico-legal orders that are now mostly discredited—those associated with colonialism, imperialism, civilized justice, orthodox development and debt—that serve strategic functions today. What is striking is how a matrix of past practices resembles suppositions relied upon at present by investment law's norm entrepreneurs (lawyers, arbitrators and scholars who articulate and promote its disciplines). It is, indeed, remarkable how salient and durable those methods remain today. These indefensible scenarios continue to 'yield new damages and renewed disparities. They are ruinous, in so far as they continue to justify the maintenance of regimes that 'lay waste' to certain peoples, social relations and environments. I characterize this matrix of practices as 'alibis' in so far as they provide cover for a set of rules and institutions—the investment law regime—that increasingly are indefensible").

[37] David Schneiderman, for example, says in his 2022 book, "The current regime has proven to be incapable of listening to voices other than those of powerful economic actors and their home states." Schneiderman, Investment Law's Alibis, at 72 (citing Nicolás M. Perrone, *The "Invisible" Local Communities: Foreign Investor Obligations, Inclusiveness, and the International Investment Regime*, 13 AJIL Unbound 16, 21 (2019).

The Current State of International Investment Law at the Global Level: Framing the Issues

The sources of international investment law are, understandably, not any different from the sources of international law in general, although the presence of a private interest in investor state disputes introduces a unique fusion between international and domestic sources of law. It is, however, broadly understood to have originated and developed in connection with the idea of the protection of alien property. In that sense, it is only a segment of international law that applies rules for the protection of aliens in general and alien property in particular. Areas of international law that are more closely linked are the law of diplomatic protection, which is the oldest, and international human rights law, which is the newest.[38] With that understanding, the primary sources are considered below not necessarily in the order of their importance.

Customary International Law

Customary international law, as a source of international investment law, raises a three-dimensional consideration. The first is whether or not it applies at all. If it applies, the second and third considerations pertain to whether it applies directly as a rule of decision or as a mere interpretive tool.

The uncertainty about its very application is linked to the very nature of investor–state dispute settlement. The innovation that gave private investors *locus standi* to directly sue states under international law does not resolve all the dilemmas of the aberration that gave private parties standing. One of them is the ascertainment of the applicable rule of law. In state-to-state disputes, customary international law indisputably constitutes the rule of decision as recognized under Article 38 of the Statute of the International Court of Justice.[39] In investor–state disputes, the rules of decision do not automatically come from custom as the treaty that offers the investor a right of action could and sometimes does explicitly or implicitly exclude customary law as a rule of decision. When the exclusion is not clear and the relevant instrument is a treaty, it leads to issues of interpretation, which could be resolved by reference to the Vienna Convention on the Law of Treaties.[40] When the exclusion is not clear and the relevant instrument is a domestic law or a contract, the resolution would require reference

[38] For a good analysis of the relevance and interaction of these areas of international law, see Ursula Kriebaum, *The Nature of Investment Disciplines*, *in* The Foundations of International Investment Law: Bringing Theory Into Practice 45–72 (Zachary Douglas, Joost Pauwelyn and Jorge E. Viñuales eds., OUP 2014). Although the law of diplomatic protection is frequently discussed in the literature on the origins of the international investment law, the international human rights dimension is a relatively recent addition.

[39] Statute of The International Court of Justice, Article 38(1)(b). United Nations, *Statute of the International Court of Justice*, Apr. 18, 1946, available at: https://www.refworld.org/docid/3deb4b9c0.html ("international custom, as evidence of a general practice accepted as law") [hereinafter ICJ Statute].

[40] *See* Article 31(3)(c) of the Vienna Convention on the Law of Treaties, United Nations, *Vienna Convention on the Law of Treaties*, May 23, 1969, Treaty Series, vol. 1155, p. 331, available at: https://www.refworld.org/docid/3ae6b3a10.html ("any relevant rules of international law applicable in the relations between the parties").

to domestic law sources of statutory interpretation. In all cases, the ascertainment of whether or not customary international law applies as a rule of decision at all could lead to controversy.

If, however, by the applicable treaty's own terms,[41] or through arbitral or judicial interpretation, customary international law is deemed applicable, the second consideration is whether it applies as a rule of decision or as an interpretive tool. If it applies as a rule of decision, its specific meaning and application would be disputed as in any legal proceeding. In international investment law, as in general international law, the ascertainment of the substance of the applicable custom must occur without the benefit of the rule of precedent.[42] In reality, however, not infrequently do ad hoc arbitral tribunals succumb to the temptation of relying on decisions of their peers in investor state arbitration creating a profound doctrinal dilemma on the issue of precedent.[43]

The third consideration of customary international law comes into play when, according to the applicable instrument's own explicit terms or otherwise, it is considered to serve as the tool of interpretation of contested applicable substantive principles.

Whether it applies as a rule of decision or as an interpretive tool, the text of Article 38 of the Statute of the International Court of Justice that gave custom the power of binding conditions its applicability on its general acceptance through state practice.[44] The determination of whether a particular norm has acquired the status of custom through state practice is a recognizably difficult undertaking. Arbitral tribunals regularly struggle to ascertain the meaning and scope of broad treaty principles such as the "fair and equitable treatment" by reference to principles of international law on a case-by-case basis.

Investment treaties frequently contain reference to principles of international law for purposes of interpretation of rules contained therein. In interpreting these treaty rules, tribunals refer to customary international law. The customary international law status of most principles of international investment law is contested. Ad hoc investor state tribunals routinely and selectively rely on each other's jurisprudence to justify a preferred outcome. Because decisions are not made within a single legal system, the status of precedent itself adds more uncertainty. As a result, customary international law as a source of international investment law is characterized by more serious doubts than just about any area of international law.[45]

41 This may be very clear from the text of the applicable treaty. An example of this is NAFTA Art. 1131(1) ("decide the issues in dispute in accordance with this Agreement and applicable rules of international law"). Text available at http://www.sice.oas.org/trade/nafta/chap-112.asp.

42 ICJ Statute, Art. 59 ("The decision of the Court has no binding force except between the parties and in respect of that particular case").

43 An example of this is the famous statement in the ICSID case of AES v. Argentina: "Each tribunal remains sovereign and may retain, as it is confirmed by ICSID practice, a different solution for resolving the same problem; but decisions on jurisdiction dealing with the same or very similar issues may at least indicate some line of reasoning of real interest; this Tribunal may consider them in order to compare its own position with those already adopted by its predecessors and, if it shares the views already expressed by one or more of these tribunals on a specific point of law, it is free to adopt the same solution." AES Corporation v. The Argentine Republic, ICSID Case No. ARB/02/17, Decision on Jurisdiction (Apr. 26, 2005), ¶ 23. Text available at https://www.italaw.com/cases/49.

44 ICJ Statute, Art. 38(1)(b).

45 Although these ad hoc proceedings occur independently of one another outside of a recognized system, the idea that propels the borrowing of principles and interpretations comes from a school of thought that says: "Where similar (if not identical) legal language is used across legal regimes that share

For example, arbitral tribunals' interpretation of the most frequently invoked principle of fair and equitable treatment ranges from "the treatment of an alien, in order to constitute an international delinquency should amount to an outrage, to bad faith, to willful neglect of duty, or an insufficiency of governmental action so far short of international standards that every reasonable and impartial man would readily recognize its insufficiency,"[46] on the one hand, to the protection of the "legitimate expectations" of the investor on the other.[47]

Apart from the uncertainty about the exact substantive meaning of some of these basic and most frequently invoked principles, questions are also raised about whether or not some of these principles, whatever their exact meanings, have acquired the status of customary international law in the first place. The inclusion of such principles as fair and equitable treatment and full protection and security in thousands of

core functional goals, there is little reason to adopt an interpretation in one that differs fundamentally from the other." Jürgen Kurtz, *Building Legitimacy Through Interpretation in Investor–State Arbitration: On Consistency, Coherence, and the Identification of Applicable Law*, in THE FOUNDATIONS OF INTERNATIONAL INVESTMENT LAW: BRINGING THEORY INTO PRACTICE 281 (Zachary Douglas, Joost Pauwelyn and Jorge E. Viñuales eds., OUP 2014). *See also* Gabrielle Kaufmann-Kohler, *Arbitral Precedent: Dream, Necessity, or Excuse? (The 2006 Freshfields Lecture)*, 23-3 ARB. INT'L (2007) 357–78. "Finally, it is important to remember that the credibility of the entire dispute resolution system depends on consistency, because a dispute settlement process that produces unpredictable results will lose the confidence of the users in the long term and defeat its own purpose. These final points lead to the overall conclusion that 'arbitral precedent' is a necessity for certain types of disputes, if not only for the sake of the rule of law." *Id.* at 378. One such type of dispute that she argues needs arbitral precedent is international investment arbitration, as opposed to commercial arbitration, which applies matured domestic laws. *Id.* at 371 ("When arbitrators apply a national law in commercial arbitration, that law is sufficiently developed to be predictable, and the arbitrators' role does not involve developing rules belonging to this national law. This is the role of the national legislators").

[46] L.F.H. Neer and Pauline Neer (U.S.A.) v. United Mexican States, 4 R.I.A.A. 60, 62 (1926). Many investor state arbitral tribunals have adopted the minimum standard of international law set forth in *Neer*. For example, in Glamis Gold v. United States, the NAFTA Tribunal stated that a breach of FET would mean "blatant unfairness, [or] a complete lack of due process . . . something far beyond the measure's mere illegality, an act so manifestly arbitrary, so unjust and surprising as to be unacceptable from the international perspective." Glamis Gold, Ltd v. United States, Award, ICC 380, ¶ 626–27 (NAFTA Ch. 11 Arb. Trib. 2009). Similarly, in Genin v. Estonia, the Tribunal held: "Any procedural irregularity that may have been present would have to amount to bad faith, willful disregard of due process of law or an extreme insufficiency of action." Alex Genin v. The Republic of Estonia, ICSID Case No. ARB/99/2, Award (June 25, 2001), ¶ 367.

[47] For example, an UNCITRAL Tribunal in International Thunderbird Gaming v. Mexico, stated: "the concept of 'legitimate expectations' relates . . . to a situation where a Contracting Party's conduct creates reasonable and justifiable expectations on the part of an investor (or investment) to act in reliance on said conduct, such that a failure by the [State] to honour these expectations could cause the investor (or investment) to suffer damages." International Thunderbird Gaming Corporation v. The United Mexican States, UNCITRAL, Award (Jan. 26, 2006), ¶ 147. Similarly, in the ICSID case Micula v. Romania, the Tribunal stated: "The crucial point is whether the state, through statements or conduct, has contributed to the creation of a reasonable expectation . . . It is irrelevant whether the state in fact wished to commit itself; it is sufficient that it acted in a manner that would reasonably be understood to create such an appearance. The element of reasonableness cannot be separated from the promise, assurance or representation, in particular if the promise is not contained in a contract or is otherwise stated explicitly. Whether a state has created a legitimate expectation in an investor is thus a factual assessment which must be undertaken in consideration of all the surrounding circumstances." Ioan Micula, Viorel Micula, SC European Food SA, SC Starmill SRL and SC Multipack SRL v. Romania, ICISD Case No. ARB/05/20, Award (Dec. 11, 2013), ¶ 669.

bilateral investment treaties is often cited as evidence of these principles' implementation into customary international law. The contrary view rests on the observation that the thousands of investment treaties formulate the principles in varied ways making the emergence of custom difficult, if not impossible,[48] presumably without a widely adopted multilateral treaty.[49]

A final consideration before treaties as sources of international investment law are discussed in the next section is the issue of the interaction between customary international law and investment treaties. A problem often arises when the rules of customary international law explicitly or implicitly incorporated into the treaty differ from the rules contained in the treaty itself. This often happens when the treaty contains a new rule on the same issue that customary international law speaks about. A good example of this is the rule on nationality for purposes of standing. A conflict of concurrent norms could in particular arise when the investor possesses the nationality of both the home and host states parties to the investment treaty. If the treaty simply grants rights to a national of the home state who has invested in the host state without consideration of whether that investor is also a national of the host state, customary international law on diplomatic protection could potentially apply to determine the dominant nationality. An Energy Charter Treaty Tribunal in 2016 addressed this issue in the *Cem Cengiz Uzan v. Republic of Turkey* case.[50] In this case, Turkey argued that the Claimant lacked standing because in addition to the relevant nationality under the treaty they also had Turkish nationality. In rejecting this argument, the tribunal opined that in the absence of an explicit exclusion in the treaty of claims by dual nationals, there is no room for the application of the customary international law rule of effective and dominate nationality doctrine.[51]

In most cases, it is fair to conclude that customary international law as a source of international investment law serves a role that is only supplemental to treaties in the order provided in Article 38 of the ICJ Statute. Africa's contribution to the development of customary international law as a rule of decision or an interpretive tool is highly significant. The details are discussed in Part II. Treaties do, however, remain the most important sources of international investment law. A brief overview of Africa's treaties at various levels is provided below as a background to the detailed discussion of the Africa-related ICSID jurisprudence in Part II. A detailed appraisal of African states' bilateral investment treaties is deferred to Part III.

48 *See* Sornarajah, The International Law On Foreign Investment, at 104–05.

49 The closest that reputable voices have come to consensus regarding the customary law status of principles regularly contained in bilateral investment treaties is that they "shaped the customary international law with respect to the rights of investors." Jeswald Salacuse, The Law of Investment Treaties (OUP 2010), at 4 (citing Mondev Int'l Ltd. v. United States, NAFTA/ICSID Case No. ARB(AF)/99/2, Award (Oct. 11, 2002), ¶ 125).

50 Cem Cengiz Uzan v. Republic of Turkey, SCC Case No. V 2014/023, Award on Respondent's Bifurcated Preliminary Objection (Apr. 20, 2016). Cited and discussed in Javier García Olmedo, *Rethinking the Relevance of Customary International Law to Issues of Nationality in Investment Treaty Arbitration, in* International Challenges in Investment Arbitration 4 (Mesut Akbaba & Giancarlo Capurro eds. 2019).

51 The doctrine comes from the Nottebohm (Liechtenstein v Guatemala), 1955 I.C.J. Rep. 4.

Treaties

The global regime for international investment is principally built upon investment treaties often called "international investment agreements" (IIA).[52] These treaties can be described in three categories: multilateral, regional, and bilateral treaties.

Multilateral Investment Related Treaties

The unrealized International Trade Organization (ITO)[53] contained investment related provisions that appear to be more than a precursor[54] to the fragments that later ended up populating the GATT/WTO system that included the Agreement on Trade-Related Aspects of Intellectual Property Rights (TRIPS),[55] Trade-Related Investment Measures (TRIMS),[56] and the General Agreement on Trade in Services (GATS).[57] All of the WTO-based investment-related substantive rules are limited to trade-related area specific rules subject to the WTO state-to-state dispute settlement mechanism.[58] At least 42 African WTO member states are bound by these multilateral treaties; however, none of these WTO related fragments purport to collectively build a coherent and robust multilateral investment protection regime.

The efforts to create a multilateral investment regime faced significant obstacles from the very inception. Opinions on why such efforts failed differ on the emphasis they place on the commonly identified factors. For example, while Salacuse puts emphasis on the advantages that developed economies saw in bilateral negotiations with weaker economies,[59] Sornarajah emphasizes the developing economies' belief that a multilateral treaty would essentially codify neo-liberal prescriptions.[60] Whatever the

[52] Salacuse, The Law of Investment Treaties, at 1.

[53] *See* Havana Charter for an International Trade Organization, U.N. Conference on Trade & Employment, Final Act and Related Documents, U.N. Doc. E/CONF. 2/78, U.N. Sales No. II.D.4 (1948), https://www.wto.org/english/docs_e/legal_e/havana_e.pdf.

[54] The Preamble for example contains this statement: "2. To foster and assist industrial and general economic development, particularly of those countries which are still in the early stages of industrial development, and to encourage the international flow of capital for productive investment." Article 12 also reads in part: "1. The Members recognize that: (a) international investment, both public and private, can be of great value in promoting economic development and reconstruction, and consequent social progress; (b) the international flow of capital will be stimulated to the extent that Members afford nationals of other countries opportunities for investment and security for existing and future investments; (c) without prejudice to existing international agreements to which Members are parties, a Member has the right: (i) to take any appropriate safeguards necessary to ensure that foreign investment is not used as a basis for interference in its internal affairs or national policies; (ii) to determine whether and, to what extent and upon what terms it will allow future foreign investment; (iii) to prescribe and give effect on just terms to requirements as to the ownership of existing and future investments; (iv) to prescribe and give effect to other reasonable requirements with respect to existing and future investments"; *Id.* at 20 (Art. 12(1)).

[55] World Trade Organization, *Agreement on Trade-Related Aspects of Intellectual Property Rights*, Apr. 15, 1994, 1869 U.N.T.S. 299, https://www.wto.org/english/tratop_e/trips_e/intel2_e.htm.

[56] World Trade Organization, *Agreement on Trade-Related Investment* Measures, Apr. 15, 1994, 1868 U.N.T.S. 186, https://www.wto.org/english/tratop_e/invest_e/trims_e.htm.

[57] World Trade Organization, *General Agreement on Trade in* Services, Apr. 15, 1994, 1869 U.N.T.S. 183, https://www.wto.org/english/tratop_e/serv_e/gatsqa_e.htm.

[58] For a discussion of WTO based investment regimes *see* Muthucumaraswamy Sornarajah, The International Law On Foreign Investment 19 (3d ed. 2010), at 309–15.

[59] *See* Salacuse, *The Emerging Global Regime for Investment*, at 464.

[60] *See* Sornarajah, The International Law On Foreign Investment, at 305–06 ("While the dissension among and within the developed states indicated that fears of losing sovereign control over an intrusive process such as foreign investment underlay the downfall of the MAI, the developing countries would have

real reasons might have been, the gap left by the absence of a WTO type global investment regime is now unsatisfactorily filled by a combination of a fairly robust procedural treaty, ICSID, and a multitude of regional and thousands of bilateral investment treaties that refer matters to ICSID arbitration and supply fragmented substantive rules of decision. Forty-five African states have ratified the ICSID Convention.[61]

Regional Investment Treaties

Globally, there are, as of this writing, 390 total regional treaties containing with investment provisions, of which 315 have entered into force.[62] Among these, 32 investment treaties include a block of states within the same region or subregion with few exceptions. Among these 32 blocks, 10 involve a group of African states.[63] Among them, at least three contain robust investment law regimes. These are (1) The Common Market for Eastern and Southern Africa (COMESA),[64] (2) Economic Community of West African States (ECOWAS),[65] and the (3) South African Development Community (SADC).[66] Whereas these three regimes are discussed in great detail in Part IV it is sufficient to note here that treaties as a sources of African international investment law come from all of these instruments that apply in their respective geographic domains.

Bilateral Investment Treaties

African states have collectively concluded a total of 854 Bilateral Investment Treaties (BITs), of which 157 are intra-Africa.[67] In the 1960s, there were more African BITs

had even greater problems with the formulations in the MAI. Some developing countries did participate in the discussions as observers. Others offered comments from sidelines, but, on the whole, developing countries could be anticipated from the comments made by developing-country officials and scholars") (citations omitted).

[61] *See Database of ICSID Member States*, Convention *on the Settlement of Investment Disputes Between States and Nationals of Other States*, 17 U.S.T. 1270, 575 U.N.T.S. 159 (Oct. 14, 1966) (containing ICSID ratification status of various States).

[62] *International Investment Agreements Navigator: Most Recent IIAs*, UNCTAD Investment Policy Hub, at https://investmentpolicy.unctad.org/international-investment-agreements (last visited Dec. 27, 2022).

[63] Those 10 blocks are: ACP (African, Caribbean and Pacific Group of States), AU (African Union), CEMAC (Economic and Monetary Community of Central Africa), CEPGC (Economic Community of the Great Lakes Countries), COMESA (Common Market for Eastern and Southern Africa), EAC (East African Community), ECCAS (Economic Community of Central African States), ECOWAS (Economic Community of West African States), SACU (Southern African Customs Union), and SADC (South African Development Community). *International Investment Agreements Navigator: IIAs by Country Grouping*, UNCTAD Investment Policy Hub, at https://investmentpolicy.unctad.org/international-investment-agreements/by-country-grouping (last visited Dec. 27, 2022).

[64] Common Market For Eastern and Southern Africa, *Investment Agreement For the COMESA Common Investment Area*, May 23, 2007, https://investmentpolicy.unctad.org/international-investment-agreements/treaties/treaties-with-investment-provisions/3225/comesa-investment-agreement.

[65] Economic Community of West African States, *The ECOWAS Supplemental Act on Investment*, Jan. 19, 2009, https://investmentpolicy.unctad.org/international-investment-agreements/treaties/treaties-with-investment-provisions/3547/ecowas-supplementary-act-on-investments.

[66] Southern African Development Community, *The SADC Protocol on Finance and Investment*, Apr. 16, 2010, https://investmentpolicy.unctad.org/international-investment-agreements/treaties/otheriia/3383/sadc-investment-protocol.

[67] *See* United Nations Economic Commission for Africa, *Investment Policies and Bilateral Investment Treaties in Africa: Implications for Regional Integration* (2016), at 18, https://repository.uneca.org/handle/10855/23035 f.

than BITs involving any other region. There were at least 110 BITs between African states and non-African states before the first intra-African BIT was signed in 1982 (between Egypt and Somalia).[68] As of the conclusion of this writing, these BITs collectively had given rise to many ICSID and UNCITRAL Investor–State cases involving African states.[69] These treaties provided both the substantive rules of decision and the jurisdictional consent. Without them, there would have been more limited ISDS cases involving African States. As such, they could rightfully be classified as the principal sources of international investment law.

Case Law as Soft Law

Case law constitutes of both international judicial and arbitral decisions. There are some decisions of the International Court of Justice (ICJ), along with the Permanent Court of International Justice (PCIJ), that have come to be considered sources of law albeit mostly for their persuasive power. In the area of international investment law, the most frequently invoked cases include the *Chorzow Factory* (on the issue of compensation),[70] *Barcelona Traction* (on the issue of corporate nationality and diplomatic protection),[71] *ELSI* (on takings and denial of justice),[72] and *Diallo v. Congo* (corporate nationality).[73]

Arbitral case law as the source of international investment law is perhaps the most contentious matter, because it goes to the heart of the nature of the global investment legal regime itself. Technically, arbitral decisions in ISDS cases are always ad hoc in nature. They derive their authority from bilateral treaties or contracts. No legal instrument links one with the other. Their existence is always parallel whether or not they are chronologically staggered. In reality, however, investor–state arbitral tribunals behave like courts of the same commonwealth. They borrow, and not infrequently rely on each other's jurisprudence. Advocates on either side selectively present arbitral case law to justify their preferred outcome. Those who hesitate ignore prior arbitral case law at their own peril. Arbitral case law is thus a source of law that could best be described as soft law—one that is "neither strictly binding nor lacking in legal significance."[74] A leading authority in the field, Sornarajah, comes very close to including

[68] *See id.* at 20–21.

[69] The most recent statistics show 111 cases, with only three UNCITRAL cases and the rest ICSID cases. *See id.* at 23–24. Compare with European BITs and cases as follows: Of the 2,337 BITs in effect as of 2020, 1,461 involve an EU member; 1,176 of which are with non-EU members. There were almost no investor state cases against an EU member state before the year 2000. There have been 421 since then with 332 pending as of Jan. 2020. Approximately 54% of these cases were decided in favor of the respondent state. Briefing, European Parliament Research Service [EPRS], Multilateral Investment Court: Overview of the Reform Proposals and Prospects (author Issam Hallak, Jan. 2020), https://www.europarl.europa.eu/RegData/etudes/BRIE/2020/646147/EPRS_BRI(2020)646147_EN.pdf.

[70] 1928 P.C.I.J. (ser. A) No. 17.

[71] 1970 I.C.J. Rep. 1.

[72] 1989 I.C.J. Rep. 15.

[73] 2008 I.C.J. Rep. 2010. These cases are identified and cited by Sornarajah as the leading cases and this author agrees. See Sornarajah, The International Law On Foreign Investment, at 107.

[74] *Soft Law*, Black's Law Dictionary, (11th ed. 2019).

them as sources of international investment law: "Yet, both the awards made by ad hoc tribunals as well as those made by institutional tribunals, particularly those made by tribunals constituted under ICSID Convention, provide evidence of possible norms which could be used for the construction of norms of international law."[75]

In reality and practice, however, the soft power of soft law could at times be more powerful than the binding nature of hard law. The availability of an increasing number of well-reasoned arbitral opinions written by highly skilled jurists seems to have taken arbitral jurisprudence generally in the direction that is least desirable: offered material to justify almost any outcome preferred by any given tribunal. This in turn has led to the current vigorous criticism of the whole ISDS system and the establishment of UNCITRAL Working Group III, which identified four areas of concern. The following section builds on those concerns in featuring the current state of the law and reform efforts and defining the analytical framework for the detailed appraisal of the African cases in the chapters that follow.

Current State of the Law, Reforms Efforts, and Directions

More than half a century of the law and practice of international investment law and dispute settlement has led to uncertainty. In recognition of this and to better understand the challenges and propose solutions, in its 50th Session in July 2017, the United Nations Commission on International Trade Law (UNCITRAL) established Working Group III and entrusted it with "[a] broad mandate to work on the possible reform of investor–State dispute settlement. . . . The Working Group would proceed to: (a) first, identify and consider concerns regarding investor–State dispute settlement; (b) second, consider whether reform was desirable in the light of any identified concerns; and (c) third, if the Working Group were to conclude that reform was desirable, develop any relevant solutions to be recommended to the Commission."[76]

Continuing its work, Working Group III identified four areas of concern requiring understanding.[77] The first of these include the following:

> Concerns pertaining to the lack of consistency, coherence, predictability and correctness of arbitral decisions by ISDS tribunals: Divergent interpretations of substantive

[75] *See* Sornarajah, The International Law On Foreign Investment, at 107.

[76] *Report of the United Nations Commission on International Trade Law*, 77 U.N. GAOR Supp. No. 17, at 46–47, U.N. Doc. A/72/17 (2017). Available at https://undocs.org/en/A/72/17.

[77] In terms of broad objectives: "The Working Group heard a general statement underlining the importance of improving the global investment environment in a way that encouraged fairness and promoted investment policies in line with the three pillars of sustainable development. It was stated that, appropriate investment policies, including transparent and fair ISDS regimes, were key components of the investment environment, and that discussions on the concerns and possible reforms of ISDS were of central importance to developing States that adopted such regimes." *Report of Working Group III (Investor–State Dispute Settlement Reform)*, United Nations Commission on International Trade Law, U.N. Doc. A/CN.9/964 (2018) at ¶ 16. Available at https://undocs.org/en/A/CN.9/964.

standards, divergent interpretations relating to jurisdiction and admissibility, and procedural inconsistency; Lack of a framework to address multiple proceedings; Limitations in the current mechanisms to address inconsistency and incorrectness of arbitral decisions.[78]

The second area includes "Concerns pertaining to arbitrators and decision makers: Lack or apparent lack of independence and impartiality; Limitations in existing challenge mechanisms; Lack of diversity of decision makers; Qualifications of decision makers"; The third area includes "Concerns pertaining to cost and duration of ISDS cases: Lengthy and costly ISDS proceedings and the lack of a mechanism to address frivolous or unmeritorious cases; Allocation of costs in ISDS; Concerns regarding the availability of security for cost in ISDS; Concerns regarding third-party funding." Finally, "Concerns pertaining to Third-party funding: lack of transparency and regulation and the impact third-party funding has on different aspects of ISDS, for instance increase in frivolous claims, costs of ISDS and security for costs."[79]

In its 36th session (October–November 2018), Working Group III further elaborated its deliberations on the causes of consistency and coherence,[80] and called upon states to undertake a more thorough study of the nature and depth of the problems of

[78] This is South Africa's summary paragraph in their submission to UNCITRAL's Working Group III's Oct. 2019 session. *Working Group III (Investment-State Dispute Settlement Reform): Submission from the Government of South Africa*, United Nations Commission on International Trade Law, U.N. Doc. A/CN.9/WG.III/WP.176 (2019) at 2. Available at https://undocs.org/en/A/CN.9/WG.III/WP.176.

[79] *See id.*

[80] Elaborated in these terms:

> 33. It was suggested that it might be useful to identify the causes or sources leading to the lack of consistency, coherence, predictability and correctness of arbitral decisions in order to develop any possible solution. In that light, it was mentioned that substantive protection standards were found in different sources of law, including investment treaties and domestic investment laws, which resulted in fragmentation. It was further pointed out that investment disputes were being resolved by tribunals constituted ad hoc for solving individual disputes.
>
> 34. Further, it was suggested that the discussion should not focus on inconsistency among decisions but on ensuring the correct interpretation of investment treaty provisions. It was explained that the main concern was not that decisions were inconsistent, but that arbitral tribunals had interpreted the treaty provisions incorrectly, sometimes not taking account of the intention of the treaty parties. It was said that in considering any reform options, it would be important to consider their possible impact on States' control over their treaties. It was also questioned whether procedural reform alone could address the question of inconsistency and unpredictability.
>
> 35. The view was expressed that the divergent interpretations and procedural inconsistency were intrinsic elements of the ISDS regime and further linked with other concerns, for instance, that arbitrators did not regard themselves as under a general duty towards an international system of justice, to act in the public interest, or to take into account the rights and interest of non-disputing parties. It was further said that related questions included how the mandate of arbitrators and their powers were determined and what limitations should apply to their decision-making and interpretative powers. It was further suggested that the concerns under consideration were closely linked to the efficiency of ISDS.

Report of Working Group III (Investor–State Dispute Settlement Reform), United Nations Commission on International Trade Law, U.N. Doc. A/CN.9/964 (2018), at 7.

the jurisprudence.[81] In this session, Working Group III focused on consistency, coherence, predictability, and correctness of decisions by arbitral tribunals as a measure of the legitimacy of the regime as a whole, and estimated the prevalence of and weighed various scenarios about the perceived inconsistencies.[82] The underlying assumption is that consistency and coherence "would support the rule of law, enhance confidence in the stability of the investment environment and further bring legitimacy to the regime."[83]

States have reported to Working Group III that inconsistencies have been (perhaps anecdotally) observed in at least two circumstances. The first, and perhaps the most common, is the differing interpretations of similar treaty provisions by different tribunals.[84] This is sometimes attributed to minor differences in textual formulations of the treaty provisions and sometimes to views and understandings of individual arbitrators.[85] The second is the different tribunals' lack of consistent application of "international rules on treaty interpretation and customary international law."[86] The Group emphasized that the lack of consistency, and predictability, is more gravely felt "where the same investment treaty standard or same customary international law was interpreted differently in the absence of justifiable grounds for distinction."[87]

Considering different scenarios, the following three anecdotal observations emerge. First, a few sets of frequently relied upon cases offer examples of different tribunal conclusions applying identical treaty standards to similar or substantially similar facts.[88] Some also exemplify different interpretations of the same ICSID Convention

[81] *See id.* at ¶ 29 ("29. In response to a suggestion that the questions of consistency, coherence, predictability and correctness of arbitral decisions deserved a more in-depth analysis, it was clarified that the focus of the discussion should be on whether the overall situation as illustrated in document A/CN.9/WG.III/WP.150 raised concerns that made reforms desirable, and not on specific examples of divergent treaty interpretations. It was further mentioned that the examples presented in that document were illustrative and not exhaustive. It was said that States were invited to conduct more in-depth analysis of those examples. It was further said that some States had conducted such an analysis and had concluded that some, but not all, of the examples were instances of unjustifiable inconsistency").

[82] *Report of Working Group (Investor–State Dispute Settlement Reform)*, United Nations Commission on International Trade Law, U.N. Doc. A/CN.9/930/Add.1/Rev.1 (2017) at 2–4. Available at https://undocs.org/en/A/CN.9/930/Add.1/Rev.1.

[83] *Id.* at p. 3, ¶ 11.

[84] *Id.* at p. 3, ¶ 9.

[85] *Id.* (citing and relying on UNCTAD, *Note No. 2: Reform of Investor–State Dispute Settlement: In Search of a Roadmap*, IIA, June 2013, at 3, finding arbitral decisions that have been made publicly available have "exposed recurring episodes of inconsistent findings . . . [including] divergent legal interpretations of identical or similar treaty provisions as well as differences in the assessment of the merits of cases involving the same facts. Sometimes, divergent outcomes can be explained by the differences in wording of a specific IIA applicable in a particular case; however, often they represent the differences in the views of individual arbitrators").

[86] *See id.* at p. 3, ¶ 13.

[87] *Report of Working Group III (Investor–State Dispute Settlement Reform)*, United Nations Commission on International Trade Law, U.N. Doc. A/CN.9/935 (2018) at ¶ 21. Available at https://undocs.org/en/A/CN.9/935.

[88] *Report of Working Group III (Investor–State Dispute Settlement Reform): Note by the Secretariat*, United Nations Commission on International Trade Law, U.N. Doc. A/CN.9/WG.III/WP.150 (2018) at ¶ 11. Available at https://undocs.org/en/A/CN.9/WG.III/WP.150 (citing the limited pairs of cases that are often cited to prove this proposition including: S. D. Myers, Inc. v. Government of Canada, UNCITRAL, Partial Award, Nov. 13, 2000; Pope & Talbot Inc. v. The Government of Canada, UNCITRAL, Award on the Merits of Phase 2, Apr. 10, 2001. And the following decisions interpreting the essential security clause differently: CMS Gas Transmission Company v. The Republic of Argentina, ICSID Case No. ARB/01/8,

jurisdiction and admissibility rules.[89] Second, another set of arbitral decisions are often cited to demonstrate instances of different tribunals constituted under different treaties arriving at different conclusions in cases arising out of the same government measures affecting related parties and under the same or similar legal standards.[90] The third set of cases is cited to support the proposition that tribunals applying the same applicable legal rules arrive at opposite conclusions in cases dealing with the same government measure affecting unrelated investors.[91]

At the more substantive level, some principles and rules are more frequently affected by inconsistent interpretation and application than others. For example, appreciable levels of inconsistent interpretations and applications were found regarding the meaning of investment, most favored nation (MFN) clauses, expropriation, the so-called umbrella clause, fair and equitable treatment (FET), and the full protection and security (FPS) clauses.[92] At the procedural level, appreciable levels of inconsistencies have been observed with respect to jurisdiction and admissibility, and procedural inconsistencies included in annulment or other post award processes.[93]

The next cluster of concerns, which are most closely related to the concerns of consistency and incoherence, pertains to arbitrators and decision-makers.[94] These concerns touch several areas, most importantly on the lack of independence and impartiality.[95]

Award (May 12, 2005); Enron Corporation Ponderosa Assets, L.P. v. The Republic of Argentina, ICSID Case No. ARB/01/3, Award (May 22, 2007); LG&E Energy Corp., L&E Capital Corp., LG&E International Inc. v. The Republic of Argentina, ICSID Case No. ARB/02/1, Decision on Liability (Oct. 3, 2006); Continental Casualty Company v. The Republic of Argentina, ICSID Case No. ARB/03/9, Award (Sep. 5, 2008)).

[89] *See id.* at ¶ 17 (citing the often relied on examples of Salini Costruttori S.p.A. and Italstrade S.p.A. v. Kingdom of Morocco, ICSID Case No. ARB/00/4, Decision on Jurisdiction (July 31, 2001); Malaysian Historical Salvors, SDN, BHD v. The Government of Malaysia, ICSID Case No. ARB/05/10, Award on Jurisdiction (May 17, 2007) (requiring economic contribution as a jurisdictional baseline) and Deutsche Bank AG v. Democratic Socialist Republic of Sri Lanka, ICSID Case No. ARB/09/2, Award (Oct. 31, 2012); Saba Fakes v. Republic of Turkey, ICSID Case No. ARB/07/20, Award (July 14, 2010) and Société Générale de Surveillance S.A. v. The Republic of Paraguay, ICSID Case No. ARB/07/29, Decision on Jurisdiction (Feb. 12, 2010) (not requiring economic contribution as a jurisdictional baseline)).

[90] *See id.* at ¶ 12 (citing the most famous Czech Republic cases: CME and Lauder (CME Czech Republic B.V. v. Czech Republic, Ad hoc UNCITRAL Arbitration Rules, Partial Award (Sep. 13, 2001), Final Award (Mar. 14, 2003) and Lauder v. Czech Republic, Ad hoc UNCITRAL Arbitration Rules, Final Award (Sep. 3, 2001). And also citing the most frequently cited umbrella clauses cases: SGS Societe Generale de Surveillance S.A. v. Islamic Republic of Pakistan, ICSID Case No. ARB/01/13, Decision of the Tribunal on Objections to Jurisdiction (Aug. 6, 2003) and SGS Societe Generale de Surveillance S.A. v. Republic of the Philippines, ICSID Case No. ARB/02/6, Decision of the Tribunal on Objections to Jurisdiction (Jan. 29, 2004); SGS Société Générale de Surveillance S.A. v. Republic of Paraguay, ICSID Case No. ARB/07/29, Award (Feb. 10, 2012)).

[91] *See id.* at ¶13 (citing examples that include: Charanne and Construction Investments v. Kingdom of Spain, SCC Case No. V 062/2012; Eiser Infrastructure Limited and Energía Solar Luxembourg Sà rl. v. Kingdom of Spain, ICSID Case No. ARB/13/36; Isolux Netherlands, BV v. Kingdom of Spain, SCC Case V2013/153; Portigon AG v. Kingdom of Spain, ICSID Case No. ARB/17/15; RREEF Infrastructure (G.P.) Limited and RREEF Pan-European Infrastructure Two Lux S.à r.l. v. Kingdom of Spain, ICSID Case No. ARB/13/30).

[92] *See id.* at p. 3–8, ¶ 14–18.

[93] *Id.*

[94] *Report of Working Group III (Investor-State Dispute Settlement Reform)*, United Nations Commission on International Trade Law, U.N. Doc. A/CN.9/964 (2018), at 64–108.

[95] *Id.*

Lack of independence and impartiality or the appearance thereof is viewed as one of the most serious concerns in this cluster. These concerns are closely associated with the uncertainties of the ethical rules of conduct that might govern the key players: arbitrators and counsel. The issues more specifically pertain to repeat appointments, which are in turn linked to possible biases, lack of diversity, conflicts of interest, and the pervasive switching of roles between arbitrator and counsel, referred to as "double-hatting."[96]

A more serious question of legitimacy, as it were, the lack of diversity is generally understood to persist primarily because of the current party-appointed ad hoc system of appointments that prioritizes ISDS experience and expertise, which necessarily leads to a limited pool of arbitrators.[97]

The concern about qualification of arbitrators is closely linked to the manners of their appointment. The overwhelming majority of treaties provide for party appointment with default appointment authority often granted to institutions. This party-appointed system provided by treaties and other laws is believed to have failed to provide the right incentives and the most effective mechanism for the appointment of the most qualified and conflict free arbitrators in each case.[98]

The other cluster of concerns pertains to the costs and duration of arbitral proceedings. There is a general recognition that the complexity of most ISDS matters and the need to ensure the quality and correctness of the decisions comes with an understandable price tag; however, there are several matters that unnecessarily inflate the cost of proceedings.[99] Among these is the willful filing of entirely frivolous or meritless claims whose dismissal is not always quick and inexpensive. In addition to the actual pecuniary cost, this is also believed to contribute to reputational damage and regulatory chill.[100]

Several other factors have been identified to contribute to potentially avoidable costs such as the lack of clear rules on precedent,[101] extensive discovery or document production, interim measures, bifurcation of proceedings, challenge of arbitrators, multiple appointments of the same individuals (which presumably leads to delays), the need for translation of documents and translation services, and delays in issuing awards.[102]

The final cluster of concerns pertains to third party funding. Beyond the several issues that it raises on its own accord as a vehicle of access to justice, concerns pertain to

[96] *See id.* at ¶ 68–72.

[97] *See id.* at ¶ 93. Although the most glaring lack of diversity pertains to gender and geographic distribution, it also concerns cultures, legal traditions, ethnicity, etc. *See id.* at ¶ 92.

[98] *See id.* at ¶ 99–106.

[99] *See id.* at ¶ 110–17.

[100] *See id.* at ¶ 111.

[101] *See id.* at ¶ 116. Although this is not directly discussed in detail in the Working Group III Report here, practitioners would understand that this could be a source of great cost because ordinarily citations in pleadings often contain reference to hundreds of cases that would need to be reviewed (for relevance, persuasive strength, rebuttal, etc.) by counsel by each side and by arbitrators and their secretaries. In domestic systems where there is a clear rule of precedent, the number of relevant cases is often limited and very well known, which could potentially reduce the cost.

[102] *See id.* at ¶ 114. Other factors that are observed under this category include inconsistency of allocation of costs. *See id.* at ¶ 124–27. And availability of security for costs, which often disadvantages Respondent states. *See* ¶ 128–31.

the "structural imbalance" that it creates as it is only available to investors not to states. Moreover, it is also believed to contribute to the inflation of the overall cost by introducing an entirely new dimension to the whole process.[103]

These four clusters of concerns have propelled the reform agenda across the development spectrum spearheaded by UNCITRAL. The reform would be informed by systematic research on each one of these areas of concern from a variety of standpoints. Although the states generally seem to consider these concerns as manifest deficiencies of the global investment law regime that they created in the aftermath of World War II needing correction, there does not seem to be a general agreement on how accurate, pervasive, inherent, deep, willful, unavoidable, and systematic these concerns are. These concerns are not universally accepted as structural or systemic. Many prominent arbitrators maintain that it is a function of misunderstanding, or even ignorance.

Whether eventually the states are right or the elite arbitrators are right, a wholesale indictment of the whole regime on the basis of a few case comparisons may not offer adequate scientific proof of a regime failure. A thorough and systematic qualitative investigation of the nature of the justice in each case and the discernment of patterns is not only the most useful tool for reform directions, but also for keeping of historical record about past regimes and systems of law that can educate future generations. The task of genetic mapping of all ISDS cases is an enormous undertaking that will need to be undertaken at the global level, but this book's attempt is limited to the African ICSID cases as the first important step in Parts II and III.

[103] *See id.* at ¶¶ 114, 120.

3

International Investment Jurisprudence and Africa

A Historical Background and Case Analysis Framework

Although the contemporary debate is primarily doctrinal in nature and seeks to find a balance between protection of investment and regulatory power regardless of the stage of development of the host or the home state, its essence and direction could only be fully understood in the context of the post–World War II economic expansion and decolonization of territories that were under the control of the advanced economies of the Global North.[1] This chapter begins with a historical note on Africa's ICSID participation and sets forth the analytical framework for the detailed analysis of the procedural and substantive principles that have emerged out of and/or consolidated in the African ICSID cases in the chapters that will follow.

Africa's Participation in the Making of ICSID

Africa's role in the making of the ICSID Convention is fairly well documented in the form of summary records of proceedings of consultations that the World Bank undertook in Addis Ababa between December 16 and 20 of 1963 with a total of 50 African delegates, most of whom were legal experts representing 29 African states.[2] These summary records offer a reasonable insight into what exactly transpired inside those consultation rooms of the Economic Commission for Africa (ECA) in Addis Ababa. These records have gotten attention only recently in the literature. They are profiled and cited to support at least two ostensibly divergent propositions. The first observation is purely textual. It builds on the congratulatory diplomatic exchange of niceties that seemed almost invariably supportive of the Bank's efforts of establishing ICSID presented by the then General Counsel, Aaron Broches. Upon return to Washington, he reported that the Addis Ababa meeting was "more constructive and more helpful and encouraging than had dared to expect."[3] The record shows how he came to this conclusion. The second proposition attempts to deconstruct the constructive comments by juxtaposing them against Africa's dire socioeconomic circumstances of the immediate postcolonial era framing it more in terms of the prisoner's dilemma. Each is described below in some detail.

[1] *See* Jeswald W. Salacuse, *The Emerging Global Regime for Investment*, 51 Harv. Int'l L. J. 427, 436–37 (2010), at 436.
[2] *See generally* History of ICSID.
[3] *Id.*. at 295, 296.

Africa's International Investment Law Regimes. Won L. Kidane, Oxford University Press. © Oxford University Press 2023.
DOI: 10.1093/oso/9780197745571.003.0003

There are numerous examples of constructive comments that the African delegates provided. At least three relatively recent writings profile some of these comments in remarkably positive light. First, Judges Charles Brower and Michael Daly, in their article "A Study of Foreign Investment Law in Africa: Opportunity Awaits," take "the optimistic view that international investment arbitration will persist as a means of peaceful dispute resolution, and that African States and nationals should maintain a healthy relationship to the field in a way that will benefit them over the long run."[4] The authors believe that the Addis Ababa records disprove the suggestion that "the capital exporting countries alone created investment arbitration for their own benefits."[5] Broches's own observations feature prominently. He is reported to have said: "No objections were expressed ... to the principles underlying the draft."[6] Broches is also quoted to have said:

> It was very fitting that the first of four regional meetings to be held by the Bank should take place in Africa. African countries [have] an urgent need to encourage that international flow of capital and skills and [have] shown a willingness to create an atmosphere conducive to financial and economic cooperation.[7]

Some of the key texts that are featured in this writing are the statements made by the Ethiopian and Nigerian representatives. The Ethiopia representative is reported to have said:

> Ethiopia favored the establishment of an International Conciliation and Arbitration Center. Ethiopian courts were empowered to hear cases against Government Ministries and Departments, but however independent the courts, the investor would always regard them as the instrument of the State. On the other hand, States might be reluctant to take action against investors because of the unfavorable impression such action might take on others. The proposed Center would therefore be of value in improving relations between investors and Governments.[8]

Judge T. O. Elias of Nigeria, who later headed the International Court of Justice (ICJ), is reported to have "warmly recommended" the draft of the ICSID Convention, saying that it "represented an attempt not only to resort the confidence of the investor but also to codify certain principles of customary law and to engage in the progressive development of international law."[9] Ultimately, he believed that the objective of the Convention was to balance the interests of the state and the investor.[10]

[4] Charles N. Brower & Michael P. Daly, *A Study of Foreign Investment Law in Africa: Opportunity Awaits*, *in* International Arbitration and the Rule of Law: Contribution and Conformity 503 (Andrea Menaker ed., 2016).

[5] *Id.* at 506.

[6] *Id.* at 506 (citing History of ICSID at 295–96).

[7] *Id.* at 507 (citing History of ICSID at 239–40).

[8] *Id.* at 508 (citing History of ICSID at 243).

[9] *Id.* at 509 (citing History of ICSID at 244).

[10] *Id.* at 509 (citing History of ICSID at 243).

In his *Global Arbitration Review* essay "The Evolution of Investment Arbitration in Africa," Benoit Le Bars also relies on the same statements given by the African delegates reproduced above to conclude that:

> Africa was in favour of an international regime for investment arbitration from the very beginning in light of their need to attract foreign investments. African states engaged actively in the negotiations prior to the conclusion of the ICSID Convention and began to conclude BITs with other capital-exporting states in order to attract foreign direct investment so as to support their economy.[11]

In particular, he restates what the Ethiopian and Nigerian representatives are reported to have said, that is, that investors would consider domestic courts as "instruments of the state," and that ICSID is not only a good idea but also that its enforcement mechanism must be strengthened, respectively.[12]

Former Deputy Secretary General of ICSID Antonio Parra has also strengthened this view in his *ICSID Review* article titled "The Participation of African States in the Making of the ICSID Convention."[13] He notes that:

> among the consultative meetings, the one in Addis Ababa stood out for its success. As Broches reported afterward to the Executive Directors, the meeting has "long and fruitful sessions [in] which a great number of comments were made dealing with matters of principles as well as details." Broches told the Executive Directors that he "had expected a good and sympathetic discussion" at Addis Ababa "but it was more constructive and more helpful and encouraging than [he] had dared to expect." Broches added special praise for the expert designated by Nigeria, its Minister of Justice and Attorney General Taslim Olawale Elias (a future President of the International Court of Justice), who "strongly welcomed the Bank's initiative."[14]

Parra goes through the records of the Addis Ababa meeting carefully and highlights the very specific contributions that the Africans made to the draft itself. It begins with the name ICSID itself. Initially, the proposed institution was supposed to be named the "International Conciliation and Arbitration Center." The term "investment" was inserted between international and conciliation "setting the drafters on a path toward the ICSID name."[15] He also goes through each change that was made and usefully documents them including the proposal for the Secretary General to be an independent and full-time employee of the institution, changing the initial idea of an employee of the Bank or even the Permanent Court of Arbitration to assume that role.[16] Other more substantive contributions pertained to rules on the standing of dual nationality,

[11] Benoit Le Bars, *The Evolution of Investment Arbitration in Africa*, GLOBAL ARBITRATION REV. (May 11, 2018), at 2.

[12] *Id.*

[13] Antonio R. Parra, *The Participation of African States in The Making of the ICISD Convention*, 34–2 ICSID REVIEW 270–77 (2019).

[14] *Id.* at 271 (citing HISTORY OF ICSID at 295, 296, 298).

[15] *Id.* at 272.

[16] *Id.* (citing HISTORY OF ICSID at 251–52).

standing of state agencies, number and challenge of arbitrators, counterclaims, seat and fees, and expenses.[17]

The December 1963 Addis Ababa meeting was not the only forum that allowed the Africans to contribute to the making of the ICSID Convention and the establishment of the Center. As Parra highlights, 16 of the 61 members of the Legal Committee of the Bank were African. He states in particular that "they helped to defeat a proposal that the Center (which had by then acquired this name) should have an intermediate organ, like the IBRD Executive Director, between the Administrative Council and the Secretariat. '[A] multiplication of organs should be avoided,' these experts maintained."[18]

Another scholar, Olabisi Akinkugbe, in his *ICSID Review* article "Reverse Contributions? African State Parties, ICSID and the Development of International Investment Law," comes to the same optimistic conclusion, building on the same passages of the records of the Addis Ababa consultative meeting including Elias's famous statements, describing the ICSID Convention as "an attempt not only to restore the confidence of the investor but also to codify certain principles of customary law and to engage in the progressive development of international law, and he warmly recommend[ed] it."[19]

Four of the above-cited authors (Brower, Daly, Le Bars, and Akinkugbe) comment on what the author of this current book has said in the past about why Africa accepted ICSID and Africa's contributions to the development of international investment law. Brower and Daly state: "Some have suggested that African States had no alternative to accepting the ICSID Convention, given their dire economic circumstances, or that they agreed to the Convention out of wishful thinking that investment treaties represented economic opportunity devoid of any risk of arbitration."[20] They selectively cite records to show that the motive was rather altruistic because their representatives made statements, such as: "The proposed center would therefore be of value in improving relations between investors and Governments,"[21] and "the aim was to strike a balance between the interests of investors and those of developing countries,"[22] and that the Convention "represented an attempt not only to restore the confidence of the investor but also to codify certain principles of customary law and to engage in the progressive development of international law."[23]

[17] *Id.* at 273–74 (highlighting the records of discussions on these issues based on his review of the preliminary draft and the record of proceedings in HISTORY OF ICSID 253–78).

[18] *Id.* at 275 (citing Summary of Proceedings of the Legal Committee Meeting (SPLCM) (Nov. 30, 1964), *reprinted in* 2 HISTORY OF ICSID (n.3) 711, 717) (featuring interventions of Mr. Kpognon (Dahomey), Mr. Bohani (Tanzania), and Mr. Manirakiza (Burundi)).

[19] Olabisi Akinkugbe, *Reverse Contributions? African State Parties, ICSID and the Development of International Investment Law*, 34-2 ICSID REVIEW 434, 438 (2019) (citing HISTORY OF ICSID, at 244).

[20] Brower & Daly, *A Study of Foreign Investment Law in Africa: Opportunity Awaits*, at 507 (quoting Won L. Kidane, *The China–Africa Factor in The ICSID Legitimacy Debate*, 35 U. PA. J. INT'L L. 559, 585–86 (2014)) ("The historical record clearly indicates that the only reason that the African states accepted ICSID is because they thought that they had to do so in order to attract private foreign investment to develop their ailing post-colonial economies").

[21] Brower & Daly, *A Study of Foreign Investment Law in Africa: Opportunity Awaits*, at 508 (citing HISTORY OF ICSID, at 243) (statement by the Ethiopian representative).

[22] *Id.*, at 509 (citing HISTORY OF ICSID, at 243) (statement by the Nigerian representative, T. O. Elias).

[23] *Id.*, at 509 (citing HISTORY OF ICSID, at 244) (statement by the Nigerian representative, T. O. Elias).

Taking a similar optimistic tone, Akinkugbe offers a more nuanced analysis using the "reverse discrimination" metaphor in characterizing Africa's contribution to international investment law by appearing before arbitral tribunals as the respondent.[24] He notes that Africa's contribution is significant and must not be overshadowed by a strong focus on its historical exclusion and subordinate position. Commenting on this author's previous suggestions, he writes:

> "Africanization" of international investment law thesis championed by Makane Mbengue, has attempted to reclaim some of Africa's role in this process, albeit not without its complexity, it is important to avoid critique that inadvertently perpetuates the "dilemmas"—as Won Kidane conceptualizes—of the role of African States in the ongoing development of international legal fields.[25]

Akinkugbe usefully goes through the notable literature on this topic and juxtaposes a few of the writings in this area such as Joost Pauwelyn's characterization of the development of international investment law being "organic and incremental"[26] and this author's previous suggestions that Pauwelyn's "organic and incremental" theory does not exactly explain Africa's story.[27] Akinkugbe then approvingly notes James Gathii's characterization of Elias's optimistic vision of "reclaim[ing] or claim[ing] a place in international legal history for Africa."[28] And that is "because Elias sought not to reject international law for its legacy and participation in the colonization of Africa, but rather sought to use these legal tools as best as he could to reform international law to serve the newly independent countries."[29] As such, "Elias's support of ICSID came at a hopeful moment for Africa—right after decolonization—and although Africa was experiencing its first series of internal challenges, Elias did not abandon his faith in the transformative potential of international law and of foreign investment."[30] This gives proper context to Elias's now famous "warm recommendation" of ICSID to Africa in a language that mimics the mandate of the International Law Commission (to which he was a member in 1963)[31] that it is "an attempt not only to restore the confidence of

[24] Akinkugbe, *Reverse Contributions? African State Parties, ICSID and the Development of International Investment Law*, (citing History of ICSID, at 244), at 436.

[25] *Id.*

[26] *Id.* at 438 (citing Joost Pauwelyn, *Rational Design or Accidental Evolution? The Emergence of International Investment Law*, *in* The Foundations of International Investment Law: Bringing Theory Into Practice 15 (Zachary Douglas, Joost Pauwelyn & Jorge E. Vinuales eds., 2014), at 10–43).

[27] *Id.* (quoting Won L. Kidane, *Contemporary International Investment Trends and Africa's Dilemmas in the Draft Pan-African Investment Code*, 50 G.W. Int'l L. Rev. 523, 526 (2018)) ("International investment law [IIL] comes with a very old and lingering historical baggage that continues to engender doctrinal confusion and outright suspicion . . . IIL is not made *by Africa*, it was made *for Africa* as a replacement for colonial rules for the protection of capital").

[28] *Id.* at 439 (quoting James Thuo Gathii, *A Critical Appraisal of International Legal Tradition of Taslim Olawale Elias*, Leiden J. of Int'l L. 317, 347 (2008).

[29] *Id.*

[30] *Id.*

[31] *See Members of the Commission at the Fifteenth Session (1963)*, International Law Commission, https://legal.un.org/ilc/sessions/15/members.shtml. Article 1 of the ICL Statute states: "1. The International Law Commission shall have for its object the promotion of the progressive development of international law and its codification." *Statute of the ICL*, G.A. Res. 174 (II), at 2 (Nov. 21, 1947), available at https://legal.un.org/docs/?path=../ilc/texts/instruments/english/statute/statute.pdf&lang=EF.

the investor but also to codify certain principles of customary law and to engage in the progressive development of international law."[32]

One of the questions that this book tries to answer is, 50 years later, what is the extent of the progress and codification? Leaving such evaluation to subsequent chapters, it is important to note that closely scrutinized in light of the power dynamics of the time, the historical record reveals a far more complicated state of mind that more closely resembles one of capitulation than the frequently cited optimistic statement by Judge Elias and repeated by all the above writers. A closer analysis of the record is offered as follows.

The World Bank conceived the idea and led the regional discussions including the now famous African discussions. The Bank's financial assistance to the African countries included, among other things, the travel and other expenses of the legal experts who traveled to Addis Ababa for the December 1943 meeting.[33] Although this seems insignificant, it not only sets the host–guest or sponsor–sponsored relationship, but also shows the economic hierarchy including the extent of the financial needs of the African states at the time. The African delegates were presented a draft that was prepared in Washington by the Bank. The *travaux preparatoire* suggests that the question of the neutrality of the Bank was raised from the very inception of the idea. "The question was asked whether the fact that the Bank can itself be regarded as an 'investor' would not tend to raise doubts as to the impartiality of a Center sponsored by, and affiliated with, the Bank."[34] The response to that was:

> The Bank is an international cooperative institution which lends funds for the benefit of its members which are also its shareholders. The fact that it is a creditor of most of its members has never put its impartiality in question. This would seem to be borne out by the requests addressed to the Bank by member governments for assistance in the solution of investment disputes. Apart from this, the administrative apparatus of the Center would not, as noted earlier, itself engage in conciliation or arbitration.[35]

In opening the Bank's Addis Ababa consultative meeting on December 16, 1963, the Executive Secretary of the ECA, Mr. Gardiner, said in language that resembles the speech that the president of the Bank gave to the Executive Council a few months before the Addis Ababa meeting on September 30, 1963, in Washington:[36]

[32] History of ICISD, at 244 (quoted Akinkugbe, *Reverse Contributions? African State Parties, ICSID and the Development of International Investment Law*, at 438).

[33] *Id.*, at 175.

[34] Note by the General Counsel Transmitted to the Executive Directors, History of ICSID, at 8–9.

[35] *Id.*

[36] Excerpt from Address by the President to the Annual Meeting of the Board of Governors, History of ICSID, at 183 ("For my part, however, I believe that, to a great extent, the attitudes of many of the less developed countries toward foreign private investment are based on the outdated past rather than on present facts. And I am convinced that those of our members who adopt as their national policy a welcome for international investment—and that means, to mince no words about it, giving foreign investors a fair opportunity to make attractive profits—will achieve their development objectives more rapidly than those who do not. For a country which is known to be hospitable to private investment will have access over the years to a much larger and more stable pool of capital than its neighbor which relies solely on government-to-government aid. It will have access, too, to a much larger pool of industrial personnel—managerial, administrative and technical—and to a much larger mass of scientific and technological information than it could possibly acquire in any other way. Most important of all, its economy will be stimulated and invigorated

> Commented on the growing realization of the power represented by properly channeled private investment as a means of promoting economic development. The importance of capital investment obtained from sources other than public funds called for the creation of a legal regime which, while fully respecting the rights of sovereign States in conformity with the recognizes principles of international law, would protect the rights of investors and provide an appropriate forum for the settlement of disputes between them.[37]

In a meeting of the Committee of the Whole on the Settlement of the Investment Disputes on December 18, 1962, exactly a year before the draft was presented to the Africans, the issue of the perception of extra-territoriality was raised. The following passage exemplifies:

> As for Mr. Krishna Moorthils point that contracting states would be subject to pressures to submit disputes to arbitration, even though they would be equally free to refrain, Mr. Broches thought this would depend in large part on how the convention was presented. Bank sponsorship, in particular, would make clear, Mr. Broches thought, that the convention was not a one-sided attempt to create a new sort of extra-territoriality for foreign private investment.[38]

In any case, it was clear from the outset that the Bank was determined to push this through one way or the other. Before any of the consultative meetings, the president of the bank had told the Board of Governors in September of 1963 that consultations would take place and that "*concrete conclusions and recommendations on this matter*" would follow.[39] The president then set the tone and all others followed. The planning was meticulous. For example, all four of the executive secretaries of the Economic Commissions of each region, Africa, Latin America, Europe, and Asia and the Far East, used the exact same text that resembled the president's speech to the Bank's Board of Governors. The following passage was repeated verbatim by each one of the

by the many different contacts, at many different levels, which a hospitable investment climate will make possible between enterprises and individuals within its own borders and those within the borders of the industrialized countries. None of these advantages is likely to be fully available to any nation whose government, however well motivated and however well administered, decides to relegate the private sector to a subordinate role").

37 Addis Ababa Meeting, History of ICSID, at 239.

38 Memorandum of the Meeting of the Whole (Dec. 28, 1962), History of ICSID, at 53.

39 This is recorded in the Excerpt of the Address of the President to the Annual Meeting of the Board of Governors of Sep. 30, 1963, in the following terms: "One proposal which we have been actively exploring with this objective in mind is the plan to establish facilities, under the umbrella of the Bank, for the conciliation and arbitration of international investment disputes. The Executive Directors, together with the staff, have had this matter under study following the request made of them by this Board of Governors at last year's Annual Meeting. The proposal has now been given the form of a draft convention. Over the next six months or so, this draft will be discussed at a series of conferences of legal experts of our member countries, to be held, through the courtesy of the four regional Economic Commissions of the United Nations, in Addis Ababa, Bangkok, Geneva and Santiago. I have high hopes that in 1964 the Executive Directors will be able to present to this Board concrete conclusions and recommendations on this matter." History of ICSID, at 183 (emphasis added).

executive secretaries of the regional economic commissions in their opening statements in their respective meetings:

> Unfortunately, private capital was not moving in sufficient volume to areas in need of capital, one of the most serious impediments to its flow being the fear of investors that their investment would be exposed to political risks such as outright expropriation, government interference and non-observance by the host government of contractual undertakings on the basis of which the investment had been made.[40]

This, of course, traces the paper prepared by the General Counsel and distributed to the members of the Committee of the Whole on February 18, 1963, which reads in relevant part:

> That private capital is not now moving to these areas in sufficient volume is not in dispute. Nor is there room for doubt that one of the most important impediments to the flow of private capital is the fear of investors that their investment will be exposed to political risks, such as outright expropriation without adequate compensation, governmental interference short of expropriation which substantially deprives the investor of the control or the benefits of his investment, and non-observance by the host government of contractual undertakings in reliance on which the investment was made.[41]

It was within this context that the Africans began to discuss the proposal. The representatives repeated one after another their support for the Center and their agreement with the Bank's suggestion that "one of the most important impediments to the flow of private capital is the fear of investors," and that the creation of the Center would alleviate that problem resulting in more private investment.[42]

On the other hand, drawing inspiration from the *Calvo Doctrine*,[43] Latin America was rather unimpressed with the whole idea and as such largely opposed ICSID altogether. Argentina's position during the consultative meeting in Santiago in February 1964 summarizes it very well:

> Mr. BARBOZA (Argentina) found great difficulty in accepting the principle underlying the draft Convention for several reasons. National sentiment could not

[40] It was first delivered as an opening for the Consultative Meeting in Addis Ababa by the Executive Secretary of the Economic Commission for Africa, Mr. Gardiner on Dec. 16, 1963. History of ICSID, at 240. It was then delivered again by the Deputy Executive Secretary of the Economic Commission for Latin America in Santiago, Chile on Feb. 3, 1964. History of ICSID, at 301. It was then delivered again by the Executive Secretary of the Economic Commission for Europe, Mr. Velebit in Geneva on Feb. 17, 1964, History of ICSID, at 369, and it was delivered again by the Executive Secretary of the Economic Commission for Asia and the Far East in Bangkok, Mr. Nyun on July 20, 1964. History of ICSID, at 461.

[41] Paper prepared by the General Counsel and distributed to the members of the Committee of the Whole on Feb. 18, 1963, History of ICSID, at 73.

[42] Examples of statements of representatives include the following: "Mr. BIGAY (Central African Republic) said that his Government attached great importance to the matter under discussion since his country was one of those which needed foreign capital." History of ICSID, at 244. And "Mr. BROWN (Tanganyika) stressed that it was necessary to attract foreign investment without prejudice to national sovereignty. He was in favor of any measures calculated to make foreign investment more of a joint international concern and bring it more directly under international control." History of ICSID, at 246.

[43] For a discussion of the doctrine, see Santiago Montt, State Liability in Investment Treaty Arbitration: Global Constitutional and Administrative Law in the BIT Generation 38–45 (2009), at 38–45.

accept the delegation to international organizations of powers belonging to national institutions. Foreign investors in Argentina had sufficient guarantees so as to make recourse to other bodies unnecessary. No shadow of suspicion must be allowed to fall on those guarantees, as would be the case were the suggested agreement ratified. There were also legal difficulties. Agreeing with the opinion expressed by the Brazilian delegate, the speaker pointed out that an unjust discrimination would exist if some persons could be excepted from the principle of equality of all before the law. From the theoretical point of view, there were no firmly established precedents for the use of arbitration between an individual and a State. While it was true that the individual had found increasing recognition in international law, especially in the field of human rights, it would still be long before he could act legally on equal terms with other international persons.[44]

Europe was highly supportive. The Statement by the representative of the Federal Republic of Germany (GDR) is illustrative of Europe's general support:

Mr. KOINZER (Federal Republic of Germany) commended the Chairman and the staff of the Bank for their work and expressed satisfaction at being given an opportunity to exchange views with his European colleagues on the Bank's proposals. His Government had invariably stressed the value of private investment in the developing countries, a form of investment which constituted an excellent means of transferring know-how and experience to those countries. Accordingly, his Government had consistently striven to create incentives for such private investment, particularly in the form of guarantees given to investors. All those efforts, however, would be in vain unless they were supplemented by a corresponding effort on the part of the recipient countries to create a favorable investment climate. His Government had endeavored to achieve that result by means of bilateral agreements, but had nevertheless favored all the initiatives taken in that connection, in particular by OECD and the Council of Europe. From the outset, therefore, his Government had welcomed the Bank's initiative in the matter; the draft which had been prepared constituted an excellent basis of discussion. He welcomed the progressive idea of giving private persons the right to be directly parties to international conciliation and arbitration proceedings. That idea was consistent with a practice which had already developed in the international sphere. It was gratifying to see that conception receive

[44] Summary of Record of Proceedings, Consultative Meeting of Legal Experts, Santiago, Chile, Feb. 1964, History of ICSID at 307–8. Bolivia's position was similar to Argentina's: "Mr. ESCOBAR (Bolivia) said that the sovereignty of States could not be subordinated to the authority of an international institution without being seriously impaired. Sovereignty could not be alienated, for any consideration whatever, without undermining the State through the dispersion of its powers. He believed that those responsible for preparing the draft had failed to appreciate its adverse effects. Thus the Bank itself seemed to be displaying a lack of confidence in the institutions of the countries wishing to attract foreign capital; moreover, the existence of the draft Convention might have caused investors to defer action pending the Governments' decision on it. In view of those ill effects, he would prefer the Bank to abandon the project. Bolivia had an investment development law in force which recognized a series of rights, privileges and safeguards in respect of foreign capital invested in the country. Any problems that might arise must be settled by Bolivia's own courts, so as to preclude any unconstitutional discrimination against its own nationals. The Bank should suggest to governments the adoption of a specific and expeditious procedural system to settle disputes with foreign investors within the legal and administrative machinery of each country. He also observed that if the draft Convention were not unanimously rejected, foreign capital might blacklist the countries that did not wish to submit their disputes with investors to international adjudication." *Id.* at 308.

> the support of the Bank with its unique prestige. He attached great importance to the fact that the proposed Center would function under the auspices of the Bank.[45]

The group of nations classified under Asia and the Far East had diverse opinions. India, for example, was opposed to the fundamental ideas more or less along the same lines as many of the Latin American nations. The following passage exemplifies India's opposition at the time:

> Mr. ADARKAR (India) said his country wished to attract private capital and to maintain a favorable investment climate, and for that purpose it was prepared to give the foreign investor the necessary safeguards including additional rights. His criticism, however, had been directed to the fact that the proposals in their present form gave investors additional rights of unspecified scope. In order to make the Convention acceptable to the developing countries, an effort should be made to clarify the precise scope of the benefits it conferred on the foreign investor. While his country might have no objection to giving the foreign investor additional rights, he believed that such rights should be given by means of specific agreements or understandings, so that the additional rights would be the counterpart of certain additional obligations undertaken by the investor. Under the Convention as it stood the investor enjoyed certain benefits while—as he was himself not a party to the Convention—it placed no obligations upon him. He felt, however, that this criticism could be met by appropriate modification of the text despite the fact that the investor would not be a party to the Convention.[46]

China was indifferent.[47] New Zealand was unsure.[48] Japan was supportive.[49] Australia's position was nuanced.[50]

[45] Summary of Record of Proceedings, Consultative Meeting of Legal Experts, Geneva, Switzerland, Feb. 1964, History of ICISD, at 374. The opinion by the representative of France was more or less to the same effect. "Mr. RODOCANACHI (France) commended the Chairman for his illuminating address which had enabled participants to have a clearer understanding of the proposed machinery and of the principles involved. The French authorities supported the Bank in its efforts to obtain maximum support for a convention of the proposed type to deal with disputes between private investors and capital-importing States." *Id.* at 373.

[46] Summary of Record of Proceedings, Consultative Meeting of Legal Experts, Bangkok, Thailand, Switzerland, Apr.–May 1964, History of ICSID, at 476.

[47] China's participation was minimalistic and technical. The following is an example of the nature of its interventions: "Mr. TSAI (China) suggested that nationals of non-member States of the Bank should not be appointed either to the offices of Secretary-General and Deputy Secretary-General, or to the Panels. His government would be unwilling to submit disputes to arbitration before a tribunal whose membership would not be limited to nationals of Contracting States and consequently might include nationals of unfriendly nations." History of ICSID, at 484.

[48] "Mr. QUILL (New Zealand) said that borrowing by New Zealand had not been subject to any restriction as to the application of the borrowed funds and that New Zealand had rarely lent money. As a State it had therefore had no experience in investment disputes of the type contemplated in the draft Convention and could approach the proposals only from a theoretical standpoint." History of ICSID, at 467.

[49] "Mr. NEMOTO (Japan) said he recognized the important role of international investment in the field of economic development and favored in principle the establishment of a new international organization for the settlement of investment disputes such as that proposed in the draft Convention. He expressed his appreciation of the efforts made by the Bank toward inaugurating this scheme since 1961." History of ICSID, at 474.

[50] "Mr. O'DONOVAN (Australia) said it was not the practice in Australia to give any extensive undertakings to foreign investors who were generally treated in the same way, received the same benefits and were

By comparison, the full record shows that Africa and Europe were the most optimistic and understandably for opposite reasons: Africa to attract capital and Europe to protect it. Africa took the first step to bring the Convention into existence,[51] was the first to answer charges,[52] and continued to answer charges for 50 years and counting.[53] As of this writing, ICSID has administered 180 cases involving African states with 36 still pending.[54] To reaffirm what this author has said in another writing in 2014, which attracted all the commentary discussed above, "The historical record clearly indicates that the only reason that the African states accepted ICSID is because they thought that they had to do so in order to attract private foreign investment to develop their ailing post-colonial economies."[55]

Case Analysis Objectives and Framework

It is against the above-stated optimistic historical context that Akinkugbe conceptualizes African states' participation as "reverse contribution" and surveys some of the most important ICSID cases involving African parties and compiles a list of contributions ranging from jurisdiction to quantum of damages.[56] He does so chronologically by subdividing the cases into three generations: first-generation, from the 1970s to 1990s; second-generation, from 2000 to 2010; and third-generation, from 2010 to 2020.[57] The survey identifies and documents a list of "reverse contributions" ranging from the "clarification of concepts" to the definition of investment in *Salini v. Morocco*[58] to the "incorporation of new themes—sustainable

under the same obligations as local investors. While the government always permitted repatriation of capital it had undertaken no obligations to do so. In accordance with the government's obligations as a member of the International Monetary Fund, it also permitted repatriation of profits." History of ICSID, at 550.

[51] *See Database of ICSID Member States*, Convention *on the Settlement of Investment Disputes Between States and Nationals of Other States*, 17 U.S.T. 1270, 575 U.N.T.S. 159 (Oct. 14, 1966) (containing ICSID ratification status and dates of various States).

[52] The first ICSID case was Holiday Inns S.A. & Others v. Morocco, ICSID Case No. ARB/72/1 (1972).

[53] *See The ICSID Caseload—Statistics*, ICSID (2020), p. 12, https://icsid.worldbank.org/sites/default/files/publications/Caseload%20Statistics/en/The%20ICSID%20Caseload%20Statistics%20%282020-1%20Edition%29%20ENG.pdf (displaying the geographic distribution of all ICSID cases as follows: Sub-Saharan Africa 15%, Middle East and North Africa 11%, Western Europe 8%). Incidentally, the breakdown for arbitrators is: Western Europe 47%, North America 21%, and Sub-Saharan Africa 2%. These statistics have not changed in any significant ways over the decades. *See id.* at 17. In 1963, 16 of the World Bank's 61 legal experts convened to deliberate the ICSID Convention were African legal experts. *See* Parra, *The Participation of African States in The Making of the ICISD Convention*, at 275. Where have they subsequently gone? Evidently, T. O. Elias later became ICJ president, but what explains the lack of African arbitrators? This issue has gotten more attention in the literature than any issue in the area of IIL, but the percentage still remains stubbornly low.

[54] A list of all concluded ICSID cases (as of Jan. 2023) is available at https://icsid.worldbank.org/cases/concluded. A list of all pending cases is available at https://icsid.worldbank.org/cases/pending.

[55] Kidane, *The China–Africa Factor in the ICSID Legitimacy Debate. But see* Brower & Daly, *A Study of Foreign Investment Law in Africa: Opportunity Awaits*, at 507.

[56] *See* Akinkugbe, *Reverse Contributions? African State Parties, ICSID and the Development of International Investment Law* (citing History of ICSID, at 244), at 441–54.

[57] *Id.*

[58] *Id.* at 445–46. Salini Construttori S.p.A and Italstrade S.p.A v. Kingdom of Morocco, ICSID Case No. ARB/00/4, Decision on Jurisdiction (July 23, 2001).

development, human rights, protection of indigenous rights and environmental standards."[59]

This survey is useful since it "reclaims" Africa's contributions by identifying principles and rules that have emerged out of these African cases. Broadening the inquiry significantly but using the same dataset of African ICSID cases, the following part takes a different approach and provides a detailed appraisal of the manifestation and development of the most important jurisdictional and substantive norms of international investment law (IIL) in these African cases. The objective is not limited to identifying the concepts and principles very emergence in one case or their use in the other but to closely appraise the reasons for their emergence, their subsequent use, and the direction that they have subsequently taken, which necessarily invites comparative analysis. Fundamentally, the analysis is designed to test whether the basic premise of Africa's "optimistic" embrace of IIL and ICSID in the 1960s was vindicated or frustrated. In particular, the critical appraisal aims at digging deeper into the metaphysics of African IIL borrowing Gary Peller's formulation in his famous article the "Metaphysics of American Law."[60] His working assumption is eloquently described in the first paragraph of this article as:

> "It is a commonplace that law is political." Ever since the realists debunked "formalism" in legal reasoning, the received learning has been that legal analysis cannot be neutral and determinate, that general propositions of law cannot decide particular cases. Some policy judgment or value choice necessarily intervenes. It is "transcendental nonsense" to believe that it could be any other way.[61]

By tracing the development of these legal norms and their application in these African cases, the following chapters also attempt to understand their metaphysics by looking into their essence and relationship with the global development and application of the same concepts and principles without losing sight of what Peller describes as "a common rejoinder to critical attacks on legal thought that, whatever the imperfections of legal analysis, a commitment to the rule of law is preferable to rule by will or passion, associated with, for example, the fascism of the Nazi regime or the lynch mobs of the American South. The purported rationality of legal discourse distinguishes it from these 'irrational' kinds of social force."[62]

Focusing on the nature and quality of the rule of law that these cases are supposed to be an integral part of, the analysis looks at each opinion of the selected cases[63] for (1) the identification and definition of the applicable rule of law, including the reasoning for the selection of the rule and definition of its scope in each individual case; (2) the epistemology of fact finding and the rationality thereof; and (3), the persuasiveness of the application of the rules to the facts, including the exercise of discretion.

[59] Akinkugbe, *Reverse Contributions? African State Parties, ICSID and the Development of International Investment Law* (citing History of ICSID, at 244), at 454.

[60] Gary Peller, *The Metaphysics of American Law*, 73 Calif. L. Rev. 1151 (1985).

[61] *Id.* at 1151 (referring to Flex Cohen's famous article *Transcendental Nonsense and a Functional Approach*, 35 Columbia L. Rev. 809 (1935)).

[62] *Id.* at 1155.

[63] The selection criteria is described in Part II.

The analysis then traces the definition and use of the rules and principles across the cases and evaluates the uniformity of application, or the lack thereof. At the macro level, these findings are then used to comment on whether the World Bank's vision of the 1960s and the African acceptance of IIL has been a net gain in ordering Africa's international economic affairs vis-à-vis the other opportunities that it might have excluded, such as the development of robust domestic legal regimes. This detailed case analysis is intended to help inform future directions that are discussed in context in Part III.

Linked to the concerns identified by Working Group III in the section above, the review also aims to (1) evaluate whether the concerns may or may not have affected each case in any notable way; (2) identify if there are any patterns of any type, and, if so, determine if there is any reason to believe that they are more common among the African cases and possibly answer the question why; (3) provide general commentary of the quality of justice in each case for historical record; and finally, (4) summarize the overall contributions that the African cases have made in the development of international investment law and identify the lessons that could be learned from these cases for the future development of international investment law generally and for African international investment law regimes in particular.

PART II
THE ANATOMY OF AFRICA'S ICSID CASES
The Development of Procedural and Substantive Norms

There are now about 144 completed African ICSID cases. Among the total 180 cases indicated above, 144 have been concluded and 36 are currently pending. The 144 cases that have been concluded were concluded with a combination of discontinuance, settlement, and rejection at the preliminary stage for lack of jurisdiction and the issuance of a final award. Of those cases that ended with a final award, 30 cases have a final award published in English. The cases that are covered in this study are the cases that ended with a final award, many of which combine decisions on jurisdiction and merits.

These cases are used to evaluate the development of Africa's international investment procedural and substantive norms chronologically beginning with the first group of cases in the 1980s and ending with the 2022 award in *Bay View Group v. Rwanda*, a case arising under the United States–Rwanda Bilateral Investment Treaty of 2004.

The development of the procedural norms is evaluated under five broad headings largely corresponding to the topics of reform discussions under the auspices of the UNCITRAL Working Group III (WGIII).

The analysis in each of the procedural and substantive chapters proceedings in chronological order classified into three eras: the initial decades during which some of the most important foundational principles were pronounced, the 2000s during which ISDS activity gained momentum, and the post-2010 era during which ISDS faced considerable backlash and showed some measure of resilience and even rebound. The analysis in each chapter follows the methodology and framework set forth under Chapter 3 and seeks to methodically understand what lies behind the superficial statistics and expressions of concerns about the decision-making process and the use or misuse of substantive principles and evaluates how the existing understating is informing or misinforming Africa's and global reform efforts.

4
Procedural History and the Evolution of the African State's Participation in Investment Arbitral Proceedings

A close reading of the procedural history of the African ICSID cases suggests that in the initial decades, which were closer in time to the postcolonial formation of many of the African states, the participation of the newly independent states in international arbitral proceedings was either totally absent, incomplete, delayed, or at best hesitant. In many of the older cases, the lack of timely, proper, and determined participation through competent counsel may have adversely affected the outcomes of many of the cases.

No matter its original merits, the dominant narrative in Africa that ISDS was an imposition on the newly independent African nations as a condition of investment, loans, and even foreign aid is progressively losing its importance as the African states continue to play by the rules and contribute to the refinement and innovation of the rules and the institutions through their active and vigorous participation as demonstrated in more recent decades.

The corpus of the published African cases spanning half a century tell a story of a continent that struggled to overcome the vestiges of colonialism and viewed foreign decision-making of all types with suspicion for good reason. Through time of independent existence and the gradual and difficult process of state building, they came to terms with the rules of the world order including its hierarchy, found their place within the modern global economic structure, and slowly began to lead in reform efforts.

The turbulent and long journey traversed by African states begins with the 1970s *Libyan Oil* cases, in which the African state lost all three cases without participation, and ends with the 2022 case of *Bay View Group LLP v. Rwanda*, in which all Western arbitrators handed a complete and resounding victory to Rwanda against investors from the United States in a case arbitrated under the 2004 US BIT Model and the ICSID Convention.[1] It tells a story of extraordinary resilience.

The Initial Decades (1970–2000)

Africa's international arbitral exposure did not begin with the ICSID cases. It began in earnest with the *Libyan Oil* cases of the 1970s that came to be regarded as

[1] These cases are discussed throughout this part and the next under both procedure and substance subtopics.

Africa's International Investment Law Regimes. Won L. Kidane, Oxford University Press. © Oxford University Press 2023.
DOI: 10.1093/oso/9780197745571.003.0004

the foundation cases[2] of the modern era.[3] In none of the foundation cases did the Respondent state participate.[4] The lack of participation no doubt contributed to the adverse nature and scale of the awards against the Respondent State. A typical passage is contained in the earliest Libyan Oil case. It reads: "No reply having been received by the Claimant, it addressed a letter of reminder to the Respondent on 11 February 1972. By a further letter dated 13 March 1972, the Claimant drew the attention of the Respondent to the fact that the period of 90 days for the nomination of it's arbitrator, stipulated in paragraph 3 of the said Clause 28, had expired and informed the Respondent of the Claimant's intention to request the President of the International Court of Justice to appoint a sole arbitrator."[5]

In *Texaco v. Libya*, the Tribunal even ordered *restitutio in integrum* because the Respondent state did not say anything about why restitution in kind would be impossible.[6] Having not heard from the State, the Tribunal could infer no particular difficulty in performing a contractual obligation that it presumably assumed voluntarily. There is almost no doubt that under the then existing political circumstances, the Respondent State, properly represented, could have presented evidence of difficulty, if not impossibility, to avoid the order of restitution in kind at that time. Indeed, it is

[2] *See* Yves Dezalay & Bryant G. Garth, Dealing In Virtue: International Commercial Arbitration And The Construction Of A Transnational Legal Order 64 (1996), at 64–65.

[3] These cases are: British Petroleum Exploration Co. (Libya) v. Libyan Arab Republic, 53 Int'l L. Rep. 297 (1973); Texaco Overseas Petroleum Co. and California Asiatic Oil Co. v. Libya, Preliminary Award (Nov. 27, 1975), 53 ILR 389; Award on the Merits (Jan. 19, 1977), 17 ILM 1 (1978).

[4] *See* Julien Cantegreil, *The Audacity of the Texaco/Calasiatic Award: René-Jean Dupuy and the Internationalization of Foreign Investment Law*, 22–2 European J. of Int'l Law 441, 452 (2011) ("As was the case in all the Libyan cases, the government refused to have the dispute settled by arbitration, as suggested by the companies in accordance with Clause 28 of the Deeds of Concession and as would happen in 1982 in the Aminoil case. As a consequence, Libya did not appoint any arbitrator, and the two companies used the arbitration clause to have the President of the International Court of Justice appoint a single arbitrator").

[5] BP Exploration Co. (Libya) Ltd. v. Libya, British Petroleum Exploration Co. (Libya) v. Libyan Arab Republic, 53 Int'l L. Rep. 297 (1973), at ¶ 3–5:

"4. On 15 March 1972, the Claimant applied to the President of the International Court of Justice for the appointment of a sole arbitrator pursuant to the provisions of paragraph 3 of the aforesaid Clause 28. Citing the BP Nationalisation Law, the Claimant stated that this premature repudiation of the Agreement, 40 years before the expiry of its term, is a fundamental breach of the Concession occasioning a claim by the Company for reparation, and giving rise to a dispute within the meaning of Clause 28.
5. The President of the International Court of Justice, Sir Muhammad Zafrullah Khan, on 28 April 1972 appointed Judge Gunnar Lagergren, President of the Court of Appeal for Western Sweden, Sole Arbitrator to hear and determine the dispute. He is qualified under paragraph 5 of Clause 28 to receive such appointment. Thus the Tribunal was duly constituted."

[6] Texaco Overseas Petroleum Company and California Asiatic Oil Company v. Libya, British Petroleum Exploration Co. (Libya) v. Libyan Arab Republic, 53 Int'l L. Rep. 297 (1973), at ¶ 112:

"In doing so, the Tribunal does not lose sight of the fact that the solution in principle which is "*restitutio in integrum* must be set aside when it is absolutely impossible to envisage performance in kind or when an irreversible situation has been created. Such does not appear, *until further information*, to be the case in this case: as far as this Court can judge, the performance of its obligations by the defendant seems to depend only on itself and it should, in all likelihood, be possible for the Libyan Government to take the necessary measures to restore the situation postulated by the application of legal principles. That if, for reasons which have not been brought to its attention, an irreversible situation beyond the control of the parties has been created, the Tribunal can only regret not having been informed of it. He must note that only the defendant would have been able to. These are the reasons, both general and specific, for which this Tribunal will invite the Libyan Government to perform its own obligations in kind."

precisely for that reason that the other two tribunals refrained from ordering restitution in kind as will be discussed later.

The first ICSID case in this study is *S.A.R.L v. Congo* (1980).[7] A commercial agreement between the parties contained an arbitration clause referring to the ICSID Convention. The Claimant submitted its request for arbitration to the Secretary General on December 15, 1977. The Secretary General registered the request the same day.[8] The Tribunal was duly constituted by June 5, 1978, with acceptance by the presiding arbitrator of his appointment by the Secretary General.[9] The Claimant submitted its Memorial on August 21, 1978, and the Respondent State submitted its countermemorial on October 20, 1978.[10]

The Tribunal characterized the latter submission as "it was in fact a denial of competence."[11] The Respondent asked for an extension of time to file a countermemorial on the merits but it was denied the extension. It sent it anyway by mail and such was received on January 4, 1979,[12] although it was due on December 29, 1978. The Tribunal characterized it as "in this document, the Government did no more than to rely upon the argument that the Tribunal lacked jurisdiction and to repeat the conclusions contained in its 'Counter-Memorial' of 20 October 1978."[13]

The Respondent missed another pleading deadline and its request for extension was denied because it was made after the submission deadline.[14] After the Tribunal fixed a date for an oral hearing, the Parties informed the Tribunal that they were attempting to settle the matter out of court. They concluded settlement agreements at least two times but the award notes that the Respondent repudiated it and the arbitral process continued. Yet again, the Respondent failed to participate in the hearing. The case was closed, and the award was issued without the Respondent's meaningful participation.[15]

As will be seen later, this is a recurring problem particularly in the early days. Note here that one of the reasons that the Respondent adduced for its lack of meeting deadlines and generally orderly conduct is change in political circumstances in the country.[16] This was not a very uncommon situation for many of the African states that had just recently won their political independence and were setting up the structure of government.

In *Klockner v. Cameroon* (1983), the request for arbitration was initially filed on April 14, 1981, and each party appointed their respective arbitrator and the tribunal

[7] S.A.R.L. Benvenuti & Bonfant v. People's Republic of Congo, ICSID Case No. ARB/77/2 (1980), 1 ICSID Rep. 330 (1993).
[8] *Id.* at ¶ 1.1.
[9] *Id.* at ¶ 1.3.
[10] *Id.* at ¶ 1.7
[11] *Id.*
[12] *Id.* at ¶ 1.9.
[13] *Id.* at ¶ 1.10.
[14] *Id.* at ¶ 1.20.
[15] *Id.* at ¶ 1.21–1.35.
[16] *See id.* at ¶ 1.29 ("The Government mentioned in telexes dated 29 and 30 October 1979 that it was in possession of certain documents relating to the case which could be remitted to the Tribunal if it was given the opportunity and that, unfortunately, the political changes which had taken place throughout the proceedings had prevented the Government from presenting to the Tribunal all the available documentation relating to the case within the time limits which had been fixed").

issued its final award in a little more than two years on October 21, 1983.[17] This case is significant for its annulment decision by Pierre Lalive in a decision issued on February 16, 1984, not to mention the fact that it was the very first ICSID annulment case. The Tribunal's award was largely favorable to Cameroon, but the Ad Hoc Annulment Committee annulled the award,[18] depriving any wins to Africa during this period. The annulment is discussed throughout various sections in great detail.

Letco v. Liberia (1986)[19] offers another example of the consequences of the State's lack of participation in the proceedings. Although Liberia had initially participated in the proceedings by appointing an arbitrator and even instructing Jan Paulsson, who was then in the Paris office of Coudert Brothers, to represent it, it failed to appear and defend itself before the Tribunal.[20] What is remarkable and indicative of the adverse consequences of lack of participation in this case is the Tribunal's finding of an outcome determinative fact on the basis of unchallenged testimony provided by the General Manager of the Claimant who testified that the land in dispute was taken from the investor, letco, and was given to "good friends" of the Liberian authorities.[21]

Although Liberia did not participate in the proceedings, government records submitted to the Tribunal indicated that the state took the land because the concessioner failed to perform its duties. The State did not pursue this line of argumentation and failed to adduce evidence to contradict the General Manager's claim that the land was taken for discriminatory or improper purposes and not as a result of the Claimant's failures to perform. This case offers another excellent example of lack of proper prosecution of the case as one of the main reasons why many of these cases were lost by the African states during the early days.

Another loss was added to the African arbitral scorecard in January 1988 when another ICISD Tribunal found Guinea liable for breach of contract under its own French inherited law in *Maritime International Nominees Establishment (MINE) v. Republic of Guinea* (1988).[22] This case is most notable for the procedural complications that predated this particular ICSID arbitration. At its core, it is a simple breach of contract

[17] Klockner Industrie-Anlagen GmbH and others v. United Republic of Cameroon and Société Camerounaise des Engrais, ICSID Case No. ARB/81/2 (1983).

[18] Decision Rendered by Ad Hoc Committee on the Application for Annulment Against the Arbitral Award in Klockner v. Cameroon, ARB/81/2 (Oct. 21, 1983), https://www.italaw.com/sites/default/files/case-documents/italaw11161.pdf. The Tribunal decided "Klockner is entitled to what it has already received, but to nothing more." *Id.* at ¶ 173. "The Arbitral Award rendered on October 21, 1983 by the Arbitral Tribunal constituted by ICSID in Case ARB/81/2 is annulled." *Id.* at 125.

[19] Liberian Eastern Timber Corporation v. Republic of Liberia, ICSID Cases No. ARB/83/2, Award (March 31, 1986).

[20] *See id.* ¶ 4–5.

[21] *See id.* at ¶ 71 ("None of these conditions is satisfied in the present case. There was no legislative enactment by the Government of Liberia. There was no evidence of any stated policy on the part of the Liberian Government to take concessions of this kind into public ownership for the public good. On the contrary, evidence was given to the Tribunal that areas of the concession taken away from Letco were granted to other foreign-owned companies: according to Mr. Alain de Marti, who was Letco's general manager in Liberia for the entire period of the concession, these foreign companies were run by people who were "good friends" of the Liberian authorities. . . . Finally, no offer of compensation has been made to Letco for the loss of its concession; to the extent that the Liberian Government has attempted any justification of its action, it has been on the basis of alleged breaches of the Concession Agreement by Letco").

[22] Maritime International Nominees Establishment v. Republic of Guinea, ICSID Case No. ARB/84/4, Award (Jan. 6, 1988).

case. Connected to its complex Bauxite resources development and marketing endeavor, Guinea had reserved a right to participate in the carriage of these resources to their receivers in Western Europe and the United States.[23] MINE, a Swiss company, entered into a joint venture with Guinea to take advantage of these reserved shipment rights. As the Tribunal noted, due to a combination of miscalculations on the market potentials on both sides and a measure of mistrust between the Parties, the joint venture never took off the ground. For reasons that the Parties did not agree on, Guinea brought in a third party to carry out the same tasks, which caused MINE to initiate a number of legal proceedings including this ICSID arbitration.[24]

MINE initially sought conciliation under the legal instrument called the Convention in April 1974.[25] The dispute settlement agreement, that is, Article 18 of the Parties' agreement called the Convention, seemed to have anticipated the escalation of conciliation to ICSID arbitration, but there was a technical problem:

> Article 18 of the Convention provided that if conciliation failed, the dispute was to be settled through arbitration in which the tribunal was to be chosen by the President of ICSID. Arbitration by ICSID provides a forum in which governments like Guinea waive their immunity to suit for alleged breach of contract with private investors. The trouble with Art. 18 was that ICSID did not and does not accept disputes for arbitration where the arbitrators are to be named in the manner stated.[26]

For this reason, in January 1975, the Parties voluntarily entered into a submission agreement correcting the initial error.[27] In January 1978, disregarding this agreement, MINE filed a lawsuit in the US District Court for the District of Columbia to compel Guinea to arbitrate before the American Arbitration Association (AAA) on the ground that Guinea reneged on its ICSID arbitration consent, although MINE never initiated an ICSID arbitration.[28] Interestingly, the District Court compelled arbitration, the AAA quickly set up a panel and within a year such panel rendered an award of $27 million in favor of MINE.[29] Although MINE attempted to enforce the award, the US Court of Appeals for the District of Columbia, however, stayed enforcement and reversed on grounds of lack of subject matter jurisdiction under the United State Foreign Sovereign Immunities Act (FSIA).[30] The Court of Appeals also ruled

[23] *Id.* at ¶ 5 ("While the Bauxite Receivers were quite capable of making all of their own transportation arrangements, only 50% of the CBG bauxite was theirs to transport. Art. 9 of the Harvey Agreement allocated to Guinea the right to have 50% of the cgb bauxite carried by ships flying the Guinean flag, or by other 'assimilated vessels,' or by ships chartered by Guinea itself in the international charter market, as long as the freight rates for Guinea's share were at or below rates obtainable in the international market for chartering vessels (the 'Art. 9 freight'). From this freight, Guinea intended to pay for creating its own merchant marine: vessels, officers, seamen, management and infrastructure").

[24] *See id.* at ¶ 1–12.

[25] *Id.* at ¶ 28–29.

[26] *Id.* at ¶ 29.

[27] *Id.* at ¶ 30.

[28] *Id.* at ¶ 30–31 ("MINE requested Guinea to execute a revised Consent to Arbitrate on September 2, 1975, but Guinea never responded").

[29] *Id.* at ¶ 31–32.

[30] *See id.* at ¶ 34.

that ICSID Arbitration was the exclusive forum under the Parties agreement. The US Supreme Court denied cert.[31]

In May 1984, following its court losses, MINE initiated this ICSID proceeding, which continued with the participation of both Parties.[32] That was not the end of the procedural maneuver. About a year after the ICSID proceedings commenced, in June 1985, Guinea submitted to the ICSID Tribunal what it titled "Emergency Request for Relief from Attachment of Its Assets by MINE" in Europe to enforce the AAA award,[33] which the Tribunal entertained.[34]

In this sense, Guinea went through what could be considered the full spectrum of dispute settlement processes with two full arbitrations and multiple judicial proceedings in Europe and the United States for a simple breach of contract claim. As indicated in the determination of facts chapter (Chapter 9), the contract never took off the ground mainly because of market conditions that both parties miscalculated. Guinea derived no benefits whatsoever from the termination and its only fault was its inability to show that its contractual partner was equally responsible for the failure of the project and that it was not able to remediate the problem. There is no indication in the awards that Guinea had any other motives in reassigning the contract to a third party (which was the source of the problem) other than getting the subject matter of the shipment contract working. This is a good example of how small errors at the level of contract formation and selection of economic partners and mismanagement of contracts could drag a nation through legal processes across continents.[35]

Southern Pacific Properties (SPP) v. Egypt (1992)[36] concerned a change of development site near the Pyramids that the investor believed breached contract and violated law.[37] The case was initiated by SPP, a Hong Kong company, on August 24, 1984, based on consent to arbitrate expressed in domestic law[38] and the tribunal was fully constituted by December 18, 1884, with the Respondent states active participation.[39] Although the Claimant asked for a sole arbitrator, in this case not only did the state appoint its arbitrator first (an Egyptian national to which the Claimant did not object

[31] *Id.*

[32] *Id.* at ¶ 35–36.

[33] *Id.* at ¶ 37–38.

[34] *Id.* at ¶ 40–41 ("40. On December 4, 1985, the Tribunal issued its Provisional Measure, ruling that MINE's litigation to enforce the AAA award in European courts constituted an 'other remedy' under Art. 26 of the ICSID Convention; that the litigation breached MINE's submission of its dispute with Guinea to ICSID for arbitration: and that at the September 3, 1985, hearing conducted to receive evidence on this issue, Guinea had demonstrated that the breach had harmed it and would continue to harm it").

[35] As the Tribunal notes, "in hindsight, the Convention failed because both parties had inflated expectations of what could be accomplished with Guinea's Art. 9 freight rights." *Id.* at ¶ 48.

[36] Southern Pacific Properties (Middle East) Limited v. Arab Republic of Egypt, ICSID Case No. ARB/84/3, Award (May 20, 1992).

[37] *See id.* at ¶ 88 ("The Respondent argues that this alteration of the agreed location of the project violated the Heads of Agreement and encroached upon an area protected by both Egyptian law and international law. According to the Respondent, the violation of the Heads of Agreement in respect of the sites was part of a larger design to transform the project into a 'housing and urban development project' and entailed the violation of other imperative laws of the are concerning the protection of antiquities, urban development and the right of foreigners to own land in Egypt").

[38] *See id.* at ¶ 3.

[39] *See id.* at ¶ 7.

although it could have under the applicable rules) but also recommended the chair, which the Claimant accepted.[40]

The Tribunal considered Egypt's jurisdictional objections first and that phase took until April 14, 1988, partly because the Tribunal had to wait for a decision from the French Court of Cassation on a related matter and conducted at least two hearings on jurisdiction.[41] Having rejected the Respondent's jurisdictional objections in its entirety after nearly four years, the Tribunal received the parties written pleadings between December 5, 1988, and February 22, 1990;[42] held the evidentiary hearing in Paris between September 3 and 11, 1990;[43] and continued to receive more comments and submissions until it closed the proceedings on February 17, 1992.[44] The posthearing submissions were unusually numerous. Although some of the submissions were not even authorized, the Tribunal nonetheless considered them.[45]

Both Parties were represented from the very beginning and indeed, the Respondent state responded to the Request for Arbitration within less than three months by November 12, 1984.[46] In many of the above-discussed cases, in the early days, there had been a lack of representation, delayed representation and delayed or absence of participation. Egypt seems to have had a record of proper participation even in the earlier cases. The significance of this case is its exposition of the expropriation standard, and that aspect of it is explored further in Chapter 9. In any case, this was yet another case that the African state lost even with proper participation.

The initial decades were periods of disorientation, misunderstanding, and suspicion. Most of the African states did not participate in the proceedings, and needless to say, they lost almost all of the cases including through default procedures. The attempted boycott did not make the cases go away and as a matter of fact, the African states faced more cases in the decades that followed.

The African Cases of the 2000s

The African states faced considerably more cases in the 2000s. The bilateral investment treaties concluded in the past decades had become an integral part of the ordering of economic affairs in the African states, and this period also saw the transition from contract-based to treaty-based ISDS cases. Indeed, most of the influential African ICSID cases, including *Salini*, were rendered during this period. The decade began with *Wena v. Egypt* (2000).[47]

[40] *Id.*
[41] *See id.* at ¶ 8–24.
[42] *See id.* at ¶ 25–28.
[43] *See id.* at ¶ 31.
[44] *See id.* at ¶ 31–41.
[45] *See id.* at ¶ 31–40 ("40. On July 9, 1991, the Claimants filed a response to the Respondent's comments of June 26,1991, and on September 18,1991, the Respondent filed a response to the Claimants' response. Although this final exchange of communications had not been requested by the Tribunal, the materials submitted by the Parties were nevertheless considered by the Tribunal").
[46] *See id.* at ¶ 5.
[47] Wena Hotels Limited v. Arab Republic of Egypt, ICSID Case No. ARB/98/4, Award (Dec. 8, 2000).

Unlike the earlier cases discussed above, in *Wena* the consent to arbitrate came not from a contract but a Bilateral Investment Treaty (BIT) between the United Kingdom and Egypt.[48] The procedural history is straightforward. The investor, Wena, filed a request for arbitration with the Secretary General of ICSID based on the BIT and the tribunal was constituted forthwith. It entertained jurisdictional objections, ruled on its own competence, received all the appropriate pleadings including memorials, conducted an oral hearing during which witnesses were heard under cross-examination, received posthearing brief, closed the evidentiary record, and rendered its award.[49] This is one of the first cases that proceeded in a way that a typical modern arbitration is expected to proceed with both parties represented. However, Egypt lost.[50]

In *Middle East Cement v. Egypt* (2002),[51] the consent to arbitrate also came from the BIT between Greece and Egypt.[52] The case proceeded with the Respondent state's participation but not without some difficulties, especially during the initial jurisdictional phase, reminiscent of the way that some of the earlier African cases had been handled by the host states.

The Tribunal was duly constituted according to the agreement of the parties and it ruled on its own jurisdiction, however, prior to such ruling, two notable Respondent state delays occurred. First, the Respondent wrote a letter asking for postponement of a procedural meeting just three days before it was supposed to happen. The Tribunal refused and counsel for the Respondent appeared by telephone from Cairo.[53] Second, the Respondent was also not represented at the hearing on jurisdiction in Paris because of visa and related travel issues, the validity of which the Tribunal did not accept.[54] Subsequently, however, the Respondent appointed counsel and fully participated in the proceedings by submitting all the required memorials and appearing for the oral hearing.[55] Two years after *Wena*, despite its participation, Egypt lost again.[56]

Semos v. Mali (2003)[57] was a contract-based arbitration involving no investment treaty claims. It is an investor–state arbitration only inasmuch as it was an

48 *Id.* at ¶ 1.

49 *Id.* at ¶ 2–15.

50 *See id.* at ¶ 88 ("Even if the Tribunal were to accept this explanation for Egypt's failure to act before the seizures, it does not justify the fact that neither the police nor the Ministry of Tourism took any immediate action to protect Wena's investments after EHC had illegally seized the hotels").

51 Middle East Cement Shipping and Handling Co. S.A. v. Arab Republic of Egypt, ICSID Case No. ARB/99/6, Award (Apr. 12, 2002).

52 *Id.* at ¶ 5 ("The request for arbitration was submitted in regard to a dispute concerning Egypt's alleged expropriation of Middle East Cement's interests in a business concession located in Egypt and Egypt's alleged failure to ensure the re-exportation of Middle East Cement's assets. The request invokes the dispute settlement provisions of the 1993 Agreement for the Promotion and Reciprocal Protection of Investments between Greece and Egypt (the BIT)").

53 *See id.* at ¶ 1416. But these types of issues were avoided for the rest of the proceedings.

54 The Respondent's complaint, the Claimant's response, and the Tribunal's decision to proceed without the Respondent's presence in the Paris meeting is captured well in *id.* ¶ 39–42. "The Hearing on Jurisdiction started on Wednesday 12 July 2000 at the announced time and place, i.e., the offices of the World Bank in Paris. The Claimant was represented in person by its three representatives. The Respondent was not represented." *Id.* at ¶ 44.

55 *See id.* at ¶ 53–62.

56 *See id.* at ¶ 178.

57 Société D'exploitation Des Mines D'or De Sadiola S.A. (Semos) v. Republic of Mali, ICSID Case No. ARB/01/5, Award (Feb. 25, 2003).

ICSID arbitration by party consent. The constitution of the Tribunal was seamless with each side appointing its own arbitrator and the two mutually selecting the chair.[58] The Tribunal set its timetable with the representation of both parties. The Parties submitted their memorials on time for each round and participated in oral hearing in Paris as agreed in the arbitration clause of the mining contract (which the parties called the Mining Convention), and the Tribunal proceeded to make its award on the basis of the law that the parties have designated.[59] In terms of procedure, this case was as uneventful as any ISDS case could get with only one postponement asked by the Respondent state and granted by the Tribunal.[60] But again, Mali lost.[61]

CDC v. Seychelles (2003)[62] decided at the end of the same year as *Semos v. Mali* also had a smooth procedural transition with both parties represented and agreeing on the appointment by ICSID of a sole arbitrator under the Parties' loan agreement.[63] The matter proceeded very swiftly with the following unusually expediated timetable:

> 16. It was agreed that CDC's request for arbitration be treated as its Memorial on the merits. The parties agreed on the following timetable:
>   (i) the Republic to file its Counter-Memorial on the merits and any objections to the jurisdiction of the Tribunal by Monday, March 24, 2003.
>   (ii) CDC to file a Reply by Thursday, April 17, 2003; and
>   (iii) the Republic to file a Rejoinder by Thursday, May 15, 2003.
>
> The parties agreed with the Sole Arbitrator's proposal that a hearing on the merits and jurisdiction be held in London on July 22–23, 2003.[64]

Although no procedural step has been skipped including an oral hearing during which witnesses were heard under cross-examination, this case was completed in less than two years. And again, the result favored the Claimant.[65]

Patrick Mitchell v. DRC (2004)[66] is one of few cases that went through the ICSID annulment procedure.[67] The consent to arbitrate came from the US–DRC BIT, which essentially expresses the contracting parties' consent in advance and admits the

[58] *See id.* at ¶ 8.

[59] *See id.* at ¶ 12–16. ("On the occasion of the preliminary hearing of 17 October 2001, the Tribunal decided that the claimant should submit its memorial by no later than 17 December 2001 and the respondent its memorial of reply by no later than February 17, 2002. In addition, it was decided that the claimant's rejoinder should be submitted by no later than 17 March 2002 and the respondent's rejoinder by no later than 17 April 2002. It will be noted that all the above-mentioned documents were submitted by the parties within the stipulated lime limits. The Tribunal further decided to hold a second hearing on 27 and 28 May 2002").

[60] *Id.* at ¶ 13.

[61] *See id.* at dispositif.

[62] CDC Group Plc v. Republic of The Seychelles, ICSID Case No. ARB/02/14 (Dec. 17, 2003).

[63] *See id.* ¶ 11–16.

[64] *Id.* at ¶ 16.

[65] *See id.* at dispositif.

[66] Patrick H. Mitchell v. Democratic Republic of the Congo, ICSID Case No. ARB/99/7, Award (Feb. 9, 2004).

[67] Patrick Mitchell v. DRC Award (Feb. 9, 2004); Annulment (Nov. 1, 2006).

claimant's submission of a claim as its expression of consent that could complete the consent requirement for purposes of ICSID arbitration.[68] Once seized of the matter, the Tribunal proceeded with the submission of the usual memorial, countermemorial, reply, and rejoinder, but it omitted oral hearings and decided the case on the pleadings alone.[69]

Otherwise, the memorials and countermemorials were submitted according to schedule with the exception that the Respondent asked for an extension after the initially scheduled date had passed, claiming that there were some changes in the Ministry of Justice,[70] which is a pattern observed in the older cases.

The Respondent raised the jurisdictional issue for the first time in its countermemorial.[71] And in fact, it turned out that the jurisdictional question was outcome determinative as it was the main ground for the Ad Hoc Committee's annulment of the award two years later in 2006.[72] Indeed, the annulment proceeding included an oral hearing conducted by some prominent members in the field.[73] The annulment decision was one of the very first victories for any African state.

The same year as the Patrick Mitchell annulment, another victory was added to the African states' arbitral scorecard. It happened in the strangest of all factual circumstances. This case was the famous *World Duty Free v. Kenya* (2006).[74] This case ended in ways that its commencement did not project because of the introduction of a new argument about the validity of the underlying contract out of which the dispute arose midway through the arbitration. The request for arbitration was received on July 7, 2000,[75] relying on an arbitration clause contained in an Investment Agreement (Article 9) signed in 1989, which states:

[68] See Patrick H. Mitchell v. Democratic Republic of the Congo, ICSID Case No. ARB/99/7, Award (Feb. 9, 2004), at ¶ 3 ("The Request refers to Article VII of the Bilateral Treaty concluded on August 3, 1984 between the Republic of Zaire and the United States of America concerning the Reciprocal Encouragement and Protection of Investments (hereinafter "BIT" or "Treaty"), which provides, in relevant part, under paragraph 4, as follows: '4. (a) The national or company concerned may consent in writing to submit the dispute to the Centre or the Additional Facility for settlement by conciliation or binding arbitration. (b) Once the national or company concerned has so consented, either party to the dispute may institute proceedings before the Centre or Additional Facility at any time after six months from the date upon which the dispute arose,. . . .'")

[69] *See, e.g.*, *id.* at ¶ 19.

[70] *See id.* at 11 ("The Respondent did not file its counter-memorial at the date initially fixed. On July 26, 2001, it requested the time limit to be extended citing a change at the head of the Ministry of justice. The President of the Tribunal acceded to this request and extended the time limit to September 10, 2001. Respondent's counter-memorial, dated September 3, 2001, was filed on September 17, 2001").

[71] *See id.* at ¶ 13.

[72] *See generally* Patrick Mitchell v. DRC Award (Feb. 9, 2004); Annulment (Nov. 1, 2006).

[73] *See id.* at ¶ 12 ("A hearing devoted to oral arguments of counsel to the parties was held in Paris on May 11, 2005, in which participated Mr. Emmanuel Gaillard assisted by Ms. Yas Banifatemi and Ms. Anna Crevon for the Claimant, and Mr. Tshibangu Kalala, Mr. Nicolas Angelet, and Mr. Joe Sepulchre for the Respondent. The hearing was conducted in French, as all the participants preferred to express themselves in that language; however, simultaneous interpretation into English was provided in accordance with item 7 of the Minutes of the first session. A transcript in French of the oral arguments was transmitted to the parties for any possible comments that they had in this respect to be submitted by June 20, 2005. The parties' comments concerned mostly questions of form and did not lead to further discussions").

[74] World Duty Free Company Limited v. Republic of Kenya, ICSID Case No. ARB/00/7, Award (Oct. 4, 2006).

[75] *Id.* at ¶ 5.

> 9. Arbitration: (1) The parties hereby consent to submit to the jurisdiction of the International Centre for Settlement of Investment Disputes, ("the Centre") all disputes arising out of this Agreement or relating to any investment made under it for settlement by arbitration pursuant to the Convention on the Settlement of Investment Disputes between States and Nationals of other States ("the Convention"). (2) It is hereby stipulated (a) that the Company is a national of the United Arab Emirates:(b) that the transaction to which this Agreement relates is an "investment" within the meaning of the Convention; (c) that any arbitral tribunal constituted pursuant to this Agreement shall apply English law; (d) that any arbitration proceeding pursuant to this Agreement shall be conducted in accordance with the Rules of Procedure for Arbitration Proceedings of the Centre in effect on the date on which the proceeding is instituted.[76]

It was thus not a treaty-based claim but an ordinary contract-based claim that became famous for bringing the issue of high level and grand bribery to light in a dispute resolution context. It was not until two years after the commencement of the claim that Kenya brought up the issue of illegality to avoid the Agreement altogether.[77] During the two years in between the initiation of the arbitration and the surfacing of the defense of illegality, the parties exchanged extensive pleadings and letters addressing many aspects of the claim and the Respondents defenses.[78]

Because both Parties were ably represented, the nature of the procedural steps were more on the side of excess of advocacy than the lack thereof that is often seen in cases when the Respondent state is not represented or is represented late.

A few procedural steps are notable in this case. The first one is just the sheer number of correspondences between the Parties and the Tribunal over an extended period addressing a wide variety of matters ranging from request of extensions to offering of new information and evidence.[79] The second notable procedural step is the Respondent's request for a provisional measure on confidentiality on January 29, 2001, more than two years before the Respondent state decided to use the defense of illegality on March 19, 2003.[80] It could be speculated that the Respondent state initially thought that the issue of bribery might be a source of embarrassment although eventually it turned out be its principal defense. The final notable procedural occurrence is the resignation of an arbitrator because of conflict, Professor James Crawford,[81] and an unsuccessful challenge by the Claimant of the Respondent's replacement appointee, Mr. V. V. Veeder.[82]

Otherwise, the Respondent state participated in the proceedings with its initial appointee resigned and its second successfully challenged and most ably represented by some of the most renowned lawyers in the field associated at the time with

[76] *Id.* at ¶ 6.
[77] *Id.* at ¶ 105.
[78] *See id.* at ¶ 3–61.
[79] *See id.* at ¶ 7.
[80] *Id.* at ¶ 12.
[81] *Id.* at ¶ 10. This was because of Professor Crawford's relationship with the law firm that was representing the Respondent, i.e., Freshfields Bruckhaus Deringer.
[82] *Id.* at ¶¶ 12, 15.

Freshfields Bruckhaus Deringer.[83] The procedural intensity and final result may partially be explained by the nature and quality of the representation that the Respondent garnered.

Champion Trading v. Egypt (2006)[84] was initially commenced by multiple corporate and individual claimants against the Egyptian state under the 1992 US–Egypt BIT,[85] but the parties that remained throughout the process were only two Delaware corporations because the Tribunal decided that it lacked jurisdiction over the individual claimants.[86]

The Tribunal bifurcated the proceedings between the jurisdictional phase and the merits phase and conducted full briefing and an oral hearing on jurisdiction before it advanced to the merits between the remaining parties because it dismissed the individual claimants for lack of jurisdiction.[87]

The Tribunal was constituted through party appointment and ICSID designation of the chair. With the jurisdictional phase taking less than a year between May 29, 2002, and October 21, 2003,[88] the merits hearing proceeded with both parties represented although the corporate entities that remained as Claimants changed counsel after the individual claimants were dismissed by the Tribunal for lack of jurisdiction.[89] The process unfolded in an unusual way with a hearing of witnesses before document production and memorials,[90] and another hearing following the submission of all pleadings including a memorial by the Claimant, a countermemorial, a Reply and a Rejoinder in that order.[91]

Significantly, the presentation of witnesses prior to document production and filing of memorials was requested by the Tribunal apparently for its own understanding of the complex cotton industry in Egypt.[92] Although the witnesses seem to

[83] *See id.* at ¶ 1 (listing Kenya's representatives to include: Mr. Jan Paulsson, Mr. Constantine Partasides and Mr. Mitesh Kotecha).

[84] Champion Trading Company Ameritrade International, Inc. v. Arab Republic of Egypt, ICSID Case No. ARB/02/9, Award (Oct. 27, 2006).

[85] *See id.* at ¶ 1 ("On May 29, 2002, the shareholders of National Cotton Company ('NCC')—Champion Trading Company, a Delaware (USA) incorporated company, Ameritrade International, Inc., another Delaware (USA) incorporated company, together with James T. Wahba, John B. Wahba and Timothy T. Wahba—submitted to the International Centre for Settlement of Investment Disputes ('ICSID' or 'the Centre') a Request for Arbitration directed against the Arab Republic of Egypt").

[86] *Id.* at ¶ 12 ("On October 21, 2003, the Arbitral Tribunal issued its Decision on Jurisdiction. The Arbitral Tribunal declared that it did have jurisdiction over the claims of the corporate Claimants—Champion Trading Company and Ameritrade International, Inc.—but did not have jurisdiction over the individual Claimants—James B. Wahba, John T. Wahba and Timothy T. Wahba. This Decision is annexed to this Award and constitutes a part thereof").

[87] *See id.* at ¶ 1–12.

[88] *See id.* at ¶¶ 1, 12.

[89] *See id.* at ¶ 13 ("On October 27, 2003, the Centre was informed that the corporate Claimants had appointed new counsel, the law firm Jones Day. On March 16, 2004, Jones Day informed the Centre that Mr. Peter E. Kirby and Ms. Ren Cadieux of the law firm Fasken Martineau DuMoulin LLP would act as co-counsel in the proceeding. Subsequently, as of September 1, 2004, Jones Day no longer acted as co-counsel for the Claimants and Prof. Todd Weiler became co-counsel").

[90] *See id.* at ¶15–16.

[91] *See id.*

[92] *Id.* at ¶ 15–16 ("15 On June 7, 2004, the corporate Claimants submitted a motion for permission to conduct limited discovery and for the production of documents. On July 9, 2004, the Respondent submitted a response to the motion, and on August 9, 2004, the Claimants filed a reply to the response by the Respondent. By letter of August 16, 2004, the Parties were informed of the Arbitral Tribunal's instructions that the Respondent produce one or several witnesses in regard to questions concerning the Egyptian

have provided testimony about the regulation and evolution of the cotton industry in Egypt, it appears that they were considered fact witnesses rather than expert witnesses. The Tribunal's lengthy discussion of the cotton industry in the award is probably a function of the witnesses' contribution.[93]

It is clear from the award that the Tribunal was highly influenced by the detailed account of what went on in the cotton industry in Egypt. More importantly, it also appears that the Tribunal relied on the pre-memorial Tribunal-called witnesses for some of the most serious contentions. For example, in its award, the Tribunal relies on the transcript of the witness hearing for the following proposition: "The marketing expenses represent all the costs involved in every activity between the acquisition of raw cotton and the sale of ginned cotton. The company engaging in these activities gets paid for these production or transformation costs."[94] The citation to this is the transcript of the witness hearing.[95] The proposition is important because it led to the following finding:

> To conclude, regarding the 1997 Settlement, the documents presented to the Arbitral Tribunal evidence that the reason for the payments was to extinguish the debts recorded for the period before 1994. Therefore, since NCC was not incorporated at the time these debts were incurred, the Arbitral Tribunal finds that the payments of the 1997 Settlements were not discriminatory.[96]

This does not indicate that the Claimant might have been prejudiced as a result of the Tribunal called witnesses, but it is a curiosity invoking procedural step as it appears to have influenced the outcome. And indeed with at least three oral hearings, one on jurisdiction and two on the merits, and document production coming in between the two hearings, it seems like the whole process was more inclined toward the investigative legal tradition of incremental steps than the more common law inclination toward one final culminating event, which most other tribunals followed. This was Egypt's first[97] and Africa's third victory of the subset of cases under review.

The year 2008 saw the rendition of final awards in three major African cases. The first of the trilogy was *Helnan v. Egypt* (2008).[98] The Tribunal bifurcated the proceedings into the jurisdictional phase and the merits phase. Commenced on March 8, 2005, the Tribunal accepted submissions on jurisdiction, conducted an oral hearing, and ruled that it had jurisdiction a year and a half later, on October 17, 2006.[99] It drew

cotton sector. The Parties subsequently agreed on the hearing of two witnesses: Mr. Samir Anis, Executive Director for Internal Cotton Trade Committee and Secretary-General of Cotton and International Trade Holding Company, and Mr. Mahmoud Karem, Member of the Cabinet of the Ministry of Finance of the Arab Republic of Egypt. 16 The hearing of the two witnesses took place in Paris on December 13, 2004").

[93] *See id.* at ¶ 41–89.

[94] *Id.* at ¶ 141.

[95] *Id.* (citing in n.104 to Transcript of the Hearing held on December 13, 2004, p. 150–52).

[96] *Id.* at ¶ 143.

[97] *See id.* at ¶ 154–56 (rejecting the discrimination claim discussed in various chapters of this part). *See also* dispositif.

[98] Helnan International Hotels A/S v. The Arab Republic of Egypt, ICSID Case No. ARB/05/19, Award (July 3, 2008).

[99] *Id.* at ¶ 9–16.

its calendar with the participation of the parties, accepted submission of memorials and counter-countermemorials on the merits, held an evidentiary hearing in Paris over a one week period during which witnesses played a significant part, declared the proceedings closed on May 16, 2008,[100] and rendered its final award on the merits in less than two months on July 3, 2008.[101] With the exception of some minor delays here and there, the proceeding was fairly straightforward.

The one unusual procedural step in *Helnan* was the Claimant's request of the production of documents from a similar hotel management case that Egypt had faced in *Wena* discussed above. The Tribunal did indeed order the production of those documents under a confidentiality agreement, and the documents were in fact produced.[102]

In *Helnan*, as in *Wena*, the Respondent state was properly and timely represented and fully participated in the proceedings including by honoring the disclosure of documents from previous ICSID legal proceedings against it.[103] Unlike in *Wena*, Egypt prevailed in Helnan,[104] giving African states the fourth victory.

The second of the 2008 trilogy was the high-profile *Biwater Gauff Tanzania (BGT) v. Tanzania* (2008) case.[105] At 242 pages long, the *Biwater* award traverses just about every aspect of international investment law.

It all began with a $140 million dollar loan that Tanzania received from international financial institutions to rehabilitate Dar es Salaam's water supply and sanitation system with the condition that it hires a private operator.[106] To meet the conditions and through a bid process, it hired a UK–German joint venture, which was the investor that eventually brought a treaty claim under the UK–Tanzania BIT signed in 1994 and entered into force in 1996.[107]

Biwater submitted its request for arbitration to the ICSID Secretariat on August 5, 2005.[108] Unlike most of the cases discussed above where the African states either failed to participate, had delayed participation, or was not properly represented at all, Tanzania was properly represented from the very beginning.[109] In that sense, the African state did not suffer the imbalance of arms in this case.

Although the proceedings unfolded in predictable steps including document production,[110] requests for interim measures,[111] and an exchange of memorials,[112] this

[100] *Id.* at ¶ 9–49.
[101] *Id.*
[102] *Id.* at ¶ 27 ("THE ARBITRAL TRIBUNAL HAS DECIDED THE FOLLOWING: 1) the following documents: Transcript of Tribunal's session held on 25 May 1999; Transcript of Tribunal's session held on 25–29 April 2000; Transcript of Tribunal's session held on 22–23 October 2001;Transcript of Tribunal's session held on 14 June 2005; All expert reports/opinions (in relation to the Egyptian Tourism industry) and any accompanying document thereof, in the ICSID Case No. ARB/98/4 Wena Hotels Ltd shall be produced by Respondent by January 16, 2007 subject to the execution by Claimant of the text of an understanding of confidentiality worded on the basis of the model attached to Procedural Order n.1").
[103] *See Id.* at ¶¶ 2, 9–49.
[104] *See Id.* at ¶ 160, and dispositif.
[105] Biwater Gauff (Tanzania) Ltd. v. United Republic of Tanzania, ICSID Case No. ARB/05/22, Final Award (July 24, 2008).
[106] *Id.* at ¶ 2.
[107] *Id.* at ¶¶ 4, 17.
[108] *Id.* at ¶ 18.
[109] *Id.* at ¶ 1–2.
[110] *See Id.* at 43 (second documents request at 55).
[111] *Id.* at 45.
[112] *Id.* at ¶ 71–75.

case was one of the first, if not the first, African case that received a petition for *amicus curie*.[113] The *amici* requested the opportunity to submit written briefs and to attend the oral hearings. The Tribunal permitted the former but not the latter, holding that it lacked the authority to permit attendance because the investor had refused to consent.[114] This issue of participation of *amici* is quite remarkable, because it was the beginning of the early signs of discomfort with ISDS processes generally. It is also notable that it was the investor who was inclined to avoid public scrutiny. Many modern BITs now make provisions for the submission of *amicus* briefs and transparency as shown in the African regional treaties and models in Part III.

In *Biwater*, having received all the memorials and documentation, as well as witness statements and expert reports, the Tribunal conducted a hearing at the Peace Palace in the Hague between April 16 and April 21, 2007.[115] Posthearing briefs were simultaneously filed with the Tribunal on June 26, 2007, and closing arguments were heard on July 6, 2007, in London.[116] Months after the close of the hearings, the Respondent State made an extraordinary submission of an arbitral award made in a related contract claim that favored the state. The Tribunal did not accept holding that the case was closed.[117] The Tribunal issued its final award on July 24, 2008.[118] The award was modern and highly nuanced. As explained further in the various sections of the chapters on the substantive principles, it found the state liable but awarded no damages because the proprietary interest that the state was said to have expropriated had no salvageable economic value. Because the relief that the Claimant received was declaratory and the state suffered no pecuniary detriment except for the costs, *Biwater* was essentially a state victory.

The third award rendered in 2008 was the *Jan de Nul N. V and Dredging International N.V v. Egypt* case (Belgian JVs case) (2008).[119] This was a dispute between a Belgian Joint Venture (the JV) and the Suez Canal Authority (SCA), an Egyptian state-owned enterprise[120] under the 1977 and 2002 bilateral investment treaties (BITs) between the Belgo-Luxembourg Economic Union and Egypt.[121] The case proceeded as orderly as any modern arbitral proceeding is expected to proceed with a smooth constitution of the Tribunal by properly represented parties. There were no signs of the types of early era lack of participation and undue delays in participation, although the proceeding took an extended period of time, until October 2008.

Within a year of the submission of the Request for Arbitration on December 23, 2003,[122] the Tribunal was fully constituted by agreement of the Parties by September

[113] *Id.* at 57. The amici were: the Lawyers' Environmental Action Team (LEAT); the Legal and Human Rights Centre (LHRC); the Tanzania Gender Networking Programme (TGNP); the Center for International Environmental Law (CIEL); and the International Institute for Sustainable Development (IISD). *Id.*

[114] *Id.* at ¶ 62 (granting the submission of briefs), 65 (rejecting attendance).

[115] *Id.* at ¶ 81.

[116] *Id.* at ¶ 64–85.

[117] *Id.* at ¶ 88–94.

[118] *Id.* at caption (front page).

[119] Jan de Nul N.V. Dredging International N.V. v. Arab Republic of Egypt, ICSID Case No. ARB/04/13, Award (Nov. 6, 2008).

[120] *Id.* at ¶ 1–2.

[121] *Id.* at ¶ 8.

[122] *Id.* at ¶ 8.

7, 2004.[123] The overall delay between the initiation of the claim and the final award on the merits appears to be a function of the bifurcation of the proceedings into the jurisdictional phase and the merits phase.

The Tribunal first considered the jurisdictional objection presented by the State. It was only in August 2007 that the Tribunal set the calendar for the merits phase.[124] Following the exchange of memorials, the Tribunal held evidentiary hearings in Paris between September 25 and 27, 2007,[125] during which it appears to have heard at least 10 fact and expert witnesses.[126] On December 19, 2007, the Parties submitted posthearing briefs and the record was closed on October 15, 2008.[127] The process unfolded in fairly predictable steps. Interestingly though, this ISDS case was preceded by 10 years of domestic litigation on the same set of factual circumstances under a breach of contract claim.[128] In any case, Egypt prevailed again,[129] giving Africa its sixth victory.

Following Africa's victory in the 2008 Trilogy, *Helnen, Biwater*, and *Jan de Nul N.V* came the first of the two Zimbabwe land expropriation cases, *Bernardus Henricus Funnekotter and Others v. Republic of Zimbabwe* (2009).[130] The Claimants were several Dutch citizens who claimed that Zimbabwe took their farmland in violation of the Netherlands-Zimbabwe BIT of 1996.[131] The proceedings took place between the filing of the claims on June 4, 2003, and the reindentation of the final award on April 22, 2009.[132]

For reasons that are not properly explained, the constitution of the arbitral tribunal took more than three years between the filing of the action until ICSID confirmed the commencement of the case on November 7, 2006.[133] In that sense, although the award came in 2009, the case itself has the indicia of the earlier ICSID cases not the least of which concerns two resignations as discussed in the next chapter.

Otherwise, the case proceeded with the parties' exchanging memorials,[134] and an oral hearing in Paris between October 29 and 31, 2007.[135] Following a submission of an additional posthearing affidavit by the Claimant and a responsive affidavit by the Respondent, the Tribunal closed the record on February 25, 2009.[136] It appears that after the constitution of the Tribunal, matters proceeded fairly regularly with both parties represented and participating at every step of the way. Needless to say, the state lost.[137]

[123] *Id.* at ¶ 13.
[124] *Id.* at ¶ 21–23.
[125] *Id.* at ¶ 32.
[126] *Id.* at ¶ 33.
[127] *Id.* at ¶ 39–41.
[128] *Id.* at ¶ 43.
[129] *See id.* at dispositif.
[130] Bernardus Henricus Funnekotter and Others v. Republic of Zimbabwe, ICSID Case No. ARB/05/6, Award (Apr.22, 2009).
[131] *Id.* at ¶¶ 1, 19.
[132] *See Id.* at ¶ 1, caption.
[133] *See Id.* at ¶ 7.
[134] *Id.* at ¶ 9–13.
[135] *Id.* at ¶ 14.
[136] *Id.* at ¶¶ 15, 17.
[137] *See Id.* at dispositif.

Initiated on May 25, 2005, *Waguih Elie v. Egypt* (2009)[138] is a claim based on the 1989 Egypt–Italy BIT.[139] This case demonstrates features that are different from those that have been discussed so far. Substantively, the expropriation claim is predicated on the Respondent State's disregard of the decisions of its own administrative and judicial organs.[140] Procedurally, it presents one of the most complicated disputes relating to the citizenship of the principal claimant[141] and his capacity to consent to an arbitration agreement because of an alleged bankruptcy-linked incapacity to accept a standing offer of arbitration under the BIT and Article 25 of the ICSID Convention.[142]

The Tribunal bifurcated the proceedings between jurisdiction and merits and was asked to further bifurcate the merits proceedings, which it refused. Several jurisdictional rulings later, the Tribunal accepted the parties' memorials and countermemorials[143] and held its merits hearing in March 2008 during which both parties were represented and witnesses from both sides were examined.[144] The Parties then submitted posthearing briefs[145] and the Tribunal rendered its award on June 1, 2009.[146]

Beyond the jurisdictional dispute, which is discussed below, the merits phase raised an interesting issue of estoppel under international law that is quasi-jurisdictional because it does not fit into any of the substantive claims under the BIT. During the jurisdictional phase, the Tribunal found that although the Claimant was born Egyptian, he had lost his Egyptian nationality by operation of law when he acquired another nationality.[147] However, on the facts of the case, it was admitted that the Claimant continued to hold himself out as an Egyptian national, including the use of an Egyptian passport. Egypt's estoppel argument was that although he might have lost his nationality under Egyptian law, which it disputed on the facts, he continued to represent himself as an Egyptian and hence must be estopped from using a treaty meant to protect foreign investors. The Tribunal did not agree with Egypt. Relying on Brownlie[148] and Lauterpacht,[149] who link the equitable principle of estoppel under international

[138] Waguih Elie George Slag and Clorinda Vecchi v. The Arab Republic of Egypt, ICSID Case No. ARB/05/15, Award (June 1, 2009).

[139] *Id.* at ¶ 175.

[140] *Id.* at ¶ 368.

[141] *Id.* at ¶ 219.

[142] *See Id.* at ¶ 175–218.

[143] *Id.* at ¶ 368–407.

[144] *Id.* at ¶ 408–18.

[145] *Id.* at ¶ 419–26.

[146] *Id.* at caption.

[147] *See id.* at ¶ 14–15 ("In his application for permission to acquire Lebanese nationality Mr Siag sought permission to maintain his Egyptian nationality pursuant to the third paragraph of Article 10 of the Nationality Law. As discussed at length in the Tribunal's Decision on Jurisdiction, the third paragraph of Article 10 contains an additional requirement, once permission to maintain Egyptian nationality is granted, to further notify the Egyptian Interior Ministry within the period of one year of the desire to retain Egyptian nationality. Mr Siag did not so notify the Ministry with the consequence, as found in the Decision on Jurisdiction, that he lost his Egyptian nationality").

[148] *Id.* at ¶ 483 (citing Ian Brownlie, Principles of International Law 616 (6th ed, 2003)) ("a considerable weight of authority supports the view that estoppel is a general principle of international law, resting on principles of good faith and consistency").

[149] *Id.* at ¶ 483 (citing Sir Hersch Lauterpacht, *Report on the Law of Treaties*, UN Doc. A/CN.4/63, Mar. 24, 1953, at p.157) ("a State cannot be allowed to avail itself of the advantages of the treaty when it suits it to do so and repudiate it when its performance becomes onerous. It is of little consequence whether that rule is based on what in English law is known as the principle of estoppels or the more generally conceived requirement of good faith. The former is probably not more than one of the aspects of the latter").

law to representations accompanied by lack of good faith, the Tribunal found on the facts that the Claimant was not estopped from using the BIT because he represented himself as Egyptian without knowing that he had actually lost it by operation of Egyptian law and that the Egyptian government should have known about the loss of citizenship.[150] This will be elaborated further in the substantive chapters, but Egypt lost this case on the merits.[151]

As seen the above discussion, unlike the decades of the 1970s, 1980s, and 1990s, in the 2000s, the African states had more meaningful participation and more victories than losses. Egypt was the major player during this period both in cases arising out of contracts and treaties, including one with the United States.

The decade of the 2000s is thus characterized by three important developments. First, the number of cases filed against African states rose considerably, with at least 12 cases ending in published awards that could be examined. Second, unlike the previous decades, the African states fully participated with proper representation in almost all of the cases. Third and more importantly, the African states won exactly half of the cases, that is, six of the twelve cases.

Interestingly, the decade began with four losses in a row: *Wena* (2000), *Middle East Cement* (2002), *Semos* (2003), and *CDC* (2003). All of the wins came after the 2004 annulment victory in the *Patrick Mitchell* case, followed by *World Duty Free* (2006), *Champions Trading* (2006), and the 2008 trilogy—*Helnan, Biwater*, and *Jan de Nul*. Two more losses came at the end of the decade: *Waguih* and *Berdanrdus*. The decade of the 2000s clearly brought Africa out of the shadows. It began shedding resentments, and suspicions of the past, played by the rules and defended itself meaningfully in a language that everybody understood.

[150] *Id.* at ¶ 483 ("The Tribunal finds that the Claimants acted in good faith in obtaining their Egyptian passports and in their subsequent business and other dealings with Egypt. As to the latter, Claimants did not know at that point, nor as lay persons could they reasonably be expected to have known, that in law they had lost their Egyptian nationality. Thus the Claimants are not estopped from now denying their Egyptian nationality").

[151] *See id.* at dispositif.

5

The Post-2010 Modern Cases

The Post-2010 period saw considerable qualitative and quantitative growth in African ICSID Cases. This chapter discusses the first half of this period followed by the second half.

The Period Between 2010 and 2020

The first of the more modern cases decided in the 2010s is *Gustave v. Ghana* (2010).[1] *Gustave* does not present serious complexity and its importance and contribution relates to the issues of attribution and umbrella clause discussed in subsequent chapters. Filed on the basis of the 1995 Ghana–Germany Treaty,[2] arising out of the Parties' joint venture agreement for cocoa trade,[3] procedurally, the case unfolded in modern and predicable steps with both parties participating and timely represented.[4] It commenced with the filing of the Request for Arbitration on September 24, 2007, and the Tribunal was fully constituted by February 4, 2008, and held its first meeting by April 2, 2008.[5] Having received written pleadings from the Parties in between,[6] the Tribunal heard oral arguments between June 28 and July 3, 2009; accepted posthearing briefs on August 17, 2009, and closed the proceedings on June 2, 2009;[7] and the award was rendered on June 18, 2010.[8] It shows all the indicia of a modern arbitral process. Ghana prevailed.[9]

The case that came next was *Malicorp v. Egypt* (2011).[10] It is a dispute submitted for arbitration by a UK investor, Malicorp, against Egypt under the 1975 UK–Egypt BIT arising out of an international airport development agreement.[11] This case followed a full-fledged contract arbitration administered by the Cairo Regional Center for International Commercial Arbitration (CRCICA) on the exact same facts between April 20, 2004, and March 7, 2006.[12] The CRCICA Tribunal held that the Malicorp obtained the contract through fraud and rejected all of its claims.[13] It did, however,

[1] Gustav F W Hamester GmbH & Co KG v. Republic of Ghana Respondent, ICSID Case No. ARB/07/24, Award (June 18, 2010).
[2] *Id.* at ¶ 1.
[3] For the facts, *see id.* at ¶ 22–28.
[4] *See id.* at caption, ¶ 1–4.
[5] *Id.* at ¶ 7–9.
[6] *Id.* at ¶ 16–18.
[7] *Id.* at ¶ 19–21.
[8] *Id.* at caption, signature page.
[9] *See id.* at dispositif.
[10] Malicorp Limited v. The Arab Republic of Egypt, ICSID Case No. ARB/08/18, Award (Feb. 7, 2011).
[11] *See id.* at ¶¶ 1, 2, 74 (referring to the 1975 BIT).
[12] *See id.* at ¶ 44–58.
[13] *Id.* at ¶ 58 ("that the Republic had been the victim of a fundamental error in signing the Contract in that it had wrongly believed that the capital registered and paid by Malicorp was 100 million pounds sterling

Africa's International Investment Law Regimes. Won L. Kidane, Oxford University Press. © Oxford University Press 2023.
DOI: 10.1093/oso/9780197745571.003.0005

award it some costs and salaries that it paid to employees for reasons that were not clear to the *Malicorp* Tribunal. The Respondents in that action took the award of costs to court for annulment but the Treaty Tribunal was not appraised of it.[14] Annulment and enforcement proceedings then followed on the amount that was awarded to Malicorp despite the finding of fraud, an issue the ICSID Tribunal did not go into in details about, essentially deeming it irrelevant to its task.[15]

It was after its commercial arbitration loss under the concession agreement that Malicorp initiated this treaty claim under the BIT. As seen in Part III, many of Egypt's BITs offer the investor a choice of arbitral fora including Cairo Regional Center as an alternative to ICSID. This is unique to Egyptian BITs. Had that been the case under the 1975 Egypt–UK Treaty (which it was not),[16] the Cairo Center would have adjudicated the treaty-based claim concurrently. This is an interesting phenomenon because nothing could have prevented the initiation of two Cairo Center proceedings—one based on contract and another one based on the BIT. Functionally, however, whether it was ICSID or the Cairo Center, the issues needing determination would have been similar as seen in this treaty case although the ICSID Tribunal had to determine all the issues including the facts de novo without any preclusive effect. Although such staggered proceedings are not uncommon, as seen from the other cases, the most common way that the contract claims are adjudicated (or not) is through the umbrella clause.

In any case, Malicorp initiated this ICSID arbitration on October 21, 2008, almost two years after its commercial arbitration loss.[17] The ICSID Tribunal was fully constituted on June 2, 2009, following regular procedures without institutional appointment.[18] The proceedings then followed predictable steps with an exchange of pleadings and an oral hearing in Paris between April 19 and 20, 2010, during which at least one witness was cross-examined.[19] It ended with the issuance of the final award on February 7, 2011, granting Egypt another full victory.[20]

Bernard von Pezold v. Zimbabwe (2015)[21] is one of the most complex and voluminous cases,[22] not only because it adjudicates two interrelated cases simultaneously

and that for this reason the Contract was void. It therefore dismissed the submissions of the Claimant claiming damages for the loss caused by the termination of the Contract"). Many persons associated with Malicorp were also found guilty of associated crimes and sentenced to varied terms of imprisonment. *See id.* at ¶ 71–73 ("73. the Cairo Court of Assizes rendered its verdict: Messrs. Chabli and Mercer were found guilty of forgery and fraud and sentenced principally to three years' imprisonment").

[14] *See id.* at ¶ 58–59.

[15] *See id.* at ¶ 60–70.

[16] *See* Agreement between the Government of the United Kingdom of Great Britain and Northern Ireland and the Government of the Arab Republic of Egypt for the Promotion and Protection of Investments (June 11, 1975) at art. 8, available at https://investmentpolicy.unctad.org/international-investment-agreements/treaty-files/1122/download [Egypt–UK BIT].

[17] *See* Malicorp Limited v. The Arab Republic of Egypt, ICSID Case No. ARB/08/18, Award (Feb. 7, 2011), at ¶74.

[18] *Id.* at ¶ 76.

[19] *See id.* at ¶ 76–85.

[20] *See id.* at caption and dispositif.

[21] Bernhard von Pezold and Others v. Republic of Zimbabwe, ICSID Case No. ARB/10/15, Award (July 28, 2015).

[22] With more than 3,000 pages of pleadings, dozens of procedural orders, and more than 300 pages of final award. *See id.* at 31 ("The voluminous nature of the Parties' pleadings and evidence cannot be overstated. The Parties have filed approximately 3,000 pages of pleadings alone").

without consolidation by an identically composed tribunal[23] under two different BITs,[24] but also substantively deals with difficult sociopolitical and historical circumstances.[25]

Initially, two cases were filed separately and were assigned two separate file numbers, although the second claimant is owned by the first claimant.[26] The first one is called *The von Pezold* Arbitration and was registered on July 8, 2010.[27] The second one is called *The Border Arbitration* registered on December 3, 2010.[28] The Tribunal dealt with both together and rendered separate awards although the factual predicates were same.[29]

The Tribunal in *The von Pezold* case was duly constituted on December 9, 2010.[30] The Parties in *The Border* case agreed that the Tribunal in their case be identically constituted, and this occurred on January 20, 2011.[31] Interestingly, the Respondent's first appointee resigned on June 6, 2011,[32] and the Respondent appointed another on July 13, 2011. The appointee refused.[33] The Respondent's third appointee was accepted on August 12, 2011,[34] and the Tribunal was reconstituted on September 15, 2011.[35] In yet another surprise, on May 19, 2013, the Respondent's third appointee also resigned.[36] The proceedings in both cases were suspended until the Respondent made another appointment. It did so on July 1, 2013.[37] The Respondent's fourth appointee saw the case through to conclusion.

[23] *See id.* at ¶ 15–16.

[24] *See id.* at ¶ 85 ("The treaties under which the Claimants advance their claims are the German BIT, signed on 29 September 1995, and which entered into force on 14 April 2002, together with the Protocol to the German BIT which was signed on 29 September 1995 (the "German Protocol"), and the Swiss BIT, signed on 15 August 1996, and which entered into force on 9 February 2001, together with the Protocol to the Swiss BIT which was signed on 15 August 1996"). That is because while all the Claimants had dual German and Swiss nationality, one had only Swiss nationality. *See id.* at ¶ 10 ("Save for Rüdiger, who is German and claims only under the German BIT, all of the von Pezold Claimants are both German and Swiss nationals, and therefore advance their claims under both the German BIT and the Swiss BIT").

[25] The Tribunal described the difficult historical background as follows in its introductory passage: "3. Following Zimbabwe's independence and the election of Robert Mugabe as President in 1980, the land policies of the Rhodesian era which favored the white minority population were reversed and replaced with land policies favouring the black indigenous population. Those policies, accompanied by the invasions of private land by settlers, feature prominently in this arbitration. 4. Oftentimes during these proceedings, members of the Tribunal had to remind themselves that their remit was not one of a commission of inquiry into what has been described as "the March of History," but rather strictly that of an Arbitral Tribunal mandated to adjudicate a dispute or disputes in accordance with the Convention of the International Centre for Settlement of Investment Disputes ("ICSID") and applicable law. This, the Tribunal has sought to do." *Id.* at ¶ 3–4.

[26] *Id.* at ¶ 15–16.

[27] *Id.* at ¶ 9–11.

[28] *Id.* at ¶ 12–14.

[29] *Id.* at ¶ 7 ("As a result of these unique conjoined and intertwined proceedings, each Tribunal now renders a separate Award which contains not only the decision of each Tribunal on every question submitted to it, together with the reasons upon which each decision is based, but also the decision of the other Tribunal on every question submitted to it, together with the reasons upon which those decisions are based").

[30] *Id.* at ¶ 15.

[31] *Id.* at ¶ 16.

[32] *Id.* at ¶ 24.

[33] *Id.* at ¶ 25.

[34] *Id.*

[35] *Id.*

[36] *Id.* at ¶ 26.

[37] *Id.* at ¶ 27.

The Tribunal accepted the Parties' written pleadings between November 15, 2011, and December 18, 2014, which amounted to a total of 25 submissions.[38] In the Tribunal's own words:

> The voluminous nature of the Parties' pleadings and evidence cannot be overstated. The Parties have filed approximately 3,000 pages of pleadings alone. The motion practice in these two cases has also been extensive, adding hundreds of additional pages to these arbitrations in procedural orders and directions and contributing to the overall lengthening of the procedure.[39]

Thirteen procedural orders and 3000 pages of written submissions later, the Tribunal held its oral hearing on jurisdiction, liability and quantum in Washington, DC, between October 28, 2013, and November 2, 2013.[40] The Tribunal heard an extraordinarily large number of expert witnesses on both sides.[41] It also heard a large number of fact witnesses on behalf of the Claimants.[42] Only one fact witness testified on behalf of the Respondent by video.[43] Because the balance on the facts was obvious, this was essentially a battle of the experts on quantum. On May 7, 2014, the Tribunal accepted posthearing submissions, closed the proceeding on February 3, 2015,[44] and issued its 305-page final award constituting 1,024 paragraphs on July 28, 2015.[45] This was an extraordinary case in every aspect. Needless to say, Zimbabwe lost.[46]

The dispute in *Standard Chartered Bank v. Tanzania Electric Supply Company Limited (TANESCO)* (2016)[47] grew out of a Power Purchase Agreement (PPA) that was plagued by dispute from the very beginning.[48] The procedural posture was complex not only because it interacted with several domestic proceedings,[49] but also because it required the review and reversal of the Tribunal's own prior decision following discovery of new evidence that the Respondent was found to have concealed.[50]

The unique aspect of this case is that the Tribunal was confronted with evidence that contradicted its previous pre-award jurisdictional decision, permitting the release of

[38] *See id.* at ¶ 30 (summary table).
[39] *Id.* at ¶ 31.
[40] *Id.* at ¶ 71.
[41] *Id.* at ¶ 74.
[42] *Id.* at ¶ 75.
[43] *Id.* at ¶ 76.
[44] *Id.* at ¶ 81–84.
[45] *Id.* at caption.
[46] *See id.* at dispositif.
[47] Standard Chartered Bank (Hong Kong) Ltd. v. Tanzania Electric Supply Company Ltd. (Tanesco), ICSID Case No. ARB/10/20, Award (Sep. 12, 2016).
[48] For a fuller procedural history, *see id.* at ¶ 79. The first ICSID case was filed in 1998 and ended in 2001. The Tribunal was composed of Mr. Kenneth S. Rokison, a national of the United Kingdom (President), Judge Charles N. Brower, a national of the United States of America, and Mr. Andrew Rogers, a national of Australia. *Id.* at ¶ 79.
[49] *See id.* at ¶ 212–19 (proceedings in Tanzania), ¶ 32–39 (English High Court), ¶ 73, n. 35 (Malaysian Hight Court).
[50] *See id.* at ¶¶ 348, 358. ("358. In short, in concluding in its Decision that it could not make an order for payment in favour of SCB HK, the Tribunal was relying on what it believed to be facts, which were not true, and assumptions based on submissions made to it that omitted relevant information and were not correct").

contested funds to an entity that it later determined should not have received them. The key procedural question was whether, under the ICSID Convention, such types of decisions are *res judicata* before they have been incorporated in the final award; and relatedly, whether the same tribunal can reopen the case and correct such error.[51]

The Tribunal had conflicting guidance. Whereas the cases cited by the Respondent, the party objecting reopening, such as *ConocoPhillips v. Venezuela*[52] and *Perenco v. Ecuador*,[53] disfavored reponing on grounds of *res judicata*, the dissent in *ConocoPhillips* by Professor Abi-Saab, relied upon by the Claimant, favored reponing.[54]

The Tribunal in this case began its analysis by acknowledging upfront that "no case has directly concluded that there is such a power although there are cases that appear to acknowledge the possibility of, or the existence of, such a power without applying it to reopen a decision."[55] It also reiterated the clear position in *ConocoPhillips* that "it is established as a matter of principle and practice that such decisions that resolve points in dispute between the Parties have res judicata effect."[56] Having clearly stated the rule that these prior tribunals announced, particularly the majority in *ConocoPhillips*, the Tribunal simply disagreed and concluded as follows:

> Decisions of tribunals are of course binding within the scope of the proceedings, but this does not make them res judicata. That is so with procedural orders and provisional measures as pointed out earlier. An essential feature of res judicata is that the judgment in question produces effects on the parties outside the proceedings in which it is granted. But decisions of tribunals only have effect within the proceedings until they have been incorporated into the final award.[57]

This is one rare example of a direct rebuff of what might be considered a fairly established rule because it does not have direct precedential force on the next ad hoc tribunal. Although on the facts of this case, the decision appears defensible because the Tribunal discovered that one of the Parties had misled it, the ad hoc interpretation of the ICSID rules necessarily leads to inconsistent results, an issue that continues to be debated and discussed in various sections of this book.

51 *See id.* at ¶ 231.

52 *Id.* at ¶ 256 (citing ConocoPhillips v. Venezuela, ICSID Case No. ARB/07/30, Decision on the Respondent's Request for Reconsideration (Mar. 10, 2014)).

53 *Id.* at ¶ 256 (citing Perenco Ecuador Limited v. Republic of Ecuador, ICSID Case No. ARB/08/6, Decision on Ecuador's Reconsideration Motion (Apr. 10, 2015)).

54 *See id.* at ¶ 304 ("The Claimant argues that the Tribunal has the power to reconsider its Decision, invoking the dissenting opinion of Professor Abi-Saab in ConocoPhillips v. Venezuela. In the Claimant's view, a decision does not become final and res judicata until it is incorporated into the final award; there is no prohibition on reopening a decision in the ICSID Convention or the Arbitration Rules; and there are pragmatic reasons for recognizing a power to reopen").

55 *Id.* at ¶ 308 (citing Antoine Biloune (Syria) and Marine Drive Complex Ltd. (Ghana) v. Ghana Investments Centre and the Government of Ghana (UNCITRAL), Award on Jurisdiction and Liability (Oct. 27, 1989); Quiborax S.A., Non Metallic Minerals S.A. and Allan Fosk Kapl n v. Plurinational State of Bolivia, ICSID Case No. ARB/06/2, Award (Sep. 16, 2015).

56 *Id.* at ¶ 310 (quoting ConocoPhillips v. Venezuela, ICSID Case No. ARB/07/30, Decision on the Respondent's Request for Reconsideration (Mar. 10, 2014) at ¶ 19).

57 *Id.* at ¶ 313.

Otherwise, the process unfolded mainly through the exchange of pleadings with both Parties receiving proper and timely representation, although the Respondent switched counsel in the middle of the proceedings.[58] Tanzania lost on the merits.[59]

Union Fenosa Gas, S.A. (UFG) v. Egypt (2018)[60] is a major Oil and Gas case that put the economic impact of the 2011 Egyptian revolutionary process on trial. The Claimant, *UFG*, a Spanish company, filed a claim against Egypt on February 14, 2014, under the 1992 Egypt–Spain BIT.[61] With both Parties properly represented, this case proceeded in predictable steps. The exchange of pleadings occurred until January 16, 2017.[62] The hearing was held between March 6 and 11, 2017, in Washington, during which fact and expert witnesses were heard from both sides,[63] and the award was rendered on August 31, 2018.[64]

The significance of this case is threefold. This was the first known African case that raised a legitimate and plausible defense of both corruption and necessity, and full restitution was awarded for violation of FET without a claim of expropriation.

Cortec Mining v. Kenya (2018)[65] doubles down on *World Duty Free v. Kenya* (2006) less dramatically, as the state sought to disavow decisions of public officials that had left office. It began with the filing of the Request for Arbitration on June 18, 2015, and the Tribunal was duly constituted on November 12, 2015, with appointments made according to the rules without any delays.[66]

For a two-year period between the constitution of the Tribunal in November 2015 and November 2017, the Parties exchanged pleadings including the Memorial, Counter-Memorial, Reply, and Rejoinder,[67] and the Tribunal held the evidentiary hearing between January 15 and 23, 2018, in Dubai.[68] It was the only African ISDS case included in this study to be heard outside of Washington or Paris.

During the hearing, several fact and expert witnesses were heard on behalf of each party.[69] The Parties then submitted their posthearing briefs on April 11, 2018,[70] and the Tribunal issued its final award on October 22, 2018.[71] This case was procedurally as modern and straightforward as any proceeding could get. Kenya prevailed,[72] and the Claimant unsuccessfully sought to annul.[73]

[58] *See id.* at ¶ 18 (Hunton & Williams withdrawing after serving between Nov. 2007 and Apr. 2014).
[59] *See id.* at dispositif.
[60] Union Fenosa Gas, S.A. v. Arab Republic of Egypt, ICSID Case No. ARB/14/4 (Aug. 31, 2018).
[61] *Id.* at ¶¶ 1.4, 2.3.
[62] *Id.* at ¶ 1.44. This was the date the Respondent's Rejoinder was filed but there were exchanges of letters and requests for additional evidence subsequent to the Joinder. *See id.* at ¶ 1.45.
[63] *Id.* at ¶ 1.58–1.60.
[64] *Id.* at caption.
[65] Cortec Mining Kenya Limited, Cortec (Pty) Limited And Stirling Capital Limited v. Republic Of Kenya, ICSID Case No. ARB/15/29, Award (Oct. 22, 2018).
[66] *Id.* at ¶ 16–18. The published version wrongly states the Request for Arbitration date as June 18, 2018.
[67] *Id.* at ¶ 19–32.
[68] *Id.* at ¶ 38.
[69] *Id.* at ¶ 39.
[70] *Id.* at ¶ 41.
[71] *Id.* at caption.
[72] *See id.* at dispositif.
[73] *See* Decision on Annulment (Mar. 19, 2021) in Cortec Mining Kenya Limited, Cortec (Pty) Limited And Stirling Capital Limited v. Republic Of Kenya, ICSID Case No. ARB/15/29, Award (Oct. 22, 2018).

In *CMC v. Mozambique* (2019)[74], the Request for Arbitration was filed on May 10, 2017, under the 1998 BIT between Mozambique and Italy claiming amounts due for works done under road rehabilitation project financed by the European Development Fund.[75] By November 29, 2017, the Tribunal was duly constituted with the Parties making timely appointments of their respective arbitrators and mutually selecting the chair.[76]

In somewhat of an uncommon practice, on August 18, 2018, the Tribunal held a hearing on the Claimant's request for bifurcation of the proceedings in Washington.[77] The Tribunal denied the bifurcation of the proceedings between jurisdiction and merits[78] and continued to receive the Parties' exchanges of pleadings, motions, and offers of evidence, and held the evidentiary hearing on jurisdiction and merits between April 29 and May 1, 2019, in Washington, during which fact and expert witnesses were presented and examined on both sides.[79] The Parties agreed not to submit any posthearing briefs but within about a week of the end of the hearing, again, highly unusually, on May 8, 2019, the Tribunal requested the Parties to comment on the relevance of a Decision of the European Court of Justice that came down on April 30, 2019,[80] and another arbitral decision rendered on May 7, 2019,[81] on the issue of jurisdiction, which appear to have been published during the time that the Tribunal was conducting the evidentiary hearings or shortly thereafter.[82] The jurisdictional aspect of this case is the most significant contribution because it involves the interaction of other treaties with the regular ICSID-BIT duo.

The Parties were timely and duly represented and participated throughout the proceedings and the Tribunal rendered its final award on October 24, 2019.[83] Mozambique faced two ISDS cases in 2019, although it managed to have the other one dismissed on jurisdictional grounds a few days after the first case. It prevailed on the merits in this case.[84]

Oded Besserglik v. Mozambique (2019)[85] was one of the first Intra-Africa cases initiated as an ICSID Additional Facilities case under the South Africa–Mozambique BIT.[86] The South African Claimant submitted an application for access to the Additional Facilities on March 24, 2014.[87] Mozambique vigorously objected to the jurisdiction

74 CMC Muratori Cementisti CMC Di Ravenna SOC. Coop. & Others v. Republic of Mozambique, ICSID Case No. ARB/17/23 (Oct. 24, 2019).
75 *Id.*
76 *Id.* at ¶ 20–24.
77 *See id.* at ¶ 34.
78 *See id.* at ¶ 35–38.
79 *Id.* at ¶ 39–77.
80 *Id.* at 79 (citing Opinion 1/17 of the Court of Justice of the European Union ("ECJ") of Apr. 30, 2019).
81 *Id.* at ¶ 79 (citing Eskosol S.p.A. in Liquidazione v. the Italian Republic, ICSID Case No. ARB/15/50, Decision on Italy's Request for Immediate Termination and Italy's Jurisdictional Objection Based on Inapplicability of the Energy Charter Treaty to Intra-EU Disputes (May 7, 2019)).
82 *See id.* at ¶ 79.
83 *Id.* at caption.
84 *See id.* at dispositif.
85 Oded Besserglik v. Republic of Mozambique, ICSID Case No. ARB(AF)/14/2, Award (Oct. 28, 2019).
86 *Id.* at ¶ 6.
87 *Id.*

of ICSID starting from before the Tribunal was constituted.[88] The Claimant appointed its arbitrator on October 9, 2014, and the Respondent reluctantly appointed its arbitrator after the 90-day period had lapsed on November 25, 2014, and replaced it with another arbitrator within two weeks on December 9, 2014.[89] The record shows that the first arbitrator later served as counsel for Mozambique.[90]

The dispute was a typical contract and corporate dispute, but the South African Claimant could not overcome the serious jurisdictional defect associated with the ratification of the BIT that would have served as the jurisdictional basis of the ICSID Additional Facilities. The Respondent's jurisdictional challenge and related motion to dismiss required a full-fledged arbitral proceeding including an evidentiary hearing that lasted until October 2019, the time of the final award. In between, the parties exchanged written pleadings and evidentiary records, and conducted telephonic and in person oral hearings in Washington.[91] Following the hearing on March 2018, the Parties exchanged several posthearing briefs between April 20, 2018, to April 30, 2019.[92] This was primarily because Mozambique raised a new but outcome determinative jurisdictional objection at the very last minute. In any case, the Tribunal issued its final award dismissing all the claims on October 28, 2019.[93] Mozambique prevailed.[94]

Post-2020 Contemporary Cases

Thomas Goslin v. Mauritius (2020)[95] is one of those cases that was rushed before a treaty tribunal without adequate facts, attempted to push the boundaries of reasonable expectations as a component of FET a little too far, and ended with the Claimant's disappointment as discussed in the relevant sections to come. Procedurally, it was initiated on September 13, 2016, by UK Claimants under the 1986 Mauritius–UK BIT.[96] It concerns pre-investment representations that were later not honored for reasons that the Parties disagreed on.

The procedural steps were regular with both Parties duly represented and participating. The Tribunal was fully constituted by January 26, 2020.[97] With the procedural calendar agreed upon after many modifications by the year's end, the Parties exchanged their written pleadings until May 10, 2019.[98] The Tribunal held its evidentiary hearing between June 17 and 25, 2019, during which several witnesses were

[88] *Id.* at ¶ 11.
[89] *Id.* at ¶ 15.
[90] *See id.* at caption.
[91] *See id.* at ¶ 17–112.
[92] *Id.* at ¶ 144–49.
[93] *Id.* at ¶ 390–96, caption.
[94] *See id.* at dispositf.
[95] Thomas Gosling, Property Partnerships Development Managers (UK) Limited & Others v. Republic of Mauritius, ICSID Case No. ARB/16/32, Award (Feb. 18, 2020).
[96] *See id.* at ¶¶ 1–3, 6.
[97] *See id.* at ¶ 8–10.
[98] *Id.* at ¶ 31.

heard on both sides.[99] The proceeding closed on February 4, 2020, and the Tribunal issued its final award on both jurisdiction and merits within two weeks on February 18, 2020.[100] Mauritius prevailed.[101]

Half a century later, Libya made important international arbitration history after its long-term leader responsible for the foundation cases of the 1970s, Colonel Muammar Gaddafi, was deposed in 2011. By historic coincidence, both his rise and fall were accompanied by ground-breaking international arbitration cases. *Strabag SE v. Libya* (2020)[102] is as pioneering as the Libyan Oil expropriation cases of the 1970s not only because it is a product of a major political change that involved a multitude of international players, but also because the claims raised rare armed conflict related substantive legal principles and proceeded under ICSID Additional Facilities Rules.[103]

The instrument of consent was the 2004 Libya-Austria BIT concluded during Colonel Gaddafi's reign. This BIT granted the investor the choice to initiate ICSID arbitration under the ICSID Additional Facilities Rules. Although Libya was not a member of ICSID, that is exactly what the Austrian infrastructure construction companies, collectively called Strabag, did: they initiated arbitration under the ICSID Additional Facilities Rules because Libya was not a member of ICSID.[104]

Strabag submitted an application for access to the ICSID Additional Facilities on June 24, 2015, which the Secretary-General approved within less than a month on July 20, 2015.[105] The access request was based on the terms of the BIT itself and the parties did not make it a point of contention, although the Tribunal addressed the jurisdictional aspect of it *sua sponte*.[106] The Parties appointed their respective arbitrator in more or less due time and the Tribunal was constituted by December 7, 2015.[107] Unlike the 1970s oil arbitration cases, which Libya essentially boycotted, after decades

99 *Id.* at ¶ 37–38.
100 *Id.* at caption.
101 *See id.* at dispositif.
102 Strabag Se v. Libya, ICSID Case No. ARB(AF)/15/1, Award (June 29, 2020).
103 *See id.* at ¶ 1–3.
104 *Id.* at ¶ 9.
105 *Id.* at ¶ 9–10.
106 *See id.* at ¶ 210 ("However, before turning to the merits of the dispute, the Tribunal must also consider whether the present dispute falls within the scope of the Additional Facility Rules. The dispute is between Strabag, a juridical person incorporated under the laws of Austria, i.e., a national of an ICSID Contracting State, and a State Party which is not an ICSID Contracting State, Libya. The Tribunal has concluded that Strabag has made an investment for the purposes of the Treaty and hence for the purposes of Articles 2(a) and 4(2) of the ICSID Additional Facility Rules. The prerequisites for Libya's consent to ICSID Additional Facility arbitration as set out in Articles I 0, 11 and 12 of the Treaty are fulfilled, i.e., consultations were requested prior to the institution of the arbitration proceedings in accordance with Article I I but there was no solution to the dispute within the prescribed time-period. In accordance with Article IO of the Treaty, the dispute refers to alleged breaches by Libya of the Treaty, which is said to have caused loss and damage to Claimant's investment. Claimant's written consent to ICSID Additional Facility arbitration is found in the Request for Arbitration. The dispute is therefore of a legal nature arising directly out of an investment in accordance with Article 2(a) of the Additional Facility Rules. Access to the Additional Facility was granted by the Secretary-General of IC SID on 20 July 2015. The Tribunal, therefore, concludes that it has jurisdiction under the Treaty to address Claimant's claims").
107 *See id.* at ¶ 11–16.

of progress including the conclusion of BITs, Libya participated in this case from the very beginning and in the Tribunal's own words, "both parties were represented by able and energetic counsel."[108]

By April 8, 2016, the Tribunal issued its second procedural order setting forth the Parties agreement to proceed in Washington[109] and the Parties exchanged their written pleadings between July 2016 and July 2018,[110] and the evidentiary hearing was conducted in Paris between July 9 and 20, 2018.[111] During the hearing, several fact and expert witnesses were heard from both sides.[112] The Parties exchanged their posthearing briefs, costs and comments on each other's costs submissions and the proceedings closed on June 2, 2020.[113] The Tribunal rendered its final award on jurisdiction and merits on July 29, 2020.[114] Libya presented a vigorous defense but eventually lost on all counts.[115]

Despite being the largest or second largest economy in Africa, Nigeria did not face an ISDS case until 2007 with the filing of the Shall case, refiled in 2021.[116] The only reported ISDS case that has gone through the entire process and resulted in a published final award is the *Interocean Oil v. Nigeria* case of 2020.[117]

The *Interocean Oil* case is an extraordinary case in which the Claimants attempted to force a quintessentially private dispute into an unlikely ISDS forum based on an offer of arbitration contained in a domestic investment legislation. Interocean filed its Request for Arbitration with ICSID on July 30, 2013.[118] Having been duly constituted by December 11, 2013, with each party timely appointing its arbitrator and the two mutually selecting their chair,[119] the Tribunal accepted memorials and countermemorials on objection on jurisdiction until April 25, 2014, and held a hearing on jurisdiction in London on June 26, 2014.[120] The Tribunal continued to accept evidence on jurisdiction after the hearing and made a partial ruling on jurisdiction on October 29, 2014.[121] It held that:

> Objection 1 (Consent) is rejected insofar as it calls into question whether Section 26 of the NIPC Act constitutes a standing offer to arbitrate. The Tribunal finds that Section 26 does indeed constitute such a standing offer. However, questions related to the adequacy of the Claimants' acceptance of that offer are joined to the merits;

[108] *Id.* at ¶ 943.
[109] *Id.* at ¶ 18.
[110] *See id.* at ¶ 19–45.
[111] *Id.* at ¶ 46.
[112] *Id.* at ¶ 48.
[113] *Id.* at ¶ 48–55.
[114] *Id.* at caption.
[115] *See id.* at dispositif.
[116] *See* UNCTAD Investment Dispute Settlement Navigator (Nigeria), available at https://investmentpolicy.unctad.org/investment-dispute-settlement/country/153/nigeria/respondent, for all Nigerian ISDS cases.
[117] Interocean Oil Development Company and Interocean Oil Exploration Company v. Federal Republic of Nigeria, ICSID Case No. ARB/13/20, Award (Oct. 6, 2020).
[118] *Id.* at ¶ 46.
[119] *Id.* at ¶ 50–51.
[120] *See id.* at ¶ 54–58.
[121] *See id.* at ¶ 58–65.

> Objections 2 (Role of the ICSID Rules), 4 (Proper Party) and 5 (Time Bars) are rejected; and Objections 3 (Registration) and 6 (Premature Filing) are joined to the merits.[122]

The key decision here was the Tribunal's affirmance that a provision contained in the Nigerian domestic investment law constituted a standing offer for ICSID arbitration.

Between February 5, 2014, and July 26, 2016, the Parties exchanged written pleadings on the merits,[123] and the Tribunal held an evidentiary hearing on the merits and remaining jurisdictional matters from August 2 to August 4, 2016, in London.[124] The Tribunal continued to accept correspondence from the Parties and held a second evidentiary hearing in London from July 19, 2017, to July 21, 2017.[125]

After the hearing, in a very unusual move, on August 16, 2017, the Respondent sought the disqualification of all three arbitrators.[126] After hearing from the Parties, on October 3, 2017, the ICSID Administrative Council rejected the Respondent's proposal for disqualification.[127] The Tribunal continued to accept correspondence from the Parties including posthearing briefs and offers of new evidence and declared the proceedings closed on September 29, 2020,[128] and rendered its final award on October 6, 2020.[129] Both Parties were ably and vigorously represented from the very beginning. Ironically, a Tribunal that the Respondent sought to disqualify handed it a complete victory.[130]

The last and the most contemporary of all the African ICSID Cases covered in this study is the *Bay View Group LLC* (BVG) *v. Rwanda* case (2022).[131] Like many of the older cases, this case also arose out of mining concession rights. The Claimants, American investors,[132] initiated this ICSID arbitration under the 2012 Rwanda–US BIT on May 18, 2018.[133] By October 3, 2018, the Tribunal was fully constituted and began its consideration of the case.[134] Between October 5, 2018, and June 17, 2021, the Parties exchanged numerous pleadings and the Tribunal issued several procedural orders, including on the issue of bifurcation and whether the hearing should be conducted in person or virtually because of the pandemic related issues.[135] The hearing on both jurisdiction and merits was conducted virtually, hosted out of London from June 21 to June 30, 2021 (excluding the

[122] *Id.* at ¶ 65.
[123] *Id.* at ¶ 66–73.
[124] *Id.* at ¶ 73.
[125] *Id.* at ¶ 74–78.
[126] *Id.* at ¶ 81.
[127] *Id.* at ¶ 85.
[128] *Id.* at ¶ 86–98.
[129] *Id.* at caption.
[130] *See id.* at dispositf.
[131] Bay View Group LLC and The Spalena Company LLC v. Republic of Rwanda, ICSID Case No. ARB/18/21, Award (Mar. 30, 2022).
[132] *Id.* at ¶ 2 ("The claimants are Bay View Group LLC ('Bay View' or 'BVG') and The Spalena Company LLC ('Spalena'), two limited liability companies organized under the laws of Delaware, United States of America (together, the 'Claimants')").
[133] *Id.* at ¶ 1–3.
[134] *Id.* at ¶ 10.
[135] *See id.* at ¶ 11–68.

weekend). Interestingly, on the first day of the hearing, the Tribunal confirmed that the hearing would be "open to the public" as required by the BIT.[136] And indeed, in an extraordinary departure from tradition, the video recording was posted on the ICSID website.[137] Following simultaneous exchange of posthearing briefs and submissions on costs in August and September 2021, the Tribunal declared the proceedings closed on February 7, 2022.[138] It issued the final award on jurisdiction and merits on March 30, 2022.[139]

This case was as contemporary in its proceeding as in its content. It is a case that hit the proverbial nail on the head in its identification of the most frequent source of the problem in many African cases when it observed:

> Rwanda hoped, no doubt, to attract experienced mining companies. The evidence suggests that it did not succeed. Instead, it attracted entrepreneurs without mining experience attracted by the possibilities of profiting from the acquisition of long-term mining licences in Rwanda. Of these Mr. Marshall was one. Mr. Marshall himself remarked that there were no mining companies among the investors. This was certainly the case so far as those behind NRD were concerned. Mr. Marshall described the Zarnacks as a plumbing company from Germany and H. C. Starck as minerals processors who had never carried out mining anywhere in the world. In the event, no less than five concessions were granted to the Zarnacks and Mr. Benzinge. NRD was founded to exploit these concessions. The Zarnacks pledged to invest some US$40 million,but did not do so. Instead, they sold NRD to Starck.[140]

This is a familiar story for most ministries of mining around Africa. This Tribunal was particularly astute in its observations of fact and was candid about its presentation. Needless to say, this observation on the facts was eventually outcome determinative. Rwanda prevailed.[141]

As the cases continue to rise in the 2010s, the African states stepped up their defense and won seven of the eleven cases of the decade. The cases they won are *Gustav v. Ghana* (2010), *Malicorp v. Egypt* (2010), *Cotec v. Kenya* (2011), *CMC v. Mozambique* (2019), *Oded Besserglik v. Mozambique* (2019), *Thomas Goslin v. Mauritius* (2020), and *Bay View Group v. Rwanda* (2022). The cases they lost were *Bernard von Pezold v. Zimbabwe* (2015), *Standard Chartered Bank v. Tanzania* (2016), *Union Fenosa Gas v. Egypt* (2018), and *Stabag SE v. Libya* (2020). To be sure, these losses represent a very serious setback for the African states' overall performance. Except perhaps *Bernard von Pezold*, in an ideal world of checks and balances, as will be seen in subsequent chapters, there is considerable room for appellate moderation of the harshness of the results, particularly in the *Union Fenosa* and *Strabag SE* cases.

136 *Id.* at ¶ 69.
137 *Id.*
138 *Id.* at ¶ 72–73.
139 *Id.* at caption.
140 *Id.* at ¶ 510.
141 *See id.* at dispositif.

Conclusion

The initial decades of the African cases were characterized by largely boycotted and irregular procedures and unmitigated losses by the African states. The 2000s saw not only increased number of cases, but also increased and robust participation by African states and more regular and modern conduct of proceedings.

The African states saw a 50% increase in wins in the 2000s, up from almost zero in the three previous decades. Despite the backlash, in the post-2010s, the African states continued to participate more fully and vigorously, winning more than 60% of the cases. The procedures continued to be more and more standardized and predictable.

Unlike the African cases of the early decades that almost exclusively arose out of contractual instruments or domestic laws, the cases of the 2000s began to apply international investment law principles enshrined in BITs. Because the principles contained in Africa's BITs have their origin in the earlier European BITs that were also concluded with the rest of the world, the African cases began to borrow and lend jurisprudence to cases originating across the world. Both the use of the ICSID platform and the substantive rules of similar origin integrated the African cases into the global international investment regime. The onset of the 2000s thus saw the integration gain traction.

The more contemporary cases suggest the increased comfort level of the African states. Some of the cases that they won are remarkable for more reasons than the fact of winning—the tribunals began to understand Africa better. They also began to increasingly question the validity of the investor claims. The exacting scrutiny of the true merits of investor claims seems to have gained momentum after the *Patrick Mitchell* annulment. It gained instructive expression in *Bay View Group v. Rwanda*. The *Bay View* Tribunal's observation of the predicaments of the African state in dealing with investors who lack the required professional competence and financial ability is the most useful development, as that is the most common problem which leads to differing expectations which escalate to disputes. Africa is now both able to explain this to ISDS tribunals, and in return ISDS tribunals appear to be increasingly solicitous of Africa's explanations. This conclusion would be incomplete without the acknowledgment that in many of the cases wherein the Claimants prevailed, although some real injuries have been identified and redressed in some of the cases, there were evident inclinations to allocate the risk of mutual loss to the states. The details of these cases are discussed in the remain chapters.

6
Decision-Makers and Representation

The identity of the decision-makers in the African cases is the subject that is discussed most frequently relative to any other topic in ISDS discourses. This section identifies all of the arbitrators and party representatives in each case. Unlike most prior studies, it presents it in a narrative form rather than in a statistical chart.

The Decision-Makers and Representatives in the African Cases of the Initial Decades

In the foundational *Libyan Oil cases* (1970s), the president of the ICJ made all the appointments based on the default appointments authority given to him under the concession agreements because the Respondent state failed to appoint its arbitrator in each of the cases. The sole appointments were Judge Gunnar Lagergren, a Swedish national, in *BP v. Libya*;[1] René-Jean Dupuy, a French national, in *Texaco v. Libya*;[2] and Dr. Sobhi Mahmassani, a Lebanese national, for *LIAMCO v. Libya*.[3] After two European appointments, it seemed that the appointing authority wanted to add some diversity and appointed Dr. Mahamassani of Lebanon.

Described in Chapter 14, his reckoning with the lawfulness of the expropriation was remarkably different from the other two, although he still awarded damages reduced under equitable principles. Judge Dupuy, by contrast, was harsher than both in his analysis of the legality of the expropriation, finding no justifiable reason for the Respondent state's failure to perform its obligations under the concession agreement. Analytically, Largergen was somewhere in between—trading more finely as between conceptions of liability and damages.[4]

In *S.A.R.L. v. Congo* (1980),[5] the Claimant appointed as arbitrator Mr. Rudolf Bystricky from the then Czechoslovakia but who at the time lived in Switzerland. The Respondent State appointed Mr. Edilbert Razafindralambo, a national of Malaysia. Because the Parties could not agree on a presiding arbitrator, the Chairman of the Administrative Council of ICSID appointed under Article 38 of the Convention and Article 4 of the Rules Mr. Alex Bonn, a national of Luxembourg as the presiding arbitrator. Mr. Bonn later resigned and was replaced under the same procedures by Mr.

[1] BP Exploration Co. (Libya) Ltd. v. Libya, British Petroleum Exploration Co. (Libya) v. Libyan Arab Republic, 53 Int'l L. Rep. 297 (1973).

[2] Texaco Overseas Petroleum Co. and California Asiatic Oil Co. v. Libya, Preliminary Award (Nov. 27, 1975).

[3] Libyan American Oil Co. (LIAMCO) v. Libyan Arab Republic, 62 Int'l L. Rep. 140; 20 ILM 1 (1981) (1977).

[4] *See* Chapter 14.

[5] S.A.R.L. Benvenuti & Bonfant v. People's Republic of Congo, ICSID Case No. ARB/77/2 (1980), 1 ICSID Rep. 330 (1993).

Africa's International Investment Law Regimes. Won L. Kidane, Oxford University Press. © Oxford University Press 2023.
DOI: 10.1093/oso/9780197745571.003.0006

Jorgen Trolle, a Danish national.[6] The award was made unanimously. The majority was European, like most of the cases that preceded it.[7]

In *Klockner v. Cameroon* (1983),[8] there were two sets of arbitrators. The 1981 Tribunal was composed of Messrs. Dominique Schmidt, a French national, appointed by the Claimant; William D. Rogers, an American national, appointed by Cameroon and the Cameroon Fertilizer Company (SOCAME S.A.), joined as the Respondent. The two mutually selected Eduardo Jimenez de Arechaga, a Uruguayan national, as President.[9] The ad hoc annulment committee (1984) was composed of Professors Ahmed El-Kosheri, an Egyptian national; Ignaz Seidl-Hohenveldern, an Austrian national; and Pierre Lalive, a Swiss national, as members of the ad hoc Committee under Article 52(3) of the ICSID Convention. Professor Pierre Lalive chaired the Committee. All of the ad hoc committee members were appointed by the Chairman of the Administrative Council of ICSID, who was also the president of the World Bank.[10]

The ad hoc annulment committee deferred to the Tribunal's decision of its own jurisdiction. That effectively means that six arbitrators including Pierre Lalive who chaired the ad hoc committee sided with the African State on jurisdiction. The annulment committee, however, sided with the investor on the substance of the Tribunal's decision and annulled the award on the merits.[11] In the annulment procedure, the investor was represented by Philippe Nouel (among others), and Cameroon was represented by Jan Paulsson (among others).[12]

Jan Paulsson, a major player in the African cases, was at about the same time temporarily appearing on behalf of Liberia in the *Liberian Eastern Timber Corporation v. Republic Of Liberia* case in 1986.[13] For reasons that the awards do not explain, he dropped out of the case soon after the case got underway in 1983, Liberia defaulted in its appearance throughout the proceedings, and both the partial award on jurisdiction and final award on the merits were made without Liberia's representation.[14] The composition of the Liberian Eastern Timber Tribunal was D. A. Redfern, a national of the United Kingdom, appointed by the State; Jorge Goncalves Pereira, a national of Portugal, appointed by the investor; and Mr. Bernardo M. Cremades, a national of Spain, appointed by the Chair of the Administrative Council of ICSID.[15]

Although Liberia appointed Allen Redfern as its arbitrator and initially retained Jan Paulsson to represent it, it later boycotted the proceedings altogether[16] and of course

6 *Id.* at ¶ 1.3.

7 *See id.* at dispositif.

8 Decision Rendered by Ad Hoc Committee on the Application for Annulment Against the Arbitral Award in Klockner v. Cameroon, ARB/81/2 (Oct. 21, 1983).

9 *Id.* at ¶ 1.

10 *Id.*

11 *Id.* at ¶ 180.

12 *Id.* at ¶ 1.

13 Liberian Eastern Timber Corporation v. Republic of Liberia, ICSID Cases No. ARB/83/2, Award (Mar. 31, 1986).

14 *See id.* at ¶ 5.

15 *Id.* at ¶ 4.

16 *See id.* at ¶ 14–15. ("... Again Liberia failed to respond to all notifications and failed to appear at the last-mentioned hearing, letco on the contrary, presented various witnesses on its behalf. Apart from the arbitrators, those present included: Mr Robert L. Simpson. Mr Robert Lasson of Sciages & Grumes (a subsidiary of letco), Mr Alan de Marti (the ex-General Manager of letco in Liberia), Mr Angel Aranda Iriarte

suffered an adverse outcome as discussed in the various sections on jurisdiction and merits. It is, however, important to note that the Tribunal was careful in addressing how it attempted to balance the inevitable one-sidedness in ways that the Tribunals before it did not articulate. It said:

> 27. In this way, the onus of testing the assertions made by the party appearing shifts onto the Tribunal itself. As it is put in the notes to Rule 42: After the Tribunal has, on the expiration of the period of grace, resumed consideration of the Request, the proceeding is no longer fully contentious in the sense that expression is used in national civil procedures; the initiative is shifted to the Tribunal as far as the substantiation of the submissions is concerned. The Tribunal must now propio motu examine:
>
> . . .
>
> (b) the substantive merit of the assertions made by both parties in order to satisfy itself whether their submissions are well founded in fact and law. To this end. it may call on the active party for observation, evidence or explanations.
>
> 28. It is this procedure which was followed by the Tribunal in the present arbitration. The Tribunal did not take for granted the assertions of law and fact made by the claimant. On the contrary, it submitted them to careful examination; and its award is made on the basis of that examination.[17]

In *MINE v. Guinea* (1988), Guinea failed to participate in the initial AAA arbitration and suffered the consequences, but in the ICSID arbitration, it fully participated by appointing David K. Sharpe, a national of the United States. The Claimant appointed Jack Berg, a national of the United States, and the two mutually selected Donald E. Zubrod, a national from the United States, as president.[18] There is no clear information about the representatives.

In *SPP v. Egypt* (1992), the Claimant had originally proposed a sole arbitrator but the Respondent State not only proposed a panel of three arbitrators but quickly appointed its own national Dr. Mohamed Arnin El Mahdi, and also recommended Dr. Jimenez De Arechaga of Uruguay to be chair. The Claimant accepted both the Respondent's designations and appointed Mr. Robert F. Pietrowski Jr., a US national, as an arbitrator.[19]

In these proceedings the Claimant was represented by Mr. Peter Munk, Mr. William Laurence Craig, Mr. Jan Paulsson, Mr. Paul D. Friedland, Mr. Jean-Claude Najar, Mr. Harvey McGregor, Q. C., Mr. Mohammed Kamel, Mr. Charles Kaplan, and Mr. Michael Polkinghorne, as Counsel; and Dr. Aron Broches.[20] It is interesting to

(a partner in Peat Marwick) and Mr Martin Igman (an American accountant practising in Paris). At this hearing the members of the Tribunal requested further information and, once such information was received, declared the close of the proceedings on 10 February 1986").

[17] Letco v. Libera, ICSID Cases No. ARB/83/2, Award (Mar. 31, 1986), at ¶ 27–28.

[18] Maritime International Nominees Establishment v. Republic of Guinea, ICSID Case No. ARB/84/4, Award (Jan. 6, 1988), at ¶ 35.

[19] Southern Pacific Properties (Middle East) Limited v. Arab Republic of Egypt, ICSID Case No. ARB/84/3, Award (May 20, 1992), at ¶ 7.

[20] *See id.* at caption.

note that one of the Claimant's representatives was Aron Broches, one of the architects of the ICSID Convention who led the deliberations of the African Union in Addis Ababa in 1964, as discussed in Chapter 3. The Respondent was also ably represented by Dr. Iskandar Ghattas, Mr. Hassan Baghdadi, Professor Fawzy Mansour, Professor Jean-Denis Bredin, Mr. Robert Saint-Esteben, Mr. Ahmed Medhat, and Professor Emmanuel Gaillard, as Counsel; and Dr. Rudolf Dolzer, as Consultant.[21] Among the representatives of the Respondent are many prominent personalities that would later go on to influence the field in the decades that followed, such as Professor Gaillard and Dr. Dolzer.

The Decision-Makers and Representatives in the 2000s African Cases

In *Wena v. Egypt* (2000), the Claimant appointed Professor Ibrahim Fadlallah, from Lebanon. Egypt appointed Hamzeh Ahmed Haddad, from Jordan. The two having failed to agree on a chair, and upon Wena's request, ICSID's Administrative Council appointed Mr. Monroe Leigh of the United States as chair.[22] Shortly after the jurisdictional phase was over, Egypt's appointee, Professor Hamzeh Ahmed Haddad, was appointed as the Minister of Justice of Jordan and had to resign. Egypt then appointed Mr. Michael F. Hoellering as a replacement.[23] Because of Mr. Hoellering'a resignation for health reasons shortly after his appointment, Egypt had to appoint another arbitrator. This time, it appointed Professor Don Wallace.[24]

Egypt appointed Professor Don Wallace yet again in its next case, *Middle East Cement v. Egypt* (2002), with the Claimant appointing Professor Piero Bernardini and the two jointly selecting Professor Dr. Karl-Heinz Bockstiegel as President of the Tribunal.[25] It is interesting to note that with the *Middle East Cement* Tribunal duly constituted on January 28, 2000,[26] it appears that Professor Don Wallace was sitting as an arbitrator appointed by Egypt in two ICSID cases concurrently because the *Wena v. Egypt* award was only issued on December 8, 2000.[27] This is just an observation of a trivia.

In *Semos v Mali* (2003), the Claimant, Semos, appointed Professor Ibrahim Fadlallah, a French and Lebanese national, and Mali, the Respondent state, appointed Batonnier Robert S. M. Dossou, a national of Benin, and the two selected Maine Bernardo M. Cremades, a Spanish national, as the presiding arbitrator.[28] Both Parties were represented from the very beginning. Semos was represented by Maitre Charles

[21] *Id.*

[22] Wena Hotels Limited v. Arab Republic of Egypt, ICSID Case No. ARB/98/4, Award (Dec. 8, 2000), at ¶ 2.

[23] *Id.* at ¶ 8.

[24] *Id.* at ¶ 11.

[25] Middle East Cement Shipping and Handling Co. S.A. v. Arab Republic of Egypt, ICSID Case No. ARB/99/6, Award (Apr. 12, 2002), at ¶ 7.

[26] *Id.* at ¶ 8.

[27] *See* Wena v. Egypt, ICSID Case No. ARB/98/4, Award (Dec. 8, 2000), at ¶ 1, caption.

[28] Société D'exploitation Des Mines D'or De Sadiola S.A. (Semos) v. Republic of Mali, ICSID Case No. ARB/01/5, Award (Feb. 25, 2003), at ¶ 8.

Kaplan and Maitre Cabrol. Mali was represented by Mrs. Bah Haoua Toumagnon and Mr. Sekou Dioro Dicko.[29]

CDC v. Seychelles (2003) was the only case thus far that was decided by a sole arbitrator. Based on the Parties' loan agreement, the Secretary General of ICSID appointed Sir Anthony Mason, AC KBE as the sole arbitrator.[30] The Parties were also represented by one counsel each. The Award lists the representatives: Mr. Stephen Jagusch of Allen & Overy, representing the Claimant; and Mr. Anthony Francis Tissa Fernando, Attorney-General of the Republic of Seychelles, representing the respondent.[31]

In *Patrick Mitchell v. DRC* (2004) and Annulment (2006), two sets of arbitrators decided the matter. At the initial stage, the Claimant, Patrick Mitchell, designated Mr. Willard Z. Estey, a national of Canada, as its arbitrator. Because the Respondent's first nominee refused to accept (the award does not indicate who it was) and it failed to nominate another, the Acting Chairman of the Administrative Council appointed Mr. Yawovi Agboyibo, a Togolese national (whose remarkable dissent set the stage for the subsequent annulment) and Professor Andreas Bucher, a Swiss national, as the presiding arbitrator.[32] With the passing of Mr. Willard Estey, the Claimant appointed its replacement, Mr. Marc Lalonde, another national of Canada.[33]

The majority, consisting of the Claimant's appointee and the presiding arbitrator, ruled in favor of the Claimant. The Respondent sought to annul the award before ICSID Ad Hoc Annulment Committee. The Committee as appointed by the Chairman of the Administrative Council was composed of Andrea Giardina (Italian), Robert S. M. Dossou (Beninese), and Antonias C. Dimolitsa (Greek) as President of the Ad Hoc Committee.[34] The end result was basically in favor of the Respondent state 4 to 2, with one dissenting at the initial stage and three Ad Hoc Committee members largely agreeing with the dissenting arbitrator at the annulment stage. At the end of it all, Mr. Patrick Mitchell's investor–state arbitral endeavor left him bearing his own costs and paying an additional $100,000, which is half of the fees that the DRC had paid for ICSID administrative and Annulment Committee expenses.[35]

World Duty Free v. Kenya (2006) saw a confluence of a high-profile tribunal and formidable representation. It took the complexity of the process and use of domestic and international jurisprudence to a higher level. The Claimant appointed the Honorable Andrew Rogers, QC, an Australian national. The Respondent reciprocated by appointing another prominent Australian, Professor James Crawford, SC. The two party-appointed arbitrators appointed none other than Judge Gilbert Guillaume, a

[29] *Id.* at ¶ 14.

[30] CDC Group Plc v. Republic of The Seychelles, ICSID Case No. ARB/02/14 (Dec. 17, 2003), at ¶ 14, caption.

[31] *See id.* at caption.

[32] Patrick Mitchell v. DRC Award (Feb. 9, 2004); Annulment (Nov. 1, 2006), at ¶ 4–6.

[33] *Id.* at ¶ 14.

[34] Patrick Mitchell v. DRC, (Feb. 9, 2004); Annulment (Nov. 1, 2006), at ¶ 6, caption.

[35] *See id.* at ¶ 67 ("Order the equal sharing of the costs of the Annulment Proceeding between the parties, with each bearing the expenses incurred for its own defense, including legal fees, which in this case, in consideration of all the circumstances of this Annulment Proceeding, appears to the ad hoc Committee to be fair and equitable. Consequently, since the DRC has solely been responsible for making the advance payments covering the costs of the Annulment Proceeding, amounting to USD 200,000, Claimant is ordered to pay the DRC the amount of USD 100,000").

French national, as the Presiding arbitrator.[36] Immediately thereafter, however, the Claimant challenged Professor Crawford for his previous relationship with the firm that was representing the Respondent, Freshfields Bruckhaus Deringer. He resigned voluntarily. Respondent then appointed Mr. V. V. Veeder, QC, a UK national.[37] The Rogers, Guillaume, and Veeder Tribunal made the final award.[38]

The Claimant was represented by Geoffrey Robertson, QC and Ms. Olivia Holdsworth, from the United Kingdom, as well as the prominent Kenyan lawyer Mr. Paul K. Muite, and Mr. Peter Buscemi Morgan of Lewis & Bockius LLP.[39] The Respondent was represented by Mr. Jan Paulsson, Mr. Constantine Partasides, and Mr. Mitesh Kotecha of Freshfields Bruckhaus Deringer.[40]

In *Champion Trading v. Egypt* (2006), the Claimants appointed Mr. L. Yves Fortier, QC, and the Respondent appointed Professor Laurent Ayn, and the Secretary-General of ICSID appointed Mr. Robert Briner as the president of the Arbitral Tribunal by the agreement of the Parties.[41] The Tribunal's composition remained the same throughout the proceedings and rendition of the final award although there had been a change in counsel on the Claimants' side after the jurisdictional decision dismissed the individual Claimants. The counsel who appeared on behalf of the Claimants for the jurisdictional phase were Mr. Emmanuel Gaillard, Ms. Yas Banifatemi, and Mr. Merwan Lomri, Shearman & Sterling; Mr. Dany Khayat; and Mr. Arif Ali. For the merits phase the Claimant was represented by Mr. Peter Kirby, Fasken Martineau DuMoulin LLP; Mr. Hilal Al Ayoubi, Fasken Martineau DuMoulin LLP; Professor Todd Weiler; Mr. Andrew Price; and Fulbright Jaworski.[42]

In *Helnan v. Egypt* (2008), the Tribunal was composed of Mr. Michael Lee, appointed by the Claimant, Prof. Rudolf Dolzer, appointed by the Respondent, and the two mutually selected Mr. Yves Derains as chair.[43] Claimant was represented by Mr. Michael P. Lennon Jr., Ms. Ania Farren, and Mr. Devashish Krishan of Baker Botts (UK); and Mr. Peter Griffin of Conyngham Advisors.[44] Egypt was represented by Counselor Milad Sidhom, President States Lawsuits Authority, Mogamaa El Tahrir, and its counsel Dr Ahmed El Kosheri of the law firm of Kosheri, Rashed & Riad and Prof. Jan Paulsson of Freshfields Bruckhaus Deringer, Dr Karim Hafez of the law firm Hafez, and Dr. Mohamed Abdel Raouf of the Abdel Raouf Law Firm.[45]

Biwater v. Tanzania (2008) brought together three of the most renowned arbitrators: Gary Born, a US national, appointed by the Claimant; Toby Landau, a UK

[36] World Duty Free Company Limited v. Republic of Kenya, ICSID Case No. ARB/00/7, Award (Oct. 4, 2006), at ¶ 6–7.

[37] *Id.* at ¶ 10–11.

[38] *See id.* at caption.

[39] *See id.* at ¶ 1.

[40] *See id.* at ¶ 2.

[41] Champion Trading Company Ameritrade International, Inc. v. Arab Republic of Egypt, ICSID Case No. ARB/02/9, Award (Oct. 27, 2006), at ¶ 3.

[42] *Id.* at ¶ 10.

[43] Helnan International Hotels A/S V. The Arab Republic of Egypt, ICSID Case No. ARB/05/19, Award (July 3, 2008), at ¶ 10.

[44] *Id.* at ¶ 1.

[45] *Id.* at ¶ 2.

national, appointed by the Respondent State; and Bernard Hanotiau, a Belgium national, selected by the party-appointed arbitrators as chair.[46]

Tanzania was represented by Julius Mallaba, Attorney-General's Chambers; Hon. Nimrod E. Mkono MP, Dr. Wilbert B. Kapinga, Carel Daele, and Bart Williams of Mkono & Co.; as well as international counsel Jan Paulsson, D. Brian King, Jonathan J. Gass, and Marijn Heemskerk of Freshfields Bruckhaus Deringer. Biwater was represented by Judith Gill, Matthew Gearing, Hannah Ambrose, Michelle de Kluyver, Autumn Ellis, and Andrew Pullen of Allen & Overy LLP.[47]

In *Jan de Nul N.V. and Dredging International N.V v. Egypt* (2008),[48] the Tribunal was constituted by the parties' consent and is composed of Professor Pierre Mayer, a national of France, appointed by the Claimant; Professor Brigitte Stern, a national of France, appointed by the Respondent; and Professor Gabrielle Kaufmann-Kohler, a national of Switzerland, selected by the two as President of the Tribunal.[49] This was one of those rare majority-women high-profile cases. Indeed, this was the only Tribunals in all of the African cases included in this study that is majority-women.

The Parties were properly and timely represented. The Claimants were represented by Prof. Antonio Crivellaro and Prof. Luca Radicati di Brozolo, who were at the time at Bonelli Erede Pappalardo.[50] Egypt was represented by Dr. Iskandar Ghattas, Under Secretary, Ministry of Justice; Dr. Mostafa Abdel Ghaffar, Director of International Cooperation, Ministry of Justice; Mr. Hosam Abdel Azim, President of the Office of State Litigation; Mr. Osama Mahmoud, Office of State Litigation; and Messrs. Robert Saint-Esteben and Louis-Christophe Delanoy, Bredin Prat.[51]

In *Bernardus v. Zimbabwe* (2009), the constitution of the Tribunal took an unusually extended period of time because the parties failed to agree on its mechanisms of constitution.[52] With the Claimant's invocation of Article 37(2)(b) of the ICSID Convention, the Tribunal was initially constituted with the Claimants' appointee Dean Ronald A. Cass, a US national; the Respondent's appointee, the Minister of Justice of Pakistan, H. E. Mr. Mohammad Wasi Zafar; and Judge Gilbert Guillaume of France, appointed by the Chairman of the Administrative Council of ICSID because the Party-appointed arbitrators failed to agree on a presiding arbitrator.[53]

The Claimant was represented from the very beginning by Mr. Charles Owen Verrill Jr., Wiley Rein LLP; and Mr. Mathew Coleman, Africa Legal.[54] Although the Respondent was initially represented by government officials, including Mrs. Virginia Mabiza, Attorney General's Office; Mrs. Mandinika, Deputy Director, Ministry of Lands, Land Reform; Mr. Mischeck C. Hove, Minister Counselor, Embassy

[46] Biwater Gauff (Tanzania) Ltd. v. United Republic of Tanzania, ICSID Case No. ARB/05/22, Final Award (July 24, 2008), at ¶ 25–27.

[47] *Id.* at ¶ 1–2.

[48] Jan de Nul N.V. Dredging International N.V. v. Arab Republic of Egypt, ICSID Case No. ARB/04/13, Award (Nov. 6, 2008).

[49] *Id.* at ¶ 13.

[50] *Id.* at ¶ 5.

[51] *Id.* at ¶ 7.

[52] Bernardus Henricus Funnekotter and Others v. Republic of Zimbabwe, ICSID Case No. ARB/05/6, Award (Apr. 22, 2009), at ¶ 5.

[53] *Id.* at ¶ 5–6.

[54] *Id.* at ¶ 8.

of Zimbabwe, Paris; and Mr. Cavins N. Mugaviri, Minister Counselor, Embassy of Zimbabwe, Paris; it added Mr. Philip Kimbrough and Mr. Tristan Moreau of Kimbrough & Associates after the submission of the written pleadings and throughout the oral hearings.[55]

In *Waguih Elie v. Egypt* (2009), the Tribunal is composed of Prof. Michael Pryles, Australian national, appointed by Claimants; Prof. Francisco Orrego Vicuna, a Chilian national, appointed by the Respondent; and Mr. David A. R. Williams, a national of New Zealand, selected as chair by the party-appointed arbitrators.[56] The Claimants were represented by Mr. Reginald R. Smith, Mr. Craig S. Miles, and Mr. Kenneth R. Fleuriet of King & Spalding LLP; and the Respondent was represented by Mr. Hazim A. Rizkana Helmy, Hamza & Partners, Baker & McKenzie International-Cairo; and Mr. Lawrence W. Newman, Baker & McKenzie LLP-New York; H. E. Counsellor Milad Sidhom Boutros, Mr. Hussein M. F. Mostafa, and Mr. Asser M. A. Harb, State Law Suites Authority, Egypt.[57]

The Decision-Makers in the Modern Post-2010s African Cases

In *Gustav v. Ghana* (2010), the Tribunal was composed of Dr. Bernardo M. Cremades, a Spanish national, appointed by the Claimant; Mr. Toby Landau QC, a British national, appointed by the Respondent; and Prof. Brigitte Stern, a French national, mutually selected as the president.[58]

The Claimant was represented by Mr. Akbar Ali, AFA Law; and by Mr. Andrew Goddard QC and Mr. Riaz Hussain, Atkin Chambers.[59] The Respondent was represented by Mr. Arthur Marriott QC, Mr. Thomas Geuther, Mr. Paul Cohen, and Ms. Christina Loucas of Dewey & LeBoeuf.[60]

The *Malicorp v. Egypt* (2011) Tribunal was composed of Claimant's appointee, Prof. Luiz Olavo Baptista, a national of Brazil; the Respondent's appointee, Maître Pierre-Yves Tschanz, a national of Switzerland; and a mutually selected chair, Prof. Pierre Tercier, a national of Switzerland.[61] The Clamant was represented by Maître Christian Bremond, Maître Sylvie Morel, Maître Yassin Tagelding Yassin, and Maître Jean-Pierre of Coutard Bremond, Vaïsse, Rambert & Associates. The Respondent was represented by Maître Thomas H. Webster, Maître Asser Harb, Paris; and H. E. Sedky Kholousy and Mr. Ahmed Saad, Egyptian State Lawsuits Authority.[62]

55 *Id.* at ¶¶ 8, 14.

56 Waguih Elie George Slag and Clorinda Vecchi v. The Arab Republic of Egypt, ICSID Case No. ARB/05/15, Award (June 1, 2009), at ¶ 92–95.

57 *See id.* at caption.

58 Gustav F W Hamester GmbH & Co KG v. Republic of Ghana Respondent, ICSID Case No. ARB/07/24, Award (June 18, 2010), at ¶ 8.

59 *Id.* at ¶ 4.

60 *Id.* at ¶ 5.

61 *See* Malicorp Limited v. The Arab Republic of Egypt, ICSID Case No. ARB/08/18, Award (Feb. 7, 2011), at ¶ 76.

62 *See id.* at caption.

The *Bernard von Pezold v. Zimbabwe* (2015) Tribunal had a remarkable task of adjudicating two cases simultaneously and suffered two resignations, as indicated above, of both appointees of the Respondent. The first appointee who resigned was Professor A. Peter Mutharika, a national of Malawi.[63] The second who resigned was Professor An Chen, a national of the People's Republic of China.[64] The Tribunal that eventually issued the final award was composed of Sir David A. R. Williams, QC, a national of New Zealand; Hon. L. Yves Fortier, a national of Canada, appointed by agreement of the co-arbitrators as presiding arbitrator;[65] and Mr. Michael Hwang, a national of Singapore, appointed as a replacement arbitrator by the Respondent.[66]

Both Parties were duly represented and participated throughout the proceedings. The external counsel that the Claimant relied on were Mr. Matthew Coleman, Mr. Kevin Williams, Mr. Anthony Rapa, Ms. Helen Aldridge, Mr. Thomas Innes, and Ms. June Booth, all of Steptoe & Johnson; and Mr. Charles Verrill Jr. of Wiley Rein.[67] The Respondent was represented by Mr. Philip Kimbrough and Mr. Tristan Moreau, Kimbrough & Associates, and a large number of government lawyers and other professionals.[68] The large representation, the high-profile Tribunal and the voluminous submissions, are indicative of the importance of the case not only from a purely investment law point of view but also the broader historical and sociopolitical background of the case, which the discussion of the merits of the substantive principles in Chapters 9 through 12 will bring out.

In *Standard Chartered Bank v. Tanzania Electric Supply Company Limited (TANESCO)* (2016), the Tribunal was composed Prof. Donald McRae, a Canadian national; President Prof. Zachary Douglas, QC, a national of Australia, appointed by the Claimant; and Prof. Brigitte Stern, a national of France, appointed by the Respondent.[69]

[63] Bernhard von Pezold and Others v. Republic of Zimbabwe, ICSID Case No. ARB/10/15, Award (July 28, 2015), at ¶ 15.

[64] *Id.* at ¶ 25.

[65] *Id.* at ¶ 15.

[66] *Id.* at ¶ 27.

[67] *Id.* at ¶ 72. A large number of others also attended the hearing on behalf of the Claimant including: Mr. Kenneth Schofield, Border Timbers Limited, Mr. Gideon Theron, Commercial Farmers' Union, Mr. Simon van der Lingen, Border Timbers Limited, Mr. George Bottger, Border Timbers Limited, Mr. Anthony Levitt, RGL Forensics, Mr. Richard Jenks, RGL Forensics, Ms. Helen Swain, RGL Forensics, Professor Stephen Chan, SOAS University, Mr. Alan Stephenson, Mills Fitchett, Mr. Paul Christopher Paul, Wintertons, Ms. Amanda von Pezold, Ms. Elba Schofield. *Id.*

[68] *Id.* at ¶ 72. The other representatives include: The Honourable Douglas T. Mombeshora, Minister of Lands and Rural Resettlement, Mr. Wellington Mvura, Aid to Minister Mombeshora, Ms. Sophia Christina Tsvakwi, Permanent Secretary, Ministry of Lands and Rural Resettlement, Ms. Elizabeth Sumowah, Legal Advisor, Ministry of Lands and Rural Resettlement, Prince Machaya, Deputy Attorney General, Civil Division Attorney General's Office, Ms. Fortune Chimbaru, Chief Law Officer, Civil Division Attorney General's Office, Ms. Fatima Maxwell, Judge, Labour Court, Minister Didymus Mutasa, Minister of State in the Office of the President and Cabinet, Mr. Onias C. Masiiwa, Chief Inspector Exchange Control, Mr. Grasiano Nyaguse, Director, Policy, Planning and Coordination, Ministry of Economic Planning and Development, Mr. Sifelani Moyo, Director, Ministry of Local Government, Public Works and National Housing, Dr. Joseph Kanyekanye, Group CEO, Allied Timbers, HE Ambassador Mapuranga Machivenyika, Embassy of the Republic of Zimbabwe in Washington, DC, Mr. Whatmore Goora, Embassy of the Republic of Zimbabwe in Washington, DC, and Mr. Richard Chibuwe, Embassy of the Republic of Zimbabwe in Washington, DC. *Id.*

[69] Standard Chartered Bank (Hong Kong) Ltd. v. Tanzania Electric Supply Company Ltd. (Tanesco), ICSID Case No. ARB/10/20, Award (Sep. 12, 2016), at caption.

The Claimant was represented by Mr. Iain Maxwell, Mr. Dominic Kennelly, Ms. Naomi Lisney, Herbert Smith Freehills LLP; and Mr. Matthew Weiniger QC, Linklaters LLP. The Respondent was represented by Mr. Richard K. Rweyongeza and Prof. Bonaventure Rutinwa, R. K. Rweyongeza & Co. Advocates; Mr. Beredy Malegesi, Crax Law Partners; and Dr. Florian Baumann, Mr. Martin Molina, Dr. Bernhard Berger, Ms. Marlen Eisenring, and Kellerhals Carrard.[70]

In *Union Fenosa Gas, S.A. (UFG) v. Egypt* (2018), the Tribunal was composed of Mr. J. William Rowley, QC, a national of Canada and the United Kingdom, appointed by the Claimant; the Respondent first appointed Mr. J. Christopher Thomas, a national of Canada, who withdrew and was replaced by Mr. Mark Alan Clodfelter, a national of the United States of America, and the two selected Mr. V. V. Veeder, citizen of the United Kingdom, as president.[71]

Both Parties were properly represented from the very beginning. The Claimant was represented by Mr. R. Doak Bishop, Mr. David H. Weiss, Ms. Anisha Sud, Ms. Sara L. McBrearty, Ms. Ginny Castelan, King & Spalding LLP (Houston); and Mr. Edward G. Kehoe, Ms. Isabel Fern ndez de la Cuesta, Mr. Aloysius Llamzon, Mr. Timothy M. McKenzie, King & Spalding LLP (NY); and Mr. James E. Castello, Mr. Rami Chahine, King & Spalding (Paris) and Ms. Sara Burns, King & Spalding LLP (Atlanta). The Respondent was represented by HE Counsellor Hussein Khalil Hamza, Counsellor Abdel Hameed Nagashy, Counsellor Mohamed Khalaf, Counsellor Amr Arafa Hassan, Counsellor Fatma Khalifa, Counsellor Yousria El Gamal, Counsellor Lela Kassem, Egyptian State Lawsuits Authority (ESLA); and (since March 17, 2015) Dr. Claudia Annacker, Mr. Robert T. Greig, Mr. J. Cameron Murphy, Ms. Laurie Achtouk-Spivak, Mr. Larry Work-Dembowski, Ms. Ariella Rosenberg, and Ms. Ellie Norton, Cleary Gottlieb Steen & Hamilton LLP.[72]

The Tribunal in *Cortec v. Kenya* (2018) was composed of Judge Ian Binnie, CC, QC, a national of Canada; president, appointed by agreement, Mr. Kanaga Dharmananda SC, a national of Australia, appointed by the Claimants; and Professor Brigitte Stern, a national of France, appointed by the Respondent.[73]

In this case, the Claimant was represented by Mr. Audley Sheppard QC, Clifford Chance London; Mr. Ben Luscombe, Dr. Sam Luttrell, Mr. Peter Harris, Mr. Nathan Eastwood, and Ms. Clementine Packer, Clifford Chance, Perth, Commonwealth of Australia; and Dr. Romesh Weeramantry, Clifford Chance, Hong Kong.[74] The Respondent was represented by Ms. Pauline Mcharo, Deputy Chief State Counsel; Mr. Emmanuel Bitta, Deputy Chief State Counsel; Ms. Christine K. Omwakwe, Prinicipal State Counsel; Mr. Charles Wamwayi, State Counsel; Mr. Guglielmo Verdirame, London; Mr. Alexander Brabant, DLP Piper France, Paris; Mr. Ben Sanderson, Ms. Elinor Thomas, Ms. Maria Scott, and Ms. Kate Cervantes-Knox, DLP Piper UK; and Mr. Kamau Karori, Ms. Milly Jalega, and Mr. Ken Melly,

[70] *See id.* at i.
[71] Union Fenosa Gas, S.A. v. Arab Republic of Egypt, ICSID Case No. ARB/14/4 (Aug. 31, 2018), at ¶ 1.6–1.16.
[72] *See id.* at caption.
[73] *See id.* at ¶ 17.
[74] *Id.* at caption.

Iseme Kamau & Maema Advocate Nairobi.[75] Both Parties were duly and timely represented.

The Tribunal in *CMC v. Mozambique* (2019) was composed of Mr. Peter Rees QC, a national of the United Kingdom, appointed by the Claimant; Mr. J. Brian Casey, a national of Canada, appointed by the Respondent; and the two mutually selected Mr. John M. Townsend, a national of the United States as chair.[76]

The Claimant was represented by Mr. Alan Del Rio and Mr. Donal Larkin, LDR Consultants, Dublin, Ireland; and Mr. Luis Gonzlez Garcia, Matrix Chambers Gray's Inn, London. The Respondent was represented by Mr. Juan C. Basombrio Esq. and Ms. Erica Chen Esq., Dorsey & Whitney, Costa Mesa, CA.[77]

In *Oded Besserglik v. Mozambique* (2019), the Claimant appointed L. Yves Fortier CC, QC, a Canadian national;[78] and the Respondent first appointed Mr. Juan C. Basombrio, a US national, but later replaced him with Dr. Claus von Wobeser, a Mexican national.[79]

The Claimant was represented from May 2018 to the rendition of the Award by Mr. Lee Caplan, Mr. Ucheora Onwuamaegbu, Arent Fox LLP, Washington; and from March 2014 to May 2018 by Mr. H. P. Jefferys, SC, Umdloti Beach, South Africa; Mr. Armando David Chissaque, Maputo; Mr. J. Maricato, of Maricato, Lima & Associados; Rua das Picoas, Lisboa; and Mr. Rui Marto, of Marto Lafitte & Associates Inc., Johannesburg.[80]

The Respondent was represented by Mr. Basombrio of Dorsey & Whitney, Costa Mesa, California, whom it first appointed as an arbitrator, and Ms. Teresa Filomena Muenda, Maputo.[81] It appears that for the hearing, the Respondent added more counsel and representatives, including Ms. Erica Haggerty of Dorsey & Whitney LLP; Mr. Angelo Vasco Matusse, Deputy Attorney-General, Republic of Mozambique; Mr. Silvestre Salom of Silindane, National Director of Legal Affairs, Republic of Mozambique; Mr. Fernando Manhi, a Director for Legal and Consular Affairs, Ministry of Foreign Affairs and Cooperation, Republic of Mozambique; Mr. Quintus van der Merwe of Shepstone & Wylie Attorneys; and Ms. Teresa Filomena Muenda.[82] Both parties were duly and timely represented.

In *Thomas Goslin v. Mauritius* (2020), the Tribunal was composed of Dr. Andres Rigo Sureda, a national of Spain, president, appointed by the co-arbitrators; Prof. Stanimir Alexandrov, a national of Bulgaria, appointed by the Claimants; and Prof. Brigitte Stern, a national of France, appointed by the Respondent.[83]

The Claimant was represented by Ms. Sophie Lamb, Mr. Samuel Pape, Ms. Shreya Ramesh, Mr. Gustavo Ruiz, and Mr. Sean Mulloy, Latham & Watkins, London; and

[75] *Id.* at caption.

[76] CMC Muratori Cementisti CMC Di Ravenna SOC. Coop. & Others v. Republic of Mozambique, ICSID Case No. ARB/17/23 (Oct. 24, 2019), at ¶ 20–23.

[77] *Id.* at caption.

[78] Oded Besserglik v. Republic of Mozambique, ICSID Case No. ARB(AF)/14/2, Award (Oct. 28, 2019), at ¶ 13.

[79] *Id.* at ¶ 15.

[80] *Id.* at caption.

[81] *Id.*

[82] *See id.* at ¶ 112.

[83] *See id.* at ¶ 8–10.

the Respondent was represented by Mr. Paul Reichler, Ms. Tafadzwa Pasipanodya, Dr. Constantinos Salonidis, Ms. Alison Macdonald QC (Essex Court Chambers), Ms. Christina Beharry, Mr. Yuri Parkhomenko, Ms. Rebecca Gerome, Mr. Antoine Lerosier, Mr. Sudhanshu Roy, Ms. Mikiko Takara, Ms. Ela Leshem, Ms. Flannery Sockwell, Ms. Nanami Hirata, Ms. Carmen de Jesus, and Ms. Nancy Lopez, all of Foley Hoag LLP, Washington.[84] Although the list of counsel might seem to have differed from those who were involved from the very beginning, the Parties were timely and duly represented and participated throughout the proceedings.

In *Strabag SE v. Libya* (2020), the Claimant appointed Professor Antonio Crivellaro, a national of Italy; the Respondent appointed Professor Nassib G. Ziade, a national of Lebanon and Chile; and the two mutually selected through a list ranking procedure Professor John Crook, a national of the United States, as the president of the Tribunal.[85]

Throughout the proceedings the Claimant was represented by Mr. Charles Claypoole, Mr. Sebastian Seelmann-Eggebert, Mr. Philip Clifford, QC, Ms. Catriona Paterson (until August 31, 2018), Mr. Robert Price, and Mr. Thomas Lane, Latham & Watkins, London. Libya was represented by Mr. Hermann Ferre and Mr. Andrew Larkin, Curtis, Mallet-Prevost, Colt & Mosle LLP, New York; Dr. Walid El-Nabal and Ms. Loujaine Kahaleh, Curtis, Mallet-Prevost, Colt & Mosle LLP, London; and Dr. Claudia Frutos-Peterson and Dr. Borzu Sabah I, Curtis, Mallet-Prevost, Colt & Mosle LLP, Washington.[86] In contrast to the Libyan Oil cases of the 1970s and despite the political transition, Libya participated fully with proper representation.

In *Interocean Oil v. Nigeria* (2020), the Claimant appointed Professor Julian D. M. Lew, a national of the United Kingdom; the Respondent appointed Justice Edward Torgbor, a national of the United Kingdom and Ghana; and the two selected Professor William W. Park, a national of the United States and Switzerland, as the presiding arbitrator.[87]

In these proceedings, the Claimant was represented by Mr. Olasupo Shasore, Senior Advocate of Nigeria (SAN); Professor Oba Nsugbe QC, SAN; and Mrs. Bimpe Nkontchou, Mr. Bello Salihu, and Ms. Fadesike Salu. The Respondent was represented by Mr. Adebayo Adenipekun, SAN, FCIArb.; Mr. Olu Daramola, SAN, FCIArb.; Mr. Robert Volterra, Mr. Christophe Bondy, Ms. Ann Babalola, Mr. Oluwasina Ogungbade, and Ms. Rose Rameau, MCIArb; Mr. Kehinde Ogunwumiju, Mr. Ola Faro, Mr. lvaro Nistal, and Mr. Chukwudi Maduka, Mrs. Yemisi Adenipekun, MCIArb.; and Ms. Maria Fogdestam-Agius, Ms. Isabella Seif, Ms. Amanda Murphy, Ms. Andrea Mauri, and Mr. Matthew Nelson.[88] Both parties were properly and timely represented. The Claimants and their representatives appear to have had significant Nigerian connection. The standing offer for ICSID arbitration also came from Nigerian domestic law and most of the Nigerian counsel were also Nigeria-based or with significant Nigerian connection. With heavy Nigerian connection on both sides

[84] *See id.* at ¶ 37. The initial list shows a slightly different composition of counsel in the caption.
[85] Strabag Se v. Libya, ICSID Case No. ARB(AF)/15/1, Award (June 29, 2020), at ¶ 12–15.
[86] *Id.* at caption.
[87] Interocean Oil Development Company and Interocean Oil Exploration Company v. Federal Republic of Nigeria, ICSID Case No. ARB/13/20, Award (Oct. 6, 2020), at ¶ 50–51.
[88] *See id.* at ¶ 73.

and an African arbitrator on the Tribunal, this was one of few, if any, cases that had its center of gravity outside of Washington, Paris, and London.

In *Bay View Group v. Rwanda* (2022), the Tribunal was composed of Mr. J. Truman Bidwell Jr., a national of the United States of America, appointed by the Claimants; Ms. Barbara Dohmann QC, a national of Germany and the United Kingdom, appointed by the Respondent; and Hon. Lord Phillips KG, PC, a national of the United Kingdom, selected by the party-appointed arbitrators as president.[89]

Appearing on behalf of the Claimant were Mr. Roderick Marshall, Bay View Group LLC and the Spalena Company LLC; Mr. Steven Cowley, Duane Morris, LLP; and Mr. Bryan Harrison, Duane Morris, LLP. The Respondent was represented by Ms. Specioza Kabibi Minijust, Government of Rwanda; Mr. Narcisse Dushiminana, Rwanda Mining Board; Mr. Richard Hill QC, Mr. Alastair Tomson, Ms. Michelle Duncan, Mr. Daniel McCarthy, Ms. Danielle Duffield, and Ms. Lucy Needle of Joseph Hage Aaronson LLP, London.[90] In this case, the United States, as the country of origin of the Claimants under the applicable BIT, was also represented by members of the US Office of International Claims and Investment Disputes and the Department of Justice.[91]

Conclusion

This chapter profiled the composition of decision-makers and representatives of 30 African cases, which is a sizable sample of all ICSID cases. Although this study does not purport to replicate or confirm previously conducted statistical studies as its main objective, is a qualitative and comprehensive review of every aspect of these selected cases, the glaring and stubborn lack of diversity among the decision-makers is a conclusion that cannot be overlooked.

With the exception of four cases—the three foundational Libyan Oil cases of the 1970s, and *CDC v. Seychelles* (2003)—all the other cases profiled above were decided by a three-member panel of arbitrators. At least two cases were decided by six decision-makers, which include ad hoc annulment committee members. That makes a total of about 88 decision-makers, that is, four sole arbitrators in the four cases that were decided by sole arbitrators, and 78 arbitrators deciding 26 cases, and 6 more deciding two annulment cases. About 80 of the 88 (including repeat appointments) have been Westerners, primarily from Australia, Canada, France, New Zealand, United Kingdom, and United States. There were only about four Africans, a Bulgarian, a Chilian, a Middle Eastern, a Mexican, and a few dual nationals. Even more astonishingly, of the 88 total arbitrators (double counting repeat appointments), there were only about four women, although Brigitte Stern was pointed by the respondent states several times. As indicated above, there was only one majority-woman tribunal. There was no majority-African tribunal. There was no tribunal chaired by an African, and

[89] Bay View Group LLC and The Spalena Company LLC v. Republic of Rwanda, ICSID Case No. ARB/18/21, Award (Mar. 30, 2022), at ¶ 9.
[90] *See id.* at ¶ 70.
[91] *Id.*

in fact, there was no tribunal chaired by a non-Western. There was only one tribunal chaired by a woman.

The more interesting fact is the evident lack of progress on the diversity front. When the president of the International Court of Justice was asked to appoint a sole arbitrator in each of the three Libyan Oil cases in the 1970s, he clearly sought to diversify by appointing a Middle Eastern as his third appointee, who brought a different perspective and helped the analytical depth of the early cases that continued to influence jurisprudence.[92] The awareness and sensitivity existed even at that time. In a way, the world of modern international arbitration involving African states began with 30% regional diversity of decision-makers in the 1970s, but did not make appreciable progress in the decades that came after that. The composition of even the most contemporary cases such as *Interocean Oil v. Nigeria* (2020) and *Bay View Group v. Rwanda* (2022) is as traditional as it could get.

The diversity deficit among the decision-makers remained a stubbornly difficult problem to resolve. Because this is a subject extensively explored in the literature,[93] no attempt is made here to add to that in any considerable way. There are, however, a few important observations that this qualitative chronological study of the African cases would permit.

The first is the role of the African states that is often discussed within the diversity topic. The study above shows that in almost all cases, the African states appointed their own arbitrators, and the appointees are mostly prominent western jurists. This is not surprising, because appointments take place in each individual case on an ad hoc basis and often follow the claimant's appointment. In those instances, for the appointing counsel or arbitrator, diversity is not always the most pressing priority. No single country or specific counsel or advisor would want to carry the burden of diversification unless that appointment makes sense for that particular case.

The second and perhaps more important and less discussed factor is the establishment's continued adoptability and refinement that makes it continually acceptable despite the lack of diversity. A very simple observation of the results and examination of the quality of the jurisprudence by the prominent arbitrators suggests a measure of care, discipline, and sophistication expected of a maturing system of decision-making.

The African states no longer find the arbitral order as frightening as they once did in the decades following independence. They won some decisive victories before all Western tribunals. Although some subtle pro-investor bias remains as seen in *Bernard von Pezold v. Zimbabwe* (2015) and *Strabag SE v. Libya* (2020), the system has maintained its resilience by rejecting nonmeritorious claims as in *Bay View Group v. Rwanda* (2022).

Like any decision-making processes, the identity of the decision-maker is vitally important, however, nationality alone is just a poor indicator of bias and predisposition. The values of cultural and gender diversity are, however, well-studied and are profound and should be considered in each case and addressed at every opportunity, step by step.

[92] *See* Chapter 12 on Dr. Sobhi Mahmassani's contributions.

[93] *See, e.g.*, A. K. Bjorklund, D. Behn, S. D., Franck, C. Giorgetti, W. Kidane, A. de Nanteuil, & E. Onyema, *The Diversity Deficit in International Investment Arbitration*, 21 J. of World Inv. & Trade, 410–40 (2020).

7
Jurisdiction and the Meaning of Investment

The difficulty that the ICSID Convention's lack of definition of "Investment" and "Investor" introduced into international investment law generally is not limited to jurisdictional complications. Because the definitions of these terms come from a multitude of legal instruments, mainly bilateral and regional investment treaties, and because substantive protection and procedural safeguards depend on whether the commitment of capital or resources qualifies as an investment by an investor, the meaning of these terms has also been a subject of immense controversy.

Many of the leading ICSID cases in this regard have involved African states. This chapter profiles some of these leading cases, understands the positions taken by African states on these issues, measures the overall influence that they have had on the general jurisprudence, and discerns how much of the jurisprudence has informed Africa's most contemporary treaty making and reform efforts.

Jurisdiction and the Meaning of Investment in the Initial Decades

The earliest African ICISD case covered under this study is the 1978 case of *S.A.R.L. Benvenuti & Bonfant v. People's Republic of the Congo.*[1] Because, like many of these ICSID cases, the State's consent to arbitrate was expressed in a contractual instrument rather than a treaty, and many of the substantive claims were akin to breach of contract claims, the jurisdictional question did not require the resolution of the meaning of investment in this case.

The Respondent State, the People's Republic of Congo, did, however, raise a jurisdictional objection on the basis of lack of exhaustion of local remedies and *lis pendis.*[2] The Tribunal rejected both not only because the contract that contained the ICSID arbitration clause[3] did not require the exhaustion of local remedies for the case to be

[1] S.A.R.L. Benvenuti & Bonfant v. People's Republic of Congo, ICSID Case No. ARB/77/2 (1980), 1 ICSID Rep. 330 (1993). The tribunal included: Jorgen Trolle (President), Edilbert Razafindralambo (Appointed by the State), and Rudolf Bystricky (Appointed by the investor).

[2] *Id.* at ¶ 1.13.

[3] The case arose out an agreement for a joint enterprise between the claimant, an Italian company and the Respondent, the Government of the Republic of Congo. There were two dispute settlement clauses. One in the Articles of Association and another one in the actual joint venture agreement. The one in the Articles of Association did contain an exhaustion of local remedies component. The other did not. The real question was the nature of the dispute, i.e., whether it was a shareholders dispute under the Articles of Association or a general breach of contract dispute under the main agreement. Although the government argued that the dispute fell under the one that required exhaustion, the Tribunal ruled in favor of exercising jurisdiction that did not require exhaustion. *See id.* at ¶ 1.13–115. The first dispute settlement clause reads: "All disputes which may arise during the existence of the Company or during its liquidation, either between the shareholders themselves over company affairs, or between the shareholders and the company, which have not

Africa's International Investment Law Regimes. Won L. Kidane, Oxford University Press. © Oxford University Press 2023.
DOI: 10.1093/oso/9780197745571.003.0007

brought before an international arbitral tribunal under the ICSID Convention, but also because the case that was said to have been pending in a local court involved related but different parties and causes of action.[4]

Although jurisdictional objections on the basis of exhaustion of local remedies did not succeed in these early days, they remained one of the most frequently raised and contentious subjects in many subsequent African ICSID cases. Regional and bilateral investment treaties as well as new models continue to struggle with the idea of exhaustion of local remedies, with the great majority appearing to have rejected it. This is discussed more fully in Part III in relation to treaty models and reform efforts.

Chronologically, the second case that raised interesting jurisdictional complications and offered durable guidance especially on the standard of review in ICSID annulment cases was *Klockner v. Cameroon*, decided on October 21, 1983.[5]

In *Klockner*, the Claimant, a German Company, initiated an ICSID arbitration claim against a Cameroonian state-owned entity on April 14, 1981, based on an arbitration clause contained in what is called Protocol of Agreement requiring the Parties to enter into a Turnkey contract for the delivery of a fertilizer factory and a management agreement for the management of the factory. Whereas the umbrella Protocol Agreement and the Turnkey Contraction Contract contained ICSID arbitration clauses, the Management Contract, signed subsequent to and in accordance with the Protocol Agreement, contained an ICC arbitration clause.[6]

The annulment action was filed by the Claimant, *Klockner*, because the ICSID Tribunal not only rejected its claims but also because it ruled against it in favor of Cameroon's counterclaims. It held that the Claimant failed in its management duties.[7] Klockner sought to annul the ICSID Tribunal's award under Article 52 of the ICSID Convention on grounds of manifest excess of jurisdiction.[8]

been resolved by the competent local courts, or by agreement, will be submitted to arbitration within the framework of the Convention of 18 March 1965 for the Settlement of Investment Disputes between States and Nationals of Other States established by the International Bank for Reconstruction and Development, the proceedings being in French." *Id.* The second one reads: "All disputes which may arise between the parties in the execution of the present protocol of agreement and which have not been resolved by agreement, will be subject to arbitration within the framework of the Convention of 18 March 1965 for the Settlement of Investment Disputes between States and Nationals of Other States established by the International Bank for Reconstruction and Development, the proceedings being in French. The parties agree to be bound by the decision of the arbitrator, undertake to ensure its execution, and renounce all rights of appeal against the decisions rendered. The arbitration costs will be shared equally by the parties." *Id.*

4 *Id.* at ¶ 1.13–1.15.

5 Decision Rendered by Ad Hoc Committee on the Application for Annulment Against the Arbitral Award in Klockner v. Cameroon, ARB/81/2 (Oct. 21, 1983).

6 For a quick reference of all these facts and procedures and timeline, *see id.* at ¶ 1–10, and for a more complete note on the key jurisdictional issues to be discussed *infra*, *see also* the ¶ 21, 22, 26, 35, 38, 40, 41, 49, 52, and 56.

7 *See id.*

8 *See id.* at ¶ 2 ("2. In its Application for Annulment, the Claimant contested the Award on several grounds. These may be grouped as follows: 'Manifest excess of powers (Article 52(1)(b)) due to the Arbitral Tribunal's lack of jurisdiction; II—Manifest excess of powers (Article 52(1)(b)) due to a violation of Article 42(1) of the Convention; III—Serious departure from a fundamental rule of procedure (Article 52(1)(d)); and IV—Failure to state reasons (Article 52(1)(e))' ").

Without going into the details, the Protocol Agreement, which contained ICSID arbitration clause, made Klockner "responsible for the technical and commercial management of the Company, to be carried out under a Management Contract."[9] The Management Contract referenced in Article 9 of the Protocol Agreement, however, contained an ICC arbitration clause.[10] The Tribunal made a nuanced jurisdictional ruling which caused this annulment process on grounds of manifest excess.

The key question was the scope of the ICSID Tribunal's jurisdiction, that is, whether it can rule that Klockner failed to perform its duties without considering the Management Contract, which contains an ICC arbitration clause for all disputes arising out of the said Management Contract.

The ad hoc Annulment Committee framed the issue as follows:

> 21. Therefore, it should first be determined whether the Tribunal assumed jurisdiction to "hear and determine the rights and obligations of the parties which constituted the raison d'tre" of the Management Contract (Application, p. 7), or whether it "examined the allegedly deficient nature of Klockner's management of SOCAME" (Application, p. 7, para. 2) and, in so doing, "necessarily applied the provisions of the Management Contract."[11]

The distinction that needed to be made was whether the Tribunal encroached upon the jurisdiction of the potential ICC Tribunal in the name of determining the rights and obligations of the parties under the Protocol Agreement.

This case is remarkable for the Annulment Committee's articulation of the deference owned to the Tribunal's decision on its jurisdiction under the ICSID Convention. The Committee disagreed with the Tribunal's determination of its own jurisdiction, but yet decided to defer to it by applying the manifest excess standard.

Consider the Committee's assessment of the validity of the Tribunal's determination of its jurisdiction:

> While the Award carefully does not cite any of the Management Contract's provisions, it obviously cannot avoid all reference to this contract. It is curious to note in this regard that, after declaring itself incompetent to interpret the Management Contract and laying down the "presumption of perfect compatibility" between this contract and the Protocol of Agreement (which, as we have seen, was the framework agreement that the Management Contract was "simply intended to carry out"), the Tribunal finds "confirmation" for this conclusion (p. 122) in a statement by Klockner "admitting on January 12, 1977 that it is the manager of the factory under the Management Contract to be signed." The following similar statement of April 8, 1978 on Klockner's responsibility for technical management is cited by the Tribunal at page 121.[12]

[9] *See id.* at ¶ 6.
[10] *See id.* at ¶ 11.
[11] *Id.* at ¶ 21.
[12] *Id.* at ¶ 42.

It further properly articulates the standard of review in the following terms:

> Summarizing, the following conclusions may be drawn from the preceding examination: (a) It is obviously not up to the ad hoc Committee constituted under Article 52 of the Washington Convention to say *whether the contested Award's interpretation is or is not the best, or the most defensible, or even whether it is correct, but only whether the Award is tainted by manifest excess of powers … Such an interpretation of the agreements and especially of the two arbitration clauses, whether correct or not, is tenable and does not in any event constitute a manifest excess of powers. To this extent, the complaint, while admissible, is unfounded.*[13]

This is a classic Chevron deference in the most familiar US administrative law parlance.[14] There are many analogous formulations of the concept of deference in Chevron. One such statement reads: "*When a challenge to an agency construction of a statutory provision, fairly conceptualized, really centers on the wisdom of the agency's policy, rather than whether it is a reasonable choice within a gap left open by Congress, the challenge must fail.*"[15]

Klockner is an extremely notable contribution to the jurisprudence on the important question of deference, a concept that recurs in a wide variety of contexts but is often misunderstood and disregarded especially as it relates to international tribunal's review and assessment of the legality of domestic administrative and judicial processes vis-à-vis international obligations. This is so whether expressed in treaties like the principles of protection of investment and nondiscrimination, or contractually on an ad hoc basis.

In international investment law, no concept is more intertwined with jurisdiction of arbitral tribunals than the meaning of investment. The first case in this study that considered the meaning of investment in relation to jurisdiction was *Liberian Eastern Timber Corporation v. Republic of Liberia (Letco v. Liberia)*.[16] The Tribunal did not engage in any sophisticated analysis of what constituted investment within the meaning of the Concession Agreement, the only instrument that expressed the Parties consent to arbitrate under the ICSID Rules.[17] Its interest was rather limited to ascertaining whether the investor spent any money in the host state in reliance on the terms of the Concession Agreement.[18] It took a very simplistic approach of whether any resources

[13] *Id.* at ¶¶ 52(a), 52(b) (emphasis added). *See also id.* at ¶ 56. ("With the exception of the latter, these various arguments do not call for any particular comments, since, as we have seen, the question is not whether they are correct or plausible, or more plausible or more correct than the Tribunal's. The only issue is whether they prove a manifest excess of powers, which is not the case. Regarding the last argument, it may be added that it is obviously not decisive, even if it is correct. It matters little in principle that the Tribunal's legal construction was different from that of one or the other of the parties, so long as the right of each to be heard was respected and, as will be seen below (infra, para. 91), so long as it remains within the "legal framework" provided by the parties. And this is indeed the case here").

[14] Chevron U.S.A., Inc. v. Natural Resources Defense Council, Inc., 468 U.S. 837 (1984).

[15] *Id.* at 866 (emphasis added).

[16] Liberian Eastern Timber Corporation v. Republic of Liberia, ICSID Cases No. ARB/83/2, Award (Mar. 31, 1986).

[17] *Id.* at ¶ 16.3. The Concession Agreement provided that "(2) The Rules of Conciliation and Arbitration of the International Centre for Settlement of Investment Disputes shall govern the conciliation and arbitration. The place of conciliation or arbitration shall be such as may be agreed by the parties and in default of Agreement shall be provided in the Rules of the Centre." *Id.*

[18] *See id.* at ¶ 16.2.

were spent. Subsequent cases have dealt with this question more carefully, including the formulation and subsequent use of the *Salini* test described below in chronological order.

The more interesting jurisdictional question in *Letco v. Liberia* pertained to the issue of the "*dispute between a Contracting State and a National of another Contracting State*" prong of Article 25(1) of the ICSID Convention because the Claimant, *Letco*, was a Liberian national.[19] The Tribunal dealt with this issue in some detail.

First, the Tribunal noted what it considered an exception to the general rule under Article 25(1) and looked for the Parties' agreement to consider what is otherwise a domestic entity as a national of another Contacting State because of foreign control. Its guidance emanates from the rule contained in Article 25(2)(b) with added emphasis:

> Any juridical person which had the nationality of a Contracting State other than the State party to the dispute on the date on which the parties consented to submit such dispute to conciliation or arbitration and *any juridical person which had the nationality of the Contracting State party to the dispute on that date and which, because of foreign control, the parties have agreed should be treated as a national of another Contracting State for the purposes of this Convention.*[20]

Second, having identified a possible exception, it had to overcome both the foreign control and party consent components. Because the host state did not participate in the proceedings and the Concession Agreement did not expressly make these facts clear, the Tribunal had to determine both prongs de novo.

Third, on foreign control, the Tribunal concluded without much difficulty that

> the evidence provided by letco clearly indicates that it was under French control at the time the Concession Agreement was signed. This control is not only a result of the fact that letco's capital stock was 100% owned by French nationals as indicated by both letco and official documents of the Liberian Government . . . French nationals dominated the company decision-making structure. It appears from the evidence presented that a majority, if not all, of letco's directors, as well as the General Manager, were at all times French nationals.[21]

Finally, although the party-consent element was a bit more problematic, the Tribunal framed the issue well and made its own conclusions based on the evidence presented to it. The framing reads:

> In order to exercise jurisdiction the Tribunal must determine that, because of French control, the Government of Liberia agreed to treat letco as a French national. This requirement raises a number of difficult questions, in particular: Must there be a causal relationship between effective control and agreement? If so, how can it be proved?

[19] *See id.* at ¶ 1.
[20] *Id.* at ¶ 16.4.
[21] *Id.* at ¶ 16.5.

> What sort of an agreement, implied or expressed, is required? If the agreement may be implied, what facts are capable of implying such an agreement?[22]

The analysis that followed is instructive not only because it was one of, if not the first, case that dealt with this issue, but also because the issue of consent needed to be determined in the absence of express agreement between the parties as indeed the Host State's arguments had to be presumed.

The Tribunal began its analysis by noting that "clearly the Convention's use of the word 'because' in Article 25(2)(b) establishes a need to show that the agreement to treat letco as a French national was motivated by the fact that it was under French control."[23] The Tribunal then said:

> However, in most instances the virtually insurmountable burden of proof in showing what motivated a government's actions might well frustrate the purpose of the Convention. Therefore, unless circumstances clearly indicate otherwise, it must be presumed that where there exists foreign control, the agreement to treat the company in question as a foreign national is "because" of this foreign control.[24]

The more difficult question was the ascertainment of the Host State's agreement to treat the domestic corporate entity as a foreign entity because of foreign control. The establishment of the foreign control was not difficult to determine as a matter of fact but the expression of agreement by the Host State was problematic not the least because the first case that considered the same issue, *Holiday Inn*, although not directly precedential, required express language to this effect.[25]

The Tribunal did, however, extrapolate such consent from the Parties' inclusion of ICSID arbitration in the Concession Agreement, categorically stating:

> When a Contracting State signs an investment agreement, containing an ICSID arbitration clause, with a foreign controlled juridical person with the same nationality as the Contracting State and it does so with the knowledge that it will only be subject to ICSID jurisdiction if it has agreed to treat that company as a juridical person of

[22] *Id.* at ¶ 16.6

[23] *Id.* at ¶ 16.7.

[24] *Id.*

[25] *See id.* at ¶ 16.11 (citing Holiday Inns S.A. & Others v. Morocco, ICSID Case No. ARB/72/1 (1972)) ("Though the Tribunal is not bound by the precedents established by other ICSID Tribunals, it is nonetheless instructive to consider their interpretations of what constitutes an agreement to treat a juridical person which had the nationality of the Contracting State party to the dispute as a national of another Contracting State. In the *Holiday Inns* case, the Tribunal indicated that 'such an agreement should therefore be explicit. An implied agreement would only be acceptable in the event that the specific circumstances would exclude any other interpretation of the intention of the parties, which is not the case here.' In *Amco-Asia et al. v. The Republic of Indonesia* the Claimant apparently applied to the Indonesian investment authorities for the establishment of a 'foreign business.' The parties also inserted an ICSID clause in their agreement. Since the Indonesian Government approved both the investment application and the ICSID clause, the Tribunal found that there was an expressed agreement. Citing the *Holiday Inns* case, the Tribunal stated: To refer to the Holiday Inns award—in spite of the same not being a binding precedent in this case here—this agreement is by no means implied; it is expressed, and clearly expressed, no formal or ritual clause being provided for in the Convention, nor needed in order for such an agreement to be binding upon the parties").

> another Contracting State, the Contracting State could be deemed to have agreed to such treatment by having agreed to the ICSID arbitration clause. This is especially the case when the Contracting State's laws require the foreign investor to establish itself locally as a juridical person in order to carry out an investment.[26]

It appears that this was the first African decision that equated the inclusion of an ICSID arbitration clause in an agreement as an expression of agreement to treat a domestic entity as a foreign one because of foreign control for purposes of arbitral jurisdiction.[27] The Tribunal did not rest its finding exclusively on such interpretation; it found many indicia of foreign treatment from the evidentiary record including registration certificates and representations indicating foreignness or more technically, a national of another Contacting State.[28]

Jurisdiction and the Meaning of Investment in the 2000s

Chronologically, a breakthrough in jurisdictional jurisprudence came in 2001. Although the cases selected for study for purposes of this case are those that went through the whole spectrum and ended with a final award on the merits, any discussion of the African cases and jurisdiction would be incomplete without a note on one of the most famous African cases that has for decades shaped the jurisprudence of ICSID jurisdiction: *Salini v. Morocco* (2001).[29] *Salini* is one of the most cited but controversial cases. A measure of misunderstanding seems to also surround it.

First, it is one of the first cases that clearly articulated the "double-barreled" jurisdictional requirement for ICSID arbitration in the following unequivocal terms:

> Insofar as the option of jurisdiction has been exercised in favour of ICSID, the rights in dispute must also constitute an investment pursuant to Article 25 of the Washington Convention. The Arbitral Tribunal, therefore, is of the opinion that its jurisdiction depends upon the existence of an investment within the meaning of the Bilateral Treaty as well as that of the Convention, in accordance with the case law.[30]

[26] *Id.* at ¶ 16.10.

[27] The Tribunal did qualify that this expression may be implicit: "In the present case, there is adequate evidence to show that there existed an agreement to treat letco as a French national. The actions of the parties indicate that, even if there was no express agreement, there was at least an implied agreement." *Id.* at ¶ 16.11.

[28] *See id.* at ¶ 16.12–16.13 ("Both actions and documents show that Liberia agreed to treat letco as a foreign national. Perhaps most indicative of such treatment are the annual certificates of registration which letco was required to file with the Liberian Ministry of Commerce, Industry and Transportation. These registrations were signed by such government officials as the Director of Domestic Trade, the Assistant Minister for Commerce and the Deputy Minister for Commerce").

[29] Salini Construttori S.p.A and Italstrade S.p.A v. Kingdom of Morocco, ICSID Case No. ARB/00/4, Decision on Jurisdiction (July 23, 2001).

[30] *Id.* at ¶ 44. It relied on cases that came before it and added "Various arbitral tribunals have ruled in this manner in rendering awards in cases in which the notion of investment was at issue (cf. Award of March 9,1998 in the Fedax N. V. vs. the Republic of Venezuela case: JDI 1999, p. 294 et seq.)." *Id.* The Tribunal also added that "there have been almost no cases where the notion of investment within the meaning of Article 25 of the Convention was raised. However, it would be inaccurate to consider that the requirement that a dispute be 'in direct relation to an investment' is diluted by the consent of the Contracting Parties. To the contrary, ICSID case law and legal authors agree that the investment requirement must be respected as an

The Tribunal's unmitigated use of the term "case law" as a source of its decision is quite remarkable, especially as early as 2001. In any case, it appears that *Salini* itself has become "soft case law" that many tribunals that came after it relied on even when they want to stretch it one way or the other.[31]

Second, and most important, is the Tribunal's framing of what has come to be known as the *Salini* factors. The exact taxonomy, often misstated and stretched, is the following with all its internal citations:

> *The doctrine generally considers that investment infers: contributions, a certain duration of performance of the contract and a participation in the risks of the transaction (cf commentary by E. Gaillard, cited above, p. 292). In reading the Convention's preamble, one may add the contribution to the economic development of the host State of the investment as an additional condition.*[32]

This is where the oft-cited *Salini* factors of contributions, duration and risk come from.[33] Applying these principles to the facts of the case, the Tribunal found that an infrastructure construction contract that was performed over a period of 36 months qualified as an investment.[34]

In the Tribunal's opinion, it was not announcing a new concept or rule; it was merely restating an existing doctrine, although it seemed utterly unsatisfied with its grounding in sound and balanced jurisprudence. It expressed its doubt in these terms:

> The criteria to be used for the definition of an investment pursuant to the Convention would be easier to define if there were awards denying the Centre's jurisdiction on the basis of the transaction giving rise to the dispute. With the exception of a decision of the Secretary General of ICSID refusing to register a request for arbitration dealing with a dispute arising out of a simple sale ... the awards at hand only very rarely

objective condition of the jurisdiction of the Centre (cf in particular, the commentary by E. Gaillard, in JDI 1999, p. 278 et seq., who cites the award rendered in 1975 in the Alcoa Minerals vs. Jamaica case as well as several other authors)." *Id.* at ¶ 52.

31 *See, e.g.*, Phoenix Action Ltd. v. The Czech Republic, ICSID Case No. ARB/06/5, Award (Apr. 15, 2009).

32 Salini v. Morocco, ICSID Case No. ARB/00/4, Decision on Jurisdiction (July 23, 2001), at 52 (emphasis added).

33 The Tribunal added, however, that "In reality, these various elements may be interdependent. Thus, the risks of the transaction may depend on the contributions and the duration of performance of the contract. As a result, these various criteria should be assessed globally even if, for the sake of reasoning, the Tribunal considers them individually here." *Id.* at 52.

34 *See id.* at ¶ 53–57. More specifically, it said:

> 56. It does not matter in this respect that these risks were freely taken. It also does not matter that the remuneration of the Contractor was not linked to the exploitation of the completed work. A construction that stretches out over many years, for which the total cost cannot be established with certainty in advance, creates an obvious risk for the Contractor.
>
> 57. Lastly, the contribution of the contract to the economic development of the Moroccan State cannot seriously be questioned. In most countries, the construction of infrastructure falls under the tasks to be carried out by the State or by other public authorities. It cannot be seriously contested that the highway in question shall serve the public interest. Finally, the Italian companies were also able to provide the host State of the investment with know-how in relation to the work to be accomplished." *Id.* (emphasis added).

> turned on the notion of investment. Notably, the first decision only came in 1997.... The criteria for characterization are, therefore, derived from cases in which the transaction giving rise to the dispute was considered to be an investment without there ever being a real discussion of the issue in almost all the cases.[35]

Despite this acknowledgment of precarious origin, the *Salini* factors dominated the ICSID jurisprudence, although with considerable revision, most notably in a 2009 decision by a prominent Tribunal in *Phoenix Action Ltd. v. The Czech Republic*.[36]

The meaning of investment in the jurisdictional context got another serious consideration in the next case against Egypt by a Greek investor in *Middle East Cement Shipping and Handling Co. S.A. v. Arab Republic of Egypt* (2002).[37] Two categories of investments were disputed by the parties. The first one was a license for the importation, storage, and distribution of cement. The second was a vessel. The license was issued for a period of 10 years, but the host state enacted a decree prohibiting the importation of certain types of cement, which the Claimant said made its business unprofitable. The vessel was auctioned off by a court order for failure to pay debts.[38] The investment, and hence the jurisdictional question, pertained to both. As to the license, the Tribunal ruled:

> The BIT, in its Art. 1 "Definitions," expressly mentions that "Investment" means every kind of asset and in particular, though not exclusively, includes: ... d) business concessions conferred by law or under contract, ... In the light of the above, *there can be no doubt that the "License" qualifies as an "Investment" under the BIT*.[39]

Although the Tribunal arrived at this conclusion quickly without much analysis, this is important because it is one of the first cases that determined that a license could, without more, be considered an investment.

As to the vessel's qualification for protection as an investment of the investor, the Respondent's only dispute was that it was owned by the parent company and not the investor for purposes of BIT protection, but the Tribunal did not have much difficulty rejecting that argument, holding that even if it was leased by the investor, it qualifies for protection under the BIT as an investment of the investor.[40].

[35] *Id.* at ¶ 52 (citations omitted).

[36] For example, in Phoenix Action Ltd. v. The Czech Republic, ICSID Case No. ARB/06/5, Award (Apr. 15, 2009), a tribunal composed of Brigitte Stern as chairperson, Andreas Bucher, and Juan Fernandez-Armesto added a few more requirements to the original Salini factors discussed below. These additions include that the assets must be invested in good faith and in compliance with the host state's laws. These cases and factors are discussed in various sections of this book.

[37] Middle East Cement Shipping and Handling Co. S.A. v. Arab Republic of Egypt, ICSID Case No. ARB/99/6, Award (Apr. 12, 2002).

[38] *Id.* at ¶ 81–84 (Summary of facts).

[39] *See id.* at ¶ 98–101 (emphasis added).

[40] *Id.* at ¶135–36 ("136. The Tribunal also notes that, as 'Investment,' Art. 1.1 of the BIT, in addition to 'property' under section a), also includes under section e) 'goods that under a leasing agreement are placed at the disposal of a lessee in the territory of a Contracting Party in conformity with its laws and regulations.' Therefore, even if the Poseidon was owned by the Claimant's mother company, as mentioned in section 5) of the letter of April 22, 1991 (C30) and the Claimant had only leased (or 'chartered' as mentioned in R II p. 24) the ship, it can still qualify as the Claimant's 'investment.' There is no evidence indicating that such lease was not in conformity with Egyptian laws and regulations (as further discussed in the following

CDC (UK) v. Seychelles (2003)[41] raised an interesting jurisdictional question tied to the meaning of investment because CDC proceeded against Seychelles for default in making loan payments.[42] As explained in subsequent sections, the host state refused to make payments because the money was used to buy a turbine which failed to work. CDC's debt collection effort having failed, it proceeded against Seychelles, which guaranteed the payment of loans made to its wholly owned public utilities company.[43]

The jurisdictional question was whether the loan to the public utilities company guaranteed by the state qualified as an investment. Although this was an interesting question, the Respondent state deprived the Tribunal of the opportunity to opine on the matter by conceding jurisdiction.[44] This was a contract-based claim, and the issue of whether or not the loan qualified as an investment was only relevant to the question of whether it fell under the ICSID Convention for purposes of ICSID arbitration.

The meaning of investment as a jurisdictional nexus got a little bit more creative and drew mainstream attention with the issuance of the award in the *Patrick Mitchell v. Democratic Republic of Congo* (DRC) (2004) case.[45] Patrick Mitchell, an American, ran a law firm in the DRC. He initiated an ICSID arbitration against the DRC under the US–DRC BIT. The undisputed facts show that the DRC military, by orders of the military court, raided his law office, seized documents, and arrested two lawyers on suspicion of illegal undertakings on behalf of a client. Mitchell fled the country and his law firm seized operations. He claimed that his investment in the DRC was expropriated.[46]

paragraph), and the same section 5) of the letter expressly confirms that 'the Vessel was used in Suez by the branch as a floating silo only.'")

41 CDC Group Plc v. Republic of The Seychelles, ICSID Case No. ARB/02/14 (Dec. 17, 2003).

42 *See id.* at ¶ 7–10.

43 *Id.*

44 *See id.* at ¶ 17–19:

> 17. CDC's activities are commercial in substance and nature. CDC's investments in the Seychelles related to the expansion of the capacity of the Baie Ste Anne Power Station on the Island of Praslin and the upgrading of Victoria A Power Station on the Island of Mah. These investments were made on a commercial basis.
>
> 18. CDC claims that each of the Loan Agreements and each of the Guarantees amount to an "investment" within the meaning of Art. 25(1) of the ICSID Convention which provides that "the jurisdiction of the Centre shall extend to any legal dispute arising directly out of an investment."
>
> 19. Although the Republic initially contested CDC's claim that the Loan Agreements and Guarantees were "investments" within the meaning of Art. 25(1), the Republic subsequently withdrew its objection to jurisdiction at the oral hearing which took place on 22–23 July 2003.

45 Patrick Mitchell v. DRC Award (Feb. 9, 2004); Annulment (Nov. 1, 2006).

46 *Id.* at Summary of Facts. The summary of the facts is provided on the first page of the excerpt as follows: "The Claimant operated a law firm in the DRC which provided legal consulting services to various clients in the DRC and abroad. In March 1999, following an order of a military court, authorities of the DRC put the law firm's premises under seal, seized documents and arrested two lawyers. These actions were based on suspected illegal activity involving the Claimant's firm and one of its clients. In November 1999, the military court rejected the charges, released the two lawyers and returned most of the seized assets to the law firm. The Claimant alleged that, as a result of the Respondent's actions, the law firm had been expropriated without compensation in violation of the BIT. He sought compensation for the damages suffered, including the loss of clients." *Id.* For a complete account, *see also* discussion on the merits at ¶ 58–95.

The jurisdictional question pertained to whether his law firm and its operations qualified as investment within the meaning of the BIT as well as the ICSID Convention.[47] The Tribunal framed the jurisdictional question as follows:

> The Tribunal is asked to decide whether Claimant's Request for arbitration comes under the jurisdiction of ICSID and the competence of this Tribunal. It is not disputed that both Parties validly expressed their consent to ICSID arbitration, as provided for in Article VII of the Bilateral Investment Treaty concluded between the Democratic Republic of the Congo and the United States of America. As Respondent has stated, its objection to jurisdiction is solely one to the qualification of Claimant's activity in the Congo as an investment.[48]

The problem partly comes from the rather deliberate omission of the definition of the term "investment" in the ICSID Convention. This was one of the first Tribunals that quoted the famous Report of the Executive Directors that said "*no attempt was made to define the term 'investment' given the essential requirement of consent by the parties, and the mechanism through which Contracting States can make known in advance, if they so desire, the classes of disputes which they would or would not consider submitting to the Centre*,"[49] essentially leaving the definition to the instrument that provides the consent to arbitrate. That is why the definition of investment in the BIT became relevant in this case as well.[50]

The BIT defines "investment" as the following: "For the purposes of this Treaty: (c) 'investment' means every kind of investment, owned or controlled directly or indirectly, including equity, debt, and service and investment contracts; and includes: (i) tangible and intangible property, including all property rights, such as liens, mortgages pledges, and real security."[51]

[47] *See id.* at ¶ 40–57.

[48] *Id.* at ¶ 32.

[49] *Id.* at 41 (quoting *ICSID Convention, Regulations and Rules*, 1 ICSID REP. 28, ICSID/15/Rev.1, Art. 25(4), p. 44) (emphasis added).

[50] The Tribunal stated this notion as follows in ¶ 43:

> 43. As indicated in the statement quoted above, an important factor in determining whether a dispute qualifies as an investment dispute under the Convention is the consent given by the Parties. The State Parties' consent to submit a certain category of disputes to the Centre's jurisdiction does contain the determination that such disputes are to be considered as related to investments within the meaning of the ICSID Convention. Even if, in a particular case, a dispute arises out of an investment within the meaning of the Convention, one must further examine, however, whether such a dispute relates to an investment as defined in the Parties' consent to ICSID arbitration.

[51] *Id.* at ¶ 45 (quoting Art. 1(c) of the US–DRC BIT). The remaining part of the definition provides:

> (ii) a company or shares of stock or other interests in a company or interests in the assets thereof;
> (iii) a claim to money or a claim to performance having economic value, and associated with an investment;
> (iv) intellectual and industrial property rights, including rights with respect to copyrights, patents, trademarks, trade names, industrial designs, trade secrets and know-how, and goodwill;
> (v) licenses and permits issued pursuant to law, including those issued for manufacture and sale of products;
> (vi) any right conferred by law or contract, including rights to search for or utilize natural resources, and rights to manufacture, use and sell products; and

To set the stage for a broader reading of the definition, the Tribunal first said that the list is merely illustrative.[52] The interpretive direction is solidified by the following expansive outlook: "Indeed, as stated expressly in the introductory part of this provision, 'investment' means every kind of investment, owned or controlled directly or indirectly. Anything that follows in the definition quoted above is included in this concept."[53] This was not what turned out to be the most contentious subject, however, it was the sentence that followed that invited an acrimonious dissent and hence contributed to the subsequent annulment: "In addition to Article I, the BIT contains in Article II, dealing with 'treatment of investment,' a list of 'associated activities,' that are to be treated like investments and include, *inter alia*, 'the making, performance and enforcement of contracts.'"[54]

Since this is one of the first cases to struggle with the concept of investment under both the ICSID Convention and the relevant BIT in any meaningful way, it is important to take a closer look at how it builds its analysis. In describing the nature of the investment, it went on stating:

> 47. The Tribunal has received ample information about the activities exercised by Mr. Mitchell in the DRC, which allow to answer the question concerning the existence of an investment of the Claimant in the DRC. These elements of information include in particular the declarations made by former clients of the firm, the agreements concluded with former associates who left the firm in 1991 and the income statements for the year 1996 to 1998.[55]

But then the Respondent introduced a difficult question based on its own domestic law, that is, that a legal firm does not qualify as a service under Congolese law. The Tribunal rejected the notion of interpretation of the ICSID Convention in reference to any domestic law and instead said that it must be interpreted in light of the Vienna Convention on the Law of Treaties.[56] Having overcome this hurdle it concluded that any materials taken from the office, the initial capital invested and the associated

(vii) returns which are reinvested. Any alteration of the form in which assets are invested or reinvested shall not affect their character as investment."

52 *Id.* at 46.
53 *Id.*
54 *Id.* at 46 (quoting 2(c) of Art. II).
55 *Id.* at 47. The remaining part reads:

> The Tribunal finds that in respect of items of Mr. Mitchell's property seized during the intervention of the military forces on March 5, 1999, the requirement listed under Article I(c)(i) of the BIT is met. This concerns movable property and any documents, like files, records and similar items. It further appears from the text of the provision as quoted that the investor's right to "know-how" and "goodwill" (iv) as well as the right to exercise its activities (vi) are elements which are stated as being covered by the protection of investments under the BIT. This concerns also the payments registered on the accounts of Mr. Mitchell in the United States to which Claimant refers in order to demonstrate his activity within the DRC. Indeed, these payments are based on bills for fees referring to legal consultations provided by Mr. Mitchell and his employees through the office "Mitchell & Associates" within the DRC. *Id.* at ¶ 48.

56 *Id.* at 49–50 ("50. On this particular question, the Tribunal has to stress firstly that the definition of an investment, as a material element of the definition of the scope of the consent to arbitration contained in Article VII of the BIT, is contained in the text of the BIT, which may have to be completed by an appropriate interpretation of this instrument. Such a concept, like any other concept retained as a matter of

activities such as performance of contracts and goodwill qualified as investment.[57] Its own summary and conclusion on jurisdiction are useful to take note of:

> The Tribunal can draw from these elements of definition the conclusion that the BIT contains a definition of the notion of investment which is as broad as the concept is used in the ICSID Convention. In addition to movable property, Claimant transferred into the Congo money and other assets which constituted the foundations for his professional activities which came to an end the day of the seizure of his firm or soon thereafter. Together with the returns on the initial investments, which also qualify as investments (see Article I(c) of the BIT), these activities and the economic value associated therewith qualify as an investment within the meaning of the BIT and the ICSID Convention.
>
> ...
>
> The Tribunal concludes, accordingly, that Mr. Mitchell's property detained in the Offices of Mitchell & Associates and the resources and activities related to this firm qualify as an investment within the meaning of the ICSID Convention and the BIT. Therefore, the Tribunal decides that this dispute is within the jurisdiction of ICSID and the competence of this Tribunal.[58]

This was but only a majority opinion. The dissent took issue with the majority's expansive interpretation of the definition of investment contained in the BIT, and in particular, the majority's use of "associated activities" in Article II as a way of getting around the issue of the *de minimis* nature of the actual capital invested if the firm's contract rights and future earnings were excluded.[59] The dissent is highly technical but cogent. The dissent makes several points but two are most important. First, the dissent contends:

> 12. Following the exchanges of views on these various issues, the Tribunal concluded that "... the resources and activities related to this firm [Patrick Mitchell] qualify as an investment within the meaning of the ICSID Convention and the BIT" (para. 57).
>
> 13. I do not share this opinion. The Tribunal, in my view, is mistaken.
>
> 14. It is true that contracts for legal assistance and the other activities referred to in the Award as constituting an investment are protected by the BIT. But Article II (2), which provides for such protection, took care to designate the activities in question by a specific term, "associated activities," to mark their difference from the notion of "investment." The nuance is not accidental. Nor is it by chance that the Treaty refers to

international law in this agreement, cannot be determined on the basis of the domestic law of one of the Parties. The principle of interpretation to be applied is contained in paragraph 1 of Article 31 of the Vienna Convention on the law of treaties of 1969, which reads as follows: 'A treaty shall be interpreted in good faith in accordance with the ordinary meaning to be given to the terms of the treaty in their context and in the light of its object and purpose'").

[57] *See id.* at 51–56.

[58] *Id.* at 55, 57.

[59] Patrick Mitchell v. DRC, Award (Feb. 9, 2004); Annulment (Nov. 1, 2006), at 6–23 (Dissenting opinion by Yawovi Agboyibo, Jan. 23, 2004).

"investment activities," not in Article I (c) concerning the definition of investment, but in Article II, devoted to the treatment of investments. Although they benefit from the same protection, the two notions are distinct.

15. Insofar as the jurisdiction of the Tribunal is dependent solely on the evidence of an investment, the Tribunal should base its analysis on this notion. Once the required investment has been established, the protection thereof rightfully extends to associated activities and products, such as goodwill, service contracts, and fees. This list of elements protected by the Treaty must be taken into account in applying the notions of expropriation and compensation.

16. The Tribunal was thus erroneous in its belief that it would attain the same result by qualifying as an "investment" activities associated with investments.[60]

Secondly, and no less vigorously, the dissent reasons that "Goods or services invested" cannot be confused with "goods or services produced."[61] The argument being "the services provided to third parties by the Claimant in the DRC and fees billed or returned for consideration are products of investment. It could be otherwise only if these fees were reinvested. Then they would constitute an investment within the meaning of Article I (c) (vii) of the Treaty."[62] The dissent then categorically states that "Likewise, ordinary goodwill is the result of investment, not an element of investment. This is the case under the Treaty."[63] It forcefully concludes with some attribution of motive of the majority as follows:

> By confusing "investment" with "associated activities," the Tribunal has given an inappropriate response to the objection to its jurisdiction, wrongly basing itself on the volume of Mr. Patrick Mitchell's activities in order to maintain that in this case there was an investment within the meaning of the BIT and the ICSID Convention.[64]

This award was subsequently annulled in 2006 for some of the same reasons that the dissent expressed as well as for the Tribunal's failure to assess the said investment's contribution to the host state in any meaningful way along the lines of the *Salini v. Morocco* factors outlined a few years before the rendition of the *Patrick Mitchell* case, to which, surprisingly no reference is made. The Ad Hoc Annulment committee did not, however, lose sight of the contribution factor.[65] Its analysis is contained in a few instructive passages reproduced in the note.[66]

[60] *Id.* at 12–16.
[61] *Id.* at 17.
[62] *Id.*
[63] *Id.* at 18.
[64] *Id.* at 23.
[65] Patrick Mitchell v. DRC, Award (Feb. 9, 2004); Annulment (Nov. 1, 2006), 38–41. In a significant and useful endorsement of the one of the Salini factors, i.e., contribution to the host state, the Ad Hoc Committee also stated that "the parties to an agreement and the States which conclude an investment treaty cannot open the jurisdiction of the Centre to any operation they might arbitrarily qualify as an investment. It is thus repeated that, before ICSID arbitral tribunals, the Washington Convention has supremacy over an agreement between the parties or a BIT." *Id.* at 31.
[66] *Id.* at 38–41. "39. As a legal consulting firm is a somewhat uncommon operation from the standpoint of the concept of investment, in the opinion of the ad hoc Committee it is necessary for the contribution to the

As the time went by, in the late 2000's, the question of jurisdiction began to increase in complexity along with the overall complexity of the cases. The jurisdictional question in *Helnan International Hotels v. Arab Republic of Egypt* (2008) is one of the first in the era.[67]

In *Helnan*, the dispute arose out of a 26-year hotel management contract signed in 1986 between Helnan, a Danish company, and the Egyptian Organization for Tourism and Hotels (hereinafter EGOTH) more than a decade before the conclusion of the Danish-Egyptian BIT of 1999.[68] In September 2003, the Egyptian Ministry of Tourism downgraded the hotel (Shepheard) from five-star to four-star after a series of inspections.[69] EGOTH initiated an arbitral proceeding in Cairo based on the management contract seeking termination. It succeeded but Helnan was also awarded a sum of money by the contract tribunal acting *amiable compositor* by the agreement of the parties.[70] Dissatisfied by the award and claiming orchestrated mistreatment by the host state, Helnan resorted to the BIT's ISDS provisions against Egypt.[71]

Egypt's jurisdictional arguments are complex. They are summarized in the following paragraphs of the final award:

> 93. EGYPT submits that there are two salient conclusions to be reached in respect of the present proceedings.
>
> 94. As regards the first, EGYPT submits that the legal consequences of the Cairo Award, which terminated the Management Contract for impossibility of performance, cannot be escaped. EGYPT submits that these legal consequences will operate on three different levels.
>
> 95. Firstly, on the jurisdictional level, EGYPT contends that following the termination of the Management Contract, HELNAN no longer had a legal interest [i.e., the Management Contract or an investment] which could form the subject matter of an agreement to arbitrate pursuant to Article 25 of the ICSID Convention or Article 1 of the Treaty. Therefore, Claimant had no investment to protect under the Treaty and thus no access to ICSID jurisdiction.
>
> 96. Secondly, on the admissibility level, EGYPT contends that due to HELNAN having filed its Request when it did not have an investment, the admission of the claim

economic development or at least the interests of the State, in this case the DRC, to be somehow present in the operation." It went on stating that "41. The ad hoc Committee thus concludes that the Award is tainted by a failure to state reasons, in the sense that the inadequacy of reasons is such that it seriously affects the coherence of the reasoning as to the existence of an investment in accordance with Article 25(1) of the Convention and the Bilateral Treaty between the United States of America and the Democratic Republic of Congo, on which relied the jurisdiction of the Arbitral Tribunal." *Id.* at 41.

[67] Helnan International Hotels A/S V. The Arab Republic of Egypt, ICSID Case No. ARB/05/19, Award (July 3, 2008).

[68] *See id.* at 3.

[69] *Id.* at 5.

[70] *Id.* at 6.

[71] *Id.* at 9.

submitted would constitute a breach of the international rule which provides that the protected investment must be existent at the date of initiation of the proceedings.

97. Thirdly, on the merits, EGYPT contends that most of the issues raised by HELNAN related to the contractual obligations found in the Management Contract. Therefore the whole dispute was to be decided by the Cairo Award which addressed the relevant issues. Since the Cairo Award is res judicata in regard to these issues, to contravene the Cairo Award would amount to a breach of Egyptian and international law."[72]

The Tribunal did not respond to these jurisdictional objections favorably. It adopted the contract-treaty claims dichotomy that previous ICSID Tribunals employed,[73] and held that it had jurisdiction over the treaty claims as distinct from contract claims even when the contract had been terminated by the contract tribunal set up by the parties.[74]

The jurisdictional question raised a combination of a contract tribunal's decision that terminated the contract itself and a host state's jurisdictional defense of *res judicata*. The Tribunal asked itself whether it would review the contract tribunal's decision on the facts as they pertained to the application of the chosen domestic law *de novo* or defer to such tribunal on those issues. Its response is instructive:

107. The precise circumstances under which the violation of a contractual right of the investor by a host state will amount to an act also unlawful under an investment treaty have not been answered in a uniform manner in arbitral practices. While some tribunals have considered that acts of the nature typical of a commercial partner will not be deemed to be a treaty violation, other decisions have been inclined, in the context of the standard of fair and equitable treatment, to protect contractual rights in a broader manner.

108. *When in the present case a Tribunal would adopt the wider approach of protection and a domestic award exists dealing solely with contractual matters, the Tribunal would have to ask whether under such circumstances it would be necessary to disregard the rule res judicata and to review the facts de novo in the light of the requirements of fair and equitable treatment. In this respect, each case will have to be reviewed in the light of the circumstances. When it is found by an international tribunal that the holding of the local award was determined strictly by considerations pertaining to contractual issues, it will not be appropriate for an international tribunal to replace the decision of the local*

[72] *Id.* at 93–97.

[73] *Id.* at 102 ("102. As regards the distinction between a contractual claim of an investor and a treaty claim subject to the jurisdiction of a competent international tribunal, this Tribunal accepts the approach adopted by a number of investment tribunals").

[74] *Id.* at 103–04 ("103. In other words, the analysis of the Claimant's rights under the BIT must on the one hand take into account the existence, or nonexistence of contractual rights of the Claimant as they exist on the level of Egyptian law. On the other hand, an exclusive focus on contractual rights will not be sufficient to determine whether or not the rights of the Claimant laid down in the Treaty have been respected. Even in the absence of a valid contract, it is possible that a certain kind of conduct of the host state is inconsistent with its obligations under a BIT").

> *court on a contractual issue subject to local law. Instead, res judicata will apply, and the outcome in this respect will be the same as that which a tribunal will reach which assumes that strictly contractual matters generally are not protected under the standard of fair and equitable treatment.*[75]

In *Biwater v. Tanzania* (2008), the key jurisdictional objection pertained to the meaning of "investment." In this regard, the host state's jurisdictional objection is unique and intriguing. The Parties did not dispute the applicability of the *Salini* factors of the assumption of risk and substantial commitment. Seizing on the requirement that the investor should have an expectation of an economic return, in this case, Tanzania argued that the investor could not have had an expectation of return in this case as the project was a " 'loss leader,' i.e., an undertaking that was not economically rational standing alone, but that might have led to other profitable opportunities later."[76] In other words, the Claimant "acquired shares in an operating company that no rational investor would have regarded as likely to produce economically valuable returns. Consequently, the Republic concludes, BGT did not make an 'investment' within the meaning of Article 25 of the Convention, and this Tribunal has no jurisdiction over BGT's claims."[77]

To be sure, in this case, the Parties' jurisdictional dispute did not pertain to whether the investor's shares constituted an investment under the BIT, which they qualified as "every kind of asset."[78] The difficulty was whether it met the *Salini* test under the ICSID Convention. Confronted with this dilemma, the *Biwater* Tribunal announced a rather significant rebuke to the *Salini* test in the following terms:

> In the Tribunal's view, there is no basis for a rote, or overly strict, application of the five Salini criteria in every case. These criteria are not fixed or mandatory as a matter of law. They do not appear in the ICSID Convention. On the contrary, it is clear from the travaux preparatoires of the Convention that several attempts to incorporate a definition of "investment" were made, but ultimately did not succeed. In the end, the term was left intentionally undefined, with the expectation (inter alia) that a definition could be the subject of agreement as between Contracting States.[79]

Applying a more flexible rule, the Tribunal rejected the host state's strict application of the *Salini* factors and found jurisdiction based not only on the BIT's more expansive

[75] *Id.* at 107–08 (emphasis added).

[76] Biwater Gauff (Tanzania) Ltd. v. United Republic of Tanzania, ICSID Case No. ARB/05/22, Final Award (July 24, 2008), at 287–89.

[77] *Id.* at 289.

[78] *Id.* at 307.

[79] *Id.* at 312. The remaining passage states: "Hence the following oft-quoted passage in the Report of the Executive Directors: 'No attempt was made to define the term "investment" given the essential requirement of consent by the parties, and the mechanism through which Contracting States can make known in advance, if they so desire, the classes of disputes which they would or would not consider submitting to the Centre (Article 25(4)).' Given that the Convention was not drafted with a strict, objective, definition of 'investment,' it is doubtful that arbitral tribunals sitting in individual cases should impose one such definition which would be applicable in all cases and for all purposes." *Id.* at 312–13.

definition of "investment" but also, on the facts of the case, rejecting the "loss lead" theory.[80] This was one of the reasons that propelled the movement toward codifying the *Salini* factors in modern BITs.

The *Jan de Nul N.V. and Dredging International N.V v. Egypt* (2008) case decided the same year raised an unusual jurisdictional issue because some of the events that gave rise to the dispute occurred before the coming into effect of the latter of the two relevant BITs, one concluded in 1997, and the other in 2002.[81] Because the Tribunal's prior jurisdictional decision was based on the 2002 BIT, the question of the Tribunal's jurisdiction over events that had occurred prior to 2002 was raised, such as the Claimant's allegation that the government agency (SCA) procured the JV's assent through fraudulent misrepresentation of the nature of the work and ground conditions for its dredge work on the Sucz canal when the contract was concluded in 1992.[82] The conditions turned out to be more difficult than the JV anticipated, hence the claim of fraudulent misrepresentation, which did not succeed.[83]

In exercising jurisdiction over events that had occurred prior to the relevant BIT's coming into effect, the Tribunal considered the challenged domestic court's decision that the investor claimed to have violated the BITs FET standard as the wrongful act although the said court adjudicated events that occurred prior to the relevant BIT.[84] The Tribunal's jurisdictional decision happens in the context of its own prior jurisdictional decision, but the key point is what is stated in the following paragraph:

> The international dispute only crystallized or arose after the date of the Ismalia Judgment which together with the conduct of other organs of the State compounded the harm caused by the alleged fraud of the SCA. As a result, the reliance on the exclusion of disputes arisen prior to the entry into force of the 2002 BIT contained in Article 12 of such treaty was inapposite and the dispute resolution clause of the BIT 2002 applied to the whole dispute brought before this Tribunal.[85]

Because the investor's main claim was that the Egyptian domestic court proceedings denied it justice and hence was a violation of FET, the Tribunal focused on the court's decision and processes rather than the events that led to the domestic claims. Although some of the events predated the applicable BIT, the Tribunal exercised jurisdiction over the question of whether the court's processes and decisions denied the Claimant justice as discussed in the FET Chapter 15. By the Tribunal's reckoning, the international claim "arose" or "crystalized" after the date of the domestic court's

80 *Id.* at 316 (The Arbitral Tribunal therefore considers that a more flexible and pragmatic approach to the meaning of "investment" is appropriate, which takes into account the features identified in Salini, but along with all the circumstances of the case, including the nature of the instrument containing the relevant consent to ICSID).

81 Jan de Nul N.V. Dredging International N.V. v. Arab Republic of Egypt, ICSID Case No. ARB/04/13, Award (Nov. 6, 2008), at 109–12, 116–17.

82 *Id.* at 70–74.

83 *See id.* at 254 ("It follows that the evidence before the Tribunal does not establish that the SCA committed a fraud. Hence, there can be no issue of substantive denial of justice based on the ground that the Ismalia Court failed to remedy a fraud that did not exist").

84 *See id.* at 128–30.

85 *Id.* at 129.

judgment and that is why what the judgment judged is only relevant to the substantive merits of the alleged substantive violations.

This jurisdictional decision is interesting because it considers the challenged decision the point of temporal departure, which is not unreasonable, but the bifurcation appears to have added complexity to the matter as the parties argued jurisdiction again during the merits phase and clearly doubled the amount of time that comparable cases have taken to complete, between 2003 and 2008. The average time is close to three years than six.

In *Bernardus v. Zimbabwe* (2009), the only jurisdictional issue pertained to the Dutch nationality of the Claimants. The issue was resolved by their furnishing of proof of their Dutch nationality. Although the Respondent disputed nationality on the facts, it later conceded its contention and the Tribunal duly exercised jurisdiction under the Zimbabwe-Netherlands BIT and Article 25 of the ICSID Convention.[86]

Waguih Elie v. Egypt (2009) was one of the first cases that presented nationality as a jurisdictional defense. It is notable for the highly technical resolution of this issue and the scale of the consequences that followed. Essentially, an award of more than $200 million dollars, including interests by and largely dependent on the resolution of whether the principal claimant lost his Egyptian nationality under Egyptian law when he acquired the nationality of a third state not covered by the BIT.[87]

The story is rather interesting. Egyptian law on nationality permitted an Egyptian citizen who acquired another nationality to keep his Egyptian nationality if permitted by the Ministry of Interior to keep it. The law also required the person to notify the Ministry of his intention to keep the nationality within a year of acquiring another nationality.[88] Although the Claimant acquired Lebanese nationality, he had never in fact sent the notification required under the law to keep his Egyptian nationality. Because this last requirement was not met, the Tribunal ruled that he had lost his Egyptian nationality for purposes of jurisdiction as a matter of law although he continued to hold Egyptian passport as a matter of fact.[89] Indeed, he invoked the Egypt–Italy BIT

[86] Bernardus Henricus Funnekotter and Others v. Republic of Zimbabwe, ICSID Case No. ARB/05/6, Award (Apr. 22, 2009), at 93–95.

[87] *See* Waguih Elie George Slag and Clorinda Vecchi v. The Arab Republic of Egypt, ICSID Case No. ARB/05/15, Award (June 1, 2009).

[88] *See id.* at 11–14 (quoting the relevant Egyptian Nationality Law ("Article 10 "An Egyptian may not gain a foreign nationality except after being permitted by virtue of a decree from the Minister of Interior; otherwise such person shall still be considered an Egyptian in every respect and under all circumstances, unless the Cabinet decides to withdraw his nationality under the provision of Article 16 of this Law. In the event an Egyptian is permitted to gain a foreign nationality, then this shall lead to the withdrawal of the Egyptian nationality. However, permission to acquire a foreign nationality may allow the person for whom such permission is given, his wife and minor children to retain the Egyptian nationality, provided he notifies his wish to take advantage of such benefit within a period not exceeding one year from the date of gaining the foreign nationality, and in such case they may retain the Egyptian nationality despite having gained a foreign nationality").

[89] *Id.* at 15 ("In his application for permission to acquire Lebanese nationality Mr Siag sought permission to maintain his Egyptian nationality pursuant to the third paragraph of Article 10 of the Nationality Law. As discussed at length in the Tribunal's Decision on Jurisdiction, the third paragraph of Article 10 contains an additional requirement, once permission to maintain Egyptian nationality is granted, to further notify the Egyptian Interior Ministry within the period of one year of the desire to retain Egyptian nationality. Mr. Siag did not so notify the Ministry with the consequence, as found in the Decision on Jurisdiction, that he lost his Egyptian nationality").

because he acquired a third nationality, Italian by marriage. His Italian nationality, the nationality covered by the BIT's protection, was not disputed.[90]

The Tribunal interpreted Egyptian law in a light most favorable to the Claimant especially because he did not deny having considered himself as an Egyptian using an Egyptian passport and availing himself of all the attendant privileges thereof. The Tribunal simply ruled that he just did not know that he had lost his Egyptian nationality by operation of Egyptian law, and that his conduct did not matter.[91] This jurisdictional decision was reached by a majority vote. The dissenting arbitrator would have applied the doctrine of effective nationality to deny jurisdiction.[92]

Although it did not determine the outcome, the issue of waiver of jurisdictional objections due to delayed presentation was raised. After the close of the jurisdictional phase, Egypt attempted to present documentation purporting to show that the Claimant's Lebanese nationality was procured through fraud. The basis of its untimely presentation was that the requirement under Article 25 that the Claimant not be a citizen of the Respondent state is an issue of subject matter jurisdiction that cannot be waived.[93]

The Tribunal rejected this contention, deeming the question one of personal jurisdiction that could be waived rather than subject matter jurisdiction that cannot be waived at least in the context similar to the US Federal Court jurisdictional rules which were raised and discussed.[94] The characterization of the citizenship requirement under Article 25 of the ICSID Convention as akin to personal jurisdiction rather than subject matter jurisdiction would seem inaccurate. In any case, the Tribunal framed the issue of fraudulent obtaining of Lebanese nationality as an issue of timeliness under ICSID Rule 41 rather than an issue of jurisdiction.[95]

It appears that the nature of the substantive violations might have prompted the majority of the Tribunal to interpret their jurisdiction a little bit more broadly than perhaps less egregious factual allegations would have urged. The Tribunal was so

[90] *Id.* at 14. ("Mr Siag acquired Italian nationality on 3 May 1993 by decree of the Italian Minister of Interior. This was obtained on the basis of his marriage to an Italian citizen and the provisions of Article 5 of the Italian nationality law Number 91 of 1992. Mr. Siag was issued with an Italian passport on 12 July 1995 and remains a citizen of Italy at the present time").

[91] *Id.* at 483 ("The Tribunal finds that the Claimants acted in good faith in obtaining their Egyptian passports and in their subsequent business and other dealings with Egypt. As to the latter, Claimants did not know at that point, nor as lay persons could they reasonably be expected to have known, that in law they had lost their Egyptian nationality. Thus the Claimants are not estopped from now denying their Egyptian nationality").

[92] *See id.* at 301.

[93] *Id.* at 231.

[94] *Id.* at 251 ("First, Egypt's contention that Mr Siag's nationality was an issue of subject-matter jurisdiction under Article 25 of the ICSID Convention and therefore could not be waived assumed that the Tribunal was bound by United States law, which was not the case. Even if the Tribunal were to adopt United States law, jurisdiction over Mr Siag was a matter of personal, not subject-matter, jurisdiction").

[95] *Id.* at 288 ("The Tribunal agrees that Article 25 does not confer jurisdiction over dual nationals. However, it does not accept the conclusions Egypt has drawn from that fact. The Tribunal does not consider that it is Article 25 that is properly under discussion as having been waived; it is ICSID Rule 41. It is that Rule which grants the right to a party to object to the jurisdiction of the Centre, and it is the right granted by Rule 41 which the Claimants assert has been waived as a result of a failure to invoke that right "as early as possible").

outraged by the facts that it chose to put the following factual narrative in the introductory passage:

> They say the case involves "undisguised bigotry and religious zealotry, governmental conduct based on contrivances, perjury by government attorneys in domestic court proceedings, blatant disrespect for the judicial branch of government and the finality of its rulings, extra-judicial seizures by brute force, the failure of the police to provide the most minimal levels of assistance or protection, governmental harassment and intimidation on multiple fronts, and corruption at the highest levels of the Government.[96]

The trouble that the Tribunal went through in the award in rejecting every defense that the State raised shows a level of determination to afford redress to the Claimant perhaps because of the perception that the administrative and judicial processes in Egypt were unfair to the Claimants as discussed under the substantive violations section.

The Tribunal's inclination is evident from what it chose to put in the introductory passages. While pertinent to its substantive rulings, they would have had no relevance to the jurisdictional decision, and this case is fundamentally a jurisdictional one. At the end of the day, Egypt was required to pay compensation to persons it considered its citizens under a BIT designed to protect foreign investors. This result required a determined arbitral majority that considered itself the best dispenser of justice under the circumstances.

[96] *See id.* at 3.

8

Post-2010 Contemporary Jurisdictional Matters

The Post-2010 period itself could be divided into the period between 2010 and 2020 and the post-2020 period. This is not only because of the sheer passage of time, but also because the changes that have occurred in the post-2020 period have been remarkable permitting a staggered appraisal in two subsections as follows.

The 2010 to 2020 Period

In *Gustav v. Ghana* (2010), as a preliminary jurisdictional matter, this BIT-based ICSID arbitration was the Claimant's second attempt as it had had its first contact based ICSID jurisdictional attempt rejected. The JV Contract out of which the dispute arose contained an arbitration agreement that read: "Where any disputes arise between the parties hereto which cannot be amicably settled, then the dispute shall be referred to the International Centre for the Settlement of Investment Disputes."[1] Interestingly, the information about the Claimant's first ICSID attempt and ICSID's decline of jurisdiction did not come out until the Claimant's submission of its posthearing brief, and even that only in response to the question raised by its own appointed arbitrator.

The brief reads:

> Arbitrator Cremades asked why Hamester had not brought an ICSID claim under the JVA. The answer is that Hamester did try to submit such a claim but the Centre declined jurisdiction on the grounds that Cocobod is not a designated constituent subdivision or agency of Ghana under Article 25(1) of the Convention.[2]

This is highly interesting because the final result primarily rested on the absence of attribution, a matter that ICSID seems to have in the previous submission weighed in on in the jurisdictional context albeit indirectly. It is not surprising that the Claimant did not volunteer that information until it was asked about it directly. It is, however, surprising that the issue was not debated more especially because of the Claimant's attempt to use the umbrella clause for its breach of contract claims.[3]

[1] Gustav F W Hamester GmbH & Co KG v. Republic of Ghana Respondent, ICSID Case No. ARB/07/24, Award (June 18, 2010), at 27 (quoting the JV Agreement, Art. 12(b)).

[2] *Id.* at 27 (quoting Claimant's posthearing brief).

[3] *Id.* at 62 of the Award suggests that this fact was indeed known, but there is no more discussion of it, which makes it even more interesting: "On May 14, 2004, Hamester submitted a Request for Arbitration against the Republic of Ghana, represented by Cocobod, to ICSID on the basis of the dispute-settlement provision of the JVA. The registration of the request was refused as the Centre found that there was manifestly

Africa's International Investment Law Regimes. Won L. Kidane, Oxford University Press. © Oxford University Press 2023.
DOI: 10.1093/oso/9780197745571.003.0008

In any case, the Respondent State challenged the jurisdiction of the court on several grounds none of which have anything to do with the competing contract-based arbitration clause, which, if accepted, would have presented a mix of advantages and disadvantages to both parties. If a contract-based jurisdiction were to have been accepted, the Claimant would have lost its treaty claims but would have gained its umbrella clause claims without the need to justify them under a treaty. The Respondent would have been relieved of the treaty claims but not the contract claims.

The underlying facts being common, it is difficult to say which party benefited by ICSD's initial rejection of the contract-based jurisdiction although the decision seems appropriate especially in view of the Tribunal's rejection of attribution on the same facts later, albeit as a part of the merits on liability.

In the treaty claim, the Respondent raises two jurisdictional objections are two: that the investor did not hold protected investment (as the JV was procured through fraud) and that the complained about breaches of obligations by the state-owned contracting partner were not attributable to the state for purpose of a treaty claim.[4] The Respondent also argued that the umbrella clause claims fell outside of the Tribunal's treaty jurisdiction.[5]

The Tribunal framed the issue of fraudulent misrepresentation as a question of jurisdiction *ratione materiae* and properly made this distinction: "Thus, on the wording of this BIT, the legality of the creation of the investment is a jurisdictional issue; the legality of the investor's conduct during the life of the investment is a merits issue."[6]

The Tribunal rejected the Respondent's allegation that the Claimant obtained interests through fraud for failure to meet its burden of proof.[7] The issue of jurisdiction relating to attribution presented a more serious dilemma because the same issue also went to the core of the merits on liability. The Tribunal thus found itself in an unenviable position of having to uphold jurisdiction on the basis of attribution but deny recovery based on lack of attribution on the merits. It does so logically and plausibly. The operative paragraph puts the resolution of the dilemma in the following terms:

> The Tribunal is not faced here with a situation where it is readily evident that the State is not involved at all, or where the issue is capable of an answer based upon a

no consent given by the ROG to ICSID arbitration under the JVA, nor any designation of Cocobod as a subdivision or an agency by the ROG for the purposes of Article 25(1) of the ICSID Convention, or any approval of Cocobod"s consent by the ROG for the purposes of Article 25(3) of the ICSID Convention."

[4] *Id.* at 81–82.

[5] *Id.* at 83.

[6] *Id.* at 127. The doctrinal foundation comes from the Phoenix formulation as the Tribunal notes: "The Tribunal considers, as was stated for example in Phoenix v. Czech Republic, that: 'States cannot be deemed to offer access to the ICSID dispute settlement mechanism to investments not made in good faith.' An investment will not be protected if it has been created in violation of national or international principles of good faith; by way of corruption, fraud, or deceitful conduct; or if its creation itself constitutes a misuse of the system of international investment protection under the ICSID Convention. It will also not be protected if it is made in violation of the host State's law (as elaborated, e.g. by the tribunal in Phoenix)." *Id.* at 123 (citing Phoenix Action Ltd. v. The Czech Republic, ICSID Case No. ARB/06/5, Award (Apr. 15, 2009), at 106.)

[7] *See Id.*. at 132, 139.

limited enquiry (akin to other jurisdictional issues). On the contrary, the evidential record in this case is more complex. In fact, the Respondent itself recognises that some acts are attributable to the Ghanaian Government, while denying that they amount to international illegal behaviour. In other words, while the extent of the State"s involvement is unclear, it is not contested that some acts are attributable to Ghana. In such a situation, the Tribunal considers that it has jurisdiction over the case brought against Ghana and jurisdiction to decide which acts are attributable and which are not.[8]

The distinction is a matter of degree and shows that jurisdiction could be exercised to decide the same set of facts and law in more depth for purposes of allocating liability. This rests the issue without contradiction. On this point, the Tribunal added: "As the Tribunal has not accepted bifurcation and has joined the jurisdictional objections to the merits, it now has the benefit of the parties' full pleadings in order to deal with the question of attribution in any event."[9] And that is exactly what it subsequently did. The Tribunal's umbrella clause discussions are deferred to Chapter 14.

Unsurprisingly, because of the findings of fraud in the local commercial arbitral proceedings involving the same parties and the same set of facts, the Respondent in *Malicorp v. Egypt* (2011) filed a jurisdictional objection on July 1, 2009, which is within a month of the constitution of the ICSID Tribunal on June 2, 2009, without even waiting for an invitation.[10] According to the Tribunal's summary, Egypt asserted that "the Contract was entered into as a result of fraud and that the Arbitral Tribunal has no jurisdiction to rule, as Egypt's consent to give the protection offered by the Agreement does not extend to fraud."[11] That became one of the key bases of the jurisdictional phase. The Tribunal's response was learned and doctrinally sound. It got into the jurisprudence of severability, one of the fundamental principles that sustains arbitration as a viable alternative to court litigation.

In its more fully developed form, the Respondent's fraud-related jurisdictional objection relies primarily on *Phoenix Action* and is articulated as follows:

> *In holding that investments marked by fraud were not entitled to such protection [the benefit or the relevant treaties, (n° 105)] as a matter or jurisdiction, the Tribunals in Inceysa, Fraport and Phoenix Action were not developing new theories. Those Tribunals were applying well-known, accepted principles to interpret jurisdictional issues regarding investment arbitrations. The principles are so well known and obvious and no one would seek to ignore them in a normal civil case or arbitration. What is perhaps more novel is that Tribunals are increasingly applying these principles of judicial common sense to deal with issues of jurisdiction at the outset of investment*

[8] *Id.* at 145.
[9] *Id.* at 146.
[10] Malicorp Limited v. The Arab Republic of Egypt, ICSID Case No. ARB/08/18, Award (Feb. 7, 2011), at 78.
[11] *Id.*

arbitrations. The Respondent respectfully submits that that is the course of action that this Tribunal should adopt.[12]

Before addressing this objection, the Tribunal had to reckon with the determination of essentially the same set of issues by the Cairo Center's commercial arbitral panel. Having recognized that breach of contract does not necessarily rise to the level of treaty violation,[13] the Tribunal, just like tribunals before it, conceived its own jurisdiction as growing out the following distinction:

> In order for a breach of contract to serve as the basis for jurisdiction of a tribunal in an investment arbitration, such breach must at the same time, and for reasons inherent in the investment protection treaty itself, amount to a violation of that treaty, one that could not be resolved by using the ordinary procedure. Among the matters falling within the scope of the jurisdiction *ratione materiae* of an arbitral tribunal in an investment case are acts by the host State in the exercise of its public powers ("actes de puissance publique") that deprive the foreign investor of its rights in violation of the guarantees offered by the Agreement.[14]

Distinguishing what it is called to adjudicate from what the contract tribunal adjudicated in this way, the Tribunal went on to examining whether its jurisdictional basis met what is often called the "double keyhole approach" or "double-barreled test," that is, meeting the requirements of both the BIT and ICSID.[15] That effectively meant the determination of whether the putative investment is covered by the BIT's definition of investment and meets the *Salini* test, where it applies under the ICSID Convention because of the lack of definition of "investment" in the Convention. This in turn meant the determination of the fraud issue for purposes of the BIT's definition and the determination of whether the *Salini* test applies and if so, whether it is met for purpose of the ICISD Convention.

The Tribunal had a plausible doctrinal response to the fraud issue as a barrier to jurisdiction and it relates the severability concept. It said that:

[12] *Id.* at 94 (emphasis by the Tribunal). The Respondent later added: "*The Respondent respectfully submits that Malicorp's claim should be rejected, promptly as an improper attempt to use BIT rights to profit from its own fraud and negligence and its own failure to perform the Concession Contract*" (emphasis by the Tribunal).

[13] *Id.*. at 103(a): "The protection afforded by investment treaties does not necessarily cover purely contractual claims where the parties to the contract have agreed on another clause granting jurisdiction, provided the parties are the same." Relying on *SGS Societe Generale de Surveillance S.A. v. Republic of the Philippines*, ICSID Case No. ARB/02/6, Decision of the Tribunal on Objections to Jurisdiction (29 Jan. 2004); Joy Mining Machinery Limited v. Egypt, ICSID Case No. ARB/03/11, Award on Jurisdiction (Aug. 6, 2004), 163; LESI S.p.A and Astaldi S.p.A v. Algeria, ICSID Case No. ARB/05/03, Award (July 12, 2006).

[14] *Id.* at 103(a). The passage that comes right before that makes this useful clarification: "It is hard to see how an investment treaty would be breached by the mere fact of a breach of contract, as long as the control mechanisms put in place by that contract are functioning normally. Investment arbitration was not set up to provide a substitute for contracting partners who refrain from following the ordinary procedure by which they have agreed to be bound, nor as a means of appeal for those who have failed to obtain satisfaction (or full satisfaction) by using that procedure." *Id.*

[15] *Id.* at 106.

> The solution derives, first, from the *principle of autonomy of the arbitration agreement*, a principle so fundamental that it also has its place in investment arbitration. According to that principle, defects undermining the validity of the substantive legal relationship, which is the subject of the dispute on the merits, do not automatically undermine the validity of the arbitration agreement. Thus, an arbitral tribunal is competent to decide on the merits even if the main contract was entered into as a result of misrepresentation or corruption. Only defects that go to the consent to arbitrate itself can deprive the tribunal of jurisdiction. In the present case, there is nothing to indicate that the consent to arbitrate, as distinct from the consent to the substantive guarantees in the bilateral Agreement, was obtained by misrepresentation or corruption or even by mistake.[16]

This is a resolute affirmance of the classic severability doctrine more fully articulated by prominent cases such as the UK House of Lords Case of *Fiona Trust v. Privalov* (2007)[17] and the US Supreme Court of *Buckeye v. Cardegna* (2006).[18] Properly applied, this principle preserves the Tribunal's jurisdiction to decide its own jurisdiction and in the absence of allegation that the arbitration agreement, rather than the underlying agreement, was tainted by fraud, the Tribunal's jurisdiction survives.

In this case, however, the Tribunal had to overcome the second-prong of the "double-barreled" test, which unavoidably meant opining on what came to be known as the *Salini* test under *Salini v. Morocco*.[19] It's endorsement of *Salini* is cautious at best:

> Consequently, in its widest, albeit disputed, meaning, there must be (i) a contribution, (ii) of a certain duration, (iii) of a nature such as to generate returns, (iv) presenting a particular risk, and (v) such as to promote the economic development of the host country. Such criteria are not at all absolute and must be regarded as attempts to pin down the notion.[20]

With this hesitation, the Tribunal had to determine what the Claimant's contribution may be. It gives the following interesting but not necessarily convincing formulation:

> It is true that Malicorp does not appear to have performed many services in connection with it. Nonetheless, the fact of being bound by that Contract implied an obligation to make major contributions in the future. That commitment constitutes the investment; it entails the promise to make contributions in the future for the performance of which that party is henceforth contractually bound. *In other words, the protection here extends to deprivation of the revenue the investor had a right to*

[16] *Id.* at 119(a).
[17] Fiona Trust & Holding Corp v. Privalov, [2007] UKHL 40 (By Lord Hoffmann).
[18] Buckeye Check Cashing, Inc. v. Cardegna, 546 U.S. 440 (2006) (By Justice Scalia)
[19] Salini Construttori S.p.A and Italstrade S.p.A v. Kingdom of Morocco, ICSID Case No. ARB/00/4, Decision on Jurisdiction (July 23, 2001).
[20] Malicorp Limited v. The Arab Republic of Egypt, ICSID Case No. ARB/08/18, Award (Feb. 7, 2011), at 109.

> *expect in consideration for contributions that it had not yet made, but which it had contractually committed to make subsequently.*[21]

This appears to be one of those result-oriented skillful *post hoc* justifications of jurisdiction. This is an excellent example of the reverence that *Salini* gained early on. The choice here was between disavowing *Salini* or inventing a detour around it. Although it came close to doing the former, it chose the latter route. This jurisdictional approach is particularly curious in view of the fact that the same Tribunal subsequently rejects the matter on the merits without much difficulty. Although analytically cogent, there is an element of futility that is not accounted for because there were clear indicia of unsustainability of the underlying claims especially in view of the commercial arbitration and the criminal convictions. As discussed in Part III, some of the most contemporary investment treaty models made provisions for the more robust screening of cases for frivolousness at the filing stage. Although by no means an easy exercise, this case might be an example of where a motion for summary judgment or some such pretrial tool would have been appropriate had the procedures permitted. The new batch of treaties and models are attempting to address some of these issues.

In *Bernard von Pezold v. Zimbabwe* (2015), the first jurisdictional challenge was *ratione personae* relating only to two of the Claimants, who the Respondent said held Zimbabwean nationality. This was defeated on the facts.[22] The other *ratione personae* jurisdictional challenge pertained to lack of corporate control, particularly as it relates to the corporate Claimant, which was incorporated in Zimbabwe.[23] The Tribunal held that it was satisfied on the facts that it was owned and controlled by Swiss nationals who enjoy the BIT's protection.[24]

The Tribunal then considered complex questions of *ratione materiae*. The Respondent State's key contention seems to focus on two of the *Salini* factors:[25] the origin of the funds and contribution to the host state.[26] It claimed the origin of the funds was primarily Zimbabwe and the nature of the investment was commercial farming that depleted the land but gave nothing back to the country in return.[27]

[21] *Id.* at 113.

[22] Bernhard von Pezold and Others v. Republic of Zimbabwe, ICSID Case No. ARB/10/15, Award (July 28, 2015), at 200–05 ("205 The Tribunal is satisfied on its review of the evidence that each of the von Pezold Claimants fulfils the nationality criteria under Article 25(2)(a) and the Tribunal therefore has jurisdiction ratione personae over the von Pezold Claimants under the ICSID Convention").

[23] *See id.* at 206–26.

[24] *Id.* at 226 ("With regard to the Border Claimants, which were incorporated in Zimbabwe, the Tribunal is satisfied that the Claimants have shown the Border Companies were "effectively controlled" by Swiss nationals and thereby satisfy the requirements of the Swiss BIT").

[25] *Id.* at 231. Among other cases, the Respondent relies on the following cases that affirm the *Salini* factors: Fedax N.V. v. Republic of Venezuela ("Fedax"), ICSID Case No. ARB/96/3, Decision of the Tribunal on Objections to Jurisdiction (July 11, 1997), Salini Costruttori S.p.A. and Italstrade S.p.A. v. Hashemite Kingdom of Jordan ("Salini"),ICSID Case No. ARB/02/13, Decision of the Tribunal on Jurisdiction (Nov. 29, 2004), Joy Mining Machinery Limited v. Egypt, ICSID Case No. ARB/03/11, Award on Jurisdiction (Aug. 6, 2004), Phoenix Action Ltd. v. The Czech Republic, ICSID Case No. ARB/06/5, Award (Apr. 15, 2009). *Id.*

[26] See Bernhard von Pezold and Others v. Republic of Zimbabwe, ICSID Case No. ARB/10/15, Award (July 28, 2015), at 243 ("because funding for the alleged investments came from Zimbabwe and remained in Zimbabwe, no foreign investments are at stake").

[27] *Id.* at 236:

Affording *Salini* only a partial endorsement and adopting a simplified version of it, the Tribunal rejected the Respondent's *ratione materiae* objection on the facts in the following terms:

> Whatever the position may be on Salini as regards the elements to be satisfied, the Tribunal finds that it is rather less clear that the Salini test is the authoritative statement on those characteristics. Indeed, there seems to be a move away from Salini to a simpler test involving contribution, duration and risk. All of these characteristics are satisfied in the present case.[28]

The Tribunal likewise rejected the Respondent's BIT based *ratione materiae* objections.[29]

The Tribunal finally considered the Respondent's *ratione temporis* challenge based on the argument that some of the events occurred before the coming into effect of the Zimbabwe-Germany BIT. The Tribunal rejected these time-based objections to jurisdiction on grounds that the BIT had provisionally entered into force based on an exchange of diplomatic notes covering the relevant period.[30]

In *Union Fenosa Gas, S.A. (UFG) v. Egypt* (2018), Egypt raised jurisdictional and admissibility defenses on the ground that the underlying NLG project contract out of which the dispute arose was procured and maintained through corruption.[31] Egypt also argued that the measures that it took following the revolution that might have affected the investor's access to natural gas were justifiable as a matter of necessity.[32]

The Tribunal addressed these issues as a matter of admissibility rather than jurisdiction. The Respondent's most serious corruption allegation was the following:

> The Respondent first contends that the Damietta project was "riddled with corruption": UFG selected Halliburton, whose bid was US$ 50 million higher than that of the next competitor, as its subcontractor; and Halliburton's CEO pleaded guilty in

The Respondent relies on the evidence of Minister Mutasa in support of its position that the Claimants made no contribution to the development of Zimbabwe and, for this reason, do not qualify for protection under the ICSID Convention or the BITs (see Rejoinder, para. 946, quoting Minister Mutasa's Witness Statement, paras. 32, 33, 34 and 42, R-12):

32. Claimants never contributed anything to Zimbabwe. They drained our land of its resources to increase their family wealth which was already considerable . . .

33. Claimants were here to reap profits for themselves only. They did not create anything useful for Zimbabwe. Their only concern was to maximise their individual family's financial gain. As they never contributed anything positive to our country, in that sense they did not make an investment which merits benefitting from the protections of a BIT in this arbitration . . . We told them "you are no longer wanted here." . . . They have exploited us, contributing nothing to our country, and drained us of our country's wealth . . . We do not like the greedy ones in any race or culture, those who are selfish, those who contribute nothing to our country but who only thing of taking. We like good people, be they white or otherwise, all good people are accepted and all bad people are not.

[28] *Id.* at 285. *See also* 286–88 (applying the simplified version to the facts of the Claimants' contribution such as employment).

[29] *See id.* at 289–316.

[30] *See id.* at 328–43.

[31] Union Fenosa Gas, S.A. v. Arab Republic of Egypt, ICSID Case No. ARB/14/4 (Aug. 31, 2018), at 2.4.

[32] *Id.* at 8.1.

> the USA to violations of the US Foreign Corrupt Practices Act, including bribes and kickbacks in connection with the Damietta Project.[33]

It also accused former Egyptian officials of conspiring with the investor to award the project in disregard of bid procedures authorized by law in exchange for personal benefits.[34]

Unlike the *World Duty Free v. Kenya* case, this Tribunal rejected the corruption defense on the ground that the State failed to carry its burden of proof under the balance of probabilities standard.[35] It held in particular that all the allegations of corruption were not proven on the facts.[36] The dissent disagreed on at least one instance of corrupt activity.[37]

The Tribunal also rejected Egypt's necessity defense, although the key source of the investor's complaint was that the Respondent reallocated natural gas supplies that left the investor's NLG plant unused was the revolution.[38] "The Respondent asserts that the prioritisation of the domestic electricity was the only way to safeguard Egypt's essential interests from a grave and imminent peril,"[39] and also that "if the Respondent had acted otherwise, it 'would thus have led to more numerous and prolonged blackouts, and even more severe accompanying violent protests and demonstrations, further aggravating the perilous security situation.' "[40]

The Tribunal first found that "the Respondent bears the legal burden of proving its defence of 'necessity' under customary international law, as a positive allegation."[41]

[33] *Id.* at 2.4.

[34] *Id.* at 2.5.

[35] *Id.* at 7.52 ("The first feature is the legal burden and standard of proof for these allegations of corruption against the Claimant. As the party making these allegations, the Respondent bears the legal burden of proof. As to the standard of proof, although these allegations amount to serious criminal misconduct, the Tribunal considers that the standard of proof remains 'the balance of probabilities.' As has long been recognised, corruption is rarely proven by direct cogent evidence; but, rather, it usually depends upon an accumulation of circumstantial evidence. Circumstantial evidence of corruption is as good as direct evidence in proving corruption. There is no reason in this arbitration, which is not a criminal proceeding, to impose a higher standard of proof").

[36] *Id.* at 7.56–7.59 ("Later, Halliburton's Chief Executive Officer, Mr Albert Stanley, pleaded guilty to corruption under the USA's Foreign Corrupt Practices Act; and the SEC (with the USA's Department of Justice) charged Halliburton (with others) with paying bribes to obtain illegally contracts worth more than US$ 6 billion.... Accordingly, the Tribunal decides that the Respondent has not discharged its legal burden of proof, on a balance of probabilities, in regard to corruption by Halliburton"). *See also id.* at 7.88 ("7.88 The Tribunal has already taken note that the several payments received by Mr El Komy and EATCO in regard to the Damietta Project seem generous. However, it is not for this Tribunal to second-guess, long after the events, upon what conditions the Claimant (with its associated companies) should have paid for the work of Mr El Komy and EATCO. Over a period of some two years, Mr El Komy, as an "investorpartner" provided personal services for the Damietta Project; and EATCO also made contributions to the Project").

[37] *See* Union Fenosa Gas, S.A v. Egypt, ICSID Case No. ARB/14/4 (Aug. 31, 2018), at 5 (Dissenting Opinion of Mark Clodfelter) ("However, I believe that Respondent did meet its burden of proof with respect to Mr. Yehia El involvement with the project. The Respondent has demonstrated that there was a huge disproportion . . ").

[38] *Id.* at 8.1.

[39] *Id.* at 8.7. Among others, the Respondent relied on the following cases: *LG&E Energy Corp., L&E Capital Corp., LG&E International Inc. v. The Republic of Argentina*, ICSID Case No. ARB/02/1, Decision on Liability (Oct. 3, 2006), Impregilo S.p.A. v. Argentine Republic, ICSID Case No. ARB/07/17, Award (June 21, 2011); and also from the Zimbabwean political crisis: Von Pezold v. Zimbabwe, ICSID Case No. ARB/10/15, Award (July 28, 2015). *Id.* at 8.8.

[40] *Id.* at 8.13.

[41] *Id.* at 8.38.

The Tribunal then rejected Egypt's revolution related necessity defense essentially on the facts:

> The Tribunal does not discount the fact of social unrest or the Respondent's reasonable concerns that serious unrest might ensue, still less the fact of the Egyptian revolution beginning in early 2011. Yet, the curtailment of gas to the Damietta Plant both pre-dated and post-dated the Egyptian revolution. It was not the proximate cause for curtailing gas supplies to the Plant. That proximate cause lay in the Respondent's long-standing policies as to the development of gas deposits, electrical power generation, the national grid and the preferential use of gas for users and consumers in Egypt.[42]

The admissibility decision on the issue of necessity was critical because the Tribunal found a violation of FET for the exact same reasons, that is, the allocation might have been necessary, but it unduly disfavored the foreign investor. The FET finding is discussed in Chapter 15.

Cortec v. Kenya (2018) was primarily a jurisdictional victory for Kenya, but the disposition required the review of factual allegations relating to the legal validity of the acquisition of the mining license the termination of which gave rise to the dispute.[43] The key jurisdictional question that the Tribunal considered was whether a mining license issued without following the legal requirements of the host state can qualify as a protected investment.[44] In this case, the license was obtained without meeting the country's Environmental Impact Assessment (EIA) requirements, which became the main jurisdictional question for the Tribunal.[45]

Although the Respondent attempted to show that the license was issued through corruption, the Tribunal was not convinced that the state met its burden of proof.[46] In any case, in *Cortec*, the Tribunal dismissed the case on jurisdictional grounds notwithstanding the lack of proof of corruption based mainly on noncompliance with domestic law requirements. The Tribunal had the benefit of a domestic court interpretation of the domestic court requirements in the same case. As quoted by the Tribunal, the Kenyan High Court ruled that "The acquisition by [CMK] of the Mining Licence

[42] *Id.* at 8.46 (8.46 "In other words, the 'act' was not 'the only way' for the Respondent 'to safeguard an essential interest against a grave and imminent peril,' using the words in Article 25(1)(a) of the ILC Articles. In contrast to the Claimant and the Damietta Plant, other commercial users of gas remained preferred by the Respondent. This is confirmed by the disproportionality in the reductions for delivered gas between the Damietta Plant and other commercial users in 2012–2013; namely: 12% reductions for Industrial users (receiving 14.8 Bcma), 14% for Power users (28.9 Bcma), 14% for Idku (5.7 Bcma) and 60% (0.3 Bcma) for the Damietta Plant (from a total production of 58.8 Bcma); and the Plant's reduction resulted in a curtailment of 96% in the Claimant's contractual volumes for export.60 In 2012–2013, if the 'act' had been 'the only way,' it would have been equally necessary for the Respondent to curtail supplies to other commercial users to a similarly minimal level as the Damietta Plant and the Claimant. That was not done").

[43] Cortec Mining Kenya Limited, Cortec (Pty) Limited And Stirling Capital Limited v. Republic Of Kenya, ICSID Case No. ARB/15/29, Award (Oct. 22, 2018), 1–13.

[44] *See id.* at 313.

[45] *Id.* ("The issue here is whether the BIT extends protection to a mining licence [SML 351] not issued 'in accord with the laws of Kenya' because the Claimants failed to satisfy statutory prerequisites such as EIA approval").

[46] *See id.* at 133.

was not in compliance with the law and the licence was *void ab initio* and liable to be revoked."[47]

Although the Tribunal said that it is not bound by the High Court's decision, it is clear that it accorded the Court's decision the kind of deference that it deserved and included the following most instructive observations:

> 222. The Tribunal is mandated to apply international law not Kenyan domestic law, yet in the Tribunal's view, the application of international law reaches the same conclusion. The alleged "investment" is a mining licence. A mining license is not bricks and mortar. It is wholly the creature of Kenyan domestic law. Its creation is governed by Kenyan law . . .
>
> 223. The Claimants were successful in bending Mr. Masibo to their will but they knew enough about the Kenyan regulatory system to know they had not yet met its requirements. The Claimants had no legitimate expectation that SML 351 was valid.[48]

Equally helpfully, it characterizes the license as: "*The special prospecting licence was not itself a licence to make money. It was a licence to spend money. Prospecting, as such, involves cost not revenue.*"[49] Linking all of the above to the core jurisdictional question, the Tribunal ruled:

> In the Tribunal's view, SML 351 was void ab initio under international law and the Tribunal is without jurisdiction: (a) for the reasons already outlined, ICSID and the BIT protects only "lawful investments." The text and purpose of the BIT and the ICSID Convention are not consistent with holding host governments financially responsible for investments created in defiance of their laws fundamental protecting public interests such as the environment. The explicit language to the effect that protected investments must be made "in accordance with the laws of Kenya" is therefore unnecessary to secure the objects and purpose of the BIT.[50]

The Claimant's efforts to annul did not succeed.[51] The Annulment Committee, chaired by Brian King, concluded in particular that:

[47] *Id.* at 213 (quoting the Kenyan High Court's Decision in Cortec Mining Kenya v. Cabinet Secretary Ministry of Mining, Judgment, Mar. 20, 2015).

[48] *Id.* at 222–23.

[49] *Id.* at 328 (emphasis added).

[50] *Id.* at 333. The remaining part reads:

> "(b) in any event, SML 351 is a piece of paper whose value, if any, lies exclusively in the consequences attached to it by Kenyan law. In this case, as the Kenyan Courts have said, Kenyan law attached no consequences to the piece of paper;
>
> (c) Mining Commissioner Moses Masibo lacked jurisdiction even to consider issuance of a special mining licence in light of the status of Mrima Hill as a nature reserve, a forestry reserve and a national monument encircled by layers of statutory protection under the Forests Act, The Environmental (Impact Assessment and Audit) Regulations 2003, the Antiquities and Monuments Act and the Mining Act and reinforced by the conditions attached to SPL 256;
>
> (d) although this Tribunal is applying international law rather than Kenyan law, the Tribunal agrees with the Kenyan Courts that SML 351 as issued was void ab initio."

[51] *See* Decision on Application for Annulment in Cortec Mining v. Kenya, ARB/15/29 (Mar. 19, 2021), at 249.

> The question thus becomes whether the Tribunal's legal analysis in relation to SML 351 was "so untenable that it cannot be supported by reasonable arguments." The Committee concludes that it was not. Having found the Claimants to be complicit in the violations of Kenyan law that occurred, it was open to the Tribunal to conclude that these violations could be attributed to the Claimants, Article 7 notwithstanding.[52]

CMC v. Mozambique (2019) raised a unique jurisdictional challenge relating to the interaction of treaties, namely the ICSID Convention, the BIT and Cotonou Convention.[53] The Respondent raised six jurisdictional objections. Some are commonly raised objections such as that the investor or investment does not qualify for protection, and that the claims are purely contractual, which the Tribunal rejected.[54] The remaining two objections are unique and are discussed here in some detail.

The first such objection was that because the project is fancied by the European Development Bank, the Cotonou Convention applies. This Convention has its own dispute settlement mechanism, and this mechanism excludes ICSID arbitration.[55]

After taking a curious detour to determine which treaty, the BIT or Cotonou, takes precedent as a matter of temporal priority,[56] the Tribunal gets to the real subject matter

[52] *Id.* at 211. The other members of the Committee were: Mr. Cavinder Bull, SC, Member Ms. Dorothy Ufot, SAN, Member. *See id.* at caption.

[53] *See Id.* at 90. What is commonly known as the Cotonou Convention is the Partnership Agreement between the members of the African, Caribbean and Pacific Group of States, of the one part, and the European Community and its Member States, of the other part (the "Cotonou Convention"), signed in Cotonou on 23 June 2000, and amended in 2005 and 2010. *Id.*

[54] See CMC Muratori Cementisti CMC Di Ravenna SOC. Coop. & Others v. Republic of Mozambique, ICSID Case No. ARB/17/23 (Oct. 24, 2019), at 156, 171 ("Since all of the Claimants qualify as 'investors,' if they had an investment in Mozambique, we turn next to whether they had such an investment"). *Id.* at 196 ("In summary, the Tribunal has no difficulty in concluding that the Claimants made an investment in Mozambique that qualified for protection under Article 25(1) of the ICSID Convention as well as under Article 1(1) of the BIT"). *Id.* at 221 ("The Claimants have asserted multiple claims under the BIT. The Claimants assert claims for denial of fair and just treatment, for unjustified and discriminatory measures, for failure to observe specific undertakings in good faith, and for treatment of their investment that is less favorable than that afforded by the Respondent to investments of nationals of third countries. Whatever merit each of those claims may have, each is stated as a claim arising under the BIT, not under the settlement agreement or any other contract. The Tribunal finds that the Claimants' claims all concern disputes 'which may arise between either Contracting Party and the investors of the other Contracting Party on investments.'") *Id.*

[55] *See id.* at 156, 223–52 ("224 Under the Cotonou Convention, according to the Respondent, both treaty claims and pure contract claims are arbitrable, but the use of other arbitration rules is excluded. According to the Respondent, the present dispute must therefore be arbitrated pursuant to the rules specified in the Cotonou Convention, to the exclusion of arbitration under the ICSID Convention and the ICSID Arbitration Rules"). ("251 The Respondent argues that this Tribunal cannot simply become a Cotonou Convention tribunal, because i) ICSID cannot administer a dispute under the Cotonou Arbitration Rules, and ii) this Tribunal does not and cannot comply with the Cotonou Arbitration Rules, which require that all arbitrators be citizens of a member state").

[56] *See id.* at 267–71 (267 "The Cotonou Convention was signed on 23 June 2000 and entered into force on 1 April 2003. The BIT was signed on 14 December 1998, and entered into force on 17 November 2003.The dates of the two treaties are important because of the rule of treaty construction stated in Article 30 of the VCLT, which provides that, "as between States parties" to "successive treaties relating to the same subject-matter,' 'the earlier treaty applies only to the extent that its provisions are compatible with those of the later treaty.' In determining which treaty is the earlier and which is the later, commentators generally refer to the date of signature of each treaty"). (citations omitted) ("271 Since predecessors of many of the provisions of the Cotonou Convention on which the Respondent relies, such as the provision for arbitrating claims arising out of the performance of contracts for projects financed by the EDF, occur in the predecessor treaties to the Cotonou Convention, which were signed before the BIT was signed, there is room for argument as

issue. It first acknowledges that both treaties deal with economic development issues,[57] but then begins to make a distinction between them. The Cotonou Convention is not only broader in its coverage but also specifically mentions that member states would enter into investment treaties.[58] It then concludes, despite the overlap:

> It would seem evident that a treaty that affirms the need for and importance of investment promotion and protection agreements, and in which the Parties undertake to study the main clauses of such an agreement, is not itself an investment promotion and protection agreement. The Cotonou Convention and the BIT thus appear to the Tribunal not to deal with "the same subject-matter."[59]

In the interest of exhaustion, the Tribunal also looked at whether there is any conflict in any case. The Tribunal found that the BIT does not exclude arbitration under the Cotonou Convention because "other international arbitration arrangements, mechanisms, or instruments adhered to and ratified by both Contracting Parties' under Article 9(3)(d) of the BIT, and both Italy and Mozambique are parties to both treaties."[60] And finally, makes the key determination that:

> The fact that the Lot 3 Contract provides for resolution of disputes arising under that contract in either the courts of Mozambique or under the Cotonou Arbitration Rules does not deprive this Tribunal of jurisdiction over claims pleaded and arising under the BIT. As the ad hoc committee in Vivendi observed: "A state cannot rely on an exclusive jurisdiction clause in a contract to avoid the characterisation of its conduct as internationally unlawful under a treaty.[61]

At the end of the day, the decision is that no matter the overlap, neither the Cotonou Convention nor the contracts can deprive the Party of its BIT rights, and as such the Tribunal would have BIT-based jurisdiction,[62] which was the Claimant's preferred forum. It is interesting to note, however, that the Respondent objected to the Tribunal's jurisdiction in favor of another tribunal, which could have had a different mix of nationality of arbitrators, but at the end, the Tribunal that it objected

to which should be considered the later treaty. The Parties did not address that question, however, and the Tribunal does not need to resolve it, because the issue arises only if the BIT and the Cotonou Convention relate to "the same subject-matter" and their provisions are not compatible in that they cannot be applied simultaneously. We therefore turn to those two questions").

[57] *Id.* at 273 ("Both treaties thus seem to include economic development among their objectives, but the scale and scope of the two is significantly different").

[58] *See id.* at 273. ("2.74 Article 78 of the Cotonou Convention, entitled 'Investment Protection,' provides that: The ACP States and the Community and its Member States, within the scope of their respective competencies, affirm the need to promote and protect either Party's investments on their respective territories, and in this context affirm the importance of concluding, in their mutual interest, investment promotion and protection agreements which could also provide the basis for insurance and guarantee schemes").

[59] *Id.* at 276.

[60] *Id.* at 279.

[61] *Id.* at 292.

[62] *See id.* at 295.

to gave the state a full victory on the merits by dismissing all of the Claimant's claims.[63]

The case that came in the last year of the decade, *Oded Besserglik v. Mozambique* (2019), was dismissed on jurisdictional grounds, but not only was the jurisdictional ground raised late, but it also required extensive evidentiary hearing for the simple question of whether the BIT had come into effect or not.[64]

Although the Parties to the dispute, the South African investor and Mozambique, contended the ratification status of the BIT by the two contracting parties according to their own national constitutional orders, the Tribunal took the higher ground in concluding "according to Respondent, the foregoing evidence establishes that both South Africa and Mozambique have unequivocally and repeatedly confirmed that the BIT is not in force. The position of the contracting States that the BIT is not (and never was) in force is conclusive for this Tribunal."[65]

More interestingly, the Tribunal dismissed the estoppel argument relating to the untimely invocation of the lack of ratification as a jurisdictional challenge. For the Tribunal, this kind of jurisdictional defect is not waivable. In its own words: "The Tribunal is of the view that the requirement of reciprocal notifications under Article 12(1) of the BIT, which, when read with Article 24 of the Vienna Convention, are essential for its entry into force, cannot be presumed to be in existence by invoking the doctrine of estoppel."[66]

More importantly, it noted that "the jurisdiction of the Tribunal and the BIT being in force is a matter of law. Just as the jurisdiction of the Tribunal cannot be created by invoking the doctrine of estoppel, neither can a treaty which is not in force be given effect by an argument based on estoppel."[67] Although the Tribunal decided to accept the Respondent's jurisdictional objection which was raised inordinately late in the process,[68] it took that into account in the award of costs discussed in Chapter 19.

The Post-2020 Cases

The Respondent state's jurisdictional objection in *Strabag SE v. Libya* (2020), while mundane as there is no investment or investor because the Claimants are mere

[63] *See id.* at 465 ("For the reasons explained above, the Tribunal finds that the Claimants have failed to prevail on any of their claims. It therefore finds in favor of the Respondent, and dismisses each of the Claimants' claims").

[64] *See* Oded Besserglik v. Republic of Mozambique, ICSID Case No. ARB(AF)/14/2, Award (Oct. 28, 2019), at 185–96.

[65] *Id.* at 196.

[66] *Id.* at 412.

[67] *Id.* at 422.

[68] *See id.* at 245. ("Claimant argues that, as far as Respondent is concerned, the obligation to raise the objection regarding the BIT arose as soon as it received Claimant's Request, i.e., prior to the constitution of the Tribunal. In fact, Claimant's attorney informed Respondent, on June 23, 2010, August 22, 2011, and June 26, 2013, that Claimant intended to institute an action against it before ICSID pursuant to the BIT. Respondent, however, failed to raise this jurisdictional objection even when it filed its Counter-Memorial on April 22, 2016. It was only on June 20, 2017 that Respondent raised this jurisdictional objection—almost six years after it was informed of this arbitration").

contractors for construction projects,[69] raised a highly interesting structural question about the applicability of the *Salini* factors.

Although the Tribunal applied the *Salini* factors and found on the facts that the investor had made an investment for purposes of jurisdiction,[70] it expressed doubt about the *Salini* factors applicability in Additional Facility cases in the following terms:

> Respondent calls for the Tribunal to give weight to the Salini criteria, which in its view show that there was no investment. Claimant denies their relevance in a case where jurisdiction does not rest on Article 25 of the ICSID Convention, the context in which the Salini criteria were first articulated. The Tribunal notes that pursuant to Article 3 of the Additional Facility Rules, none of the Convention provisions, including its Article 25, are applicable to Additional Facility arbitrations. However, the Tribunal does not need to decide whether the Salini criteria have legal relevance here to determine whether an investment for the purposes of Article 2(a) of the Additional Facility Rules exists, because the record shows that if they were to be applied in assessing whether there is an investment for the purposes of the Additional Facility Rules, they are satisfied.[71]

This statement is more remarkable for the inference that it leaves behind than its refusal to extend the *Salini* factors to Additional Facilities cases. The inference is that where Article 25 applies, the *Salini* factors apply although *Salini v. Morocco* was an ad hoc case like all ICSID cases. By no means a novel pronouncement, the noncommittal stance adds to the lingering doubt about the applicability of *Salini* in all non-ICSID cases where the instrument of consent fails to clearly define investment or investor.

The other notable jurisdictional challenge pertains to the umbrella clause claims under Article 8(1) of the BIT, which provides: "Each Contracting Party shall observe any obligation it may have entered into with regard to specific investments by investors of the other Contracting Party."[72] This raises a very common problem of the disregard of the dispute settlement rules contained in the actual contracts out of which the dispute arises.

The Tribunal did not have any difficulty rejecting the Respondent's claim of inappropriate forum on the ground that at the end of the day, it is a matter of treaty interpretation: "In the Tribunal's view, this issue cannot be resolved by comparing the number of awards expressing one view or another."[73] As both Parties acknowledged in

[69] *Id.* at 101.

[70] *Id.* at 101–09.

[71] *Id.* at 109.

[72] *Id.* at 137.

[73] *See id.* at 155–58, summarizing the competing positions:

> 155. The Tribunal is of course mindful that the interpretation and application of umbrella clauses is a much discussed and disputed subject, and that tribunals have taken varying positions regarding these clauses. In the wake of *SGS v. Pakistan*, some tribunals including many cited by Respondent have interpreted these provisions narrowly, for example by limiting their effectiveness to a narrow range of obligations involving sovereign conduct, or by limiting them to agreements concluded directly between the State and the investor. Such awards often involve tribunals' rejection of alternative interpretations, either because they are thought to have unacceptably broad practical implications, or because they would expand the scope of international jurisdiction to matters that should be left to national law and courts.

their arguments, it is the words of a particular treaty that matter. Hence, the meaning of Article 8(1) of the Treaty is ultimately a question of treaty interpretation."[74]

Having certified it for its own unconstrained discretion that way, the Tribunal interpreted Article 8(1) to permit the exercise of a treaty tribunal's jurisdiction primarily because the Respondent state was involved in the conclusion of the contract and was responsible for its performance in its public capacity.[75]

Interocean Oil v. Nigeria (2020) raised unique jurisdictional issues because the standing offer of arbitration came from the following ambiguous domestic investment law provision.

(1) Where a dispute arises between an investor an any Government of the Federation in respect of an enterprise, all efforts shall be made through mutual discussion to reach an amicable settlement.

(2) Any dispute between an investor and any Government of the Federation inrespect of an enterprise to which this Act applies which is not amicably settled through mutual discussions, may be submitted at the option of the aggrieved party to arbitration as follows—

(a) In the case of a Nigerian investor, in accordance with the rules of procedure for arbitration as specified in the Arbitration and Conciliation Act; or

(b) In the case of a foreign investor, within the framework of any bilateral or multilateral agreement on investment protection to which the Federal Government and the country of which the investor is a national are parties; or

(c) In accordance with any other national or international machinery for the settlement of investment disputes agreed on by the parties.

(3) Where in respect of a dispute, there is disagreement between the investor and the Federal Government as to the method of dispute settlement to be adopted, the International Centre for Settlement of Investment Disputes Rules shall apply.[76]

158. However, there is also a substantial cohort of cases that comes at the matter differently, and gives broader effect to umbrella clauses. Soon after *SGS v. Pakistan*, a second investment tribunal addressed the same issue in *SGS v. Philippines*. In its Decision on the Objections to Jurisdiction, the *SGS v. Philippines* tribunal emphasized the specific language of the umbrella clause in the Swiss-Philippines BIT. Comparing it with the analogous provision in the Swiss-Pakistan BIT, the *SGS v. Philippines* tribunal found the umbrella clause in the Swiss-Philippines BIT to be much clearer. Article X(2) of the latter treaty did indeed offer treaty protection to "any obligation [each Contracting Party] has assumed with regard to specific investments in its territory by investors of the other Contracting Party." The tribunal found these terms to be "clear and categorical" and to require an "effective interpretation" consistent with the object and purpose of the treaty, which was made for the promotion and reciprocal protection of investments.

These are the most frequently cited cases to support the jurisprudential inconsistency and incoherence, but this tribunal attempted to explain it by the differences of the texts of the treaties.

[74] *Id.* at 159.

[75] *See id.* at 175.

[76] Interocean Oil Development Company and Interocean Oil Exploration Company v. Federal Republic of Nigeria, ICSID Case No. ARB/13/20, Award (Oct. 6, 2020), at ¶ 99 (quoting §26 of Nigerian Investment Promotion Commission Act (NIPC Act)).

The Respondent's first objection to jurisdiction was based on the last subsection. It said that the reference to ICSID Rules does not mean that the dispute shall be referred to ICSID but that it shall be arbitrated under ICSID Rules.[77] The Tribunal quickly rejected that argument, saying that "Section 26 did indeed constitute such a standing offer to arbitrate under the ICSID Rules."[78]

While this objection appeared the main structural challenge, the Respondent added several other objections relating to the adequacy and capability of acceptance of the offer of arbitration by the Claimant,[79] which the Tribunal dismissed in the merits phase devoting a considerable amount of energy and time across about 78 paragraphs.[80]

Most importantly, the Tribunal found that the actions of the persons and entities that the Claimant claims were against were not attributable to the state,[81] a finding which killed the case on the merits as discussed in Chapter 13. That said, the actual claims of liability were highly intertwined with the factual contention of who did what on whose behalf and when. The Tribunal attempted to unpack those questions in the merits phase.[82]

In the *Bay View Group v. Rwanda* (2022) case, there were two Claimants, BVG and Spalena, both Delaware Corporations.[83] The Respondent raised at least four objections to the Tribunal's jurisdiction: lack of *ratione temporis*, *ratione personae*, *ratione materiae* and *ratione voluntatis*.[84]

Quickly dismissing the *ratione temporis* challenge on technical grounds,[85] the Tribunal addressed the *ratione personae* challenge more carefully because the objection under that heading was essentially that the Claimants did not hold protected investment in Rwanda and as such did not have *locus standi*.[86] On the facts, the Tribunal ruled that one of the Claimants, BVG, did not make any investment in Rwanda and as such lacked standing. It said in particular that:

[77] *See id.* at 100 ("Section 26 of the Nigerian Investment Protection Commission Act ("NIPC") does not provide a basis for finding consent on the part of Respondent as it merely provides that disputes should be conducted in accordance with the ICSID Rules [Objection 2 (Role of the ICSID Rules)]")

[78] *Id.* at 101.

[79] *See id.* at 107 ("Subject to the comments below on 'Further Jurisdictional Objections' (infra) the Tribunal has grouped Respondent's challenges to the Tribunal's jurisdiction into five (5) bases, some of which overlap: (i) the adequacy of acceptance of Respondent's offer to arbitrate under the NIPC Act, which implicates registration and premature filing; (ii) Pan Ocean's lack of registration under the NIPC Act; (iii) the premature nature of the filing of claims, due to Claimants' alleged failure to seek amicable settlement; (iv) whether the scope of consent to ICSID arbitration under the NIPC Act includes expropriation claims and claims based on customary international law, and (v) attribution to Respondent of actions of private individuals").

[80] *See id.* at 108–86.

[81] *See id.* at 186 ("The alleged wrongdoings are not attributable to Respondent or do not form part of a concerted effort involving Respondent to deprive Claimants of their investment").

[82] *See id.* at 187.

[83] *See* Bay View Group LLC and The Spalena Company LLC v. Republic of Rwanda, ICSID Case No. ARB/18/21, Award (Mar. 30, 2022), at ¶ 2.

[84] *See id.* at 121–22.

[85] *See id.* at 124–47.

[86] *See id.* at 148–915.

> The onus of proving that BVG has *locus standi* as an investor in respect of the investments that form the subject of the claims in this arbitration lies on BVG. For the reasons given BVG has failed to discharge that onus. The Tribunal finds that BVG has no standing to claim in this Arbitration.[87]

It did, however, reject the Respondent's jurisdictional objection vis-à-vis the other Claimant, Spalena, because it determined on the facts that although the amount of funds that Spalena spent to acquire the holder of the Rwandan mining license, NDR, was modest, it met all the *Salini-Phoenix* factors.[88] In its own words:

> The Tribunal has concluded that NRD satisfied the six criteria of an investment identified by the tribunal in Phoenix v. Czech Republic by way of refinement of the Salini criteria. There was a contribution in money or other assets. Spalena aspired to a duration of NRD's activities of thirty years. The venture involved risk. The object of the venture was the development of an economic activity in Rwanda. The assets were invested in accordance with the law of Rwanda and they were invested bona fide.[89]

As discussed in the next section on the determination of facts and the substantive expropriation and discrimination cases, the Tribunal rejects all the claims on the merits primarily because it understood that the Claimants' design was to invest a very small amount of money to acquire a mining license and raise funds using the license, and thus if the license is lawfully terminated, they would have no claim.[90] The decision that dismisses the claims on the merits may not technically be inconsistent with the jurisdictional decision, which also requires the determination that there be a protected investment no matter how small, however a more robust reading of the *Salini* factors could have disposed this case off on jurisdictional grounds. The Tribunal's chosen means of dismissal is also respectable.

[87] *Id.* at 193.

[88] *See id.* at 224–26:

> 224. On 23 December 2010, Spalena acquired indirect ownership and control of NRD for a price of only . . . The Tribunal accepts the observation of the tribunal in Phoenix v. Czech Republic that such a modest price raises a question as to whether the transaction was bona fide. Rwanda has not, however, challenged the propriety of the transaction. The price plainly reflected a desire by Starck to abandon involvement in mining in Rwanda.
>
> 225. It is not disputed that Spalena, as personified by Mr. Marshall, hoped that NRD would obtain long-term licences for the Five Concessions, enabling Spalena to raise finance to exploit those licences on the international money market. In this NRD was unsuccessful. NRD continued to operate, albeit with poor returns, as a mining company, up to, at least, 19 May 2015 and remained in existence, and in Occupation of the Concessions, after that date and after the Cut-off Date of 15 June 2015. There is no evidence of any significant external funding being provided to NRD by or through Spalena during this period. NRD's costs were funded from the proceeds of the mining carried on. The Tribunal does not consider that this detracts from the status of NRD as an investment.

[89] *Id.* at 227.

[90] *See* discussion in Part III.

Conclusions

In an unchanged approach to advocacy over the decades, the African states have challenged the treaty tribunal's jurisdiction in all of the reviewed cases while succeeding only in a handful of them. The above cases offer incontrovertible evidence that treaty tribunals interpret their jurisdiction generously, preferring the dismissal of nonmeritorious cases on the merits.

The meaning of investment as a jurisdictional concept is more prominent in ICSID cases because of the double-barreled requirement. The post-*Salini* cases have considered *Salini* the center of gravity, while not always honoring it.

The most common jurisdictional objection appears to be a combination of the lack of investment by the investor and fraudulent procurement of the underlying project or contract—objections that almost never succeeded. That is ironically for opposing reasons: the tribunals set the burden of proof of investment so low while setting the standard of the proof of fraud so high. In most cases, the smallest tokens are held to qualify as an investment although *Cotec v. Kenya* (2018) seems to be an exception in this regard. The Tribunal famously ruled: "*The special prospecting licence was not itself a licence to make money. It was a licence to spend money. Prospecting, as such, involves cost not revenue.*"[91] Although fraudulent procurement of the underlying contract was raised as a jurisdictional objection in many of the above cases, it had no appreciable jurisdictional success because of the difficulty of proof of fraud.

One more observation is worthwhile: There is some anecdote that suggests that in cases where the tribunals felt the precarious nature of their jurisdiction, they tend to make up for it through a more exacting scrutiny of the claimant's case on the merits. But again, this is no more than an anecdotal observation. It is raised here to suggest that a nonfrivolous pursual of jurisdictional objections is not always futile even when the jurisdictional objection is unsuccessful. At a minimum, it educates members of the tribunal about the case and helps the tribunal's assessment of the merits, allowing it to weigh the overall background of the case more fully.

[91] Cortec v. Kenya, ICSID Case No. ARB/15/29, Award (Oct. 22, 2018), at 328 (emphasis added).

9
Determination of Facts

In many of the cases under review, the outcome often depended exclusively or partially on the determination of contested facts. The determination of facts is a particularly difficult task for treaty tribunals for several reasons. First, most treaty claims are preceded by ordinary domestic disputes. By the time the treaty tribunal gets to the disputed facts, in many cases, the facts had already been muddled by prior processes often accompanied by vagarious advocacy. Second, the treaty tribunal does not only need to understand the facts as they are presented to it but also consider the effects of prior juridical, arbitral, or administrative determinations of fact and decide the level of deference it should accord them mostly without specific legal guidance. Finally, and perhaps more importantly, there is often a cultural disconnect between the parties and the decision-makers, which makes the determination of certain culturally engrained facts more difficult than in purely domestic cases where the judges and the judged share a common cultural background.

The cases profiled in this study contain numerous examples of what kinds of facts are litigated in ISDS cases and how the various tribunals undertake the task of determining dispositive facts. It also shows how facts, although less frequently talked about, are perhaps more important determinants of outcome than just about anything else, even in treaty cases. In a related sense, this chapter shows that the determination of facts is truly as essential in treaty cases as it is in any domestic judicial or arbitral proceedings.

Determination of Facts in the African Cases of the Early Decades (1980–2000)

One of the earliest cases that offers a good example of the determination of facts in treaty cases and the nature of the factual disputes is the the *Letco v. Liberia* case (1986).[1] In this case, Letco, the Concessioner, had been granted 470,00 acres of land for harvesting timber with numerous obligations under the Agreement. The Host State took back a significant portion of the originally allocated land under the Concession Agreement on grounds of the concessioner's alleged failure to perform.[2] The list of failures as described by the Tribunal included:

[1] Liberian Eastern Timber Corporation v. Republic of Liberia, ICSID Cases No. ARB/83/2, Award (Mar. 31, 1986).

[2] *Id.* at 43 ("After a period of normal relations between the contracting parties, certain problems began to appear in 1979. At first, the Forestry Development Authority of Liberia (hereinafter "FDA") began to request a renegotiation of the concession granted to letco. Later, in July 1980, the fda accused letco of abandoning quantities of logs in the concession area. Finally, in a letter dated 18 November 1980. the fda indicated to LETCO that its concession area would be reduced by 279,000 acres "with immediate effect." In support of this decision, the fda alleged a number of breaches of the Concession Agreement by letco").

Africa's International Investment Law Regimes. Won L. Kidane, Oxford University Press. © Oxford University Press 2023.
DOI: 10.1093/oso/9780197745571.003.0009

> Letco had failed to annually exploit 4% of the total area of the concession, [a]s a result of inadequate investments in its installations, letco was forced to abandon logs and permit them to be wasted, letco had used an overly selective process of exploitation; letco failed to process 33 1/3% of its annual production, letco had used inadequate technology, as compared with other companies, in the exploitation of its concession, letco had employed an inadequate number of Liberian workers (less than 200 workers), letco had made inadequate investments in the concession allegedly 2 million US dollars).[3]

Immediately following this list, the Tribunal concluded: "The Tribunal has determined that none of these allegations is adequately supported by facts. On the contrary, the Tribunal has found, to the extent possible, that Letco has substantially complied with its obligations."[4]

Apart from stating these facts, Liberia never made any effort to submit evidence to the Tribunal in any form or shape. As such, the Tribunal's factual determination was necessarily based on one sided submission. The Tribunal took note of and analyzed various letters that Liberia had written to the Claimant, which were presumably submitted to the Tribunal by the Claimant itself. Since it had no evidence submitted to it by Liberia, the Tribunal had to make a decision on the bases of these unilateral submissions.

Interestingly, in justifying a finding of no fault on the part of the Claimant, it opined about how some default would be excusable on the basis of its own (apparently *sua sponte*) observation of political circumstances,[5] but without explaining the possible

[3] *Id.* at 60. The grounds of termination under the Concession Agreement are:

> Article VII.4. of the Concession Agreement recognizes the right of the Government of Liberia to revoke the Agreement in the event that:
>
> (a) The concessionaire fails to commence operations within the months as required by Article I of this Agreement or fails to meet its expenditure obligations within the period specified in Article I of this Agreement, or
> (b) No commercial shipment of logs, timber or timber products is made within four years of the effective date of this Agreement, or
> (c) Any rent, stumpage fee or income tax payable by the concessionaire under this Agreement shall be in arrear or unpaid for a period of six calendar months next after any of the days on or before which the same ought to have been paid, or
> (d) The concessionaire assigns to a third party the whole or part of the rights held by it under this Agreement without the previous written consent of the government as provided in this Article VII. or
> (e) The concessionaire has knowingly submitted to the government any false statements which were a material consideration for the execution of this Agreement, or
> (f) The concessionaire intentionally extracts any natural resources other than timber and other forest products without the express authorization by the government, or
> (g) The CONCESSIONAIRE fails to comply with any final decision by the Arbitral tribunal in a controversy arising with the government under this Agreement, or
> (h) There be any other breach or non-observance by the concessionaire of any of the terms, obligations or conditions of this Agreement, or any law of Liberia not superseded by this Agreement, or
> (i) The concessionaire shall make or enter into any agreement or composition with its creditors or shall go into liquidation whether compulsory or voluntary (other than for the purpose of reconstruction) or if a receiver is appointed the government may, subject to the provisions of this section, revoke this agreement. *Id.* at 48.

[4] *Id.* at 61.

[5] *Id.* at 63.

motive or reason behind the Host State's withdrawal of a segment of the land without the Claimant's fault. The Tribunal concluded:

> Again, the Tribunal stresses the fact that, according to the Concession Agreement, Letco should not be obligated to demonstrate its compliance with the Concession Agreement in order to prove its right to recovery. Nonetheless, this Tribunal has sought such proof both for reasons of prudence and to assist it in determining the award of possible damages. The evidence which was produced to the Tribunal demonstrates Letco's compliance with the Concession Agreement.[6]

The Tribunal mentions the need for prudence in a default proceeding of this type. Its analysis, however, suggests that it focused on matters that could possibly justify the outcome without considering why the host state would want to takeaway concessions that it voluntarily granted if it was not dissatisfied with the grantee's performance or had other more nefarious motives. In other words, a question that needed to be answered was whether or not the State's claims were false as a matter of fact.

Because the Respondent submitted no evidence to support its allegations, the Tribunal was confronted with a serious dilemma but chose to resolve it in favor of the moving party, the Claimant. That in essence is what a default judgment is all about. If the host state had proven the existence of some of the Claimant's breaches, the result could have been different.

A commonsense observation could be made that some of the State's allegations, if not all, might have actually been true. But if the State fails to make its case properly, the result cannot be complained about. In the early days of these ICSID cases, the nature and consequences of default proceedings may not have become clear. In fact, the Tribunal did no more than make a normative choice without articulating any standard that would guide its determination of fact when one party is in default.

Subsequent cases have also struggled with this. It should be emphasized here that the *Lecto v. Liberia* case is one of those cases that was totally decided on the facts of the case. In other words, the factual determination was outcome determinative. In the Tribunal's own words:

> It should be emphasized that the Government of Liberia has not sought to justify its action on this basis; rather, it has consistently claimed that its action was taken because of failure on the part of the claimant to properly carry out its obligations under the Concession Agreement—an argument which the Tribunal has rejected on the facts.[7]

The factual contention in *MINE v. Guinea* (1988) related to why a joint project failed. The Tribunal was quick to recognize that both sides miscalculated the potential returns of their joint undertaking. Indeed, it said: "In hindsight, the Convention failed because both parties had inflated expectations of what could be accomplished with Guinea's Art. 9 freight rights."[8] This refers to a freight right that Guinea negotiated

[6] *Id.* at 69.
[7] *Id.* at 70.
[8] *Id.* at 48.

attached its Bauxite deals. It brought in MINE for the shipping venture, which never materialized. In the award, the Tribunal did not attempt to explain why, despite its recognition that both parties miscalculated the feasibility of the deal, the host state bore the exclusive responsibility of loss. The reassignment of some of the rights of the Claimant to a third party was the principal source of the liability.[9]

Guinea's contention, which is very common in many of these and similar African cases, is that the investor lacked the financial resources and professional competence.[10] Many projects fail because small groups willing to take risks of developing markets oversell their capacities and consider arbitration as an alternative way of gaining their aspired gains. *Bay View Group v. Rwanda* discussed below exemplifies this better, but in *MINE*, as the Tribunal summarized, Guinea contended that:

> (2) While Guinea relied upon MINE and its expert partners to provide financial strength, technical know-how, and a program that would have permitted Guinea and SOTRAMAR to take advantage of the freight opportunities offered by Art. 9. MINE's proposals were unrealistic, unworkable, and unfair, and MINE never delivered a single contract of affreightment with any Bauxite Receiver or identified a single charter party opportunity.[11]

The Tribunal did not directly confront the truth or falsity of this factual contention. It is reemphasized here because it seems like this was the main reason why Guinea had to look for another partner as the Tribunal does not explain and indeed MINE never claimed that there was any other motive. Although it is difficult to determine facts by simply reading an award, the similarity of Guinea's assertion with many other cases on the issue of investor's lack of proper financial and professional competencies is recurring and quite remarkable across these African cases as will be discussed in some more detail below.

But again, the key factual contention in this case would have been whether MINE lacked the competence and relatedly whether that caused Guinea to find another partner who could do the work. Avoiding this question, the Tribunal framed the contention as whether MINE breached its part of the bargain in the agreement. It did not find any breach on the part of the Claimant but found a breach on the part of the Respondent, but the kind of breach it found was one that did not require it to determine the key factual contention, that is, whether MINE had the financial and professional competence as it claimed.[12] This, again, is a very serious problem in Africa. If one may speculate from experience, MINE might have exaggerated its competencies, and by the Tribunal's own reckoning miscalculated the feasibility of the project. This 17-page award is just too shallow to exhaustively deal with the factual contentions in a satisfactory way. It might have been purposeful as the result finally rested on a

[9] *See* Maritime International Nominees Establishment v. Republic of Guinea, ICSID Case No. ARB/84/4, Award (Jan. 6, 1988), at 55.

[10] *Id.* at 43.

[11] *Id.*

[12] *See id.* at 53.

third-party issue and the Respondent's failure to inform MINE before it brought in a third party which seemed to have done a better job.[13]

In both of the above-profiled early cases, the facts were determined in the least favorable way to the African state, and it would seem that the lack of robust representation and the early tribunal's propensity to disbelieve the African part of the story might have contributed to the losses.

The Determination of Facts in the African Cases of the 2000s

The facts of *Wena v. Egypt* (2000) might at first seem uncontested, but the findings of treaty violations rested on facts that were assumed rather than determined. The uncontested facts include EHC's (the state-owned entity) physical takeover of the hotels that Wena was managing under contract on the allegation that Wena failed to make the necessary payments.[14] Instead of going to court to enforce its rights under the contract, EHC forcibly overtook the properties. The facts as determined through witness testimony include the following narrative:

> 48. According to a subsequent statement to the Luxor police by Mr. Bahia El Din Abdel Hadi El Wakeel, a security guard at the Luxor Hotel, "more than 100 people from the EHC seized the Wena Hotel by force in spite myself and others responsible for the security and guards in the hotel presence at the time." Mr. Wakeel also stated that "EHC forced their entry through by force ... which caused panic, fear, and hysteria for the guests and employees ... Two other guards, Messrs. Ismael Ahmed Hefni and Ahmed Hamza Mostafa, made short statements, agreeing with Mr. Wakeel's description of events.
>
> 49. Mr. Muhammad Nagib Al-Sayyid, Wena's General manager of the Luxor Hotel, also filed a police statement, asserting that, at approximately 7:00 p.m., EHC personnel entered his office, seized the hotel's papers and ordered him to leave the hotel. 108 Mr. Nagib reported the incident to the Luxor Tourist Police, who accompanied Mr. Nagib back to the hotel and subsequently opened an investigation into the seizure.
>
> 50. These contemporaneous descriptions comport with the subsequent report by the Advocate General at the Office of the Assistant Attorney General for Upper Egypt, which concluded that EHC "broke into the Hotel ... entered by force into the

[13] *Id.* at 54 ("the Tribunal finds that Guinea's entering the AFROBULK agreement was contrary to the spirit and express provisions of the Convention, because SOTRAMAR was the only organization represented to the Bauxite Receivers as authorized user of the Art. 9 freight rights. Guinea's conduct in secretly negotiating the AFROBULK arrangement, and in denying its existence to MINE thereafter, exhibits bad faith on its part, violating the principle of good faith set forth in the French Civil Code. 7 Guinea's subsequent offer, to 'cut the pear in half' and permit MINE to share the AFROBULK agreement, did not restore the possibility of performance, and MINE reasonably rejected the offer").

[14] *See* Wena Hotels Limited v. Arab Republic of Egypt, ICSID Case No. ARB/98/4, Award (Dec. 8, 2000).

> management office, broke open the doors and Offices of the Hotels Ltd. [and] forced the personnel they found there to quit the Hotel.[15]

These facts show that EHC acted arbitrarily and took the law into its own hands. The key treaty violation question was, however, whether the Egyptian state violated the Bilateral Investment Treaty with the United Kingdom by expropriating Wena's property and denying such property FET and FSP. While EHC's actions are relevant, the Claimant had to have proven the government's participation or at least indifference as a matter of fact. There are bits and pieces of evidence that the Tribunal thought collectively proved the government's culpability:

> Despite all these warnings, Egypt took no action to protect Wena's investment. Minister Sultan sought to defend Egypt's failure to prevent the seizure by explaining he was not aware that EHC planned to illegally seize the hotels, and that "if I had the slightest idea about that incident, I would have immediately stopped it. . . . ," Even if the Tribunal were to accept this explanation for Egypt's failure to act before the seizures, it does not justify the fact that neither the police nor the Ministry of Tourism took any immediate action to protect Wena's investments after EHC had illegally seized the hotels.[16]

It is clear that the Tribunal did not find the Egyptian Minister's statement credible and sought explanation for why it did not want to believe him, and went on stating:

> 91. Instead, neither hotel was restored to Wena until nearly a year later, after decisions by the Chief Prosecutor of Egypt, which Wena asserts were only obtained as a result of diplomatic pressure on Egypt. Even after the Chief Prosecutor's first decision (concerning the Nile Hotel) was issued on January 16, 1992, in which he found the seizures "illegal," the Ministry of Tourism delayed returning control of the Nile

[15] *Id.* at 48–50.

[16] *Id.* at 88. The details of the incidents are contained in 89–90.

> 89. For example, despite the convincing evidence that a large number of people forcibly seized the Nile Hotelat approximately 7:00 p.m., it is undisputed that the Kasr El-Nile police (located only a few minutes away) did not begin an investigation until four hours later and it is not evident that the Ministry of Tourism police (also located nearby) ever responded to Wena's request for assistance. Moreover, even after the Kasr El-Nile police began their investigation, they took no steps to remove EHC and restore Wena to control of the hotel. The Luxor police, although more prompt in their response, also declined to expel EHC and restore the Luxor hotel to Wena.
>
> 90. The Ministry of Tourism also failed to take any immediate action to protect Wena's investments. Although he testified that he "was furious" at EHC's decision to seize the hotels and that EHC's actions were "wrong," Minister Sultan also acknowledged that he did not take any action to return the hotels to Wena, to punish EHC or its officials, or to withdraw the hotel's licenses so that EHC could not operate the hotels. Under Law Number 97 of 1983 governing Public Sector Companies and Organizations, Minister Sultan was empowered to dismiss the Chairman and the members of the Board of EHC if "it appears that the continued presence of these persons would affect the proper functioning of the company." Also, given its power as the sole shareholder in EHC, with several of its senior officials participating in and one of them chairing EHC's shareholder assembly, and with "EHC operat[ing] within broad policy guidelines laid down by the Egyptian Government, Egypt could have directed EHC to return the hotels to Wena's control and make reparations.

> Hotel to Wena. For example, on February 21, 1992, Mr. Webster wrote to the British Embassy in Cairo, complaining of Minister Sultan's "uncooperative stance" and the delays that Wena was experiencing in recovering the hotels: "if he [Minister Sultan] wishes to press settlement of account, then we too will press for settlement of monies outstanding to Wena." Mr. Webster concluded his letter by saying that" we are of the impression that the Minister is either poorly informed or part of the entire scheme.
>
> 92. Moreover, neither hotel was returned to Wena in the same operating condition that it had been in before the seizures. According to Wena's witnesses, both hotels had been vandalized.[17]

The Tribunal gave more credence to Mr. Webster's letter to the British Embassy in Cairo than Minister Sultan's witness statement offered in the presence of all three arbitrators. Eventually, the standard that the Tribunal applied for the finding of a treaty violation was one of negligence although it does not expressly say that. It is notable that the Tribunal does not make a determination that Egypt condoned EHC's behavior but that it failed to timely act to prevent or reverse the violation. To arrive at that conclusion, it must have disbelieved the Egyptian witnesses including the Minister and rely on contemporaneous correspondence between Wena and third parties.

Consider these two conflicting factual narratives: According to Wena correspondence: "We are of the impression that the Minister is either poorly informed or part of the entire scheme." Under this narrative, the writer speculates that the Minster is either ignorant or complicit. The Minister's narrative: "If I had the slightest idea about that incident, I would have immediately stopped it." This obviously supports the "poorly informed" narrative, but the Tribunal does not rest its conclusion on the "poorly informed" narrative. It was inclined to believe that Egypt knew but failed to prevent or remediate. This could be discerned from the following factual conclusion:

> Egypt also refused to compensate Wena for the losses it had experienced. On November 11, 1992, Mr. Malins wrote to the Honorable Lee Hamilton, a senior member of the U.S. House of Representatives, complaining that "the Minister of Tourism, Dr. Fouad Sultan, will not consider our requests" and that "it is clear that subsequent to any perceived movement, Dr. Sultan personally intervenes to obstruct a solution."[18]

It is thus clear that the Tribunal's factual conclusions almost entirely discredit or disregard all testimonial evidence from the Respondent state's high-ranking officials and exclusively relies on the Claimant's own correspondence with third parties whose relevance and involvement is not explained. More importantly, there is no explanation in the award on the purpose and authenticity of these self-serving letters and why they deserved total credit. The Tribunal used these letters not only to prove the truth of what they assert (total hearsay), but also discredit contradictory witness statements offered before it presumably under cross-examination. This could be a function of the civil law orientation of giving more credit to contemporaneous correspondence or an

[17] *Id.* at 88–92.
[18] *Id.* at 93.

overall disbelief of the particular witnesses who appeared before the Tribunal. Like many of the other ICSID cases that came before it, the award does not sufficiently explain why the Tribunal gave some form of evidence more credence than others.

In *Middle East v. Egypt* (2002), the Tribunal determined all of the disputed facts based on a combination of documents and party admission. There is no reference to testimonial evidence at all. The outcome of the case was essentially determined by the Respondent's own admission that a Decree that it enacted might have invalidated or rendered ineffective a license that the government issued to the investor four months prematurely. The Respondent's admission was for the purpose of showing the insignificance of the impact on the investor because of the brevity of the time left on the license, but the Tribunal took that as an admission of guilt and made the dispute about the extent of the taking rather than the occurrence of the taking. In other words, the Tribunal took the admission as proof of expropriation, no matter how small. The factual dispute then became about quantum rather than about liability.[19]

The Tribunal had to determine the duration of the license that the investor was given as a matter of fact. The evidence that was submitted to it was the text of the instrument itself. The dispute was a function of textual ambiguity amplified by translation problems. Having considered the various texts and some agreed upon translations, the Tribunal endorsed the Claimant's version without consideration of any other form of evidence.[20] As such, the factual dispute was resolved on the basis of the reading of the contractual instruments alone.

This would ordinarily have been a question of contract interpretation had it not been relevant to the determination of the issue of whether the Respondent took the Claimant's property. A proper inquiry should have looked at whether there was an intent to take, whether the action was discriminatory, whether there were domestic remedies and other matters that make government regulations rise to the level of expropriation. The simplistic outlook on the issue of the occurrence of expropriation also simplified the evidentiary standard for the determination of the relevant facts. In the final analysis, the factual determination might have been accurate, but the steps appear highly simplified and incomplete.

[19] *See* Middle East Cement Shipping and Handling Co. S.A. v. Arab Republic of Egypt, ICSID Case No. ARB/99/6, Award (Apr. 12, 2002), at 107–09.

[20] Middle East v. Egypt, ICSID Case No. ARB/99/6, Award (Apr. 12, 2002), at 110–11:

> 110. Respondent argues that the License only lasted for the duration of the contract to supply cement to the Egyptian Cement Office (ECO), i.e., the Contract between the Claimant and Petra Navigation and International Trading Co., LTD, Amman, Jordan (Petra) (C37) of September 20, 1988 for 12 months, that is till September 20, 1989").
>
> 111. The Tribunal is not persuaded by that argument. The last sentence of Art. (1) of the License expressly permits importation of cement "dispatched within the country for the Public and Private Sectors." Under the above mentioned agreed correct English translation of Art. (9), the fact that the actual contract concluded in September 1988 lasted only till September 20, 1989, does not limit the period of the License to that date as well, because it does not exclude that further quantities "may be contracted" with ECO for up to 10 years. For the same reason, neither the conclusion nor the performance of such other contracts must take place before September 20, 1989. The reference to ECO in Art. (9) can, therefore, not be understood to mean that other contracts, particularly with the Private Sector, should be excluded. Taking into account the agreed corrected translation of Art. (9), that provision must be interpreted to the effect that also supplies which may be contracted for the Private Sector fall under the License and its duration as long as supplies to both the Public and Private Sectors do not exceed ten years, i.e., till January 18, 1993.

The Tribunal's determination of an important fact and its application of the same to the expropriation and FET provisions relating to another factual contention, that is, the auctioning of the investor's vessel is more interesting. The Tribunal found that the Claimant's vessel was expropriated exclusively because the notice of seizure and auction did not follow the procedures set forth under the applicable domestic procedural rules. The factual dispute also pertains to the order of the notice requirement and why the Respondent used one and not the other. The notice rule provides as follows:

> 1.... A copy of each of the notice, warning and distraint report shall be handed to the Debtor, or the person signing for him, and another copy to the sequester.
>
> 2. A copy of the distraint report shall be put on the door of the police post, ... in whose circle the distraint is levied...
>
> 3. If the Debtor or the person deputising for him are absent, this absence shall be recorded in the distraint report, and a copy thereof shall be handed to the superintendant of the Police Section... Another copy shall be put at the locations set forth in the previous clause. Such procedures shall stand for the notice itself.[21]

There was no dispute that notice was served under the third option.[22] The question then was whether or not skipping steps one and two was justified. The more specific factual contention was whether or not the party that was supposed to receive direct notice was absent.[23] The Tribunal's attempt to determine whether the party that was supposed to receive notice was absent seems limited to the following:

> While the minutes of the attachment show that the Claimant was not represented on the Poseidon on November 15, 1999, it seems doubtful whether this already justified the "absent" procedure. As the activities on the Poseidon [the vessel] had stopped some time before due to the discontinuance of the import activities, it could not be expected that there was always somebody on the ship. The address of the Claimant and his attorney in Egypt were well known to the Authority from its many contacts with the Claimant as can be seen from the letter of the Chairman of the Authority of March 31, 1996.[24]

The Tribunal goes directly from this to a finding of liability:

> Therefore, a matter as important as the seizure and auctioning of a ship of the Claimant should have been notified by a direct communication for which the law No. 308

[21] *Id.* at 141 (quoting the notice requirements of Art. 7 of "Law No. 308 of 1955 concerning Administrative Distraint" (R7 to RIV)).

[22] *Id.* at 143.

[23] *Id.* at 142 ("It seems that, regarding the Poseidon, the procedure under the 3rd paragraph of Art. 7 was applied: according to the Respondent, on November 15, 1999, the attachment order and notice for an auction on November 28, 1999 were applied by a lawyer of the Authority on board of the Poseidon (R9) having not found the debtor or his representative (RIV 3), notified to the chief of the Suez port's Police (R10), and published in the newspaper Al Safeer of November 22, 1999 (RII 23)").

[24] *Id.* at 143.

> provided under the 1st paragraph of Art. 7, irrespective of whether there was a legal duty or practice to do so by registered mail with return receipt requested as argued by Claimant (CV 4).[25]

That means the provision of notice under sub-3, while it should have happened under sub-1 and 2, amounted to expropriation and denial of FET. Indeed, the Tribunal was explicit in its finding of expropriation: "Thus, the Tribunal concludes that the Poseidon was taken by a 'measure the effects of which would be tantamount to expropriation' and that the is entitled to a compensation as provided for under Art. 4. c) of the BIT."[26]

The ultimate result was that notice under what the Tribunal considered the wrong provision of domestic notice law amounted to expropriation entitling the investor to the award of the market value of the vessel that was auctioned off to meet the investor's debt obligations.[27] But the key factual issue that the Tribunal seems to have conveniently ignored is whether the investor was "absent," justifying indirect alternate notice such as service to the police or by publication. The Tribunal does not describe what other inquiries that it had conducted to find out whether or not the investor was in fact absent, and whether it deliberately avoided notice or did otherwise know the pendency of the proceeding. One would expect an elaborate evidentiary hearing on this matter especially if the Tribunal was willing to find expropriation for lack of notice.

In *Semos v. Mali* (2003), the facts that needed to be determined were inextricably linked with the interpretation of the contract and identification of the temporal fit of the law. The Tribunal had to determine which version of the law applied to which version of the contract, but the key question of fact was whether or not the Parties intended to exempt the exportation of minerals by the investor to be duty free for the validity of the license.[28] That question, albeit a mainly factual one, was determined exclusively on the basis of the Tribunal's reading of the law and contract rather than any evidentiary records or testimony.[29] As such, the factual question effectively merged into the interpretation of the contract.

CDC v. Seychelles (2003) was one of the first cases that addressed witness testimony as a form of proof in any meaningful way although its decision turned out to be the opposite of what all three witnesses who appeared before it sought to achieve. The Claimant, CDC (the financier seeking to collect its money which it lent to Seychelles so that it could buy a turbine, which failed), did not produce any testimonial evidence but cross-examined all three of the Respondent's witnesses produced to prove the Respondent state's contention that it took the loan in reliance on the lender's representation that the turbine that they used the money to buy with was suitable for the purpose it was bought for.[30]

[25] *Id.*
[26] *Id.* at 144.
[27] *See id.* at 146–51.
[28] *See* Société D'exploitation Des Mines D'or De Sadiola S.A. (Semos) v. Republic of Mali, ICSID Case No. ARB/01/5, Award (Feb. 25, 2003), at 75.
[29] *Id.* at 67–93.
[30] CDC Group Plc v. Republic of The Seychelles, ICSID Case No. ARB/02/14 (Dec. 17, 2003), at 34–42.

The first witness, an engineer who was part of the negotiating team, testified that the state paid CDC 1.25% of the project amount for the analysis of the project, and that the borrower had no prior experience with the turbine and that they relied on CDC's representation, which had more experience than they did.[31] The witness testified that "if CDC had not done an appraisal of the project, PUC would not have bought the turbine from EGT."[32] But the key part of the testimony that the Tribunal seized on was the last sentence of the following paragraph:

> Mr. Morin then stated that the gas plant never operated properly, that it was plagued with numerous problems, that it was not used after 1999 and was replaced by four small generator sets at substantial extra cost. The breakdown and the incapacity of the plant had a very significant adverse impact on the tourist industry and was detrimental to the Seychelles economy. When asked whether there was anything about the loan which was unfair or unreasonable, leaving aside the problems with the turbine, Mr. Morin's answer was "No."[33]

The last fact being admitted, the rest of his testimony became irrelevant as a matter of the applicable English law. Counsel for the Claimant, CDC, drove this point home when asking the witness the following question under cross-examination, which the Tribunal reproduces:

> "Are you saying one of them [officers of CDC] said to one of you that they were appraising the project in terms of its suitability or viability, or did they merely tell [you] that they were conducting their own assessment of the project?" His answer was "They were conducting their own assessment of the project."[34]

The Tribunal further noted that "Mr. Morin stated in reexamination that CDC had 'not directly' ever represented to PUC the quality and suitability of the turbine. He was not aware that it had ever been asked to do so."[35]

The second witness, who was the governor of the host state's central bank, testified that given his country's long-standing relationship with CDC, it was justified in relying on its implicit representation that it was lending money for a viable purpose. Because it admitted under cross-examination that he was not a part of this particular loan negotiation, the Tribunal did not lend his testimony any weight.[36] The third witness, an engineer, simply said that the CDC should have known that this particular turbine was not suitable for Seychelles and shouldn't have lent the money in the first place.[37]

None of the witnesses advanced the Respondent's case in any positive direction. These testimonies were very useful for the Tribunal's decision, but were not exactly

[31] *Id.* at 35–36.
[32] *Id.* at 36.
[33] *Id.* at 37.
[34] *Id.* at 38.
[35] *Id.* at 39.
[36] *Id.* at 40–41.
[37] *Id.* at 42.

useful for the Respondent state, which might have been better off without them. Its own witnesses confirmed that the loan assessment was done for the benefit of the lender and not the borrower, and the law simply did not hold the lender vicariously liable for the borrower's reliance without express warranty and contractual commitment.

In fact, the Respondent relied on testimonial evidence because there was no documentary evidence showing that CDC made any direct representation to the borrower that the project was feasible or that the turbine was a good choice. But the justice of the matter is also clear that a developing country that lacked the expertise relied on the lender's confidence to lend the money as evidence of the viability of the underlying project for which the money is lent. In the end, the host state lost when it contracted to buy a turbine that it did not understand without an express warranty from the lender or a performance guarantee from the supplier. The award suggests that the host state failed to recover its losses from the supplier because it did not have the resources to proceed against it,[38] and instead chose to default on its loan obligations, something that appeared cheaper at first. This is a recurring problem in many of the cases. It is essentially a developmental challenge.

The essential facts in *Patrick Mitchell v. DRC* (2004) were not disputed: Mr. Mitchell's law office was raided by the DRC military under a military court warrant and that documents and people were seized. Some nonessential facts were disputed such as whether the documents were indeed returned or reclaimed. For the majority, the only question pertained mainly to what legal consequences must flow from these established facts. The dissent, however, focused on two facts that it considered essential: whether Mitchell had a proper license to practice law in the DRC and whether he accepted payment in the United States for works performed in the DRC without paying DRC taxes. Although these are not facts that the Tribunal properly determined on the record, the dissent seems to have taken the position that those facts needed to be determined for an accurate outcome. On the issue of whether the practice of law was authorized, the dissent remarks:

> 8. The DRC contends, among other things, that the activity as an attorney or legal counsel does not qualify as a service within the meaning of Article I (c) of the BIT which provides a definition of the term investment. It also argues that the license to operate delivered to the Claimant is not in conformity with the Congolese Investment Code. It contends, moreover, that the profession of attorney-at-law or legal counsel is not considered as a commercial activity falling under the scope of the BIT.
>
> 9. The Tribunal is correct in rejecting the various facets of the argument. I should simply like to note that I do not understand why the Tribunal insisted on including among the grounds for the Award that it "does not have to examine, in relation to the question of its jurisdiction, whether Mr. Mitchell's firm had or did not have the

[38] *Id.* ("Mr Morin said that he was not aware that PUC had ever made a claim against CDC in connection with the project before CDC made its request for arbitration. He also said that PUC had not taken action against EGT, the supplier of the gas turbine, on account of the expense involved. It seems that PUC had decided on a gas turbine, though not an EGT turbine, before PUC sought finance from CDC. Mr Morin stated in reexamination that CDC had 'not directly' ever represented to PUC the quality and suitability of the turbine. He was not aware that it had ever been asked to do so").

> permission to perform activities as attorney-at-law or legal consultant" (Award, para. 51). It could have omitted these grounds, especially since it responded immediately thereafter to the concern expressed by the DRC. In reality, I find it surprising that the Tribunal implies that the Claimant could have set up business in the host country without conforming to the regulations and administrative procedures referred to in Articles II (9) and IX (a) of the BIT.[39]

It is clear that the Tribunal did not determine this seemingly important fact, or at least the record does not show such a determination and hence the dissent's complaint above. Likewise, according to the dissent, the Tribunal failed to determine another inconvenient fact relating to the assessment of damages, that is, the collection of fees in the United States for work performed in the DRC without paying DRC taxes under DRC law. In the dissent's own words: "Secondly, the action will have serious consequences in that it constitutes an open and inadmissible means of supporting a mechanism invented by Mr. Patrick Mitchell to illegally transfer abroad the income generated by his office in the DRC."[40]

Although these may be facts that could be extrapolated from the parties' pleadings and submission of evidence, it does not appear that the specific facts—such as income subject to DRC tax regime not having been paid—were determined as a matter of fact in these proceedings.

The *World Duty Free v. Kenya* (2006) case presented most interesting facts relating to bribery and culture. The fact of giving of money to the former president was not disputed. Indeed, it was the Claimant himself who first confessed this fact, which was later used against him by the State whose former president took the money, although the purpose was disputed.[41] The Tribunal notes that:

[39] *Id.* at 8–9.

[40] *Id.* at 35–38. The paragraphs that follow state:

> 35. If Article V (1) (a) of the Bilateral Treaty of August 28, 1984 guarantees Mr. Patrick Mitchell the free transfer of his returns in the DRC, it is on the express condition that he conform with the prescribed procedures in Congolese law and that he pay income taxes (Article V (3)).
>
> 36. However, by his method of billing and collecting fees abroad, Mr. Patrick Mitchell has, over the years, shielded the bulk of his revenues from the application of these regulations.
>
> 37. The Tribunal cannot close its eyes to such practices without betraying the objectives of the BIT and the ICSID Convention.
>
> 38. It is legally and morally unacceptable for Mr. Patrick Mitchell to be demanding with respect to the provisions of the BIT that favor him while his own behavior is detrimental to the development of the host country.

[41] World Duty Free Company Limited v. Republic of Kenya, ICSID Case No. ARB/00/7, Award (Oct. 4, 2006), at 11–18. The admission, contained in the witness statement of the Chief Executive Officer and shareholder of the Claimant describes the famous "fresh corn" incident as follows:

> 11. As a leading businessman in Dubai, I met in normal business circles, one Rashid Sajjad, a Kenyan, who would come to Dubai frequently in order to buy goods for export to Kenya for his company, Bawazir & Co.
>
> 12. From my discussions with Sajjad, I came to understand that he was politically and powerfully connected in the Kenya Government. Wishing to diversify my business from perfumes into the duty-free market, I raised my interest with Sajjad and asked his advice on arranging the necessary licences and authorisation for the establishment of duty free complexes in Nairobi and Mombassa airports. Sajjad informed me that he would arrange meetings for me with the relevant officials in Kenya.

132. The Respondent does not deny Mr. Ali's payments to President Moi in the circumstances related by the witness in his written statement. Such a payment must then be considered as established.

133. Nevertheless, the Parties differ on the way in which they qualify that payment. Kenya considers that it is a bribe given in order to obtain the Agreement on which the claims are based. World Duty Free considers it a gift of protocol or a personal donation made to the President to be used for public purposes within the framework of the Kenyan system of Harambee; the Claimant recalls that this system is "largely anchored in cultural practices when people are able to pull whatever resources they have, 'in particular' to finance community projects."[42]

The Tribunal further notes:

134. The Tribunal is aware of the fact that, on the occasion of visits to heads of State, gifts are often exchanged as a matter of protocol. It has also noted the report of the Task Force on Public Collections or "Harambees" presented in December 2003 to the Minister of Justice of Kenya. According to this report "the concept of Harambee had its root in the African culture where societies made collective

13. In March 1989 Sajjad informed me that the necessary appointments had been arranged. The first was an audience with His Excellency Daniel arap Moi (HEDAM). Sajjad informed me that although my concept for establishing duty-free complexes at Nairobi and Mombassa airports to an international standard would require heavy investment, which I believed would be for the national benefit of Kenya, Protocol in Kenya required that I should in addition make a "personal donation" to HEDAM. I was given to believe, that this was payment for doing business with the Government of Kenya.

14. Sajjad advised me that the appropriate donation, given the estimated value of the investment, was US$2 million. I was further advised by him that the donation should be in cash.

15. Sajjad arranged a letter of credit for the value US$2 million from his bank, Banque Indosuez, London Branch, dated 7 February 1989 in the name of Mr. Sajjad of Bawazir & Co. Against this letter of credit I remitted US$ 2 million cash in his favour at Banque Indosuez on 16 February 1989. (See copy of letter of credit and supporting documents at Exhibit 5(b).

16. I travelled to Nairobi from Dubai in March 1989 in order to attend my audience with HEDAM. I flew into Nairobi airport and was greeted by Sajjad and two official vehicles. Sajjad drove me to HEDAM's Kabarak Residence In Nakuru District of Kenya, which is approximately 150 kilometres from Nairobi.

17. I was received by one Joshua Kulei (JK), who introduced himself as the Personal Assistant to the President. Sajjad and I met the President and I presented and explained my proposed investment to him. I realise that Sajjad was in fact very close to HEDAM. I refer to a copy of photograph showing Sajjad, seated to the left and behind HEDAM at a critical political meeting on 14 October this year at Exhibit 5(a).

18. I understood that Sajjad had received the cash worth US$500,000 against the letter of credit on 16 February 1989. He had then arranged for this to be exchanged into Kenyan Shillings (KSh). He brought the KSh in cash to my meeting with HEDAM in a brown briefcase. When we entered the room where the President received us, he put the briefcase by the wall and left it there. After the meeting we collected the briefcase from where we had left it. On the departing journey I looked in the briefcase and saw that the money had been replaced with fresh corn.

[42] *Id.* at 132–33.

> contribution toward individual or communal activities" and this practice became popularised by President Kenyatta just after Kenyan independence. However, the report adds that "over the years, the spirit of Harambee has undergone a metamorphosis which has resulted in gross abuses. It has been linked to the emergence of oppressive and extortionist practices and entrenchment of corruption and abuse of office."[43]

It chose to believe this last version, concluding:

> 136. Under these circumstances, such as described by Mr. Ali himself, the Tribunal has no doubt that the concealed payments made by Mr. Ali on behalf of the House of Perfume to President Moi and Mr. Sajjad could not be considered as a personal donation for public purposes. Those payments were made not only in order to obtain an audience with President Moi (as submitted by the Claimant), but above all to obtain during that audience the agreement of the President on the contemplated investment. The Tribunal considers that those payments must be regarded as a bribe made in order to obtain the conclusion of the 1989 Agreement.[44]

But again, although the facts are determined on the basis of admission against interest, the Claimant's point of view of making a donation as a cultural matter and the consequences of the president's behavior under the color of law, particularly its impact on the investor, remained largely unexplained.

In *Champion Trading v. Egypt* (2006), the various rules that affected the Claimant's interests were themselves facts that needed to be ascertained. What was disputed was not their existence or nonexistence, but the impact of their application on the investor's interests. In other words, whether they were applied in a discriminatory manner to similarly situated entities because of nationality.

The Claimant, an American company, claimed that the Egyptian authorities, through a combination of rules and regulations, favored their own entities over the American investor. The favor was admitted as a matter of fact. What was denied was that the American investor was similarly situated as a matter of fact. The Claimant's main argument was rather interesting—that it was denied the opportunity to be similar.

> 95. The Claimants refer to a set of events that allegedly led to violation of the non-discrimination clause by Egypt. On August 7, 1995, a Coordination Committee was established by Decree to supervise the cotton operations of the affiliated companies and of the private companies who chose to supply their cotton to the collection centres. The Committee also drafted and adopted a Uniform Contract to govern the transactions between buyers and sellers. According to the Claimants, NCC sought to negotiate concessions and special terms with the Coordinating Committee. Its requests were unsuccessful and, according to Mahmoud Wahba, NCC was ordered,

[43] *Id.* at 134.
[44] *Id.* at 136.

> by letter of March 11, 1996, from the Coordinating Committee, to deliver a certain quantity of cotton to certain spinning mills.
>
> 96. During the 1995/1996 season, NCC made several requests to the Government to receive an export authorization; all of the requests were unsuccessful.
>
> 97. In 1996, NCC was forced to sell its stocks within a short period of time in order to comply with the regulations of the Ministerial Decree. In August 1996, NCC was left with huge amounts of cotton because of the export prohibition and needed to sell its stocks urgently, before the beginning of the new season. NCC was finally able to sell its cotton in September 1996, at the time when the new crop for the 1996/1997 season was introduced. The price paid for NCC's stocks by the Government-owned mills being very low, NCC sustained losses. By the end of the 1995/1996 season, NCC had lost huge amounts of money as a result of Government actions designed to reverse the 1994 privatisation Laws.[45]

The fact that the investor lost as a result of government decision was not disputed as a matter of fact, and indeed the claim of discrimination does not directly rest on that, but rather on what happened next. The domestic entities obtained government payment, but the investor did not. The Respondent's argument is that the investor was excluded not because it was a foreigner but because it failed to participate in a qualifying government program. The question of fact that the Tribunal needed to determine was exactly this last one, and it did so in the affirmative based on its review of decrees, settlement agreements, and other related documents.[46] But again the key question of whether the investor's failure to participate in qualifying government programs was induced or simply a poor business decision on the part of the investor is not clear from the award although the latter is what the Tribunal seems to suggest.

The Clamant in *Helnan v. Egypt* (2008) set out to prove a particularly grave set of factual allegations against the Egyptian state but failed. It claimed that a number of Egyptian government agencies including the Ministry of Tourism orchestrated a downgrading of its hotel from five-start to four-star so that they could terminate the management contract to pave the way for privatization. The factual allegation is summarized in the following paragraph:

> The core of HELNAN's position is that EGYPT wanted to terminate the contractual relationship because it considered the Management Contract an obstacle for the privatization of the Shepheard given that in the case of a sale of the hotel, the 15 October 2002 Amendment allowed the sale of the hotel, but also gave HELNAN the right either to remain as the manager or to be adequately compensated. For this reason, making an improper use of its authority over the holding company HOTAC,

[45] Champion Trading Company Ameritrade International, Inc. v. Arab Republic of Egypt, ICSID Case No. ARB/02/9, Award (Oct. 27, 2006), at 95–97.

[46] *Id.* at 148–56 ("156 Since the Arbitral Tribunal came to the conclusion that the companies were not in a like situation, it does not need to analyze the other requirements which prohibit discrimination on the grounds of nationality").

> EGOTH and the Ministry of Tourism, EGYPT proceeded to orchestrate a series of events which ultimately lead to HELNAN's eviction from the Hotel.[47]

To support its allegation, the Claimant alleges:

> HELNAN alleges that in order to allow and implement such a strategy, EGYPT, through EGOTH, rejected the numerous renovation and upgrade plans for the Shepheard prepared and submitted by HELNAN. For the same reason the Ministry of Tourism carried out the 2003 inspections in a way which did not conform to accepted policy and practice. After an inspection was conducted in a hostile fashion on 14 June 2003, an unjustifiably harsh report was issued which did not even provide HELNAN with a grace period to cure any alleged violations. A further inspection took place on 4 September 2003, followed by a second inspection report filed on that same day. The decision to downgrade the hotel was issued three days later, on 7 September 2003.[48]

Having examined the parties' documentary evidence including letters showing the deteriorations of the hotel and reports of inspection results, the Tribunal seemed convinced that the hotel had a problem, but the inspection and termination process also had some irregularities.[49] Although the result finally rested on the lack of proof of attribution to the state of the various agencies' behavior, the Tribunal's evaluation of the testimonial evidence presented to it is worth highlighting.

The award summarizes the testimonies of some of the witnesses. One of the Claimant's allegations was that the downgrade gave the Egyptian agency that contracted with the Claimant, EGOTH, the contractual right to initiate an arbitration seeking termination of the Management Contact. Indeed, that is exactly what EGOTH did in a domestic Cairo arbitration. One of the factual questions was whether the arbitration was part of an elaborate plan to push Helnan out. One of EGOTH's witnesses was its legal advisor who testified about the arbitration in the Cairo proceedings. The key question was when she knew that there would be an arbitration proceeding against Helnan.

Here is what she testified under cross-examination:

Q. When did you first learn of the downgrade of the Shepheard Hotel?
A. Before initiating the procedures for the arbitration by a very, very short time. Approximately 60 days before.
Q. I'm sorry, you learnt of the downgrade 60 days before initiating the arbitration?
A. Approximately, yes.

[47] Helnan International Hotels A/S v. The Arab Republic of Egypt, ICSID Case No. ARB/05/19, Award (July 3, 2008), at 132.

[48] *Id.* at 134. *See also id.* at 135–36 ("135. The Cairo arbitration proceedings were initiated 25 days after the downgrading, a move which HELNAN believes to have been actually planned even before the decision to downgrade the hotel was made. After the Cairo Award terminated the Management Contract, EGYPT pursued its enforcement in a way that HELNAN considers to be unfair. 136. According to HELNAN, this series of actions amounts to abusive actions by Egyptian government officials who used the inspections and the downgrade to ensure HELNAN's eviction from the Shepheard").

[49] *See id.* at 134–52.

Q. Who told you about the downgrade?
A. The sector concerned within the organisation told me. There is a sector that is concerned with the survey and monitoring of the hotels, and from that I knew about this[50]

The point was that the arbitral proceeding was initiated 25 days after the downgrade suggesting that the legal department had knowledge of the downgrade before it happened. It appears that upon redirect, the testimony was somewhat rectified, but the Tribunal did not consider the retraction credible. In its own words:

> The indication by Mrs Dorreya Refaat in re-examination that she was mistaken in her answers to Claimant's counsel was far from being convincing, since the way the question was put by EGYPT's counsel, if not leading, allowed the witness to understand the consequences of her first, candid, answer. Moreover, a period of 60 days to prepare a request for arbitration seems to be more realistic than the period of 25 days.[51]

Indeed this, along with other forms of evidence, essentially led to the conclusion that there was a concerted effort among some agencies to evict the Claimant[52] although ultimately there was no proof of a plan that could be attributed to the state itself. This case is most notable for its finding of enough evidence of conspiracy among government agencies and its failure to find attribution to the state for lack of enough evidence. Its analysis of evidence of attribution is also interesting.

One of the Claimant's witnesses, who was a former government official testifying against the government, said in his witness statement:

> *The first undersecretary to the ministry of Tourism told him that Mr Moustafa Eid the then President of the Holding Company for Housing, Tourism and Cinemas had specifically ordered that the Shepeard Hotel be downgraded by one star to provide EGOTH with an excuse to cancel the management contract with Helnan.*[53]

[50] *Id.* at 154.

[51] *Id.* at 155.

[52] *Id.* at 156–57 ("156. Thus, the Arbitral Tribunal is satisfied that EGOTH and various Egyptian authorities, including the Ministry of Tourism, played a significant role in the implementation of a plan aiming at terminating the Management Contract. There is no doubt that the 4 September 2003 inspection, the report of the same date containing the recommendation that the Shepheard hotel be downgraded, the preparation for the Minister of Tourism, on that same day as well, of a Memorandum by his Legal Counsellor with the same recommendation, attaching a draft Decree ordering the downgrade of the hotel to four stars, were part of such an overall plan. 157. Together, these manoeuvres evidence a plan aiming at terminating the Management Contract, with the active participation of the Ministry of Tourism in the implementation of the plan. The decisive question is whether this plan was adopted by EGYPT to get rid of HELNAN to be able to privatize the Shepheard hotel more easily. The only evidence of intervention of the administration to obtain, directly or indirectly, the termination of the Contract is based on hearsay, with no further corroborating evidence").

[53] *Id.* at 158 (quoting from Witness Statement of Mr Bahi Nasr, a former Chairman of the Egyptian Hotels Company (EHC), the predecessor of EGOTH, from 1985 to 1989) (italics in original).

The Tribunal did not consider this credible at all for reasons stated in this paragraph:

> At the hearing, Mr Nasr was far from being convincing. He did not remember precisely the conversation he reported, but explained that he suspected that Mr Moustafa Eid wanted to get rid of the Management Contract so that EGOTH might sell the Shepheard hotel to a Libyan company of which he also happened to be the Chairman. Mr Moustafa Eid testified and denied having ordered the downgrade of the Shepheard Hotel. He was not cross-examined on this point. Another reason to doubt the accuracy of Mr Nasr's testimony is that he indicated to have informed at the time Mr El Galaly, HELNAN's President and a close friend, of the reported conversation with the undersecretary to the Ministry of Tourism. If such has been the case, it is even less understandable that HELNAN abstained from challenging in the administrative courts the downgrade decision.[54]

More importantly, the Tribunal noted that:

> even if the conversation referred to by Mr Nasr did actually take place, it would not necessarily prove that EGYPT had engineered a plan to get rid of HELNAN in order to be able to privatize the Shepheard hotel more easily. Mr Nasr's suspicions that Mr Eid was acting in his own interest, if confirmed, would indicate a completely different scenario, in particular, since HELNAN, informed by Mr Nasr, chose not to challenge the downgrading Decree in the competent administrative jurisdiction. any event, Mr Nasr's version of Mr Eid's plan has not been proven to be correct in the proceedings.[55]

At the end, none of the testimonial evidence moved the case one way or the other because the Tribunal found that the records of the domestic arbitral proceeding for the termination of the Management Contract in which the present Claimant won compensation had determined many of the contentions and that its decisions must not be disturbed in the absence of proof that the proceeding itself violated the treaty, which was not established.[56]

In *Biwater v. Tanzania* (2008), there was no serious contention relating to material facts because the State's termination of the investor's lease was admitted and in fact announced by officials on TV. Likewise, the government's takeover of management and deportation of the investor's senior manager were not disputed.[57] The host state's contention pertained to the value of the lease at the time of termination—that the investor had already breached the lease agreement and that the agreement had no economic value at the time of termination.[58] The outcome ultimately depended not

[54] *Id.* at 158 (second half).

[55] *Id.* at 159.

[56] *Id.* at 163 ("The Management Contract was terminated by the Cairo Award on 30 December 2004 pursuant to the arbitration clause included in the Management Contract. This award was rendered by three arbitrators enjoying the powers of amiable compositeur as expressly agreed by the parties. It is final and binding. It has been enforced and has res judicata effects in the Egyptian legal order. As Egyptian law was applicable to the Management Contract, the present Arbitral Tribunal cannot ignore its effect, unless it would be established that the rendering of the Award was made in breach of the Treaty, or general international law").

[57] Biwater Gauff (Tanzania) Ltd. v. United Republic of Tanzania, ICSID Case No. ARB/05/22, Final Award (July 24, 2008), at 393.

[58] *Id.* at 424.

on the truth or falsity of the factual allegations but what, if any, value the leasehold retained at the time of the termination.[59]

The *Jan de Nul N.V. and Dredging International N.V v. Egypt* (2008) case required the determination of serious factual contentions, primarily whether the Egypt state agency (SCA) fraudulently induced the JV's assent to the terms of the agreement that it concluded for the Suez Canal project.[60] The fraud claim more particularly alleged that the Egyptian agency withheld information on geology and volumes to be dredged, in particular it "failed to disclose that it had encountered rocks in pre-dredged areas."[61] The Tribunal considered the documentary evidence, heard fact and expert witnesses and concluded that the Claimant did not prove the existence of fraud.[62]

The Tribunal arrives at this conclusion even if it was convinced that SCA had relevant information but failed to disclose it.[63] That is primarily because the investor had the duty and opportunity to investigate.[64] Generally, the facts were viewed most favorably to the SCA, which eventually helped the government win the treaty claim on the merits.

In *Bernardus v. Zimbabwe* (2009), the key factual basis of the Claimants' claims was the dispossession of land through a combination of constitutional, legislative, and judicial and extra-legal means. None of the essential facts were disputed.[65] Indeed, Zimbabwe admitted that land was taken and that its laws required the payment of compensation but that compensation was not offered.[66] On the facts, it did, however, contend among other minor procedural matters, that the failure to pay compensation was a result of a state of emergency that existed during the relevant time.[67]

[59] *See id.* at 485.

[60] Jan de Nul N.V. Dredging International N.V. v. Arab Republic of Egypt, ICSID Case No. ARB/04/13, Award (Nov. 6, 2008), at 208. In the Tribunal's framing: "The Tribunal understands, however, from the Egyptian rules on fraud that intent is a necessary element and that there is no fraud when the alleged victim could have known about the relevant facts by another means33. For this reason, the Tribunal will proceed to an assessment of the facts and review whether the SCA has intentionally withheld material information leading the JV to enter into the Contract on wrong premises and whether the JV had no other means of knowing the relevant facts."

[61] *Id.* at 210.

[62] *Id.* at 211.

[63] *Id.* at 221 ("The SCA did not provide all the information it had. Was it obliged to do so? The Tribunal would be inclined to think so. This said, the Tribunal must also examine whether the Claimants were nevertheless in a position to know of the pre-dredging works").

[64] *Id.* at 226 ("Article 5 of the GCC especially provided that 'each tenderer must under his full responsibility, take all necessary steps and make all required investigations to be able to estimate exactly the nature and extent of his obligations.' Thus, the Claimants were aware of the importance of the preparation period").

[65] Bernardus Henricus Funnekotter and Others v. Republic of Zimbabwe, ICSID Case No. ARB/05/6, Award (Apr. 22, 2009), at 97 ("Zimbabwe, although it denies any responsibility in the farm occupation by settlers and war veterans 'concede[s] that compulsory acquisition ... done in terms of the Land Acquisition Act and the Constitution of Zimbabwe ... is tantamount to expropriation.' It contends however that the measures it then took did not violate Article 6").

[66] *Id.* at 97–101.

[67] *Id.* at 102 ("Zimbabwe then invokes the defense that a state of necessity or emergency existed, which, in its submission, relieved Respondent of responsibility for complying with otherwise applicable provisions of the BIT. It submits that such state 'began on 20 March 2000 and continued until 13 September 2005,' and that 'this rightfully suspended Respondent's obligation to evaluate compensation at the date of such evaluation until 14 September 2005.' In this respect, it invokes Zimbabwe domestic law, Article 7 of the BIT and customary International Law").

Although the main argument was a legal one that invoked the BIT's state of emergency provision, the Tribunal did not determine on the facts whether the said state of emergency existed, but instead ruled that the Respondent did not explain how the existence of the emergency, if there was one, prevented it from offering the required compensation.[68]

Although the nationality issue in *Waguih Elie v. Egypt* (2009) was largely determined on the law, the factual predicates were also important. For example, the Parties disputed whether the Claimant did indeed acquire Lebanese nationality, which would have been the only way that he could have lost his Egyptian nationality. Egypt categorically claimed that the Claimant used fraudulent documentation to show his Lebanese nationality. To support this claim, Egypt submitted a letter from the Lebanese authorities that said that the Claimant had never been a Lebanese citizen.[69]

> Egypt claimed that this new evidence demonstrated that the documents Mr. Siag had proffered in support of his Lebanese nationality were fraudulent and probably also forged, and that it was more than sufficient to prove that Mr. Siag had made false claims as to his Lebanese nationality. Egypt noted that Mr. Siag had claimed that he lost his Egyptian nationality as a result of obtaining Lebanese nationality and failing to apply within one year to retain Egyptian nationality.[70]

The factual contention got little bit more interesting. The Tribunal had at least four documents, including a passport that the person used to travel in and outside of Lebanon in the record. That is when the Tribunal said the government's theory shifted to fraudulent procurement rather than the documents themselves being forged. In weighing the evidence, the Tribunal said:

> 327.... At the March 2008 hearing, when asked by Mr Newman whether Mr Khouly, the man Mr Siag asked for assistance in obtaining Lebanese nationality, told Mr Siag that he was going to obtain Mr Siag's Individual Record by bribery Mr Siag responded "Of course not, sir ... I will never accept it, we had no reason to do this, and I absolutely deny anything like this." As noted earlier the Tribunal found Mr Siag to be an honest and credible witness and it accepts his denials as truthful, but it is nevertheless appropriate to examine each example presented by Egypt as evidencing fraud or other dishonest behaviour.
>
> 328. Before doing so it is appropriate to note that on the last day of the hearing, in response to direct questioning from the President, Egypt abandoned its earlier

[68] *Id.* ¶106 ("In the present case, Zimbabwe is invoking state of necessity, first, to explain its difficulties to face the situation resulting from the invasion of commercial farms by settlers and war veterans; second, to justify the measures of expropriation it took in the public interest. However, it never explains why such a state of necessity prevented it from calculating and paying the compensation due to the farmers in conformity with the BIT. The argument drawn on that point by the Respondent from the alleged state of necessity, therefore, cannot be upheld").

[69] Waguih Elie George Slag and Clorinda Vecchi v. The Arab Republic of Egypt, ICSID Case No. ARB/05/15, Award (June 1, 2009), at 219–20.

[70] *Id.* at 31.

allegation that Mr Siag had "forged" the contemporaneous documents of his Lebanese nationality.

The theory then became that it was the underlying file that was forged, and that the other documents were authentic but were issued either because of oversight or due to corrupt activity. The Tribunal did not find the new theory plausible and rejected it on the facts.[71] There were, however, two curious facts that the Tribunal also did not consider indicia of fraud. It was undisputed that the reason why the Claimant wanted Lebanese nationality was to avoid military service and that he paid $5,000 to someone to process the nationality application process. Egypt suggested that the Tribunal should infer from the payment of this large sum that it must have included bribes. The Tribunal rejected the invitation for inference, saying that it is not uncommon to pay money for immigration services.[72]

The above passages make it very clear that the Tribunal was highly influenced by the credibility of the witnesses who appeared before it, especially the principal claimant whom it repeatedly praised as a "credible and innocent" man.[73] Related to its appreciation of the witness's candor, it might have taken a result-oriented approach, particularly to clear the jurisdictional obstacles, which were the state's main line of defense.

[71] *Id.* at 312–32 ("Egypt's argument further required the Tribunal to accept that the three other contemporaneous documents, the Lebanese nationality certificate and the two passports, were all exclusively based on the allegedly fraudulent Individual Record. The other three documents, while neither fraudulent nor forged, were to be characterised as mistakes issues by careless officials at the Lebanese Embassy in Cairo. It is against this background that the Tribunal passes to consider Egypt's contentions").

[72] *Id.* at 352.

[73] *See id.* at 214 ("Mr Siag impressed the Tribunal as an honest and credible witness"), 327 ("As noted earlier the Tribunal found Mr Siag to be an honest and credible witness and it accepts his denials as truthful").

10
Determination of Facts in the Modern Post-2010 Cases

The outcome of some cases is more dependent on the facts than others, but in all cases, the facts are almost always important. Whenever the facts are disputed, their determination require the tribunal's weighing of the evidence presented by the parties no matter whether it adopts an adversarial or investigative method, or a combination thereof. The cases profiled here in two temporal scopes, i.e., the decade of the 2010 and post-2020, offer a good insight into the arbitral fact finding process.

The 2010–2020 Period

In *Gustav v. Ghana* (2010), the most serious factual contentions pertained to the Respondent's allegations that the Claimant obtained the contract through fraud, which was sustained throughout the lifecycle of the JV. Tribunal did not determine this allegation as a matter of fact because it chose to decide the claim on the basis of the law of attribution, finding that the alleged breach is not attributable to the state as a matter of law, and even if it were, it would not have constituted breach of any treaty provisions. In that sense, the decision rested on the uncontested facts.[1]

In *Malicorp v. Egypt* (2011), the key factual contention pertained to whether the investor misled the state about its financial abilities to carry out the airport development project at the project bidding phase. A local commercial arbitral tribunal had already determined the issue in the affirmative.[2] The Tribunal examined the relevant documents and found that:

> it suffices to find that the nature and content of the information supplied to the Respondent by Malicorp's representatives was such as to give rise to an essential mistake; for a project as monumental as that of the Ras Sudr airport, knowing whether the company awarded the project is an empty shell or a company with exceptional resources is obviously fundamental, and any error on that point justifies calling the Contract into question.[3]

[1] *See* Gustav F W Hamester GmbH & Co KG v. Republic of Ghana Respondent, ICSID Case No. ARB/07/24, Award (June 18, 2010), at 350 ("Given the analysis above and the conclusion that no responsibility can be incurred by Ghana under the BIT, there is therefore no need to address the Respondent's defences based upon the alleged fraudulent acts and violations of fiduciary duties by the Claimant during the life of the investment").

[2] *See* Malicorp Limited v. The Arab Republic of Egypt, ICSID Case No. ARB/08/18, Award (Feb. 7, 2011), at 136.

[3] *Id.*

Africa's International Investment Law Regimes. Won L. Kidane, Oxford University Press. © Oxford University Press 2023.
DOI: 10.1093/oso/9780197745571.003.0010

This type of investor behavior is a common issue that many tribunals have encountered. Because outright fraud must often be pled with particularity and is difficult to prove, it is not uncommon for tribunals to view them as merely inducing mistake. In this case, the Tribunal looked at the evidence carefully—perhaps more carefully than the government officials who awarded the contract to the investor. The Tribunal uncovered traces of misrepresentations from the investor's bid submissions. The financials were presented in a misleading way, as follows:

> In its bid, the Claimant submitted its Memorandum of Association, which showed that it had a capital of 1000 pounds sterling divided into 1,000 shares of one pound sterling each (see above, no. 7; Exhibit R-2, p. 23, no. 5: 'The Company's share capital is 1000 divided into 1000 shares of 1 each"). It is true that Malicorp decided on 15 September 1999 to increase its capital to 100 million pounds sterling, but that was not subscribed capital, but authorised capital (see above, no. 6). The difference is substantial, because in the first case there are shareholders who have made a firm commitment to pay it, while in the second, there is only a power given to the company's organs to decide when they will look for shareholders willing to commit.[4]

It is not surprising then that the Claimant's claim was rejected. Again, this type of lack of financial and professional qualifications of the claimants is the most common source of investment trouble in many of these cases.

The *Bernard von Pezold v. Zimbabwe* (2015) case presented one of the most complicated sets of factual circumstances, but most of the essential facts were undisputed, as the government's actions were taken by law and through institutions. The Tribunal had no difficulty ascertaining the basic facts to its satisfaction relying on documentary evidence, experts and fact witnesses.[5] The Tribunal offers an excellent summary of the important facts. A paragraph from the Respondent's only and key fact witness, Minister Didiymus Mutasa, puts the perineal matter in perspective:

> Our existence in our own country, on our own land in the days before liberation, was a very sad existence indeed. Our land was taken away, our friends, who were talking about farms, are talking about farms which didn't come from heaven for them, but farms which they expropriated from our forefathers, from our ancestors, many not so long ago, where many of us were already living. They did not expect us to sit back and smile and enjoy what they were doing, and indeed, we did not sit back and enjoy. We had to mount a liberation struggle, and I am happy to say that I am one of those who participated in the liberation struggle.[6]

At the most basic level, the legal proceedings were about how this liberation should be pursued and who should bear the burden. As observed by the Tribunal, a long and complicated land reform process reduced the number of white farmers in Zimbabwe

[4] *Id.* at 133(b).

[5] *See* Bernardus Henricus Funnekotter and Others v. Republic of Zimbabwe, ICSID Case No. ARB/05/6, Award (Apr. 22, 2009), at 91.

[6] *Id.* at 93.

from 6,000 owning all the commercial land when Zimbabwe won its independence in 1979,[7] to about 400 by the time the Tribunal was deciding this case in 2015.[8] This was achieved through a combination of constitutional and legal processes and extra-legal measures. The Tribunal's task was to determine exactly how the present Claimants lost their property and if they can get redress under the applicable BITs.

The BITs come into play in highly interesting ways. Although the case appears to be about historic colonial landholdings, the Claimant['s] acquisition was a more recent phenomenon: they acquired the landholdings and related property from 1988 through 2007.[9] The historical background of these holdings is not clear from the award, but the interests that were the subject of the expropriation and other BIT claims were not historical rights, although the owners were European.

Most importantly, in its land reacquisition effort, Zimbabwe had attempted to make a clear distinction between these two types of holdings. The Tribunal goes through the various reform efforts as a matter of fact relying on an expert testimony on how change was effectuated. It began with compensated dispossession, regressed to compensation for improvements only and ended up with uncompensated dispossession of the historic holdings over a period of more than four decades.[10] However, the final 2013 constitutional amendment that allowed dispossession of land owned by non-Indigenous owners[11] without compensation exempted those who had BIT protection, which formed the basis of these cases. As identified by the Tribunal:

> On the matter of agricultural land, addressed in Chapter 16 of the 2013 Constitution, the principles relating to compensation for land acquired by the Respondent were again changed, this time to provide expressly for the full compensation of any "indigenous Zimbabwean" whose agricultural land was acquired, in contradistinction to the compensation of non-indigenous Zimbabweans. The 2013 Constitution also reaffirmed that foreign nationals protected by a BIT whose agricultural land had been acquired are entitled to full compensation for that land pursuant to the terms of the BIT.[12]

Although clouded by difficult history, at the end of the day, when the law is read and the facts understood, the contentions in these cases were rather typical and they ask

[7] *Id.* at 96 ("As at 1980, 15.5 million hectares ("ha") of Zimbabwe's total area (i.e., 39.6 million ha) were dedicated to large scale commercial farming. Title to this land was held by approximately 6,000 white farmers. 6.4 million ha were comprised of Communal Land, largely devoted to subsistence farming by the indigenous population, and the remaining land was divided between small scale commercial operations, national parks, State land and urban settlements").

[8] *See id.* at 160 ("It is estimated that there are approximately 400 white farmers remaining in Zimbabwe today, farming 117,409 ha of land. This may be compared to the approximately 4,500 white farmers on 4,800 large scale commercial farms, covering 11.9 million ha of land, present in Zimbabwe in 1999. Save for a few instances, it is not really disputed by the Parties that the majority of land farmed by white farmers was compulsorily acquired without compensation pursuant to the LRP").

[9] *See id.* at 121–39.

[10] *See id.* at 97–163.

[11] *See id.* at 163 ("During the Hearing, Ms. Tsvakwi, a fact witness for the Respondent, confirmed that an 'indigenous Zimbabwean' within the meaning of the 2013 Constitution is a black farmer or black Zimbabwean (see Tr. Day 4, p. 1191)").

[12] *Id.* at 162. The referenced constitutional provision states:

16.8 Compensation for acquisition of previously-acquired agricultural land

the same fundamental question as the other BIT cases: did the host state keep its promise to foreign investors?

Cortec v. Kenya (2018) raised an important factual contention pertaining to the allegation of corruption by some officials who were responsible for the issuance of the investor's license. The Tribunal did not believe that, despite the seriousness of the allegations, the Respondent did enough to carry its burden of proof. Indeed, in response to one of the allegations of corruption the Tribunal surmised: "Mr. Juma is dead and cannot defend himself."[13] It also reprimanded the Respondent for not cross-examining the other person accused of corruption who appeared before the Tribunal to testify. It said: "Mr. Masibo provided a detailed witness statement which denied any wrongdoing. The government did not put to Mr. Masibo while in the witness box the so-called 'incriminating' evidence."[14] Unimpressed with the Respondent's presentation of evidence of corruption, the Tribunal dismissed the corruption defense for lack of proof.[15]

This is not an isolated problem. Allegations of corruption are extremely difficult to prove. *World Duty Free* is just about the only African case that has succeeded because the Claimant itself admitted to the essential facts believing that they were helpful to it, a serious strategic mistake.

The Post-2020 Cases

The *Strabag SE v. Libya* (2020) Tribunal had one of the most difficult tasks of determining facts in the fog of war. As a matter of fact, it appears that the co-arbitrators might have selected Professor John Crook as chair because of his nine years of experience on the Eritrea-Ethiopia Claims Tribunal adjudicating claims for wartime losses. The Tribunal framed the legal issues in such a way that the finding of liability depended on highly specific factual findings. In each particular instance, the Tribunal

(1) Any indigenous Zimbabwean whose agricultural land was acquired by the State before the effective date is entitled to compensation from the State for the land and any improvements that were on the land when it was acquired.
(2) Any persons whose agricultural land was acquired by the State before the effective date and whose property rights at that time were guaranteed or protected by an agreement concluded by the Government of Zimbabwe with the government of another country, is entitled to compensation from the State for the land and any improvements in accordance with that agreement.
(3) Any person, other than a person referred to in subsection (1) or (2), whose agricultural land was acquired by the State before the effective date is entitled to compensation from the State only for improvements that were on the land when it was acquired."

[13] *Id.* at 184.

[14] *Id.* at 184 ("to pursue its allegations of corruption, that Mr. Masibo be given the opportunity to explain his conduct. This opportunity was not given. The Tribunal does not accept the Government's explanation that it did not wish by cross-examination to further complicate Mr. Masibo's existing legal jeopardy in Kenya. Mr. Masibo's lawyer, not the Government, was present to protect Mr. Masibo. Nevertheless, the Government seeks to persuade the Tribunal to draw the conclusion that "this arrangement involved corruption. On that basis alone, the Government says, the claim should be dismissed, as investment treaty protection does not extend to investments procured by corruption and/or made in bad faith").

[15] *See id.* at 185 ("The Tribunal rejects the allegations of corruption against Mr. Masibo as unproven").

had to find who committed what distraction when and why. Because there were numerous players including NATO forces, the Tribunal had to find in each case whether the Libyan forces caused the damage to the exclusion of others and whether that damage was not justifiable by military necessity.[16]

In that sense, it took a creative solution to the very difficult task of determining facts under these circumstances. For example, it adopted a percentage allocation methodology for some of the claims. Consider the following:

> The Tribunal is therefore again left to make its best assessment of how much damage is attributable to actions by Libya's armed forces, in particular, soldiers of the 32nd Reinforced Brigade, in conditions not potentially implicating military necessity. In doing so, it is again guided by the principles applied in the previous claim for equipment lost/destroyed in 2011, recognizing that some compensation is due, but that the evidence does not allow of precise determination. Based on the Sadaoui Report, especially the detailed chronology of events from page 11 onwards, the Tribunal determines that approximately one-third of the damage is attributable to Libyan State forces for purposes of liability under Article 5(2)(b) with a reasonable degree of certainty. Consequently, the damages for which Libya is liable amount to €858,000, approximately one-third of the €2,573, 186 claimed.[17]

One important matter of fact caused a two-to-one split of the members of the Tribunal, and it concerned a potentially significant setoff opportunity for the Respondent. Interestingly, the split between the members of the Tribunal was caused not by matters of legal principle but primarily by matters of appreciation of fact. The Tribunal awarded a significant amount of money for the Claimant's losses sustained during the revolution, however, the Claimant, as a construction company, had taken tens of millions of dollars as advance payment against performance guarantees. These guarantees had their own expiry dates. The Parties disputed whether the bank guarantees expired or not. Two members of the Tribunal considered this a matter outside of this arbitration and did not want to get to the bottom of it for purposes of setoff. The dissenting arbitrator, however, thought that the evidence showed that these guarantees may not be recoverable by the Respondent and as such the Respondent should have been permitted to setoff against some of the award of damages. "Respondent contends, however, that Al Hani still holds EUR 98,128,159 in unearned advance payments under the Tajura, TIAR, TIAR-NE, and Garaboulli contracts, 17 and that Al Hani has an obligation to repay those unearned amounts since they pertain to work that was never performed by Al Hani under the contracts."[18]

The dissent imparts a very serious indictment of the majority for failing to get to the bottom of the issue of advance payment,[19] stating in strong terms:

16 *See, e.g.*, Strabag Se v. Libya, ICSID Case No. ARB(AF)/15/1, Award (June 29, 2020), at 320.
17 *Id.* at 321.
18 *Id.* at 13 (Partial Dissenting Opinion of Professor Nassib G. Ziade).
19 The Tribunal does acknowledge the lack of clarity of the facts surrounding the advance payment in the following terms: "The Tribunal notes that the Parties' recent exchange of correspondence leaves some matters of fact unclear. Inter alia, there is a lack of clarity regarding the advance payment guarantees for the TIAR, TIAR-NE and Garaboulli Contracts. Respondent appears to regard the unrecovered advance payments under these three contracts as relevant in determining the amount of its claimed set-off." *Id.* at 894.

> 41. While Respondent and its expert provide detailed figures for advance payments that they consider not yet to have been earned, Claimant states vaguely, with little supporting documentation, that the full advance payments had been fully used up to finance "significant costs that Strabag incurred upfront at the outset of the projects (for example, in recruiting and mobilising personnel, constructing site facilities, purchasing equipment and machinery, and engaging sub-contractors)." By its own admission, Claimant used unearned portions of the advance payments to buy equipment and supply the joint venture with cash.
>
> 42. The Tribunal nonetheless awards Claimant Compensation for some of the aforementioned up front costs, including for lost or damaged equipment and damages caused by delay. Without proper consideration of the issue of advance payments, it may well turn out that the Award compensates Claimant for equipment and other costs that, by Claimant's own admission, have already been covered using unearned portions of the advance payments, i.e., monies from Respondent.[20]

Not satisfied with this, it continued:

> A task partially completed may prove in practice to be more problematic than a task not initiated at all. The majority's decision to summarily deny Respondent's requested setoff fails to recognize that the issues of the advance payments, the bank guarantees, and Claimant's claims for damages are intertwined and cannot be resolved separately. This fragmentation is not conducive to "good order and fundamental fairness," to which the majority and indeed the entire Tribunal aspired.[21]

It is clear that the majority of this Tribunal viewed the facts in the light most favorable to the Claimant and showed no sympathy for the Respondent's war-caused predicaments.

In *Interocean Oil v. Nigeria* (2020), the factual contentions were numerous and were primarily of private and corporate nature.[22] The Tribunal determined the relevant facts based on extensive documentary and testimonial evidence.[23] At the end of the day, however, the actual determination of who did what and when and when turned out to be less important than which actors' conduct was attributable to the state, as it is presented as an ISDS case. The Tribunal's finding of lack of attribution made the factual contentions less important.[24]

[20] *Id.* at 41–42.

[21] *Id.* at 44.

[22] *See* Interocean Oil Development Company and Interocean Oil Exploration Company v. Federal Republic of Nigeria, ICSID Case No. ARB/13/20, Award (Oct. 6, 2020), at 237.

[23] *See id.* at 74.

[24] *See id.* at 176 ("The Tribunal can have no jurisdiction over harms that are not attributable to Respondent. As the Parties have also recognized, however, that analysis is based on the context of each event"). *Id.* at 186 ("The Tribunal has determined that under either interpretation of the scope and extent of that customary law, the result of this award would be the same. The Tribunal does not find a breach of customary international law. The alleged wrongdoings are not attributable to Respondent or do not form part of a concerted effort involving Respondent to deprive Claimants of their investment"). *Id.* at 296 ("No evidence demonstrates attribution to Respondent of any actions that might have been taken").

Bay View Group v. Rwanda (2022) attracted extraordinary commentary about the credibility of witnesses. The Tribunal was so dissatisfied with the lack of credibility of the principal of the Claimant companies that it could not even wait until it got to the details of the facts in the awards section to say how incredible it found the testimony:

> The Tribunal's appraisal of the witnesses will be dealt with in due course, in the context of the evidence that they have given. It is right, however, to observe at the outset that Mr. Marshall's perception that he was the victim of injustice appears to have led him to give evidence that was repeatedly at odds with contemporary documents and manifestly inaccurate. His response to documents that conflicted with his evidence was frequently to suggest that they were fabricated—suggestions that were not put by counsel to the relevant witnesses in cross-examination. On other occasions Mr. Marshall made, for the first time, allegations of fact that one would have expected to feature in the pleadings or in witness statements and which the Tribunal has not been able to accept. *In short, Mr. Marshall was not a reliable witness.*[25]

This is a rare express indictment of witnesses, but once the Tribunal had made this type of factual finding, the result became obvious. The Tribunal's assessment of all the other testimonial and evidentiary evidence painted a picture of adventurous businessmen who sought to profit in a frontier market with little to no investment. Indeed, the Tribunal went as far as saying: "The Tribunal has concluded that the development over the course of this arbitration of the allegation that Rwanda was bent on a campaign of creeping expropriation in order to further smuggling of minerals from the DRC was the product of Mr. Marshall's imagination."[26] The Tribunal further found that:

> Mr. Marshall had, however, the *idèè fixe* of obtaining long-term licences for all Five Concessions, and persisted in attempting to obtain these. It may be that he believed that the pro bono assistance that he had provided to Rwanda, and was perhaps still providing, in areas that had nothing to do with mining, would result in NRD's applications being afforded preferential treatment. Such treatment would have been improper. In the event, NRD's applications were

[25] Bay View Group LLC and The Spalena Company LLC v. Republic of Rwanda, ICSID Case No. ARB/18/21, Award (Mar. 30, 2022), at 78 (emphasis added). The preceding two paragraphs read:

> 76. The Claimants allege that the Rwanda breached obligations owed to them under the BIT.
>
> 77. The driving force behind the initiation and conduct of this arbitration on behalf of the Claimants has, unquestionably, been Mr. Marshall. He is the founder, principal shareholder in, and Managing Director of, each of the Claimants. He also acted as the Managing Director of NRD and directed its activities once it had been acquired by Spalena. As the Claimants' principal witness, Mr. Marshall was cross-examined over a period of some four days. It appeared to the Tribunal that Mr. Marshall was labouring under a burning sense that he—in person and the Claimants' investments, in the form of NRD and its mining business—had been unfairly treated by Rwanda.

[26] *Id.* at 482.

> fairly and thoroughly assessed by Rwanda, with the inevitable result that they were rejected.[27]

This is one of few cases that completely collapsed on the facts. The Tribunal simply did not believe that the Claimants made any *bona fide* investment.

Conclusion

The degree of egregiousness of the facts is perhaps the single most important indicator of the outcome of these cases. It appears that where the claimants suffered more serious and real injuries on the facts such as in the Zimbabwe cases, the tribunals are more inclined to find the legal basis for liability. Where the facts suggest a degree of investor adventurism as in *Bay View Group v. Rwanda*, they strengthen the legal scrutiny.

In the earlier cases, lack of participation or proper and timely representation appeared to have resulted in the findings of fact more favorable to the investors. However, the trend continued in the decades that followed. Most tribunals found facts in favor of the investors in significantly more cases than in favor of the state. Of the two post-2020 most recent cases, the tally on the facts is equal—with one case going in each direction.

Beyond superficial comparing of results, however, a few useful observations could be made. First, there are two most frequently raised defenses by the Respondent state: lack of financial and professional qualifications of the investor and fraudulent misrepresentations. Both defenses were rarely accepted. The only case that has properly acknowledged the investor's lack of abilities and speculative involvement is *Bay View Group v. Rwanda* (2022), although *Gustav v. Ghana (2000), Malicorp v. Egypt*

[27] *Id.* at 514. The paragraphs preceding this also provide proper context:

> 507. For the reasons given above, the Tribunal finds that Rwanda did not discriminate against NRD in favour of other investors in breach of its obligations under Articles 3.1 and 3.2 of the BIT.
>
> 508. The prolix allegations made by the Claimants of breach by Rwanda of the BIT have resulted in a lengthy analysis in this Award. At the end of the day, however, the picture is a simpleone.
>
> 509. When Rwanda set about privatizing its mining industry, it offered short-term, four-year contracts to investors to enable them to demonstrate not only their aspirations but their abilities to revolutionize Rwanda's mining industry by introducing industrial methods of extracting and processing minerals in place of the artisanal methods under which extraction was done by the wielding of picks and shovels by individual miners, to the detriment of the environment.
>
> 510. Rwanda hoped, no doubt, to attract experienced mining companies. The evidence suggests that it did not succeed. Instead, it attracted entrepreneurs without mining experience attracted by the possibilities of profiting from the acquisition of long-term mining licences in Rwanda. Of these Mr. Marshall was one. Mr. Marshall himself remarked that there were no mining companies among the investors. This was certainly the case so far as those behind NRD were concerned. Mr. Marshall described the Zarnacks as a plumbing company from Germany and H.C. Starck as minerals processors who had never carried out mining anywhere in the world. In the event, no less than five concessions were granted to the Zarnacks and Mr. Benzinge. NRD was founded to exploit these concessions. The Zarnacks pledged to invest some US$40 million, but did not do so. Instead they sold NRD to Starck.

(2011), *Interocean Oil v. Nigeria* (2020) also favored the state on grounds of lack of attribution.

The fraud or bribery defense was successful in only one case, *World Duty Free v. Kenya*, because the proof presented to the Tribunal was direct and incontrovertible. Allegations of fraud and bribery have been raised in a disproportionate number of the cases but have never succeeded in showing the difficulty in sustaining the burden of proof relating to these defenses. Even when the existence of some fraudulent behavior is clear, the tribunals tend to avoid the subject and rule on legal grounds rather than confronting the factual allegations as in *Malicorp v. Egypt* (2011).

Overall, the results on the factual determinations tend to show that the tribunals in these cases were much more likely to disbelieve the respondent states' stories than the claimants. They rule in the respondent states' favor when the investor's behavior falls below a very low threshold, as in *Malicorp v. Egypt* (2011) and *Bay View Group v. Rwanda* (2022).

11
Duration of the Proceedings

One of the most frequently raised concerns about ISDS is the length of time that the proceedings take. This chapter surveys the duration of the proceedings of the cases under study to evaluate if the concerns of inordinate delay are accurate in light of the nature of the disputes and the procedural steps that need to be followed to ensure due process.

The Early Decades

To start with the foundation cases, *BP v. Libya* commenced on December 11, 1971, and concluded with the issuance of the final award on the merits on October 10, 1973.[1] *Texaco v. Libya* commenced on September 2, 1973, and concluded on January 19, 1977, with the issuance of the final award.[2] *LIAMCO v. Libya* was commenced on July 2, 1974[3] and concluded on April 12, 1977, with the issuance of the final award.[4] These foundational cases took between two and four years. Although the one that took four years seems on the longer side of the spectrum, these cases seem to have set the standard for the cases that followed with most cases falling within this range. It is important to note from the outset that the nature of the claims have inherent attributes that make a quick resolution difficult because, with the exception of purely umbrella clause claims, they often require the resolution of the existence of a breach of some domestic type and the evaluation of those under international law.

S.A.R.L v. the Republic of Congo commenced on December 15, 1977,[5] and concluded with a final award on August 8, 1980.[6] With two and a half years, it falls right in the middle of the duration spectrum set by the foundational cases.

In *Klockner v. Cameroon*, there were two legal proceedings. The first case was initially filed on April 14, 1981, and the final award was rendered on October 21, 1983.[7] The application for annulment was lodged with ICSID on February 10, 1984,[8] and the

[1] Texaco Overseas Petroleum Co. and California Asiatic Oil Co. v. Libya, Preliminary Award (Nov. 27, 1975), 53 ILR 389; Award on the Merits (Jan. 19, 1977), 17 ILM 1 (1978), at caption.

[2] Texaco Overseas Petroleum Company and California Asiatic Oil Company v. Libya, Preliminary Award (Nov. 27, 1975), 53 ILR 389; Award on the Merits (Jan. 19, 1977), 17 ILM 1 (1978), at caption.

[3] *See id.* at 1.

[4] *See id.* at caption, 208.

[5] S.A.R.L. Benvenuti & Bonfant v. People's Republic of Congo, ICSID Case No. ARB/77/2 (1980), 1 ICSID Rep. 330 (1993), at 1.2.

[6] *Id.* at caption.

[7] Klockner Industrie-Anlagen GmbH and others v. United Republic of Cameroon and Société Camerounaise des Engrais, ICSID Case No. ARB/81/2 (1983), at 1.

[8] *Id.* at 1.

Africa's International Investment Law Regimes. Won L. Kidane, Oxford University Press. © Oxford University Press 2023.
DOI: 10.1093/oso/9780197745571.003.0011

final annulment decision was rendered on May 3, 1985.[9] This was still largely within the four-year range, even with the second annulment proceedings.

In the *Letco v. Liberia* case, the request for arbitration was filed on June 16, 1983,[10] and the final award was rendered on March 31, 1986. This is a period of about three years and as such generally falls within the range.

In *MINE v. Guinea*, although the actual ICSID arbitration commenced on May 7, 1984,[11] and concluded on January 6, 1988.[12] MINE actually initiated conciliation 10 years prior to the ICSID arbitration on March 11, 1974,[13] followed by domestic court litigation in the United States in June 1978,[14] four-year arbitration between February 5, 1979, and April 14, 1980.[15] Although because of the multitude of proceedings and many procedural complications the length of time for the overall resolution of the *MINE v. Guinea* dispute has taken an exceptionally long period of time, the actual ICSID proceeding took a little longer than the outer limit of the four year range.

The Duration of the Africa's ICSID Cases of the 2000s

The first of the cases in this period is *Wena v. Egypt*. The request for arbitration in this case was filed with ICSID on July 10, 1998,[16] and the final award was issued on December 8, 2000.[17] With close to two and a half years of proceedings, this case was also completed within the normal range.

The duration of the next Egyptian case within the same decade, *Middle East Cement v. Egypt* (2002), is also within the same four-year general range. The case was initiated on November 19, 1999,[18] and concluded with the issuance of the final award on April 12, 2002.[19]

Semos v. Mali (2003) was initiated on May 24, 2001,[20] and concluded with the rendition of the final award on February 25, 2003.[21] With less than two years of proceedings, *Semos* qualifies as one of the shortest durations. The reason for that appears to be that the contentions were more of the interpretation of law and contract that did not depend on the development of factual records. The fact that the state imposed and collected mineral export duties of some type was not disputed. The dispute pertained

9 *Id.* at 180.
10 Liberian Eastern Timber Corporation v. Republic of Liberia, ICSID Cases No. ARB/83/2, Award (Mar. 31, 1986), at 1.
11 Maritime International Nominees Establishment v. Republic of Guinea, ICSID Case No. ARB/84/4, Award (Jan. 6, 1988), 35.
12 *See id.* at caption.
13 *Id.* at 27.
14 *Id.* at 31.
15 *Id.* at 32.
16 Wena Hotels Limited v. Arab Republic of Egypt, ICSID Case No. ARB/98/4, Award (Dec. 8, 2000), 1.
17 *See id.* at caption.
18 Middle East Cement Shipping and Handling Co. S.A. v. Arab Republic of Egypt, ICSID Case No. ARB/99/6, Award (Apr. 12, 2002), at 4.
19 *See id.* at caption.
20 Société D'exploitation Des Mines D'or De Sadiola S.A. (Semos) v. Republic of Mali, ICSID Case No. ARB/01/5, Award (Feb. 25, 2003), at 1.
21 *Id.* at caption.

to whether there was legal basis for the taxes under the relevant domestic tax laws and contracts. The Tribunal could have considered these domestic law issues as questions of Malian domestic law and seek to prove them through expert opinion, which would have taken more time and perhaps improved accuracy, but the Tribunal seemed comfortable enough to apply Malian law without Malian law experts and shortened the proceedings to less than two years although it recognized the difficulty of the legal issues in its award of costs.[22]

CDC v. Seychelles (2003) had one of the shortest durations. The request for arbitration was filed on August 22, 2002,[23] and the award was rendered on December 17, 2003.[24] With less than a year and a half, it holds the record for being the shortest duration.

Patrick Mitchell v. DRC (2004) took longer than average even excluding the annulment proceeding. The initial request for arbitration was filed with ICSID on October 6, 1999,[25] but the final award was not rendered until February 9, 2004,[26] which is a period of more than four years. This is not explained by the passing of the Claimant's first arbitrator because the replacement took less than two weeks.[27] This case was decided on the pleadings and evidence thereof without oral hearing. There is no one obvious delaying event, but it seems like the Tribunal continued to accept small scale exchanges of letters and materials beyond the major memorials.[28]

On June 7, 2004, about five months after the rendition of the final award, the DRC sought a stay of enforcement under Article 52(5) of the ICSID Convention and annulment under Article 52(1) of the Convention.[29] The Ad Hoc Committee was expeditiously set up on August 24, 2004,[30] and rendered its final decision on the application more than two years later on November 1, 2006.[31] This appears to be because the case was suspended for about a year between September 2005 and September 2006 as a result of DRC's failure to pay the tribunal's fees.[32] Because the delay was caused toward the end of the process, it appears that the Tribunal might have withheld the award until payment was effected as it was entitled to. It turned out that it was certainly

[22] *See id.* at dispositif.

[23] CDC Group Plc v. Republic of The Seychelles, ICSID Case No. ARB/02/14 (Dec. 17, 2003), at 11.

[24] *See id.* at caption.

[25] Patrick Mitchell v. DRC Award (Feb. 9, 2004); Annulment (Nov. 1, 2006), at 1.

[26] *Id.* at caption.

[27] *See id.* at 14 ("14. On January 29, 2002, all concerned learned with deep regret that Mr. Willard Z. Estey, the arbitrator appointed by Claimant, had passed away on January 25, 2002. In accordance with Arbitration Rule 10(2), the proceeding was suspended until the vacancy on the Tribunal was filled. On February 13, 2002, the Tribunal was reconstituted and the proceedings were resumed when Mr. Marc Lalonde, a national of Canada, accepted his appointment as an arbitrator designated by Claimant pursuant to Arbitration Rule 11(1)").

[28] *See, e.g., id.* at 19.

[29] Patrick Mitchell v. DRC Award (Feb. 9, 2004); Annulment (Nov. 1, 2006), at 4.

[30] *Id.* at 6.

[31] *Id.* at caption.

[32] *Id.* at 13 ("Due to the non-payment by the DRC of the amounts requested by the Centre in accordance with Regulation 14(3) of the Administrative and Financial Regulations, the proceeding was suspended on September 21, 2005 by virtue of the above Regulation. The requested payment was finally made by the DRC and the proceeding was resumed on September 19, 2006. As the presentation of the case by the parties had been already completed, the proceeding was declared closed on September 26, 2006 in accordance with Rule 38 of the Arbitration Rules, applied in accordance with Rule 53 of the Rules").

cheaper for the DRC to pay and get the award released, but it may not have been certain that the annulment decision went its way. In the meantime, it appears that it continued to benefit from a stay of enforcement during the suspension of the annulment proceedings. This, of course, raises an interesting question of what happens to a stay order if the party that brought the annulment application gets a stay of enforcement and fails to pay causing an indefinite hold on enforcement, an issue that was avoided in this case.

World Duty Free v. Kenya (2006) commenced on June 16, 2000,[33] and ended on October 4, 2006.[34] With nearly six years of process, it stands as one of the most delayed ICSID cases. There was not any particular procedural infirmity or complexity that caused the delay. If anything, it is probably a function of the oversupply of legal skills and procedural and doctrinal erudition.

The corporate and individual Claimants in *Champion Trading v. Egypt* (2006) commenced the ICSID arbitration on May 29, 2002,[35] and the Tribunal rendered its final award on the merits on October 27, 2006.[36] That is a period of four and a half years, a little longer than the four-year window.

Helnan v. Egypt commenced on March 8, 2005,[37] and concluded on July 3, 2008.[38] Although this proceeding was bifurcated into the jurisdictional and the merits phases, it was completed within the average three-year period. The record was closed on May 16, 2008, and the award on the merits was issued on July 3, 2008, although the hearing was conducted about nine months earlier in October 2007.[39]

Biwater v. Tanzania (2008) commenced on August 5, 2005, and ended with the rendition of the final award on July 24, 2008.[40] With almost exactly three years of duration, it qualifies as a typical case in terms of the time taken.

The *Jan de Nul N.V. and Dredging International N.V v. Egypt* (2008) case commenced on December 23, 2003,[41] and ended with a final award on November 6, 2008,[42] almost exactly five years later, mainly because there was a jurisdictional phase in between. The wisdom of the bifurcation is questionable in this case not only because it almost doubled the amount of time and perhaps the costs, but also because the Parties brought back some of the jurisdictional issues in the merits phase so much so that the Tribunal had to address jurisdiction again in its final award on the merits.

33 World Duty Free Company Limited v. Republic of Kenya, ICSID Case No. ARB/00/7, Award (Oct. 4, 2006), at 4.

34 *Id.* at caption.

35 Champion Trading Company Ameritrade International, Inc. v. Arab Republic of Egypt, ICSID Case No. ARB/02/9, Award (Oct. 27, 2006), at 1.

36 *See id.* at caption.

37 Helnan International Hotels A/S V. The Arab Republic of Egypt, ICSID Case No. ARB/05/19, Award (July 3, 2008), at 9.

38 *Id.* at caption.

39 *Id.* at 45, 49.

40 *See* Biwater Gauff (Tanzania) Ltd. v. United Republic of Tanzania, ICSID Case No. ARB/05/22, Final Award (July 24, 2008), at 18, caption.

41 Jan de Nul N.V. Dredging International N.V. v. Arab Republic of Egypt, ICSID Case No. ARB/04/13, Award (Nov. 6, 2008), at 8.

42 *Id.* at caption.

Bernardus v. Zimbabwe (2009) commenced on June 4, 2003,[43] and concluded on April 22, 2009, with the rendition of the final award.[44] Taking almost six years, its lifespan was almost double the average time. As indicated above, almost half of that time was taken to constitute the Tribunal.

Waguih Elie v. Egypt (2009) commenced on May 26, 2005,[45] and the Tribunal issued its final award on June 1, 2009.[46] The proceedings were bifurcated between jurisdiction and merits. Although the Tribunal had rejected Egypt's request for the bifurcation of the merits phase to deal with the quasi-jurisdictional estoppel argument, which, if accepted, could have destroyed jurisdiction, the Tribunal still considered it separately during the merits phase.[47] With the complexity of the matter and the various jurisdictional objections, its more than average duration of about four years appears within a reasonable range. As a matter of fact, the actual controversy began a decade earlier in 1995 before the Egyptian domestic court system.[48]

Modern Post-2010 Cases

The first of the 2010s case, *Gustav v. Ghana* (2010), commenced with the filing of the Request for Arbitration on September 24, 2007,[49] and ended with the rendition of the award on June 18, 2010.[50] With less than three years of duration, it falls squarely within the normal range.

The *Malicorp v. Egypt* (2011) case commenced on October 21, 2008,[51] and concluded with the issuance of the final award on February 7, 2011.[52] Taking approximately two and a half years, its duration is below average.

In *Bernard von Pezold v. Zimbabwe* (2015), the first of the two cases, the von Pezold Claimants, was filed on June 11, 2010, and the second case of the Border Claimants was filed on December 3, 2010.[53] The Tribunal issued its final award for both on July 28, 2015.[54] For the volume and complexity of the case this is not an exceptionally long duration, taking about five years since the first filing, although it is significantly higher than the average duration.

Standard Chartered Bank v. Tanzania Electric Supply Company Limited (TANESCO) (2016) has a rather complex genesis dating back to the first ICSID case initiated in

[43] Bernardus Henricus Funnekotter and Others v. Republic of Zimbabwe, ICSID Case No. ARB/05/6, Award (Apr. 22, 2009), at 1.
[44] *Id.* at caption.
[45] Waguih Elie George Slag and Clorinda Vecchi v. The Arab Republic of Egypt, ICSID Case No. ARB/05/15, Award (June 1, 2009), at 88.
[46] *Id.* at caption.
[47] *Id.* at 113–16.
[48] *See id.* at 2.
[49] Gustav F W Hamester GmbH & Co KG v. Republic of Ghana Respondent, ICSID Case No. ARB/07/24, Award (June 18, 2010), at 7–9.
[50] *Id.* at last caption and signature page.
[51] *See* Malicorp Limited v. The Arab Republic of Egypt, ICSID Case No. ARB/08/18, Award (Feb. 7, 2011), at 74.
[52] *See id.* at caption.
[53] Bernard v. von Pezold v. Zimbabwe, ICSID Case No. ARB/05/6, Award (Apr. 22, 2009), at 9–10.
[54] *Id.* at caption.

1998 and a jurisdictional and liabilities phase that preceded the case under consideration here which is the second phase that grew out of the jurisdictional decision of February 12, 2014, and ended with a final award issued on September 12, 2016.[55] The case was first filed on October 1, 2010.[56] The same Tribunal bifurcated the proceeding. The Decision on jurisdiction and liability was rendered on February 12, 2014.[57] The total duration of the proceedings including both phases is close to six years, not counting the previous ICSID proceeding dating back to 1998.[58]

Cortec v. Kenya is modern in all senses. It commenced on June 18, 2015,[59] and concluded with a final award on October 22, 2018.[60] With less than three years of proceedings, it took less time than the average. The structure of the award itself tells a story of efficacy and care.

CMC v. Mozambique (2019) was filed on May 10, 2017,[61] and concluded with an award on the merits on October 24, 2019.[62] Although this case ran a full course, it took less than half the time that the next Mozambique case that was dismissed on jurisdictional grounds took.

Oded Besserglik v. Mozambique commenced on March 24, 2014,[63] and concluded with a total dismissal on jurisdictional grounds on October 28, 2019.[64] Although it was a jurisdictional dismissal, it involved intense factual disputes relating to the ratification status of the applicable South Africa–Mozambique BIT, and as such took as much time as those cases that ran the full course did.[65] Incidentally, the above two Mozambique cases came down within a few days of each other and both handed the Respondent state total victory.

Strabag SE v. Libya (2020) commenced on June 24, 2015, with the Claimant's filing of an application for access to the ICSID Additional Facilities,[66] and concluded with the issuance of the final award on June 29, 2020.[67] That is a total of exactly five years. Although it took more time than most cases, there is no noticeable unnecessary delay at any point during the five years.[68] The numerosity of the written submissions including Tribunal sought clarifications appear to be a function of the factual complexity of the conflict and revolution-related claims.

[55] *See* Standard Chartered Bank (Hong Kong) Ltd. v. Tanzania Electric Supply Company Ltd. (Tanesco), ICSID Case No. ARB/10/20, Award (Sep. 12, 2016), at 5, caption.

[56] *See id.* at 5.

[57] *See id.* at caption.

[58] *See id.* at 21 ("The Tribunal has been charged with the daunting task of settling a dispute that traces back to 1998 and which has already generated two ICSID arbitration proceedings and an interpretation proceeding as well as an LCIA arbitration and multiple domestic proceedings in Tanzania and Malaysia").

[59] *See* Cortec Mining Kenya Limited, Cortec (Pty) Limited And Stirling Capital Limited v. Republic Of Kenya, ICSID Case No. ARB/15/29, Award (Oct. 22, 2018), at 16 (error in the published version).

[60] *Id.* at caption.

[61] CMC Muratori Cementisti CMC Di Ravenna SOC. Coop. & Others v. Republic of Mozambique, ICSID Case No. ARB/17/23 (Oct. 24, 2019), at 20.

[62] *Id.* at caption.

[63] Oded Besserglik v. Republic of Mozambique, ICSID Case No. ARB(AF)/14/2, Award (Oct. 28, 2019), at 6.

[64] *Id.* at caption.

[65] *See id.* at 6–112.

[66] Strabag Se v. Libya, ICSID Case No. ARB(AF)/15/1, Award (June 29, 2020), at 9.

[67] *Id.* at caption.

[68] *See id.* at 9–55 (listing all the procedural activities in chronological order).

Interocean Oil v. Nigeria (2020) commenced on July 30, 2013,[69] and concluded with the issuance of the final award on October 6, 2020.[70] This case took more than seven years. The jurisdictional phase took an inordinate amount of time. It was also characterized by many irregular submissions. The result on the merits would have been clear from the very beginning, but the Tribunal chose to exhaust the jurisdictional objections only to find the merits unsustainable because of lack of attribution although it went through the whole process of adjudicating complex facts. That clearly contributed to the amount of time it took. This was one of those cases that did not fit the forum in every aspect and bordered wastefulness. This might be an excellent example of where a more robust institutional screening could have helped.

Bay View Group v. Rwanda (2022) was filed on May 18, 2018,[71] and concluded on March 30, 2022.[72] Although this case fell in the middle of the pandemic, the tribunal conducted its business as economically as possible, conducted the evidentiary hearings virtually and concluded in less than four years.

Conclusion

Although there are examples of cases that have taken an inordinate amount of time and suggest wastefulness such as *Interocean*, there are few, if any, glaring examples of delays that are not justified by the complexities and due process necessities of the case. Most of the cases were completed within the four-year range. This was particularly true in the earlier period. There are more recent cases that took more than four years than older ones. As indicated above, however, the delays are mostly explicable and often justifiable.

Although a more concerted effort of shortening the time could potentially avoid excesses and expediate the rendition of justice, a careful look at each step in the process and its function shows that there is often little room for improvement in many of these cases. The typical countermemorial in a typical ISDS case responds to grave allegations of violations of treaty and customary law by acts of agents whose conducts are allegedly attributable to the state. Because the state is the Respondent, it needs to investigate facts from its agents and instrumentalities, interview witnesses, collect documentary evidence, analyze domestic and international rules, seek representation, find expert witnesses, organize the information, and respond in writing often running in the hundreds of pages accompanied by hundreds, if not thousands, of exhibits and legal authorities. This is not something that could easily be accomplished within a couple of months. This is just one step in the process. Due process requires that each party gets the same amount of time. The exchange of written pleadings itself takes at least two years in the typical case. With the evidentiary hearing and posthearing

[69] Interocean Oil Development Company and Interocean Oil Exploration Company v. Federal Republic of Nigeria, ICSID Case No. ARB/13/20, Award (Oct. 6, 2020), at 46.

[70] *Id.* at caption.

[71] *See* Bay View Group LLC and The Spalena Company LLC v. Republic of Rwanda, ICSID Case No. ARB/18/21, Award (Mar. 30, 2022), at 6.

[72] *See id.* at caption.

submissions and time for the tribunal's deliberations, three to four years is a reasonable and justifiable range depending on the complexity of the matter.

Most of the cases reviewed have been completed within this range. The few that were not completed within this range seem to have valid reasons for delay relating to the specific circumstances of the case, although unnecessary bifurcation seems to have contributed to delay in more than a couple of cases.

Overall, the frequently raised complaint about the duration of ISDS cases seems to be more of a myth than a reality. For context and at the risk of digression, it is not difficult to conclude on the basis of the above review and anecdotal observation of domestic court processes in many advanced jurisdictions that ISDS still takes less time than cases of comparable complexity in domestic court proceedings.

PART III
THE DEVELOPMENT OF SUBSTANTIVE PRINCIPLES, NORMS, AND RULES

Beginning with the foundation *Libyan Oil* cases, the substantive principles, norms, and rules of international investment law developed with considerable African involvement. This part methodically documents the development and use of the most important substantive principles of expropriation (Chapters 12 and 13); the umbrella clause (Chapter 14); fair and equitable treatment, full security and protection, and non-discrimination (Chapter 15 and 16); choice of law (Chapter 17); damages (Chapter 18); and the allocation of costs and interests (Chapter 19).

12
Expropriation

Expropriation in international investment law is generally the most frequently invoked, intensely debated, and best understood principle. Some of the most frequently cited expropriation rules involve Africa treaties and cases. This section conducts a deeper inquiry into the evolution of the African states' position on expropriation in light not only, of investment treaty cases, but also in reference to the *Libyan Oil* cases, as they are considered the foundation cases of the modern law of expropriation in international arbitration. Tracing the evolution, this chapter seeks to underscore the communality of positions of the African states on this issue and how the jurisprudence influenced contemporary legal doctrine and textual articulation in modern treaties.

Expropriation in the Early African Cases (1970–2000)

The earliest ICSID expropriation case in the subset of cases under study applied a combination of national constitutional protection against expropriation and principles of international law without comprehensive justification. This seems partly because the parties had agreed to decisions *ex aequo et bono.* This was the 1980 case of *S.A.R.L. Benvenuti & Bonfant v. People's Republic of the Congo.*[1] The Tribunal's entire expropriation discussion is limited to a few paragraphs of the Award,[2] and it did not take much for it to find expropriation based on limited uncontested

[1] S.A.R.L. Benvenuti & Bonfant v. People's Republic of Congo, ICSID Case No. ARB/77/2 (1980), 1 ICSID Rep. 330 (1993).

[2] *Id.* at 4.56–6.65:

> 4.56. B&B has stated that the Government, by means of the administrative memorandum mentioned in para. 2.22 and the use of the military occupation of the property and the premises of PLASCO mentioned in para. 2.23. dispossessed it of its share in PLASCO and appropriated it to itself.
>
> 4.57. The Government denies, for its part, in the Memorial in Defence, that it carried out any confiscation or nationalization and maintains that the Italian party is free at any time, to return and recover its share (pp. 17–20).
>
> 4.58. The Tribunal considers that it is difficult to accept this line of reasoning. First of all. a whole series of facts are contrary to the Government's case. In its Administrative Memorandum (Annexe 33-M) the Government treats PLASCO as a State company.
>
> 4.59. Secondly, by instituting criminal proceedings against Mr Bonfant, the latter was induced to follow the advice of the Italian diplomatic representative and to leave the Congo, without the Tribunal having been presented with any evidence enabling it to establish whether those criminal proceedings were well-founded. The fact that the Government did not react to B&B's subsequent request for the resumption of negotiations must also be noted.
>
> … 4.62. The Tribunal therefore considers that the Government did, in fact, appropriate B&B's share in PLASCO and owes it damages. […]
>
> … 6.63. Furthermore, the Government recognized in the Memorial in Defence: the obligation not to carry out any confiscation, whether overt or covert, and certainly not to nationalize the share of the Italian investor, without just compensation (p.5).

Africa's International Investment Law Regimes. Won L. Kidane, Oxford University Press. © Oxford University Press 2023.
DOI: 10.1093/oso/9780197745571.003.0012

facts and many inferences that the Tribunal drew from contested facts. Some of the inferences are interesting. For example, it is uncontested that the investor and the state embarked on a joint enterprise shareholding arrangement in which the government held the majority. It is also clear that the enterprise required a preferential government treatment to be profitable. It also appears from the facts that the government was either not willing or able to provide such preference. That is where the uncontested facts end. Because the government did not properly participate, let alone be properly represented, it offered limited information to the tribunal. As such, the Tribunal adopted many of the Claimant's version of the facts as established.[3]

Although the Claimant did not claim that there was a formal expropriation, the Tribunal adopted the Claimant's position that the series of economic measures rose to the level of expropriation. One of the key disputes was whether Mr. Bonfant's departure and nonreturn was justified. The government had a slightly different take on what was going on. It said that Mr. Bonfant and others misused their privilege as investors including using its duty-free privileges to import commodities and selling them to third parties, overpricing, and failing to pay taxes (for which the government counterclaimed).[4] At least two serious allegations against the Claimant in this regard were rejected for lack of proof.[5]

The government was not even able to prove that there was a duty-free privilege, which appears to be a common incentive, let alone fraudulent acts. Nothing in the fact pattern suggests that such allegations are made up out of nothing, but the government was not able to prove it, a very common problem when there is no or half-hearted participation.

The government also disputed the fact that Mr. Bonfant was at any risk and that the investor could have returned and reclaimed its share of the company or even resumed their work.[6] The sequence of events as described by the Tribunal do not necessarily suggest that there was harsh treatment. The only evidence of possible danger was

> 6.64. This principle of compensation in case of nationalization is in accordance with the Congolese Constitution and constitutes one of the generally recognized principles of international law as well as of equity.
>
> 6.65 By reason of the above, the Government must therefore be ordered to pay B&B damages, the quantum of which will be determined *ex aequo et bono* by the Tribunal in the following paragraphs.

[3] *See id.* at 2.1–2.24.

[4] *See id.* at 3.5.

[5] *Id.* at 4.106–4.107.

> 4.106 The Tribunal recalls in this respect that, as mentioned above, it has not been established that PLASCO obtained privileged tax status. Furthermore, it has not been conclusively proven that the company in fact enjoyed preferential customs rights.
>
> 4.107 None of the documents lodged with the Tribunal established that Mr. Bonfant perpetrated fraudulent acts against the Customs Division. In these circumstances, the Tribunal must dismiss the Government's claim under this head, without it being necessary to examine the question of whether the plaintiff should be considered as responsible for possibly fraudulent acts perpetrated by Mr. Bonfant.

[6] *See id.* at 4.57.

information received by Mr. Bonfant from the Italian Embassy.[7] There were no previous incidents. The Tribunal obviously believed the Claimant's version of the story, which is not surprising because the government did not appear to have presented its version of events properly. Overall, the tribunal's exposition of the expropriation claim was fact intensive and not guided by any jurisprudence.

Interestingly, however, by 1980, when this case was under consideration, the trilogy of the foundation *Libyan Oil* cases had already been decided and at least two of the decisions had already been published.[8] The *S.A.R.L.* case does not mention the *Libyan Oil* arbitration cases although their jurisprudence was a matter of public record. It appears that at that time ICSID tribunals were rather uncertain as to what jurisprudence played what role in the newly conceived legal framework of investor–state dispute settlement. Notwithstanding the initial confusion about the role of outside jurisprudence to ICSID cases in the early days, any appraisal of the international investment law of expropriation must begin with these foundation cases.

The most recent of the three Libyan Oil Arbitration cases was *Libyan American Oil Co. v. The Government of the Libyan Arab Republic*.[9] By the time this case was filed against it in July 1974,[10] Libya had been an independent state for about 25 years, having been recognized by the United Nations in January 1949;[11] however, the oil concessions were granted under the postcolonial Petroleum Law of 1955, which seems to have begun the gradual process of increasing the state's autonomy over its natural resources. The Petroleum Law of 1955, as amended several times before the case was filed in July 1974, contained the two most important provisions that made the arbitral case itself possible: an international arbitration clause and an expropriation clause.

The relevant dispute settlement clause in its modified form and as adopted by the Tribunal states:

> (1) If at any time during or after the currency of this contract any difference or dispute shall arise between the Government and the Company concerning the interpretation or performance of the provisions of this contract, or its annexes, or in connection with the rights and liabilities of either of the contracting parties hereunder, and if the parties should fail to settle such difference or dispute by agreement, the same shall, failing any agreement to settle it in any other way, be referred to two Arbitrators, one

[7] *See id.* at 2.23 ("Considering that their personal safety was no longer guaranteed and on the advice of Mr Corradello, Charge d'Affaires at the Italian Embassy in Brazzaville, according to whom the arrest of Mr Bonfant was imminent, the latter and most of the Italian personnel of PLASCO hastily left the Congo in February 1976 (Annexe 4 to the declarations of the representatives of B&B at the hearing in Geneva). The registered office of PLASCO was subsequently occupied by the Army. His hasty departure from the Congo prevented Mr Bonfant from taking with him all the documents of PLASCO and EDICO relating to this case").

[8] These cases and their publication dates are: (1) British Petroleum Exploration Co. (Libya) v. Libyan Arab Republic, 53 Int'l L. Rep. 297 (1973), (2) Texaco Overseas Petroleum Co. and California Asiatic Oil Co. v. Libya, Preliminary Award (Nov. 27, 1975), 53 ILR 389; Award on the Merits (Jan. 19, 1977), 17 ILM 1 (1978), (3) Libyan American Oil Co. (LIAMCO) v. Libyan Arab Republic, 62 Int'l L. Rep. 140; 20 ILM 1 (1981) (1977).

[9] Libyan American Oil Co. (LIAMCO) v. Libyan Arab Republic, 62 Int'l L. Rep. 140; 20 ILM 1 (1981) (1977).

[10] *See id.* at 1.

[11] *See id.* at 13.

> of whom shall be appointed by each party, and an Umpire who shall be appointed by the Arbitrators immediately after their appointment.[12]

The application of this provision led to the appointment of a sole arbitrator, Dr. Sobhi Mahmassani of Lebanon,[13] because the Respondent State, Libya, refused to participate.[14] Dr. Sobhi Mahmassani saw the case through completion and issued the final award on the merits on April 12, 1977.[15]

The key substantive question pertained to the meaning of expropriation under Libyan and international law. This case is notable for its contribution to such inquiry. Dr. Mahamassani analyzed a combination of the Concession Agreement and the applicable Petroleum Law in light of international law. The source of the problem was a series of Nationalization Decrees by the Libyan Administrative Council led by Colonel Muammar el Qadhafi, which overtook government power from Kind Indriss I, the post-independence monarch.[16] These Decrees gradually transferred the Concessioner's interests to the government beginning with a demand to transfer 51% and culminating in the total takeover.[17] The final act is described by the Tribunal as follows:

> By Decree effective February 11, 1974, the Revolutionary Command Council of Libya issued Law No. 10 of 1974, nationalizing LIAMCO's remaining concession interests. Article 1 provides as follows:
>
> "The ownership of all property, rights, assets, portions, shares, activities and interests in any form, owned by Libyan American Oil Company in connection with petroleum Concession Deeds Nos. 16, 17 and 20 shall be nationalized and transferred to the State."[18]

The Nationalization Law did, however, contain a provision on compensation in Article 2, which reads:

> The State shall compensate people concerned for the property, rights and assets that have reverted to it under Article 1. Such compensation shall be assessed by a committee or committees which shall be formed by a decision from the Minister of Petroleum, in the following manner:

[12] *Id.* at 4.

[13] *Id.* at 3.

[14] *Id.* at ¶12 ("As the Respondent did not appear, the Arbitral Tribunal had to admit the best evidence available and to rely chiefly on the basic facts as supported by copies of the various official documents and by conclusive technical reports or expert testimony presented by the Claimant").

[15] *See id.* at caption.

[16] *See id.* at 53 ("On September 1, 1969, a Revolutionary Command Council, headed by Colonel Muammar el Qadhafi, overthrew the Government of King Idriss, and announced the formation of the Libyan Arab Republic").

[17] *See id.* at ¶53. *See also id.* at 64 ("The relevant articles for said nationalization were the following: "Article 1 The ownership of 51 % of all property, rights, assets, portions, shares, activities and interests in any form . . . as regards petroleum concession deeds . . . shall be nationalized and transferred to the State").

[18] *Id.* at 69.

(a) One of the Judges of the Courts of Appeal, being Chairman, to be nominated by the Minister of Justice,
(b) A representative of the National Oil Corporation, being a member, to be nominated by the Minister of Petroleum
(c) A representative of the Ministry of Treasury being a member, to be nominated by the Minister of Treasury.

In carrying out its task, the committee may seek assistance of any employee or others whose assistance it considers necessary.[19]

As determined by the Tribunal, the Libyan government proceeded to liquidate all interests of LIAMCO, but offered no compensation.[20] The Tribunal noted with approval the US government's diplomatic note expressing its understanding of the law of expropriation articulated as "under the principles of international law, measures taken by a State against the interests of foreign nationals, which are motivated not by reason of public utility, but of political retaliation against the State of which those nationals are citizens, are invalid and are not entitled to recognition by other States."[21] It further noted the position of the US government as:

> Under international law, the United States has a right to expect:
> - That any taking of American private property will be nondiscriminatory;
> - That it will be for a public purpose; and
> - That its citizens will receive prompt, adequate and effective compensation from the expropriating country.
>
> ... The State Department wishes to place on record its view that foreign investors are entitled to the fair market value of their interests. Acceptance by U.S. nationals of less than fair market value does not constitute acceptance of any other standard by the United States Government.[22]

The Tribunal continues its analysis by approvingly quoting the State Department's articulation of what is known as the Hull Rule, which requires prompt, adequate, and effective compensation with the fair market value as the measure of damages, although such measure is not typically considered part of the Hull Rule.[23]

[19] *Id.* at 67–72.
[20] *Id.* at 78–80.
[21] *Id.* at 83 (quoting diplomatic note from the State Department to the Government of Libya).
[22] *Id.* at 84 (quoting US State Dep't Press Release of Dec. 30, 1975, No. 630 on Foreign Investment and Nationalization).
[23] The Rule is articulated by US Secretary of State Cordell Hull in his famous letter to the Mexican Foreign Minister of the time. The essential part of it reads: "The taking of property without compensation is not expropriation. It is confiscation ... We cannot question the right of a foreign government to treat its own nationals in this fashion if it so desires. This is a matter of domestic concern. But we cannot admit that a foreign government may take the property of American nationals in disregard of the rule of compensation under international law. Nor can we admit that any government unilaterally and through its municipal legislation can, as in this instant case, nullify this universally accepted principle of international law, based as it is on reason, equity and justice ... The right of prompt and just compensation for expropriated property is a part of this [international legal] structure." Letter from Cordell Hull, US Secretary of State, to Francisco Castillo Nájera, Mex. Ambassador to the US (July 21, 1938), *as reprinted in* ANDREAS F. LOWENFELD, INTERNATIONAL ECONOMIC LAW 536–37 (2nd ed. 2008), at 476.

The Agreement as amended contained a choice of law clause which reads as:

> This Concession shall be governed by and interpreted in accordance with the principles of law of Libya common to the principles of international law, and in the absence of such common principles then by and in accordance with the general principles of law as may have been applied by international tribunals.[24]

In the Tribunal's interpretation, "the proper law governing LIAMCO's Concession Agreements, as set forth in the amended version of said Clause 28, para.7, is in the first place the law of Libya when consistent with international law, and subsidiarily the general principles of law."[25] In addition, the Tribunal sought guidance from the Libyan Civil Code of 1953, which states in relevant part: "(2) If there is no legal text to be applied the judge will adjudicate in accordance with the principles of Islamic law, failing which in accordance with custom, and failing that in accordance with natural law and the rules of equity."[26]

The two fundamental questions on the merits of the claims were "unlawful taking of property by unlawful nationalization, and breach of contract."[27] The Tribunal then considered the lawfulness of the nationalization measure and the taking of proprietary interest as well as the breach of contract and consequent damages and compensation.[28]

Having gone through the classic conception of the private ownership of property[29] and the evolution of the conception through the emergence of the right to nationalization, including in states that adopted the communist conception of the right to private property[30] and newly decolonized states,[31] and seeking support from writings

[24] LIAMCO v. Libya, 62 Int'l L. Rep. 140; 20 ILM 1 (1981) (1977), at 123.

[25] *Id.* at 132.

[26] *Id.* at 136.

[27] *Id.* at 173.

[28] *Id.* at 174.

[29] *See id.* at 178 ("One of the fundamental rights universally recognized is the right of private ownership or property (Dominium). The Classical concept of this right defines it as the right to the use, exploitation and disposal (usus, fructus, abusus) of the object owned. Although this classical definition has been tempered and limited sometimes by reason of public interest, nonetheless the inviolability of the right of property has remained throughout history as a sacred proposition confirmed and reaffirmed by a succession of constitutional and international declarations and charters. The most famous instances of such basic documents are:the English Magna Charta of 1215, the French Declaration des droits de l'homme et du citoyen" of 1789 which was recently incorporated in the Preamble to the French constitution of 1958, the Fifth amendment to the American constitution of 1789, the two Hague Conventions of 1890 and 1907, the Declarations of the International Law Association of Vienna in 1926 and of Oxford in 1932, and last but not least the United Nations Bill of Human Rights of 1948, the Pan-American Bill of the same name and date, and the Protocol of 1952 annexed to the Convention of Rome on Human Rights of 1950").

[30] *See id.* at 187 ("From the outset of this century and especially after World War I, new political and economic trends have tempered the absolute character of the aforementioned classical meaning of property [188] Gradually, property came to be viewed as having a dominant 'social function or role,' and has as such to be subservient to the public interest of the Community represented by the State. The old sacred character of property has become subject to the influence of social objectives. Its protection has thus been attenuated in domestic as well as in international law").

[31] *See id.* at 198–99 ("Moreover, during that period and afterward, many new nations, in particular those forming the so-called Third World, have emerged and attained their independence. Motivated by a

of publicists and United Nations Resolutions, the Tribunal concluded that "a State possesses as an attribute of its sovereignty and supreme power the right to nationalize all things belonging to any person within its jurisdiction."[32] The Tribunal, however, noted that "it is clear and undisputed that non-discrimination is a requisite for the validity of a lawful nationalization. This is a rule well established in international legal theory and practice. Therefore, a purely discriminatory nationalization is illegal and wrongful."[33]

More importantly, the Tribunal noted that "the said right is always subject to the respect for contractual agreements and to the obligation of compensation."[34] Remarkably, the Tribunal then observed that *"nationalization of concession rights, if not discriminatory and not accompanied by a wrongful act or conduct, is not unlawful as such, and constitutes not a tort but a source of liability to compensate the concessionaire for said premature termination of the concession agreements."*[35]

Rejecting the request for restitution on a number of grounds,[36] the Tribunal held that "under that proper law, that is according to principles commonly accepted by municipal and international laws the obligation to compensate a nationalized concessionaire is a necessary consequence of the right of nationalization."[37] As to the measure of damages, the Tribunal held that "the indemnity should include as a minimum the *damoun emergens*, e.g., the value of the nationalized corporeal property, including all assets, installations, and various expenses incurred."[38]

The most controversial question that remained was whether lost profit would be a part of the compensation under the circumstances. The Tribunal canvased various views on this issue and approvingly cited the famous Permanent Court of

nationalistic spirit to stress their prestige and to control their national economy, many of these new States as well as some other old ones had recourse, especially since 1950, to general measures of nationalization covering 'chiefly oil concessions and other natural resources and public utilities. [199]. Among such measures were those taken by: Iran in 1951, Egypt in 1956, Indonesia in 1957, Irak, Ceylon and Cuba in 1961, Algeria from 1963, Syria in 1964, Peru in 1968, Bolivia and Zambia in 1969, Chile in 1970, Libya from 1970, Saudi Arabia in 1972, and Kuweit since 1973. Some of these nationalizations will be discussed hereafter").

[32] *See id.* at 201.

[33] *Id.* at 244 (citations omitted).

[34] *Id.* at 206.

[35] *Id.* at 254 (emphasis added). *See also* at 255 ("Examined in the light of the above propositions, LIAMCO's Concession Agreements are binding, and cannot validly be terminated except on one of the following grounds: (a) -Expiry of their contractual period as set out in Clauses 1 and 3 of the Agreements; (b) -Mutual consent of the contracting parties, in compliance with the said principle of the sanctity of contracts and particularly with the explicit terms of Clause 16 of the Agreements; (c) -Revocation by the Libyan Government for non-fulfilment by LIAMCO of its contractual obligations, with the latter's right of recourse to arbitration as specified and regulated in Clause 27 of same; (d)- Non-discriminatory nationalization coupled with the required compensation").

[36] *Id.* at 269 ("Restitution has thus been considered in international law as against the respect due for the sovereignty of the nationalizing State").; *Id.* at 271 ("Further, restitution presupposes the cancellation of the nationalization measures at issue, and such cancellation violates also the sovereignty of the nationalizing State. Moreover, nationalization is sometimes qualified as an "Act of State," which is immune from control, judicial or otherwise").

[37] *Id.* at 280. *See also id.* at 286 ("Thus, the principle of the necessity indemnification, being unanimously and equally supported by municipal and international legal theory and practice, should be applied in this dispute, as being the proper law of the concession agreements, in compliance with Clause 28 thereof").

[38] *Id.* at 287.

International Justice's 1922 case of *Chorzow Factory*, making a distinction between remedies for wrongful and lawful expropriation:

> Whereas in a wrongful taking the injured party must be restored to its original rights,—on the contrary in a lawful expropriation where the only wrongful act was the failure to pay the just price of what had been expropriated, the compensation due should be the value of the undertaking at the time of dispossession.[39]

The Tribunal further noted that:

> 310. The classical doctrine required the payment of "prompt, adequate and effective" compensation for the nationalized property of an alien. This is the formula adopted by the U.S. State Department in its various statements to which it was alluded in a previous section. "Adequate" compensation, in particular, had to include "lucrum cessans, namely the loss of future profits from property such as invested capital or a concessionary right granted for a specific number of years
>
> . . .
>
> 312. In conclusion, it may be safely laid down that it is lawful to nationalize concession rights before the expiry of the concession term, provided that the measure be not discriminatory nor in breach of treaty, and provided that compensation be duly paid.
>
> 313. But the question whether or not the concessionaire may claim compensation for all the loss of future profits for the unexpired term is still a controversial point which has not been definitely settled.[40]

It further added:

> The same trend is noticeable in some recent publications, where it is asserted that the rule of "full and prior" compensation is no more imperativa, and that only "convenient and equitable" compensation is required in cases of nationalization. This trend has been justified by the necessity of taking into consideration not only the interest of the owner of the property nationalized, but also those of the Society (Community) and of the nationalizing State.[41]

LIAMCO was the latest of the three Libyan cases that attempted to give context-based meaning to expropriation of foreign interests by an African state. The *LIAMCO* Tribunal helpfully outlined its understanding of the classic and evolved conception of nationalization as a means of expropriating foreign interest. It is notable for its recognition of the state's right to lawfully nationalize foreign interest if it is done in a nondiscriminatory manner. It is also remarkable for its qualification of the Hull Rule as it relates to the third element, the adequacy of the compensation. The second half, the assessment of compensation for lawful expropriation or the adequacy of the

[39] *Id.* at 300.
[40] *Id.* at 309–13 (citations omitted).
[41] *Id.* at 317.

compensation, was more problematic and required a creative solution. The *LIAMCO* Tribunal resolved the dilemma in favor of equity, which gave it a great latitude in shaping the eventual remedy. As such, its utility as a principled way of assessing damages where lawful expropriation had taken place remained marginal.

LIAMCO was where matters stood by the time *S.A.R.L. Benvenuti & Bonfant v. People's Republic of the Congo*[42] was decided. Although *S.A.R.L* did not cite *LIAMCO*, its basic analysis, particularly its use of equitable principles for the assessment of damages, was consistent with *LIAMCO*'s approach. In the Tribunal's own words: "By reason of the above, the Government must therefore be ordered to pay B&B damages, the quantum of which will be determined *ex aequo et bono* by the Tribunal in the following paragraphs."[43] It is important to note, however, while the *LIAMCO* Tribunal arrived at an equitable assessment of damages by applying legal principles, the *S.A.R.L* Tribunal arrived at that conclusion by somewhat convincing the Parties to agree to decision *ex aequo et bono*. The result was the same: giving the tribunal broad discretion in the assessment of damages with due regard to the circumstances as an important part of the expropriation jurisprudence.

The first two Libyan Oil cases did, however, found the Libyan nationalization measures to be unlawful expropriation. The *BP* case, which was the first of all three, found that:

> No elaborate reasons are required to resolve the third issue in this case. The BP Nationalisation Law, and the actions taken thereunder by the Respondent, do constitute a fundamental breach of the BP Concession as they amount to a total repudiation of the agreement and the obligations of the Respondent thereunder, and, on the basis of rules of applicable systems of law too elementary and voluminous to require or permit citation, the Tribunal so holds. Further, the taking by the Respondent of the property, rights and interests of the Claimant clearly violates public international law as it was made for purely extraneous political reasons and was arbitrary and discriminatory in character. Nearly two years have now passed since the nationalisation, and the fact that no offer of compensation has been made indicates that the taking was also confiscatory.[44]

Although the Tribunal found unlawful expropriation, it did not go as far as awarding restitution as a remedy. Indeed, it usefully opined that *restitutio in integrum* is merely a useful tool to measuring damages. It said in particular:

> The survey of cases and other relevant materials presented above demonstrates that there is no explicit support for the proposition that specific performance, and even less so restitutio in integrum, are remedies of public international law available at the option of a party suffering a wrongful breach by a co-contracting party. An analysis of the cases shows instead that while declaratory awards have often been made in terms

[42] S.A.R.L. Benvenuti & Bonfant v. People's Republic of Congo, ICSID Case No. ARB/77/2 (1980), 1 ICSID Rep. 330 (1993).

[43] *Id.* at ¶¶ 4.58–4.64, 6.63–6.65.

[44] British Petroleum Exploration Co. (Libya) v. Libyan Arab Republic, 53 Int'l L. Rep. 297 (1973), at 111.

> of defining the rights and obligations of parties to a concession contract, these cases have never involved the total expropriation or taking by the State of the property, rights and interests of the concessionnaire; and indeed in the most important of the cases the validity and continued existence of the contract has not been questioned. The case analysis also demonstrates that the responsibility incurred by the defaulting party for breach of an obligation to perform a contractual undertaking is a duty to pay damages, and that the concept of restitutio in integrum has been employed merely as a vehicle for establishing the amount of damages. This becomes nowhere more apparent than in certain remarks on the concept made in 1927 by the late Sir Hersch Lauterpacht.[45]

On the merits of whether there was expropriation, and if so, whether it is unlawful, the extraneous political circumstances were precisely the reasons that gave Dr. Mahmassani in *LIAMCO* pause. As discussed above, he found the nationalization to be lawful and computed damages on an equitable basis.

It is worth remembering that neither Dr. Sobhi Mahmassani in *LIAMCO* nor Judge Gunnar Lagergren in *BP* were as bold as René-Jean Dupuy in *Texaco*.[46] The former two may have had a better reckoning of the complexities of the postcolonial sociopolitical circumstances of the region. They both ordered the payment of damages. Dupuy essentially found that the expropriation was unlawful and concluded that "neither the notion of sovereignty nor the nature of the nationalization measures taken against the plaintiff companies provide a legal justification for these measures."[47] Lagergren

[45] *Id.* at 175. The quoted Lauterpacht passage reads: "A problem of a similar kind is involved in the question as to how far the general principle of private law, that in awarding damages restitutio in integrum should, as a rule, be aimed at, applies in cases when damages are to be awarded under international law. That principle means that the injured person is placed in the position he occupied before the occurrence of the injurious act or omission; it means that, to use the Roman law terminology, not only the damnum emergens but also lucrum cessans is taken into consideration. (Lauterpacht, Private Law Sources and Analogies of International Law, 1929, p. 147.)"

[46] Texaco v. Libya (1977), Preliminary Award (Nov. 27, 1975), 53 ILR 389; Award on the Merits (Jan. 19, 1977), 17 ILM 1 (1978).

[47] *See id.* at 79. The reasoning is elaborate and the core of his opinion in this regard instructively reads: "Thus, with regard to international contract law, nationalization cannot prevail against an internationalized contract concluded between a State and a foreign private company and comprising stabilization provisions. It could only be otherwise if one were to consider that the exercise by a State of its right to nationalize situates it on a plane external and superior to the contract as well as to the international legal order itself and constitutes an "act of government" escaping any contentious recourse as well as any criticism." *Id.* at 73. Incidentally, Dupuy's opinion is notable for its endorsement of US Secretary of State Cordell Hull's 1938 famous letter to the Mexican Foreign Minister, almost verbatim:

> However, if, for a State, its decision to nationalize is the expression of its sovereignty, which this Tribunal fully recognizes, does its exercise know no limits in the international order? In particular, does the act of sovereignty constituted by nationalization empower it to disregard the international commitments it has also subscribed to within the framework of its sovereignty? It is quite obvious that a measure of nationalization concerning nationals of the State cannot be internationally criticized any more than those affecting foreigners in respect of whom it has made no particular commitment to guarantee the maintenance of their situation. In the event that the nationalizing State has concluded a contract with a foreign company originating in the internal law of this State and entirely governed by it, the settlement of the new situation, created by the nationalization, will fall under the legal provisions and regulations in force.

similarly found the nationalizations to be unlawful expropriation.[48] Mahmassani, on the other hand, found a lawful expropriation. The differences in the nature of the violations manifested themselves only in the award of remedies because all three found the Respondent State liable under different expropriation theories. The jurisprudence that they generated continued to be standard citations for expropriation, although they are not necessarily coherent internally or across all three cases. In any case, these African cases set the stage for the modern law of expropriation.

Temporally, the closest African ICSID case as indicated above was the 1980 case of *S.A.R.L. Benvenuti & Bonfant v. People's Republic of the Congo.*[49] *S.A.R.L's* contribution to expropriation jurisprudence remained modest as it came to conclusion without much legal analysis. That is partly because there was a lack of competing views as the government was not properly represented although all three of the Libyan Oil cases did a better appraisal of the law of expropriation as it existed at the time without the Respondent State's participation.

The next case was *SPP v. Egypt* (1992). The expropriation claim arose out of the cancellation of an investor-owned tourist development project by a decree purporting to protect antiquities near the pyramids.[50] The Tribunal had no difficulty finding that the state had the right to cancel any investment projects for the protection of antiquities in the exercise of its power of eminent domain under its own laws, but the issue pertained to the consequences that must follow.[51]

On the facts of the case, a post hoc decree required the investor to relocate with some offer of compensation. The state argued that the investor's contractual rights to develop are incapable of being expropriated as a matter of law. Moreover, the investor chose not to take the offer and left the country. As such, there was no expropriation.[52] The Claimant argued that "the Respondent's arguments ignore economic reality . . . the cancellation of the Pyramids Oasis Project and the publicity engendered thereby created a climate of opinion which made it impossible for the Claimants to

. . . Thus the decision of a State to carry out nationalization measures constitutes the exercise of a jurisdiction of internal law but it has international consequences when these measures reach a legal relationship of international law in which the State is engaged. nationalizing state. . . . In order to assess the scope of nationalization measures, it is therefore necessary to ascertain whether the State which carried them out has subscribed to international obligations which had the effect of prohibiting it . . . " *Id.* at 61–63. Letter from Cordell Hull, US Secretary of State, to Francisco Castillo Nájera, Mex. Ambassador to the US (July 21, 1938), *as reprinted in* LOWENFELD, INTERNATIONAL ECONOMIC LAW 536–37 (2d ed. 2008), at 476.

[48] *See id.* at 79.

[49] S.A.R.L. Benvenuti & Bonfant v. People's Republic of Congo, ICSID Case No. ARB/77/2 (1980), 1 ICSID Rep. 330 (1993).

[50] *See* Southern Pacific Properties (Middle East) Limited v. Arab Republic of Egypt, ICSID Case No. ARB/84/3, Award (May 20, 1992), at 158.

[51] *See id.* at 158 ("Clearly, as a matter of international law, the Respondent was entitled to cancel a tourist development project situated on its own territory for the purpose of protecting antiquities. This prerogative is an unquestionable attribute of sovereignty. The decision to cancel the project constituted a lawful exercise of the right of eminent domain. The right was exercised for a public purpose, namely, the preservation and protection of antiquities in the area. Nor have the Claimants challenged the Respondent's right to cancel the project. Rather, they claim that the cancellation amounted to an expropriation of their investment for which they are entitled to compensation under both Egyptian law and international law").

[52] *See id.* at 160.

raise additional funds in international financial markets and to undertake fix their investments."[53]

The Tribunal determined that contractual rights are capable of being expropriated as a matter of law. It noted in particular that "there is considerable authority for the proposition that contract rights are entitled to the protection of international law and that the taking of such rights involves an obligation to make compensation therefore."[54] More importantly, it concluded that "it follows that the duty to compensate in the event of expropriation cannot be evaded by contending that municipal regulations give a narrow meaning to the term 'expropriation' or apply the concept only to certain kinds of property."[55] These concepts may seem standard now but they were important pronouncements at the time.

As far as the relocation option was concerned, the Tribunal determined on the facts that the parties' agreement for the development of the initial location had many underlying assumptions, including the attraction of financing that were not easily transferable and as such the decision effectively rendered the initial contract ineffective and hence expropriated.[56]

Having established that a lawful expropriation had occurred, the Tribunal then looked at the consequences that must follow and determined that the investor must be compensated as a matter of Egyptian law. It relied on two such laws. The first is the Constitution, which provided that:

> Private ownership shall be safeguarded and may not be put under sequestration except in the cases specified in the law and with a judicial decision. It may not be expropriated except for a public purpose and against a fair compensation in accordance with the law. The right of inheritance is guaranteed in it.[57]

It also relied on the Antiquities Law of 1951, which also recognizes the right to compensation of a private party who may have to be relocate because of the discovery of antiquities.[58] Predicated on these domestic laws, the Tribunal determined that the cancellation of the project amounted to expropriation but the award of compensation is not for breach of contract but "fair compensation for what was expropriated," not reparation.[59]

[53] *Id.* at 161.

[54] *Id.* at 164–65 (citing the Judgment of the Permanent Court of International Justice concerning *Certain German Interests in Polish Up Silesia*, P.C.I.J., Series A, No. 7, 1926, at p. 44); *Id.* at 166 ("by taking possession of a factory, Poland had also "expropriated the contractual rights" of the operating company").; *Amoco Int'l Finance Cop v. Iran* (15 Iran-US CTR, p. 89, 108) ("Expropriation, which can be defined as a compulsory transfer of property rights, may extend to any right which can be the object of a commercial transaction"); *Phillips Petroleum Co Iran v. Iran* (21 Iran-US CTR, p. 79, 76) ("whether the expropriation is formal or de facto and whether the property is tangible, such as real estate or a factory, or intangible, such as the contractual rights involved in the present Case").

[55] SPP v. Egypt, ICSID Case No. ARB/84/3, Award (May 20, 1992), at 168.

[56] *Id.* at 170–72.

[57] *Id.* at 159 (quoting Art. 34 of the Egyptian Constitution).

[58] *Id.* at 59 (quoting Art. 11 of Law No. 215 of 1951 for the Protection of Monuments and Antiquities).

[59] *Id.* at 183.

The Development of the International Investment Law of Expropriation of the African Cases of the 2000s

It was not until the turn of the twenty-first century that the issue of expropriation began to be directly addressed in earnest by ICSID tribunals in the African cases based on provisions contained in investment treaties. All of the older expropriation cases discussed above arose out of domestic contracts or constitutional law claims. Chronologically, one of the very first cases that raised the question of expropriation based on a treaty was *Wena Hotels Limited v. Arab Republic of Egypt* (2000).[60] *Wena* was decided on the basis of one of the earliest Egyptian BITs, the June 1975 UK–Egypt treaty.[61] This BIT contained modern investment protection provisions including a nonexpropriation provision, which reads in Article 5:

> Investments of nationals or companies of either Contracting Party shall not be nationalised, expropriated or subjected to measures having effect equivalent to nationalisation or expropriation (hereinafter referred to as 'expropriation') in the territory of the other Contracting Party except for a public purpose related to the internal needs of the Party and against prompt, adequate and effective compensation. Such compensation shall amount to the market value of the investment expropriated immediately before the expropriation itself or before there was an official Government announcement that expropriation would be effected in the future, whichever is the earlier, shall be made without delay, be effectively realizable and be freely transferable. The national or company affected shall have a right under the law of the Contracting Party making the expropriation, to prompt review, by a judicial or other independent authority of that Party, of whether the expropriation is in conformity with domestic law and of the valuation of his or its investment in accordance with the principles set out in this paragraph.[62]

Wena, a UK national, entered into a "Lease and Development Agreement" with the government owned Egyptian Hotels Company (EHC)[63] for Luxor Hotel on August 8, 1989, and for El Nile Hotel on January 28, 1990.[64] These deals did not work. Wena defaulted in its payment of the agreed sums. After an extended period of negotiations, EHC took the law into its own hands and forcibly evicted Wena.[65] The events

[60] Wena Hotels Limited v. Arab Republic of Egypt, ICSID Case No. ARB/98/4, Award (Dec. 8, 2000).

[61] *Id.* at 16.

[62] *Id.* at 96.

[63] *Id.* at 66 ("As explained by Minster Sultan during his testimony, under Law Number 97 of 1983, the sole shareholder of EHC was Egypt").

[64] *Id.* at 17–18.

[65] *Id.* at 19–50. For example, 48 states: "According to a subsequent statement to the Luxor police by Mr. Bahia El Din Abdel Hadi El Wakeel, a security guard at the Luxor Hotel, "more than 100 people from the EHC seized the Wena Hotel by force in spite myself and others responsible for the security and guards in the hotel presence at the time."los Mr. Wakeel also stated that "EHC forced their entry through by force ... which caused panic, fear, and hysteria for the guests and employees ... Two other guards, Messrs. Ismael Ahmed Hefni and Ahmed Hamza Mostafa, made short statements, agreeing with Mr. Wakeel's description of events." 49 states: "Mr. Muhammad Nagib AI-Sayyid, Wena's General manager of the Luxor Hotel, also filed a police statement, asserting that, at approximately 7:00 p.m., EHC personnel entered his office, seized the hotel's papers and ordered him to leave the hotel. Mr. Nagib reported the incident to the

of EHC's forcible eviction without due process are not disputed. The claim pertains to the Egyptian government's role in failing to protect and offering prompt, effective and adequate compensation. In fact, the government restored Wena to its place within a year. But the Tribunal found expropriation anyway because it said that "an expropriation also exists merely by the state withdrawing the protection of its courts from the owner expropriated, and tacitly allowing a *de facto* possessor to remain in possession of the thing seized."[66]

On the facts of this case, the extra-judicial violations that the investor, Wena, suffered in the hands of the government owned EHC was no doubt egregious, but the Tribunal's bridge from there to a finding of liability on the part of the Egyptian state under the BIT was the failure to offer "prompt, adequate and effective compensation." To be sure, the Tribunal did not find that Egypt took Wena's property, but it merely found that it failed to protect it. This last part is a finding of FET and FSP violations discussed below, but it is important to note here (as it is a recurring problem) that the remedy for those violations appear to have been found under expropriation: prompt, adequate, and effective compensation.

The problem with the *Wena* expropriation decision is not limited to the linkage that it implicitly attempts to make between distinct grounds of liability (i.e., FET, FSP, and expropriation) and mixing and matching remedies for different types of violations. The violation was found not because of a finding of a taking but a lack of offering of timely compensation because the process of restoring Wena to its place took a year, and Wena believed that a government minister obstructed the offering of compensation.

The award makes reference to one letter that Wena's representatives wrote to a US House Representative claiming that Egypt's tourism minister obstructed the offering

Luxor Tourist Police, who accompanied Mr. Nagib back to the hotel and subsequently opened an investigation into the seizure."

[66] *Id.* at 97 (quoting from *Amco Asia v. Indonesia*). *See also id.* at 99–100:

> 99. Here, the Tribunal has no difficulty finding that the actions previously described constitute such an expropriation~ Whether or not it authorized or participated in the actual seizures of the hotels, Egypt deprived Wena of its "fundamental rights of ownership" by allowing EHC forcibly to seize the hotels, to possess them illegally for nearly a year, and to return the hotels stripped of much of their furniture and fixtures. Egypt has suggested that this deprivation was merely "ephemeral" and therefore did not constitute an expropriation. The Tribunal disagrees. Putting aside various other improper actions, allowing an entity (over which Egypt could exert effective control) to seize and illegally possess the hotels for nearly a year is more than an ephemeral interference "in the use of that property or with the enjoyment of its benefits.
>
> 100. Moreover, even after the hotels were returned to Wena, Egypt failed to satisfy its obligation under the IPPA, and international norms generally, by refusing to offer Wena "prompt, adequate and effective compensation" for the losses it had suffered as result of Egypt's failure to act. For example, as already noted, on November 11, 1992, Mr. Malins wrote to U.S. Congressman Lee Hamilton, complaining that "the Minister of Tourism, Dr. Fouad Sultan, will not consider our requests" and that "it is clear that subsequent to any perceived movement, Dr. Sultan personally intervenes to obstruct a solution. "
>
> 101. For all these reasons, the Tribunal concludes that Egypt violated its obligation under Article 5 of the IPPA, by failing to provide Wena with "prompt, adequate and effective compensation" for the losses it suffered as a result of the seizures of the Luxor and Nile Hotel.

of compensation.[67] The only source of evidence is this letter but nothing more. It appears otherwise that Egyptian officials condemned EHC's actions, investigated the matter, and even punished some officials although it appeared from the record that the punishment was rather symbolic.[68] It is clear that the Tribunal felt that Egypt at a minimum tolerated the unlawful conduct by EHC, which it owned, but the analytical steps do not necessarily build the grounds for the finding of expropriation. They not only skip the first step of the finding of a taking, but also predicate the finding of a lack of compensation on what appears to be a hearsay statement contained in a self-serving letter written to a third party. At a minimum, this finding should have a more robust evidentiary basis. While the outrage about the fact of a forcible eviction is understandable, a finding of expropriation without following the necessary analytical steps and accumulation of adequate evidentiary support affects the credibility of this particular award, not to mention the impact on subsequent cases. As indicated below, the FET and FPS analysis seems to have better grounding in law and evidentiary record than the expropriation analysis.

The *Middle East Cement v. Egypt* (2002) case advanced the regulatory creeping expropriation doctrine a little bit further. The alleged taking was effectuated by a government decree that prohibited the importation into the host country of certain types of cement affecting the investor's core business.[69] The Decree that the investor claimed expropriated its interests (license to import and distribute cement) provided:

> Article 1: To prohibit the import of all kinds of Grey Portland Cement either through the Public of the Governmental Sector or the Private Sector.
> Article 2: This resolution does not affect the remainder of the existing contracts relating to the Egyptian Cement Sale Office for the Balanced Transactions and Protocols.
> Article 3: This resolution does not affect the Thermal and White Portland Cement.
> Article 4: This resolution is effective from the date of its issuance and be published in the Egyptian Gazette.[70]

[67] *See id.* at 93 ("Egypt also refused to compensate Wena for the losses it had experienced. On November 11, 1992, Mr. Malins wrote to the Honorable Lee Hamilton, a senior member of the US House of Representatives, complaining that 'the Minister of Tourism, Dr. Fouad Sultan, will not consider our requests' and that 'it is clear that subsequent to any perceived movement, Dr. Sultan personally intervenes to obstruct a solution.'")

[68] *See id.* at 94 ("Finally, neither EHC nor its senior officials were seriously punished for their actions in forcibly expelling Wena and illegally possessing the hotels for approximately a year. Although several representatives of EHC—including Messrs. Kandil and Munir—were convicted for their actions, neither Mr. Kandil nor Mr. Munir was sentenced to serve any jail time. Instead, both were fined only EGP 200, which Mr. Munir stated that he has never paid. Also, neither official appears to have suffered any repercussions in their careers. As noted above, the Ministry of Tourism chose not to exercise its authority to remove Mr. Kandil as Chairman of ECH and, according to Ms. Jelcic, he currently is serving as an advisor to a senior member of the Egyptian parliament.Since the seizures, Mr. Munir has been promoted to become the Head of the Legal Affairs Division at EHC and is expecting a further promotion in the near future. This absence of any punishment of EHC and its officials suggest that Egypt condoned EHC's actions").

[69] Middle East Cement Shipping and Handling Co. S.A. v. Arab Republic of Egypt, ICSID Case No. ARB/99/6, Award (Apr. 12, 2002), at 81–84.

[70] Decree No. 195 of May 28, 1989 (C6) provides the following relevant wording (English translation): "Arab Republic of Egypt Ministry of Construction The Minister's Office ministerial Decree No. 195 of 1989 in respect of the Import of Grey Portland Cement" (quoted in *id.* at 106).

The Tribunal noted that to qualify for relief against the adverse impacts of this Decree on its cement business, the Decree must violate the expropriation provision of the Greece-Egypt BIT, which reads:

> Expropriation
> Investments by investors of either Contracting Party shall not be expropriated, nationalized or subjected to any other measure the effects of which would be tantamount to expropriation or nationalization in the territory of the other Contracting Party except under the following conditions:
>
> a) the measures are taken in the public interest and under due process of law,
> b) the measures are clear and not discriminatory, and
> c) the measures are accompanied by provisions for the payment of prompt, adequate and effective compensation. Such compensation shall amount to the market value of the investments affected immediately before the measures referred to above in this paragraph occurred or became public knowledge and it shall be freely transferable in convertible currencies from the Contracting Party, at the bank rate of exchange applicable on the dated used for the determination of value. The compensation shall be transferable without delay and shall include interest until the date of payment.[71]

The Tribunal had no difficulty finding that the Decree expropriated the investor's investment, which was the license. The Tribunal based its finding on the Respondent's own admission that the Decree ended the usefulness of the license granted for 10 years four months earlier than it was supposed to expire.[72]

The Parties disputed the remaining time on the license. The government insisted that there was only four months remining on the license. Most interestingly, the Tribunal considered this factual contention to be relevant only to the determination of the extent of the expropriation rather than for the determination of whether an expropriation had taken place in the first place.[73] This appears to be a fundamental

[71] Greece-Egypt BIA, Art. 4 (reproduced in *id.* at 104).

[72] Middle Eastern Cement v. Egypt, ¶107:

> 107. As also Respondent concedes that, at least for a period of 4 months, Claimant was deprived, by the Decree, of rights it had been granted under the License, there is no dispute between the Parties that, in principle, a taking did take place. When measures are taken by a State the effect of which is to deprive the investor of the use and benefit of his investment even though he may retain nominal ownership of the respective rights being the investment, the measures are often referred to as a "creeping" or "indirect" expropriation or, as in the BIT, as measures "the effect of which is tantamount to expropriation." As a matter of fact, the investor is deprived by such measures of parts of the value of his investment. This is the case here, and, therefore, it is the Tribunal's view that such a taking amounted to an expropriation within the meaning of Art. 4 of the BI and that, accordingly, Respondent is liable to pay compensation therefor.

[73] *Id.* at 112 ("To find out the extent of the taking by Decree No. 195, the Tribunal, therefore, has to examine which supplies, either to the Public or the Private Sector, Claimant may have contracted for during that 10 year period and which profits were lost from those contracts due to the taking. This examination will have to be done on the basis of the evidence submitted to the Tribunal and taking into account, as this is disputed by Respondent, that Claimant has the burden of proof in this respect").

flaw in the analysis. The Tribunal concludes, rather implausibly, that a decree of general applicability that terminates the investor's license four months earlier than it was supposed to expire amounted to "measure the effects of which would be tantamount to expropriation or nationalization" under Article 4 of the BIT. To be sure, the Tribunal did determine on the facts that the period of validity without the Decree would have been longer but this affected only the extent of the expropriation for purposes of damages.[74] For purposes of finding expropriation, the Tribunal does not consider whether the Decree was discriminatory or not, why it was enacted, who else it affected, what motivated it, and to what extent it impacted the investor. In that sense, it did not advance the jurisprudence in any measurable way. It was distracted by a small admission and went straight to quantum of damages without justifying its finding on liability.

The Tribunal's finding of expropriation relating to the court seizure and auctioning of the investor's vessel for debts that the investor did not pay is more interesting. There was no dispute that the investor owed money and that the seizure took place under a court order, but the Tribunal's finding of expropriation pertained to the sufficiency of notice of the legal process under Egyptian law:

> 143. . . . Therefore, a matter as important as the seizure and auctioning of a ship of the Claimant should have been notified by a direct communication for which the law No. 308 provided under the 1st paragraph of Art. 7, irrespective of whether there was a legal duty or practice to do so by registered mail with return receipt requested as argued by Claimant (CV 4). The Tribunal finds that the procedure in fact applied here does not fulfill the requirements of Art. 2.2 and 4 of the BIT.
>
> 144. Thus, the Tribunal concludes that the Poseidon was taken by a "measure the effects of which would be tantamount to expropriation" and that the Claimant is entitled to a compensation as provided for under Art. 4. c) of the BIT.[75]

The Tribunal merged its expropriation analysis with the denial of FET, and essentially considered the defect in providing notice singularly amounted to expropriation.

The next case with a significant expropriation component was *Patrick Mitchell v. DCR* (2004).[76] This case involved the application of the expropriation provision of US BIT model that was signed with the DRC (then Zaire) in 1984. The text reads:

> No investment or any part of an investment of a national or a company of either Party shall be expropriated or nationalized by the other Party or subjected to any

[74] *Id.* at 112–30.
[75] *Id.* at 143–44.
[76] Patrick Mitchell v. DRC Award (Feb. 9, 2004); Annulment (Nov. 1, 2006).

other measure or series of measures, direct or indirect, tantamount to expropriation, unless the expropriation:

(a) is done for a public purpose;
(b) is accomplished under due process of law;
(c) is not discriminatory;
(d) does not violate any specific provision on contractual stability or expropriation contained in an investment agreement between the national or company concerned and the Party making the expropriation; and
(e) is accompanied by prompt, adequate and effectively realizable compensation.[77]

Applying this to the facts of the *Patrick Mitchell* case, the Tribunal concluded the following:

> 71. In the Tribunal's view, the measures taken by the military authorities of the DRC are tantamount to an expropriation of Mr. Mitchell's investment, including the loss of clients who no longer made use of the services provided by the firm. Done as it was under dramatic circumstances, as is the case in a sudden intervention of military forces, the search and the sealing of the premises of the firm, the detention of two employees for the purported reason of the security of the State, the intervention of March 5, 1999 ended up with the total loss of the firm's clients. That loss is to be explained not only by the fact that the firm ceased to offer services and by the circumstances relating to the intervention on March 5, 1999, but also by the fact that many clients had been asking the firm for counseling in relation to requests to be presented to State authorities, for which Mitchell & Associates was no longer a credible reference after March 5, 1999.
>
> 72. The arrest of two employees lasted more than eight months and Mr. Mitchell considered preferable to stay abroad waiting for the situation to improve in respect of his safety. The expropriation initiated by the intervention of March 5, 1999 has, therefore, not produced results that could be qualified as being of an exclusively transitory nature. The loss of clients was definitive. It is correct to say that the Military Court ordered the restitution of the documents which had been seized. Such restitution has not been evidenced before this Tribunal. Even if it had occurred, such return would manifestly not have been an incentive for the clients to return. The Tribunal cannot, therefore, share Respondent's view that the removal of the seals, the release of the two employees and the restitution of the items seized for the purpose of the inquiry did re-establish the Claimant in his rights.[78]

[77] Reproduced in *id.* at 59.

[78] *Id.* at 70–72. The passage before this quotation states:

70. An expropriation of an asset invested is a measure by which the host State, acting for a public purpose, deprives the investor of his title in respect of such asset, totally or in part. Such title can be property or a receivable or any other right which constitutes an asset qualified as an investment by the definition given in Article I of the BIT. As indicated in Article III(1) of the BIT, the notion of an expropriation is not a formal one, which would imply that a decision of an authority of the

Because the dissent did not agree with the majority's finding of the existence of investment in the first place, it simply concluded that where there is no investment there could be no expropriation, although conceptually, it agreed with the Tribunal's overall expropriation analysis, including indirect expropriation.[79]

The famous *World Duty Free Company Limited v. Republic of Kenya* (2006)[80] case raised so many unusual issues including the issue of contract invalidity because of fraudulent procurement,[81] but it all began with a contract-based expropriation claim by a UK (Isle of Man)–registered United Arab Emirates based investor in Kenya.[82] The facts of this case are extremely complicated, as they involve allegations of elaborate politically motivated and government sponsored misuse of a foreign corporate entity for different types of illicit transfers of funds with or without the knowledge of investor.[83] Many of the factual allegations, except the bribe allegedly paid to the president of the Republic for the initial procurement of the contract for two duty free shops in the Nairobi and Mombasa airports for the benefit of the investor (World Duty Free Limited, formerly called House of Perfume), did not need to be determined.

The core of the expropriation claim, which is exclusively based on contract and domestic law (and without the benefit of an investment treaty) is summarized by the Tribunal in the following terms:

> In short, "the Claimant's contention is that the Government of Kenya expropriated the Claimant's property and destroyed its rights under the [1989] Agreement in using its executive, judiciary and agents like Kamlesh Pattni and his hand picked purported receivers." In this respect, the Claimant identifies several breaches of the agreement: i) use of World Duty Free in the Goldenberg fraud; ii) illegal expropriation of the Company; iii) placing of World Duty Free in receivership; iv) damage suffered from Court-appointed "receiver"; v) Court refusal to protect World Duty Free from

State would be needed in order to qualify a taking of title as an expropriation. This notion is to be understood as substantial in nature, which means that it covers any measure which is, directly or indirectly, tantamount to an expropriation. The Protocol added to the Treaty further stipulates that "direct or indirect measures tantamount to expropriation" may include "the levying of taxes equivalent to indirect expropriation, the compulsory sale of all or part of an investment, or the impairment or deprivation of the management, control, or economic value of an investment.

79 Patrick Mitchell v. DRC, Award (Feb. 9, 2004); Annulment (Nov. 1, 2006), at 4 (Dissenting opinion by Yawovi Agboyibo, Jan. 23, 2004) ("Without prejudice to the comments I shall now make with regard to the precondition of jurisdiction, I think that the Tribunal rightly applied the above-mentioned rules to the issue of whether or not Mr. Patrick Mitchell was the victim of expropriation of his law firm in the DRC. I believe that, in view of their consequences, the measures applied to the firm are tantamount to an expropriation, even though the Congolese authorities may have acted legally or did not intentionally seek the effects produced").

80 World Duty Free Company Limited v. Republic of Kenya, ICSID Case No. ARB/00/7, Award (Oct. 4, 2006).

81 *See id.* at 128.

82 *See id.* at 62–79 (The Claimant describes its corporate identity and entitlement to ICSID arbitration as: "75. The Claimant stresses that 'this case is a classic example of the type of investment dispute that ICSID was established to resolve' under the Washington Convention. In this respect, the Claimant recalls that it is incorporated in the United Kingdom (ICSID Convention ratified on 18 January 1967), that it is resident and headquartered in the United Arab Emirates (ICSID Convention ratified on 22 January 1982), and that it operates in Kenya (ICSID Convention ratified on 2 February 1987). The Claimant adds that the consent relied upon as the basis for instituting proceedings is contained in Clause 9 of the 1989 House of Perfume Contract").

83 *See id.* for the details of the factual allegations of the complex fraudulent scheme.

> crime; vi) unlawful deportation of the company's Chief Executive Officer; vii) final judgment in defiance of ICSID; and viii) registration of a duplicate World Duty Free during the pendency of the ICSID proceedings.[84]

Many of the factual allegations did not need to be determined because the proceeding took an unusual and interesting turn on March 19, 2003, two years after the initiation of the proceeding, when Kenya introduced a claim of invalidity of the 1989 Agreement, which gave rise to the claim of expropriation due to allegation of fraudulent procurement.[85] As such, the allegation of invalidity of the contract preempted the resolution of whether or not an expropriation had taken place. Because the Tribunal resolved that the Agreement was illegally procured,[86] the expropriation question did not have to be answered at all.

The main claim in the *Helnan v. Egypt* case (2008) was expropriation. As the Tribunal summarized:

> As will be recalled, HELNAN's contractual thesis is that EGYPT considered the Management Contract an obstacle for the privatization of the Shepheard hotel and that, making an improper use of its authority over the holding company HOTAC, EGOTH and the Ministry of Tourism, it orchestrated a series of events which ultimately led to HELNAN's expropriation of its investment in breach of Article 5 of the Treaty.[87]

Because the expropriation claim largely depended on whether or not the steps that the government took were deliberately designed to push Helnan out as a factual matter, the Tribunal's critical task became the determination of fact. The discussion of what, as a matter of law, constitutes expropriation was rather limited. The Tribunal concludes:

> In any case, and whatever be the real explanation, the Arbitral Tribunal is bound to conclude as a result of all these observations, that HELNAN did not discharge its burden to prove that EGYPT had engineered a plan to get rid of HELNAN in order to be able to privatize the Shepheard hotel more easily.[88]

[84] *Id.* at 74.

[85] *Id.* at 105 ("105. On 19 March 2003, Kenya submitted to the Tribunal an application alleging that the 1989 Agreement is unenforceable and requesting the dismissal of the claims with prejudice on that basis. In that application, the Respondent states that "it is the Claimant's case that the Contract upon which its claims in these proceedings are based was procured by paying a bribe of US$2 million to the then President of Kenya, Daniel arap Moi." It adds that "the payment of a bribe is criminal," and "as a matter of Kenyan, English and International ordre public, the resulting Contract does not have the force of law").

[86] *See id.* at 188 ("In conclusion: 1. The Respondent, Kenya, was legally entitled to avoid and did avoid legally by its Counter-Memorial dated 18 April 2003 the "House of Perfume Contract," namely the Agreement of 27 April 1989 as amended on 11 May 1990, under its applicable laws, the laws of England and Kenya; 2. The Respondent, Kenya, did not lose its right to avoid the said contract by affirmation or otherwise before 18 April 2003 under these applicable laws; and 3. The Claimant is not legally entitled to maintain any of its pleaded claims in these proceedings as a matter of ordre public international and public policy under the contract's applicable laws").

[87] Helnan International Hotels A/S V. The Arab Republic of Egypt, ICSID Case No. ARB/05/19, Award (July 3, 2008), at 153.

[88] *Id.* at 160.

As such, the decision was essentially a factual one. Had Helnan proven that there was an orchestrated plan and that the plan was attributable to the state, the Tribunal would have had to reckon with whether it constituted an indirect expropriation by outlining the elements of expropriation, which it did not do in this case. It did, however, very helpfully outline its opinion of the rule on attribution. Some of the most recent cases such as *Gustav v. Ghana* (2010) and *Interocean Oil v. Nigeria* (2020), discussed in the following section, have elaborated and applied the concept of attribution in more concrete terms.

Biwater v. Tanzania (2008) elevated the concept of causation in expropriation to outcome determinative heights in ways that no other African case that came before it did. It introduced a level of nuance that justified the finding of uncompensated indirect expropriation that did not cause damage. It decoupled causation as an element of expropriation; in fact, it introduced the idea that something that is not there could be taken. Consider the Tribunal's analysis on this point: the simple idea is that by the time Tanzania terminated the investor's lease contract, the contract had no residual economic value but nonetheless it was capable of being expropriated in a symbolic way.[89] The rationale, which is the key contribution of this Tribunal, whether convincing or not, is stated in clear terms as follows:

> 464. Equally, whilst accepting that effects of a certain severity must be shown to qualify an act as expropriatory, there is nothing to require that such effects be economic in nature. A distinction must be drawn between (a) interference with rights and (b) economic loss. A substantial interference with rights may well occur without actually causing any economic damage which can be quantified in terms of due compensation. In other words, the fact that the effect of conduct must be considered in deciding whether an indirect expropriation has occurred, does not necessarily import an economic test.
>
> 465. In the Arbitral Tribunal's view, the absence of economic loss or damage is primarily a matter of causation and quantum—rather than a necessary ingredient in the cause of action of expropriation itself. Thus, the suffering of substantive and quantifiable economic loss by the investor is not a pre-condition for the finding of an expropriation under Article 5 of the BIT. There may have been a substantial interference with an investor's rights, so as to amount to an expropriation, even if that interference has been overtaken by other events, such that no economic loss actually results, or the interference simply cannot be quantified in financial terms. In

[89] *See* Biwater Gauff (Tanzania) Ltd. v. United Republic of Tanzania, ICSID Case No. ARB/05/22, Final Award (July 24, 2008), at 519 ("We therefore conclude that, on a cumulative basis, the public announcement of the termination of the contract by Minister Lowassa on 13 May 2005; the subsequent political rally of 17 May; the withdrawal of the VAT certificate by the TRA on 24 May; and finally, the seizing of the assets of City Water, the immediate installation of DAWASCO, and the deportation of City Water's management on 1 June, amount to an expropriation of BGT's investment on the basis of Article 5 of the BIT"). It is clear that the deportation of the management members concerned the tribunal particularly seriously. Indeed, it cited African cases where the state deported someone of the investor and ended up with a liability including Biloune v. Ghana, Award on Jurisdiction and Liability (Oct. 27, 1989) at 209 (cited at 512) and Benvenuti & Bonfant v. Congo, Award (Aug. 8, 1980) at 357 (cited at 513).

> such circumstances, there may still be scope for a non-compensatory remedy for the expropriation (e.g. injunctive, declaratory or restitutionary relief).[90]

Biwater essentially changed the definition of "taking" to include a non-economic loss: "*In this case, the BIT does not include "economic damage" as a requirement for expropriation, and the Arbitral Tribunal does not consider that it must or should be imported.*"[91] This approach obviously encourages claims even when there is no prospect of recovery. In ordinary domestic civil legal proceedings, this case would have been appropriate for dismissal for failure to state a claim upon which relief may be granted; for example, under US Federal Rules of Civil Procedure Rule 12(b)(6).[92] In domestic law, these kinds of motions exist to avoid the excesses of litigation. Typically, these kinds of motions are granted if there is no point in going forward with the litigation in the first place. New BIT models have begun introducing provisions akin to these kinds of motions for the dismissal of nonmeritorious claims. To be fair, arriving at the conclusion that the Tribunal arrived at might, in earnest, have required the development of the record and proper exposition of the competing points of view before this kind of nuanced award is issued.

The principal complaint in *Bernardus v. Zimbabwe* (2009) was also expropriation. The Respondent state did not deny that the actions constituted expropriation, but disputed that they violated the BIT's expropriation provision because they were authorized by the State's constitutional and legislative rules. As the Tribunal framed it:

> Zimbabwe, although it denies any responsibility in the farm occupation by settlers and war veterans "concede[s] that compulsory acquisition … done in terms of the Land Acquisition Act and the Constitution of Zimbabwe … is tantamount to expropriation." It contends however that the measures it then took did not violate Article 6.[93]

Article 6 of the Zimbabwe-Netherlands BIT reads:

> Neither Contracting Party shall subject nationals of the other Contracting Party to any measures depriving them, directly or indirectly, of their investments unless the following conditions are complied with:
>
> a) the measures are taken in the public interest and under due process of law;
> b) the measures are not discriminatory or contrary to any undertaking which the former Contracting Party may have given;
> c) the measures are accompanied by provision of just compensation. Such compensation shall represent the genuine value of the investments affected and shall, in order to be effective for the claimants, be paid and made transferable, without delay, to the country designated by the claimants concerned and in

90 Biwater, ICSID Case No. ARB/05/22, Final Award (July 24, 2008), at 464–65.
91 *Id.* at 468 (emphasis added).
92 Fed. R. Civ. P. 12(b)(6) ("failure to state a claim upon which relief can be granted").
93 Bernardus Henricus Funnekotter and Others v. Republic of Zimbabwe, ICSID Case No. ARB/05/6, Award (Apr. 22, 2009), at 97.

> the currency of the country of which the claimants are nationals or in any free convertible currency accepted by the claimants. The genuine value of the investments shall include, but not exclusively, the net asset value thereof as certified by an independent firm of auditors.[94]

The Tribunal noted that to be considered lawful, any measure of expropriation must meet all of the requirements of Article 6 cumulatively. That means if any one of the requirements is missing, the expropriation would be considered unlawful.[95] Zimbabwe did not deny that the takings took place, albeit through due process, and that the Claimants were not compensated. It did, however, advance reasons such as the Claimants failed to take advantage of local processes and that there was a state of emergency at the time that excused the lack of compensation. The Tribunal did not accept any of these the excuses.[96]

One of the excuses led the Tribunal to the discussion of one of the rarely invoked provisions in BITs: the war and armed conflict provision, which often incorporates a national treatment rule. The relevant one here provided that:

> nationals of the one Contracting Party who suffer losses in respect of their investment in the territory of the other Contracting Party owing to war or other armed conflict, revolution, a state of national emergency, revolt, insurrection or riot shall be accorded by the latter Contracting Party treatment, as regards restitution, indemnification, compensation or other settlement, no less favourable that that which that Contracting Party accords to its own nationals or nationals of any third State, whichever is more favourable to the nationals concerned.[97]

In a remarkable analytical twist, the Tribunal showed how the National Treatment and MFN rule contained herein was rather unhelpful to the Respondent even if it were to accept the national emergency rationale on the facts.[98] Unconvinced by the Respondent's defenses and taking note of the admission that the taking took place without compensation, the Tribunal rather categorically ruled that "Zimbabwe breached its obligation under Article 6© of the BIT to pay just compensation to the Claimants."[99] It took the very simple approach that if any one of the elements of Article 6 (a provision that mimics the Hull Rule) is missing, there is expropriation.

As to the quantum of damages, although the Tribunal offered a good analysis on the distinction between the lawfulness or unlawfulness of the expropriation,[100] its own

[94] *Id.* at 96 (quoting Art. 6 of the Zimbabwe-Netherlands BIT).

[95] *Id.* at 98 ("The Tribunal observes that the conditions enumerated in Article 6 are cumulative. In other terms, if any of those conditions is violated, there is a breach of Article 6. The Tribunal will first examine whether or not subparagraph (c) relating to the provisions of a just compensation has been breached. If it arrives to the conclusion that it has, it will not be necessary for it to consider whether, as alleged by the Claimants, the other conditions provided for in that Article or the provisions of Article 3 have also been breached").

[96] *Id.* at 99–103.

[97] *Id.* at 104 (quoting Art. 7 of the Zimbabwe-Netherlands BIT).

[98] *Id.*

[99] *Id.* at 107.

[100] *See id.* at 108 ("It remains for the Tribunal to fix the damages due to the Claimants. In this respect Zimbabwe submits that the damages must be calculated as specified in Article 6(c). For their part, the

application of the rules seemed to have merged these notions at the end, because it simply said "it will accordingly proceed to the evaluation of the damages suffered in each case at the date of dispossession on the basis of the market value at that date."[101]

The expropriation analysis of this case is notable for its linkage with the war and emergency provisions of the applicable BIT and its observation of the distinction between lawful and unlawful expropriation, although its result did not exactly reflect the distinction like most tribunals that came before it, including the famous Libyan Oil cases.

In *Waguih Elie v. Egypt* (2009), the undisputed facts indicate that land initially granted to the investor for resort development was reallocated to a government owned gas pipeline company through a series of government actions after the investor had commenced work.[102] The Respondent conceded that the expropriation had occurred but argued that it was for a public purpose.[103] However, the Tribunal found on the facts that the expropriation did not qualify as one for public purpose.[104] Egypt also accepted the obligation to pay compensation and said that its domestic judicial processes were still undertaking that task, although the expropriation occurred some 12 years earlier.[105]

The Tribunal held that although the applicable BIT (Egypt–Italy) does not contain the word "prompt" in the expropriation provision alongside adequate and effective, "the absence of that word ought not to be seen to permit Egypt to refrain from paying compensation indefinitely."[106] The Tribunal concluded that "even the most charitable of impartial observers would not, in the Tribunal's view, contend that a 12-year delay (at the least) was 'prompt.' The Tribunal finds on all the evidence that Egypt has not paid 'adequate and fair' compensation to the Claimants."[107] In fact, the Tribunal found that Egypt failed to show that it met any of the lawful expropriation prongs of the BIT's provision, including the procedural due process component.[108]

The main question then became how to quantify the damages. Once the Claimants overcame the jurisdictional obstacle relating to the nationality dispute, on the merits, the Tribunal had no difficulty finding liability under many of the BITs substantive protection provisions, primarily expropriation.

Claimants contend that the standard of compensation provided for in Article 6(c) is the standard applicable in case of lawful expropriation. By contrast, compensation due in case of unlawful expropriation must be calculated according to customary international law as decided by the Permanent Court of International Justice in the Chorzow Factory case").

[101] *See id.* at 124.

[102] Waguih Elie George Slag and Clorinda Vecchi v. The Arab Republic of Egypt, ICSID Case No. ARB/05/15, Award (June 1, 2009), at 427.

[103] *Id.* at 429.

[104] *Id.* at 432–33.

[105] *Id.* 434.

[106] *Id.* 434–35.

[107] *Id.* 435.

[108] *Id.* 443.

13
Development of Expropriation Rules in the Post-2010 Period

The modern developments in the post-2010 period could themselves be analyzed in two temporal categories with the period between 2010 to 2020 setting the stage for the most contemporary developments that occurred in the post-2020 period.

The Period between 2010 and 2020

In the post-2010 period, expropriation continued to be the main source of claims and liability, although FET began to gain momentum in the period. *Gustav v. Ghana* (2010) was the first case in this period. The main expropriation claim is linked to the Claimant's loss of managerial power under the JV due to the Respondent's takeover plan.[1] The Respondent argued that the managerial takeover was because the Claimant abandoned its post.[2] Notwithstanding the factual contention about who did what and when, the Tribunal focused on the issue of attribution as the key component of the expropriation claim. It identified two relevant sets of allegations: first, whether the acts of the JV's Board chair could be attributed to the state; and second, whether the actions of some Ghanaian officials could also be attributed to the state.[3]

> To the Tribunal, these letters are clearly part of a general corporate battle, between the shareholders of Wamco. On one side was the majority shareholder, Hamester, which expressed a desire to withdraw from the company and whose representative (the Managing Director of Wamco) had, at a certain point in time, physically abandoned his post, and had given orders to shut down Wamco. On the other side was the minority shareholder, Cocobod, which was trying to keep the business going. Not one of these letters contains an act of *puissance publique* which could be attributed to

[1] Gustav F W Hamester GmbH & Co KG v. Republic of Ghana Respondent, ICSID Case No. ARB/07/24, Award (June 18, 2010), at 270–71 ("This is more precisely described in the following manner: 'The JVA expressly gave Hamester a majority shareholding in Wamco and thereby management control. The management control was two-fold. Firstly, under Article 4.3 (b) of the JVA Hamester"s appointed Managing Director shall have responsibility for the day to day management of the Company to enable it to perform as a viable commercial enterprise. Secondly, under Article 4.11 of the JVA, decisions by the Board of Directors required a simple majority; Hamester's appointed directors formed a majority under Article 4.1 of the JVA. 271. The Claimant's thesis is that it was deprived of its management rights in early 2003, and it submits that: 'Cocobod"s strategy was now to make Wamco its effective puppet and to emasculate Hamester.' ")

[2] *Id.* at 272 (quoting the Respondent's Counter-Memorial: "Hamester's voluntary and wrongful repudiation of the JVA and its abandonment of its management responsibilities in relation to Wamco in early 2003 because Mr. Opferkuch found that he could no longer plunder Wamco and hoped to make higher profits in the European chocolate market").

[3] *Id.* at 279–80.

Africa's International Investment Law Regimes. Won L. Kidane, Oxford University Press. © Oxford University Press 2023.
DOI: 10.1093/oso/9780197745571.003.0013

> the State. All of these letters could have been written by a frustrated private minority shareholder who was compelled to run the company, faced with the withdrawal of the majority shareholder. Corporate life is replete with such examples of shareholder disputes. The position is akin to that in Jan de Nul, where it was held that certain acts of SCA complained of by the investor could not be attributed to Egypt on the basis that: "(a)ny private contract partner could have acted in the same way."[4]

In terms of the attribution of the conducts of government officials, the Tribunal found three matters worth considering: alleged police investigation and harassment, acts of a Ghanaian Minister, and an export ban that allegedly affected the bottom-line.[5] Rejecting the police investigation and acts of the some alleged instructions of the Minister of Finance on the facts alone,[6] the Tribunal found that the imposition of export ban by the customs authority in response to the requests made by the minority shareholder of the JV (which is the government owned entity) is attributable to the government.[7] That became the main expropriation question.

Having found attribution, the Tribunal had to determine the question of whether the said ban amounted to expropriation as a matter of law. In somewhat of an extraordinary appreciation of the government's concerns, the Tribunal offered the following mix of fact and law as its final disposition of the expropriation issue:

> Without entering into sophisticated discussions on the contours of indirect expropriation, it is sufficient for the Tribunal to state its conclusion that the export ban was an act of protection of the joint-venture, in view of the fact that Hamester had already made known its desire to withdraw, and considering that there was a legitimate fear that before withdrawal, as much value as possible would be taken out of the country by the foreign partner. More importantly, the ban was a temporary decision, which was only in force for six weeks. The Tribunal agrees with the Respondent that "(i)t is impossible for Hamester to base its Expropriation Claim on these temporary export restrictions." Moreover, it was only a partial ban, as a temporary agent, CMC, Cocobod's trading company, was allowed to market and export Wamco's products.[8]

The facts of this case demonstrate that a treaty tribunal is not always the best forum for grievances that grow out of contractual relationships. As shown in the next chapter, the Tribunal was also not sympathetic to the Claimant's umbrella clause claims.

The expropriation claim in *Malicorp v. Egypt* (2011) is highly fact dependent, because the government's recension of the investor's contract for the development of an international airport was on allegations of the investor's fraudulent procurement

[4] *Id.* at 283 (quoting from Jan de Nul N.V. Dredging International N.V. v. Arab Republic of Egypt, ICSID Case No. ARB/04/13, Award (Nov. 6, 2008), at 170).

[5] Gustav F W Hamester GmbH & Co KG v. Republic of Ghana Respondent, ICSID Case No. ARB/07/24, Award (June 18, 2010), at 291.

[6] *See id.* at 297–300 (on police investigation) and 301–04 (on Minster's instructions).

[7] *See id.* at 294–95.

[8] *Id.* at 309.

of the contract in the first place.[9] Because the Tribunal ruled on the facts that the investor did indeed mislead the government about its financial abilities, the contract that it obtained through mistaken belief could not be expropriated. In the Tribunal's words: "The principal reason given by the Respondent in its letter rescinding the Contract was sufficiently well founded, and gave the Respondent the right to withdraw from the Contract. It follows that the rescission of the Contract cannot be considered as a form of expropriation under international law."[10]

The essential and somewhat unique feature of the expropriation claim[11] in *Bernard von Pezold v. Zimbabwe* (2015) relates to the defenses of proportionality, margin of appreciation, and necessity, because the underlying actions that caused the disposition of the Claimant's land and other properties were essentially admitted.[12] The Tribunal dismissed the margin of appreciation argument quickly, saying that it is a concept alien to international investment law inappropriately borrowed from human rights law without context and proper development.[13] It also rejected the proportionality

[9] *See* Malicorp Limited v. The Arab Republic of Egypt, ICSID Case No. ARB/08/18, Award (Feb. 7, 2011), at 133 ("However, in the light of the evidence on the record, none of the founding members of Malicorp could produce such large sums of money, either from their own resources or from partners prepared to take a risk of that magnitude").

[10] *Id.* at 137.

[11] For a summary of the key factual bases of the expropriation claims, *see* Bernardus Henricus Funnekotter and Others v. Republic of Zimbabwe, ICSID Case No. ARB/05/6, Award (Apr. 22, 2009), at 471:

> The Zimbabwean Properties were directly expropriated as of 14 September 2005, when the Constitutional Amendment vested in the State title to the 10 Forrester Properties, 21 of the 28 Border Properties, and six of the nine Makandi Properties66. The Claimants note that, without title, they are no longer able to sell or otherwise realise the properties, they face criminal prosecution for continuing to occupy them, and certain parts of the Estates are now controlled by Settlers/War Veterans (see Cl. Skel., para. 116). The Residual Properties were indirectly expropriated as of 14 September 2005 by the Constitutional Amendment, as they are not viable without the directly expropriated properties. The Claimants say that the operations of the Residual Properties would be disjointed and economically unviable when compared to their original unified investment, which used scale to produce returns, and their rights in the assets have been rendered useless (citations omitted).

[12] *Id.* at 460. *See also id.* at 473 ("Cross-Examination of Minister Mutasa (see Tr. Day 5, pp. 1403, 1384):

Q. And do you accept that compensation has not been paid to the von Pezolds with regard to the expropriation of their land?
A. They don't need it. I would—I would protest very violently that these people are being paid unfairly. They have lost absolutely nothing. They did not bring anything with them from Germany that should be compensated.
Q. And do we agree that up until the Constitutional Amendment of 2005, you agreed to provide due process in regards to expropriation?
A. Well, with the difference that we stated publicly that Land Reform problems should not be referred to courts. They should be settled by the Ministry of Lands, and that understanding still exists.
Q. Okay. And, again, I'm assuming you're familiar with the laws. Okay. So you're saying that the issue is being taken to the Ministry of Lands as opposed to the courts. So the Courts' jurisdiction in this regard no longer applies?
A. It doesn't apply at all.
Q. But only from 14 September 2005 onwards?
A. Uh-huh.

[13] *Id.* at 465 ("As to 'margin of appreciation' and the Respondent's argument that it should be given a wide margin when determining what is in the Zimbabwean public interest, the Tribunal is of the opinion that due caution should be exercised in importing concepts from other legal regimes (in this case European

argument on the facts by applying the *Tecmed* standard that "if the State instituted measures because of social or political pressures, such measures will not be proportional unless they are in response to a serious emergency, and unless the investor's conduct is a cause of that social or political pressure."[14]

The Tribunal did, however, consider the necessity defense more seriously. The essence of the necessity defense is that the overall weakening of the economy and sanctions called the very "ongoingness" of the state in question, and the only way that the state could have continued is through land reform.[15] The state relied on Article 25 of the ILC Articles of the State Responsibility, claiming:

> Necessity is invoked by the State of Zimbabwe as a ground for precluding any wrongfulness of acts not in conformity with an international obligation of that State because the act of land reform: a) is the only way for the State of Zimbabwe to safeguard an essential interest against a grave and imminent peril; and b) land reform in Zimbabwe does not seriously impair an essential interest of Germany and/or Switzerland, or of the international community as a whole.[16]

It further claimed that "the mass movements of the landless Zimbabweans presented a serious and imminent danger to an essential interest."[17] It also argued:

> The Respondent notes that all of the major economic indicators of the Zimbabwean economy reached catastrophic proportions in 2007, 2008 and 2009; multilateral financial institutions suspended all forms of balance of payments support, technical assistance, grants, and infrastructural development flows to government and the private sector in Zimbabwe, and stopped all lending operations to the country.[18]

human rights law) without a solid basis for doing so. Balancing competing (and nonabsolute) human rights and the need to grant States a margin of appreciation when making those balancing decisions is well established in human rights law, but the Tribunal is not aware that the concept has found much support in international investment law. The Respondent has only referred the Tribunal to European human rights cases in its arguments").

[14] *Id.* at 461–63.

[15] *See id.* at 612 ("Prior to 2000, the Respondent highlights that it had no issues with servicing its foreign debts and was well regarded in the financial markets with its capital account traditionally in surplus (see *id.*). However, by 2006, the opposite held true. From 2007 to 2009 the economy had entered a crisis of catastrophic proportions (see *id.*, paras. 913–18). This crisis had been the result of a number of factors, namely: (i) a decline in export performance and reduced capital inflows; (ii) a corresponding decline in foreign exchange reserves, and a significant build-up of external payments arrears, which had reached US$2.5 billion by the end of 2006; (iii) the suspension of all forms of payments support from multilateral financial institutions; (iv) the implementation of sanctions; (v) the suspension of technical assistance, grants, and infrastructure development inflows to both the Government and private sector; and (vi) the cessation of lending to the State. This also had the effect of degrading the international community's perceptions of the State and affected the ability of Zimbabwean companies to access affordable credit, forcing them to pay above-market interest rates. Accordingly, unemployment increased and standards of living decreased, leading to large outflows of skilled labour").

[16] *Id.* at 613.

[17] *Id.* at 614.

[18] *Id.* at 615.

The Claimants did not dispute that Article 25 of ILC Articles applies, but based their argument on the state's lack of declaration of emergency under its constitution, which they said contains the same standards as Article 25, and its own complicity in the acts of deprivation.[19]

The Tribunal identified the core of Article 25 of the ILC Articles as follows:

> Article 25. Necessity
>
> 1. Necessity may not be invoked by a State as a ground for precluding the wrongfulness of an act not in conformity with an international obligation of that State unless the act:
>   (a) is the only way for the State to safeguard an essential interest against a grave and imminent peril; and
>   (b) does not seriously impair an essential interest of the State or States towards which the obligation exists, or of the international community as a whole.
> 2. In any case, necessity may not be invoked by a State as a ground for precluding wrongfulness if:
>   (a) the international obligation in question excludes the possibility of invoking necessity; or
>   (b) the State has contributed to the situation of necessity.[20]

The crux of the Respondent's argument was that its choices were either to use deadly force and aggravate the political situation, or do nothing, and allow the continuation of the land "invasions."[21] The Tribunal questioned the wisdom of the state's choice of not doing anything about it, and indeed agreed with the Claimants that the state was complicit. Its final conclusion is captured in the following paragraph very well:

> The Tribunal finds that there has been a total failure on the part of the Respondent to divorce the politics of the situation from the underlying necessary duty of the State to protect its citizenry. It is the Respondent's burden to prove that it took the "right" or "correct" decision by doing nothing. The Respondent has submitted that there were no alternative means, except that of appeasement, on the one hand, or "Rhodesian style security" on the other (which would have resulted in bloodshed and loss of life).... The Respondent has not demonstrated that it carried out a rigorous process of assessing all possible alternatives, and it failed to take control of the situation by

[19] *See id.* at 617–23 ("619. Minister Mutasa stated that the Government had transported Settlers/War Veterans onto the farms, provided them with food and allocated them with units of land, thereby acknowledging that the State 'contributed to the situation of necessity' ").

[20] *Id.* at 624 (quoting Art. 25 of ILC Articles of State Responsibility).

[21] *See, e.g., i.* at 639 ("Prince Machaya also notes at para. 3 of his first Witness Statement that when the police: Went on the ground to try and stop the invasions and as events continued unfolding, it became obvious that the situation had become volatile and the problem monumental as more and more landless Zimbabweans took up land. [The land invaders] were no longer impressed by the law which they perceived to be the continuation of colonial times and which was stopping them from getting land").

> maintaining law and order. Instead, it instructed the police and other officials not to act. The Tribunal finds on the evidence that the Government was assisting and encouraging the Settlers/War Veterans after the Invasions. Indeed, in the short period of "ten days to two weeks of the beginnings of the land invasions, [President Mugabe] declared himself in favor of these land invasions."[22]

This was the essence of the 2015 Zimbabwe case. The Respondent unsuccessfully attempted to annul the award on grounds of denial of due process.[23]

The Post-2020 Cases

Interocean Oil v. Nigeria (2020) is one of those rare cases in which the underlying deprivation of preparatory interest was proven on the facts, but failed to qualify as expropriation because of lack of attribution: "Below, the Tribunal accepts that Claimants have been deprived of their investment in Nigeria and of Pan Ocean. This loss alone, however, does not implicate international responsibility. Rather, in order for this Tribunal to find that an expropriation has occurred, the actions alleged must be attributable to Respondent."[24] Moreover, "the Tribunal is not persuaded that Claimants' loss is due to breaches of Nigerian law (including customary international law) for which Respondent is responsible."[25] The Tribunal further noted that "if the alleged conspiracy involving Respondent is not established, Claimants will be found to have filed unfounded claims."[26] And indeed that is what seems to have happened in this case.

The claim of expropriation was based on a domestic Nigerian investment law rather than a BIT or any other kind of investment agreement. The relevant domestic law reads:

> 25. Guarantees against expropriation
>
> (1) Subject to subsections (2) and (3) of this section—
>
> (a) no enterprise shall be nationalized or expropriated by any Government of the Federation; and
>
> (b) no person who owns, whether wholly or in part, the capital of any enterprise shall be compelled by law to surrender his interest in the capital to any other person.

[22] *Id.* at 645. More specifically, the Tribunal decided that "The argument that Zimbabwe was in a state of emergency from 16 February 2000 to 16 March 2013, so that the Government had no other reasonable choice but to expedite the LRP and expropriate land without compensation, is unconvincing. The Respondent cannot invoke ILC Article 25." *Id.* at 668.

[23] An ad hoc annulment committee composed of Jean E. Kalicki, Azzedine Keffani, and Vejio A Keiskanen rejected Zimbabwe's annulment application on July 24, 2018. A copy of the annulment decision is available at https://jusmundi.com/en/document/decision/en-bernhard-von-pezold-and-others-v-republic-of-zimbabwe-decision-on-annulment-wednesday-21st-november-2018#decision_2406.

[24] Interocean Oil Development Company and Interocean Oil Exploration Company v. Federal Republic of Nigeria, ICSID Case No. ARB/13/20, Award (Oct. 6, 2020).

[25] *Id.* at 192.

[26] *Id.* at 191.

(2) There shall be no acquisition of an enterprise to which this Act applies by the Federal Government, unless the acquisition is in the national interest or for a public purpose and under a law which makes provision for—
   (a) payment of fair and adequate compensation; and
   (b) a right of access to the courts for the determination of the investor's interest or right and the amount of compensation to which he is entitled.

(3) Any compensation payable under this section shall be paid without undue delay, and authorization for its repatriation is convertible currency shall where applicable, be issued.[27]

The Tribunal rejected all of the Claimant's expropriation claims primarily because, on the facts, it considered the dispute primarily between private parties. For example, it noted that

> the expropriation of their investment "has led directly to the inability to receive any dividends, profits or other proceeds from their asset." The Tribunal agrees with Respondent's position that Section 24 of the NIPC Act cannot be used to enable or require Respondent intervene into payment disputes between two private parties. Thus, Claimants have not suffered a violation of Section 24 of the NIPC Act.[28]

The Tribunal further suggested that this case could have been more suitably resolved in Nigerian domestic courts through the appeals process.[29]

In *Bay View Group v. Rwanda* (2022), the Claimants' sought $95 million for what they called creeping expropriation.[30] The basic claim is that the American investors bought a five-year mining license from a local company with the belief that they would get a 35-year extension on the license, but the state refused to extend. "The reason alleged by the Claimants for Rwanda's wish to drive NRD to abandon the Five Concessions was to facilitate 'smuggling,' this being the marketing or minerals originating in the RDC, sometimes described as the Belgian Congo, as being mined in Rwanda, to the profit of the latter country."[31] The Tribunal rejected this on the facts as follows:

> Had NRD been occupying the Five Concessions under long-term licences and had Rwanda wished to remove NRD from the Concessions, it is possible to envisage

[27] *Id.* at 193 (quoting Sec. 24 of NIPC Act).

[28] *Id.* at 309.

[29] *Id.* at 315 ("As indicated in the previous section, the JOA did not give the NNPC the authority to intervene in the internal disputes of Pan Ocean's shareholders. In this case, Claimants' remedy would have been to challenge the decision in the courts. Initially, this is what happened. It is, however, unclear why the case was withdrawn and did not go on appeal. In principle, this case and its merits could have been presented before the Nigerian Court of Appeal. Even if Dr. Fadeyi and NNPC raised procedural issues such that the case could never proceed, as alleged, the Tribunal is not persuaded that Respondent was responsible for any action that was taken in the courts as part of an alleged intention to enable Dr. Fadeyi to take over Pan Ocean and deprive Claimants of their ownership of Pan Ocean").

[30] *See* Bay View Group LLC and The Spalena Company LLC v. Republic of Rwanda, ICSID Case No. ARB/18/21, Award (Mar. 30, 2022), at 88–95.

[31] *Id.* at 90.

> Rwanda repeatedly treating NRD unfairly in an attempt to get them to relinquish their licences. But NRD had no right to remain in occupation of the Concessions after 2012 other than that voluntarily conferred by Rwanda. On the facts of this case it would have been open to Rwanda simply to have rejected the 2012 Application. Instead, over a period of about three years, Rwanda first granted NRD repeated extensions of the Special Licences granted in 2007, then invited NRD to make a new application under the 2014 Law and, when a deficient application was made, gave NRD a series of opportunities to remedy the deficiencies. This behaviour was wholly at odds with a wish on the part of Rwanda to get NRD out of the Concessions.[32]

In this sense, the Claimant could not sustain its creeping expropriation claim because the Tribunal was not convinced that the state took any adverse and unlawful measures to deprive the investor of its proprietary interest. The most serious claim pertained to FET violation as discussed in Chapter 11.

Conclusion

Expropriation is the most fundamental international investment law concept. As described at length in Part I, investment law essentially originated and acquired doctrinal exposition in the context of expropriation. The 1970s foundation cases were also exclusively expropriation cases. Most of the cases that came in the decades that followed were also expropriation cases. The jurisprudence of expropriation is essentially a bridge that connects the old-world order of colonial means of the protection of capital with the new rules-based world order. The inertia is evident in the old cases. In the 1970s and 1980s, the recently independent state of Libya exercised the power of eminent domain but it was harshly reprimanded, and other newly independent states took note of the limits of state power vis-à-vis foreign capital.

All of the African states that were called on to answer charges of expropriation before ICSID tribunals gave their consent voluntarily, and many participated in the proceedings but none of them accepted liability in any individual case. They presented a view of expropriation that is often quite different from the view of expropriation held by the investors. Indeed, in most cases, the tribunals agreed with the Claimants and

[32] *Id.* at 478. The paragraphs immediately preceding that offer context:

> 477. In his opening address at the Hearing, Counsel for Rwanda submitted that it was difficult to understand the smuggling conspiracy theory and there was a total absence of evidence to support it. The case was evidentially nonsensical for three reasons:
>
> (1) It was possible to see on the evidence what in fact happened to NRD's application for long-term licences. There was a contemporaneously documented transparent process. This involved teams analysing NRD's applications and explaining why they were deficient;
> (2) There was no conceivable basis for suggesting that Rwanda was promoting or even condoning smuggling. On the contrary, Rwanda had put in place well observed and thorough processes to prevent smuggling; and
> (3) The Claimants sought, inferentially, to support their theory by misinterpreting or drawing incorrect conclusions from bits of data and statistics.
>
> 478. The Tribunal endorses these submissions, but considers that there are additional reasons for rejecting the "*creeping expropriation*" allegation.

not the respondent states. It appears from the discussion of the cases above that most tribunals interpreted the concept of expropriation more expansively than the African states were willing to accept. However, the results have been mixed and nuanced. While in most of the early cases the tribunals found the African states responsible for expropriation, in the more recent cases beginning with *Gustav v. Ghana* (2010) and continuing through to *Bay View Group v. Rwanda* (2022) the results have been mixed, with many of the tribunals rejecting claims of creeping expropriation on both legal and factual grounds.

As a matter of law, the expropriation standards that all of the tribunals have adopted and employed are almost identical and are largely based on the Hull Rule. The most common formulation, whether it comes from contract, domestic law or treaty is this taxonomy:

> Investments of investors shall not be subject to any measures depriving them, directly or indirectly, of their investments or value unless the following conditions are complied with:
> a) the measures are taken in the public interest and under due process of law;
> b) the measures are not discriminatory;
> c) the measures are accompanied by provision of prompt adequate and effective compensation.

Although there might be variations in the textual renditions, there is no example that shows that outcome depended on the actual variation in terminology employed in the underlying instrument.

Overall, perhaps with the exception of the *Strabag v. Libya* (2020) case in which the umbrella clause is inappropriately used to justify a result that bypassed a proper expropriation analysis discussed in Chapter 15, it is fair to conclude that none of the tribunals appear to have stretched the concept beyond the limit that the concept could reasonably shoulder.

As indicated above, some tribunals seem to have done a better job than others, but one matter remains true in all of these cases: the severity of the facts are the single most important indicator of outcome, begging the question of how much of the exposition of legal doctrine is a pathway to *ex aquo et bono*. To the extent there be any inconsistencies, they are almost invariably a function of the appreciation of the facts, preferences of the particular arbitrators, or the perceived justice of the matter than differences of opinion on the law of expropriation. Beyond that, these cases do not seem to present any greater inconsistency and incoherence than any domestic jurisprudence on the taking of private property.

14

The Umbrella Clause as a Concept of International Investment Law in the African Cases

General obligations that state entities assume under domestic law and contract are often elevated to international obligations under provisions of investment treaties, often referred to as the umbrella clause. Many tribunals have defined the contours of this principle. This chapter examines the prevalence and use of this principle in the African cases in temporal classification corresponding to the previous chapters.

The Umbrella Clause in the Early African Cases

The umbrella clause is a modern invention, at least in the African cases. Because most of the early African cases arose out of concession agreements, the umbrella clause, being a treaty law concept, had no applicability. In fact, it was not until the *Gustav v. Ghana* case in 2010 that it got express treatment. However, in some of the contract-based cases, what would have been considered contract-based umbrella clause claims had been raised and decided in close connection with expropriation, which was the main source of liability in the early days.

A good example of this is *Letco v. Liberia* (1986).[1] Its expropriation analysis, mostly called nationalization, focused on the existence or nonexistence of a nondiscriminatory legislative act of nationalization along the lines of the Libyan Oil cases. Because Liberia was not represented and its defense for taking back part of the land that it had granted to the Claimant was based on allegations of the Claimant's lack of performance, the Tribunal's discussion of expropriation was primarily based on breach of contract under the applicable domestic law under the Concession Agreement, that is, Liberian law. The following paragraph captures the main part of the expropriation issue:

> As part of its consideration of this case, the Tribunal considered whether the action taken by the Liberian Government in depriving letco of its concession might be considered as an act of nationalization, which might be justifiable both under the law of Liberia and under international law, if accompanied by payment of appropriate compensation. It should be emphasized that the Government of Liberia has not sought to justify its action on this basis; rather, it has consistently claimed that its

[1] Liberian Eastern Timber Corporation v. Republic of Liberia, ICSID Cases No. ARB/83/2, Award (Mar. 31, 1986).

Africa's International Investment Law Regimes. Won L. Kidane, Oxford University Press. © Oxford University Press 2023.
DOI: 10.1093/oso/9780197745571.003.0014

> action was taken because of failure on the part of the claimant to properly carry out its obligations under the Concession Agreement—an argument which the Tribunal has rejected on the facts. However, even if the Government had sought to justify its action as an act of nationalization, it would have had to first point to some legislative enactment, embodying the act of nationalization. It would then have had to show that its action was taken for a bona fide public purpose; that it was non-discriminatory; and that it was accompanied by payment (or at least the offer of payment) of appropriate compensation.[2]

This was a proper restatement of the Hull Rule as applied by many of the Tribunals before it; however, in applying it to the facts of this case, it comes to a quick conclusion that even if the State had made the argument that it was a lawful expropriation—nationalization under generally applicable nationalization law or decree—it would have been discriminatory.[3]

The Tribunal's decision on expropriation was underdeveloped because the decision eventually rested on breach of contract. Although the breach of contract issue also raised the question of whether a breach by a governmental agency with a regulatory power *ipso jure* amounted to direct or indirect expropriation, the Tribunal did not travel that path, instead choosing to rest its decision exclusively on breach of contract under Liberian domestic contract law. In this sense, this case is an investment case only inasmuch as it was arbitrated under the ICSID Convention. Otherwise, as indicated above, no effort was made to link breach of contract with expropriation, but it raised the same kinds of issues that a classic umbrella clause case would have raised.

In any case, none of the pre-2010 cases under review raised a pure umbrella clause claim, making those claims the most contemporary additions to the jurisprudence.

Umbrella Clause Claims in the Post-2010 Period

Gustav v. Ghana (2010) is one of the first and few African cases that featured the umbrella clause more prominently than other claims, because the dispute was essentially a contract dispute. The Tribunal quite instructively begins by proclaiming "as a general rule, a violation of contract is not a violation of international law":[4]

[2] Letco v. Liberia, ICSID Cases No. ARB/83/2, Award (Mar.31, 1986), at 70 (relying on the following authorities: UN Res. 1803 (XVII) of 1962 (relating to Permanent Sovereignty over natural resources); Higgins, *The Taking of Property by the State: Recent Developments in International Law*, Recueil des Cours, 176, 305 (1982—III); Aminoil v. The Government of Kuwait, 21 ILM 976, Final Award (Mar. 24, 1982).

[3] Letco v. Liberia, ICSID Cases No. ARB/83/2, Award (Mar.31, 1986), at 72.

[4] Gustav F W Hamester GmbH & Co KG v. Republic of Ghana Respondent, ICSID Case No. ARB/07/24, Award (June 18, 2010), at 327–28. The Tribunal lists a collection of quotes that support this well-established rule. It is important to document them for reference here as well:

> Waste Management v. Mexico:
> "In the Tribunal's view, an enterprise is not expropriated just because its debts are not paid or other contractual obligations towards it are breached. There was no outright repudiation of the transaction in the present case, and if the City entered into the Concession Agreement on the basis of an over-optimistic assessment of the possibilities, so did Acaverde. It is not the function of Article 1110 to compensate for failed business ventures, absent arbitrary intervention by the State amounting to a virtual taking or sterilising of the enterprise." Waste Management, Inc.

> It may be that there were violations of the JVA committed by the Claimant, and it may be that Cocobod violated the JVA in failing or refusing to deliver the requested amount of cocoa beans, but these are contractual matters and not treaty matters. As a result, the commercial acts of Cocobod, even if they had been attributable to the Respondent, could still not have constituted a breach of the BIT engaging the international responsibility of the ROG. This constitutes a complete answer to the Claimants allegations with regard to Articles 2(1), 4(2) and 4(3) of the BIT (FET and expropriation).[5]

In a board stroke, the Tribunal properly disposed of all the important claims, including expropriation and FET. It did, however, add a few analytical steps to the legitimate expectations prong of the FET clause distinguishing it from expectations arising out of contractual relationships.[6]

It took another decade before any tribunal in the African cases took the umbrella clause claims more seriously. *Strabag SE v. Libya* (2020) is one of few cases that based a substantial part of the finding of liability and award of damages on the umbrella clause. The Tribunal first found jurisdiction to adjudicate the purely contractual claims of the contractors by interpreting the generic umbrella clause under Article 8(1) of the applicable Libya-Austria BIT.[7] It then considered each and every breach

v. United Mexican States (Number 2), ICSID Case No. ARB(AF)/00/3, Final Award (April 30, 2004), at 160.

Joy Machinery Limited v. Egypt:

"A basic general distinction can be made between commercial aspects of a dispute and other aspects involving the existence of some forms of State interference with the operation of the contract involved." Joy Mining Machinery Limited v. Egypt, ICSID Case No. ARB/03/11, Award on Jurisdiction (August 6, 2004), at 72.

Impregilo v. Pakistan:

Only the State in the exercise of its sovereign authority ("puissance publique"), and not as a contracting party, may breach the obligations assumed under the BIT. In other words, the investment protection treaty only provides a remedy to the investor where the investor proves that the alleged damages were a consequence of the behaviour of the Host State acting in breach of the obligations it had assumed under the treaty." Impregilo S.p.A. v. Islamic Republic of Pakistan, ICSID Case No. ARB/03/3 (Italy/Pakistan BIT), Decision on Jurisdiction (April 22, 2005), at 260.

Noble Venture v. Romania:

"The Tribunal recalls the well established rule of general international law that in normal circumstances per se a breach of a contract by the State does not give rise to direct international responsibility on the part of the State. This derives from the clear distinction between municipal law on the one hand and international law on the other, two separate legal systems." Noble Ventures, Inc. v. Romania, ICSID Case No. ARB/01/11, Award (Oct. 12, 2005), at 53.

Azurix v. Argentina:

"The Tribunal agrees that contractual breaches by a State party or one of its instrumentalities would not normally constitute expropriation. Whether one or series of such breaches can be considered to be measures tantamount to expropriation will depend on whether the State or its instrumentality has breached the contract in the exercise of its sovereign authority, or as a party to a contract." Azurix v. Argentine Republic, ICSID Case No. ARB/01/12, Award, July 14, 2006, para. 315.

[5] *Id.* at 331.

[6] *See id.* at 335–36, *see also* Chapter 12 (discussing legitimate expectations as it relates to the FET standard and contract rights).

[7] Strabag Se v. Libya, ICSID Case No. ARB(AF)/15/1, Award (June 29, 2020), at 165 ("While the Tribunal has great respect for the proponents of such views, it is not able to agree that arguments regarding

of contract claim under the umbrella clause by referring back to its jurisdictional decision without any analysis of its substantive content. The only reference in the substantive merits part about the application of the umbrella clause for the substantive breach of contract claims was this: "Claimant advances substantial claims on the basis of Article 8(1) of the Treaty, the umbrella clause. Interpretation and application of this provision are discussed supra, in connection with Respondent's objections to the Tribunal's jurisdiction."[8]

The next time Article 8(1) appears in the award is the finding of liability for a very specific claim of unpaid certificate of work: "On this basis, FTI assesses and the Tribunal accepts that Al Hani is entitled to receive an additional € I,092,078 on its payment certificates claim pursuant to Article 8(1) of the Treaty."[9]

Likewise, the next time Article 8(1) appears is also in connection with a finding of liability and allocation of damages: "Accordingly, on the basis of Article 8(1) of the Treaty, the Tribunal awards 90% of the amount claimed with respect Payment Certificate No. 3, € 1.04 million."[10]

There seems to be a tremendous analytical gap between the finding of jurisdiction to adjudicate umbrella clause claims and the finding of liability under the umbrella clause. Technically, the finding of jurisdiction under the umbrella clause permits the Tribunal to assess whether the state failed to honor specific international commitments, which in this case might have been expressed in construction contracts.

While the Tribunal has assessed the various payment certificates on the facts, it seems to have skipped an essential analytical step of whether or not they were considered breaches of obligation under Libyan law, and if so, whether each unpaid payment certificate represented a dishonored international obligation under the umbrella clause.

The Tribunal took a shortcut by relying on its jurisdictional analysis of the umbrella clause for its finding of liability and assessment of damages. Its use of the umbrella clause was indeed more generous than would be expected from a post-backlash contemporary tribunal. As indicated in next chapter, the Tribunal, at least the majority, gave a noticeably sympathetic consideration to the investor's wartime disruptions and losses, perhaps subscribing to the view that the state is more blameworthy for its predicaments and is in a better position to absorb wartime or conflict produced losses. For that, it used the umbrella clause highly effectively.

puissance publique or on the perceived inherent limits of international jurisdiction can amend or condition the plain language of the treaty-makers in Article 8(I). In any case, although the requirement of *puissance publique* is absent in Article 8(1) of the Treaty, as discussed more fully infra, the factual circumstances clearly show that Al Hani's contracts were all made for significant public infrastructural projects in the interest of Libya. Contracting for such public works contracts is in fact a typical State function, not a commercial activity carried out *Jure privatorum*. Further, their performance involved actions by a range of State organs exercising their governmental powers") ("166. Accordingly, the Tribunal finds that Respondent's first and second objections to jurisdiction under Article 8(1) of the Treaty must be rejected").

[8] *Id.* at 237.
[9] *Id.* at 363.
[10] *Id.* at 391.

Conclusion

The use of the umbrella clause is a rarity in the African cases. Even when it was used, as in *Strabag v. Libya* (2020), it is poorly reasoned and used to justify a preferred outcome. It generally sits uncomfortably as a concept of treaty law. It encourages jurisdictional conflict and unduly duplicates grounds of substantive claims. It converts treaty tribunals into commercial tribunals. As such, it is fair to conclude that the wholesale elevation of breach of contract claims to the level of treaty violation is as unintended and uncomfortable as it is exorbitant. The umbrella clause is the least defensible international investment law concept, one that has found no positive example in the African cases.

15

Fair and Equitable Treatment, Full Protection and Security, and Nondiscrimination

Innocuous sounding terms such as "fair and equitable," "legitimate expectations," and "nondiscrimination" have over the decades been subjects of immeasurable acrimony and resulted in more controversy than any other substantive principles of international investment law. Following the claims of expropriation, the second most common claims labeled against the African states have been the denial of Fair and Equitable Treatment (FET) and/or Full Protection and Security (FPS), and to a lesser extent, principles of nondiscrimination such as Most Favored Nation (MFN) treatment and national treatment.

This chapter examines the nature and scope of the assertion of these principles against African states, identifies the various defenses that these African states have advanced, and analyzes the jurisprudence that has emerged out of them. It also synthesizes the specific rules that have emerged and evaluates whether there is any evidence of the abuse of the FET standard that justifies the fear of FET that continues to inform the existing reform efforts.

The Full Protection and Security principle is often countenanced in relation to and sometimes in addition to the Fair and Equitable Treatment. Although some tribunals and more contemporary treaties conceive it as the protection of physical property, some cases have over the years given it a broader meaning analogous to the Fair and Equitable Treatment principle. This chapter also identifies those instances.

The nondiscrimination principles of MFN and National Treatment have been invoked infrequently. Indeed, there is only one case in the subset of cases that used these principles as a rule of decision. The principles are discussed in connection with relevant cases in this chapter.

Because all of these principles are necessarily based on treaty law and because almost all of the early African cases were not based on BITs, these principles did not begin to occur until the 2000s, at least not in the published English cases. As such, the discussion begins with the cases decided in the 2000s.

The Fair and Equitable Principles in the African Cases of the 2000s

One of the first treaty-based African cases that considered claims based on FET and FSP was the *Wena v. Egypt* case of December 2000.[1] In *Wena*, the FET and FSP provisions were contained in one of the earliest African BITs, the 1974 UK–Egypt BIT.

[1] Wena Hotels Limited v. Arab Republic of Egypt, ICSID Case No. ARB/98/4, Award (Dec. 8, 2000).

Africa's International Investment Law Regimes. Won L. Kidane, Oxford University Press. © Oxford University Press 2023.
DOI: 10.1093/oso/9780197745571.003.0015

Article 2(2) of this BIT states:

> Investments of nationals or companies of either Contracting Party shall at all time be accorded fair and equitable treatment and shall enjoy full protection and security in the territory of the other Contracting Party. Each Contracting Party shall ensure that the management, maintenance, use, enjoyment or disposal of investments in its territory of nationals or companies of the other Contracting Party is not in any way impaired by unreasonable or discriminatory measures. Each Contracting Party shall observe any obligation it may have entered into with regard to investments of nationals or companies of the other Contracting party.[2]

The Tribunal discusses FET and FSP in tandem. As indicated in the expropriation section above, the undisputed facts show that the wholly Egyptian owned enterprise, EHC, forcibly evicted the UK hotel management entity, Wena, the investor in this case, for failure to pay its lease. Wena claimed against Egypt for its failure to stop the violations and take timely and appropriate remedial measures.[3] The Tribunal's summary of the findings of what went wrong reads as follows:

> There is substantial evidence that, even if Egyptian officials other than officials of EHC did not participate in the seizures of the hotels on April 1, 1991, 1) Egypt was aware of EHC's intentions to seize the hotels and did nothing to prevent those seizures, 2) the police, although responding to the seizures, did nothing to protect Wena's investments; 3) for almost one year, Egypt (despite its control over EHC both before and after April, 1991) did nothing to restore the hotels to Wena; 4) Egypt failed to prevent damage to the hotels before their return to Wena; 5) Egypt failed to impose any substantial sanctions on EHC (or its senior officials responsible for the seizures), suggesting its approval of EHC's actions; and 6) Egypt refused to compensate Wena for the losses it suffered.[4]

The evidence shows that EHC acted unlawfully by taking over the properties that Wena was managing under management contract on allegations of withholding of payment due to it. The takeover was ordered by EHC leadership and involved a large number of individuals who used some level of force against Wena's personnel. Police arrived late and investigated the matter poorly. Offenders were treated with leniency. A legal process took one year to return the properties to Wena. Egypt, as a state, offered no compensation.[5] Although the award offers no discussion of what domestic contractual and other remedies were anticipated to make the injuries good, it appears that the investor was reinstated without the offer of compensation by the state itself.

Under these facts, the Tribunal had no difficulty finding a violation of both FET and FPS in the following paragraphs containing a partial list of the wrongful conduct:

[2] *Id.* at 84.
[3] *See id.* at 82–95.
[4] *Id.* at 82.
[5] *See id.* at 82–95.

> Finally, neither EHC nor its senior officials were seriously punished for their actions in forcibly expelling Wena and illegally possessing the hotels for approximately a year. Although several representatives of EHC—including Messrs. Kandil and Munir—were convicted for their actions, neither Mr. Kandil nor Mr. Munir was sentenced to serve any jail time. Instead, both were fined only EGP 200, which Mr. Munir stated that he has never paid. Also, neither official appears to have suffered any repercussions in their careers. As noted above, the Ministry of Tourism chose not to exercise its authority to remove Mr. Kandil as Chairman of ECH and, according to Ms. Jelcic, he currently is serving as an advisor to a senior member of the Egyptian parliament. Since the seizures, Mr. Munir has been promoted to become the Head of the Legal Affairs Division at EHC and is expecting a further promotion in the near future. This absence of any punishment of EHC and its officials suggest that Egypt condoned EHC's actions:
>
> 95. For all of these reasons, the Tribunal concludes that Egypt violated its obligation under Article 2(2) of the IPPA, by failing to accord Wena's investments "fair and equitable treatment" and "full protection and security.[6]

Although the mistreatment appears clear, there is no discussion of the standard of protection that FET and FSP offer. The investor was unlawfully disposed of its rights for a year but the host state's legal process seems to have worked in returning the property to the investor in a year. However, the Tribunal was more interested in assessing the host state's efforts to punish those who violated the investor's rights. Whether that directly constituted a violation of FET or FSP or both is not clear from the discussion. Not only are the two are lumped together, but the relevance of the punitive steps is also not explained. Subsequent cases attempted to expound what acts constitute a violation of FET and/or FSP and the level of severity of the wrongful act. In this case, however, it is clear that the Tribunal was merely troubled by the disregard of the legal process by EHC in enforcing its contractual rights against Wena.

In that sense, the FET/FSP analysis is simplistic. The evidentiary record clearly focused on the nature of the violation by EHC rather than on the host state's failures. There is no discussion of why it took one year and how the host state accomplished that result within its own legal process. The fault appears to have been one of failure to prevent an unlawful act by its own enterprise, but the finding appears to be a cumulative effect of both the failure to prevent and the delay in restoration. That being the most important inquiry, the description of the evidence is scant at best.

For the *Middle East Cement v. Egypt Tribunal* (2002), FET was remarkably an aspect of the expropriation inquiry, not an independent violation. Consider the nexus that the Tribunal attempts to create between expropriation and FET in the following passage:

> 143. Art. 2.2 of the BIT requires that "Investments by investors of a Contracting Party shall, at all times, be accorded fair and equitable treatment and shall enjoy full protection and security, in the territory of the other Contracting Party." This BIT

[6] *Id.* at 94–95.

> provision must be given particular relevance in view of the special protection granted by Art. 4 against measures "tantamount to expropriation," and in the requirement for "due process of law" in Art.4.a). Therefore, a matter as important as the seizure and auctioning of a ship of the
>
> Claimant should have been notified by a direct communication for which the law No. 308 provided under the 1st paragraph of Art. 7, irrespective of whether there was a legal duty or practice to do so by registered mail with return receipt requested as argued by Claimant (CV 4). The Tribunal finds that the procedure in fact applied here does not fulfill the requirements of Art. 2.2 and 4 of the BIT.
>
> 144. Thus, the Tribunal concludes that the Poseidon was taken by a "measure the effects of which would be tantamount to expropriation" and that the Claimant is entitled to a compensation as provided for under Art. 4. c) of the BIT.[7]

For this Tribunal, the denial of due process simultaneously violates the expropriation and FET provisions. Or perhaps a more accurate characterization would be that the violation of due process is a violation of FET, and the violation of FET is a violation of protection against expropriation. Such approach merges all violations into expropriation and unduly simplifies the assessment of damages because then the Tribunal does not have to worry about quantifying an FET violation, which many tribunals found difficult.

The *Patrick Mitchell v. DRC* (2004) Tribunal mentions the FET principle in passing as a prelude to its more detailed expropriation analysis. The full FET reference is contained in this introductory passage under the title the applicable provisions of the BIT.[8] Having quoted the FET provision in full, it goes straight to the expropriation analysis without adding more.

As indicated in the expropriation section above, the Tribunal finds that the DRC expropriated Patrick Mitchell's law firm, but makes no ruling on whether the said events such as the removal of documents and property and arrest of lawyers by the military amount to the denial of FET or FPS within the meaning of the BIT. Although the award's annulment was primarily because of the lack of a qualifying investment, a finding of an FET and/or FPS violation and a modest award of compensatory damages akin to moral damages would probably have attracted less acrimony in terms of dissent and would have avoided an annulment proceeding altogether. Up until this time, FET was less utilized and the Claimants' cases were primarily based on expropriation claims.

[7] *Id.* at 143–44.

[8] Patrick Mitchell v. DRC Award (Feb. 9, 2004); Annulment (Nov. 1, 2006), at 58:

> 58. The Investment Treaty concluded in 1984 between the United States of America and the Democratic Republic of Congo ("Zare" at that time) contains a number of provisions on the protection of investments that can be found in many other Treaties of this kind. Article II of this BIT is dealing with the "Treatment of Investment" and it provides under paragraph 4 as follows:
>
> "Investments of nationals and companies of either Party shall at all times be accorded fair and equitable treatment and shall enjoy protection and security in the territory of the other Party. The treatment, protection and security of investment shall be in accordance with applicable national laws, and may not be less than that recognized by international law. Neither Party shall in any way impair by arbitrary and discriminatory measures the management, operation, maintenance, use, enjoyment, acquisition, expansion, or disposal of investment made by nationals or companies of the other Party. Each Party shall observe any obligation it may have entered into with regard to investment of nationals or companies of the other Party."

The *Champion Trading v. Egypt* (2006) case was remarkable for its omission of an FET claim, but maintained a transparency and discrimination claim under a provision that said: "The treatment, protection and security of investments shall never be less than that required by international law and national legislation."[9] It would appear that the Tribunal assumed that FET is implicit in this broad protection and security provision because the 1992 US BIT Model that the US and Egypt concluded did not contain an independent FET clause.[10]

In this BIT, FET is expressly made only a part of the tax exception provision, which reads:

> With respect to its tax policies, each Party should strive to accord fairness and equity in the treatment of investments of nationals or companies of the other Party. Nevertheless, all matters relating to the taxation of nationals or companies of a Party, or their investments in the territories of the other Party or a subdivision thereof shall be excluded from this Treaty, except with regard to measures covered by Article III and the specific provisions of Article V.[11]

In any case, the *Champion Trading* Tribunal applied the transparency doctrine as a part of the general nondiscriminatory treatment and security provision under Art. (4) although it found no violation on the facts of the case.[12] This was one of the earlier cases that entertained the doctrine of transparency as an aspect of investment protection. Subsequent cases developed it further as a component of legitimate expectations, which in turn became a contentious component of FET.

More Developments in the Concepts of Non-Discrimination and FET

Champions Trading is just about the only case under review that contains useful discussion of the nondiscrimination principles. The examination of the African ICSID cases suggests that the principles of nondiscrimination, that is, MFN and National Treatment (NT) are invoked surprisingly infrequently and succeed even more infrequently. It was not until *Champions Trading* that the issue of discriminatory treatment independent of the expropriation context got serious consideration at least in the published English cases.

The MFN and NT question came about in the following context. The Claimants, Champion Trading and Ameritrade International, Inc., were Delaware companies holding shares in the Egyptian National Cotton Company (NCC).[13] Along with other individual shareholders who were later dismissed due to the Tribunal's lack of

[9] *Id.*

[10] *See* US–Egypt BIT (entered into force in 1992), at https://investmentpolicy.unctad.org/international-investment-agreements/treaty-files/1123/download.

[11] *Id.* at Art. XI.

[12] *See* Champion Trading Company Ameritrade International, Inc. v. Arab Republic of Egypt, ICSID Case No. ARB/02/9, Award (Oct. 27, 2006), at 157–64.

[13] *Id.* at 1 ("On May 29, 2002, the shareholders of National Cotton Company ("NCC")—Champion Trading Company, a Delaware (USA) incorporated company, Ameritrade International, Inc., another Delaware (USA) incorporated company, together with James T. Wahba, John B. Wahba and Timothy T. Wahba—submitted to the International Centre for Settlement of Investment Disputes ("ICSID" or "the Centre") a Request for Arbitration directed against the Arab Republic of Egypt").

jurisdiction over them,[14] they initiated the proceeding on the basis of the 1992 United States–Egypt Bilateral Investment Treaty.[15] The Claimants' specific claim was based on national treatment contained in Article II(2) of the BIT, which reads:

> Article II (2)(a) of the BIT provides:
>
> Each Party shall accord investments in its territory, and associated activities in connection with these investments of nationals or companies of the other Party, treatment no less favorable than that accorded in like situations to investments and associated activities of its own nationals and companies, or nationals and companies of any third country, whichever is the most favourable.[16]

This was supplemented by reference to Article II (4) of the BIT, which also reads: "The treatment, protection and security of investments shall never be less than that required by international law and national legislation."[17]

The factual predicate of the claim is a complex mix of numerous legislative and regulatory efforts by the Egyptian government taken to streamline its important cotton industry.[18] In its simplest form, the foundational claim was that the state implemented its economic plan in the cotton industry in a discriminatory way, causing the Claimants quantifiable injury.[19]

Because this was in the early days of the development of BIT jurisprudence (at least in the African cases), there was some level of conceptual confusion toward the beginning of the proceedings. For example, the legal basis of the Claimants' position merges different notions in the following way:

> The Claimants allege that the Respondent has violated its obligations to provide non-discriminatory treatment under Article II (2)(a) of the BIT (i.e., discrimination/ national treatment claim, cf. infra 4.1.1) and to provide treatment in accordance with international law including full protection and security and fair and equitable treatment under Article II (4) of the BIT.[20]

The Claimants later dropped their FET and FPS claims,[21] but maintained what the Tribunal continued to call treatment in accordance with international law, a concept that it analyzed independently of FET as discussed below.[22]

[14] *Id.* at 12 ("On October 21, 2003, the Arbitral Tribunal issued its Decision on Jurisdiction. The Arbitral Tribunal declared that it did have jurisdiction over the claims of the corporate Claimants—Champion Trading Company and Ameritrade International, Inc.—but did not have jurisdiction over the individual Claimants—James B. Wahba, John T. Wahba and Timothy T. Wahba. This Decision is annexed to this Award and constitutes a part thereof").

[15] *Id.* at 40.

[16] Reproduced in *id.*

[17] *Id.*

[18] The Tribunal offers an unusually detailed description of the industry and the measures in *id.* at 41–89.

[19] *See id.* at 90–108.

[20] *Id.* at 90.

[21] *See id.* at 158 ("158 Because the Claimants withdrew their claim based on the alleged violation of the fair and equitable treatment and the full protection and security obligations, the Arbitral Tribunal will not further analyze this facet of the claim").

[22] *Id.* at 159 ("159 However, the Claimants maintained their claim based on the lack of transparency of the Settlements, pursuant to Art. II (4) of the BIT, which will be analyzed hereunder").

The Tribunal stated the elements of a discrimination claim and the burden shifting scheme as follows:

> 125. The non-discrimination principle is found in Art. II (2)(a) of the BIT, which prohibits discrimination based on nationality and requires the State to treat equally investments that are in like situations.
>
> 126. The purpose of Art. II (2)(a) is to promote foreign investment and to guarantee the foreign investor that his investment will not because of his foreign nationality be accorded a treatment less favourable than that accorded to others in like situations.
>
> 127. The Parties are in agreement that the application of this clause requires that a foreign company make an investment and/or any associated activity in connection with this investment, in the territory of a Contracting State.
>
> 128. To comply with the non-discrimination provision, the following requirements need to be met: there shall be no treatment less favourable—i.e., no discrimination—between foreign and national investments when they are in like situations. This standard requires the Arbitral Tribunal to first determine whether the parties involved—NCC and the companies who received payments from the Government under the various Settlements—were in like situations, and then to compare the treatment being received by foreign investments with the treatment received by local investors to determine whether there was a violation of the provision.
>
> 129. Were the parties involved—NCC and the companies who received payments from the Government—in like situations?
>
> 130. The national treatment obligation does not generally prohibit a State from adopting measures that constitute a difference in treatment. The obligation only prohibits a State from taking measures resulting in different treatment in like circumstances91. A like situation has been defined as a similar situation that should be assessed within the same business or economic sector.[23]

On the facts, the Tribunal found that there was disparate treatment, but such was justified because the disparately treated parties were not similarly situated.[24] In particular, the Tribunal found that there was a legitimate nondiscriminatory purpose for

[23] *Id.* at 125–30.

[24] *Id.* at 131–34:

> 131 In the present case, the Parties agree that NCC and the other publicly—or privately—owned cotton trading companies were prima facie in similar situations: both purchased cotton from farmers, and both ginned their cotton and sold it.
>
> 132 According to the Respondent, the payments made by the Government to some cotton trade companies were based on objective criteria: the payments aimed either to reimburse debts for pre-1994 operations or to reimburse price differentials for operations post-1995/96 in which NCC did not participate93. Therefore, the payments did not violate the national treatment obligation.
>
> 133 According to the Claimants, the payments made by the Government did discriminate. An analysis of the intent of the Government of Egypt is irrelevant. Because the Claimants did demonstrate a prima facie difference in treatment, the burden had shifted to the Respondent to demonstrate that a reasonable non-discriminatory policy justification existed that would explain the differences in treatment received by NCC and the other cotton companies94.

treating the American companies differently from the Egyptian companies because the American companies did not participate in some of the programs that qualified for government payment.[25]

Although this was a case that was primarily decided on the facts, it articulated the proper discrimination standard very well as reproduced above. In practice, it is not uncommon to see Tribunal confusion on the issue of disparate treatment of dissimilar circumstances, which may give the impression that there is discrimination, whether it is analyzed as a component of MFN, NT, or FET.

Apart from the discrimination claim, the Tribunal analyzed a lack of transparency claim as a component of general international law but not based on FET. Subsequent tribunals considered transparency as a component of legitimate expectations, which is a component of FET, but, as shown above, this Tribunal analyzed transparency independently of those notions under Article II (4) of the BIT, that is, general international law and domestic law on nondiscrimination.

The Tribunal said in particular that "the non-discrimination principle can also be found more generally in Art. II (4) of the BIT, which provides for a general non-discrimination principle, as required by international law and national legislation."[26] The Tribunal also reconfirmed that it was not analyzing transparency as a part of the FET claim as the Claimant had actually withdrawn such claim.[27] As such, transparency, as a rule of decision, came not from FET or NT, but from general international law as indicated in Art. II (4).[28]

The Claimant attempted to source the rule of international law on transparency by reference to WTO Appellate Body Decisions and ISDS jurisprudence, the latter of which incidentally was an FET analysis.[29] The Tribunal did not doubt that

> 134 Under Art. II (2)(a) of the BIT, the Government of Egypt should not treat differently NCC and other cotton trading companies on the grounds of their different nationality, if they were in like situations. The question would remain whether a difference of treatment in like situations could be permissible based on other objective grounds. It is, however, not necessary for the Arbitral Tribunal to answer this question since the Arbitral Tribunal, as shown hereafter, finds that NCC and the companies which received the payments were not in a like situation.

[25] *Id.* at 154–56:

> 154 Although both kinds of companies operate in the same industry and are subject to same kind of rules, there is a significant difference between a company which opts to buy cotton from the Collection Centres at fixed prices and a company which opts to trade on the free market, whether or not the company is privately-owned or State-owned or whether the company is national or foreign.
>
> 155 The first requirement to be fulfilled in order to receive compensation payments from the Government is the participation in the trading of cotton through the Collection Centres. The Parties are in agreement that NCC did not participate in this system. Therefore, NCC cannot be compared with other cotton trading companies regarding the Settlements.
>
> 156 Since the Arbitral Tribunal came to the conclusion that the companies were not in a like situation, it does not need to analyze the other requirements which prohibit discrimination on the grounds of nationality."

[26] *Id.* at 157.

[27] *Id.* at 158.

[28] *Id.* at 158–60.

[29] *See id.* at 161–62 ("161 The transparency principle was developed by the Claimant by reference to the principle of transparency as it has been addressed by the WTO Appellate Body, and recalled the U.S.-Underwear case in which the Appellate Body described how the principle of transparency finds expression in the GATT agreement: 'The essential implication is that Members and other persons affected, or likely to

transparency is a part of Art. II (4), which reads "the treatment, protection and security of investments shall never be less than that required by international Law and national legislation,"[30] but denied relief because it was not convinced on the facts that the relevant Egyptian laws, regulations and government decisions lacked transparency.[31] Evidently, subsequent cases developed the concept of transparency as a component of FET rather than a general nondiscrimination rule of international law.

By 2008, a sizable body of ICSID jurisprudence in non-African ICSID cases had begun to accumulate. *Biwater v. Tanzania* (2008) drew from that accumulation and as such was one of the first African cases to explore the parameters of modern FET doctrine. In doing so it went through many of the most frequently cited FET cases,[32] and distilled the following defining characteristics of FET as the rule of decision:

> Protection of legitimate expectations: the purpose of the fair and equitable treatment standard is to provide to international investments treatment that does not affect the basic expectations that were taken into account by the foreign investor to make the investment, as long as these expectations are reasonable and legitimate and have been relied upon by the investor to make the investment.
> - Good faith: the standard includes the general principle recognised in international law that the contracting parties must act in good faith, although bad faith on the part of the State is not required for its violation.
> - Transparency, consistency, non-discrimination: the standard also implies that the conduct of the State must be transparent, consistent and non-discriminatory, that is, not based on unjustifiable distinctions or arbitrary.[33]

be affected, by Governmental measures imposing restraints, requirements and other burdens, should have a reasonable opportunity to acquire authentic information about such measures and, accordingly, to protect and adjust their activities, or alternatively to seek modification of such measures'").

[30] *Id.* at 40.

[31] *Id.* at 163–64.

> 163 According to the Respondent, the payments were known, public and transparent. The payments were published and the reimbursements were decided on the grounds of a report drafted by the independent Central Audit Agency. Evidence was produced by the Respondent to this effect.
>
> 164 The parties are in agreement that each Party has the burden to prove the facts on which it relies to support its claims and defenses. It was therefore the obligation of the Claimants to prove that the Settlements were not made in a transparent manner. The Tribunal notes that the Laws and Decrees regarding the organization of the cotton trading structures, the prices and the Government Centres' purchase and sale mechanism were public, available, or have been published or produced by the Respondent upon the request of the Claimants. The Claimants were in a position to know beforehand all rules and regulations that would govern their investments for the respective season to come. The Claimants have not produced any evidence or even pertinent arguments that Egypt violated the principle of transparency under international law and this claim therefore also has to be denied.

[32] These cases include: Waste Management, Inc. v. United Mexican States (Number 2), ICSID Case No. ARB(AF)/00/3, Final Award (Apr. 30, 2004); Middle East Cement Shipping and Handling Co. S.A. v. Arab Republic of Egypt, ICSID Case No. ARB/99/6, Award (Apr. 12, 2002); Saluka Investments BV v. Czech Republic, UNCITRAL, Partial Award (Mar. 17, 2006); CME Czech Republic B.V. v. Czech Republic, UNCITRAL, Partial Award (Sep. 13, 2001), 9 ICSID Rep. 121 (2006); Maffezini v. Spain, Award (Nov. 13, 2000), and Metalclad v. Mexico, Award (Aug. 30, 2000). These cases are cited in Biwater Gauff (Tanzania) Ltd. v. United Republic of Tanzania, ICSID Case No. ARB/05/22, Final Award (July 24, 2008), at n. 257–58.

[33] Biwater Gauff (Tanzania) Ltd. v. United Republic of Tanzania, ICSID Case No. ARB/05/22, Final Award (July 24, 2008), at 602.

Clearly inclined toward a more liberal reading of the FET standard than the pure minimum standards of treatment under customary international law, which the Tribunal attempts to suggest is the same standard,[34] it went on applying it to the facts of the case and found that Tanzania denied the investor FET by terminating the lease and deporting the managers[35] although the actions caused no economic damage.[36]

At the end of the day, the violation was not a measure that caused economic damage to the investor but it was the state's failure to follow process that was deemed to be a violation of FET, an international wrongful act. On the same facts, although no physical force was used, the Tribunal found a violation of FSP.[37] The Tribunal spared no deference to the Respondent State although it finally exonerated it from the payment of damages.

Analytically, *Biwater v. Tanzania* (2008) is notable for its approval of the fusion of the consequences of expropriation and violation of FET especially in the context of the award of damages.[38]

The last of the 2008 trilogy, *Jan de Nul N.V. and Dredging International N.V v. Egypt* (2008), runs into the same dilemma and surveys the same line of cases ranging from *Tecmed* to *Saluka* to *West Management*, emphasizing the latter.[39] Comprised of Professors Stern and Koufmann-Kohler, the Tribunal firmly establishes the denial of justice as the core component of FET,[40] and adopts a flexible standard as to what it means:

[34] *Id.* at 592 ("Having said this, the Arbitral Tribunal also accepts, as found by a number of previous arbitral tribunals and commentators, that the actual content of the treaty standard of fair and equitable treatment is not materially different from the content of the minimum standard of treatment in customary international law").

[35] *Id.* at 605 ("The Arbitral Tribunal concludes that the following conduct on the part of the Republic was in violation of Article 2(2) of the BIT: (a) Minister Lowassa's press conference on 13 May 2005, and his address to the staff on 17 May 2005; (b) the withdrawal of the VAT exemption on 24 May 2005; (c) the seizing of control of City Water's offices; the immediate installation of DAWASCO; and the deportation of senior management on 1 June 2005").

[36] *Id.* at 606.

[37] *Id.* at 731.

[38] *Id.* at 776 ("For claims other than expropriation (breach of fair and equitable treatment, unreasonable and discriminatory measures, violation of full protection and security, and of the principle of unrestricted transfer of funds), the BIT does not offer any guidance for evaluating the damages arising from such breaches. On the basis that this does not mean that compensation is excluded, the common starting point is the broad principle articulated in the well known Factory at Chorzow case, according to which any award should: 'as far as possible wipe out all the consequences of the illegal act and re-establish the situation which would, in all probability, have existed if that act had not been committed.' ")

[39] Jan de Nul N.V. Dredging International N.V. v. Arab Republic of Egypt, ICSID Case No. ARB/04/13, Award (Nov. 6, 2008), at 187 ("For example, the Waste Management tribunal considered that fair and equitable treatment could be denied 'if the conduct is grossly unfair or idiosyncratic, discriminatory and exposes the claimant to sectional or racial prejudice or involves lack of due process leading to an outcome which offends judicial propriety—as might be the case with a manifest failure of natural justice in judicial proceedings or a complete lack of transparency and candour in an administrative process.' ") (quoting Waste Management, Inc. v. United Mexican States (Number 2), ICSID Case No. ARB(AF)/00/3, Final Award (Apr. 30, 2004), at 98).

[40] *Id.* at 188 ("It considers, however, that the fair and equitable treatment standard encompasses the notion of denial of justice. The Parties and their experts are in agreement on that point").

193. Denial of justice may occur irrespective of any trace of discrimination or maliciousness, if the judgment at stake shocks a sense of judicial propriety. A reference to the test formulated by the Mondev tribunal is useful in this context:

In the ELSI case, a Chamber of the Court described as arbitrary conduct that which displays "a willful disregard of due process of law... which shocks, or at least surprises, a sense of judicial propriety." It is true that the question there was whether certain administrative conduct was "arbitrary," contrary to the provisions of an FCN treaty. Nonetheless (and without otherwise commenting on the soundness of the decision itself) the Tribunal regards the Chamber's criterion as useful also in the context of denial of justice, and it has been applied in that context, as the Claimant pointed out. The Tribunal would stress that the word "surprises" does not occur in isolation. The test is not whether a particular result is surprising, but whether the shock or surprise occasioned to an impartial tribunal leads, on reflection, to justified concerns as to the judicial propriety of the outcome, bearing in mind on the one hand that international tribunals are not courts of appeal, and on the other hand that Chapter 11 of NAFTA (like other treaties for the protection of investments) is intended to provide a real measure of protection. In the end the question is whether, at an international level and having regard to generally accepted standards of the administration of justice, a tribunal can conclude in the light of all the available facts that the impugned decision was clearly *improper and discreditable*, with the result that the investment has been subjected to unfair and inequitable treatment. This is admittedly a somewhat open-ended standard, but it may be that in practice no more precise formula can be offered to cover the range of possibilities.

194. Albeit rendered in the context of Article 1105(1) of the NAFTA and the minimum standard of customary international law, the Tribunal finds this test appropriate.[41]

The most instructive aspect of this Tribunal's reckoning with the FET standard is its characterization of its own role in judging the conducts of the domestic administrative and judicial organs of the host state. It clearly stated that it does not sit as an appeals court to correct errors of the host state's court's application of their own laws, but rather "the task of the Tribunal is to determine whether the Judgment is "*clearly improper and discreditable.*"[42] Applying these standards, the Tribunal found for the host state on all counts.[43] This case as a whole is highly instructive for other tribunals in

[41] *Id.* at 193–94 (quoting Mondev Int'l Ltd. v. United States, NAFTA/ICSID Case No. ARB(AF)/99/2, Award (Oct. 11, 2002), 125, at 127). The Tribunal emphasized the "improper and discreditable" phrase and used it in its analysis.

[42] *Id.* at 209. The whole passage is highly instructive: "There is no evidence on record of any discrimination, bias or malicious application of the law based on a sectional prejudice. In this instance, it is not the role of the Tribunal to review whether the Isma lia Court conducted a correct contractual analysis or correctly applied Egyptian law. Whether under Egyptian law the Court could (as argued by the Respondent's expert, Prof. Hossam El-Ehwany, Exh. R-12) or on the contrary could not (as alleged by the Claimants' expert, Mr. Hosni Abdelwahed, Exh. C-178) invoke the provisions of the Contract in its Judgment is not for this Tribunal to decide. It is not the role of a tribunal constituted on the basis of a BIT to act as a court of appeal for national courts. The task of the Tribunal is rather to determine whether the Judgment is "clearly improper and discreditable" in the words of the Mondev tribunal."

[43] See *id.* at 282.

understanding their role as to the finding the denial of justice, rather than quarrelling with domestic courts on the application of their own laws.

The *Waguih Elie v. Egypt* (2009) case offers a good example of the denial of justice as a component of FET. In that case, although the Respondent state admitted liability and offered to compensate, the fact that the state ignored no less than nine different administrative and judicial rulings in favor of the Claimant over a period of 12 years prompted the Tribunal to find "an egregious denial of justice to the Claimant."[44] Although the Tribunal also considered the same set of facts in its analysis on the question of unlawful expropriation, it summarized what it considered the core of the FET standard as follows:

> The general, if not cardinal, principle of customary international law that States must act in good faith is thus a useful yardstick by which to measure the Fair and Equitable standard. While its precise ambit is not easily articulated, a number of categories of frequent application may be observed from past cases. These include such notions as transparency, protection of legitimate expectations, due process, freedom from discrimination and freedom from coercion and harassment.[45]

[44] Waguih Elie George Slag and Clorinda Vecchi v. The Arab Republic of Egypt, ICSID Case No. ARB/05/15, Award (June 1, 2009).

[45] *Id.* at 450 (citing See Rudolf Dolzer & Christoph Schreuer, Principles of International Investment Law 5 (2d ed. 2012), at 133–47).

16
Fair and Equitable Treatment and Nondiscrimination Principles in the Post-2010 Cases

The evolution of the fair and equitable treatment and related non-discrimination principles evolved more rapidly in the years since 2010 with more notable developments in the more contemporary cases in the post-2020 period.

The Period between 2010 and 2020

The various elements of FET discussed in the previous chapter continued to gain momentum over the years and began crystalizing as time passed. *Gustav v. Ghana* (2010) came next, to clarify the relationship between legitimate expectations as an element of FET and ordinary performance expectations under contract.

The Tribunal first rejected the Claimant's attempt to frame a breach of contract claim as a breach of treaty in the following categorial terms:

> The Tribunal wishes to make clear that it considers this analysis as no more than one of several attempts to present what are in truth "contract claims" as "treaty claims." It agrees with the Respondent that: "Hamester's approach to an FET clause is striking, for it appears to equate every FET clause into an umbrella clause interpreted in the most extreme 'transformative' manner."[1]

Unsatisfied, the Tribunal wanted to make its position abundantly clear as if it were talking to other tribunals that confused these issues: "*It is important to emphasise that the existence of legitimate expectations and the existence of contractual rights are two separate issues.*"[2] It sought support from the *Parkerings v. Lithuania* tribunal, and said that that tribunal "made a clear distinction between contractual obligations under national law and legitimate expectations under international law." It did so in the following terms:

> It is evident that not every hope amounts to an expectation under international law. The expectation a party to an agreement may have of the regular fulfilment of the obligation by the other party is not necessarily an expectation protected by international

[1] Gustav v. Ghana (2010) at 334 (quoting from the Respondent's Counter-Memorial, 315).
[2] *Id.* at 335 (emphasis added).

Africa's International Investment Law Regimes. Won L. Kidane, Oxford University Press. © Oxford University Press 2023.
DOI: 10.1093/oso/9780197745571.003.0016

law. In other words, contracts involve intrinsic expectations from each party that do not amount to expectations as understood in international law.[3]

Bringing it back to the attribution issue for the purpose of disposition of the controversy before it, it made a narrower ruling:

> Applying the actual words of Article 9(2) of the BIT, the contractual obligations which the Claimant seeks to impose upon the ROG were not "assumed by it." Given that the umbrella clause in this BIT is specifically delimited by reference to obligations that have been "assumed by the State," the Tribunal sees no basis to ignore these words, and to extend the ambit of the provision to contractual obligations assumed by other separate entities.[4]

The Tribunal's focus was on attribution, and at the end of the day all allegations of treaty violations including legitimate expectations as a component of FET failed for lack of attribution, and the umbrella cause could not elevate any possible breaches of contractual promise to a level of treaty violation. This seems to be a genuine interpretation of the BIT by an informed tribunal.

The *Bernard von Pezold v. Zimbabwe* (2015) case is mainly an expropriation case, but it had a significant FET and FSP component. The factual predicates of these claims are identical with the expropriation claims discussed in Chapter 10, but the FET and FSP claims are notable for the Tribunal's endorsement of the FET standard proposed by the Claimant.[5] The Tribunal stated its understanding of the FET standard as follows:

> In particular, the jurisprudence supports the Claimants' contention that a breach of FET can be based on State actions that are "arbitrary, grossly unfair, unjust, idiosyncratic, discriminatory, expose the investor to sectional or racial prejudice, coerce or harass the investor, or lack due process" and/or a breach of specific representations made to the investor (legitimate expectations). A State is thus expected to behave, as the Claimants submit, in a "consistent, even handed, unambiguous, transparent, candid" manner. To the extent FET incorporates the

[3] *Id.* (quoting Parkerings-Compagniet AS v. Republic of Lithuania, ICSID Case No. ARB/05/8, Award (Sep. 11, 2007), 344).

[4] Gustav F W Hamester GmbH & Co KG v. Republic of Ghana Respondent, ICSID Case No. ARB/07/24, Award (June 18, 2010), at 347(i). *See also id.* at 348 ("In these circumstances, the contractual commitments of Cocobod, being a separate entity from the State, cannot be considered as elevated—and transformed in nature—by Article 9(2) of the BIT, into treaty commitments of the State itself. It follows that a violation by Cocobod—if such a violation had been found—could not have constituted a violation of the BIT").

[5] Bernardus Henricus Funnekotter and Others v. Republic of Zimbabwe, ICSID Case No. ARB/05/6, Award (Apr. 22, 2009), at 525 ("The Claimants state that they had basic and legitimate expectations at the time they made their investments that the Respondent would treat them and their investments in a just, consistent, transparent, even-handed, nonarbitrary and nondiscriminatory manner, "follow due process and act in good faith proportionately without coercion or harassment and pay compensation upon expropriation" The Claimants assert that President Mugabe recognized these norms when he made speeches at the time the Republic of Zimbabwe gained its independance, which caused the von Pezolds to invest in Zimbabwe over other African States "that were less progressive").

> minimum standard of treatment under international law, it is clear that this standard has moved on since the Neer case.[6]

Applying this standard to the facts, the Tribunal had no difficulty finding a violation of the FET standard.[7] Like most Tribunals do, it appeared to have merged the FSP standard with either the expropriation or FET standard as it did not go into the details separately.

The *Union Fenosa Gas, S.A. (UFG) v. Egypt* (2018) case is one of those rare cases that found an FET violation without finding expropriation and awarded full reparation exclusively on the basis of the finding of discrimination as a component of FET.

It concerned the Respondent state's inability to supply natural gas that the investor's NLG plant required to operate. The Tribunal found that the reallocation of limited resources due to the Egyptian revolution did not absolve the state of its nondiscrimination obligation.[8] The Claimant's principal claim was that the Respondent violated the FET provision of the relevant BIT by "failing to ensure an adequate gas supply to the Damietta Plant and prioritising the domestic market and other gas consumers at the Claimant's expense."[9]

In explaining the FET standard under the BIT, the Claimants proposed the following analytical framework: "(i) Did the host State's conduct create legitimate expectations on the part of the investor? (ii) Did the investor rely on the State's conduct at the time it invested? And (iii) did the host State subsequently fail to honor the expectations it created?"[10] In response, the Respondent argued for the *Waste Management v. Mexico* (2004) standard of "arbitrary, grossly unfair, unjust or idiosyncratic... conduct."[11]

The Tribunal combined the suggestions by the two the parties and said: "The Tribunal is content to apply under Article 4(1) the customary international law standard as prohibiting (inter alia) conduct by the host State 'which is unjust, arbitrary, unfair, discriminatory or in violation of due process,' including conduct that frustrates an investor's "legitimate expectations," as decided by the NAFTA tribunal in Merrill v. Canada (2010).[12] Explaining its middle ground further, the Tribunal noted that:

> (i) its expectations were reasonable in the circumstances; (ii) it relied upon such undertaking or representation when it made its investment in Egypt; and (iii) that

[6] *Id.* at 546.

[7] *See id.* at 561 ("Accordingly, the Tribunal finds that the Claimants have established a breach of the FET standard contained in Article 2(1) of the German BIT and Article 4(1) of the Swiss BIT by failing to accord the Claimants FET in connection with (a) the Zimbabwean Properties; (b) the Residual Properties, Zimbabwean Company Shares and Income-Generating Assets; (c) the Forrester Water Rights; (d) the Forrester Loans; (e) the Forrester Tobacco Value Shortfall; (f) the Forester Conversion Amount; and (g) the Border Liquidation Shortfall").

[8] Union Fenosa Gas, S.A. v. Arab Republic of Egypt, ICSID Case No. ARB/14/4 (Aug. 31, 2018), at 9.1.

[9] *Id.* at 9.7.

[10] *Id.* at 9.9.

[11] *Id.* at 9.30 (quoting Waste Management, Inc. v. United Mexican States (Number 2), ICSID Case No. ARB(AF)/00/3, Final Award (Apr. 30, 2004), 98).

[12] *Id.* at 9.51 (citing Merrill v. Canada, ICSID Case No. UNCT/07/1, Award (Mar. 31, 2010), 208).

> the Respondent's non-compliance with its undertaking or representation violated the FET standard in Article 4(1) of the Treaty. The Tribunaldoes not consider that such a representation or undertaking amounts to a free-standing part of the FET standard but, rather, that it is "a relevant factor" in assessing whether or not the Respondent violated the FET standard, as was decided in Mobil v. Canada (2012).[13]

The Tribunal found on the facts that there was a clear representation by the government to the investor that it would get natural gas for its plant, and that:

> it was essential for the Claimant to receive natural gas under the SPA. There was no other source of natural gas for the Plant. It was to be connected to the national grid; and it was not to be supplied from its own gas field. Without such supply, the Plant would become a "white elephant."[14]

The decision eventually rested on the factual finding that Egypt discriminated against the investor. In the Tribunal's own words:

> During the same period, the Damietta Plant's supply of gas was curtailed by 96%, whereas foreign-owned industrial plants were curtailed by 15% to 34%; namely EFC (Netherlands) as to 28%, EBIC (Netherlands) as to 34%, Emethanex (Canada) as to 25%, and Lafarge (France) as to 15%.169 As to Egyptian-owned industries, there were no curtailments or only minor curtailments.[15]

This is a concrete example of what types of quantifiable discriminatory disfavors could rise to the level of FET violation on the basis of discrimination. Although the Tribunal appears not to have given sufficient attention to the background economic and security considerations, on the distilled facts, the result does not seem surprising.

CMC v. Mozambique (2019) is a failed attempt to elevate an unpaid invoice in a simple construction agreement to a treaty violation. The Claimant claimed that "a state's conduct is inconsistent and contradictory when it amounts to a willful refusal

[13] *Id.* at 9.53 (citing Mobil v. Canada, Decision on Liability and on Principles of Quantum (May 22, 2012), 152; CMS Gas Transmission Company v. The Republic of Argentina, ICSID Case No. ARB/01/8, Award (May 12, 2005), at 89; Waste Management v. Mexico II, ICSID Case No. ARB(AF)/00/3, Final Award (Apr. 30, 2004), at 98; MTD v. Chile, Decision on Annulment (Mar. 21, 2007), 67).

[14] *Id.* at 9.65. *See also id.* at 9.84 ("From the time when the Plant's commercial operations began on 15 October 2006 to the end of 2010, the shortfall was 190 million BTUs;117 and from 2012 to 2014, the supply was too limited to comprise even a single cargo. The Damietta Plant has lain idle since 2014; and it remains idle to the present day").

[15] *Id.* at 9.142 ("9.138 In the Tribunal's view, as regards both phases, the Respondent's decisions to cut and curtail gas supply to the Damietta Plant was, by its nature and purpose, a sovereign act by the Respondent under international law. It was also, of course, a political decision by the Respondent in the broadest sense. It was not a decision required by Egyptian law; and it was not a commercial or operational decision originating with EGAS. It was, in fact, a decision against EGAS' commercial interest, given the higher prices under the SPA and the lower prices for the subsidised Egyptian electricity sector. Nor was the decision the enforced result of the Global Financial Crisis of 2007–2008 or the Egyptian revolution during 2011–2014: the decision would have been made without these events or their consequences, given the Respondent's earlier long-term policies on the development of new gas field, compounded by gas subsidies favouring domestic users, well established before 2010").

by a government authority, not based on reasonable grounds, to abide by its contractual obligations."[16]

The factual predicates were essentially that the government first promised to enter into a settlement agreement for unpaid invoices but changed its mind because there was a change in government officials.[17] Interestingly, the Claimant admitted that bad faith was a part of the FET standard, but argued that the state acted in bad faith.[18]

The Tribunal first noted that bad faith alone is not sufficient to show a violation of FET and relied upon an ICJ statement that "good faith, as a concept, 'is not in itself a source of obligation,' "[19] but rejected the Claimant's claim of FET violation on the facts in the following terms:

> The Claimants have not established that the Respondent shifted its position on settlement at all, much less that it did so in bad faith. ANE extended a settlement offer to CMC on 30 October 2009, but CMC did not accept that offer. The offer expired by its terms seven days after it was made, and ANE never made another offer. It is true that a new administrator of ANE, Mr. Grachane, took over as General Director of ANE in January of 2011, and Mr. Grachane made it clear that he felt that it had been a mistake for ANE to make the settlement offer in the first place.535 But the offer made in 2009 had expired long before Mr. Grachane took office. It is not bad faith for two successive holders of the same office to hold different views, and that is all that the Claimants have established on this point.[20]

While *CMC v. Mozambique* is an excellent example of a case that should not have been brought before a treaty tribunal, *Thomas Goslin v. Mauritius* (2020) is remarkable for similar reasons and perhaps also for being too inchoate because the Claimant could not even prove that there were representations that could have given rise to reasonable expectations. According to the Tribunal, even if there were any representations, the government was entitled to change its policy without violating FET because the investors knew the possibility existed.[21]

[16] CMC Muratori Cementisti CMC Di Ravenna SOC. Coop. & Others v. Republic of Mozambique, ICSID Case No. ARB/17/23 (Oct. 24, 2019), at 397.

[17] *See id.* at 398 ("Mozambique offered to enter into a settlement agreement on 30 October 2009, made the Claimants believe that the settlement agreement would be honored after it was accepted on 2 November 2009, and then repudiated that commitment on 8 August 2011. b. Mozambique failed to respond to the Claimants' repeated requests for payment during the period from 2010 until 2017 and refused to engage in good faith discussions during that time period. c. More specifically, the Government failed to inform the Claimants in a timely manner that its position regarding the settlement agreement had changed after a new Minister of Public Works and a new Director General of ANE took office following the 2009 elections, instead waiting for 20 months to reply to the Claimants' requests for payment").

[18] *Id.* at 402 ("The Claimants argue that Mozambique violated the FET standard by acting in bad faith, which they contend is an inherent component of that standard. The Claimants argue that Mozambique acted in bad faith by shifting its position with regard to the settlement agreement after the new political appointees assumed their offices at ANE and the Ministry, by waiting more than 20 months to reply to a request for payment, by revisiting the settlement agreement, and by failing to engage in meaningful discussions to resolve outstanding issues").

[19] *Id.* at 415.

[20] *Id.* at 417.

[21] *See* Thomas Gosling, Property Partnerships Development Managers (UK) Limited & Others v. Republic of Mauritius, ICSID Case No. ARB/16/32, Award (Feb. 18, 2020), at 249 ("The Respondent's objective had always been to inscribe Le Morne as a heritage site. The Claimants were aware of this objective.

In rejecting the Claimant's underdeveloped and unsupported claims, the Tribunal did weigh in on the FET standard. It is important to take note of it. The Tribunal questioned the utility of distinguishing between FET as an expression of the minimum standard of treatment under customary international law or as a treaty created autonomous obligation in the following terms:

> The Parties differ on whether the FET is an autonomous standard or it requires merely the minimum standard of treatment under international law. The Tribunal questions the relevance of the differentiation. Whether it is considered equivalent to the minimum standard of treatment or an autonomous standard, the level of the treatment required to breach the standard has evolved.[22]

This is remarkable because many tribunals do puzzle over this, and indeed in certain cases, it could make a difference. However, in this Tribunal's view, the distinction is meaningless because the minimum standard of treatment has evolved beyond this distinction in any case: "What was considered minimum treatment in the nineteenth century is not the minimum required in the twenty-first, particularly in the context of a treaty specifically providing for fair and equitable treatment."[23] Remarkably, however, having said that, it went on outlining what it considers the elements of FET as it has evolved. First, it said that

> given the wide variety of situations to which fair and equitable treatment may be applicable, there is no comprehensive definition of the FET standard. The standard is "a flexible one which must be adapted to the circumstances of each case." However, flexibility does not mean that treatment will be determined by the subjective expectations of the investors. Their expectations "to be protected, must rise to the level of legitimacy and reasonableness in light of the circumstances."[24]

Second, "as pointed out by other tribunals, the fair and equitable treatment obligation needs to be interpreted in a balanced manner."[25] As to balance, the Tribunal borrows from the *El Paso* Tribunal, which stated "this Tribunal considers that a balanced interpretation is needed, taking into account both State sovereignty and the State's responsibility to create an adapted and evolutionary framework for the development

The Claimants pressed BOI to issue the LOI for their own internal arrangements and those of Mr. Giraud with his family. The Respondent was entitled to change its policy in respect of development in Le Morne and had never given any assurance that it would not change it. The change in policy as regards the buffer sub-zones needs to be assessed in the context of the progress made by the Claimants in obtaining all the permits required for the Le Morne Project. By the time Revised PPG2 was issued, the Claimants had not obtained the permits necessary for BOI to consider the issuance of an Investment Certificate. In fact, the LOI had expired more than a year earlier, and the Claimants had not obtained the permits from the local authorities in charge of issuing development rights").

[22] *Id.* at 243.
[23] *Id.*
[24] *Id.* at 244.
[25] *Id.* at 245.

of economic activities, and the necessity to protect foreign investment and its continuing flow."[26]

Finally, it adds its own instructive note as follows: "*To sum up, the Tribunal understands fair and equitable treatment to mean treatment that objectively will be considered just by an impartial observer bearing in mind the circumstances.*"[27] This last part is the most valuable contribution of this Tribunal. No matter what the evolution looks like and no matter how differently stated, at the end of the day, FET is what an impartial decision-maker objectively considers *just* under the circumstances. It is a sensible conclusion, but it makes the issue of impartiality and sense of justice of the arbitrators ever more important as it delegates too much power to the arbitrators' sense of justice. In this case, seeing no injustice, the Tribunal dismissed Thomas Goslin's claim against Mauritius.[28]

The Post-2020 Period

In *Strabag SE v. Libya* (2020), the principles of fair and equitable treatment and full security and protection competed with the infrequently invoked MFN rule contained in a War and Conflict provision of the Libya-Austria BIT.[29] The key question was whether the War and Conflict losses provision[30] was *lex specialis* replacing FET and FSP.[31] The Respondent relied on such cases as *Venezuela Holdings and others v. Venezuela* and *ConocoPhillips and others v. Venezuela* cases that carved tax and fiscal matters out of FET.[32] The idea is that where the War and Conflict clause applies, the

[26] *Id.* at 245 (quoting El Paso Energy International Company v. Argentine Republic, ICSID Case No. ARB/03/15, Decision on Jurisdiction (Apr. 27, 2006), 70).

[27] *Id.* at 246 (emphasis added).

[28] *See, e.g., id.* at 261, rejecting the claim of discrimination as it did all other claims: "The Tribunal concludes that there is no basis for the discrimination claim. The review of the instances on which the Claimants have based their claim of discrimination shows that each of the cases can be distinguished from the case before the Tribunal and also shows that there was no practice of extending routinely the period to start construction. The Claimants were aware of the risk that they ran. BOI's letter of February 16, 2006 (nine days after the deadline had expired) drew the attention of the Claimants to 'the fact that amendment of the Pointe Jerome Project at this stage may question the validity of the Letter of Intent issued by BOI and the various permits and clearances granted by different Government bodies.' Mr. Gosling himself was aware that the Government had cancelled or attempted to cancel leases in 'a large number of cases.' For this reason, he requested that the LMB property be exchanged against freehold State land." *Id.*

[29] *See* Strabag Se v. Libya, ICSID Case No. ARB(AF)/15/1, Award (June 29, 2020), at 221.

[30] *Id.* at 213 (quoting Art. 5(2) of the Treaty) ("Article 5 of the Treaty provides: (I) An investor of a Contracting Party who has suffered a loss relating to its investment in the territory of the other Contracting Party due to war or to other armed conflict, state of emergency, revolution, insurrection, civil disturbance, or any other similar event, or acts of God or force majeure, in the territory of the latter Contracting Party, shall be accorded by the latter Contracting Party, as regards restitution, indemnification, compensation or any other settlement, treatment no less favourable than that which it accords to its own investors or to investors of any third state, whichever is most favourable to the investor. (2) An investor of a Contracting Party who in any of the events referred to in paragraph (I) suffers loss resulting from: (a) requisitioning of its investment or part thereof by the forces or authorities of the other Contracting Party, or (b) destruction of its investment or part thereof by the forces or authorities of the other Contracting Party, which was not required by the necessity of the situation, shall in any case be accorded by the latter Contracting Party restitution or compensation which in either case shall be prompt, adequate and effective and, with respect to compensation, shall be in accordance with Article 4(2) and (3)").

[31] *Id.* at 221.

[32] *Id.* at 222 (citing these two cases) (citations omitted).

ordinary FET clause is overridden just like the tax carveouts in the above-cited cases. The Tribunal, however, categorically ruled that "Article 5 [War and Conflict] does not have the preclusive effect urged by Respondent,"[33]and added that "Nothing in the language of Article 5(2) or in other provisions of the Treaty indicates that it operates in the limiting manner urged by Respondent."[34]

The Tribunal then went on considering the parameters of the FSP standard. In an attempt to reconcile the Parties' positions, the Tribunal adopted a reasonableness standard suggested by Dolzer and Schreuer that "the standard of liability under the full protection and security standard requires a host State 'to take such measures to protect the foreign investment as are reasonable in the circumstances.' "[35]

As is very rarely the case, the FET provision took the back seat in the *Strabag* because the Tribunal considered it duplicative of the FSP and War and Conflict clause.[36] And as such, none of the awards were based on FET.

Although the Tribunal ruled that the War and Conflict Clause was not *lex specialis*, it devoted a considerable amount of analysis to it. There were at least two broad categories of claims for damage or loss. The first category is damage and loss the Libyan forces have caused unjustified by military necessary, and damage that they were not able to prevent.[37]

Article 5(2)(b) of the BIT assimilates losses sustained by the investor in times of war to expropriation unless justified by military necessity. It reads in relevant part:

> Destruction of its investment or part thereof by the forces or authorities of the other Contracting Party, which was not required by the necessity of the situation, shall in any case be accorded by the latter Contracting Party restitution or compensation which in either case shall be prompt, adequate and effective and, with respect to compensation, shall be 1naccordance with Article 4 (2) and (3).[38]

[33] *Id.* at 224.

[34] *Id.*

[35] *Id.* at 235 (citing RUDOLF DOLZER & CHRISTOPH SCHREUER, PRINCIPLES OF INTERNATIONAL INVESTMENT LAW 5 (2d ed. 2012), at 161). "The Tribunal concluded that 'In light of both Parties' extensive evidence showing circumstances of widespread conflict, violence and disorder in Libya at relevant times, the Tribunal is compelled to agree with the thrust of Respondent's assessment: In the circumstances prevailing in Libya during and since the Revolution, it was not reasonably possible for the Libyan authorities to take consistent and effective measures to protect Claimant's investment.272 The Tribunal has accordingly assessed Claimant's claims of failure to accord full protection and security in light of what both Parties' evidence shows regarding the security situation existing at the relevant place and time.' " *Id.* at 236.

[36] *Id.* at 239–40 ("239. These claims drew much less attention by the Parties in their written and oral submissions and involve the same conduct and facts as the Tribunal considers in connection with Claimant's other claims under the Treaty dealing with full protection under Article 3, compensation for losses under Article 5, and other obligations under Article 8. The Tribunal finds that they overlap or duplicate claims more fully developed by the Parties under these other provisions of the Treaty, without adding clarity to the case or providing bases for additional relief. 240. As other tribunals have observed, considerations of economy both jurisprudential and financial may lead a tribunal to conclude it need not consider in detail issues that are duplicative and do not contribute to a full and proper decision, or that would not alter a decision reached on other grounds. This is such a case."

[37] *Id.* at 264.

[38] *Id.* at 265.

The Tribunal first framed the issues properly as follows:

> A claimant can recover under Article 5(2)(b) of the Treaty only for losses from "destruction of its investment or part thereof by the forces or authorities of the other Contracting Party, which was not required by the necessity of the situation." Thus, two conditions must be met. First, the claimant must demonstrate that its property was destroyed "by the forces or authorities" of the respondent State. Second, it must be shown that such destruction "was not required by the necessity of the situation." Article 5(2)(b) of the Treaty thus presents the challenge of establishing responsibility for wartime damage by forces of the State party to the investor's property in violent and often chaotic circumstances.[39]

Applying this principle, the Tribunal found Libya liable for some of the Claimant's losses of equipment and properties that were taken or destroyed by Libyan forces without military necessity.

This was an intensely factual determination.[40] The biggest challenge was the determination of who was responsible for what in the fog of war, especially when the government now defending the claims was not the same government responsible for the losses. Indeed, that issue was raised. Libya claimed that the "Military forces for which the Respondent is responsible under the BIT were present. However, as Respondent also points out, those forces were loyal to the previous regime and no longer exist."[41] It is also noted that "Respondent advances an alternative argument to the effect that if damage was inflicted by Libya's military forces, it resulted from unauthorized conduct by forces acting outside of their orders, for which it was not responsible."[42] The Tribunal concludes, however that "this argument fails,"[43] and that is because "as a matter of international law, the International Law Commission affirms that the responsibility of a State under Article 91 of Geneva Protocol I—that the State 'shall be responsible for all acts by persons forming part of its armed forces' clearly covers acts committed contrary to orders or instructions."[44]

Applying these principles, the Tribunal found liability on the part of the Libyan state on the facts of some of the claims and rejected others. As a matter of principle, however, the Tribunal was guided by the following:

> As with Claimant's other claims for loss of property during the Revolution, the evidence shows that there was some damage to Al Hani's property and facilities for which there is a right to compensation under Article 5(2)(b) of the Treaty. The evidence also shows, however, that during this period, Al Hani's property and facilities were also damaged or looted by others including rebels, NATO, looters, and Al Han i's own employees. Respondent is not responsible under Article 5 of the Treaty for damage from these other causes.[45]

[39] *Id.* at 270.
[40] *See id.* at 271.
[41] *Id.* at 316.
[42] *Id.* at 319.
[43] *Id.*
[44] *Id.* at 319 (citations omitted).
[45] *Id.* at 320.

Considering these factual uncertainties, the Tribunal allocated responsibility on a percentage basis and filled the gap in the evidentiary record that way. In any case, this Tribunal did not advance the FET jurisprudence in any measurable way.

Interocean Oil v. Nigeria (2020) presented a weak domestic law-based FET case that the Tribunal had no difficulty dismissing in few paragraphs on grounds of lack of attribution just like it dismissed the expropriation case.

> 354. Claimants invite the Tribunal to assess this case pursuant to the minimum standard of treatment established in the *Neer v. Mexico* case. Under those criteria, action violates international law when it is "[...] sufficiently egregious and shocking—gross denial of justice, manifest arbitrariness, blatant unfairness, a complete lack of due process, evident discrimination, or a manifest lack of reasons."
>
> 355. Even if the Tribunal were to accept Claimants' position regarding the international minimum standard and its applicability, however, the Tribunal has concluded that Dr. Fadeyi's actions are not attributable to Respondent.[46]

What is extraordinary in this case is the Claimant's invitation of the application of the *Neer* standard, which is extremely deferential to the state. In any case, the claim was dismissed for lack of attribution,[47] denying the Tribunal the opportunity to opine on what standard of FET should apply.

In *Bay View Group v. Rwanda* (2022), the main claim was the frustration of the investor's expectation that by buying a five-year mining license it would get a 35-year mining right.[48] The Tribunal accepted that the principal of the Claimant companies entered Rwanda with the expectation of gaining a long-term mining license, but it had to determine whether the expectation of gaining a long term right was legitimate.[49] That question allowed the Tribunal to weigh in on the intense debate about the outer limits of the FET standard. This case being the most recent of all and of course involving one of the most recently modified BITs (although this was the 2004 US Model rather than the 2012), its expositions are useful. As a matter of fact, its analysis was also informed by the submission from the US government as the country of origin of the investor although the submission appears on a matter of principle that did not advance the Claimant's position.

[46] Interocean Oil Development Company and Interocean Oil Exploration Company v. Federal Republic of Nigeria, ICSID Case No. ARB/13/20, Award (Oct. 6, 2020), at 354–55.

[47] *See id.* at 357 ("The Tribunal, likewise, cannot find a violation of the fair and equitable treatment standard, including a duty to provide full protection and security. Claimants have not shown that there was any connection between Respondent's detention of Mr. Rooks (which Claimants have also stated was 'in connection with a disagreement over termination of a crude oil lifting contract and to enforce its rights as a joint venture partner') and Dr. Fadeyi or his potential concerns of termination. Claimants have likewise not met their burden of establishing the elements of a fair and equitable treatment or full protection and security claim").

[48] Bay View Group LLC and The Spalena Company LLC v. Republic of Rwanda, ICSID Case No. ARB/18/21, Award (Mar. 30, 2022), at 316.

[49] *See id.* at 316 ("The Tribunal is able to accept that Mr. Marshall became involved in mining in Rwanda in the hope of obtaining valuable longterm mining concessions. The Tribunal turns to consider whether any expectations that Mr. Marshall had that NRD would receive such concessions were 'legitimate.'")

It began with a historical note:

> The doctrine of "*legitimate expectation*" has been developed by English Courts and adopted by some other common law jurisdictions as part of the growth of administrative law over the last 50 years. Where an authorized agent of government has made a lawful representation or undertaking, that an individual will receive a benefit the State may be held bound to that representation in public law proceedings.[50]

The Tribunal goes on citing to two more authorities that are not necessarily consistent. The first is the submission in these proceedings by the United States, which reads:

> The concept of "legitimate expectations" is not a component element of "fair and equitable treatment" under customary international law that gives rise to an independent host State obligation. The United States is aware of no general and consistent State practice and *opinio juris* establishing an obligation under the minimum standard of treatment not to frustrate investors' expectations; instead, something more is required. An investor may develop its own expectations about the legal regime governing its investment, but those expectations impose no obligations on the State under the minimum standard of treatment.[51]

This cogent articulation has been the consistent position of the United States progressively enshrined in its most contemporary BIT models. However, the Tribunal also cited to a proposition that is not directly in line with this in the paragraph that follows this one. It is the opinion by Prof. Zachary Douglas who wrote:

> Where there is no specific rule of decision to apply, which is invariably the case in investment treaty arbitrations, the tribunal should search for principles of law. For instance, a tribunal would be on safer ground by making reference to the principle of estoppel or legitimate expectations to give content to the fair and equitable standard of treatment rather than appealing to the policy of achieving "greater economic cooperation."[52]

Without attempting to reconcile the above two propositions, the Tribunal then refers to Rwanda's understanding of the concept as follows:

> In its Rejoinder, Rwanda accepts that Article 5 of the BIT can be infringed by a failure by a State to satisfy the legitimate expectations of an investor provided that (i) failure to comply with the expectations infringed the minimum standard of treatment required by Article 5; (ii) the expectations were founded on a representation that

[50] *Id.* at 317.
[51] *Id.* at 318 (quoting USA Submission, 50).
[52] *Id.* at 319 (quoting Zachary Douglas, The International Law of Investment Claims (2009), 148).

> was made or subsisted at the time of the investment; (iii) the representation was reasonably relied upon by the investor in making his investment.[53]

The Tribunal then adds: "The Tribunal endorses these propositions and adds that an expectation will not be reasonable unless based on a representation that was lawful and was made by an official who was authorized to make it."[54] That was the entirety of the FET jurisprudence that the Tribunal was guided by.

Although this relatively incoherent use of legal authority is totally understandable for this particular Tribunal because it had already made up its mind on the facts, no matter how broadly or narrowly the FET standard was interpreted, as a matter of the hierarchy of the use of authorities, however, the interpretation of the United States and Rwanda as the contracting parties should have been given primacy and indeed there was no place for a legal treatise where there is direct evidence of the intent of the parties. This offers an excellent example of how ISDS jurisprudence could sometimes be guided by the preferences of the arbitrators rather than any principles of treaty interpretation. To be sure, this was one of the most sensible Tribunals in its analysis of the facts, as such, it may be because the facts were so clear that it did not see reason to spend any amount of time and energy to offer a sensible and coherent exposition of the FET standard. This could be blamed on "judicial" economy.

In any case, on the facts, the Tribunal found that the Claimants' expectations were not legitimate. Because the facts of this case are so similar to so many other African mining cases, it is important to reproduce the Tribunal's findings as follows:

> 329. Mr. Marshall refers to an email from Mr. Mucyo dated 12 December 2006. This provided advice as to how to obtain a Four-Year Contract for the Bisesero Concession but does not suggest that obtaining this would guarantee a long-term concession. Nor would Mr. Mucyo have had authority to give such an assurance on behalf of Rwanda.
>
> 330. In summary, the Claimants have failed to prove that, prior to their acquisition of NRD, any authorized Government official represented that long-term licences would be guaranteed to any company that succeeded in obtaining a Four-Year Contract. Nor would such a guarantee have been lawful, for it would have purported to abrogate the preconditions to entitlement to long-term licences contained in the Four-Year Contracts themselves.[55]

This was a decision that the facts made easy.

[53] *Id.* at 320.

[54] *Id.* at 321.

[55] *Id.* at 329–30. The paragraphs that follow state:

> 331. Paradoxically, the Claimants have sought to rely in support of their alleged legitimate expectation on the wording of the Contract itself, inasmuch as Article 4 states that NRD "will be granted the mining concessions" following the expiration of the Contract. But as the Memorial goes on to recognize, it was only after compliance with its obligations under the Contract that NRD would be entitled to the long-term licences.
>
> 332. For all these reasons the Tribunal finds that when Spalena acquired indirect ownership and control of NRD in December 2010 the Claimants had no legitimate expectation that NRD would be granted long-term licences.

Conclusion

The Stern-Koufmann-Kohler coalition-endorsed formulation of the FET appears to be the best articulation of the contemporary standard albeit with all its uncertainties:

> In the end the question is whether, at an international level and having regard to generally accepted standards of the administration of justice, a tribunal can conclude in the light of all the available facts that the impugned decision was clearly *improper and discreditable*, with the result that the investment has been subjected to unfair and inequitable treatment. This is admittedly a somewhat open-ended standard, but it may be that in practice no more precise formula can be offered to cover the range of possibilities.[56]

A critical mass of the African ICSID cases have addressed the FET and nondiscrimination principles. All tribunals in these cases have attempted to reckon with the uncertainties of the doctrine, but none have appreciably abused it. As a matter of fact, the FET standard presented no greater difficulty than the expropriation standard. Indeed, in many cases the two were analytically merged. In all cases, the most important indicator of the outcome of the cases was the gravity of the factual circumstances. The FET standard has been used as a scale for gauging how bad, how unfair, how improper the facts, and how "discreditable" the governments decisions were. In whatever language it is defined, at the end of the day, it is a principle that invites the arbitrators' sense of justice. The way that the various tribunals have articulated it over the years has created a useful template that they each use to structure the weighing of the facts.

A comparison of the pre-2000 contract-based African ICSID cases that did not involve FET with the more recent batch of FET-based African cases suggests that the tribunals have struggled with the same set of considerations of justice and fairness. Considerations of fairness and equity are inherent and implicit in all legal proceedings whether they are expressly called for in written text or not.

Moreover, as indicated above, the use of the FET standard in the African cases does not provide any evidence of the misuse of the principle. In fact, the respondent states have been able to have most FET-based claims rejected. These cases are a considerable proportion of all of the African ICSID cases. As such, it is not clear where the African fear of FET comes from. As will be demonstrated in Part IV, this fear seems to have affected the reform efforts ranging from new BIT models, regional treaties, and even the Draft Pan-African Investment Code.

A few observations could be added in summary. First, FET is a newcomer to the African ISDS jurisprudence because the pre-2000 ISDS cases were primarily expropriation cases based on contracts and domestic law. Second, even if many of the post-2000 cases have involved FET claims, none of the reviewed cases suggest discreditable use of the FET standard. Third, most of the FET based claims against African states have failed. In fact, there is no evidence that FET has been the exclusive source of

[56] Jan de Nul N.V. Dredging International N.V. v. Arab Republic of Egypt, ICSID Case No. ARB/04/13, Award (Nov. 6, 2008), at 193–94 (quoting Mondev Int'l Ltd. V. United States, NAFTA/ICSID Case No. ARB(AF)/99/2, Award (Oct. 11, 2002), 125), at 127).

liability except in one case discussed above. Fourth, although uncertainty in the standard is recognized by the various tribunals, they all agree that there is a common standard of justice, fairness, and judicial and administrative propriety. Indeed, they all repeat the same version of the standard of fairness and due process more or less verbatim even though they tinker with the outer limits. Finally, the range of matters of fairness and equity that the tribunals consider under the FET rubric are inherent matters of fair play that would be considered even without any express textual obligation or guidance.

Therefore the quarrel with the FET standard, at least in the African context, seems misplaced. The textual elimination of the standard will not eliminate its fundamental considerations. Problems with the decision-making process itself cannot be cured by eliminating the substantive standard. In fact, eliminating the standard would deprive future tribunals of a well-developed analytical template. A good fix needs to first identify the weak link. There is no evidence that the FET standard is inherently more prone to abuse than any other standards including expropriation.

As discussed fully in Part IV, the better option is to define the rule more fully and accurately following the more recent Canadian model, rather than taking the radical measure of eliminating the FET standard altogether. Such action will not resolve any structural problems particularly in the Intra-Africa context. As repeatedly expressed throughout this book, the key to correction lies in the decision-makers and in accountability throughout the decision-making processes.

17
Choice of Law
The Concurrent Application of Host State Laws and Principles of International Law

The selection of the applicable law is often one of the most important decisions that any tribunal could make. Many of the African ICSID cases applied a combination of the host country's domestic laws, treaties, and principles of international law. The selection and ascertainment of the applicable rule of law is often a subject of contention. This chapter explores the various tribunals' concurrent application of the host state's laws and principles and rules of international law.

Choice of Law: The Concurrent Application of Domestic and International Law in the Early African Cases

This issue of the role of the host state's domestic law arose in the very first ICSID annulment case, *Klockner v. Cameroon* (1983).[1] In *Klockner*, the Tribunal had ruled in favor of Cameroon rejecting a substantial portion of the Claimant's claims. The Ad Hoc Annulment Committee did, however, annul the award. Interestingly, the Committee found excess of authority for the Tribunal's reliance on general equitable principles and failure to ascertain and apply the host state's law as required under Article 42 of the ICSID Convention.

Although the Committee deferred to the Tribunal's decision on its own competence, it did not show the same level of deference when it comes to the applicable law. It engaged in a detailed and exacting scrutiny of the Tribunal's identification and application of the substantive law. It began with this general observation:

> It is undeniable that this conclusion is presented by the Award as having been reached by applying the applicable law in accordance with Article 42 of the Convention, i.e., the law of the Contracting State, 'Cameroonian law based on French law or even French civil law.' (p. 105, paras. 2 and 3). According to the Application for Annulment (p. 12), however, the Tribunal actually based itself 'not on a principle of French law,

[1] Decision Rendered by Ad Hoc Committee on the Application for Annulment Against the Arbitral Award in Klockner v. Cameroon, ARB/81/2 (Oct. 21, 1983), at 80 ("In view of this case's importance, the fact that this is the first Application for Annulment ever lodged against an ICSID award and, finally, because it may be of interest to the parties and to the new Tribunal that may be constituted under Article 52(6) of the Washington Convention to have additional indications, it would nonetheless be appropriate to examine, albeit in less depth, the main arguments raised and discussed in the course of the annulment proceeding").

Africa's International Investment Law Regimes. Won L. Kidane, Oxford University Press. © Oxford University Press 2023.
DOI: 10.1093/oso/9780197745571.003.0017

> but on a sort of declaration, as general as it is imprecise, of principles which are allegedly universally recognized' "[2]

What the Committee expected the Tribunal to do was identify the exact provision of Cameroonian law that said the Claimant, as a contracting party, had the contractual obligation of good faith and full disclosure.[3] To be sure, the Committee found that Cameroonian law on the duty of full disclosure in the pre-contractual phase was clearly identified and applied, but the same legal duty in the postcontract formation stage as an ongoing obligation was not proven.[4] It is precisely because no textual or jurisprudential support could be found under Cameroonian law that the Tribunal applied general equitable principles of good faith and disclosure.[5]

The committee found that such failure to identify the host state's law on this point and reliance on general equitable principles amounted to manifest excess of authority.[6] Relatedly, this first ICSID Annulment Committee also offered its thoughts on the "failure to state a reason" prong in the annulment grounds. It made it clear that the

[2] *Id.* at 65.

[3] *Id.* at 72 ("72. In the latter case, is it possible to hold that the Award has 'applied the law of the Contracting State' as required in Article 42(1)? It is true that the principle of good faith is 'at the basis' of French civil law, as of other legal systems, but this elementary proposition does not by itself answer the question. In Cameroonian or Franco-Cameroonian law does the 'principle' affirmed or postulated by the Award, the 'duty of full disclosure,' exist? If it does, no doubt flowing from the general principle of good faith, from the obligation of frankness and loyalty, then how, by what rules and under what conditions is it implemented and within what limits? Can a duty to make a 'full disclosure,' even to one's own prejudice, be accepted, especially without limits? Is there a single legal system which contains such a broad obligation? These are a few of the questions that naturally come to mind and that the Award provides no basis for answering"). *Id.* at 75 ("75. In any event, in the absence of any information, evidence or citation in the Award, it would seem difficult to accept, and impossible to presume, that there is a general duty, under French civil law, or for that matter other systems of civil law, for a contracting party to make a 'full disclosure' to its partner. If we were to 'presume' anything, it would instead be that such a duty (the basic idea of which may, of course, be accepted as it follows from the principle of good faith; cf. Article 1134, para. 3 of the French Civil Code) must, to be given effect in positive law, have conditions for its application and limits!").

[4] The arbitrators may have recourse to the "principles of international law" only after having inquired into and established the content of the law of the State party to the dispute (which cannot be reduced to one principle, even a basic one) and after having applied the relevant rules of the State's law. Article 42(1) therefore clearly does not allow the arbitrator to base his decision solely on the "rules" or "principles of international law." *Id.* at 69.

[5] *Id.* at 71 ("71. Does the 'basic principle' referred to by the Award (p. 105) as one of 'French civil law' come from positive law, i.e., from the law's body of rules? It is impossible to answer this question by reading the Award, which contains no reference whatsoever to legislative texts, to judgments, or to scholarly opinions. In this respect the contrast is striking between Section 2 (on the 'duty of full disclosure') and Section 3 (on the exceptio non adimpleti contractus, pp. 109–14 and pp. 118, 124, 126, etc). Section 3 contains a great number of references to scholarly opinion (doctrine) as well as, directly or indirectly, to case law (jurisprudence). One could therefore assume that in the case of Section 2, regarding the duty of frankness, the arbitrators either began a similar search for authorities but found it unproductive or, more likely, thought that a search for positive law was unnecessary").

[6] *Id.* at 79 ("79. In conclusion, it must be acknowledged that in its reasoning, limited to postulating and not demonstrating the existence of a principle or exploring the rules by which it can only take concrete form, the Tribunal has not applied 'the law of the Contracting State.' Strictly speaking, it could not be said that it made this decision without providing reasons, within the meaning of Articles 48(3) and 52(1)(e). It did, however, act outside the framework provided by Article 42(1), applying concepts or principles it probably considered equitable (acting as an amicable compositor, which should not be confused with applying 'equitable considerations' as the International Court of Justice did in the Continental Shelf case). However justified its award may be (a question on which the Committee has no opinion), the Tribunal thus 'manifestly exceeded its powers' within the meaning of Article 52(1)(b) of the Washington Convention").

Committee does not purport to review the award for error of law or fact, but somehow found a way to annul[7] on this ground as well, because the Tribunal had some confusion about the applicable rule of law.[8] Consider this instructive passage on what was wrong with the Tribunal's reasoning, which relates to the applicable rule of law again:

> The Award also observes that Cameroon expressly requested that, if it were found obliged to pay the price of the factory, it should not be required to pay the entirety of the price, "taking into account Cameroon's claim arising from Klockner's failure to perform its obligations ... and this on the grounds of the exceptio non adimpleti contractus and of judicial setoff." (p. 110)
>
> After citing several French authors on the exception based on nonperformance (pp. 110 and 111), the Award continues: 'In view of the parties' divergence of views as to the applicable law under Article 42 of the ICSID Convention, it is appropriate to note that English law and international law reach similar conclusions.' (p. 111) This superfluous observation is rather difficult to reconcile with the Tribunal's previous decision (p. 105) that, as the Claimant argued, 'only that part of Cameroonian law that is based on French law should be applied in the dispute.' "[9]

This was instructive for the Tribunals that followed.

In *Letco v. Liberia* (1986), the Tribunal discussed the question of the applicable procedural and substantive laws in turn. Its discussion of the procedural rules is brief and concerns only the arbitral procedure. There is no meaningful discussion of the seat of the arbitration and the *lex arbitri loci*. This is rather unsurprising, because unlike commercial arbitration, the ICSID Convention assigns no significance to the concept of the seat of arbitration.[10] Not only are the grounds of annulment potentially more limited than those under *lex arbitri loci* of any New York Convention member states,[11]

[7] *See id.* at 171 ("In summary, while the Award contains some reasoning on the conditions for applying the exception based on nonperformance, the question may be asked whether these reasons are sufficient or 'sufficiently relevant.' It is not necessary to answer this, since on the question of the effects of the exception based on nonperformance, the Award does not state the legal grounds nor does it state the rules of civil law (reinforced by references to scholarly opinion and case law comparable to those which the Award cited on the general principle) which could justify its conclusion. In reality, everything occurs as if the Arbitral Tribunal had considered the exceptio non adimpleti contractus as a ground for extinguishing obligations under French law. On the basis of the Award's own citations, this conclusion does not necessarily follow, nor does it conform to the understanding the ad hoc Committee may have of this area of law, but in any case it should have been expressly justified. The complaint that there was a failure to state reasons therefore appears to be not only admissible but well founded").

[8] *See id.* at 165–71.

[9] *Id.* at 167–68.

[10] ICSID Art. 54 ("(1) Each Contracting State shall recognize an award rendered pursuant to this Convention as binding and enforce the pecuniary obligations imposed by that award within its territories as if it were a final judgment of a court in that State. A Contracting State with a federal constitution may enforce such an award in or through its federal courts and may provide that such courts shall treat the award as if it were a final judgment of the courts of a constituent state").

[11] Although the New York Convention itself does not make any provisions limiting grounds of annulment, states that have adopted the Model UNCITRAL Rules limit grounds of annulment to grounds of refusal of enforcement under Article V of the New York Convention:

> 1. Recognition and enforcement of the award may be refused, at the request of the party against whom it is invoked, only if that party furnishes to the competent authority where the recognition and enforcement is sought, proof that:

but the only possible procedural recourse that it anticipates under Article 52 is annulment before an ad hoc committee constituted by the Chair of the Administrative Council.[12]

The Tribunal's four paragraph discussion of procedural rules centers on the Parties selection of the ICSID Rules.[13] Relying on Article 44 of the ICSID Convention, the Tribunal ruled that the proceedings will be governed by the ICSID Regulations and Rules with the Tribunal retaining the power to fill any gaps.[14]

The applicable substantive law invited a more serious inquiry. The starting point is obviously Article 42 of the ICSID Convention: "The Tribunal shall decide any dispute in accordance with such rules of law as may be agreed by the parties."[15] In this

> (a) The parties to the agreement referred to in article II were, under the law applicable to them, under some incapacity, or the said agreement is not valid under the law to which the parties have subjected it or, failing any indication thereon, under the law of the country where the award was made; or
> (b) The party against whom the award is invoked was not given proper notice of the appointment of the arbitrator or of the arbitration proceedings or was otherwise unable to present his case; or
> (c) The award deals with a difference not contemplated by or not falling within the terms of the submission to arbitration, or it contains decisions on matters beyond the scope of the submission to arbitration, provided that, if the decisions on matters submitted to arbitration can be separated from those not so submitted, that part of the award which contains decisions on matters submitted to arbitration may be recognized and enforced; or
> (d) The composition of the arbitral authority or the arbitral procedure was not in accordance with the agreement of the parties, or, failing such agreement, was not in accordance with the law of the country where the arbitration took place; or
> (e) The award has not yet become binding on the parties, or has been set aside or suspended by a competent authority of the country in which, or under the law of which, that award was made.
>
> 2. Recognition and enforcement of an arbitral award may also be refused if the competent authority in the country where recognition and enforcement is sought finds that:
> (a) The subject matter of the difference is not capable of settlement by arbitration under the law of that country; or
> (b) The recognition or enforcement of the award would be contrary to the public policy of that country.

12 ICSID Art. 52.

13 *Id.* at 30–34.

14 *Id.* at 32–33:

> 32. Article 44 of the ICSID Convention states: Any arbitration proceeding shall be conducted in accordance with the provisions of this section and except as the parties otherwise agree, in accordance with the Arbitration Rules in effect on the date on which the parties consented to arbitration. If any question of procedure arises which is not covered by this section or the Arbitration Rules or any rules agreed by the parties, the Tribunal shall decide the question.
>
> 33. This [*sic*] Article 44 clearly calls for the application of the Arbitration Rules in the case at hand. In the event of any procedural gaps in the Arbitration Rules (which is not the case here), the arbitrators are granted the power to fill these gaps. No agreement by the parties has been reached concerning procedural rules. Therefore, given the clear mandate of the icsid Convention and its support in international law, this Tribunal concludes that there is no need to resort to any other procedures whether based on national law or not.

15 ICSID Art. 42. The reminder of the provision reads: "(1) The Tribunal shall decide a dispute in accordance with such rules of law as may be agreed by the parties. In the absence of such agreement, the Tribunal shall apply the law of the Contracting State party to the dispute (including its rules on the conflict of laws) and such rules of international law as may be applicable. (2) The Tribunal may not bring in a finding of non liquet on the ground of silence or obscurity of the law. (3) The provisions of paragraphs (1) and (2) shall not prejudice the power of the Tribunal to decide a dispute ex aequo et bono if the parties so agree." *Id.*

case, the Parties' choice of law had some ambiguity. The Concession Agreement only said: "Agreement is made 'under the General Business Law, Title 15 of the Liberian Code of Laws of 1956.' "[16] The Tribunal was not troubled by this apparent ambiguity and even politely mocked what appears to be the Claimant's counsel's initial enthusiastic argument and subsequent concession that the Parties made no choice of law, notwithstanding this statement.[17]

The only question for the Tribunal as to the applicable substantive law was whether or not such choice of domestic law was exclusive or if it includes principles of international law as envisioned under Article 42 of the ICSID Convention.[18] Having ruled that the Parties have indeed selected Liberian law to govern the Concession Agreement, it avoided answering the question of whether Liberian law applies exclusively or in tandem with principles of international law as envisioned under subparagraph 2 of Article 42, which suggests such is the case only when the Tribunal is unable to find party selection of the applicable law. Here is how the Tribunal avoided answering the real question of whether principles of international law applied and answered a question that it was not asked on the consistency of Liberian law with principles of public international law:

> The law of the Contracting State is recognized as paramount within its own territory, but is nevertheless subjected to control by international law. The role of international law as a "regulator" of national systems of law has been much discussed, with particular emphasis being focused on the problems likely to arise if there is divergence on a particular point between national and international law. No such problem arises in the present case; the Tribunal is satisfied that the rules and principles of Liberian law which it has taken into account are in conformity with generally accepted principles of public international law governing the validity of contracts and the remedies for their breach.[19]

Having made determinations on the applicable law[20] and found the facts, the Tribunal finally concluded that "by its failure to follow the procedure laid down in

[16] Liberian Eastern Timber Corporation v. Republic of Liberia, ICSID Cases No. ARB/83/2, Award (Mar. 31, 1986), at 35.

[17] *See id.* at 35 ("This appears to indicate an express choice by the parties of the Law of Liberia as the law governing the Concession Agreement. However, counsel for the claimant, who put his arguments skillfully and persistently throughout the proceedings, suggested at one stage that there had been no express choice of law by the parties (transcript of the hearing on 9 December 1985 at p. 67). Later he appeared to concede (at p. 72) that Liberian law was 'probably applicable' ").

[18] *Id.* at 36.

[19] *Id.* at 37.

[20] *See id.* at 73–79:

> 76. The Liberian Code of Laws defines a contract in a manner which, with its reference to consideration, is readily familiar to a common lawyer; then, in relation to breach of contract, the Liberian Code of Laws states: If the person omits to do an act which he legally contracted to do, or does an act which he legally contracted not to do. he commits an injury and an action for damages will lie against him. (Liberian Code of Laws, para. 2)
>
> 77. The Liberian Code of Laws also contains provisions dealing with "injury" which it defines as unlawful damage (para. 1); in its classification of injuries (para. 8) it distinguishes between "personal injuries" and "injuries to property," stating that "injuries to property are divided into

the Concession Agreement, as well as by its subsequent actions, the Government of Liberia has acted in plain breach of the terms of the Concession Agreement. Its breach of the Agreement entitles letco to the recovery of damages."[21]

Choice of Law: The Concurrent Application of Host State Law and International Law in the African Cases of the 2000s

All of the above-discussed cases applied the host state's domestic substantive laws and principles of international law generally. It was only in 2000 that the *Wena v. Egypt* (2000) case applied more specific substantive principles emanating from an investment treaty, namely, the FET and FSP as well as expropriation standards contained in the UK–Egypt BIT concluded in June 1975.[22] In the Tribunal's own words:

> The Tribunal finds that, beyond the provisions of the IPPA, there is no special agreement between the parties on the rules of law applicable to the dispute. Rather, the pleadings of both parties indicate that, aside from the provisions of the IPPA, the Tribunal should apply both Egyptian law (i.e., 'the law of the Contracting State party to the dispute') and such rules of international law as may be applicable. The Tribunal notes that the provisions of the IPPA would in any event be the first rules of law to

breaches of contract and other injuries to property." It thus adopts the notion of a contract as apropprietorial right. As to measure of damages, the Liberian Code of Laws provides, in paragraph 11:The object of a civil action for injuries is to indemnify the injured person, not to punish the injurer; therefore it follows that the measure of damages is the actual amount of the loss or inconvenience sustained by the injured person without any reference to the degree of misconduct of which the injurer may have been guilty.

78. There are then set out certain exceptions to this rule, which relate to injuries which are said to be "of a particular nature and partake of a criminal character": the only exception relevant to the context of the dispute would seem to be that for "injuries to the reputation for which an action will lie without alleging and proving special damages."

79. It is clear that under the law of Liberia (as under most, if not all, developed systems of law) the binding force of contracts is recognized, so long as the contracts in question are validly made and do not offend public policy (l'ordre publique). No doubt has been raised as to the validity of the original grant of the concession to foreign persons and corporations (see Berlowitz, Concessions and Incentives in Liberia).

[21] *Id.* at 87. *See also id.* at 88 ("Having determined letco's right to damages, it is now necessary to determine the nature of these damages and the extent to which they must be compensated. It is necessary to determine whether letco is entitled to receive compensation for both the amounts invested in the forestry concession and subsequently lost due to the confiscation and those profits lost that letco would have obtained had the Concession Agreement not been revoked." See also 100 ("This Tribunal therefore determines that both according to international law and, more importantly, Liberian law, letco is entitled to compensation for damages for both its lost investments and its foregone future profits"). *See also id.* at 105 ("1) The determination of damages assumes that the Concession Agreement would have lasted for a total of 35 years; 20 years which correspond to the initial period (from 1972 to 1992) and a second period, available at letco's option, of 15 years (from 1992 to 2007). As a result, the calculation of lost profits corresponds to a period beginning with the initial revocation to the end of the optional renewal (from 1980 to 2007)").

[22] Wena Hotels Limited v. Arab Republic of Egypt, ICSID Case No. ARB/98/4, Award (Dec. 8, 2000), at 16.

> be applied by the Tribunal, both on the basis of the agreement of the parties and as mandated by Egyptian law as well as international law.[23]

The starting point being Article 42 of the ICSID Convention that requires the tribunal to apply the law that the parties have selected, the *Middle East v. Egypt* (2002)[24] Tribunal excluded the applicability of Egyptian law in a very interesting way. First, it identified the BIT between Greece and Egypt as being selected by the parties, although it only applies because the two states have signed it for the benefit of their respective investors, but more interestingly, the Tribunal used *argumentum a contrario* to exclude all Egyptian laws that are unfavorable to the investor. That was based on Article 11 of the BIT, which provides that in addition to the provisions of the BIT, the investor is also entitled to more favorable rules under principles of international law and domestic law.[25] The Tribunal's *a contrario* reading of this provision was sweeping all unfavorable domestic laws do not apply.[26]

Having limited the applicable substantive law that way, the *Middle East* Tribunal somewhat unusually offered a description of the burden of proof and evidentiary standards. It stated:

> In order to accept a claim under the BIT, a breach of its provisions by the Respondent must be found leading to a claim, as for example under Art. 4 (Expropriation). The respective provisions of the BIT confirm what can be considered as a general principle of international procedure—and probably also of virtually all national

[23] *Id.* at 76.

[24] Middle East Cement Shipping and Handling Co. S.A. v. Arab Republic of Egypt, ICSID Case No. ARB/99/6, Award (Apr. 12, 2002).

[25] *Id.* at 86 ("An important limitation of this framework is that, in its Decision on Jurisdiction of November 28, 2000, the Tribunal found that it only had jurisdiction on the basis of the Bilateral Investment Treaty of 1993 between Egypt and Greece. Art. 11 of this BIT provides that, in addition to the rules of the BIT, obligations for a more favorable treatment stemming from the national law of the Contracting Parties or existing under international law between the Contracting Parties shall prevail. But there are no such additional obligations relevant for this case. Therefore, the Tribunal can only consider and accept claims of the investor under this BIT").

[26] *Id.* at 87 ("Convention. The first sentence of Art. 42 (1) requires the application of rules of law agreed by the Parties. The above-mentioned Art. 11 of the BIT provides such an agreement and thus has to be respected. While that provision requires the application of additional provisions of the national law if more favorable for the investor—which the Tribunal does not find to exist in this case -, by argumentum a contrario it does not permit application of provisions of national law limiting any claims found by the Tribunal to exist under the BIT. As expressly mentioned in the beginning of the 2nd sentence of Art. 42 (1) of the ICSID Convention, only 'in the absence of such an agreement' regarding the rules of law to be applied, that 2nd sentence provides that'"the Tribunal shall apply the law of the Contracting State party to the dispute (including its rules on the conflict of laws) and such rules of international law as may be applicable.' While, thus, this Tribunal takes into account the law of Egypt where appropriate, consistent with its decision to consider and accept only claims under the BIT, the Tribunal shall apply the substantive provisions of the BIT for all matters regulated by the Treaty and cannot apply any provisions of national Egyptian law limiting claims found to exist under the BIT. Thus, Egyptian law will be taken into account by the Tribunal when it is not overridden by the application of provisions of the BIT. On the other hand, both according to the 1st sentence of Art. 42 (1) as the rules of law chosen by the Parties in Art. 11 of the BIT and according to the 2nd sentence of Art. 42 (1) of the ICSID Convention as 'rules of international law as may be applicable,' the reference to and application of the BIT implies that the Tribunal may have recourse to the rules of general international law to supplement those of the BIT").

procedural laws—namely that it is the Claimant who has the burden of proof for the conditions required in the applicable substantive rules of law to establish the claim.[27]

The Tribunal also stated that it considers that it is established under international law that the party who has the burden of proof also has the burden of persuasion.[28] The Tribunal also helpfully outlined some fundamental rules of evidence relying on a previously decided ICSID case: It summarized the basic rules as follows:

> Rule (J)—The international responsibility of the State is not to be presumed. The party alleging a violation of international law giving rise to international responsibility has the burden of proving the assertion.
>
> Rule (K)—International tribunals are not bound to adhere to strict judicial rules of evidence. As a general principle the probative force of the evidence presented is for the Tribunal to determine . . .
>
> Rule (L)—In exercising the free evaluation of evidence provided for under the previous Rule, the international tribunals decided the case on the strength of the evidence produced by both parties, and in a case a party adduces some evidence which prima facie supports his allegation, the burden of proof shifts to his opponent.[29]

As indicated earlier, however, proof of the Respondent's admission that the economic value of the cement license was affected for four months was enough for the Tribunal to hold that the Claimant had carried its burden of proof and persuasion that the Respondent expropriated the Claimant's property.[30]

Semos v. Republic of Mali (2003)[31] did not raise any of the substantive issues that would ordinarily arise out of BITs such as expropriation or FET, but it applied a series of domestic tax laws in an ISDS context.

The dispute pertained to the state's ability to impose duties on export of minerals lawfully exploited under an exploration and exploitation license subject to a series of evolving laws and contractual instruments.[32] The Tribunal decided the cases exclusively on the basis of its own reading of Malian law and the contracts that governed the relationship between the investor and the state.[33] The Tribunal's task was limited

[27] *Id.* at 89.

[28] *Id.* at 90 ("the Tribunal also considered as an established international law rule that ' . . . a Party having the burden of proof must not only bring evidence in support of his allegations, but must also convince the Tribunal of their truth, lest they be disregarded for want, or insufficiency, of proof' ") (citing Asian Agricultural Products Ltd. v. Republic of Sri Lanka, ICSID Case No. Arb/87/3, Award (1991), at 527).

[29] *Id.* at 94 (quoting Asian Agricultural Products Ltd. v. Republic of Sri Lanka, ICSID Case No. Arb/87/3, Award (1991), at 549–50).

[30] *See id.* at 107 ("107. As also Respondent concedes that, at least for a period of 4 months, Claimant was deprived, by the Decree, of rights it had been granted under the License, there is no dispute between the Parties that, in principle, a taking did take place.)

[31] Société D'exploitation Des Mines D'or De Sadiola S.A. (Semos) v. Republic of Mali, ICSID Case No. ARB/01/5, Award (Feb. 25, 2003).

[32] *Id.* at 17–22.

[33] *See id.* at 23–46.

to analyzing Malian tax, mining, and related laws in light of the Parties' arguments without any reference to international law or even international standards. In that sense, it essentially acted like a domestic court of law. It first identified the dispute as purely arising out of domestic law and contract as follows:

> The dispute between Semos and the Republic of Mali arose when Mali's Tax Administration and, more particularly, the National Tax Department, decided to impose stamp duty on the gold export applications made by Semos, relying on Article 9.3 of the Amended Convention which stipulates that "after the first three years of production," the operating company (i.e. Semos) would be required, inter alia, to pay stamp duty. As the date of the first production was fixed at 4 March 1997, the Administration intended to impose stamp duty on export applications, as stipulated in Article 993 of the General Tax Code, with effect from 4 March 2000.[34] It then identified the applicable laws as consisted of the mining law that was in effect at the time of the signing of the original contract and the various amendments to it along with the domestic tax code as amended several times during the validity of the exploration and exploitation license.[35]

The Tribunal then engaged in a detailed analysis of the host state's laws based on the arguments of the Parties.[36] There is no indication that any experts on Malian law offered evidence on the domestic tax laws perhaps because the parties did not dispute the state of the law except its application to the facts of the case. Although it engaged in a lengthy legal analysis, the outcome was eventually decided on the finding of the intent of the parties like any ordinary contract dispute.

In the Tribunal's own words:

> Though, as already stated, the Tribunal is of the view that there is a difference between the two texts, it will now proceed to examine, in the light of the Convention, what was the common intention of the parties with respect to the imposition of stamp duty on export operations.[37]

And concludes:

> A combined reading of Article 9.3 and Article 7.3 of the Amended Convention leads the Tribunal to conclude that the stamp duty laid down in the General Tax Code is payable at the end of the exemption period of three years stipulated in Article 9.3, with the exception of stamp duty on operations concerning the export of minerals such as gold. This applies irrespective of the name given to the documents subject to stamp duty, since payment of the duly constitutes a formality which is essential for the export procedure. Therefore, slump duty must be equaled with a duly imposed

[34] *Id.* at 23.
[35] *See id.* at 46–66.
[36] *See id.* at 67–75.
[37] *Id.* at 75.

> upon exit within the meaning, of Article 7.3 of the Amended Convention, payment of which is subject to exemption throughout the term of the Convention.[38]

The only reference that it makes to international standards is in a comparative light:

> Interpreting the contract in the same spirit, if need be, it may also be pointed out that, within the international framework of fiscal policy with regard to mining, a comparative study of the legislation of a number of developing countries has shown that, in order to encourage foreign investments, these countries have instituted an exemption from exit duties on the mining products.[39]

What is remarkable about this purely domestic approach is not that the case was fully disposed of on the basis of domestic law, but the total lack of any discussion as to any level of deference to the host state's interpretation of its own domestic tax laws as a regulatory matter. The Tribunal basically reviewed the host state's own administrative tax decisions *de novo* and substituted its own judgment for the administrative agencies who imposed the tax. This question would have been even more important had it been asked to determine a treaty breach such as FET, rather than adjudicate a pure breach of contract case in an international forum. The issue of deference is a matter that arises frequently, but is also one that gets the least attention in ISDS jurisprudence with only a few tribunals even addressing it. The notable ones are *Klockner* in the context of the Ad Hoc Annulment Committee's deference to the Tribunal's decision of its own jurisdiction, and the *Cortec* Tribunal's deference to the factual determinations and interpretation of Kenyan law to the Kenyan High Court.

Some of the ICSID cases involve neither the host state's laws nor principles of international law. They are decided on the basis of a different body of law selected under the contract, just like any commercial arbitration matter. A good example of this is *CDC v. Seychelles* (2003).[40] The dispute arose out of a couple of loan agreements between CDC, a UK public corporation and the Seychelles, because the host state refused to pay the principal and interest of the loans which it guaranteed for the benefit of its public utilities corporation (PUC) to purchase a gas turbine that failed to work properly.[41]

The host state's substantive defenses included: "The Respondent would be relying for its defence on the principles of equity, contractual fairness, inequality of bargaining power, contributory negligence and the emerging jurisprudence in relation to international trade and investments between developed and developing countries."[42] The validity of these defenses had to be decided under the law that the parties selected: the laws of England.[43] As the Tribunal noted: "Although the Republic made

[38] *Id.* at 91.
[39] *Id.* at 90.
[40] CDC Group Plc v. Republic of The Seychelles, ICSID Case No. ARB/02/14 (Dec. 17, 2003).
[41] *See id.* at 7–9.
[42] *Id.* at 29.
[43] *Id.* at 43.

reference in its Rejoinder to 'the emerging jurisprudence in relation to international trade and investments between developed and developing countries,' no argument based in such jurisprudence was presented to the Tribunal."[44] As such, the decision was made exclusively on the basis of English law.

In applying English contract law, the Tribunal cited to a combination of cases and scholarly writings. The key legal issue was whether by lending money the lender implicitly warrants the feasibility of the project that it is underwriting. This issue arose because the host state made the argument that as CDC approved the loan, it represented to the borrower that it was a worthy project and that the state guaranteed the loan relying on this implicit representation. In ejecting this argument, the Tribunal relied on Lord Millett's opinion in the UK case of *National Commercial Bank (Jamaica) Ltd v Hew*,[45] stating:

> There is a useful illustration of the truism that the viability of a transaction may depend on the vantage point from which it is viewed; what is a viable loan may not be a viable borrowing. This is one reason why a borrower is not entitled to rely on the fact that the lender has chosen to lend him the money as evidence, still less as advice, that the lender thinks that the purpose for which the borrower intends to use it is sound.[46]

Although the facts relating to the extent of the representation and justifiableness of the reliance were also important, the decision in this case essentially rested on this and related English law rules. This is thus an investor–state case that was fully decided by the application of a third country's domestic law, much like a commercial case.

The *Patrick Mitchell v. DRC* (2004) Tribunal made an interesting observation about the relationship between domestic law and the BIT that the host state concluded with the sending state. It advanced an interesting legal theory that the BIT is indeed an integral part of the domestic law of the host state:

> As the Parties to this dispute have not concluded an agreement in respect of the applicable law, the Tribunal, pursuant to Article 42(1) of the ICSID Convention, shall apply the law of the Contracting State party to the dispute and such rules of international law as may be applicable. The most prominent rules of international law applicable to investment disputes are the rules embodied in investment treaties to which the host State is a party. The BIT concluded in 1984 contains the rules of

44 *Id.* The full paragraph reads: "43. Clause 7.8 of the Amending and Rescheduling Agreement provides: 'This Agreement and its performance shall be governed by and construed in all respects in accordance with the laws of England . . . ' Although the Republic made reference in its Rejoinder to 'the emerging jurisprudence in relation to international trade and investments between developed and developing countries,' no argument based in such jurisprudence was presented to the Tribunal. The submissions presented by the parties proceeded on the footing that CDC's claim was to be resolved in accordance with English law."

45 National Commercial Bank (Jamaica) Ltd v Hew [2003] UKPC Appeal No. 65 of 2002, June 30, 2003. Cited in *id.* at 53.

46 National Commercial Bank (Jamaica) Ltd v Hew, UKPC Appeal No. 65 of 2002, June 30, 2003, at 22 (quoted in CDC v. Seychelles, ICSID Case No. ARB/02/14 (Dec. 17, 2003), at 53).

> international law applicable to the merits of this dispute. As the DRC is a party to the BIT, the rules of this Treaty are equally to be considered as part of the law of the State party to this dispute.[47]

Although the Tribunal offers no further comments on this, its discussion suggests that the BIT is not only a part of the host state's law for purposes of Article 42(1) of the ICSID Convention on the applicable law, but also that it preempts any contrary state law. This approach is clear from its rejection of the Respondent's argument that because legal services are not considered investment under DRC law, they are not capable of being expropriated.[48] The decision on preemption is of course fundamentally flawed under the Tribunal's own theory because if the BIT is considered a part of the domestic law, the issue of hierarchy of the laws and hence preemption need to be decided in reference to the domestic law including perhaps the constitution that defines the position of international law. The Tribunal makes no effort to ascertain this from the domestic law of the host state.

World Duty Free V. Kenya (2006) raised an interesting and unusual interaction between domestic and international legal principles relating to illegality and public order. As indicated in the expropriation section above, two years into the proceedings, in March 2003, Kenya introduced a claim that the Agreement that gave rise to the dispute was tainted by illegality and as such was *void ab initio*.[49] The Tribunal summarized the claim of illegality and under domestic law as follows:

> Kenya, for its part, submits that the 1989 Agreement was procured by paying a bribe to the then President of Kenya, Daniel Arap Moi. It adds that the payment of such a bribe is criminal and that the resulting contract does not have the force of law. It is unenforceable and the claims cannot be heard as a matter of public policy. Furthermore, as a matter of applicable law, the contract is voidable and has been validly avoided by Kenya. Consequently, the claims must be dismissed with prejudice.[50] The Tribunal then said that it would consider whether or not a bribe had been paid as a matter of fact, and, if so, determine the consequences that must follow under both domestic Kenyan and English law chosen by the Parties as well as notions of

[47] Patrick Mitchell v. DRC Award (Feb. 9, 2004); Annulment (Nov. 1, 2006), at 60.

[48] *Id.* at 67–68. The Tribunal said in particular:

> 67. Respondent's main objection to the claim is that the Mitchell & Associates firm has not been victim of any measure of expropriation and that, therefore, no compensation is due under such title. For the Respondent, indeed, the BIT uses the term expropriation, but it does not contain any definition. Such definition, it says, has therefore to be found by reference to national law, which is in this case the law of the Congo. As stated by Respondent, the law No. 77-001 of February 22, 1977 does provide for expropriation for a public purpose, but it can relate to immovable property only. Even if one would consider that the seizure of movable property would be tantamount to an expropriation, this could be of concern, in the instant case, for the seized documents only. However, these documents have been the subject of a regular seizure which cannot be assimilated to an expropriation. Respondent contends that, as a consequence of the decision of the Military Court, these documents have been returned.

[49] World Duty Free Company Limited v. Republic of Kenya, ICSID Case No. ARB/00/7, Award (Oct. 4, 2006), at 105.

[50] *Id.* at 128.

international public order.[51] The applicable laws chosen in the Agreement were both Kenyan and English law due to what appears to be a drafting problem, but that did not present any obstacles for the Tribunal because substantively there was no consequential difference between the two common law rules of contract.[52]

Having found that the Agreement was procured through bribery as a matter of fact, the Tribunal turned its analysis to international public order and the applicable English and Kenyan laws.[53] Because the Tribunal was significantly disturbed by bribery that it ascertained as a matter of evidentiary record, it engaged in an elaborate exposition of illegality of contracts under principles of international public order seeking support from sources ranging from "universal standards and accepted norms of conduct that must be applied in all fora"[54] to " 'good morals,' 'bonas mores,' 'ethics of international trade' or 'transnational public policy' "[55] to anti-corruption conventions, General Assembly Resolutions, arbitral and domestic court decisions.[56] The Tribunal concluded:

> In light of domestic laws and international conventions relating to corruption, and in light of the decisions taken in this matter by courts and arbitral tribunals, this Tribunal is convinced that bribery is contrary to the international public policy of most, if not all, States or, to use another formula, to transnational public policy. Thus, claims based on contracts of corruption or on contracts obtained by corruption cannot be upheld by this Arbitral Tribunal.[57]

Having established that international public policy applies to the resolution of this particular dispute just because it is there, the Tribunal then turned to the more concrete party-chosen applicable domestic law regimes. Having established the overlap between English and Kenyan laws, it went on stating the basic principle of English law on the avoidance of contracts on the basis of illegality, as:

> illegality may affect a contract in a number of ways but it is traditional to distinguish between (1) illegality as to formation and (2) illegality as to performance ... Where a contract is illegal as formed, ... the courts will not enforce the contract, or provide any other remedies arising out of the contract.[58]

[51] *Id.* at 129 ("The Tribunal will consider first whether a bribe has been paid by Mr. Ali to President, Moi in the present case, and whether the 1989 Agreement has been procured as a result of such a payment. If so, the Tribunal will have to examine the consequences of the bribe on the enforceability and the validity of the Agreement, both under ordre public international and the applicable laws").

[52] *Id.* at 158. ("The Tribunal now turns to the applicable laws chosen by the Parties in their Agreement of 27th April 1989, as required by Article 42(1) of the ICSID Convention. As already recorded above, Article 9(2)(c) of this Agreement provides that 'any arbitral tribunal constituted pursuant to this Agreement shall apply English law'; and Article 10(A) provides that 'This Agreement shall be governed by and construed in accordance with the law of Kenya.' ").

[53] *Id.* at 137–57 (international public order) and 158–87 (English and Kenyan laws)

[54] *Id.* at 139.

[55] *Id.* at 141.

[56] *Id.* at 143–57.

[57] *Id.* at 157.

[58] *Id.* at 161 (citing Public Policy—General Principles, Chitty on Contracts, Vol. 1, at 17–007 (28th edition)) (noting that it is cited by Kenya as the leading English treatise). The full passage reads: "Illegality may

Although the Tribunal could have ended it there, it went on adding more authorities and elaboration[59] before it got to the inevitable conclusion: "The Respondent, Kenya, was legally entitled to avoid and did avoid legally by its Counter-Memorial dated 18 April 2003 the 'House of Perfume Contract,' namely the Agreement of 27 April 1989 as amended on 11 May 1990, under its applicable laws, the laws of England and Kenya."[60]

The difficulty, of course, was the defense of illegality was raised by the party whose former president took the "bribe," which experts said had a complex cultural and situational nuance rather than a simple *quid pro quo*.[61] Despite the admirable explanation of international public order and national laws against bribery, this anomaly remained unexplained as a matter of law.

In *Champion Trading v. Egypt* (2006), the Tribunal strictly applied the national treatment nondiscrimination provision of the US–Egypt BIT, but the discriminatory measure that the US investor Claimant presented was based on Egyptian domestic rules and regulations of the cotton industry. The domestic laws were thus assessed in the context only of their disparate application. There was, however, some nuance that the Tribunal decided to defer to an already commenced domestic administrative court litigation. The Tribunal's final decision was that the Claimant failed to meet its burden of proving that it was similarly situated to the domestic cotton traders who received the Egyptian government subsidy, because the disparate treatment was admitted.

The Claimant's more serious argument, which the Tribunal elected not to decide, was that the neutral rules and regulations themselves had the overall exclusionary impact that made the Claimant look less like the domestic entities that eventually benefited from the payouts. The award does not make this argument readily clear, but a closer reading shows that. For example, the Tribunal identifies issues that it is deferring to Administrative Court determination:

affect a contract in a number of ways but it is traditional to distinguish between (1) illegality as to formation and (2) illegality as to performance." *Id.*

59 *See id.* at 163–87.

60 *Id.* at 188.

61 *See id.* at 133–34:

> 133. Nevertheless, the Parties differ on the way in which they qualify that payment. Kenya considers that it is a bribe given in order to obtain the Agreement on which the claims are based. World Duty Free considers it a gift of protocol or a personal donation made to the President to be used for public purposes within the framework of the Kenyan system of Harambee; the Claimant recalls that this system is "largely anchored in cultural practices when people are able to pull whatever resources they have, 'in particular' to finance community projects."
>
> 134. The Tribunal is aware of the fact that, on the occasion of visits to heads of State, gifts are often exchanged as a matter of protocol. It has also noted the report of the Task Force on Public Collections or "Harambees" presented in December 2003 to the Minister of Justice of Kenya. According to this report "the concept of Harambee had its root in the African culture where societies made collective contribution toward individual or communal activities" and this practice became popularised by President Kenyatta just after Kenyan independence. However, the report adds that "over the years, the spirit of Harambee has undergone a metamorphosis which has resulted in gross abuses. It has been linked to the emergence of oppressive and extortionist practices and entrenchment of corruption and abuse of office" (emphasis added).

> This Tribunal has not been asked to examine the reasons for the losses incurred by NCC resulting, according to the Claimants, from acts and omissions of the Egyptian authorities. All these alleged acts and omissions are the object of a lawsuit commenced by NCC against the Egyptian Government before the Egyptian Administrative Courts. In any case, the acts and omissions occurred before the investment of the two corporate Claimants in NCC and would therefore be outside the jurisdiction of this Tribunal based on the Bilateral Investment Treaty between Egypt and the USA.[62]

Although it may have had a jurisdictional component as the Tribunal identifies, a major issue is that the content and application of domestic regulations seem to have produced the dissimilarity of situations undermining a discrimination claim. By deferring certain key domestic law questions for domestic administrative and US court litigation,[63] the Tribunal might have avoided answering some key domestic law questions that might have interacted with the BIT rules on discrimination that might have impacted the outcome.

The *Jan de Nul N.V. and Dredging International N.V v. Egypt* (2008)[64] Tribunal applied principles of domestic law *sua sponte* to resolve an extremely important contention that the parties had treated as factual:

> The Parties did not discuss the standards on which the alleged fraud must be measured. They have argued their case on the basis of the facts. The Tribunal understands, however, from the Egyptian rules on fraud that intent is a necessary element and that there is no fraud when the alleged victim could have known about the relevant facts by another means. For this reason, the Tribunal will proceed to an assessment of the facts and review whether the SCA has intentionally withheld material information leading the JV to enter into the Contract on wrong premises and whether the JV had no other means of knowing the relevant facts.[65]

This is significant not only because the Parties never argued this point, but also because the domestic law that the Tribunal identified and applied on its own motion was outcome determinative. The Tribunal's application of Egyptian law's requirement of intent to include the notion of discoverability of the vital information from other sources and the investor's obligations to have done so is not totally unindicated by the parties' arguments, but the Tribunal used the domestic law to structure its analysis in a credible and cogent manner as a part of its denial of justice analysis.

62 Champion Trading Company Ameritrade International, Inc. v. Arab Republic of Egypt, ICSID Case No. ARB/02/9, Award (Oct. 27, 2006), at 118.

63 *See id.* at 105 ("Initially, the Claimants claimed that the Claimants' major shareholder, Mr. Wahba, was compelled, under threats by the Government, to agree to the sale to the Claimants of the shares in NCC held by the NBE and the Pension Fund. As a consequence, the Claimants claim, the agreement relating to the purchase of the shares by the Claimants was made under duress. In the Claimants' Reply, the Claimants withdrew all claims based on the relationship between the NBE and the Socialist Prosecutor and the resulting agreements with the NBE, since these issues are currently pending in U.S. courts").

64 Jan de Nul N.V. and Dredging International N.V v. Egypt, ICSID Case No. ARB/04/13, Award (Nov. 6, 2008).

65 *Id.* at 208.

The fate of another Egyptian case decided a year later, *Waguih Elie v. Egypt* (2009), was also by and large decided on the application of Egyptian domestic law, albeit in the jurisdictional context. The question of whether the principal Claimant in this case had lost his nationality as a matter of Egyptian law was outcome determinative in this case because if he had retained his Egyptian nationality, this ICSID Tribunal would not have had jurisdiction to hear the case.[66] Because the Claimant had struggled for 12 years through the domestic legal processes to get compensation, the Tribunal's rejection of jurisdiction would have returned him to the same legal processes that the Tribunal found to have denied him justice on the merits.[67]

Although the Tribunal determined the issue of the Claimant's loss of the host state's nationality exclusively on the basis of Egyptian law, the Claimant had to also overcome the issue of the Claimant's possession of the nationality of the other contracting state, Italy. The Tribunal had to address the latter under international law, the *Nottebohm* effective nationality doctrine.[68] The Tribunal distinguished this case from the *Nottebohm* case and found the presence of effective nationality.[69] The resolution of a key jurisdictional issue thus depended on the concurrent application of the domestic and international law sources.

Choice of Law: The Concurrent Application of Host State Law and International Law in the Post-2010 African Cases

Gustav v. Ghana (2010) reckoned with the balance of domestic law created contractual rights and their implications under international law, particularly in light of the Claimant's umbrella clause claim discussed in Chapter 14. Primarily, however, the Tribunal conceived the interaction between domestic and international rules as the Claimant's attempt to reorient what is quintessentially a domestic law-based contract claim into a breach of international law. Although the Tribunal disposed the case on attribution grounds, its analysis of the relationship between the two sets of rules is instructive:

> If the municipal law obligations which were negotiated between the parties to the JVA, and assumed by Cocobod in this case, are to be taken as obligations assumed by the State to Hamester, this would—in effect—completely transform their nature, extent, and governing law. The Tribunal considers that nothing in Article 9(2) of

[66] Waguih Elie v. Egypt, ICSID Case No. ARB/05/15, Award (June 1, 2009), at 15 ("In his application for permission to acquire Lebanese nationality Mr Siag sought permission to maintain his Egyptian nationality pursuant to the third paragraph of Article 10 of the Nationality Law. As discussed at length in the Tribunal's Decision on Jurisdiction, the third paragraph of Article 10 contains an additional requirement, once permission to maintain Egyptian nationality is granted, to further notify the Egyptian Interior Ministry within the period of one year of the desire to retain Egyptian nationality. Mr Siag did not so notify the Ministry with the consequence, as found in the Decision on Jurisdiction, that he lost his Egyptian nationality").

[67] *See id.* at 449–56.

[68] *Nottebohm Case* (second phase), Judgment (Apr. 6, 1955), I.C.J. Reports 1955, p.4 (articulating the principle of dominant and effective nationality doctrine.)

[69] Waguih Elie George Slag and Clorinda Vecchi v. The Arab Republic of Egypt, ICSID Case No. ARB/05/15, Award (June 1, 2009), at 468–80.

> the BIT here would justify this. Put the other way, given the wording of Article 9(2) of this BIT, the Tribunal concludes that the Contracting States did not intend to so transform domestic law contractual obligations concluded by separate entities.[70]

In *Bernard von Pezold v. Zimbabwe* (2015), as discussed extensively in the various procedural and substantive section above, the host state's laws including the constitutional amendments that permitted the dispossession of the land were said to have contributed or directly resulted in violations of the various provisions of the BITs as well as other relevant rules of international law. As such, the Tribunal's task in that case was not the application of domestic laws but it was the evaluation of the laws themselves in light of international law. In that sense, their interaction was one of hierarchy and preemption more than anything else.

Oded Besserglik v. Mozambique (2019) raised an interesting interaction between domestic and international laws for the determination of whether the BIT relied on by the Claimant had acquired the force of law through the ratification process under the contracting parties' domestic legal processes.

The Tribunal had to determine whether each state had properly ratified the BIT under its own laws. This raised domestic constitutional issues. Having considered the domestic constitutional laws and the provisions of the relevant BIT, the Tribunal concluded: "The Tribunal is of the view that the signature of the President, approval of Parliament and publication in the Gazette prove that the BIT was ratified by Respondent. This was also not contested by Respondent."[71] Having exhausted the constitutional requirements, the Tribunal cross-referred to the BIT and said:

> Ratification, however, was not what was required for the entry in force of the BIT under its Article 12(1). The requirement was reciprocal notifications from Respondent to South Africa and vice versa that the BIT had been ratified. The BIT was to enter in force only a day after the last such notification was received. The Tribunal is of the view that ratification and the publication in the Official Gazette that the BIT was ratified, by Respondent, was, therefore, a step toward the entering into force of the BIT.[72]

Having not been satisfied that the Claimant proved the occurrence of the BIT's mutual notification requirement under the domestic laws of each party, the Tribunal concluded that the BIT had not come into effect as a matter of both domestic and international law, the BIT's own provision on notification.[73]

[70] Gustav F W Hamester GmbH & Co KG v. Republic of Ghana Respondent, ICSID Case No. ARB/07/24, Award (June 18, 2010), at 347.

[71] Oded Besserglik v. Republic of Mozambique, ICSID Case No. ARB(AF)/14/2, Award (Oct. 28, 2019), at 341.

[72] *Id.*

[73] *See id.* at 369 ("In this case, not only Respondent but also South Africa has contested that the BIT is in force. Both States have denied that the notifications in question were issued. South Africa has also resisted the litigation commenced by its citizen, Claimant, in its courts to discover evidence with regard to any notification of the fulfillment of the constitutional requirements for entry into force for the BIT. Its officials and a Minister have sworn affidavits in that litigation which cast doubt on the circumstantial evidence produced by Claimant. Even if the Tribunal were to give some weight to the circumstantial evidence about Respondent issuing the notification, that would not take matters very far. There is no evidence by anyone

In *Bay View Group v. Rwanda* (2022), the host state's law played a curtail role. The mining contract, out of which the dispute arose, was subject to interpretation under Rwandan law. The parties disagreed about the meaning of certain terms in the mining contract which was the legal basis of the mining license. The relevant portion of the contract reads: "Article 4: The Rights: After positive evaluation of the submitted feasibility study Natural Resources Development Rwanda Limited will be granted the mining concessions."[74] Because the Contract expressly provides that it is governed by Rwandan law,[75] the Tribunal went on ascertaining the meaning of the last paragraph, that is, the rights of the investor under Rwandan law.

It received and considered expert reports and testimony on Rwandan law. It found that the expert testimony by the Respondent's expert witness was credible and useful, but the Claimant's expert was neither credible nor useful.[76]

The substantive question was whether the contract promised the investor the grant of a long-term mining concession, and if so, under what conditions. This relates to the overall question of the legitimate expectations of the investor under the BIT, which

who can claim to have seen either or both notifications in the records of either of the two States. No plausible explanation has been offered as to why South Africa would go to such lengths to support Respondent and undermine the claim of its citizen"). *See also id.* at 371 ("The Tribunal, therefore determines that it cannot, on the basis of the evidence on the record, conclude that the BIT is in force. This conclusion suffices to resolve the case before it").

[74] Bay View Group LLC and The Spalena Company LLC v. Republic of Rwanda, ICSID Case No. ARB/18/21, Award (Mar. 30, 2022), at 245. The provision of the law that precedes this one reads:

> Article 1: Purpose of the contract
> The Government of Rwanda authorizes Natural Resource Development Rwanda Ltd. To explore and run mining operations within RUTSIRO, MARA, SEBEYA, GICIYE and NEMBA Perimeters for a period of four (4) years. [. . .]
>
> Article 2: Obligations
> The Company Natural Resources Development Rwanda Ltd has the following obligations:
>
> 1. Make a geographical demarcation of the perimeters;
> 2. Provide the following documents as part of the contract:
>   - The action plan.
>   - The environmental protection plan.
>   - The investment plan.
> 3. Proceed immediately to the industrial exploitation in all given sites.
> 4. Provide progress reports on research activities after two years.
> 5. Provide evaluation reports of reserves and the feasibility study after 4 years.

[75] Bay View Group v. Rwanda, ICSID Case No. ARB/18/21, Award (Mar. 30, 2022), at 245.

[76] *See id.* at 246 ("Expert evidence on Rwandan law was given on behalf of Rwanda by Mr. Richard Mugisha, a member of the Rwanda Bar Association and founding senior partner of Trust Law Chambers. The Tribunal is satisfied that he is well qualified to give evidence on Rwandan law and that he gave his evidence carefully and with proper objectivity"). *See also id.* at 247 ("Evidence of Rwandan law was also given by Mr. Olivier Rwamasirabo, on behalf of the Claimants. He is also a member of the Rwandan Bar Association, having been admitted on 24 October 2017 and is the Managing Partner of Legal Wise Chambers Ltd. He was not tendered as an expert witness although he did not give any admissible evidence of fact. His precise role is not clear to the Tribunal. It appears from his evidence that he has given general advice to Mr. Marshall. In the view of the Tribunal he appeared to be acting more as an advocate than an impartial legal expert. In particular, he produced a Third Witness Statement dated 13 March 2020 that expressed views favourable to the Claimants on almost every issue in dispute, most of which depended critically on facts that were not within his knowledge, but which he asserted were based on his analysis of the documents and on conversations with Mr. Marshall. The Tribunal has not been assisted by this evidence").

was the key treaty question that needed to be determined in reference to the domestic law of the host state.

Applying Rwandan law, the Tribunal arrived at an important conclusion that "under Article 4, as interpreted by the Tribunal, it was a condition of any contractual entitlement on the part of NRD to long-term licences that the feasibility study should receive a positive evaluation from Rwanda."[77] It concluded that "the Tribunal finds that NRD failed to acquire a right to long-term licences under the Contract."[78] Although the Tribunal had to apply certain facts to come to this conclusion, it was essentially an interpretation of the contract under the host state's law as proven through expert testimony.

Conclusion

In most of the African cases, the host state's domestic laws have played as vital a role as the rules of international law, if not more. In the majority of these cases, the domestic laws applied concurrently with the rules of international law. The tribunals sometimes used expert testimony to ascertain the contents of the applicable domestic laws, and sometimes relied on texts of the laws suppled to them by the parties. No uniform rule of ascertainment of the rules of domestic law seems to have emerged.

At the technical level, they used the domestic laws for at least three purposes. First, they used the rule of decision to adjudicate contract-based controversies. Second, they judged the compliance of the state's behavior with its treaty obligations or standards of international law that it is subject to. Finally, they determined the enforceability of the invoked treaty. These cases show that the host state's domestic laws are extremely important in the adjudication of ISDS cases even when they are exclusively based on treaty standards. This might be one of the least appreciated aspects of ISDS.

[77] *Id.* at 295.
[78] *Id.* at 297.

18
Damages

The award and assessment of damages is often no less contentious than the finding of liability. While some tribunals bifurcate the proceedings, most tribunals consider damages in a unified proceeding. Depending on the nature of the proceeding, damages could be assessed under domestic law standards, international law standards, or under a combination of domestic and international law standards. Many of the African cases demonstrate the difficulties of the articulation of these standards and their application to specific factual circumstances. This chapter canvases the various tribunals' articulation of legal standards for the assessment of damages and their application of these standards to the African cases under review.

The Assessment of Damages in the Early African Cases (1970–2000)

In *MINE v. Guinea* (1988), the contract that gave rise to the claim was never performed at all. The finding of liability was essentially based on lost opportunity because Guinea reassigned the Claimant's rights to another contactor, although it claimed that it was temporary and that it was because the Claimant failed to perform. That may as well have been true, but the state was asked to compensate the nonperforming contractual partner because of its decision to prematurely reassign.

The measure of damages was assessed under the following legal theory:

> The Tribunal accepts the general principle that MINE is entitled to be compensated for the profits that it would have earned if Guinea had not breached the Convention. The lost profits need not be proven with complete certainty, nor should recovery be denied simply because the amount is difficult to ascertain.[1]

Although this closely resembles the measure of damages under many civil law jurisdictions, the Tribunal does not cite to any authority. Applying this principle, the Tribunal found as follows:

> The Tribunal finds that MINE's loss of profits may be measured adequately by the AFROBULK agreement: the 50 cents per ton which Guinea received from AFROBULK for the right to carry bauxite under Art. 9 during a two-year period rightfully belongs to SOTRAMAR. In addition, it seems fair to conclude that such an arrangement could have been extended, or negotiated with others, to a total period of

[1] Maritime International Nominees Establishment v. Republic of Guinea, ICSID Case No. ARB/84/4, Award (Jan. 6, 1988), at 65.

Africa's International Investment Law Regimes. Won L. Kidane, Oxford University Press.
DOI: 10.1093/oso/9780197745571.003.0018

> 10 years. While the Convention was to last 30 years, the Bauxite Receivers under the Harvey Agreement were bound to CBG for only 20 years, and 10 years appears to be a reasonable period considering that the Convention contained provisions for early termination.[2]

In that sense, the Tribunal awarded to the Claimant all the benefits that Guinea had gotten and any potential benefits that Guinea would have gotten over a 10-year period. The Tribunal made no considerations as to Guinea's expenses to earn those funds. And indeed, in what appears to be a punitive measure, it also awarded interests, fees, and expenses, as indicated in the next section. This is an excellent example of how heavy-handed litigation tactics and tenacious multijurisdiction pursual could sometimes pay off. As to the justice of the matter, however, the measure of damages might have been too favorable to the Claimant.

In *SPP v. Egypt* (1992), the Tribunal found that Egypt lawfully expropriated the contractual rights of the investor without offering compensation and as such must offer fair compensation for what was expropriated. This is not what would have been considered restitution for unlawful expropriation.[3] In its own words: "The cardinal point to be borne in mind, then, in determining the appropriate compensation is that, while the contracts could no longer be performed, the Claimants are entitled to receive fair compensation for what was expropriated rather than damages for breach of contract."[4]

The Tribunal rejected the Claimant's proposed Discounted Cash Flow (DFC) method because the project had no history of operation[5] and essentially awarded out of pocket expenses, costs, and related interests, which amounted to a total of about $27 million.[6]

The Assessment of Damages in the African Cases of the 2000s

In *Wena v. Egypt* (2000), the Tribunal found Egypt liable for violation of at least three investor protection provisions of the 1975 UK–Egypt BIT including expropriation, FET, and FSP,[7] and awarded Wena, the investor, what it considered the market value of its investment right before the expropriation.[8] At the technical level, the Tribunal

[2] *Id.* at 69.

[3] Southern Pacific Properties (Middle East) Limited v. Arab Republic of Egypt, ICSID Case No. ARB/84/3, Award (May 20, 1992), at 183.

[4] *Id.*

[5] *See id.* at 188 ("the DCF method is not appropriate for determining the fair compensation in this case because the project was not in existence for a sufficient period of time to generate the data necessary for a meaningful DCF calculation").

[6] *Id.* at 257.

[7] Wena Hotels Limited v. Arab Republic of Egypt, ICSID Case No. ARB/98/4, Award (Dec. 8, 2000), at 77 ("77. Despite the able representation of Egypt's counsel, the Tribunal concludes that Egypt did violate its obligations under the IPPA by failing to provide Wena's investments in Egypt 'fair and equitable treatment' and 'full protection and security' and by failing to provide Wena with 'prompt, adequate and effective compensation' following the expropriation of its investments").

[8] *Id.* at 118 ("118. Article 5 of the IPPA between Egypt and the United Kingdom provides that in the event of an expropriation, the private investor shall be entitled to 'prompt, adequate, and effective compensation'

was confronted with a wide disparity in the Parties' assessments of how much money was actually spent by the investor. While Wena claimed that it spent more than $8 million on its ventures, Egypt claimed that the investor spent no more than $750,000.[9] The Tribunal did not need to resolve this as it assessed damages on the basis of what it considered the market value of the investment that it determined was expropriated. But it was also not willing to either use a Discounted Cash Flow (DCF) method, as there was no proven record of profitability consistent with the *Metalclad* decision that came before it.[10] The Tribunal focused on the amount that the investor spent in Egypt despite the factual contentions about the quantum. The Tribunal believed the investor's version of the investment, although it cites to no evidence except to summarize the Parties' contentions.[11] In terms of the standard of the measure of damages, the Tribunal stated it as follows:

> Rather, the Tribunal agrees with the parties that the proper calculation of "the market value" of the investment expropriated immediately before the expropriation is best arrived at, in this case, by reference to Wena's actual investments in the two hotels. As noted above, Wena pleads in the alternative for award of at least the amount of Wena's proven investment in the Egyptian hotel venture. Similarly, Respondent pleads in the alternative that if any award were made it should not be more than the amount of Wen a's proven investment.[12]

Once the standard was set this way, the result depended on which side of the story the Tribunal believed in terms of how much money was spent. Believing the investor more, the Tribunal awarded what the investor claimed to have spent with minor deductions. It also awarded a 9% interest to be compounded quarterly.[13] The Tribunal used the interest rate for the purpose of "restor[ing] the Claimant to a reasonable

and 'such compensation shall amount to the market value of the investment immediately before the expropriation.' The Tribunal shall apply this standard to the determination of damages").

[9] *See id.* at 121, 124.

[10] *Id.* at 123 ("123. The Tribunal agrees with Egypt that, in this case, Wena's claims for lost profits (using a discounted cash flow analysis), lost opportunities and reinstatement costs are inappropriate- because an award based on such claims would be too speculative. As another ICSID panel recently noted in the Metalclad decision: Normally, the fair market value of a going concern which has a history of profitable operation may be based on an estimate of future profits subject to a discounted cash flow analysis. However, where the enterprise has not operated for a sufficiently long time to establish a performance record or where it has failed to make a profit, future profits cannot be used to determine going concern or fair market value").

[11] *Id.* at 124 ("Finally, the Tribunal is disinclined to grant Wena's request for lost profits and lost opportunities given the large disparity between the requested amount (GB 45.7 million) and Wena's stated investment in the two hotels (US$8,819,466.93)").

[12] *Id.* at 125.

[13] *Id.* at 128–29 ("128. To this should be added an appropriate sum for interest. Claimant has claimed interest but neither specified a rate nor whether interest should be compounded. Moreover, the IPPA, the lease agreements, and the ICSID Convention and Rules are all silent on the subject of interest. The Panel is of the view that in this case interest should be awarded and that it would be appropriate to adopt a rate of 9%, to be compounded quarterly. 129. Like the distinguished panel in the recently-issued *Metalclad* decision, this Tribunal also has determined that compounded interest will best 'restore the Claimant to a reasonable approximation of the position in which it would have been if the wrongful act had not taken place.'")

approximation of the position in which it would have been if the wrongful act had not taken place."[14] It is essentially an award of lost profits measured by what was spent not what was expected. In that sense, this decision added more confusion than clarification to the ever-elusive issue of the assessment of damages. At the end, an investor that Egypt claimed to have only spent $750,000 walked away with an award of more than $20 million.[15]

Beyond the assessment of the quantum of damages, there was a missing link in the analysis of damages—not an unusual omission. The Tribunal's main finding of liability was the denial of FET and FSP but the assessment damages pertained only to expropriation which in fact was not even established. In terms of quantum, the award of more than $20 million is to be contrasted with what Wena received as a full measure of damages in Egyptian domestic arbitration, which was limited to a total of about $436,000.[16]

In *Middle East Cement v. Egypt* (2002), the Tribunal calculated damages on the basis of lost profit predicated on the Greece-Egypt BIT's expropriation provision's reference to market value in the following terms: "... compensation shall amount to the market value of the investments affected immediately before the measures referred to above in this paragraph occurred or became public knowledge."[17] Having found the Respondent liable for expropriation of the investor's property, which was the cement license overtaken by a Decree (determined on the facts that the remaining period of validity would have been 44 months rather than four months as alleged by the Respondent), the Tribunal awarded only lost profit that the Claimant could prove on the basis of existing supply contracts that were interrupted. The Claimant had sought more than $42 million in lost profit, but the Tribunal only awarded about $1.7 million.[18] It reasoned that:

> 127. The License being the "expropriated" investment, its earning capacity during the remainder of its life may well come into consideration for assessing its "market value" under the BIT. Nothing would have prevented Claimant from concluding other cement supply contracts or contracts providing for the use of its terminal facilities. The circumstance that some of the cement supply contracts take into consideration possible increases in quantities and/ or extension of duration lends support to the conclusion that the License had not exhausted its potentiality of yielding further

[14] *Id.* at 129.

[15] *Id.* at 130 ("Thus, including the Claimant's attorney's fees and costs, the grand total to be awarded Claimant is US$20,600,986.43. This award will be payable within 30 days from the date hereof. Thereafter, it will accumulate additional interest at 9% compounded quarterly until paid").

[16] *Id.* at 127. The exact amount received was $435,570.38.

[17] *See* Middle East Cement Shipping and Handling Co. S.A. v. Arab Republic of Egypt, ICSID Case No. ARB/99/6, Award (Apr. 12, 2002), at 105.

[18] *Id.* at 118–19 ("118. The total amount of lost profits claimed by Claimant is equal therefore to US$ 21,175,500 (C II 20).

> 119. In its Reply Memorial Claimant has requested, in addition to the foregoing, the amount of profits lost under the Halkis Agreement, totaling US$ 42,240,000 (C III 20)"). *See also id.* at 125 ("125. The total amount of lost profits under the three cement supply agreements still in force on the date of Decree No. 195 of May 28, 1989 is therefore determined to be equal to US$ 1,712,712").

> profits to Claimant's benefit and that, accordingly, Claimant had a legitimate expectation that it could have earned additional profits under the License.
>
> 128. However, in order to add such expectations to the "market value" of the investment (Art.4.c) of the BIT), it would have been necessary for the Claimant to provide proof of concrete contracts missed and of the profit lost from them. The Tribunal concludes that the Claimant has not fulfilled that burden of proof and that, therefore, no additional compensation is due in this regard.[19]

By limiting the amount of damages this way, the Tribunal mitigated its generous finding of liability. In that sense, its damages opinion relating to the expropriation of the license might be its most enduring contribution.

The Tribunal's assessment of damages with respect to the vessel that it found to have been expropriated (because it was auctioned off without due process) was creative. The vessel was auctioned for the equivalent of $90,000.[20] The Claimant said it was worth $5 million, showing insurance for that much, but also suggested that it should at least be paid the scrap price for bulkers of US $864,500.00.[21]

The Tribunals said that because the amount is too small to warrant the hiring of a valuation expert, it would just simply take the average between the Respondents valuation and the Claimant's valuation and awarded $477,718 for the expropriation of the vessel.[22] This was just a rule of convenience with no discernable jurisprudential value beyond the disposition of this particular case. And indeed, the Tribunal's handling of the issue of the auctioning of the vessel as expropriation and FET violation for lack of proper notice does not seem to have inspired appreciation and following in subsequent cases.

Semos v. Mali (2003) did not involve a difficult damages analysis because what the Claimant sought in the form of relief was exemption from readily quantifiable mineral export duties. As such, the Tribunal's award of relief is limited to the reimbursement of known amounts of duties already collected and the prohibition of future collection of duties,[23] as the prospective relief was essentially declaratory in nature.

[19] *Id.* at 127–28.

[20] Middle East Cement v. Egypt, Award (Apr. 12, 2002), at 150.

[21] *Id.* at 149.

[22] *Id.* at 150 ("150. Using the discretion it has under ICSID Rule 34 regarding evidence, the Tribunal holds that—even if it were possible—it would be too time consuming and costly, related to the amount in dispute, to seek some independent expert opinion on the value of the Poseidon at the time of the auction, and that it is thus the best procedural method, under the circumstances, to reach an estimate of the value of the Poseidon from the evidence available in the file. Taking into account that the Respondent alleges the auction price as the correct value, i.e., EP 301,000.00, which was equivalent to US$ 90,936.00 at the contemporaneous rate of 3.31 used by both Parties (C I 26 and R II 26) at that time, and that the Claimant has shown the scrap value to be US$ 864,500.00, the Tribunal concludes that at least the average between these amounts, i.e., US$ 477,718.00 can be taken as the market value due under Art. 4. c) of the BIT").

[23] Société D'exploitation Des Mines D'or De Sadiola S.A. (Semos) v. Republic of Mali, ICSID Case No. ARB/01/5, Award (Feb. 25, 2003), 96–99:

> 96. In view of all of the foregoing, the documents produced and the claims made by the parties, the Arbitral Tribunal has decided as follows:
>
> 97. The pursuit by the State of Mali of the proceedings instituted with a view to collecting stamp duties on the gold exports made by Semos since 4 March 2000 is contrary to its obligations under the Convention;

The assessment of damages in the *Patrick Mitchell v. DRC* (2004) case was a point of contention not only between the parties but also between the arbitrators, eventually causing a split that led to annulment. Having found that the host state expropriated the Claimant's law firm, the majority of the Tribunal faced a problem of quantifying the amount of damages. The legal basis for the quantification of the damages is contained in Article III(1) of the US–DRC BIT:

> Compensation shall be equivalent to the fair market value of the expropriated investment. The calculation of such compensation shall not result in any reduction in such fair market value due to either prior public notice or announcement of the expropriatory action, or the occurrence of the events that constituted or resulted in the expropriatory action. Such compensation shall include interest at a rate equivalent to current international rates from the date of expropriation, and be freely transferable at the prevailing market rate of exchange on the date of expropriation.[24]

The road to the award of lost profit in three offices was treacherous. It required the consideration of varied methodologies. The Claimant offered two expert reports on quantum. Although each used different methodologies, they seem to have assigned a similar value to the firm based on the income statements, earning reports, bank statements, invoices, contracts, and other indicia of annual income for a few years preceding the event.[25] It was not the use of these indicia and quantum methodology that caused the split within the decision-makers. It was rather the inclusion of income received in offices outside of the DRC, that is, in the United States and South Africa, that raised the question of both BIT coverage and linkage to what is deemed expropriated.[26]

The majority satisfied itself that the closure of the firm due to the raid caused the loss of expected income for three years measured by the earnings of the previous years. Although it considered the expert reports, in the end, the valuation was no more complicated than that.[27] The Tribunal awarded the Claimant a total of $750,000 as the fair market value of the firm, representing three years' worth of expected

> 98. Semos is entitled to be exempt from stamp duty on gold export applications, licences or certificates throughout the term of the Amended Convention;
>
> 99. In consequence, the Tribunal:—orders the Republic of Mali to reimburse to Semos the stamp duty unduly collected on the export applications already submitted by Semos which, as at 13 September 2002, amounted to CFA 1,800,024,000.

24 Patrick Mitchell v. DRC Award (Feb. 9, 2004); Annulment (Nov. 1, 2006), at 77 (reproducing the text of Article III(1) of the BIT).

25 *See id.* at 78–95.

26 *See id.* at Dissent 29 ("29. Why did the Tribunal choose to base itself on the consolidated revenue of the three offices? It would certainly not have done so if the income accrued by the Kinshasa office for the fiscal year 1998 had been substantial").

27 *See* Patrick Mitchell v. DRC, (Feb. 9, 2004); Annulment (Nov. 1, 2006), at 91 ("91. Claimant contends that in order to assess the level of profitability which would have occurred in the future, the appropriate figure is determinable by averaging the three years 1996 to 1998 either by simple average or weighted average. In the Tribunal's view, such an approach is reasonable in light of the important variations in the annual results. The variations in the annual results are considerable. The decrease in profit in 1998 has not been explained as being exceptional, apart from the fact that the bonus paid to [. . .] was particularly high that year. It has been noted also that certain expenses are included in the loss registered in the RSA. In addition, some weight has to be given to the lack of more structured and readable accounts, despite the repeated

profits calculated on the basis of past earnings in all three offices.[28] Its assessment was as simple as that.

The *World Duty Free v. Kenya* (2006) Tribunal did not have to worry about damages because the claims were dismissed in their entirety, as the Agreement that gave rise to the dispute was found to be void.[29] The final decision reads:

In conclusion:

1. The Respondent, Kenya, was legally entitled to avoid and did avoid legally by its Counter-Memorial dated 18 April 2003 the "House of Perfume Contract," namely the Agreement of 27 April 1989 as amended on 11 May 1990, under its applicable laws, the laws of England and Kenya;
2. The Respondent, Kenya, did not lose its right to avoid the said contract by affirmation or otherwise before 18 April 2003 under these applicable laws; and
3. The Claimant is not legally entitled to maintain any of its pleaded claims in these proceedings as a matter of ordre public international and public policy under the contract's applicable laws.[30]

This appears to be one of the first major fully litigated cases that an African state decisively won on the merits. It did so in the strangest of circumstances: blaming its own former president for taking a bribe to allow the investment. The finding of illegality at the stage of contract formation deprived it of any legal effect and whatever violation that the investor might have suffered had no legal remedy. As such, whatever damages were caused, they were simply not compensable as a matter of law.

In *Champion Trading v. Egypt* (2006), the Tribunal did not have to assess damages because it dismissed the Claimants' claims entirely on the merits because the Claimants failed to carry their burden of proof that the disparate treatment they suffered (lack of government payment in the cotton industry) was because of their foreign nationality rather than a function of their own business decision not to participate in qualifying government program.[31] As the case against the government was

queries addressed to Claimant. The Tribunal therefore concludes that an amount of US$ [. . .] could reasonably be retained as an expected annual benefit as from 1999").

[28] *Id.* at 93 ("93. The Tribunal acknowledges that the mining and banking sector in which the Claimant was particularly involved, are among the most profitable parts of the Congo's economy, despite a lack of political stability in that country. However, the commercial value that Claimant identifies essentially as his know-how and client-basis can hardly be given an asset-value of more than four years. First of all, the capitalization rate of 24% used by [. . .] might be valid in the South African context; however, one cannot assimilate the economic and political environment of the Congo to that of South Africa. A higher capitalization rate would clearly be required in the case of the Congo. Secondly, it has been established that Mr. Mitchell visited the Congo some time in 2002, without being interfered with. In the circumstances, the Tribunal finds that a shorter period would be more realistic, which it establishes at three years. It results from this that the "fair market value" of Mitchell & Associates was at the relevant time US$ 750,000").

[29] World Duty Free Company Limited v. Republic of Kenya, ICSID Case No. ARB/00/7, Award (Oct. 4, 2006), at 188.

[30] *Id.*

[31] *See* Champion Trading Company Ameritrade International, Inc. v. Arab Republic of Egypt, ICSID Case No. ARB/02/9, Award (Oct. 27, 2006), at 156 ("Since the Arbitral Tribunal came to the conclusion that the companies were not in a like situation, it does not need to analyze the other requirements which prohibit discrimination on the grounds of nationality").

dismissed and the government did not have counterclaims, no damages assessment was necessary.

Biwater v. Tanzania (2008) is most remarkable for its finding of liability for FET and denial of the award of any damages showing that not all damages are reparable. Having proven liability to the satisfaction of the Tribunal, the investor failed to earn any compensation because of a lack of causal nexus between the international wrongful act and the injuries it sustained.[32] The award of damages was thus zero.[33] The relief that the investor got was declaratory.[34] In this regard, the Tribunal instructively noted that:

> the Arbitral Tribunal considers that an expropriation may take place by reason of a substantial interference with rights, even if no economic loss is caused thereby, or can be quantified. In such cases, non-pecuniary remedies (e.g. injunctive, declaratory or restitutionary relief) may still be appropriate. Whether any economic loss has in fact been caused by the "taking" in question is a matter to be considered in the context of a claim for compensation, rather than being a necessary ingredient in the cause of action of unlawful expropriation itself.[35]

Although the Tribunal indicated that the assessment of damages for the finding of liability under expropriation and the other protection principles such as FET may be similar in the sense of restitution under *Chorzow* factory, the disposition of the case did not require a determination in this case, as it rested on lack of causation.[36] This is a good example of the state's unnecessary and untimely reaction even when the action itself is justified. It could clearly have been managed better to avoid the case against the state altogether. As indicated in the facts chapter, it is the combination of some unnecessary steps such as the deportation of managers that gave the appearance of

[32] Biwater Gauff (Tanzania) Ltd. v. United Republic of Tanzania, ICSID Case No. ARB/05/22, Final Award (July 24, 2008), at 485 ("On the basis of a careful consideration of the full evidential record and all submissions by all parties, the Arbitral Tribunal has reached the conclusion that BGT's investment, as embodied in the Lease Contract, was the subject of an expropriation by the Republic. However, as explained later in this Award, by the time that this expropriation took place, the termination of the Lease Contract was inevitable in any event, and the losses and damage for which BGT claims in these proceedings had already been (separately) caused").

[33] *Id.* at 792 ("In the Arbitral Tribunal's view, by 1 June 2005, being the date BGT states its investment was expropriated by the Republic, the said investment was of no economic value. This, indeed, had been the position since well before this date, and well before 13 May 2005").

[34] *See Id.* at 807 ("Given that none of the Republic's violations of the BIT caused the loss and damage for which BGT now claims compensation, it follows that each of BGT's claims for damages must be dismissed, and that the only appropriate remedies for the Republic's conduct can be declaratory in nature").

[35] *Id.* at 781.

[36] *Id.* at 776–77 ("776. Other Claims: For claims other than expropriation (breach of fair and equitable treatment, unreasonable and discriminatory measures, violation of full protection and security, and of the principle of unrestricted transfer of funds), the BIT does not offer any guidance for evaluating the damages arising from such breaches. On the basis that this does not mean that compensation is excluded, the common starting point is the broad principle articulated in the well known Factory at Chorzow case, according to which any award should: "as far as possible wipe out all the consequences of the illegal act and re-establish the situation which would, in all probability, have existed if that act had not been committed" 777. The application of this broad principle has been the subject of detailed analysis in many commentaries and decisions, albeit that in many BIT cases, arbitral tribunals appear to have simply deployed the fair market value of the investment in question as the measure of damages both for claims of expropriation and breaches of other treaty standards").

irrational government behavior that were found to have violated fundamental principles of international investment law.

Bernardus v. Zimbabwe (2009) confronted the perineal question of the difference in the evaluation of damages for lawful expropriation and unlawful expropriation. The Respondent did not deny that it was liable for takings but disagreed with the Claimant's on the legality of the taking. Having deemed the taking unlawful, the Tribunal had to struggle as to how the quantum of compensation defers from lawful expropriation that the Respondent admitted:[37]

> As the Iran–United States Claims Tribunal rightly observed in the Amoco case, "obviously, the value of an expropriated enterprise does not vary according to the lawfulness or the unlawfulness of the taking.... The difference is that, if the taking is lawful the value of the undertaking at the time of the dispossession is the measure and the limit of the compensation, while if it is unlawful, this value is or may be, only a part of the reparation to be paid." In general, as the same Tribunal stated in the Phillips Petroleum case, "the lawful/unlawful taking distinction ... is relevant only to two possible issues: whether restitution of the property can be awarded and whether compensation can be awarded for increase of the value of the property between the date of the taking and the date of the judicial or arbitral decision awarding compensation."[38]

Applying these principles, it calculated damages based on quantum expert reports and awarded the Claimant's varying amounts corresponding to their losses "at the date of dispossession on the basis of the market value at that date."[39]

The Tribunal in *Waguih Elie v. Egypt* (2009) had no difficulty finding Egypt liable for violations of several investment protection rules such as expropriation and FET, but, like the tribunals that came before, it was confronted with competing theories of recovery.

The Claimant sought "full compensation" under customary international law.[40] The Respondent state sought to limit the damages to what is prescribed in the applicable BIT, which states: "Where the market value [of the investment] cannot be readily ascertained, the compensation shall be determined on equitable principles taking into account, inter alia, the capital invested, depreciation, capital already repatriated, replacement value, goodwill and other relevant factors."[41]

The Tribunal rejected Egypt's contention on the application of the BIT's rule on compensation, arguing that it only apples for lawful expropriation.[42] It did so

[37] Bernardus Henricus Funnekotter and Others v. Republic of Zimbabwe, ICSID Case No. ARB/05/6, Award (Apr. 22, 2009), at 108–24.

[38] *Id.* at 111.

[39] *Id.* at 124.

[40] Waguih Elie George Slag and Clorinda Vecchi v. The Arab Republic of Egypt, ICSID Case No. ARB/05/15, Award (June 1, 2009), at 535.

[41] *Id.* at 537.

[42] *Id.* at 539 ("Reading Article 5 of the BIT as a whole, it is plain that subclause (iii) is concerned with lawful expropriation, which is to say expropriation permitted in terms of subclause (ii). Pursuant to Article 5(ii), investments may not be nationalised or expropriated except on the specific terms stated. Those terms include that the expropriation must be '... for a public purpose in the national interest of [the] State, for adequate and fair compensation ... and in accordance with due process of law.' For the reasons given in

relying on *Vivindi v. Argentina*, which categorically rules that the BIT's compensation provision "does not purport to establish a *lex specialis* governing the standards of compensation for wrongful or unlawful expropriations."[43] Having made this major announcement on the applicable rule, it said in reality there is essentially no difference between compensation for lawful expropriation and unlawful expropriation in this case because, unlike *Vivindi*, there is no claim for lost profit but fair market value of what was expropriated.[44] Relying on expert valuation, the Tribunal finally fixed the Claimant's compensation at $74,550,794.75.[45]

The Assessment of Damages in the Post-2010 African Cases

Bernard von Pezold v. Zimbabwe (2015) presented highly complex damages assessment issues. According to the Tribunal, "in a case such as the present one, where there are complex valuations and extensive evidence, absolute certainty is an aspiration unlikely to be achieved."[46]

Guided primarily by the principle of restitution,[47] and assisted by expert witnesses, the Tribunal employed a variety of assessment methodologies including DCF for some[48] and income-based valuation for going concerns,[49] and awarded damages amounting a total of close to $200 million,[50] which included a modest amount of $1 million in moral damages.[51] In that sense, the Tribunal essentially took fact and equity based assessment of damages rather than any particular legal theory.

Union Fenosa Gas, S.A. (UFG) v. Egypt (2018) is notable for both the size of the award and its exclusive reliance on the FET violation as a source of *Chorzow Factory* level restitution. The Tribunal found Egypt liable for its violation of FET and said the following relating to the award of damages:

> 10.95 Standard of Compensation: The Treaty does not set out a standard of compensation to be applied in the case of any violations of the Treaty, save as regards expropriation under Article 6 of the Treaty. Expropriation is not alleged by the

paragraphs 427 to 443 above, the Tribunal is strongly of the view that the expropriation in this case did not satisfy those conditions, and that accordingly it was not a lawful expropriation to which Article 5 of the BIT applied").

43 *Id.* at 540 (citing Compania de Aguas del Aconquija S.A. and Vivendi Universal S.A. v Argentine Republic, ICSID Case No. ARB/97/3 (Resubmission Proceeding), Award (Aug. 20, 2007).

44 *Id.* at 541.

45 *Id.* at 631.

46 Bernardus Henricus Funnekotter and Others v. Republic of Zimbabwe, ICSID Case No. ARB/05/6, Award (Apr. 22, 2009), at 809.

47 *See id.* at 813 ("The sum of compensation that the Tribunal arrives at should reflect the value of the Estate that would have been received if restitution had been successful; that is, the value at the date of the Award.)

48 *See, e.g., id.* at 814.

49 *See, e.g., id.* at 815.

50 *See id.* at 924.

51 *See id.* at 923.

> Claimant to have taken place, at least for the purpose of its present claims in this particular arbitration.
>
> 10.96 It follows that any compensation to be awarded by this Tribunal is to be decided by applying principles of customary international law, namely "full reparation" to wipe out, as far as possible, the consequences of the Respondent's international wrongs under the general principle long established in the PCIJ's judgment in Chorzow Factory (1928), as also confirmed by Articles 31 and 36 of the ILC Articles on State Responsibility.[52]

Relying on this and similar related authorities, the Tribunal found Egypt liable for "total principal sum of US$ 2,013,071,000 (after tax, but before interest)."[53] This corresponded to "lost cash flow."[54] This in a way considers the violation of FET as a source of the assessment of damages independently of the expropriation standard and elevates it to full reparations that many tribunals reserved for unlawful expropriation under customary international law. The award does not properly explain what in the nature of an FET violation warrants full reparation without an actual taking.

The assessment of damages in *Strtabag SE v. Libya* (2020) proceeded in a classic breach of contract sense because most of the findings of liability related to breach of contract under the umbrella clause.[55] The tribunal followed the Parties classification of damages into 12 categories of losses that included equipment requisition, damage and destruction, unpaid work certificates, and financial charges.[56] The damages assessment required no greater exposition of legal doctrine than the valuation of lost equipment and the amount of unpaid work certificates, just like any ordinary construction works contract.

The Tribunal assessed a total of €124,895,006, and because the Claimant was the owner of only 60% of the enterprise, it was awarded a total of €74,937,003.60.[57] Although a significant proportion of this was for unpaid works certificates, the Tribunal by majority vote chose not to apply a set-off for the advance payment of at least €51 million because of the factual uncertainty surrounding the validity of the bank guarantees.[58] In that sense, the majority of the Tribunal erred on the side of placing the potential risk of loss of the performance guarantee amount of more than €50 million on the Respondent state. The Tribunal decided that "for the forgoing reasons, the Tribunal decides, by majority, that Respondent's requested set-off is denied.

[52] Union Fenosa Gas, S.A. v. Arab Republic of Egypt, ICSID Case No. ARB/14/4 (Aug. 31, 2018), at 10.95–.96 (citing Chorzow Factory, PCIJ Rep Series A, No. 17 (1928)).

[53] *Id.* at 10.133.

[54] *Id.* 10.134.

[55] *See* Strabag Se v. Libya, ICSID Case No. ARB(AF)/15/1, Award (June 29, 2020), at 363, 373 391, 399, 485, 486, 590, 591, 645, 707, 720, 722, 735, 756, 768, 778, and 874.

[56] *See id.* at 245–46.

[57] *Id.* at 977–80.

[58] *See id.* at 22 (Partial Dissenting Opinion of Professor Nassib Ziadi) ("However, the evidence on the record regarding the Tajura advance payment guarantee in the amount of EUR 51,905,971.53 (by far the most substantial guarantee) casts serious doubt on its continuing validity. The record shows that both Gumhouria Bank and ABC International Bank regarded at least the fronting guarantee component of the Tajura advance payment guarantee as having expired").

In the view of the majority, this is a matter that must be addressed by the Parties, if it is to be addressed, outside the context of this arbitration."[59]

It is obvious that the majority preferred that the Respondent bear the potential risk of not recovering the advance payment than the Claimant risks additional losses if the guarantees were honored, because it had spent at least some of the advance payment for works. The most prudent course of action would have been to get to the bottom of the validity of the bank guarantee, which is essentially what caused the split among members of the Tribunal.

Conclusion

There appears to be more uncertainty and inconsistency in the rules for the assessment of damages than in the rules that apply for the finding of liability. The uncertainty relates to three broad categories. First, the tribunals are uncertain about the distinction between the damages due to unlawful expropriation and lawful expropriation. Some held that such distinction is inconsequential for the assessment of damages, but others held that the remedy for lawful expropriation is an award of damages equal to the value of what was expropriated, such as the value of the equipment taken but the remedy for unlawful expropriation should be full restitution.

The second uncertainty relates to the measure of damages for nonexpropriation violations such as FET. Many tribunals treated the measure of damages for FET violation just like expropriation. At least one tribunal awarded restitution, which other tribunals reserved for unlawful expropriation.

The third category of uncertainties relates to the finding of liability under the umbrella clause. Although technically it is a treaty violation, the tribunal that found a violation of the umbrella clause essentially assessed damages just like any breach of contract claim without regard to the treaty nature of the violation.

Overall, just like the various tribunals use the FET rule to exercise their own sense of justice, most of the tribunals attempt to articulate the rules of law for the assessment of damages that seemed like the most appropriate measure of compensation under the circumstances. More than anything else, the tribunals seem to have been guided by the principle of awarding the claimant what it has lost in reality—although some have gone beyond that and offered what could be classified as punitive, as indicated above.

Finally, the uncertainties of the assessment of damages in these ISDS cases do not seem to be any greater than uncertainties faced by any adjudicator asked to assess damages in any domestic legal proceeding for breach of obligations. The core difficulty is inherent in the law of damages generally, although ISDS often faces additional difficulties because of the overlap of national and international standards and issues of quantity and quality of proof.

This conclusion would be incomplete without the mention of the particularly concerning award of full restitution for an FET violation that the *Union Fenosa Gas v. Egypt* tribunal awarded. It equates the violation of FET to unlawful expropriation. It

[59] *Id.* at 921.

is a doctrinally unsound shortcut. This award did not sit comfortably and indeed annulment, enforcement, and related arbitral and judicial proceedings followed.[60]

The potential acceptability and enforceability of awards must always be a serious consideration. Certain tribunals do not consider the potential enforceability of their award their job, which is reminiscent of Justice Holmes' famous response to Judge Learned Hand's plea—"Do justice, Sir!" The response was: "It is not my job."[61]

[60] For reports on what happened after the award, see Jack Ballantyne, *Defeats US$3 Billion Claim*, GAR (Feb. 11, 2020), at https://www.shearman.com/-/media/files/news/2020/02/gar--20200211--egyptian-state-entity-defeats-us3-billion-claim.pdf?la=en&hash=2F0CB19BE130D78008B3490827FA6D435 11ADF28.

[61] This is reported in slightly different ways, but Judge Learned Hand's own recollection is this: "I remember once I was with [Justice Holmes]; it was a Saturday when the Court was to confer. It was before we had a motor car, and we jogged along in an old coupé. When we got down to the Capitol, I wanted to provoke a response, so as he walked off, I said to him: "Well, sir, goodbye. Do justice!" He turned quite sharply and he said: "Come here. Come here." I answered: "Oh, I know, I know." He replied: "That is not my job. My job is to play the game according to the rules." Learned Hand, *A Personal Confession*, *in* THE SPIRIT LIBERTY 302, 306–07 (Irving Dillard 3d ed., 1960) (cited in Michael Herz, *Do Justice!: Variations of a Thrice-Told Tale*, 82 VIRGINIA L. REV. 111, 111 (1996)).

19
Allocation of Costs and Interests

Each proceeding ends with the allocation of costs and interests. These decisions are taken on the basis of substantive rules that apply specifically to the allocation of costs and interests. These rules are a combination of the arbitral rules' choice of law and relevant domestic laws addressing these matters. Collectively, these rules often delegate broad authority to the tribunal. As a result, the approaches have been as varied as the tribunals themselves although the choices they have are not exactly unlimited. This chapter surveys the allocation of costs and the award of interests in the African cases.

The Allocation of Costs and Interests in the Early African Cases

The stage on the allocation of costs and interests was set by the foundation cases that invariably allocated the costs of the proceedings on the Respondent state and awarded interests albeit under slightly different theories of liability.

In *BP v. Libya*, the Tribunal declared "the Claimant is entitled to be restored to the full enjoyment of its rights under the Concession Agreement," and ordered the payment of damages and full costs but deferred the actual assessment to subsequent proceedings.[1]

In *Texaco v. Libya*, the Tribunal awarded the extraordinary remedy of restitution in kind and decided that the Respondent state must pay full costs and interests if it fails to reinstate the Claimant. The award gave the state five months to comply or risk the payment of all damages and costs if it failed to do so.[2] The award did not fix those damages.

In *LIAMCO v. Libya*, although the Claimant asked for 12% interest as of the commencement of the arbitral proceeding, the Tribunal reduced it to 5% as of the time of the award, which it said was fair and equitable and consistent with the applicable Libyan law inspired by principles of Islamic law prohibiting usurious interests.[3] The LIAMCO

[1] *See* British Petroleum Exploration Co. (Libya) v. Libyan Arab Republic, 53 Int'l L. Rep. 297 (1973), at 206–07.

[2] *See* Texaco Overseas Petroleum Co. and California Asiatic Oil Co. v. Libya, Preliminary Award (Nov. 27, 1975), at 114.

[3] Libyan American Oil Co. (LIAMCO) v. Libyan Arab Republic, 62 Int'l L. Rep. 140; 20 ILM 1 (1981) (1977), 363–65:

> According to Article 229 of the Libyan Civil Code;
>
> "If the object of the obligation is a sum of money whose amount is known at the time of the claim and the debtor is delaying payment, he shall be liable to pay to the creditor, by way of compensation for the delay, an interest at the rate of 4 % in civil cases and 5 % in commercial cases. This interest accrues from the date of its judicial demand, unless the contract or the commercial usage fix another date for its accrual, always provided that the law does not stipulate otherwise."

Africa's International Investment Law Regimes. Won L. Kidane, Oxford University Press. © Oxford University Press 2023.
DOI: 10.1093/oso/9780197745571.003.0019

Tribunal also awarded Claimant some of its costs guided by equitable principles and limitations and discretions contained in Libyan law.[4] It was with this background that the African ICSID cases began to confront the issue of the allocation of costs and interests.

In *S.A.R.L.v. DRC* (1980), the Tribunal ordered the payment of interests ranging from 6% to 10% on different categories of awards of damages essentially commencing from the time of the wrongful act as found by the Tribunal.[5] The Tribunal did, however, allocate the Tribunal's costs 50% and for the parties to bear their own costs.[6] Interestingly, the Tribunal also awarded interest on the Respondent's portion of the Tribunal's cost that was paid by the Claimant and fixed it at a lower rate of 6%.[7]

In *Klockner v. Cameroon* (1983), the Annulment Committee annulled the Tribunal's award on grounds of manifest excess of authority and required each party to bear its own costs evidently because each party had presented serious and what appeared to be genuine legal arguments.[8]

In *Letco v. Liberia* (1986), having determined that "both according to international law and, more importantly, Liberian law, letco is entitled to compensation for damages

[364]. This rule should be applied in the light of the recent trend in Libyan legislation which tends to be in conformity with Islamic legal principles. Interest in Islam is prohibited if it has a usurious(riba) character.

[365]. Pursuant to that trend and to equitable general principles of Law, and taking into consideration the discount rate which was applied by the Claimant in its evaluations, the Arbitral Tribunal has reached the conclusion that it is just and equitable to consider the interest claimed not as usury (riba), but as a compensatory equivalent consideration of the said discount rate, after reducing it, in harmony with the Libyan Code, to the most usual rate of 5%, applicable to commercial matters.

[366]. But as, in general law, interest on damages is due on claims of money whose amount is known (above mentioned terms of the Libyan Civil Code), it cannot accrue for unliquidated damages before their judicial ascertainment and liquidation. Consequently, this Tribunal has to apply it only from the time of the final assessment of damages at the date of this Award.

4 *Id.* at 268–70:

Article 284 of the Libyan Code of Civil Procedure prescribes that:

"If each of the litigants fails in some of his claims, it may be decreed that each (litigant) should support the costs he has defrayed, or that the costs be apportioned among them according to the appreciation of the Court, or that one of them be condemned to support all the costs."

[369]. Moreover, Clause 28, para.8, of the Concession Agreements, based on Schedule II to the Libyan Petroleum laws of 1955 and 1965, provides that: "The costs of the arbitration shall be borne by the said two parties in such proportion and manner as may be fixed in the award."

[370]. Pursuant to said provisions and taking into consideration the circumstances of the present case, the Arbitral Tribunal deems equitable to award the sum of $203,000(two hundred and three thousand American dollars) towards the costs and expenses of the Claimant."

5 S.A.R.L. Benvenuti & Bonfant v. People's Republic of Congo, ICSID Case No. ARB/77/2 (1980), 1 ICSID Rep. 330 (1993), at dispositif, (a)(II)(D,E,F) ("(E) As compensation following the dissolution of EDICO: CFA 1,000,000 and interest torun from 9 November 1975 at the annual rate of 10%. (F) As compensation for intangible loss: CFA 5,000,000 and interest to run from 3 February 1976 at the annual rate of 10% and (iii) in addition the Government is ordered to pay B&B as supplementary damages, the sum of US $15,000. plus interest on this sum at the annual rate of 6% to run from the date of the present award").

6 *Id.* at dispositif, (c).

7 *Id.* at dispositif, (c)(1).

8 Klockner Industrie-Anlagen GmbH and others v. United Republic of Cameroon and Société Camerounaise des Engrais, ICSID Case No. ARB/81/2 (1983), at 180 ("Taking into account the nature of the present proceeding, its outcome and all circumstances, it is justifiable to divide the costs equally and to leave each party responsible for its own expenses").

for both its lost investments and its foregone future profits,"[9] the Tribunal awarded the Claimant the costs of the proceedings. What is interesting about the allocation of costs in this case is that the Tribunal expressly said that it was penalizing the host state for not taking part in the proceedings, considering it a demonstration of bad faith.[10]

In *MINE v. Guinea* (1988), the Tribunal not only ordered the state to pay interests and costs it also back dated the interests from the time of the initial contractual agreement.[11] Most notably, the Tribunal awarded fees relating to the various judicial and arbitral proceedings that preceded the ICSID arbitration. The Tribunal took the exclusivity of its jurisdiction seriously and penalized the Claimant for exploring various other fora seeking redress.[12] After all, the Claimant initiated a lawsuit compelling an arbitration without consent only to be reversed by an appeals court and sought the attachment of assets on the basis of an overturned award. Although technically that might have been possible under Article V(1)(e) of the New York Convention,[13] the Tribunal took the Claimant's efforts outside this particular ICSID arbitration into account in the allocation of costs and interests.

[9] Liberian Eastern Timber Corporation v. Republic of Liberia, ICSID Cases No. ARB/83/2, Award (Mar. 31, 1986), at 100.

[10] *Id.* at 119 ("4) The Tribunal awards letco the costs incurred for carrying out this arbitration (Article 27 of the Arbitration Rules) as well as those costs incurred for legal representation by LETCO (Article 47 of the Arbitration Rules). This decision is based largely on Liberia's procedural bad faith. Not only did Liberia fail to partake in these arbitral proceedings, contrary to its contractual agreement, but it has also undertaken judicial proceedings in Liberia in order to nullify the results of this arbitration. The foregoing decision of the Tribunal is made pursuant to Article 61(2) of the icsid Convention and based on the criteria described in the preceding paragraphs of this part B)").

[11] Maritime International Nominees Establishment v. Republic of Guinea, ICSID Case No. ARB/84/4, Award (Jan. 6, 1988), at 71–72 ("The Tribunal also awards simple interest on each year's estimated lost profits from 1975 through 1987 calculated at the average United States prime interest rate for each year that is published by the Chase Manhattan Bank, a total of $5,457,986. until the date of this award. The Tribunal also awards MINE costs toward its fees and expenses in the ICSID arbitration in the amount of $275,000").

[12] *Id.* at 79 ("The Tribunal considers that MINE's actions in those nations were contrary to the exclusive jurisdiction granted ICSID in this proceeding. Nevertheless, Guinea's lack of response to prior proceedings, the decision of the United States Court of Appeals for the District of Columbia Circuit that left the AAA award at large, and the lack of precedent for the Tribunal's order to discontinue the European attachments, all excused MINE somewhat in seeking to enforce what it argued was a valid AAA award. Upon consideration of the arguments on this counterclaim, the Tribunal awards Guinea the sum of $210,000 toward its costs and legal fees relating to the attachment proceedings in Belgium and Switzerland").

[13] NY Convention, Art. V(1)(e) ("1. Recognition and enforcement of the award may be refused, at the request of the party against whom it is invoked, only if that party furnishes to the competent authority where the recognition and enforcement is sought, proof that:

(a) The parties to the agreement referred to in article II were, under the law applicable to them, under some incapacity, or the said agreement is not valid under the law to which the parties have subjected it or, failing any indication thereon, under the law of the country where the award was made; or
(b) The party against whom the award is invoked was not given proper notice of the appointment of the arbitrator or of the arbitration proceedings or was otherwise unable to present his case; or
(c) The award deals with a difference not contemplated by or not falling within the terms of the submission to arbitration, or it contains decisions on matters beyond the scope of the submission to arbitration, provided that, if the decisions on matters submitted to arbitration can be separated from those not so submitted, that part of the award which contains decisions on matters submitted to arbitration may be recognized and enforced; or
(d) The composition of the arbitral authority or the arbitral procedure was not in accordance with the agreement of the parties, or, failing such agreement, was not in accordance with the law of the country where the arbitration took place; or

In *SPP v. Egypt* (1992), the Tribunal awarded full costs and interests as a part of the compensation primarily because what it sought to award, for what it considered a lawful expropriation, was the actual expenditures plus interests.[14] The costs included the costs of representation amounting to about $5 million in legal fees and a simple interest of 5% on loans that the investor had taken out for the project, and all other monies that the Respondent was asked to pay to apply 30 days after the date of the Respondent's receipt of the award.[15]

The Allocation of Costs and Interests in the African Cases of the 2000s

In *Wena v. Egypt* (2000), the Tribunal awarded costs and compound interests to the Claimant. It relied on *Metalclad* for its award of compound interest[16] and added its own rationale. Indeed, it appears that it used compound interest as a measure of damages, writing: "Almost all financing and investment vehicles involve compound interest.... If the claimant could have received compound interest merely by placing its money in a readily available and commonly used investment vehicle, it is neither logical nor equitable to award the claimant only simple interest."[17] The Tribunal endorses the idea that, barring exceptional circumstances, compound interest be awarded in all cases where liability is found.[18]

In addition to compound interest, the Tribunal also awarded costs and attorney's fees that it said were "for losses sufficiently related to its central claims and in keeping with common practice in international arbitration."[19] It did not award costs associated with the jurisdictional phase.[20] Although it did not state the reasons in clear terms, it did so presumably because it considered the jurisdictional objections nonfrivolous.

(e) The award has not yet become binding on the parties, or has been set aside or suspended by a competent authority of the country in which, or under the law of which, that award was made."

See also Chromalloy Aeroservices v. Arab Republic, 939 F. Supp. 907 (1996) (holding that an award annulled in the place where it was made may still be enforced). *But see* TermoRio S.A. E.S.P. v. Electranta S.P., 487 F.3d 928 (2007) (casting serious doubt about Chromalloy's theory).

14 Southern Pacific Properties (Middle East) Limited v. Arab Republic of Egypt, ICSID Case No. ARB/84/3, Award (May 20, 1992), at 188.

15 *See id.* at 257.

16 Wena Hotels Limited v. Arab Republic of Egypt, ICSID Case No. ARB/98/4, Award (Dec. 8, 2000), 129 ("Like the distinguished panel in the recently-issued Metalclad decision, this Tribunal also has determined that compounded interest will best "restore the Claimant to a reasonable approximation of the position in which it would have been if the wrongful act had not taken place")..

17 *Id.* at 129 (quoting John Y. Gotanda, *Awarding Interest in International Arbitration*, 90 Amer. J. Int'l L. 40, 61 (1996)).

18 *Id.* ("For similar reasons, Professor Mann has" submitted that ... compound interest may be and, in absence of special circumstances, should be awarded to the claimant as damages by international tribunals." (quoting F. A. Mann, *Compound Interest as an Item of Damage in International Law*, 21 Univ. of California, Davis L. J. 577, 586 (1988))).

19 *Id.* at 130.

20 *Id.*

The Tribunal in *Middle East Cement v. Egypt* (2002) followed *Wena v. Egypt*'s (2000) in awarding compound interest at the capital market's rate as of the time of the taking of the property, that is, the cement license and the vessel that was auctioned off.[21] It relied on *Wena* and *Metalclad* considering them as expressions of the rule of international law on the award of interests as follows:

> Regarding such claims for expropriation, international jurisprudence and literature have recently, after detailed consideration, concluded that interest is an integral part of the compensation due after the award and that compound (as opposed to simple) interest is at present deemed appropriate as the standard of international law in such expropriation cases.[22]

As to costs, the *Middle East Cement* Tribunal held that each party should bear its own costs as each had succeeded in some of its claims and lost on some.[23] It did, however, require Egypt to pay its portion of the arbitration fees that were paid by the Claimant on its behalf.[24]

In *Semos v. Mali* (2003), the Tribunal ordered the losing party, the Respondent state, to bear the full cost of the arbitration with the exception of the attorneys' fees of the Claimant because it said that the case involved some difficult legal issues suggesting that the Respondent state was justified in defending itself.[25] In its own words: "However, in view of the seriousness and the difficulty of the issue resolved by this award, the Tribunal has decided to leave Semos to pay the costs and fees of its lawyers."[26]

The legal issues were indeed very difficult and as indicated in the applicable law section above, the Tribunal did not defer the interpretation of Malian tax laws and their application to the contracts at issue to the Malian administrative agencies although this was a purely domestic administrative law matter. Its exclusion of the award of the costs of representation of the Claimant is an indication of its reckoning with the reality that the state imposed the said duties with the belief that its laws permitted it, and that it did not create them for any improper purpose that are often alleged in ISDS cases.

With a total administrative and tribunal cost of $80,000, the *CDC v. Seychelles* case[27] qualified as one of the most efficient and inexpensive resolutions of an investment dispute. With a sole arbitrator and one person representing each side, this case was done very economically. Indeed, the award of costs shows this. The Tribunal ordered each party to bear its own cost of representation but asked the Respondent to pay the costs of the proceedings other than the cost of party representation. As the Award indicates, half of the cost of ICSID plus the tribunal was a mere $40,000.[28] This may

21 Middle East Cement Shipping and Handling Co. S.A. v. Arab Republic of Egypt, ICSID Case No. ARB/99/6, Award (Apr. 12, 2002), at 175.

22 *Id.* at 174 ("See the distinguished ICSID Tribunals in Wena v. Egypt (Award of December 8, 2000, paragraphs 128 to 136) Metalclad v. Mexico (Award of 30 August 30, 2000, paragraphs 128 to 129)").

23 *Id.* at 176.

24 *Id.* at 177.

25 Société D'exploitation Des Mines D'or De Sadiola S.A. (Semos) v. Republic of Mali, ICSID Case No. ARB/01/5, Award (Feb. 25, 2003), at 94–95.

26 *Id.* at 95.

27 *See* CDC Group Plc v. Republic of The Seychelles, ICSID Case No. ARB/02/14 (Dec. 17, 2003), at 63.

28 *See id.*

be a function of the small amount in controversy, but the legal and factual issues were probably no less complex than some of the other cases that took longer and cost more.

Interests in the *Patrick Mitchell v. DRC* (2004) case raised a question of hierarchy of laws, which the majority resolved in the following terms:

> Claimant submits that the rate of interest applicable to this amount is the Federal Reserve Board of Governors Bank prime loan rate which was at 7.75 percent in March 1999. Respondent argues that this matter is governed by the law of the DRC, which provides for a rate not higher than 6% in respect of civil law claims and 8% in commercial matters, to be determined as from the date of the filing of the claim with the court. In reply, Claimant, without arguing about the applicable law, contends that Congolese law gives power to the courts to determine the rate of interest in a range between 6% and 12% and that in tort actions, the injured party may recover interest on the damages from the date of the loss. Respondent rejects this explanation, adding in particular that under Congolese law, a tort claim cannot produce interest before it comes into legal existence by a court order awarding the principal amount. The Tribunal, however, has to apply the pertinent provisions of the BIT which prevail over Congolese domestic law. Pursuant to the second paragraph of Article III(1) of the BIT (corresponding to the third paragraph of the same provision in the French version), "compensation shall include interest at a rate equivalent to current international rates," to be fixed as "from the date of expropriation." The Tribunal is of the view that the rate indicated by Claimant is appropriate. Therefore, the annual rate of 7.75% shall apply to the amount of US$ 750,000 as from March 6, 1999.[29]

The Tribunal essentially required each party to bear its own costs and share the Tribunal's cost equally, with the exception of a relatively small contribution that it asked the Respondent to make to the Claimant's legal fees for losing on jurisdiction,[30]

[29] *Id.* at 94; *see also* 95 ("In conclusion, the Tribunal decides that Respondent has to pay to Claimant the amount of US$ 750,000 plus interest thereon at a rate of 7.75% per annum from March 6, 1999 until the date of payment").

[30] Patrick Mitchell v. DRC Award (Feb. 9, 2004); Annulment (Nov. 1, 2006), at 98–100:

> 98. Claimant requests that Respondent be required to reimburse to him all his costs incurred in undertaking this arbitration, including the arbitrators' fees, the fees of any expert, the legal costs incurred by Mr. Mitchell and any administrative costs. Claimant's costs have been identified as US$ 206,560 (divided in US$ 172,337.40 and R 243,223.81).
>
> 99. Respondent requests that Claimant be required to pay the DRC all costs incurred as expenses in the present litigation, including fees of arbitrators and experts. Respondent's costs have been identified as US$ 307,907.50.
>
> 100. Taking into account that Respondent did oppose without success the Tribunal's jurisdiction and that its objections to the merits of the claim have been rejected by the Tribunal, as well as its counter-claim, while Claimant has been successful with respect to a part of his claim only, the Tribunal finds appropriate that Respondent shall bear its own costs, expenses and counsel fees and that it shall contribute to Claimant's costs by the amount of US$ 35,000. Claimant shall bear its own costs, expenses and counsel fees above this amount of US$ 35,000. The costs incurred by the Arbitral Tribunal and ICSID have been settled by Claimant in the amount of US$ 110,000 and by Respondent in the amount of US$ 70,000. The Tribunal decides that Respondent shall bear its share and shall further pay to Claimant the amount of US$ 60,000, who will bear the costs of the Tribunal he paid above the latter amount.

notably a matter that was reversed by annulment. At the end of it all, Mr. Patrick Mitchell's investor–state arbitral endeavor left him bearing his own costs and an additional $100,000, which is half of the fees that the DRC had paid for ICSID administrative and Annulment Committee expenses.[31]

In *World Duty Free v. Kenya* (2006), the issue of interest did not have to be determined as the claim was dismissed on grounds of illegality in the formation of the Agreement that gave rise to the dispute.[32] Unsurprisingly, due to the complexity of the case and good arguments on both sides, the Tribunal allocated the costs of the Tribunal equally and asked the Parties to bear their own costs.[33]

In *Champion Trading v. Egypt* (2006), indicating that it lacked specific guidance about the allocation of costs and interests in any governing instrument including the ICSID Arbitration rules, the Tribunal decided that the "costs follow the event."[34] Most notably, the Tribunal seems to have been particularly concerned by the Claimants' repeated document production requests and made it a point to mention that in its allocation of costs. It said:

> In this Award, the Arbitral Tribunal comes to the conclusion that the claims of the remaining Claimants are without any merit. The Tribunal notes that the Respondent produced a great number of documents based on repeated production requests by the Claimants after having already produced two witnesses for the hearing in Paris on December 13, 2004.[35]

Consequently, it required the Claimant to bear the full cost of the Tribunal and ICSD and pay half of the Respondent's costs,[36] because the Respondent prevailed although it unsuccessfully contested the jurisdiction of the Tribunal.[37] Indeed, the Tribunal made

[31] *See id.* at 67 ("Order the equal sharing of the costs of the Annulment Proceeding between the parties, with each bearing the expenses incurred for its own defense, including legal fees, which in this case, in consideration of all the circumstances of this Annulment Proceeding, appears to the ad hoc Committee to be fair and equitable. Consequently, since the DRC has solely been responsible for making the advance payments covering the costs of the Annulment Proceeding, amounting to USD 200,000, Claimant is ordered to pay the DRC the amount of USD 100,000").

[32] *See* World Duty Free Company Limited v. Republic of Kenya, ICSID Case No. ARB/00/7, Award (Oct. 4, 2006), at 188.

[33] *Id.* at 189–91.

[34] Champion Trading Company Ameritrade International, Inc. v. Arab Republic of Egypt, ICSID Case No. ARB/02/9, Award (Oct. 27, 2006), at 176.

[35] *Id.* at 175.

[36] *Id.* at 176 ("The Tribunal is of the opinion that it is appropriate in this case that basically the costs follow the event. Taking all factors into consideration, especially the fact that the claim was denied, the Arbitral Tribunal comes to the conclusion that the Claimants shall assume the total amount of the fees and expenses of the Arbitral Tribunal and of ICSID. They are therefore ordered to pay an amount of USD 225,000 to the Respondent").

[37] *Id.* at 177 ("With respect to the costs of the Parties, the Arbitral Tribunal holds that the Claimants have to carry their own costs and expenses as their claims were denied. Especially in view of the fact that the Respondent contested the jurisdiction of the Tribunal and as the Tribunal did allow the claims of the two Corporate Claimants to go forward, it would seem appropriate that the Claimants pay to the Respondent one half its expenses. The amounts claimed by the Respondent (at the September 2006 rates of exchange approximately USD 775,000) seem reasonable also when compared to the total costs claim of the Claimants. The Claimants shall therefore pay to the Respondent the amount of USD 334,037.50; EGP 194,350; and Euro 14,765").

the original individual Claimants who failed at the jurisdictional stage responsible for their share of the Respondents costs up to the jurisdictional phase.[38]

In *Biwater v. Tanzania* (2008), although it was an elaborate proceeding involving numerous issues that ended with a lengthy award of close to 250 pages, the Tribunal did not order any payment of interests and costs because: (1) although there was a finding of liability, the Tribunal found that the wrongful acts did not cause any damages because the investor's investment had no economic value at the time it was deemed taken. That essentially excluded the award of interests as a matter of law; and (2) the Tribunal required each party to bear their own costs because each succeeded in at least one respect, that is, Claimant on liability and Respondent on damages. It was well balanced. This is likely a function of the equality of arms and proper coalescing of high-level analytical prowess.

In *Bernardus v. Zimbabwe* (2009), the Tribunal ordered the Respondent state to pay 10% interest compounded every six months[39] and ordered the Respondent to pay the costs of the proceedings, excluding the costs of the Claimant's representation.[40]

In *Waguih Elie v. Egypt* (2009), the Tribunal awarded compound interest as of the time of the occurrence of the expropriation although the Tribunal did not split the findings of individual violations for purposes of computing damages.[41] The Tribunal also awarded a significant proportion of the costs that the Claimant sought with interest including the costs of representation and experts in the amount of $6 million dollars, but it apportioned the costs of the Tribunal and ICSID equally.[42]

In *Bernard von Pezold v. Zimbabwe* (2015) case, the Tribunal awarded pre- and postaward compound interest, emphasizing "as this is a clear expropriation case, the Tribunal finds that the Claimants should be awarded compound interest. In order to reflect business and economic reality, the Tribunal finds that it is appropriate for both Pre- and Post-Award interest to be compounded at six-month intervals."[43]

The Tribunal also decided that the Respondent should bear all of the costs of its own representation, the costs of the Tribunal, administrative and the costs of the Claimant's representation,[44] plus interest as of the date of the award at the rate of LIBOR plus 2%.[45] The Tribunal was unforgiving in this case, and indeed it said: "In

[38] *Id.* at dispositif.

[39] Bernardus Henricus Funnekotter and Others v. Republic of Zimbabwe, ICSID Case No. ARB/05/6, Award (Apr. 22, 2009), at 146 ("146. The Tribunal does not share that appreciation. As stated rightly by an ICSID Tribunal, 'it is not the purpose of compound interest to attribute blame to, or to punish, anybody for the delay in the payment made to the expropriated owner; it is a mechanism to ensure that compensation awarded to the Claimant is appropriate in the circumstances.' This explains why, in many ICSID cases, such compound interests have been granted. In the present case, it seems to the Tribunal appropriate to decide that the 10% interest will be compounded every six months").

[40] *Id.* at 147.

[41] Waguih Elie George Slag and Clorinda Vecchi v. The Arab Republic of Egypt, ICSID Case No. ARB/05/15, Award (June 1, 2009), at 631(VI) ("The Claimants are entitled to recover interest from Egypt and Egypt is ordered to pay interest on all sums of damages awarded under paragraph 631 (IV) above, at the six month LIBOR rates applicable from time to time since 23 May 1996 through until the date of payment, with such interest being compounded six-monthly").

[42] *Id.*

[43] Bernardus Henricus Funnekotter and Others v. Republic of Zimbabwe, ICSID Case No. ARB/05/6, Award (Apr. 22, 2009), at 953.

[44] *See id.* at 1003–11.

[45] *Id.* at 1011.

the present proceedings, it is clear to the Tribunal that the Claimants have prevailed and have been successful in respect of both jurisdiction and merits. The Tribunal can see no reason why the Respondent, the unsuccessful party, should not bear the costs of the arbitrations."[46]

In *Union Fenosa Gas, S.A. (UFG) v. Egypt* (2018), the Tribunal noted that because the BIT does not give guidance about interests, it would apply a reasonableness standard consistent with the *Chorzow* restitution regime at the rate of Three-Month LIBOR plus 2% compounded quarterly.[47] The interest included pre-award as of January 1, 2016.[48] The Tribunal also allocated the total cost to the losing party, the Respondent, saying that it had no reason to depart from the general rule that most ICSID tribunals followed: "loser pays."[49] On that basis the Tribunal awarded the Claimant $10 million in legal fees and reimbursed the Claimant's share of the Tribunal's cost, $700,000.[50]

In allocating costs in *Oded Besserglik v. Mozambique* (2019), the Tribunal considered the Respondent's delayed invocation of an outcome determinative jurisdictional objection. It said: "As is apparent from the procedural history of this case, Respondent vociferously objected to the jurisdiction of the Tribunal and raised multiple objections but did not, until the filing of the Motion to Dismiss, contest that the BIT was in force."[51]

In that sense, although the Respondent prevailed, the Tribunal held that each side should bear its own costs and split the costs of the arbitration.[52] The lack of the BIT's entry in to force is an incurable jurisdictional defect that cannot be waived (much like subject matter jurisdiction), the Tribunal could have used its inherent cost allocation discretion to sanction the Respondent and/or its lawyers even more for waiting too long before they raised a jurisdictional objection as important as the coming into force of the treaty that makes the basis of the Tribunal's jurisdiction.

[46] The total costs amounted to more than $10 million, with the Claimant's legal fees of more than $7 million and the Tribunal's cost of $1.3 million. *Id.* at ¶¶ 1003, 1010.

[47] Union Fenosa Gas, S.A. v. Arab Republic of Egypt, ICSID Case No. ARB/14/4 (Aug. 31, 2018), at 10.138–10.139 ("10.138 The Tribunal considers that rate to reflect a reasonable rate of interest applicable to the Project as an investment by the Claimant, in concordance with the principles in Chorzow Factory (1928) and Article 36 of the ILC Articles on State Responsibility").

[48] *Id.* at 13.9.

[49] *Id.* at 12.14 ("The Tribunal bases this decision on the 'loser pays' principle applied by the majority of ICSID tribunals to compensate a successful claimant for the expenses of bringing a meritorious claim against a respondent. Without such compensation, a successful claimant would be penalised for resorting to ICSID arbitration. In this case, the Tribunal can see no reason to depart from the general principle that a successful claimant should be reimbursed for its legal costs by an unsuccessful respondent").

[50] *Id.* at 13.13.

[51] Oded Besserglik v. Republic of Mozambique, ICSID Case No. ARB(AF)/14/2, Award (Oct. 28, 2019), at 439–40. The remaining passage reads: "Objections to jurisdiction were raised in the very first session of the Tribunal on December 15, 2015 and continued to be raised. It was on Respondent's insistence that the proceedings were bifurcated with the first phase being restricted to objections to jurisdiction and liability. Respondent filed an extensive Counter-Memorial on Jurisdiction and Liability on April 22, 2016 without a word on the BIT not being in force. Six months later, when Respondent filed its detailed Rejoinder on Jurisdiction and Liability, the position remained unchanged. The Hearing on Jurisdiction and Liability was twice derailed by agreement of the Parties. It was only on June 20, 2017 when Respondent filed its Motion to Dismiss, that it, for the first time, raised the objection that the Tribunal lacked jurisdiction on the basis that the requirements of Article 12 of the BIT had not been complied with, and hence the BIT was not in force").

[52] *Id.* at 449.

In *Strabag Se v. Libya* (2020), the Claimant submitted a cost of about €10 million,[53] the Respondent submitted a total of about €6 million,[54] and the Tribunal's and administrative costs were determined to be about € 1.4 million.[55] The Tribunal imposed 75% of the Claimant's costs and legal fees on the Respondent "given the overall outcome of the case."[56] By the same reasoning, the Tribunal also imposed 75% of the Tribunal's and administrative costs on the Respondent.[57]

Moreover, the Tribunal awarded simple interest at the rate of EURIBOR plus 4% as of the date of loss for the award of damages and as of 60 days for the award of costs.[58] In avoiding the award of compound interest, the Tribunal seems to have been influenced by Judge Crawford's suggestion that the award of compound interest requires "special circumstances which justify some element of compounding as an aspect of full reparation."[59]

Finally, although in awarding simple interest rather than compound interest, the Tribunal recognized "the unusual circumstances of this case, where it has found that Respondent has been subject to a protracted period of *force majeure* from early 2011 to the present day," such consideration does not seem to have influenced its overall appraisal of all the claims. It appears that it simply lacked the sympathy toward a new government that was struggling to emerge out of a devastating war that was caused by a multitude of international actors.

The Tribunal's findings of liability and assessment of damages including costs and interests were rather proforma. This case would have offered a great opportunity for the exposition of the functions and limits of investment treaties in times of war and revolutionary succession. The award paints a picture of avoidance of the real legal issues pretending that these were normal circumstances. The percentage allocation methodology is an unexplained shortcut.

In *Interocean Oil v. Nigeria* (2020), although the Respondent state won on all counts in a case that should not have been brought to ICSID in the first place, the Tribunal applied the "costs follows the event" principle, but only ordered the Claimant to reimburse the Respondent's share of the costs of the arbitration of about $660,000.[60] The Tribunal did, however, make certain interesting observations about the Respondent's submission of costs. First, it considered the Respondent's submission of

[53] Strabag Se v. Libya, ICSID Case No. ARB(AF)/15/1, Award (June 29, 2020), at 933.

[54] *Id.* at 939.

[55] *Id.* at 940.

[56] *Id.* at 945, 944 ("At the end of the day, Claimant has been largely successful. The Tribunal has not accepted Respondent's multiple objections to jurisdiction, or its claimed set-off for the contract claims. However, Claimant has not prevailed in all respects. The Tribunal has accepted only a portion of its claims for losses relating to actions by Respondent's military forces under Article 5 of the Treaty. Its claim for the disappearance of a large quantity of property from the Tweisha yard in 2014 failed for lack of proof. While Claimant's claims under the road and Tajura Contracts have largely been upheld, portions of its 'Article 36' claims and claims for delay and additional work on the Tajura project have not been accepted. Thus, Claimant's success is less than total").

[57] *Id.* at 947.

[58] *Id.* at 963–64.

[59] *Id.* at 962 (quoting Crawford's Commentary on ILC State Responsibility Articles, Art. 38, Sec. IO).

[60] Interocean Oil Development Company and Interocean Oil Exploration Company v. Federal Republic of Nigeria, ICSID Case No. ARB/13/20, Award (Oct. 6, 2020), at 338.

$1.2 million for travel and accommodation of the Nigerian delegation as excessive. In its own words:

> The Tribunal finds the amount claimed under the Travelling and Accommodations Expenses category, USD 1,270,000.00, to be unreasonably high. The Tribunal understands that a Nigerian delegation had to travel to and stay in London on four different occasions, and that the resulting costs would necessarily be higher than that of Claimants, but the amount claimed is over 10 times higher than Claimants' and seems to reflect opulent, if not sumptuous choices made by Respondent. The Tribunal considers that it would be unfair to order Claimants to bear the financial consequences of the travelling and accommodation choices made by Respondent when such choices have driven the costs to over a million dollars.[61]

The Tribunal also said that it found the costs for witnesses to be odd:

> The Tribunal finds the amounts claimed under the Witness Costs category to be odd. Not only are the costs claimed for Engr. Bello and Prof. Atsegbua identical, i.e. USD 50,986.59 each, which seems highly unlikely, but they each are exactly half of the costs claimed with respect to Justice Ayoola, i.e. USD 101,973.18. It is as if the Respondent has divided by two the costs of Justice Ayoola to establish and claim the costs of Engr. Bello and Prof. Atsegbua. In addition, the fact that the costs claimed with respect to Daniel Harris is a round figure of USD 400,000 seems artificial and therefore unlikely to reflect reality. The Tribunal is unable to order the reimbursement of these costs when the amounts claimed are so obviously odd.[62]

It also found:

> The Tribunal also finds the amounts claimed under the Disbursements category to be odd. First, they all are round figures, which seems artificial and therefore unlikely to reflect reality. Second, the amount claimed as "Hyperlink of processes and documents," i.e. USD 30,000 seems greatly exaggerated, especially when it does not appear than any of the Respondent's submissions or even lists of supporting documents were hyperlinked at all. The Tribunal is unable to order the reimbursement of these costs when the amounts claimed are so obviously odd.[63]

The Tribunal also disallowed the Respondent's request for legal representation fees because:

> The Attorney General on 27 October 2016 confirmed that "Afe Babalola & Co offered their services to the Respondent in relation to this present proceedings at no cost for the Respondent. […] As earlier stated in my letter of 4 August 2016, in proffering

[61] *Id.* at 385.
[62] *Id.* at 386.
[63] *Id.* at 387.

> a robust defence to the Respondent, Are Afe Babalola of Afe Babalola & Co has also engaged the firm of Volterra Fietta and Ms. Rameau at no cost to the Respondent."[64]

The submissions on costs might be a function either of poor recordkeeping, differing expectations, or lack of seriousness because of the belief that the Claimant would not pay anyway. In any case, just about everything, starting from the source of jurisdiction to the decision and comments on costs was just extraordinary in this case.

In *Bay View Group v. Rwanda* (2022), exercising its discretion under Article 61(2) of the ICSID Convention, the Tribunal imposed most of the costs on the Claimants who lost the case. The Tribunal's words were duly reprimanding of the Claimant:

> The Tribunal considers that this is pre-eminently a case where the successful party should recover its costs. The Claimants' claims against Rwanda have been demonstrated to be without foundation. Serious and groundless allegations have been made against the probity of Rwanda and its officers. These have ranged over a wide canvas and have been thoroughly addressed by the lawyers acting for Rwanda.[65]

Accordingly, it ordered the Claimant to pay the full costs of the arbitration and a significant portion of the Respondent's costs of representation with interest at the rate of Sterling Overnight Index Average (SONIA) for GBP as of the date of the award.[66]

Conclusion

A majority of the Tribunals adopted the principle of "costs follow the event," awarding the winning party various measures of costs. Although the allocation of full costs of representation were extremely rare, in most of these cases and without variability in era, the tribunals have awarded the wining party at least some portion of the cost of representation.

Some tribunals have viewed the award of costs as a component of the measure of damages while others treated it independently and assessed it under domestic and international rules that they have identified in each individual case. Although mainly remarkable for its ad hoc exercise of broad discretion in designing the specifics, the normative development is clearly in the direction of the "costs follow the event" direction. That said, only the angriest tribunals, such as *Union Fenosa Gas v. Egypt* and *Bernard von Pezold v. Zimbabwe*, imposed the full costs of the arbitration and the winning side's costs of representation on the losing party. These tribunals consider total loss sufficient to impose total costs on the losing party.

In *Bernard von Pezold*, for instance, the Tribunal said that if a party loses, there is no reason why it should not bear the total costs: "In the present proceedings, it is clear to the Tribunal that the Claimants have prevailed and have been successful in respect of

[64] *Id.* at 381.

[65] Bay View Group LLC and The Spalena Company LLC v. Republic of Rwanda, ICSID Case No. ARB/18/21, Award (Mar. 30, 2022), at 548.

[66] *Id.* at 553–56.

both jurisdiction and merits. The Tribunal can see no reason why the Respondent, the unsuccessful party, should not bear the costs of the arbitrations."[67] But this simplifies the difficult question of the function of the award of costs, especially when the normative guidance is scant. Is the award of costs part of the assessment of damages? Is it a sanction for defending oneself or a sanction for bad behavior during the proceedings? Many of the tribunal took many considerations into account, but those that imposed full costs did not justify their imposition plausibly other than saying loser pays all.

In fact, there is no universal consensus on this: what is often referred to as "the American rule," for example, requires that each party pays its own expenses win or lose, although there are exceptions.[68] None of the tribunals seem to have applied the American rule in any meaningful way. Even when they split the costs, they do so more as a matter of equity and pragmatism than as a matter of the application of specific rules.

The award of interests consistently raised at least four issues: (1) whether it should be awarded at all; (2) if so, at what rate; (3) as of when; and (4) simple or compound. Where any monetary awards were made, interests followed. The tribunals, however, differed on the rate, the time, and rate of accumulation. No principled rule has emerged as to each of these components. Tribunals awarded rates of interest ranging from 2% to 10% as of the time of the violation or as of the time of the award in different combinations.

The choice between simple interest and compound interest attracted the most serious doctrinal division. The tribunals that awarded compound interest regarded it as the default rule, claiming that "international jurisprudence and literature have recently, after detailed consideration, concluded that interest is an integral part of the compensation due after the award and that compound (as opposed to simple) interest is at present deemed appropriate as the standard of international law in such expropriation cases."[69] Other tribunals disagreed, and following Crawford's ILC Commentary, held that the award of compound interest requires "special circumstances which justify some element of compounding as an aspect of full reparation."[70]

In the final analysis, however, the choice between award of simple or compound interests seems to correspond more to the tribunal's own appreciation of the gravity of the violation and the behavior of the parties than the rules of law that they identify in a systematic and coherent manner.

Overall, the allocation of costs and interests in these cases might qualify as being both the least disciplined in terms of the applicable rules of law and perhaps, with few exceptions, the most sensible as a matter of fact at the same time.

[67] The total costs amounted to more than $10 million, with the Claimant's legal fees of more than $7 million and the Tribunal's cost of $1.3 million. *Id.* at ¶¶ 1003, 1010.

[68] For a good comparative discussion of the American Rule and English rule, *see generally* Theodore Eisenberg & Geoffrey P. Miller, *The English versus the American Rule on Attorney Fees: An Empirical Study of Public Company Contracts*, 98 Cornell Law Review 327 (2013). "The American rule for attorney fees requires each party to pay its attorney, win or lose; the English rule (applicable in most of the world) requires the losing party to pay the winner's reasonable attorney fees." *Id.* at 327.

[69] Middle East Cement Shipping and Handling Co. S.A. v. Arab Republic of Egypt, ICSID Case No. ARB/99/6, Award (Apr. 12, 2002), at 174 (relying on ICSID Tribunals in *Wena v. Egypt* and *Metalclad v. Mexico*).

[70] *See* Strabag v. Libya, ICSID Case No. ARB(AF)/15/1, Award (June 29, 2020), at 962 (quoting Crawford's Commentary on ILC State Responsibility Articles, Art. 38, Sec. IO).

The African regional and subregional investment legal regimes are some of the most complex regimes in the world today, but unfortunately, they are also the least studied. The complexity comes from their interactions with other regimes including bilateral, other subregional, regional, and multilateral regimes. Although they may eventually get absorbed into the continent-wide community, they will continue to have vitality for the foreseeable future. This part documents and critically analyzes the African Union's recognized regional investment regimes in some detail.

PART IV
AFRICA'S REGIONAL INVESTMENT LAW REGIMES

Unlike the multilateral investment regime unified by a common procedural platform for the resolution of disputes yielding jurisprudence only by accidental formation of custom,[1] the African regional investment regimes are characterized by uniform substantive norms (rather than substantive norms supplied by bilateral treaties), and mostly with institutional mechanisms of enforcement of the rights and obligations of the investors and host states. Many of the investment related regional arrangements, despite their own fragmentation, contain various types of innovations requiring a close look not only because they need to be analyzed on their own accord, but also because they are serving as building blocks for the development of a continent-wide investment regime.

Their methodical documentation and analysis are even more important because of the technical and substantive obstacles of harmonization and residual overlaps that will linger for the foreseeable future. This part will therefore chart the existing regional arrangements and analyze their continued vitality and eventual harmonization both in terms of substance and procedure.

There are eight Regional Economic Communities recognized by the African Union.[2] Among these, at least four have meaningful investment related regimes: COMESA, EAC, ECOWAS, and SADC. Indeed, three of them, COMESA, EAC, and SADC, have created a Tripartite Free Trade Area (TFTA).[3] This part brings forth a detailed exposition of these regional instruments. In particular, Chapter 20 surveys the eight Regional Economic Communities, followed by a closer look at COMESA (Chapter 21), ECOWAS (Chapter 22), and SADC (Chapter 23).

[1] Whether the ICSID platform has concretized into a system rather than a mere framework for the resolution of diverse disputes remains a subject of immense controversy. For a summary of the opposing views, *see* Won L. Kidane, The Culture of International Arbitration 88–89 (2017).

[2] These are: Arab Maghreb Union (UMA); Common Market for Eastern and Southern Africa (COMESA); Community of Sahel-Saharan States (CEN-SAD); East African Community (EAC); Economic Community of Central African States (ECCAS); Economic Community of West African States (ECOWAS); Intergovernmental Authority on Development (IGAD); Southern African Development Community (SADC). See *Regional Economic Communities*, African Union, at https://au.int/en/organs/recs, for more information.

[3] Texts available at https://www.tralac.org/resources/by-region/comesa-eac-sadc-tripartite-fta.html.

20
The Eight African Regional Economic Communities in Context

The proliferation of Regional Economic Communities is not unique to Africa; however, the number of regional communities with investment chapters or protocols in Africa is large by any standard. Of the many such communities, the African Union has recognized eight. This chapter offers a brief background on these communities to set the stage for a more detailed discussion of the selected three that are profiled separately in the next three chapters.

Although temporally neither the earliest nor the latest, the key legal instrument that connects all the RECs and gives them futuristic purpose is the Treaty Establishing the African Economic Community (AEC) of June 1991 (called the Abuja Treaty),[1] and Protocol on Relations Between the African Economic Community and the Regional Economic Communities (RECs).[2]

The Abuja Treaty aimed at establishing the AEC over a period of 34 years in six stages.[3] It seeks to do so by integrating the RECs primarily in the area of

[1] Treaty Establishing the African Economic Community (Abuja Treaty), signed on June 3, 1991, entered into force May 1994, at https://au.int/sites/default/files/treaties/37636-treaty-0016_-_treaty_establishing_the_african_economic_community_e.pdf.

[2] Protocol on Relations Between the African Economic Community and the Regional Economic Communities (1997), available at https://wits.worldbank.org/GPTAD/PDF/annexes/AEC_protocols.pdf.

[3] *See id.* at Art. 6:

Article 6 Modalities for the establishment of the Community

1. The Community shall be established gradually in six (6) stages of variable duration over a transitional period not exceeding thirty-four (34) years.
2. At each such stage, specific activities shall be assigned and implemented concurrently as follows:

(a) First Stage:

Strengthening of existing regional economic communities and, within a period not exceeding five (5) years from the date of entry into force of this Treaty, establishing economic communities in regions where they do not exist;

(b) Second Stage:

(i) At the level of each regional economic community and within a period not exceeding eight (ii) years, stabilizing Tariff Barriers and Non-Tariff Barriers, Customs Duties and internal taxes existing at the date of entry into force of this Treaty; there shall also be prepared and adopted studies to determine the time-table for the gradual removal of Tariff Barriers and NonTariff Barriers to regional and intra-Community trade and for the gradual harmonisation of Customs Duties in relation to third States; (ii) Strengthening of sectoral integration at the regional and continental levels in all areas of activity particularly in the fields of trade, agriculture, money and finance, transport and communications, industry and energy; and

Africa's International Investment Law Regimes. Won L. Kidane, Oxford University Press. © Oxford University Press 2023.
DOI: 10.1093/oso/9780197745571.003.0020

trade.[4] Indeed, the term "investment" appears only three times in the text of the Treaty

(iii) Co-ordination and harmonisation of activities among the existing and future economic communities.

(c) Third Stage:

At the level of each regional economic community and within a period not exceeding ten (10) years, establishment of a Free Trade Area through the observance of the time-table for the gradual removal of Tariff Barriers and Non-Tariff Barriers to intra-community trade and the establishment of a Customs Union by means of adopting a common external tariff.

(d) Fourth Stage:

Within a period not exceeding two (2) years, co-ordination and harmonisation of tariff and non-tariff systems among the various regional economic communities with a view to establishing a Customs Union at the continental level by means of adopting a common external tariff.

(e) Fifth Stage:

Within a period not exceeding four (4) years, establishment of an African Common Market through:

(i) The adoption of a common policy in several areas such as agriculture, transport and communications, industry, energy and scientific research;
(ii) The harmonisation of monetary, financial and fiscal policies;
(iii) The application of the principle of free movement of persons as well as the provisions herein regarding the rights of residence and establishment; and
(iv) Constituting the proper resources of the Community as provided for in paragraph 2 of Article 82 of this Treaty.

(f) Sixth Stage:

Within a period not exceeding five (5) years:

(i) Consolidation and strengthening of the structure of the African Common Market, through including the free movement of people, goods, capital and services, as well as, the provisions herein regarding the rights of residence and establishment;
(ii) Integration of all the sectors namely economic, political, social and cultural; establishment of a single domestic market and a Pan-African Economic and Monetary Union;
(iii) Implementation of the final stage for the setting up of an African Monetary Union, the establishment of a single African Central Bank and the creation of a single African Currency;
(iv) Implementation of the final stage for the setting up of the structure of the Pan-African Parliament and election of its members by continental universal suffrage;
(v) Implementation of the final stage for the harmonisation and co-ordination process of the activities of regional economic communities;
(vi) Implementation of the final stage for the setting up of the structures of African multinational enterprises in all sectors; and
(vii) Implementation of the final stage for the setting up of the structures of the executive organs of the Community.

[4] The Protocol on Relations Between The African Economic Community And The Regional Economic Communities (February 25, 1998), at https://wits.worldbank.org/GPTAD/PDF/annexes/AEC_protocols.pdf, is designed to facilitate the integration process. The objectives are stated in *id.* at Art. 2:

> "The objectives of this protocol shall be: a) to strengthen the existing regional economic communities in accordance with the provisions of the Treaty, treaties and this Protocol; b) to promote the coordination and harmonization of the policies, measures, programmes and activities of regional economic communities to ensure that the provisions of paragraph 2 (a) through (d) of Article 6 of the Treaty are implemented in a harmonious manner to facilitate, at stage five set out in Article 6 of the Treaty, an efficient integration of the regional economic communities into the African Common Market; c) to promote closer co-operation among the regional economic communities; and d) to provide an institutional structure for the coordination of relations between the Community and the regional economic Communities on the implementation of the stages 1 through 4 set out in Article 6 of the Treaty." The specific undertakings are very ambitious. They are stated in ibid. at Art. 5 as follows: "1. The Regional Economic Communities shall take steps to

itself, making only a passing reference.[5] It is clear that regulating and harmonizing investment regimes was not the principal objective of the Treaty, although economic integration, by default, entails the minimization of barriers to cross-border investment

review their treaties to provide an umbilical link to the Community and in particular provide: a) in the treaties as their final objective, the establishment of the Community; b) legal links to this Protocol, the Treaty and the treaties of the Regional Economic Communities; and c) for the eventual absorption, at stage 5 set-out in paragraph 2 (f) of Article 6 of the Treaty, of the Regional Economic Communities into the African Common Market as a prelude to the Community. 2. The Community undertakes to discharge fully, and as the first priority, its responsibility of strengthening the existing Regional Economic Communities and establishing new ones where none exist, within the time framework set-out in Article 6 of the Treaty as well as of coordinating and harmonizing the activities of the regional economic communities."

[5] The first reference appears in Art. 4 of the Abuja Treaty, *supra* note 1423. Since the objectives provision is important in putting the REC's investment regimes in context, it is reproduced as follows, *id.* at Art. 4:

Objectives 1. The objectives of the Community shall be: (a) To promote economic, social and cultural development and the integration of African economies in order to increase economic selfreliance and promote an endogenous and self-sustained development; (b) To establish, on a continental scale, a framework for the development, mobilisation and utilisation of the human and material resources of Africa in order to achieve a self-reliant development; (c) To promote co-operation in all fields of human endeavour in order to raise the standard of living of African peoples, and maintain and enhance economic stability, foster close and peaceful relations among Member States and contribute to the progress, development and the economic integration of the Continent; and (d) To coordinate and harmonize policies among existing and future economic communities in order to foster the gradual establishment of the Community. 2. In order to promote the attainment of the objectives of the Community as set out in paragraph I of this Article, and in accordance with the relevant provisions of this Treaty, the Community shall, by stages, ensure: (a) The strengthening of existing regional economic communities and the establishment of other communities where they do not exist; (b) The conclusion of agreements aimed at harmonising and coordinating policies among existing and future sub-regional and regional economic communities; (c) The promotion and strengthening of joint investment programmes in the production and trade of major products and inputs within the framework of collective self-reliance; (d) The liberalisation of trade through the abolition, among Member States, of Customs Duties levied on imports and exports and the abolition, among Member States of Non-Tariff Barriers in order to establish a free trade area at the level of each regional economic community; (e) The harmonisation of national policies in order to promote Community activities, particularly in the fields of agriculture, industry, transport and communications, energy, natural resources, trade, money and finance, human resources, education, culture, science and technology; (f) The adoption of a common trade policy vis-à-vis third States; (g) The establishment and maintenance of a common external tariff; (h) The establishment of a common market; (i) The gradual removal, among Member States, of obstacles to the free movement of persons, goods, services and capital and the right of residence and establishment; (j) The establishment of a Community Solidarity, Development and Compensation Fund; (k) The granting of special treatment to Member States classified as least developed countries and the adoption of special measures in favour of land-locked, semi-land-locked and island countries; (l) The harmonisation and rationalisation of the activities of existing African multinational institutions and the establishment of such institutions, as and when necessary, with a view to their possible transformation into organs of the Community; (m) The establishment of appropriate organs for trade in agricultural and cultural products, minerals, metals, and manufactured and semimanufactured goods within the Community; (n) The establishment of contacts and the promotion of information flow among trading organisations such as State commercial enterprises, export promotion and marketing bodies, chambers of commerce, associations of businessmen, and business and advertising agencies; (o) The harmonisation and co-ordination of environmental protection policies; and (p) Any other activity that Member States may decide to undertake jointly with a view to attaining the objectives of the Community.

and harmonization of investment and private law regimes. As such, the investment regime that may attach to or follow the economic integration of AEC would not be by original specific design but by gradual harmonization of the separate regimes contained in the RECs.

In fact, the newer and the more modern Agreement Establishing the African Continental Free Trade Area (AfCFTA) of March 21, 2018,[6] has also deferred the investment regime to an additional protocol, which has not seen the light of day as of this writing. Much like the Abuja Treaty, the AfCFTA text mentions the term "investment" exactly twice, and even that for the purpose of deferring it for an additional protocol.[7]

These principal economic integration instruments are primarily aimed at trade regulation and treat investment only incidentally. This gives the RECs primacy in the area of investment regulation.

Not all RECs treat investment equally. Only the three discussed in the following chapters have given it deeper treatment. The others have accorded it varied levels of importance. These are discussed in the following subsections.

Arab Maghreb Union (AMU)

Chronologically, AMU qualifies as the earliest African REC by inception. Although the African Union has recognized it, the only description contained on the AU official website is the following historical account:

> The first Conference of Maghreb Economic Ministers in Tunis in 1964 established the Conseil Permanent Cunsultatif du Maghreb (CPCM) between Algeria, Libya, Morocco, and Tunisia, to coordinate and harmonize the development plans of the four countries as well as interaregional trade and relations with the EU. However, for a number of reasons, the plans never came to fruition. It was not until the late 1980s that new impetus began to bring the parties together again. The first Maghreb Summit of the five Heads of State, held at Zeralda (Algeria) in June 1988, resulted in a decision to set up the Maghreb High Commission and various specialized commissions. Finally, on February 17, 1989 in Marrakech, the Treaty establishing the AMU was signed by the Heads of State of the five countries.[8]

[6] Agreement Establishing the African Continental Free Trade Area, signed on Mar. 21, 2018, entered into force Jan. 2021. Comprehensive information on AfCFTA is available on its official website at https://au-afcfta.org/, the text of the Agreement is available at https://au-afcfta.org/afcfta-legal-texts/, and more information is available at https://www.worldbank.org/en/topic/trade/publication/the-african-continental-free-trade-area.

[7] *See* AfCFTA at Preamble ("ALSO CONSCIOUS of the need to establish clear, transparent, predictable and mutually-advantageous rules to govern Trade in Goods and Services, Competition Policy, Investment and Intellectual Property among State Parties, by resolving the challenges of multiple and overlapping trade regimes to achieve policy coherence, including relations with third parties;... CONFIDENT that a comprehensive Protocol on Trade in Goods will deepen economic efficiency and linkages, improve social welfare, progressively eliminate trade barriers, increase trade and investment with greater opportunities for economies of scale for the businesses of State Parties").

[8] *Union du Maghreb Arabe (UMA)*, African Union, at https://au.int/en/recs/uma (containing AU's description of the AMU).

The Institute for Security Studies describes AMU's predicaments as follows: "The AMU has not met at the level of Heads of State since April 1994, and has effectively been paralysed by the dispute over the status of Western Sahara, annexed by Morocco in 1975, but claimed as an independent state by the Polisario Front with Algerian backing."[9]

It also notes that "the AMU has no relations with the African Economic Community (AEC) and has not yet signed the Protocol on Relations with the AEC. It was, however, originally designated a pillar of the AEC and is still recognized by the AU as one of its eight RECs."[10]

However, despite these challenges, the AMU states have signed more than 30 multilateral agreements including one on investment guarantee and double taxation.[11] Concluded on July 23, 1990, the AMU Agreement to Encourage and Guarantee Investment Between the Countries of the Arab Maghreb Union[12] contains some basic investment protection and dispute settlement provisions, many with slightly unusual formulations. For example, although the expropriation[13] and MFN[14] provisions appear standard, the FET provision is unique. The closest to an FET standard is the following provision:

> The investor shall be entitled to compensation for the damage caused to his investment as a result of the contracting party or one of the general or local authorities or its institutions, including the following:
> A) Prejudice to any of the rights and guarantees accorded to the investor in this agreement, for any decision issued by a competent authority;
> B) Breach of any of the international obligations and commitments imposed on the responsibility of the contracting party emerging from this agreement for the benefit of the Maghreb investor and a failure to do what is necessary to implement them, whether intentionally or negligently;
> C) Refrain from implementing an enforceable judgement, directly related to the investment;

9 *Profile: Arab Maghreb Union (AMU)*, Institute for Security Studies (ISS), at https://issafrica.org/profile-arab-maghreb-union-amu#:~:text=The%20Heads%20of%20State%20of,%2C%20social%2C%20and%20cultural%20areas.

10 *Id.*

11 *Id.*

12 English Text of the AMU Investment Guarantee Agreement (1990) is available at https://edit.wti.org/document/show/0be1b608-3de3-42b7-b068-94a1013595ce.

13 *See id.* at Art. 15 ("1 The investments of nationals of any Contracting Party cannot be nationalized or expropriated and such investment may not be subject to any action having a similar effect on the territory of the other Contracting Parties unless the following conditions are met: A) Such measures shall be taken for the benefit of the public interest and in accordance with the modalities prescribed by the law in the host country for the investment; B) The said measures shall be taken without discrimination; C) Such procedures shall be accompanied by prompt, fair and effective compensation, within a period not exceeding one year from the date on which the expropriation decision has been become definitive and the property can be freely transferred. 2 the provisions of the first paragraph of this chapter also apply to the proceeds derived from the investment").

14 *Id.* at Art. 6 ("The investment made by investors in the countries of the Arab Maghreb Union shall enjoy any advantages provided by the Contracting Party to the citizens of the State of any other State").

D) Causing harm in any other way by action or inaction to the Maghreb investor, violating the legal provisions in force in the country where the investment takes place.

The value of the compensation shall be equal to the damage suffered by the investor, depending on the type and amount of the damage.[15]

Beyond its deviation from the standard FET textual formulation, this provision not only elaborates the types of possible violations in the kind of detail that often comes from cases as seen in Parts II and III of this book, but also attempts to prescribe rules on the value of compensation just like expropriation. Again, most of the ICSID tribunals struggled with the notion of damages as it pertains to FET, often conflating it with the expropriation standard itself. Although this is not a model of clarity, it is an attempt to avoid the contentious FET formulations, though it came too early in the history of the FET jurisprudence to be regarded as a corrective measure.

The dispute settlement provision also cannot be characterized as common. It offers the investor a wide range of choice of forums including international arbitration based on relevant treaties depending on the investor's state's and the host state's membership.[16]

Community of Sahel-Saharan States (CEN-SAD)

Established on February 4, 1998, the Community of Sahel-Saharan States[17] had its Treaty revised in February 2013.[18] Among other reasons, the revision was aimed at "[giving] concrete expression to the desire for economic, political, cultural and social integration in accordance with the relevant provisions of the Constitutive Act of the African Union and the Abuja Treaty of 1991."[19]

"Economic, commercial, scientific and socio-cultural cooperation" is just one of six objectives of the Community. Peace and security are given primacy, followed by political dialogue and cross border crimes and the movement of persons, not necessarily in that order.[20]

[15] *Id.* at Art. 12.

[16] *Id.* at Art. 19 ("The Contracting Parties shall accept the presentation of any dispute of a legal nature that arises between one of them and an investor of one of the other Parties, in respect of an investment to the jurisdiction of the countries of the Arab Maghreb Union and the Arab Investment Court in accordance with the Convention on the Unified Agreement for the Investment of Arab Capital in Arab States, or to conciliation or arbitration specialized in the settlement of investment disputes, in accordance with the relevant conventions ratified by the Contracting Parties to the dispute").

[17] The member States of CEN-SAD are Benin, Burkina Faso, Central African Republic, Chad, the Comoros, Côte d'Ivoire, Djibouti, Egypt, Eritrea, the Gambia, Ghana, Guinea-Bissau, Libya, Mali, Mauritania, Morocco, Niger, Nigeria, Senegal, Sierra Leone, Somalia, the Sudan, Togo and Tunisia. See list at https://archive.uneca.org/oria/pages/cen-sad-community-sahel-saharan-states.

[18] *Id.*

[19] *See* English Version of the Community of Sahel-Saharan States Revised Treaty (2013) at https://edit.wti.org/document/show/5dbd7174-6ed3-403d-a5ed-9b1de76cd34e.

[20] *See id.* at Art. 3 ("Article 3. CEN-SAD shall focus its action in two major areas: regional security and sustainable development. To this end, it shall pursue in particular the following objectives: a. the preservation and consolidation of peace, security and stability in the CEN-SAD zone; b. Promotion of political dialogue and the fight against cross-border crime and its related scourges such as trafficking in drugs, arms and human beings, money-laundering and terrorism; c. combating desertification, drought and climate change

This is to indicate that although it is an economic community, unlike the other RECs, trade and investment are not the principal focus of the CEN-SAD. As a matter of fact, the term "investment" appears only twice in the Treaty and even that not for the purpose of regulation, but in connection with the investment bank it creates as one of the institutions.[21]

It does, however, recognize itself as one of the building blocks of the African Economic Community and aspires to contribute its share. The preambular passage indicates as much:

> Bearing in mind the Plan of Action and the Lagos Final Act of April 1980, in particular the measures aimed at the economic, social and cultural development of Africa and defining, inter alia, those relating to the creation of subregional structures and the strengthening of existing structures with a view to the gradual and progressive establishment of an African Economic Community;
>
> Recognizing that efforts towards regional co-operation should neither hinder nor impede other similar efforts to promote the economic integration of the continent and an African common market as a prelude to an African Economic Community.

The term "economic" appears a few more times in the Treaty, but all in reference to the African Economic Community and the Economic Council that the Treaty establishes as one of its organs. Otherwise, its security and sociopolitical focus is also evident from the statement of its fundamental principles.[22]

Overall, although the CEN-SAD is one of the AU recognized RECs, its contribution to economic integration aspired under the AEC Treaty comes only indirectly through improvements in security and related cooperation, which in turn are expected to create conducive grounds for economic integration. As such, there are limited rules of direct economic significance, such as the elimination of trade and investment barriers in the Revised Establishment Treaty itself.

through the preservation of natural resources and research in the field of renewable energies; d. economic, commercial, scientific and socio-cultural cooperation; e. infrastructure development; f. the promotion of the free movement of persons, goods and services. These objectives will be attained by all appropriate means, including through Community sectoral policies adopted by the Conference of Heads of State and/or Government by means of an additional protocol").

[21] *Id.* at Art. 2 ("2. Institutions: a. The Economic, Social and Cultural Council; b. The Sahel-Saharan Bank for Investment and Trade").

[22] These principles are stated in Art. 4 as follows: "Article 4. Fundamental Principles of the Community: In pursuit of the objectives set out in Article 3 of this Treaty, and in accordance with Article 4 of the Constitutive Act of the African Union and the relevant provisions of the Treaty establishing the African Economic Community signed in Abuja (Nigeria) on 3 June 1991, the Member States agree to adhere to the following principles: a. Equality and interdependence of Member States: b. Solidarity among Member States; c. Inter-State cooperation, harmonization of policies and programmes among Member States; d. non-aggression among Member States; e. recognition, promotion and protection of human and peoples' rights, in accordance with the provisions of the African Charter on Human and Peoples' Rights; f. Accountability, Economic Justice and Popular Participation in Development; g. Recognition and respect for the rule of law; h. Promotion and maintenance of a democratic system of government in each Member State; i. maintenance of peace and regional stability through the promotion and strengthening of the policy of good neighbourliness; j. peaceful settlement of disputes between Member States and the promotion of a peaceful environment as a basis for the development of the region." *Id.* at Art. 4.

East African Community (EAC)

The East African Community (EAC) is a seven member REC that was set in motion in 1999 by the signing of the Treaty for the Establishment of EAC.[23] Investment promotion and private sector development is a significant part of its objectives. The most relevant objective stated in the Treaty is Article 5(2):

> In pursuance of the provisions of paragraph 1 of this Article, the Partner States undertake to establish among themselves and in accordance with the provisions of this Treaty, a Customs Union, a Common Market, subsequently a Monetary Union and ultimately a Political Federation in order to strengthen and regulate the industrial, commercial, infrastructural, cultural, social, political and other relations of the Partner States to the end that there shall be accelerated, harmonious and balanced development and sustained expansion of economic activities, the benefit of which shall be equitably shared.[24]

Although the Treaty does not contain specific rules on investment promotion and protection, it refers to investment at least nine times in the following order and manner:

> Article 80(f) (f) harmonise and rationalise investment incentives including those relating to taxation of industries particularly those that use local materials and labour with a view to promoting the Community as a single investment area.
>
> Article 83(d) (d) liberalise their financial sectors by freeing and deregulating interest rates with a view to achieving positive real interest rates in order to promote savings for investment within the Community and to enhance competition and efficiency in their financial systems;
>
> Article 89(d) (d) maintain, expand and upgrade communication facilities to enhance interaction between persons and businesses in the Partner States and promote the full exploitation of the market and investment opportunities created by the Community;
>
> 114(2)(b) (iii) the establishment of common fisheries management and investment guidelines for inland and marine waters;
>
> 114(2)(c)ii) (ii) to pursue the creation of an enabling environment for investment in the mining sector;
>
> 127(2)(a) (a) improve the business environment through the promotion of conducive investment codes, the protection of property rights and other rights and the proper regulation of the private sector;

[23] The Treaty Establishing the East African Community (EAC), signed on Nov. 3, 1999, entered into force July 7, 2000, at https://www.eac.int/overview-of-eac. The seven members are the Democratic Republic of the Congo, the Republics of Burundi, Kenya, Rwanda, South Sudan, Uganda, and the United Republic of Tanzania. *Id.*

[24] EAC Treaty, Art. 5(2). Text of the Treaty is available at https://investmentpolicy.unctad.org/international-investment-agreements/treaty-files/2487/download.

> 129(1)(a) (a) support joint activities which will promote trade and investment among the Partner States;[25]

Referring to some of these provisions, the official website of EAC features the promotion of investment and private sector development prominently and states one of its objectives as "providing an enabling environment for the private sector to take full advantage of the Community through the promotion of a continuous dialogue with the private sector to help create an improved business environment and enhancing investor confidence in the region."[26]

Although the EAC does not yet have a set of investment promotion and protection rules whether in the form of a protocol or otherwise, the many references in the constitutive Treaty and the notable description on the website suggest that investment is certainly an area that is given significant attention.[27] Indeed, in 2002, the EAC had drafted a Model Investment Treaty and Model Investment Code seeking to harmonize the investment codes of the seven member states.[28]

Drafted in 2014–2015, the Model Investment Treaty appears to have benefited from several contemporary treaties and model BITs.[29] It contains some of the most common investment promotion and protection provisions.

[25] All of these are provisions of the EAC Treaty; *see id.*

[26] *Investment Promotion & Private Sector Development*, East African Community, at https://www.eac.int/eac-sectors.

[27] *See, e.g.*, *Investment Framework: Key Features*, East African Community, at https://www.eac.int/investment/75-sector/investment-promotion-private-sector-development ("Investment Promotion and Private Sector Development as contained in the third EAC Development Strategy (2006–2010) aims to: achieve free movement of people, capital, labour, services and right of establishment and residence; promote balanced and competitive industrial / manufacturing sector in the region; promote participation of the citizenry (civil society, women and private sector) and having them fully aware of the EAC affairs, and strengthen relations with other regional and international organisations").

[28] The Model Investment Code is a model designed to help the harmonization of the domestic codes. *See EAC Report of the Committee on Communication, Trade and Investments on the Workshop on Investment Policies and Strategies in EAC The Region*, p. 4–5, Apr. 23–24, 2015, Kigali—Rwanda, at https://www.eala.org/uploads/Report%20of%20the%20Wrkshp%20On%20Investment%20in%20KGL%20April%202015%20(2)%20-%20Tabled%20on%2018th%20Aug%202015.pdf.

> 4.1.4 The Existing EAC Policy Framework on Investment It was presented that the EAC's current policy and strategy on investment is contained in the EAC Treaty article 79, the Common Market Protocol and the EAC Model Investment Code. The EAC Treaty obliges the Partner States to cooperate on investment cooperation. The more substantive instrument on investment, the EAC Investment Code was formulated in 2006 as one of the tools for investment and private sector promotion as envisaged in the EAC Development Strategy 2011/12–2015/16. The Code is designed to be a non-binding guide to the Partner States for use in attracting investments into the region. The objective of the EAC Model Investment Code is to enhance qualitative and quantitative local, regional and foreign investment into the region. The Model Investment Code intends to facilitate adoption of transparent, predictable regulations and laws to the potential investors, especially in matters relating to compensation for loss of investment and dispute settlement mechanisms. The Model Code thus introduces the need to nurse private investments well beyond the initial period of attracting and facilitating the new investors.

[29] *The EAC Model Investment Treaty*, EDIT, available at https://edit.wti.org/app.php/document/show/062e9278-4383-4ff9-97b4-a8bbff3eb21c. On the preparation of the draft, the introductory passage of the treaty itself states: "The preparation of the EAC Model Investment Treaty has been undertaken in an interactive process by EAC Experts from the Partner States. For the most part, the EAC Model Investment Treaty draws from the approaches set out in the 2012 Model Bilateral Investment Treaty Template of the Southern African Development Community (the SADC Model BIT), the COMESA Common Investment Area Agreement and the Model Text for the Indian Bilateral Investment Treaty (Indian Model BIT). The

The objectives are stated as follows:

> The main objective of this Treaty is to promote, facilitate, protect and increase investments between investors of one State Party into the territory of the other State Party that supports: employment generation, increased production and productivity, technology and skills transfer for local value addition, synergies with local firms and ultimately contribute to poverty reduction in the host State in a sustainable way.[30]

A review of the text of the Draft suggests that the drafters attempted to address many of the criticisms of the basic principles of international investment law such as national treatment,[31] most favored nation (MFN),[32] and

International Institute for Sustainable Development (IISD) also provided input toward the development of the EAC Model Investment Treaty. The EAC Secretariat facilitated the process of development of the Model Investment Treaty." *Id.*

[30] *Id.* at Art. 1.

[31] *Id.* at Art. 4:

> 4.1 Subject to paragraphs 4.3–4.5, each State Party shall accord to Investors and their Investments treatment no less favourable than the treatment it accords, in like circumstances, to its own investors and their investments.
>
> 4.2 For greater certainty, references to "like circumstances" in paragraph 4.1 requires an overall examination on a case-by-case basis of all the circumstances of an Investment including, inter alia:
>
> a. its effects on third persons and the local community;
> b. its effects on the local, regional or national environment, including the cumulative effects of all investments within a jurisdiction on the environment;
> c. the sector the Investor is in;
> d. the aim of the measure concerned;
> e. the regulatory process generally applied in relation to the measure concerned; and
> f. other factors directly relating to the Investment or Investor in relation to the measure concerned.
>
> The examination referred to in this paragraph shall not be limited to or be biased toward any one factor.
>
> 4.3 Non-conforming measures and excluded sectors:
>
> a. This Article shall not apply to future measures or to sectors and activities set out in the Schedules to this Treaty.

[32] *Id.* at Art. 5:

> 5.1 Subject to Article 4, each State Party shall accord to Investors and their Investments treatment no less favourable than the treatment it accords, in like circumstances, to investors of any other State and their investments with respect to the management, operation and disposition of Investments in its Territory.
>
> 5.2 Notwithstanding any other provision of this Treaty, the provisions of this Article shall not apply to concessions, advantages, exemptions or other measures that may result from:
>
> (i) bilateral investment treaty or free trade agreement that entered into force prior to this Treaty; or
> (ii) any multilateral or regional agreement relating to investment or economic integration in which a State Party is participating or may participate.
>
> 5.3 For greater certainty, the "treatment" referred to in Paragraph 5.1 and 5.2 does not include dispute settlement procedures provided for in other treaties, including those provided for in other investment treaties. Substantive obligations in other treaties, including other investment treaties, do not in themselves constitute "treatment," and thus cannot give rise to a breach of this article.

expropriation,[33] providing detailed guidance in what appears to be a restatement of rules emerging out of preferred jurisprudence. But, most importantly, they not only

[33] *Id.* at Art. 7:

7.1 Neither Party may nationalize or expropriate an Investment (hereinafter "expropriate"), or take Measures having an effect equivalent to expropriation, except for reasons of:

i. public purpose or interest,
ii. in accordance with due process of the Law,
iii. on anon-discriminatory manner, and
iv. on payment of just and adequate compensation.
The determination of whether a measure or a series of measures have an effect equivalent to expropriation requires a case-by-case, fact-based inquiry, and usually requires evidence that there has been:
i. permanent and complete or near complete deprivation of the value of Investment;
ii. permanent and complete or near complete deprivation of the Investor's right of management and control over the Investment; and
iii. an appropriation of the Investment by the Host State which results in transfer of the complete or near complete value of the Investment to that Party or to an agency or instrumentality of the Party or a third party.

7.2 Just and adequate compensation shall normally be assessed in relation to the fair market value of the expropriated investment immediately before the expropriation took place ("date of expropriation") and shall not reflect any change in value occurring because the intended expropriation had become known earlier. In no event shall the valuation date be moved to any future date. The computation of the fair market value of the property shall exclude any consequential or exemplary losses or speculative or windfall profits claimed by the Investor, including those relating to moral damages or loss of goodwill. However, where appropriate, the assessment of fair and adequate compensation shall be based on an equitable balance between the public interest and interest of those affected, having regard for all relevant circumstances and taking account of:

a. current and past use of the Investment, including the history of its acquisition and purpose;
b. the duration of the Investment and previous profits made by the Investment;
c. compensation or insurance payouts received by the Investor or Investment from other sources;
d. the value of property that remains subject to the Investor or Investment's disposition or control,
e. options available to the Investor or Investment to mitigate its losses, including reasonable efforts made by the Investor or Investor towards such mitigation, if any;
f. conduct of the Investor that contributed to its damage;
g. any obligation the Investor or its Investment is relieved of due to the expropriation,
h. liabilities owed in the Host State to the government as a result of the Investment's activities,
i. any harm or damage that the Investor or its Investment has caused to the environment or local community that have not been remedied by the Investor or the Investment, and
j. any other relevant considerations regarding the need to balance the public interest and the interests of the Investment.

7.3. Any payment shall be made in a freely convertible currency. Payment shall include simple interest at the current commercial rate of the Host State from the date of expropriation until the date of actual payment. On payment, compensation shall be freely transferable.

7.4. Awards that are significantly burdensome on a Host State may be paid over a period as agreed by the parties to the arbitration, subject to interest at the rate established by agreement of the parties to the arbitration or by an arbitral tribunal failing such agreement.

7.5. This Article shall not apply to the issuance of compulsory licenses granted in relation to intellectual property rights, or to the revocation, limitation or creation of intellectual property rights, to the extent that such issuance, revocation, limitation or creation is consistent with applicable international agreements on_ intellectual property.

7.6. A non-discriminatory measure of general application shall not be considered an expropriation of a debt security or loan covered by this Treaty solely on the ground that the measure imposes costs on the debtor that cause it to default on the debt.

replaced the standard of fair and equitable treatment (FET) language with an elaborate set of nondiscrimination and denial of justice principles,[34] but they also avoid mentioning international arbitration as a means of dispute settlement. It does, however, mention the UNCITRAL Rules and ICSID in the definition of terms. This is not surprising, because of the controversy surrounding international arbitration in recent times, and indeed, even the drafters of the Pan African Investment Code (PAIC) could not manage to propose a workable dispute settlement mechanism.

Finally, the EAC has a Protocol for the Establishment of the East African Common Market.[35] Although the Protocol defines investment[36] and investor,[37] it mentions investment in a total of seven places, and each reference, other than the definition

> 7.7. | Anon-discriminatory measure of a State Party that is designed and applied to protect or enhance legitimate public welfare objectives, such as public health, safety and the environment, does not constitute an indirect expropriation under this Treaty.
>
> 7.8. The Investor affected by the expropriation shall have a right under the law of the State Party making the expropriation to a review by a judicial or other independent authority of that State Party of his/its case and the valuation of his/its investment in accordance with the principles set out in this Article.

[34] *Id.* at Art. 6:

> 6.1 The State Parties shall ensure that their administrative, legislative, and judicial processes do not operate in a manner that is arbitrary or that denies administrative and procedural [justice][due process] to investors of the other State Party or their investments taking into consideration the level of development of the State Party.
>
> 6.2. Investors or their Investments, as required by the circumstances, shall be notified in a timely manner of administrative or judicial proceedings directly affecting the Investment(s), unless, due to exceptional circumstances, such notice is contrary to domestic law.
>
> 6.3 Administrative decision-making processes shall include the right of administrative review, appeal of decisions, commensurate with the level of development and available resources at the disposal of State Parties.
>
> 6.4 The Investor or Investment shall have access to government-held information in a timely fashion and in accordance with domestic law, and subject to the limitations on access to information under the applicable domestic law.
>
> 6.5 State Parties will progressively strive to improve the transparency, efficiency, independence and accountability of their legislative, regulatory, administrative and judicial processes in accordance with their respective domestic laws and regulations.
>
> 6.6 A determination that there has been a breach of another provision of this Treaty, or of a separate international agreement, does not establish that there has been a breach of this Article.

[35] *Protocol On The Establishment Of The East African Community Common Market*, East African Community, at https://www.unhcr.org/4d5259759.pdf.

[36] *Id.* at Art. 4 ("For the purpose of this Article: 'cross-border investment' means any investment by a national of a Partner State in the territory of another Partner State; 'investment' means any kind of asset owned or controlled by an investor of a Partner State in another Partner State in accordance with the national laws and investment policies of that Partner State and includes: (a) an enterprise; (b) shares, stock, and other forms of equity participation in an enterprise; (c) bonds, debentures, other debt instruments and loans; (d) futures, options and other derivatives; (e) turnkey, construction, management, production, concession, revenue-sharing and other similar contracts; (f) intellectual property rights; (g) licenses, authorizations, permits and similar rights conferred pursuant to applicable national laws; and (h) other tangible or intangible, movable or immovable property, and related property rights such as leases, mortgages, liens and pledges").

[37] *Id.* at Art. 4 ('Investor' means a national of a Partner State who has made an investment in the territory of another Partner State").

sections, is for a specific purpose relating to specific areas such as taxation,[38] cooperation in industrial development,[39] and cooperation in agriculture and food security.[40]

Economic Community of Central African States (ECCAS)

The Economic Community of Central African States (ECCAS) was conceived in October 1983; however, it stayed dormant for a variety of factors affecting the region for decades until it regained vitality in October 1999, having been recognized as one of the RECs by the AU.[41]

Aspiring to create a "unified economic and political space," ECCAS,[42] more so than the RECs discussed above, prioritizes matters of peace and security because of the challenges of the region.[43] The objectives of the Treaty establishing ECCAS are, however, ambitious and robust in their effort to create an economic community through the building of customs unions and elimination of trade barriers.[44] Although there is only one reference to the term "investment" in the entire Treaty, there are at least 40 references to trade. The objectives are stated in Article 4 of the Treaty as follows:

> 1. It shall be the aim of the Community to promote and strengthen harmonious cooperation and balanced and self-sustained development in all fields of economic and social activity, particularly in the fields of industry, transport and communications, energy agriculture, natural resources, trade, customs, monetary and financial matters, human resources, tourism, education, further training, culture, science and technology and the movement of persons, in order to achieve collective self-reliance, raise the standard of living of its peoples, increase and maintain economic stability, foster close and peaceful relations between Member States and contribute to the progress and development of the African continent,

[38] *Id.* at Art. 32 ("The Partner States undertake to progressively harmonize their tax policies and laws to remove tax distortions in order to facilitate the free movement of goods, services and capital and to promote investment within the Community").

[39] *See id.* at Art. 44.

[40] *Id.* at Art. 45.

[41] Economic Community of Central African States (ECCAS), African Union, at https://au.int/en/recs/eccas.

[42] *See* ECCAS's official website at https://ceeac-eccas.org/en/#presentation. The members are Angola, Burundi, Cameroon, Central African Republic, Chad, Congo, Democratic Republic of the Congo, Equatorial Guinea, Gabon, Rwanda, and Sao Tome and Principe. *Id.*

[43] *See id.* at Introduction ("The Economic Community of Central African States—mobilizes all its resources and energy to make Central Africa a region of peace, prosperity and solidarity based on a unified economic and political space where each citizen moves freely in order to 'thus ensures sustainable and balanced development. The ECCAS Commission, for its part, covers all the activities of public institutions, private companies, civil society and the populations of the region in an integrative dynamic perspective based on five pillars: peace and security; common market; environment and natural resources; land use planning and infrastructure; gender and human development. Thus, economic growth, social well-being and preservation of nature are being built through the regional integration that ECCAS is developing among its eleven member countries. Preserving peace and collective security is indeed a strong focus of the Commission's missions in a hostile environment combining terrorism, organized crime and religious radicalism against which ECCAS and its partners have structured an early warning mechanism, multinational force and protocol, action").

[44] *See generally* Treaty Establishing the Economic Community of Central African States (CEEAC), at https://investmentpolicy.unctad.org/international-investment-agreements/treaty-files/2401/download.

> 2. For the purposes set out in paragraph 1 of this Article and in accordance with the relevant provisions of this Treaty, the aims of the Community shall be as follows: a) The elimination between Member States of customs duties and any other charges having an equivalent effect levied on imports and exports; b) The abolition between Member States of quantitative restrictions and other trade barriers; c) The establishment and maintenance of an external common customs tariff; d) The establishment of a trade policy vis-à-vis third States; e) The progressive abolition between Member States of obstacles to the free movement of persons, goods, services and capital and to the right of establishment; f) The harmonization of national policies in order to promote Community activities, particularly in industry, transport and communications, energy, agriculture, natural resources, trade, currency and finance, human resources, tourism, education, culture, science and technology; g) The establishment of a Cooperation and Development Fund; h) The rapid development of States which are landlocked, semi-landlocked, island or part-island and/or belong to the category of the least advanced countries; i) Any other join activities by Member States for achieving Community aims.[45]

The only reference to investment is in Article 46(1). It suggests that the Community aims to harmonize the domestic investment codes by providing: "To achieve rational and harmonious industrial development, Member States shall: a) harmonize measures for stimulating industrial development by gradually establishing a homogenous industrial environment in the sub-region, inter alia by the preparation of a common investment code."[46]

Although it is a singular mention, it requires the member states, as a matter of international obligation under the Treaty, to prepare "a common investment code." It is not just a model. This anticipated "common investment code" does not appear to be available in any discoverable way as of the writing of this book.

There are, however, some important provisions with direct investment protection role though they are not presented in the traditional investment protection language. For example, the same provision that requires the member states to prepare a common investment code also contains the following nontraditional substantive investment protection rules:

> b) promote the establishment of large industrial units of a Community character and of an industrial development center;
> c) allocate Community projects in a balanced and harmonious manner among all Member States;
> d) forbid the establishment of national industries which might compete with Community industries satisfactorily meeting the needs of Member States of the Community;[47]

[45] *Id.* at Art. 4.
[46] *Id.* at 46(1)(a).
[47] *Id.* at 46(1)(b–d).

Subsection (b) favors the "establishment of large industrial units of a Community character." Presumably, if implemented correctly, Community developers should get some kind of preferential treatment. This is a substantive investment rule. Moreover, while subsection (c) incorporates somewhat indirectly the MFN principle, subsection (d) aims at forbidding discrimination or even a slight preference for Community investment.

Although this interpretation is generally accurate, the Treaty's principal way of handling investment matters was through the preparation of a common investment code, which would presumably clarify the investment rules whether they are given effect as a model law or are concluded as an investment protocol.

Intergovernmental Authority on Development (IGAD)

The Intergovernmental Authority on Development (IGAD) is one of the AU recognized RECs of eight Eastern African nations which include Djibouti, Ethiopia, Eritrea, Kenya, Somalia, Sudan, South Sudan, and Uganda.[48] It was established in 1996 by replacing its predecessor, the Intergovernmental Authority on Drought and Development (IGADD), founded a decade earlier to deal with serious predicaments of underdevelopment in the region.[49]

The constitutive document called the Agreement Establishing the Intergovernmental Authority on Development[50] is above all "inspired by the noble purpose of promoting peace, security and stability, and eliminating the sources of conflict as well as preventing and resolving conflicts in the sub-region."[51]

[48] *See IGAD: Its History and Development*, Intergovernmental Authority on Development, at https://igad.int/about/.

[49] *Id.*

[50] Agreement Establishing the Intergovernmental Authority on Development (IGAD), at https://www3.nd.edu/~ggoertz/rei/rei475/rei475.01tt.pdf.

[51] *Id.* at Preamble. The whole of the preambular section states:

> Considering the well established ties of brotherhood and fruitful co-operation existing among our peoples and governments;
>
> Cognizant of the wide ranging similarities of present and future challenges and interdependence of our countries as well as the extensive complementarities of our natural resource endowments;
>
> Convinced that Africa's ability to meet the challenges for promoting sustained economic growth, its ability to interact and compete in the global economy on behalf of its inhabitants will depend on collective self reliance and on its determination and ability in pooling its considerable natural endowments and human resources through appropriate, sustainable and practical arrangements for co-operation as stipulated in the Treaty Establishing the African Economic Community;
>
> Recalling further the spirit, principles and objectives of the Treaty Establishing the Common Market for Eastern and Southern Africa (COMESA);
>
> Mindful of our responsibility to guarantee the economic security and development of our peoples in order to minimize the vulnerability of our States;
>
> Confident that the development of economic cooperation and integration between the countries of the region will contribute to the achievement of the purposes set forth in the Charters of both the OAU and the United Nations; Resolved to pursue comprehensive cooperation on the basis of equality and mutual benefit with the view to achieving economic integration;
>
> Convinced of the need for concerted efforts to combat drought and other natural or man-made disasters; Inspired by the noble purpose of promoting peace, security and stability, and eliminating the sources of conflict as well as preventing and resolving conflicts in the sub-region;

The Agreement states among other things that:

the Aims and Objectives of the Authority shall be to:

a) Promote joint development strategies and gradually harmonize macro-economic policies and programmes in the social, technological and scientific fields;
b) Harmonize policies with regard to trade, customs, transport, communications, agriculture, and natural resources, and promote free movement of goods, services, and people and the establishment of residence;
c) Create an enabling environment for foreign, cross-border and domestic trade and investment.[52]

In addition to the reference to investment contained in the above provision, another one makes a more serious reference to investment as one area of cooperation in the following broad terms: "create an enabling environment for cross border investment and gradually harmonize their investment policies."[53]

Although the gradual harmonization of investment policies and facilitation of cross border investment is clearly made a part of the cooperative framework, the progress in this area has been slow. Given the existing circumstances of the region, the type of harmonization that has been given priority seems to be the harmonization of remittance policy. According to a 2021 UNCDF Inception report related to IGAD, project development for the harmonization of remittance policies seems to be underway. For example, this report envisions legal and regulatory frameworks. It states in relevant part:

The main objective of this project is to elaborate a conducive gender-responsive policy and regulatory framework and supporting infrastructure to facilitate

Recalling our Declaration of 18 April 1995 in Addis Ababa, Ethiopia on the vital need for a more expanded cooperation among our countries within the framework of an expanded and revitalised IGADD.

[52] *Id.* at Art. 7. The rest of the objectives are:

d) Achieve regional food security and encourage and assist efforts of Member States to collectively combat drought and other natural and man-made disasters and their consequences;
e) Initiate and promote programmes and projects for sustainable development of natural resources and environment protection;
f) Develop and improve a coordinated and complementary infrastructure, particularly in the areas of transport and energy;
g) Promote peace and stability in the sub-region and create mechanisms within the sub-region for the prevention, management and resolution of inter and intra-State conflicts through dialogue;
h) Mobilize resources for the implementation of emergency, short term, medium-term and long-term programmes within the framework of sub-regional cooperation;
i) Promote and realize the objectives of the Common Market for Eastern and Southern Africa (COMESA) and the African Economic Community;
j) Facilitate, promote and strengthen cooperation in research, development and application in the fields of science and technology.
k) Develop such other activities as the Member States may decide in furtherance of the objectives of this Agreement."

[53] *Id.* at Art. 13A.

> affordable and accessible cross-border remittances, that will drive remittance costs down and increase flows through formal channels. Harmonized policies form anchors upon which legal and regulatory frameworks can be developed to guide and oversee markets for the ultimate benefit of vulnerable people while also promoting trade and enterprise. Such policies have to promote common interests and address common challenges to ease adoption and implementation at regional and national levels. The project is assessing policy and regulatory regimes to identify areas for possible convergence in areas such as licensing and authorization regimes, prudential supervision, anti-money laundering and combating the financing of terrorism (AML/CFT) laws and regulations, consumer protection, complaints resolution mechanisms and transparency, and disclosures and foreign exchange regimes.[54]

The regulatory and investment policy harmonization appears a key component of the IGAD efforts, but so far, this remittance related undertaking is the main one that could be discovered from publicly available sources.

The most recent Handbook of IGAD (2020) indicates that the region has not been able to attract significant FDI.[55] Although the Handbook does not indicate the breakdown, that appears to be the case for both intra-IGAD investment or otherwise. The Handbook makes several references to investment but mainly to indicate steps that will need to be undertaken. In one instance it states:

> Trade in services with several components of the 2008 Minimum Integration Plan and the 2016–2020 Strategic Plan are being implemented such as the IGAD Sustainable Tourism Master Plan being rolled out in Ethiopia and Djibouti. However, there is need to operationalise the regional tourism master plan, marketing the region as a single tourism destination and common investment area.[56]

In another instance, it states: "IGAD has been championing improvement of small- and medium-sized enterprise (SME) competitiveness and enhancing trade and investment climate. Priority has been given to promoting product development and value addition in agriculture, services sectors, minerals, infrastructure and energy." In yet another instance, "the idea to create the IBF was mooted in 1998 to facilitate trade and investment in the IGAD region in view of IGAD's objectives, particularly those on regional economic cooperation and integration."[57]

The Handbook puts the progress in the priority areas in the following terms: "The Drought Resilience Initiative is well and truly underway with evidence to demonstrate

[54] *Harmonization of Remittance Policies in the Intergovernmental Authority on Development (IGAD) Region Inception Report* (Sep. 2021), IGAD and UNCDF, at https://migrantmoney.uncdf.org/wp-content/uploads/2021/12/IGAD-Inception-Report-2_updated_Pr3-incl-FC.pdf, at 27.

[55] *Handbook of the Intergovernmental Authority on Development (IGAD)*, IGAD (2020), available at https://igad.int/wp-content/uploads/2021/07/IGAD-Handbook-2020.pdf, at 52 ("The IGAD region has not been able to attract the significant investment levels required to support higher levels of economic growth, although there is indeed the need to increase infrastructure access and particularly transport infrastructure").

[56] *Id.* at 54.

[57] *Id.* at 55.

the seriousness with which countries and the region's development partners are determined to expeditiously end drought emergencies in the region."[58]

For these obvious priority related reasons, just like many of the African RECs discussed above, the investment related harmonization progress of IGAD has so far remained minimal.

Conclusion

The Constitutive treaties of all the AU-recognized RECs discussed in this chapter consider investment as a significant aspect of the creation of an economic community. Although they vary in their approaches, they all set out their aspirations for the creation of harmonized and orderly investment regimes. The priorities for each being what they are in terms of the development of international investment law regimes, even the most advanced have not gone beyond the creation of model domestic investment codes and model investment treaty drafts that have not been used in any meaningful way.

Among the eight AU-recognized RECs, however, three have advanced African regional international law regimes considerably by creating binding investment protocols that have already begun to influence discourse and jurisprudence. The following three chapters are devoted to the detailed discussion of these regimes: COMESA, ECOWAS, and SADC.

[58] *Id.* at 83.

21

The Common Market for Eastern and Southern Africa

The Common Market for Eastern and Southern Africa (COMESA) is a full-fledged regional community integrating the economies of 21 African countries with a separate and elaborate Investment Agreement signed in 2007. This chapter provides an in-depth analysis of the investment regime that the Agreement seeks to establish, including the dispute settlement mechanism. It will also situate this community within the broader Pan-African investment regime context.

Background

COMESA is a quintessential economic organization as a matter of inception, evolution, and existing mandate. Growing out of the 1981 three-nation Preferential Trade Area (PTA) in 1994,[1] it now stands as the largest economic organization in Africa with 21 members states and a combined population of more than 600 million and GDP of about $900 billion.[2] Its priority areas are the promotion of trade and investment. Indeed, as of 2001, the FTA was attained when nine of its members eliminated all tariffs on all *COMSEA*-originating products.[3]

The principal legal instrument is the COMESA Treaty.[4] Article 3 of the Treaty sets forth the aims and objectives of COMESA as follows:

> (a) to attain sustainable growth and development of the Member States by promoting a more balanced and harmonious development of its production and marketing structures; (b) to promote joint development in all fields of economic activity and the joint adoption of macro-economic policies and programmes to raise the standard of living of its peoples and to foster closer relations among its Member States; (c) to co-operate in the creation of an enabling environment for foreign, cross border and domestic investment including the joint promotion of research and adaptation of science and technology for development; (d) to

[1] *See* COMESA Objectives and Priorities, COMESA, at https://www.comesa.int/what-is-comesa/.

[2] See Member States, COMESA, at https://www.comesa.int/members/. The members are Burundi, Comoros Congo (Dem. Republic), Djibouti, Egypt, Eritrea, Eswatini, Ethiopia, Kenya, Libya, Madagascar, Malawi, Mauritius, Rwanda, Seychelles, Somalia, Sudan, Tunisia, Uganda, Zambia, and Zimbabwe.

[3] See *id*. The nine members are: Djibouti, Kenya, Madagascar, Malawi, Mauritius, Sudan, Zambia, and Zimbabwe.

[4] Treaty Establishing the Common Market for Eastern and Southern Africa (COMESA), signed Nov. 5, 1993, entered into force Dec. 8, 1994, available at https://www.comesa.int/wp-content/uploads/2020/07/Comesa-Treaty.pdf.

Africa's International Investment Law Regimes. Won L. Kidane, Oxford University Press. © Oxford University Press 2023.
DOI: 10.1093/oso/9780197745571.003.0021

> co-operate in the promotion of peace, security and stability among the Member States in order to enhance economic development in the region; (e) to co-operate in strengthening the relations between the Common Market and the rest of the world and the adoption of common positions in international fora; and (f) to contribute towards the establishment, progress and the realisation of the objectives of the African Economic Community.[5]

Unlike the establishment treaties of the various RECs discussed in the previous sections, the COMESA Treaty mentions investment 54 times and indeed devotes an entire chapter to investment promotion and protection. Chapter 28 recites some of the foundational and traditional principles of international investment law.

Substantive Investment Law Principles

One of the principal objectives of RECs is the prescription of substantive economic rules in various areas that the member states must follow. This section profiles the COMESA Treaty's substantive rules.

COMESA Treaty

First, it commits the members "to adopt harmonised macro-economic policies that shall attract private sector investment into the Common Market."[6] Second, it incorporates the principle of fair and equitable treatment in its most elaborate fashion. It states:

> In order to encourage and facilitate private investment flows into the Common Market, Member States shall: (a) accord fair and equitable treatment to private investors; (b) adopt a programme for the promotion of cross-border investment; (c) create and maintain a predictable, transparent and secure investment climate in the Member States; (d) remove administrative, fiscal and legal restrictions to intra-Common Market investment; and (e) accelerate the deregulation of the investment process.[7]

Interestingly, the COMESA Treaty's FET formulation goes beyond the traditional "shall accord Fair and Equitable Treatment" taxonomy and adds a restatement of expansive and more modern but contentious jurisprudence along the lines of legitimate expectations such as maintaining predictability and transparency, removal of fiscal and legal restrictions, and acceleration of deregulation. This is unsurprising and seems appropriate, because the beneficiaries are intra-COMESA states who aspire to create a common market with elimination of all barriers.

[5] COMESA Treaty, at Art. 3.
[6] *Id.* at Art. 158.
[7] *Id.* at Art. 159(1).

The problem arises when the same principles are utilized by more resourced investors from the Global North through MFN or other legal doctrines that might in some cases open the possibility. To avoid that kind of possibility and perhaps also as a matter of normative choice, the more contemporary African investment law related instruments such as the Pan-African Investment Code have opted for more restrictive inclusion or total elimination of the FET provision, even for the benefit of African investors. This matter is still being debated in connection with the formulation of the investment protocol of the AfCFTA.

The COMESA Treaties, third notable inclusion of investment law principles is the one that relates to expropriation. The formulation has aspects that are both common and somewhat uncommon. The text reads:

> 3. The Member States agree that part of the conducive climate to investment are measures aimed at protecting and guaranteeing such investment. To this end, the Member States shall: (a) subject to the accepted principle of public interest, refrain from nationalising or expropriating private investment; and (b) in the event private investment is nationalised or expropriated, pay adequate compensation.
>
> 4. For the purposes of paragraph 3 of this Article, expropriation shall include any measures attributable to the government of a Member State which have the effect of depriving an investor of his ownership or control of, or a substantial benefit from his investment and shall be interpreted to include all forms of expropriation such as nationalisation and attachment as well as creeping expropriation in the form of imposition of excessive and discriminatory taxes, restrictions in the procurement of raw materials, administrative action or omission where there is a legal obligation to act or measures that frustrate the exercise of the investors rights to dividends, profits and proceeds of the right to dispose of the investment.[8]

The exception to expropriation is stated as "principles of public interest." This introduces a relatively unusual terminology that would inevitably attract controversy about its exact limits in cases where the exception matters. Beyond that, the obligation is to refrain from nationalizing or expropriating private investment. This does not inject any new confusion, although the compensation prong is limited to "adequate," omitting the usual Hull Rule of "Prompt and Effective." Unlike most investment treaties, it also makes no rules on how and as of when the losses should be measured. It focus in the third paragraph is on what constitutes expropriation and incorporates the traditional creeping expropriation while adding some unusual explanatory specifics such as discriminatory tax treatment, a subject often singled out in investment treaties for the opposite reason—that is, for purposes of exemption.[9] Overall, this expropriation

[8] *Id.* at Art. 159(3–4).

[9] Many investment treaties contain independent tax provisions and they often give the state boarder latitude in its regulatory power relating to taxation. For example, they omit FET from tax related matters. *See, e.g.*, Netherlands-Ethiopia Bilateral Investment Treaty, at Art. 4:

> Article 4 Taxes and other Fiscal Matters
> With respect to taxes, fees, charges and to fiscal deductions and exemptions, each Contracting Party shall accord to nationals of the other Contracting Party who are engaged in any economic

formulation expands the exception, limits compensation to "adequate," and adds unusual specifics to the meaning of creeping expropriation.

The fourth notable substantive obligation that members have undertaken in the COMESA Treaty is the obligation to accede to ICSID and other investment related multilateral treaties, which presumably would include the New York Convention, as most investment awards are enforced through the New York Convention.[10] In that sense, because this Treaty was pre-backlash, unlike some of the more contemporary African investment related instruments, it principally envisioned quicker integration into the established global investment regime. Relatedly, even the limited digression from standard language does not appear to be a challenge to status quo. Such an approach is indeed not only more predictable and less disruptive, but also avoids the quagmire that reform efforts have confronted for more than a decade as of this writing.

Agreement for COMESA Common Investment Area (CCIA-2007)

Although the COMESA Treaty initially took a more conservative and perhaps traditional approach, COMESA entered the foray of reform efforts in 2007 by unveiling its Investment Agreement for COMESA Common Investment Area (CCIA).[11] This instrument is officially described as "a promotional tool meant to guide Member States in harmonizing best practices in investment and facilitating private sector development."[12] Ten years after its initial adoption, in 2017, a revised ICCA was unveiled. It appears that the International Institute for Sustainable Development (IISD) and UNCTAD participated in the revision and that the revision was informed by the Pan African Investment Code (PAIC).[13] The 2007 version of the CCIA was not exactly

activity in its territory, treatment not less favourable than that accorded to its own nationals or to those of any third State who are in the same circumstances, whichever is more favourable to the nationals concerned. For this purpose, however, there shall not be taken into account any special fiscal advantages accorded by that Party:

a) under an agreement for the avoidance of double taxation; or
b) by virtue of its participation in a customs union, economic union or similar institution; or
c) on the basis of reciprocity with a third State.

Text available at https://investmentpolicy.unctad.org/international-investment-agreements/treaty-files/1172/download.

[10] *See* COMESA Treaty, at Art. 162 ("The Member States agree to take necessary measures to accede to multilateral agreements on investment dispute resolution and guarantee arrangements as a means of creating a conducive climate for investment promotion. To this end, the Member States undertake to accede to: (a) the International Convention on Settlement of Investment Disputes Between States and Nationals of Other States, 1965; (b) the Convention Establishing the Multilateral Investment Guarantee Agency; and (c) any other multilateral agreements designed to promote or protect investment").

[11] Investment Agreement for the COMESA Common Investment Area (2007). The Agreement has not yet entered into force. Text available at https://investmentpolicy.unctad.org/international-investment-agreements/treaty-files/3092/download.

[12] *See Plans Afoot to Publicize a Common Investment Area Agreement*, COMESA Official Website (Apr. 27, 2020), at https://www.comesa.int/plans-afoot-to-publicize-common-investment-area-agreement/.

[13] *See id.* ("The International Institute for Sustainable Development (IISD) and UNCTAD, worked with the Secretariat in the review, which was finally adopted by the Council of Ministers in November 2017. The revised CCIA is aligned to the Pan African Investment Code championed by the African Union. This Framework will provide a platform for the investment chapter that is the integral part of the Continental Free Trade Area (ACFTA)").

consistent in all material terms with the COMESA Treaty,[14] but the discrepancy now only has historic significance, as the 2007 version was transient and unratified with no force to make any changes to the Treaty. Hence that version requires no deeper inquiry. However, the revised CCIA, which, should it come into force, will constitute a significant part of the existing African investment law regime, requires a closer look.

Revised Agreement for *COMSEA* Common Investment Area (CCIA-2017)

The Revised CCIA[15] is an extremely complex document both in its structure and content. This section offers a detailed review because it is now an important part of the African investment law regimes, which will only increase in significance both as a source of law for a large cross-section of Africa when ratified, and as a source of doctrinal experimentation for some of the innovations that it contains.

Structure, Objectives, and Member State Obligations

Structurally, the CCIA grows out of Article 159 of the COMESA Treaty, which among other things states:

> 1. In order to encourage and facilitate private investment flows into the Common the Market, Member States shall: (a) accord fair and equitable treatment to private investors; (b) adopt a programme for the promotion of crossborder investment. (c) create and maintain a predictable, transparent and secure investment climate in the Member States; (d) remove administrative, fiscal and legal restrictions to intra-Common Market investment; and (e) accelerate the deregulation of the investment process.[16]

[14] *See, e.g.*, Art. 59(3) of the COMESA Treaty on expropriation and compensation, which reads: "3. The Member States agree that part of the conducive climate to investment are measures aimed at protecting and guaranteeing such investment. To this end, the Member States shall: (a) subject to the accepted principle of public interest, refrain from nationalising or expropriating private investment; and (b) in the event private investment is nationalised or expropriated, pay adequate compensation." *See also* Art. 20 of CCIA (2007 version) ("1. Member States shall not nationalize or expropriate investments in their territory or adopt any other measures tantamount to expropriation of investments except: (a) in the public interest; (a) on a non-discriminatory basis; (b) in accordance with due process of law; and (c) on payment of prompt adequate compensation. 2. Appropriate compensation shall normally be equivalent to the fair market value of the expropriated investment immediately before the expropriation took place ("date of expropriation"), and shall not reflect any change in value occurring because the intended expropriation had become known earlier. Compensation may be adjusted to reflect the aggravating conduct by a COMESA investor or such conduct that does not seek to mitigate damages"). The latter adds "prompt" and fixes the time of the appraisal of the damages. It does not appear that the initial omissions were legislative oversight and thus this was a proposed fix to the Treaty's binding provisions. Although they may appear minor, these are sensitive changes that often cause serious difficulty in adjudication of real cases. And indeed, the Treaty being the only binding instrument, the rule that is contained therein is the rule of the game for Member States until is formally amended.

[15] Revised Investment Agreement for the COMESA Common Investment Area (CCIA), available at https://www.comesa.int/wp-content/uploads/2020/10/English-Revised-Investment-agreement-for-the-CCIA-28.09.17-FINAL-after-Adoption-for-signing.pdf.

[16] COMESA Treaty, Art. 159(1).

The Preamble to the CCIA confirms that its legal basis is Article 159 of the Treaty when it states: "RECALLING that the Member States have agreed under paragraph 1 of Article 159 of the Treaty Establishing COMESA to encourage and facilitate private investment flows into COMESA."[17]

At the technical level, the text of the CCIA is adopted by the COMESA Council, but it is an independent legal instrument that requires each member state's ratification to have binding effect on that member.[18] Once ratified, however, it gives the Council the power to issue regulations for the implementation of the CCIA.[19]

The objectives are ambitious: they seek to establish a common investment area for the purpose of sustainable development by striking the optimal balance between the rights and obligations of the host state and foreign investors from other Member States of COMESA.[20]

The obligations that the states have undertaken in this Agreement are twofold. They are divided between Part Two (compliance) and Part Three (specific host state and inventor rights and obligations).

The compliance rules are broader obligations such as overall liberalization,[21] encouraging Members to ratify relevant multilateral treaties such as the ICSID Convention and the New York Convention,[22] creating institutional mechanism of implementation,[23] implementing programs and plans of action,[24] and overall

[17] Revised CCIA, Preamble.

[18] *See id.* at Arts. 42 and 43:

> ARTICLE 42 Entry into Force 1. This Agreement shall enter into force when signed and ratified by at least two thirds Member States. 2. This Agreement shall enter into force in relation to an acceding Member State on the date its instrument of accession shall be deposited.
>
> ARTICLE 43 Accession Any Member State that has not ratified this Agreement on the date of its entry into force may accede to this Agreement.

[19] CCIA, Art. 41 ("ARTICLE 41 Adoption of Regulations the Council may on the recommendation of the CCIA Committee adopt additional regulations to this Agreement, which shall come into force in accordance with the provisions of Article 43 of this Agreement").

[20] The text of the objectives provision reads in full: "ARTICLE 2 Objective The parties to this agreement hereby designate the COMESA region as a common investment area with the following objectives: (a) promote investments that support sustainable development in Member States; (b) encourage the gradual elimination of investment restrictions and conditions, which may impede investment flows and the operation of investment projects in COMESA and promote a more transparent investment environment; (c) provide COMESA investors, in the conduct of their business, with an overall balance of rights and obligations between investors and Member States, in accordance with this Agreement; (d) strengthen and increase the competitiveness of COMESA's economic activities; and (e) promote COMESA as an attractive investment area."

[21] *See id.* at Art. 5, which reads in part: "To realize the objectives referred to in Article 2, the Member States shall: (a) undertake appropriate actions to promote transparency and consistency in the application and interpretation of their investment laws, regulations and administrative procedures; (b) strengthen the process of facilitation, promotion and liberalisation which would contribute continuously and significantly to achieving the objective of a more liberal and transparent investment environment; (c) take appropriate actions to enhance the attractiveness of their investment environment for direct investment flows; (d) promote, maintain and encourage competition to enhance economic efficiency in investment and consumer protection; (e) prohibit any anti-competitive investment conduct that prevents, restricts or distorts competition at the national and regional levels."

[22] *See* CCIA, Art. 6.

[23] *See* CCIA, Art. 7. For example, among other things, this provision requires in subsection (d): "(d) making recommendations to the Council on any policy issues that need to be made to enhance the objectives of this Agreement. For example the development of common minimum standards relating to investment in areas such as: (i) environmental impact and social impact assessments; (ii) labour standards; (iii) respect for human rights; (iv) conduct in conflict zones; (v) corruption; and (vi) subsidies and incentives."

[24] *See* CCIA, Art. 8.

liberalization programs.[25] Although as a matter of textual formulation the obligations undertaken in Part Two seem obligatory,[26] the CCIA expressly exempts them from the dispute settlement provision, which means that Member States may not initiate proceedings complaining about any violation of obligations undertaken under Part Two.[27] The more innovative investment and investor protection provisions are discussed next.

Investment Protection

The Revised CCIA has introduced several new provisions with the objective of balancing the rights and responsibilities of the host states and the investors. As experimental as it were, it could not avoid the pitfalls that previous attempts such as the PAIC (discussed in Chapter 26), have encountered.

Helpfully, however, CCIA resorted to textual elaboration rather than confusion by silence. As such, the drafters have made their choices express. There are two categories of provisions that require serious treatment: the investor protection provisions and the investor obligation provisions. CCIA has made many changes to the foundational principles of international investment law in Part Three of the Agreement.

National Treatment

At least three provisions deal with different aspects of National Treatment (NT). CCIA begins its incorporation of an extremely broad domestic industry support exception to all nondiscrimination rules in the following swiping and indeterminate and discretionary terms:

> Support to domestic investors
> Notwithstanding any other provision of this Agreement, Member States may support the development of local and regional industries that provide, inter alia, up-stream and down-stream linkages and have a favourable effect on attracting investments and generating increased employment in Member States. The support covered by this paragraph include: (a) measures to grant preferential treatment to any qualifying enterprise under the domestic law of a Member State in order to achieve national or regional development goals; (b) measures to support the development of local entrepreneurs; (c) measures to enhance productive capacity, increase employment, increase human resource capacity, research and development including, new technology, technology transfer, innovation and other benefits of investment through the use of specified requirements on investors; or (d) measures to address historically

[25] *See* CCIA, Art. 9.

[26] *See, e.g.*, the use of obligatory language in CCIA, Art. 1: "1.The parties *shall* adopt a liberalisation programme, whereby they *shall*: (a) unilaterally reduce and eliminate restrictive investment measures and review their investment regimes regularly towards further liberalization. In this context, Member States may undertake actions to liberalise, among others" (emphasis added).

[27] *See* CCIA, Art. 10 ("Relation to Dispute Settlement No recourse to dispute settlement shall be initiated for any matter relating to Part Two of this Agreement").

> based economic disparities suffered by identifiable ethnic or cultural groups due to discriminatory or oppressive measures against such groups.[28]

Several steps removed comes the National Treatment provision, which reads in generic terms as: "1. Subject to Article 19, each Member State shall accord to COMESA investors and their investments treatment no less favourable than the treatment it accords, in like circumstance, to its own investors and to their investments with respect to the management, operation and disposition of investments in its territory." Although it only cross-refers to Article 19 on the temporal scope of application of the Agreement and considerations of legitimate affirmative action rules, the main substantive exception is Article 13, which gives the host state enormous power to prefer its own nationals and industries provided it offers some plausible reason that it is doing so to "achieve national or regional development goal[s]." Although the idea seems to have grown out of the legitimate objective of affirmative action to remediate historic injustice in certain communities, the breadth in which Article 13 is drafted carries the potential that the anticipated narrow exception could potentially swallow the National Treatment rule, which is the bedrock of any common investment area.

Indeed, because the drafters were not satisfied that they made themselves clear about the exception to National Treatment in Article 13, they repeat the same affirmative action exception more elaborately in the second part of Article 19:

> 2. Notwithstanding any other provision of this Agreement, a Member State may take measures necessary to address historically based economic disparities suffered by identifiable ethnic or cultural groups due to discriminatory or oppressive measures against such groups prior to the signing of this Agreement. 3. The implementation of these exceptions shall not entitle any investor or investment to compensation for any competitive disadvantages he may suffer. 4. For greater certainty, non-discriminatory measures taken by a Member State to comply with its international obligations under other treaties shall not constitute a breach of this Agreement.[29]

While this level of care and repetition is understandable to deal with the vestiges of history, permitting discrimination against investors of Member States of the Community on the basis of expansive grounds does not facilitate the expeditious building of a common investment area. It encourages the opposite.

Ironically, it appears that these exceptions are inspired by South Africa's experience and insistence in different fora, but its enterprises are most likely to be the most affected by it as South Africa (although not a member of *COMSEA*) is the largest investor in Africa in relative terms.

Most Favored Nation Treatment (MFN)

CCIA's Most Favored Nation Treatment (MFN) provision is also irremediably burdened with exceptions to the point of irrelevance. The protection language comes with a prior warning about the exception but is fairly standard. It reads:

[28] CCIA, Art. 13.
[29] CCIA, Art. 19(2).

> 1. Subject to the exceptions provided for under paragraph 3 of this Article, each Member State shall accord to COMESA investors and their investments treatment no less favourable than that it accords, in like circumstances, to investors and their investments from any third country with respect to the management, operation and disposition of investments in its territory. This paragraph shall not apply to investment agreements entered into by Member States with non-Member States prior to the entry into force of this Agreement.[30]

Then it imposes two restrictions. First, it defines "like circumstances" in such a way that it would be difficult to find any two things to be said to be alike. Then it adds a broad general exception. The definition of "like circumstances" is clearly inspired by the desire to clarify the confused jurisprudence around it, but it takes it further than that. It states:

> 2. For greater certainty, references to "like circumstances" in paragraph 1 of this Article requires an overall examination on a case by case basis of all the circumstances of an investment including, inter alia: (a) its effects on third persons and the local community; (b) its effects on the local, regional or national environment, including the cumulative effects of all investments within a jurisdiction on the environment; (c) the sector the investor is in; (d) the aim of the measure concerned; (e) the regulatory process generally applied in relation to the measure concerned; or (f) other factors directly relating to the investment or investor in relation to the measure concerned, and the examination shall not be limited to or be biased towards any one factor.[31]

In a dispute where a violation of MFN is alleged, unless the disparate treatment involved twins operating car dealerships next to each other, it is difficult to see how able lawyers arguing dissimilarity would fail to find nonfrivolous grounding in one or more of these factors in almost any real-life cases of discrimination.

As if this is not enough, the CCIA adds a swiping and express exception as follows:

> 3. Nothing in paragraph 1 of this Article shall oblige a Member State to extend to COMESA investors the benefits of any treatment, preference or privilege resulting from: (a) any customs union, free trade area, common market or monetary union, or any similar international convention or other forms of regional preferential arrangements, present or future, of which any of the Member States is or may become a party; (b) any matter, including international agreements, pertaining wholly or mainly to taxation; (c) any other international agreements, or chapters of international agreements, pertaining to the promotion or protection of investment; or (d) any dispute settlement procedures in any other treaty.[32]

[30] CCIA, Art. 18(1).
[31] CCIA, Art. 18(2).
[32] CCIA, Art. 18(3).

The first subsection treats COMESA investors less favorably than all other customs unions, free trade areas, common markets, or similar groupings under international agreements not only existing at the time, but also future ones. The second subsection excludes taxation measures. The third, broader than the first, prioritizes investors under "any other international agreement ... pertaining to the promotion or protection of investment," which necessarily includes BITs. Finally, the MFN exception excludes dispute settlement procedures.

Under these circumstances, it is virtually impossible to qualify any COMESA investor for a more favorable treatment under the CCIA MFN provision. Any advocate who can do that in a real-life case deserves a prize. Because all other investors are almost always favored, the CCIA's MFN clause should, without irony, be renamed the Least Favored Nation Treatment, as is often said in trade law. It appears that the drafters of the MFN provision disfavored MFN but decided to keep it in the Agreement in a debilitated shape just for decorum, out of respect for one of the oldest principles of international economic law.

Fair and Equitable Treatment (FET) and Full Security and Protection (FPS)

Blamed beyond its share of contribution to the perceived injustices of ISDS, the Fair and Equitable (FET) principle did not even receive the courtesy of keeping its name. CCIA not only changes the standard of Fair and Equitable Treatment and Full Security and Protection, but also even the name itself. Calling it "fair judicial and administrative treatment," CCIA's FET standard carefully distills and keeps only the most fundamental due process protections. It states:

> 1. Member States shall ensure that investments of investors of another Member State are not subjected to measures that constitute: (a) denial of justice in criminal, civil or administrative proceedings; (b) un-remedied and egregious violations of due process; (c) targeted discrimination on manifestly unjustified grounds, such as gender, race or religious belief; or (d) manifestly abusive treatment, such as coercion, duress and harassment. 2. A determination that there has been a breach of another provision of this Agreement, or of a separate international agreement, does not establish that there has been a breach of this Article.

This is CCIA's best improvement. The FET standard contained in many bilateral, regional, and other investment agreements has given rise to the many dimensional problems discussed in Parts Two and Three of this book. The drafters of the CCIA clearly aimed at addressing all these problems that host states have complained about for so long. What they kept is what needed to be kept. It disavows the excesses of arbitral jurisprudence of the last two decades, including the principles of legitimate expectations that many arbitral tribunals abused, and limited due process to real injury because of invidious discrimination and system failure.

In that regard, the protection is against real host state investor abuse that the state itself cannot correct. The use of the terms "egregious," "manifest," "unjustified," and "unremedied" suggests a movement toward the traditional *Neer* standard,[33] rather than the more contemporary legitimate expectations standard that has caused serious backlash against ISDS in recent decades.

Expropriation

CCIA's expropriation provision is a careful restatement of what has emerged from honorable jurisprudence over an extended period of trials and tribulations. The conceptualization of expropriation predated the Libyan Oil Cases discussed in Parts II and III, but those cases were the beginning of postcolonial jurisprudence related to Africa. The great majority of African ICSID cases discussed in those parts also showed the development of the concept of expropriation in a wide range of cases over the years. This 2017 CCIA codification of the concept is essentially the restatement of what most African states appearing before the many arbitral tribunals considered to be the parameters of the principle. It begins with the most common and simplest expression of the principle as:

> Member States shall not nationalize or expropriate investments in their territory or adopt any other measures tantamount to expropriation of investments except: (a) in the public interest; and (b) in accordance with due process of law. 2. Where expropriation has been carried out, prompt and adequate compensation shall be paid.[34]

Although not necessarily a significant departure, it noticeably separated the payment prong from the reason and process prongs. This, of course, is not an insignificant drafting choice because it goes directly to the issue of lawfulness or unlawfulness of expropriation that many tribunals have struggled with, especially as a factor in the determination of the quantum of damages.

It appears that the drafters wanted to avoid the whole debate about what difference, if any, the lawfulness of the expropriation makes in assessing the amount of damages by simply bifurcating the inquiry between expropriation for a legitimate purpose and payment of prompt and adequate compensation for all expropriations. This avoids any type of punitive addition of damages when the expropriation is not exactly for public purpose or failed to follow due process, injuries that may have other types of remedies under other provisions, including the due process provision that replaced FET.

[33] The standard comes from dictum in the The Neer Claim (1926) in which the U.S.—Mexico Claim Commission included this frequently quoted passage: "The propriety of governmental acts should be put to the test of international standards … the treatment of an alien, in order to constitute an international delinquency should amount to an outrage, to bad faith, to willful neglect of duty, or to an insufficiency of governmental action so far short of international standards that every reasonable and impartial man would readily recognize its insufficiency. Whether the insufficiency proceeds from the deficient execution of a reasonable law or from the fact that the laws of the country do not empower the authorities to measure up to international standards is immaterial." UN Reports of International Arbitral Awards, 1926, Vol. IV, p. 60 (quoted in *Fair and Equitable Treatment Standard in International Investment Law*, OECD Working Papers on International Investment (Sep. 1, 2004), at 37, https://www.oecd.org/daf/inv/investment-policy/WP-2004_3.pdf.).

[34] CCIA, Art. 20(1).

Formulating the core principle this way, the provision goes on stating the principle on the assessment of compensation. Note that the Hull Rule's term "effective" is deleted, presumably for fear of redundancy, ambiguity, and previous jurisprudential confusion. In any case, the compensation must be assessed "in relation to the fair market value of the expropriated investment immediately before the expropriation took place ("date of expropriation") and shall not reflect any change in value occurring because the intended expropriation had become known earlier."[35] While so far there is no appreciable deviation from standard expropriation language, it begins to inject fairly new prudential explanatory texts.

The first such injection is a part of the assessment of compensation provision. It goes on to state:

> However, where appropriate, the assessment of fair and adequate compensation shall be based on an equitable balance between the public interest and interest of those affected, having regard for all relevant circumstances and taking account of the current and past use of the property, the history of its acquisition, the fair market value of the investment, the purpose of the expropriation, the extent of previous profit made by the foreign investor through the investment, and the duration of the investment. Compensation may be adjusted to reflect the aggravating conduct by a COMESA investor or such conduct that does not seek to mitigate damages.[36]

While on the one hand it appears to suggest that unlawfulness of the expropriation may shift the balance on the side of the investor when it says "having regard for all relevant circumstances," all other considerations in the provision including the history of acquisition, the duration, the over profits that the investor might have made, and the fair market value of the investment seem to reckon with the extended history of undue compensation that arbitral tribunals have awarded investors on the basis mainly of expected profits as a punishment for breach of investment contracts as many of the ICSID cases detained in Parts Two and Three demonstrated. This provision goes further and requires the adjustment of damages for the investor's aggravating conduct and failure to mitigate damages. In that context, it hopes to restore some sense of equilibrium.

Carving out intellectual property matters[37] and debt instruments[38] for specific treatment, it states the most important substantive exception as follows:

> Bona fide regulatory measures taken by a Member State or awards by judicial bodies of a Member State that are designed and applied to protect or enhance legitimate

[35] CCIA, Art. 20(3).

[36] CCIA, Art. 20(3).

[37] CCIA, Art. 20(7) ("This Article shall not apply to the issuance of compulsory licences granted in relation to intellectual property rights, or to the revocation, limitation or creation of intellectual property rights, to the extent that such issuance, revocation, limitation or creation is consistent with applicable international agreements on intellectual property").

[38] CCIA, Art. 20(8) ("8. A measure of general application shall not be considered an expropriation of a debt security or loan covered by this Agreement solely on the ground that the measure imposes costs on the debtor that cause it to default on the debt").

> public welfare objectives, such as public health, safety and the environment, shall not constitute an expropriation or measures tantamount to expropriation under this Article.[39]

If an expropriation is made for public purpose under due process of law, it is still expropriation and as such prompt and adequate compensation must be paid; however, if the measure is taken to enhance public safety and protect the environment, such measure is not deemed expropriation at all and as such the investor expects no compensation, at least not for expropriation. This is a broad exception especially in view of what comes next, that is, the meaning of creeping or indirect expropriation.

The expropriation provision includes an elaborate explanation of what the Parties consider indirect expropriation, a matter often left for explanatory notes in some BIT models such as the Canadian Model:

> The Parties confirm their shared understanding that: (a) expropriation may be direct or indirect: (i) direct expropriation occurs when an investment is nationalised or otherwise directly expropriated through formal transfer of title or outright seizure; and (ii) indirect expropriation occurs if a measure or series of measures of a Party has an effect equivalent to direct expropriation, in that it substantially or permanently deprives the investor of the fundamental attributes of property in its investment, including the right to use, enjoy and dispose of its investment, without formal transfer of title or outright seizure.[40]

This is more or less a verbatim codification of the definition that has emerged out of the oft-cited ICSDS cases. The provision contains more elaborations to ensure that tribunals are properly instructed on the Parties' intentions as to what they consider indirect expropriation because of the infinite contentions of the past.

> (b) the determination of whether a measure or a series of measures have an effect equivalent to expropriation requires a case-by-case, fact-based inquiry, that takes into consideration: (i) the economic impact of the measure or series of measures, although the sole fact that a measure or series of measures of a Party has an adverse effect on the economic value of an investment does not establish that an indirect expropriation has occurred; (ii) the duration of the measure or series of measures of a Party; (iii) the character of the measure or series of measures, notably their object, context and intent; and (iv) whether a measure by a Party breaches the Party's prior binding written commitment to the investor whether by contract, licence or other legal document.[41]

These explanations are obviously designed to counter decades of expansive jurisprudence that neglected the nature of the measures and the intent of the host state in taking the measures. Moreover, it also seems to counter the contentious view that

[39] CCIA, Art. 20(8).
[40] CCIA, Art. 20(10)(a).
[41] CCIA, Art. 20(10)(b).

unwritten and casual oral representations could give rise to legitimate expectations, a concept that might have spilled over from the uncertain jurisprudence of FET. This provision makes it clear that investor expectations need to be grounded on formal and ascertainable commitment to be actionable. Although the nature and source of the commitment is often a matter of FET analysis, it was expressed here in the expropriation context. In any case, the objective remains the circumscription of the instances of government measures that rise to the level of indirect expropriation.

Other Protection Provisions

CCIA includes other provisions that are not typically considered a part of the investor protection provisions discussed above. The most notable ones include provision on movement of labor and compensation for war and conflict related losses.

The movement of labor provision is not surprising because the COMESA Treaty itself seeks to facilitate the movement of persons within the COMESA Free Trade Area, and as such its inclusion in the Free Investment Area is only consistent with that. If anything, it is not as sweeping as it ought to have been. It permits the hiring of expatriates in limited circumstances with some local employment safeguards:

> Movement of Labour
>
> Taking account of the need to facilitate labour resources, in the CCIA and subject to the laws in force in the host state, Member States shall accord to investors the right to hire technically qualified persons, necessary for investment from any Member State. Such persons shall have the right to enter and receive the necessary authorisations to reside in the Member State. However, COMESA investors shall accord a priority to workers who possess the same qualifications or expertise and are available in the host Member State or any other Member State.[42]

It permits investors to hire "technically qualified persons" without qualifying that requirement, but only if domestic workers who could do the work are not available. This is very common in immigration laws, and as such is unsurprising at early stages of the development of any common investment area. The aspirations of the COMESA Treaty in this regard are more robust: they seek to "(e) remove obstacles to the free movement of persons, labour and services, right of establishment for investors and right of residence within the Common Market."[43] This might be the first step in the gradual opening up of the employment market for cross border economic interactions within COMESA.

The second provision relates to compensation for losses that follow armed conflict and other related types of national emergency other than natural disaster. It accords the COMESA investor national treatment or MFN, as the case may be.[44] Although not a very common part of many investment treaties, it is also not entirely unusual. Where it is incorporated, its terms are more or less similar to the formulation in the CCIA. As

[42] CCIA, Art. 16.
[43] COMESA Treaty, Art. 4(6)(e).
[44] CCIA, Art. 21.

such, it has no remarkable features expect perhaps its exclusion of losses as a result of natural disaster.[45]

Investor Obligations and Counterclaims

Guided by *PIAC's* innovations and in a remarkable departure from traditional investment treaties, the Revised CCIA most notably incorporates elaborate investor obligations in an independent section titled "Investor and Investment Obligations."[46]

The basic principle states the obvious in broad terms: "COMESA investors and their investments shall comply with all applicable domestic laws and measures of the host state,"[47] although "measures" injects a measure of uncertainty about the nature, content, and legality. More importantly, however, the remaining provisions impose affirmative obligations ranging from corporate governance, labor, and environmental care to compliance with anti-corruption rules.[48]

Some of these obligations are worth highlighting for their breadth. The first seeks to regulate the core of internal corporate transactional behavior by stating, for example, "COMESA Investors and their investments shall ensure that all transactions with related or affiliated companies shall be arm's length transactions at fair market price. Investors and their investments shall not undertake any transfer pricing practices

[45] *Id.* It reads in full:

> 1. COMESA investors whose investments in the territory of the Member States suffer losses owing to war or other armed conflict, revolution, a state of national emergency, revolt, insurrection or riot shall be accorded treatment, as regards restitution, indemnification, compensation or other settlement, not less favourable than that which Member States accord to their own investors or to investors of any third State. Resulting payments shall be freely transferable at the exchange rate applicable on the date of transfer pursuant to the exchange regulations in force. 2. Without derogating from the provisions of paragraph (1) of this Article, any investor who, in any of the situations referred to in that paragraph, suffers losses in a Member State resulting from: (a) requisitioning of their property by the forces or authorities of the Member States, acting under and within the scope of the legal provisions relating to their competences, duties and command structures; or (b) destruction of their property by the forces or authorities of the Member States, which was not caused in combat action or was not required by the necessity of the situation or observance of any legal requirement; shall be accorded restitution, or adequate compensation not less favourable than that which the Member States accord to their own investors or to investors of any third State. 3. For the purposes of this Article, state of emergency excludes natural disaster.

[46] CCIA, Part Four (Art. 25–33).

[47] CCIA, Art. 25.

[48] *See* CCIA, Art 26–33. The anti-corruption provision reads, for example, "Bribery and Corruption 1. COMESA Investors and their investments shall not offer, promise or give any undue pecuniary or other advantage, whether directly or through intermediaries, to a public official of a Member State, or to an official's relative or business associate or other person in close proximity to an official, for that official or for a third party, in order that the official or third party act or refrain from acting in relation to the performance of official duties, in order to achieve any favour in relation to a proposed investment or any other rights in relation to an investment. 2. COMESA Investors and their investments shall also not be complicit in any act described in paragraph 1 of this Article, including through incitement, aiding and abetting or conspiracy to commit or authorize such acts. 3. Member States shall adopt such legislative and other measures as may be necessary to establish jurisdiction and enforce laws and procedures against any criminal offence committed in whole or in part in their territory by a national, or a COMESA investor and investment or its agent, or by any other person acting in relation to an investment in a Member State. 4. A breach of this article by a COMESA investor or its investment is deemed to constitute a breach of the domestic law of the Host State concerning the establishment and operation of an investment." *Id.* at Art. 28.

between themselves or any other related or affiliated companies."[49] Transfer pricing has been a subject of great controversy over the years because it has the tendency to deprive host states of tax and related revenues. However, the implementation of the obligation "not to undertake any transfer pricing practices" would require domestic legislation that would hold the investor responsible and also perhaps also permit the host state to impose taxation and other measures on the investor without risking claims of denial of justice or even expropriation. This is clearly a pro-regulation provision that could potentially disadvantage COMESA investors over third-state investors without such obligation.[50]

The second notable investor obligation is a part of corporate social responsibility. It states that "investors and their investments should act in accordance with fair business, marketing and advertising practices when dealing with consumers and should ensure the safety and quality of goods and services they provide."[51] This is a blanket warranty of safety and merchantability of goods and services that are often dealt with under domestic laws of obligations—contractual and extra-contractual. It is unclear what meaning this provision adds as a matter of treaty obligation imposed on the investor. It may just be that where the Member States make or preserve and enforce domestic laws to this effect, they could use these provisions as a shield from investor claim under investment protection provisions. In any case, it is notable for its presence in a treaty even if it adds nothing to the regular domestic laws of obligation that regularly sanction safety and quality matters.

The most meaningful and implementable investor obligations the CCIA has included are those relating to the environment. It dedicates two separate provisions, one relating to environmental protection and social impact and another relating to environmental management and improvement.

The first states in full:

> Environmental Protection and Social Impact Assessment
>
> COMESA Investors and their investments shall, in performing their activities, protect the environment and where such activity causes damages to the environment; take reasonable steps to restore it as far as possible, and to ensure fair compensation is paid to those impacted by the environmental damages. 2. COMESA Investors or their investments shall comply with environmental and social assessment screening criteria and assessment processes applicable to their proposed investments prior to their

[49] CCIA, Art 26(2).

[50] The same provision contains several corporate governance obligations in subsection 3 ("3. COMESA Investors and their investments shall, in accordance with domestic laws and regulations: (a) ensure the equitable treatment of all shareholders, in accordance with national laws; (b) encourage active co-operation between corporations and stakeholders in creating wealth, jobs and the sustainability of financially sound enterprises; (c) ensure that timely and accurate disclosure is made on all material matters regarding a corporation, including the financial situation, performance, ownership, and governance of the company, risks related to environmental liabilities, and any other matters in accordance with the relevant regulations and requirements; and (d) provide information relating to human resource policies, such as programs for human resource development"). Were these to be implemented by domestic legislation, monitoring the performance of these types of obligations seems both cumbersome and perhaps also unnecessarily intrusive and hence a disincentive to investment.

[51] CCIA, Art. 30(2).

> establishment, as required by the laws of the host state for such an investment. 3. The impact assessments required under paragraph 2 shall include assessments of the impacts on the human rights of the persons in the areas potentially impacted by the investment. 4. COMESA Investors or their investments shall make the environmental and social impact assessments: (a) public; and (b) accessible to the local communities, or other areas with potentially affected interests, in an effective and sufficiently timely manner so as to allow comments to be made to the investor, investment and/or government prior to the completion of the host state processes for establishing an investment. 5. COMESA Investors, their investments and the host state authorities shall apply the precautionary principle to their environmental impact assessment and to decisions taken in relation to a proposed investment, including any necessary mitigating or alternative approaches to the investment, or precluding the investment if necessary. The application of the precautionary principle by investors and investments shall be described in the environmental impact assessment.[52]

The importance of this principle is twofold. First, it imposes a full range of environmental obligations on the investor including due diligence, transparency, the inclusion of human rights in environmental impact assessments, and the application of the precautionary principle in making choices in favor of the environment in cases of ambiguity. Secondly, and most notably, it imposes such broad obligations prior to establishment of the investor. This is important in avoiding postestablishment environment related disputes that has been characteristic of many ISDS cases.

A question about when exactly before establishment this obligation may attach would inevitably arise because the investor may not be considered an investor before establishment. But this is a matter that could be regulated by contract and/or the host states domestic laws as long as the treaty obligations are clear. In practice, however, the way it is likely to come up is when disputes arise because of the host state's decision to disallow certain activities and/or demands relocation because of environmental concerns causing the investor financial losses. This provision has the potential of immunizing the host state in ways that existing investment treaties do not. It may even open up the avenue for counterclaims as discussed in the follow section.

The second, relating to environmental management, is mostly aspirational. The core of the provision incorporates "recognized international environmental management standards and good business practice standards"[53] and requires that the investor "strive to exceed legally applicable standards and always maintain high levels of environmental performance consistent with best industry practice."[54]

The most important investor obligation provision comes last. It is on how these obligations may be enforced. Titled "Implications of breach of investors' obligations," it states in full:

> Without prejudice to other rights and remedies of a host state or its population, a host state may initiate a proceeding against a COMESA investor or its investment in the

[52] CCIA, Art. 31.
[53] CCIA, Art. 32(1).
[54] CCIA, Art. 32(4).

> courts of the host state for breaches of its obligations under this Agreement. By specific written agreement, the disputing parties may submit the dispute to an arbitral tribunal in accordance with Article 36.[55]

Under this provision, the default forum being the host state's courts, the provision does not preclude and in fact seems to anticipate that the investor and the state would by contract submit investor obligation matters to arbitral resolution. What this does as a matter of practice is probably the interpretation of regular investor state arbitration clauses that say "disputes arising out of this treaty" to include claims or counterclaims by the host state on the basis of these investor obligations.

It is not difficult to imagine that in the great majority of cases, these investor obligation issues would be presented for judicial or arbitral resolution in the form of counterclaims, which traditional investment treaties have for ages precluded because of the one-way nature of the substantive obligations and the lack of investor consent in investment treaties that merely make investors third-party beneficiaries. CCIA's attempt to resolve the more technical challenges of counterclaims is discussed below.

Interaction with Existing Treaties

CCIA contains an express provision on its interactions with other preexisting and future treaties. Unsurprisingly, it claims supremacy, but not without ambiguity, deliberate or not. Consider the text's last paragraph more carefully:

> Other Agreements
>
> This Agreement or any action taken under it shall not affect the rights and obligations of the Member States under existing agreements to which they are party. 2. Nothing in this Agreement shall affect the rights of the Member States to enter into other agreements not contrary to the principles, objectives and terms of this Agreement. 3. In the event of inconsistency between this Agreement and such other agreements between Member States mentioned in paragraph 2 of this Article, this Agreement shall prevail to the extent of the inconsistency, and in so far as it is more favorable to the investor.[56]

The comma before the last sentence is not an editorial error, and injects some ambiguity. The practical situation whose resolution may depend on the meaning of this comma where a preexisting or new treaty contains a rule that favors the host state is real. Would CCIA prevail in that instance? Without the comma, the answer appears clear—it would not. But with the comma, the first general rule seems to have definitively come to an end and an add-on follows for emphasis. It won't be surprising if this issue is litigated at some point after the coming into force of the CCIA, assuming the choice is made to maintain the ambiguity.

[55] CCIA, Art. 33.
[56] CCIA, Art. 38.

Procedural Rules and Dispute Settlement

COMESA Treaty

The COMESA Treaty establishes a Court of Justice under Chapter V.[57] The Court's jurisdiction extends to all matters arising out of the Treaty referred to it by member states. Necessarily limited to state-to-state disputes under the Treaty, the Court's jurisdiction extends in particular to matters referred to it by a Member State or the Council, or the Secretary General as stated under the following provisions:

1. A Member State which considers that another Member State or the Council has failed to fulfill an obligation under this Treaty or has infringed a provision of this Treaty, may refer the matter to the Court.
2. A Member State may refer for determination by the Court, the legality of any act, regulation, directive or decision of the Council on the grounds that such act, regulation, directive or decision is ultra vires or unlawful or an infringement of the provisions of this Treaty or any rule of law relating to its application or amounts to a misuse or abuse of power.[58]

Presumably, therefore, not only can the Member States sue each other for violations of the Treaty before the Court of Justice, but each one of them can sue the Council for ultra vires.

The more interesting *locus standi* that the Treaty creates is one that gives the power to initiate an action before the court to "residents." Article 26 provides:

> Any person who is resident in a Member State may refer for determination by the Court the legality of any act, regulation, directive, or decision of the Council or of a Member State on the grounds that such act, directive, decision or regulation is unlawful or an infringement of the provisions of this Treaty: Provided that where the matter for determination relates to any act, regulation, directive or decision by a Member State, such person shall not refer the matter for determination under this Article unless he has first exhausted local remedies in the national courts or tribunals of the Member State.[59]

[57] Chapter V is comprised of Arts. 19–27.

[58] COMESA Treaty, Art. 24. A matter may also be referred to the Court by the Secretary General under circumstances set forth in Article 25 ("ARTICLE 25 Reference by the Secretary-General 1. Where the Secretary-General considers that a Member State has failed to fulfill an obligation under this Treaty or has infringed a provision of this Treaty, he shall submit his findings to the Member State concerned to enable that Member State to submit its observations on the findings. 2. If the Member State concerned does not submit its observations to the Secretary-General within two months, or if the observations submitted are unsatisfactory, the Secretary-General shall refer the matter to the Bureau of the Council which shall decide whether the matter shall be referred by the Secretary General to the Court immediately or be referred to the Council. 3. Where a matter has been referred to the Council under the provisions of paragraph 2 of this Article and the Council fails to resolve the matter, the Council shall direct the Secretary-General to refer the matter to the Court").

[59] CCIA, Art. 26.

This is an extremely useful remedy of last resort for persons, including foreign investors, who could resort to the court for a Member State's violations of the substantive provisions of the Treaty including the FET and expropriation provisions discussed above. But of course they have to be "residents" first, which is almost always the case if they have invested in the host state, although the Treaty does not offer a specific definition of the term. They must then exhaust all domestic remedies before resorting to national courts or tribunals. Whether the term "tribunals of the Member State" includes arbitral tribunals and, if so, whether it is limited to domestic arbitration is difficult to say, as no interpretation has so far been given by the Court; however, the resort to international arbitration by foreign investors seems to be the primary reason why the COMSA Court of Justice is underutilized. If investors resort to domestic legal processes and exhaust remedies and still believe that the Member state has violated the Treaty, including the investment provisions, they could potentially seek redress from the Court under these provisions. This may even follow international arbitral proceedings if such deny the investor from COMESA the kind of justice that the Treaty anticipates under the substantive provisions.

Beyond its judicial power, the Treaty confers some circumscribed arbitral power to the Court of Justice. Article 28 states such conferral as follows:

> The Court shall have jurisdiction to hear and determine any matter: (a) arising from an arbitration clause contained in a contract which confers such jurisdiction to which the Common Market or any of its institutions is a party; and (b) arising from a dispute between the Member States regarding this Treaty if the dispute is submitted to it under a special agreement between the Member States concerned.[60]

The Court's arbitral jurisdiction is thus limited to matters that concern COMESA itself as a juridical entity and its institutions and only if they had concluded an arbitral agreement with a third party designating the COMESA Court as the arbiter. The second basis of arbitral jurisdiction is even more attenuated. It applies only when the Member States conclude an arbitration agreement granting the Court arbitral jurisdiction instead of submitting their dispute for judicial resolution by the same court under Article 19-27 of the Treaty. The rationale behind the conferral of both types of arbitral jurisdiction is difficult to understand.

CCIA Dispute Settlement

At the initial stage, the CCIA's state-to-state dispute settlement provision refers the matter to the Court of Justice that the COMESA Treaty establishes but only in its arbitral capacity, not judicial capacity. The exact words are: "Any dispute between Member States as to the interpretation or application of this Agreement not satisfactorily settled through amicable means in the cooling-off period may be referred for decision to the COMESA Court of Justice sitting as a court of arbitration, in accordance with

[60] COMESA Treaty, Art. 28.

Article 28(b) of the COMESA Treaty."[61] The cross-referenced provision is the one that says: "The Court shall have jurisdiction to hear and determine any matter:... (b) arising from a dispute between the Member States regarding this Treaty if the dispute is submitted to it under a special agreement between the Member States concerned."[62]

What this provision anticipates is an arbitral resolution of matters referred to the Court by a member state based on an arbitral agreement between one or more member states for a dispute that arises out of the COMESA Treaty—hence the reference to "regarding this Treaty." The CCIA attempts to use this infrastructure for the resolution of disputes arising out of the CCIA itself, an agreement independent of the COMESA Treaty. The idea seems to be that because the CCIA grows out of the COMESA Treaty, a dispute arising out of CCIA arises out of the COMESA Treaty by progeny. Be that as it may, it appears that the drafters believed that the CCIA qualifies as the "special agreement" referenced in 28(b) of the Treaty. It is unclear why the drafters thought that a state-to-state dispute arising out the CCIA would not be appropriate for judicial resolution before the COMESA Court. It would seem to fit very well under the Treaty's grant of judicial power which states: "A Member State which considers that another Member State or the Council has failed to fulfill an obligation under this Treaty or has infringed a provision of this Treaty, may refer the matter to the Court."[63]

The investor–state dispute settlement provision begins with a cooling off period and escalates from negotiations and mediation[64] to binding arbitration, but does so in an unusual and convoluted way. There is no better demonstration of this than the text itself. The first segment staggers possibilities as follows:

> In the event that a dispute between a COMESA investor and a Member State has not been resolved, pursuant to Article 34, a COMESA investor may, subject to the exhaustion of local remedies in the host state, submit a claim to the COMESA Court of Justice under Article 26 (1) of the Treaty. 2. Paragraph 1 shall apply unless the disputing parties, by specific written agreement, submit the dispute to the following arbitral fora: (a) an African international arbitration institution; or (b) under any other arbitration institution or under any other arbitration rules, as both parties to the dispute agree.[65]

The first possibility is the submission of the case to the COMESA Court's resolution under Article 26(1) of the COMESA Treaty, which reads:

> Any person who is resident in a Member State may refer for determination by the Court the legality of any act, regulation, directive, or decision of the Council or of a Member State on the grounds that such act, directive, decision or regulation is unlawful or an infringement of the provisions of this Treaty: Provided that where the

[61] CCIA, Art. 35(1).
[62] COMESA Treaty, Art. 28(b).
[63] COMESA Treaty, Art. 24(1).
[64] CCIA, Art. 34.
[65] CCIA, Art. 36(1).

> matter for determination relates to any act, regulation, directive or decision by a Member State, such person shall not refer the matter for determination under this Article unless he has first exhausted local remedies in the national courts or tribunals of the Member State.[66]

The reference in CCIA to this particular provision clarifies the original intent that investors could make use of the COMESA Court for judicial resolution. The importance of this clarification goes beyond the CCIA, an agreement that is still waiting for ratification, and permits COMESA investors to access the COMESA Court for violations of the investor protection provisions in the COMESA Treaty are more protective of investment than the CCIA protection provisions that are not yet in force.

The obstacle for both the COMESA Treaty-based and CCIA-based investor claims to the Court of Justice is, however, the exhaustion of local remedies. In this regard, the Treaty's provisions are more categorical than the CCIA, which at least recognizes futility as an exception to exhaustion. It states in relevant part:

> A COMESA investor or its investment may submit a claim to arbitration pursuant to this Agreement, provided that the COMESA investor or investment, as appropriate: (a) has first submitted a claim before the domestic courts of the Host State for the purpose of pursuing local remedies, after the exhaustion of any administrative remedies, relating to the measure underlying the claim under this Agreement, and a resolution has not been reached within a reasonable period of time from its submission to a local court of the host state; or (b) demonstrates on a motion to permit arbitration that there are no reasonably available legal remedies capable of providing effective remedies for the dispute concerning the underlying measure, or the legal remedies provide no reasonable possibility of such remedies in a reasonable period of time.[67]

It is guided by a reasonableness standard for both the availability of the local remedy and the period of time that it would take. Although that much is clear, there is an inherent ambiguity in the structure of this provision. While subsections 1 and 2 cross-refer to each other and make it clear that exhaustion of local remedies is required before the investor resorts to the Court of Justice, subsection 3 follows an exhaustive set of provisions and inserts conditions to subsection 2 without cross-referencing. It seems a function of the drafter's discomfort rather than inartful drafting because what they have done is virtually abolish international arbitration as a means of investor–state dispute settlement even when the parties have expressly agreed in a contract, which subsection 2 seems to permit before subsection 3 takes it all away.

The only compromise that the drafters seem to have agreed on is the insertion of a futility doctrine at the end of subsection 3(b). However, what this provision does not do is identify the decision-maker to whom the said "motion" for futility may be submitted. The most sensible interpretation is that such motion should be submitted to the arbitral tribunal constituted by the parties' agreement as there is structurally

[66] COMESA Treaty, Art. 26(1).
[67] CCIA, Art. 36(3).

no other authority that could undertake this task. Clearly, it cannot be the domestic courts that are asked to determine that there is no point in submitting a case to them.

Finally, beyond its inclusion of a three-year statute of limitation[68] and a fork-in-the-road rule,[69] the CCIA innovatively creates avenues for host state counterclaims. Although that is mainly a function of the substantive investor obligations, the articulation of the procedural mechanism is also important. Consider if the CCIA gets the mechanics right:

> Each Member State consents to the submission of a claim to arbitration under this Agreement in accordance with its provisions. *Each COMESA investor or its investment, by virtue of establishing or continuing to operate or own an investment subject to this Agreement, consents to the terms of the submission of a claim to dispute resolution under this Agreement.*[70]

Under this formulation, the expression of consent to arbitrate by the investor comes from the act of "establishing or continuing to operate or own an investment," presumably no matter what the arbitration agreement might say. But the question remains: which arbitration? Two possible scenarios could be conceived. The first and more common way that this could work is in the form of host state counterclaims when the investor seeks arbitration under Article 36(2) and (3), which require the exhaustion or showing of futility of local remedies. Because all of these provisions directly and expressly address the investor's course of action, none of them requires the host state to exhaust domestic judicial remedies.

If the host state initiates an arbitral proceeding, it would appear that the investor could counterclaim without exhausting domestic remedies. The most common possibility is, however, an investor's judicial claim and dissatisfaction followed by arbitration. In that sense, if the host state submits a counterclaim for arbitral resolution, it would mean either that it chose not to raise the same issues in the judicial proceedings as it is not required to exhaust judicial remedies unlike the investor, or that it was equally dissatisfied by them. Because counterclaims are a new addition to the treaty text, the drafter's omission of the exhaustion requirement for counterclaims may be an oversight rather than an imbalance deliberately left because there are instances in which the host state would simply prefer an arbitral award over its own court's judgment against the investor for obvious reasons of better enforceability in multiple fora under the New York Convention.

Another imbalance relates to access to the COMESA Court of Justice under Article 36(1). If the investor utilizes this provision and submits a claim for judicial resolution, the admissibility of the host state's counterclaims by the Court seems doubtful because

[68] *See* CCIA, Art. 36(4) ("No claim shall be submitted to arbitration if more than three (3) years have elapsed from the date on which the COMESA investor or its investment first acquired, or should have first acquired, knowledge of the breach and knowledge that the COMESA investor or its investment has incurred loss or damage").

[69] CCIA, Art. 36(5) ("If the COMESA investor elects to submit a claim at one of the fora set out in paragraph 1 of this Article, that election shall be definitive and the investor may not thereafter submit a claim relating to the same subject matter or underlying measure to other fora").

[70] CCIA, Art. 36(6) (emphasis added).

the relevant provision refers to the investor only: "A COMESA investor may, subject to the exhaustion of local remedies in the host state, submit a claim to the COMESA Court of Justice under Article 26 (1) of the Treaty."[71] Granted that Article 26 of the COMESA Treaty also contains a domestic remedy exhaustion requirement, the drafters might have thought that the host state could bring its actions in domestic court proceedings, but that is a limited view because the host state might prefer, just like an arbitral award, an international court award for purposes of enforceability and other reasons.

For all these reasons, although the substantive investor obligation provisions of the ICCA are elaborate and well-conceived, the procedural mechanisms of their enforcement lack clarity, consistency, and focus and rely primarily on unwarranted presumptions of what the host state might consider appropriate in all cases. This requires careful review and rectification.

Conclusion

The COMESA investment regime covers the biggest Regional Economic Community in such a robust, modern, and innovative way. The COMESA Treaty started out with a more traditional investor protection and dispute settlement regime. The Revised CCIA clarified contentious principles such as FET and expropriation, but it does so by an independent agreement that ranks lower in the hierarchy of instruments. The COMESA Treaty permits amendment through a lengthy process and adoption by two-thirds of the Member States.[72]

Technically, the investment related provisions of the Treaty remain in effect until the Member States bring them into compliance with the CCIA provisions (when it comes into effect) through the correct amendment procedure. It could be argued that because the coming into force of the CCIA requires the ratification of two-thirds of the same Member States, it is the functional equivalent. Although the required votes are there, the Treaty sets for amendment procedures and any amendment that fails to follow such may not be effective as a matter of law.

Beyond the procedures, and assuming that the inconsistency would not subject investors and host states to conflicting commands in the interim, the CCIA's addition of investor obligation is quite remarkable at least in substantive terms although, at the end, it most certainly is a policy choice that vigorously pushes the pendulum toward state rights rather than investment attraction and protection.

There is no doubt that the policy decision is a reaction to Africa's perceived unfavorable experience with investment treaties and investor–state arbitration. However, the compatibility of unusually restrictive investment protection rules and the excessive expansion of host states' rights with the creation of a common investment area is a dilemma that remains unresolved.

[71] CCIA, Art. 36(1).

[72] *See* COMESA Treaty, Art. 190(1–5) ("(5) Any amendment to this Treaty shall be adopted by the Authority and shall enter into force when ratified by two-thirds of the Member States, provided that in exceptional cases the Authority may provide for an Amendment of the Treaty to come into force upon adoption by the Authority").

22
The Economic Community for West African States

The Economic Community for West African States (ECOWAS) is a union of 15 West African countries. ECOWAS includes a comprehensive Supplementary Act on Investment that entered into force in January 2009. This chapter examines this Act and related instruments as a part of Africa's international investment law regimes and in light of its contributions to the emerging Pan-African investment regime.

Background on ECOWAS

The Economic Community of West African States (ECOWAS) is a regional economic community of 15 West African states[1] established on May 28, 1975, by a treaty that came to be known as the Treaty of Lagos.[2]

The aims and objectives of the Community is the promotion of development in all economic fields.[3] Although the aim is predominantly focused on the elimination

[1] *See* ECOWAS's official website at https://ecowas.int/?page_id=40. The members are Benin, Burkina Faso, Cape Verde, Cote d' Ivoire, The Gambia, Ghana, Guinea, Guinea Bissau, Liberia, Mali, Niger, Nigeria, Sierra Leone, Senegal, and Togo.

[2] Treaty of the Economic Community of West African States (ECOWAS), concluded at Lagos on May 28, 1975, at https://investmentpolicy.unctad.org/international-investment-agreements/treaty-files/5560/download.

[3] ECOWAS Treaty, Art. 2:

> It shall be the aim of the Community to promote co-operation and development in all fields of economic activity particularly in the fields of industry, transport, telecommunications, energy, agriculture, natural resources, commerce, monetary and financial questions and in social and cultural matters for the purpose of raising the standard of living of its peoples, of increasing and maintaining economic stability, of fostering closer relations among its members and of contributing to the progress and development of the African continent. 2. For the purposes set out in the preceding paragraph and as hereinafter provided for in this Treaty, the Community shall by stages ensure: (a) the elimination as between the Member States of customs duties and other charges of equivalent effect in respect of the importation and exportation of goods; (b) the abolition of quantitative and administrative restrictions on trade among the Member States; (c) the establishment of a common customs tariff and a common commercial policy towards third countries; (d) the abolition as between the Member States of the obstacles to the free movement of persons, services and capital; (e) the harmonisation of the agricultural policies and the promotion of common projects in the Member States notably in the fields of marketing, research and agro-industrial enterprises; (f) the implementation of schemes for the joint development of transport, communication, energy and other infrastructural facilities as well as the evolution of a common policy in these fields; (g) the harmonisation of the economic and industrial policies of the Member States and the elimination of disparities in the level of development of Member States; (h) the harmonisation, required for the proper functioning of the Community, of the monetary policies of the Member States; (i) the establishment of a Fund for Co-operation, Compensation and Development; and (j) such other activities calculated to further the aims of the Community as the Member States may from time to time undertake in common.

Africa's International Investment Law Regimes. Won L. Kidane, Oxford University Press. © Oxford University Press 2023.
DOI: 10.1093/oso/9780197745571.003.0022

of trade barriers and the establishment of a customs union, it contains an unusually robust provision on the movement of capital with significant implication on investment.[4]

Having the unimpeded flow of capital as its main objective, this provision seems to have opened up the avenue for further permissive investment rules in the Community. Based on this underlying principle, in 2008, ECOWAS adopted the Supplementary Act on Investment.[5]

The preambular language offers context:

> NOTING that national investment codes in force in Member States offer investors different incentives and protection measures; CONVINCED of the need to establish within the ECOWAS region, reliable, transparent, stable and predictable conditions for investments; DESIROUS of adopting common regional rules on investments and defining the modalities for their implementation, in order to achieve the aforementioned objectives.[6]

The objective of the Community rule is stated as the promotion of "investment that supports sustainable development of the region."[7] In furtherance of such objectives, the Supplementary Act sets forth detailed substantive investor and

[4] ECOWAS Treaty, Art. 39:

> For the purpose of ensuring the free flow of capital between the Member States consistent with the objectives of this Treaty, there is hereby established a Capital Issues Committee, which shall consist of representatives designated one each by the Member States and shall, subject to this Treaty, determine its own procedure. 2. The Member States, in designating their representatives referred to in paragraph 1 of this Article, shall designate persons with financial, commercial, banking or administrative experience or qualifications. 3. In the exercise of its functions under paragraph 1 of this Article, the Capital Issues Committee shall: (a) seek to achieve the mobility of capital within the Community through the inter-locking of any capital markets and stock exchanges; (b) ensure that stocks and shares floated in the territory of a Member State are quoted on the stock exchanges of the other Member States; (c) ensure that nationals of a Member State are given the opportunity of acquiring stocks, shares and other securities or otherwise investing in enterprises in the territories of other Member States; (d) establish a machinery for the wide dissemination in the Member States of stock exchange quotations of each Member State; (e) organise and arrange the quotation of prices, timing, volume and conditions of issue of securities of new enterprises in the Member States; if) ensure the unimpeded flow of capital within the Community through the removal of controls on the transfer of capital among the Member States in accordance with a time-table, to be determined by the Council Ministers; and (g) seek to harmonise the rates of interest on loans prevailing in the Member States so as to facilitate the investment of capital from a Member State in profitable enterprises elsewhere within the Community. 4. The capital envisaged in the provisions of this Article is that of Member States or their citizens. 5. With regard to capital other than that referred to in paragraph 4 of this Article, the Capital Issues Committee shall determine its movement within the Community.

[5] Supplementary Act A/SA.3/12/08 Adopting Community Rules on Investment and the Modalities for their Implementation with ECOWAS, entered into force Jan. 9, 2009, available at https://investmentpolicy.unctad.org/international-investment-agreements/treaties/treaties-with-investment-provisions/3547/ecowas-supplementary-act-on-investments.

[6] *Id.* at Preamble.

[7] *Id.* at Art. 2.

investment protection rules alongside investor obligations and unusually detained host state rights. It seeks to create a balance between the investor and state's rights and obligations. It also attempts to craft procedural mechanisms of enforcement and redress.

A decade after the adoption of the Supplemental Act, in July 2018, ECOWAS added the more detailed and elaborate Common Investment Code (ECOWIC).[8] Its rendition is "MINDFUL of the Supplementary Act A/SA.3/12/08 Adopting Community Rules On Investment and the Modalities for their Implementation within ECOWAS."[9] ECOWAS officially describes this Code's function as one of operationalization of the Supplemental in the following terms:

> The ECOWAS Common Investments Code mark the fulfilment of the Common market of investment within West Africa. It is designed to operationalize the ECOWAS Supplementary Act adopting Community Rules on Investments and Modalities for their Implementation (adopted in 2008), ahead to the harmonization of national investment policies and regimes for greater investment climate in the region.[10]

It is thus essentially an elaborate version of the Supplemental Act.

The following sections address the substantive and procedural rules contained in each of these instruments in turn.

Substantive Investment Law Principles

Both the Supplemental Act (the Act) and the ECOWIC (the Code) enshrine all known investment law principles in some modified form. The most fundamental ones are discussed below.

[8] ECOWAS Common Investment Code (ECOWIC), at https://nipc.gov.ng/wp-content/uploads/2019/12/ecowiccode.pdf.

[9] *Id.* at Preamble.

[10] See ECOWAS's official website at https://ecotis.projects.ecowas.int/policy-development/agreemenst-under-negotiations/#:~:text=The%20ECOWAS%20Investment%20Code%20provides,for%20implementation%20of%20the%20policy. It also adds that

> in particular, the code aligns the Member States into a single economic space and provides:
>
> a clear definition of investment and investors that qualify for benefits under the code.
>
> a full-fledged set of provisions aimed at providing policy space for Member States in the operation of investment in their countries and within the region.
>
> a wide set of sectoral policy tools for economic and social development, poverty reduction, and for the advancement of the ECOWAS integration agenda.
>
> an innovative dispute settlement arrangement, aligned with the current development on investment governance policy discussions and reform process.
>
> a mechanism for implementation of the code by Member States in line with their respective national interests.
>
> full coherence with the continental framework on investment as envisaged in the African Continental Free Trade Area (AfCFTA)." *Id.*

Meaning of Investment

The Act defines investment as:

> "investment" means i) a company; ii) shares, stock and other forms of equity participation in a company, and bonds, debentures and other forms of debt interests in a company; iii) contractual rights, such as under turnkey, construction or management contracts, production or revenue-sharing contracts, concessions or other similar contracts; iv) tangible property, including real property; and intangible property, including rights, such as leases, mortgages; liens and pledges on real property; v) rights conferred pursuant to law, such as licences and permits provided that:—such investments are not in the nature of portfolio investments which shall not be covered by this Supplementary Act;—there is a significant physical presence of the investment in the host State;—the investment in the host State is made in accordance with the laws of that host State;—the investment is part or all of a business or commercial operation; and—the investment is made by an investor as defined herein.[11]

The Code reincorporates the whole definition verbatim and adds interpretive text that goes beyond the *Salini* factors. It offers them for greater clarity as follows:

> For greater certainty, investment does not include: (i) Debt securities issued by a government or loans to a government; (ii) Portfolio investments; (iii) Claims to money that arise solely from commercial contracts for the sale of goods or services by a national or enterprise in the territory of a Member State to an enterprise in the territory of another Member State, or the extension of credit in connection with a commercial transaction, or any other claims to money that do not involve the kind of interests set out in Subparagraphs (i) through (v) above; (iv) Investments of a speculative nature; (v) Investments in any sector sensitive to its development or which would have an adverse impact on its economy; (vi) Commercial activities. In order to qualify as an investment under this Code, the investment must have the following characteristics: substantial business activity according to Paragraph e, commitment of capital or other resources, the expectation of gain or profit, the assumption of risk, and a significant contribution to the host State's economic development. Substantial business activity requires overall examination, on a case by case basis, of all the circumstances, including, inter alia: the amount of investment to be brought into the host state; the number of jobs to be created; its effect on the local community; the length of time the business has been in operation.[12]

The characteristics that the investment must have to qualify for protection are quantitatively and qualitatively cumbersome, as they need to be substantial in scale and significant in contribution. Moreover, qualitatively, the Code's added definition excludes, among other things, loans to government, portfolio investments, investments of

[11] Supplemental Act, Art. 1(c).
[12] ECOWIC, Art. 1(h).

speculative nature and more interestingly "investments in any sector sensitive to its development or which would have an adverse impact on its economy." These exclusions grant the host state broad authority to exclude many sectors and economic undertakings from protection. The breadth of discretionary exclusion is such that it narrows the class of investments that qualify for undoubted protection, which is key for investment attraction. It is unclear why the drafters believed that an investment attraction and encouragement regime would benefit from this kind of broad discretionary exclusion.

Substantive Investment Protection Rules

The investment protection provisions encompass foundational principles of national treatment, most favored nation treatment, a modified version of fair and equitable treatment, and nonexpropriation principle.

National Treatment

The national treatment provision combines national treatment with MFN treatment while also deferring MFN to a different provision in an unusual way. It states in part:

> (1) Each Member State shall accord to investors of another Member State treatment no less favourable than that, which it accords, in like circumstances to any other investor operating in its territory, with respect to the management, conduct, operation, expansion and sale or other disposition of investments. (2) Each Member State shall accord to investments of investors from another Member State treatment no less favourable than that which it accords, in like circumstances, to investments of its own investors with respect to the managements, conduct, operation, expansion and sale or other disposition of investments. (3) The treatment accorded by a Member State under Paragraphs (1) and (2) means, with respect to a local authority, treatment no less favourable than that which it accords, in like circumstances, to investors within the Community.[13]

Subsections (1) and (2) cumulatively grant all Community investors not only national treatment but also treatment that may theoretically be better than national treatment if the better of the two is ever granted to an investor from anywhere in the world. That seems to be the correct reading of this provision, although it is unclear from the text alone what prompted this kind of unusual measure of protection.

The definition of "like circumstances" sets a highly broad standard that cannot easily be met by anyone complaining of discrimination.[14] But more importantly, in

[13] *Id.* at Art. 5.

[14] *Id.* ("(4) The concept of 'in like circumstances' requires an overall examination, on a case by-case basis, of all the circumstances of an investment, including notably: a) its effects on third persons and the local community; b) its effects on the local, regional or national environment, the health of the populations, or on the global commons; c) the sector in which the investor is active; d) the aim of the measure in question; e) the regulatory process generally applied in relation to a measure in question; and f) other factors directly relating to the investment or investor in relation to the measure in question").

what seems to be a reversal of policy on national treatment, the ECOWIC includes exceptions that have the potential to swallow the rule. Among other things, the Code permits exception to national treatment for "any regulatory measure taken by a Member State that is designed and applied to protect or enhance legitimate public welfare objectives, such as national interests, public health, safety and the environment, does not constitute a breach of the National Treatment principle."[15]

Most Favored Treatment (MFN)

The MFN protection included under national treatment notwithstanding, the Act dedicates another provision to another version of MFN, this time MFN for investors of Community states:

> Each Member State shall accord to investors of another Member State treatment no less favourable than that it accords in like circumstances, to investors of any other state within the Community with respect to the management, conduct, operation, expansion, sale or other disposition of investments. (3) Each Member State shall accord to investments made by investors of another Member State treatment no less favourable than that it accords in like circumstances, to investments made by investors of any other Member State of the Community or of a third party with respect to the management, conduct, operation, expansion, sale or other disposition of investments. (4) Each Member State shall accord to investors of another Member State and to investments made by investors from other Member States, the better of the treatment required by this Article, and the national treatment obligation.

Recognizing the duplication with the National Treatment provision, this MFN provision gives priority to the rule that offers the investor the better of the treatments. Read together, the end result is offering a Community investor the better of MFN or National Treatment as the case may be. In terms of textual representation, it seems that this result could have more economically been achieved.

[15] ECOWIC, Art. 7 ("Article 7: -Exceptions to National Treatment 1. Member States may adopt measures that derogate from the National Treatment principle provided such measures are not arbitrary and subject to the conditions set out in this Article. 2. Any regulatory measure taken by a Member State that is designed and applied to protect or enhance legitimate public welfare objectives, such as national interests, public health, safety and the environment, does not constitute a breach of the National Treatment principle. 3. Member States may, in accordance with their respective domestic legislation, grant preferential treatment to qualifying investments and investors in order to achieve national development objectives. 4. A Member State reserves the right to deny an investor the benefits of this Code where: (a) The investor does not have substantial business activities in the Member State; or (b) The investor is engaged in activities inimical to the economic interest of Member States. 5. A Member State may deny national treatment if advantages available within the Member State's economy are made for the exclusive benefit of its own nationals within the framework of its national development programs or its List of scheduled investment sectors where applicable. 6. The National Treatment principle shall not apply: (a) to subsidies or grants provided to a government or a State enterprise, including government-supported loans, guarantees and insurance; or (b) to taxation measures aimed at ensuring the effective collection of taxes, except where this results in arbitrary discrimination. 7. In accordance with national laws and regulations, Member States may accord more favourable treatment to address the internal needs of designated disadvantaged persons, groups or regions. 8. The implementation of these exceptions shall not entitle any investor to compensation for any competitive disadvantages they may suffer").

Although the Code maintained the MFN provision's text, it added elaborate exceptions that would effectively undermine the basic MFN rule. One of the exceptions, for example, states: "Nothing in this Code shall be construed to prevent the adoption or enforcement by any Member State of measures taken in good faith and designed and applied ... (c) to secure compliance with the national laws or regulations which are not inconsistent with this Code."[16] The addition of broad exceptions such as this[17] is sure to be a rich source of dispute. Relatedly, if a dispute arises out of the application of these unusual exceptions, such disputes are likely to be resolved without precedent for at least the first few times. Simply put, these exceptions do not demonstrate simplicity and are contrary to the objectives of transparency and harmonization. They are also indications of Africa's continued struggle to make sense of existing international investment law principles.

Fair and Equitable Treatment (FET)

No principle has wrestled the African investment law regime as much as the FET principle. The way the Act and ECOWIC handled it is a good demonstration of the struggle. The Act splits various components of the FET standard into various provisions. First, under investment protection, it approves the minimum standards of treatment under customary international law.

The first provision, titled "Minimum Regional Standards," goes on stating that it is essentially the minimum standards of treatment under international law, which appears to suggest the minimum standard of treatment under customary international law. In that sense, it reflects the policy choice to limit the meaning of the FET away from the modern iteration of FET, which includes the expansive notion of legitimate expectations. This is achieved with reasonable clarity in the following terms:

[16] *See* ECOWIC, Art. 9. To made matters a little bit more complicated, there is another provision titled "Non-discrimination" that further undermines the nondiscrimination provisions of National Treatment and MFN treatment. It states: "(1) The rights and obligations under Articles 6 & 7 (National Treatment and Most Favoured Nation Treatment principles) do not apply to subsidies or grants provided to a government or a State enterprise, including government-supported loans, guarantees and insurance. (2) Exceptions and exemptions from the most-favoured nation and from the national treatment obligations within the context of incentives shall apply only if Member States make due commitments in this respect in their Annexes schedules of excluded sectors. (3) The rights and obligations under Articles 6 & 7 (National Treatment and Most Favoured Nation Treatment principles) do not apply with regard to taxation measures aimed at ensuring the effective collection of taxes, except where this results in arbitrary discrimination duly noted and reported by the investor." ECOWIC, Art. 20.

[17] Some of the other exceptions include measures that a state may take "(a) to protect public morals or to maintain public order; (b) to protect human, animal, or plant life or health; (c) to secure compliance with the national laws or regulations which are not inconsistent with this Code, including those relating to: (i) for the prevention of deceptive and fraudulent practices to deal with the effects of a default on a contract; (ii) to the protection of the privacy of individuals in relation to the processing and dissemination of personal data and the protection of confidentiality of individual records and accounts; or (iii) for safety reasons; (d) to ensure the equitable or effective imposition or collection of direct taxes in respect of investors of another Member State and their investments; (e) to protect national treasures of artistic, historic, or archaeological value; (f) for the conservation of exhaustible natural resources if such measures are made effective in conjunction with restrictions on domestic production or consumption. (g) to promote the achievement of equality in its territory, land planning, or designed to protect or advance categories of disadvantaged persons. (h) to preserve and promote cultural and linguistic diversity. (i) to preserve and protect the biodiversity and the rights of local communities, in conformity with the relevant multilateral instruments." *Id.* There are also more exceptions relating to security, financial and economic circumstances. *Id.*

> (1) Each Member State shall accord to investors from a Member State or their investments, treatment in accordance with customary international law, including fair and equitable treatment and reasonable protection and security under the domestic law. This obligation shall be understood to be consistent with the obligation of ECOWAS Member States. (2) Paragraph (1) prescribes the customary usage of international law minimum standard of treatment of aliens as the minimum standard of treatment to be accorded to investments. The concepts of "fair and equitable treatment" and "full protection and security" are included within this standard, and do not create additional substantive rights.[18]

Whereas this appeared to have denied recognition to the "progressive" development of the FET principle, another provision under Obligations of the State (rather than the rights of the investor) brings back some of the contentious elements of the FET principle under the title "Host State Obligations: Procedural Fairness":

> In accordance with the requirements of Article 7 (1) Host Member States shall ensure that their administrative, legislative and judicial processes do not operate in a manner that is arbitrary or that does not deny administrative and procedural fairness to investors and their investments. Investors or investments shall be notified in a timely fashion of administrative or judicial proceedings and changes thereof directly relating to them, unless such notice is contrary to domestic law on an exceptional basis. (2) Hosts Member States shall act in a manner that does not create a denial of justice in judicial and administrative proceedings. (3) Administrative decision-making processes shall include the right of administrative appeal of decisions, commensurate with the level of development of the host Member State. Judicial review of administrative decisions should also be available through domestic or regional judicial review processes. (4) Notwithstanding the differences in administrative, legislative and judicial systems, Member States shall strive to improve the transparency, efficiency, independence and accountability of their legislative, regulatory, administrative and judicial processes, and shall provide review or appeal procedures to ensure that they operate in accordance with applicable domestic laws.[19]

This is a rather modern codification of the established minimum standards of treatment without the exorbitant legitimate expectations rule, although the last part comes close to recognizing at least the transparency and accountability prongs of the legitimate expectations principle when it states: "Member States shall strive to improve the transparency, efficiency, independence and accountability of their legislative, regulatory, administrative and judicial processes."[20]

The splitting of the FET principle between investment protection and host state obligation provisions is only successful in adding more confusion for the adjudication of real cases.

[18] *Id.* at Art. 7.
[19] *Id.* at Art. 19.
[20] *Id.*

Whereas the Act's reckoning with the FET principle and its maintenance of the core principles of denial of justice and due process generally appeared a reasonable restatement of the FET principle as it has historically been understood, albeit in split provisions suggesting discomfort, the ECOWIC took the radical step of eliminating any reference to the FET principle including the denial of justice and due process altogether. It maintained some protections that are ordinarily understood to be part of the FET standard in a highly diluted manner in an unusual way across many provisions. For example, it adds a provision on transparency, which reads:

> A Member State shall endeavour to ensure that its laws, policies, regulations, procedures, administrative rulings and judicial decisions of general application, as well as international agreements after their entry into force, which may affect investments in its territory, including among others, exchange regimes and those of fiscal nature, are promptly published, or otherwise made publicly available. Such information shall be regularly updated and published at least annually.[21]

Even the/this state transparency obligation comes with a corresponding investor disclosure obligation including the publication of how much taxes they have paid.[22]

The ECOWIC's conspicuous omission of any reference to such core principles of the denial of justice or due process is clear indication of the policy choice to eliminate the concept of the FET principle including perhaps the minimum standards of treatment under customary international law that the Act seemed to have codified in reasonable detail. This policy shift between the Act's adoption in 2008 and the Code's rendition in 2018 is undoubtedly an overreaction to the widespread indictment of the application of these principles in arbitral cases during the decade.

Expropriation

The Act includes a traditional expropriation provision without any notable modification, as follows:

> (1) No Member State may directly or indirectly nationalize or expropriate an investment in its territory ("expropriation"), except: a) for a public purpose; b) on a non discriminatory basis; c) in accordance with due process of law; and d) on payment of compensation in accordance with Paragraphs (2) to (6). (2) Appropriate compensation shall normally be equivalent to the fair market value of the expropriated investment immediately before the expropriation took place ("date of expropriation"), and shall not reflect any change in value occurring because the intended expropriation had become known earlier. Valuation criteria shall include going concern value, asset value including declared tax value of tangible property, and other criteria, as appropriate, to determine fair market value; (3) Compensation shall be paid without delay and be fully realizable; (4) Payment should be made in

[21] *Id.* at Art. 15(1)(a).

[22] *Id.* at Art. 15(4)(a) ("(a)... investors shall make available to the public in the Member State where they are operating information relating to payments made to the Member State's public authorities, including taxes, royalties, surcharges, fees and all other payments relating to the investment contract or agreement").

> a convertible currency and compensation shall include interest at a commercially reasonable rate for that currency from the date of expropriation until the date of actual payment. (5) On payment, compensation shall be freely transferable. Awards that are significantly burdensome on a host State may be paid yearly over a period of three (3) years or such other period as may be agreed by the Member States, subject to interest at the rate established by mutual consent. (6) This Article does not apply to the issuance of compulsory licences granted in relation to intellectual property rights, or to the revocation, limitation or creation of intellectual property rights, to the extent that such issuance, revocation, limitation or creation is consistent with applicable international agreements on intellectual property. (7) A non-discriminatory measure of general application shall not be considered an expropriation of a debt security or loan covered by this Supplementary Act solely on the ground that the measure imposes costs on the debtor that cause it to default on the debt.[23]

The Code makes limited modifications to this, only relating to the assessment of compensation. It injects an equitable balance principle, the application of which is likely to further complicate an already complicated damages assessment process:

> 6. Where appropriate, the assessment of fair and adequate compensation shall be based on an equitable balance between the public interest and interest of those affected, having regard for all relevant circumstances and taking account of: the current and past use of the property, the history of its acquisition, the fair market value of the investment, the purpose of the expropriation, the extent of previous profit made by the foreign investor through the investment, and the duration of the investment.[24]

Investor Obligations

Both the Act and the ECOWIC contain detailed investor obligation provisions. Substantively, the Act's inclusion of investor obligations is modest covering such uncontroversial areas as compliance with the laws of the host state,[25] pre-establishment environmental impact assessment and publication of same,[26] anti-corruption,[27] post-establishment best practices and human rights protection,[28] good corporate governance,[29] and corporate social responsibility.[30] To enforce all of these obligations, the Act contains a civil liabilities provision with an accompanying judicial remedy presumably separate from the liability that could be redressed under the dispute settlement

[23] Act, Art. 8.
[24] ECOWIC, Art. 11 (6).
[25] Act, Art. 11.
[26] Act, Art. 12.
[27] Act, Art. 13.
[28] Act, Art. 14.
[29] Act, Art. 15.
[30] Act, Art. 16.

clause discussed below. The investor liabilities clause states: "Investors shall be subject to civil actions for liability in the judicial process of their host State for acts or decisions made in relation to the investment where such acts or decisions lead to significant damage, personal injuries or loss of life in the host State."[31]

The ECOWIC took this to the next level and spread the obligations across many provisions. The first cluster of investor obligations pertain to environmental care. This provision is robust and proper. Among other things, it requires the application of the precautionary principle, stating: "(c) apply the precautionary principle to their environmental and social impact assessments and to decisions taken in relation to a proposed investment, including any necessary mitigating or alternative approaches to such investment."[32] It also imposes such related environmental obligations as the following:

> (d) make the investor environmental and social impact assessments available to the general public and accessible to the affected local communities and to any other affected interests in the Member State of the proposed investment; (e) perform the restoration, using appropriate technologies, for any damage caused to the natural environment and to pay adequate compensation to all affected interested persons; (f) provide to the competent national environmental authorities, in respect of the products, processes, and services of the investor's enterprises, all relevant environmental information, together with measures and costs necessary to avoid and mitigate against any potentially harmful effects.[33]

Some of these are additional to the list of obligations under the Act.

The next investor obligation pertains to what are called "development obligations." These obligations are shared between the state and the investor. The investor's obligation is stated as:

> (3) Investors doing business in the ECOWAS territory shall in pursuit of their economic objectives, proceed in ways that do not conflict with the social and economic development of host countries in particular, they shall be sensitive to changes in the social and economic goals of their hosts. Accordingly, there should be no conflict between the obligations of the parties in the investment agreement and the sovereign right of countries to pursue other key policy objectives.[34]

The next cluster of obligations are titled "Socio-political Obligations." They are elaborate and unusual in any investment treaties, stating:

> (1) Investors conducting business in the ECOWAS territory shall adhere to the following principles including but not limited to: a) respect for national sovereignty and observance of domestic laws, regulations and administrative practices; b)respect

[31] Act, Art. 17.
[32] ECOWIC, Art. 27.
[33] *Id.*
[34] *Id.* at Art. 31(3).

> for socio-cultural objectives and values; c)non-interference in internal political affairs; and e)non-interference in intergovernmental relations; (2) Investors shall not influence the appointment of persons to public office or finance political parties or organisations; (3) The investor shall be bound by the laws and regulations in force in the host state and shall refrain from all acts that may disturb public order or morals or that may be prejudicial to the public interest. The investor is also to refrain from exercising restrictive practices and from trying to achieve gains through unlawful means.[35]

The politics of neighboring countries might have prompted this, but the imposition of more and more elastic investor obligations such as these could potentially be antithetical to the core objective of investment promotion and protection.

The next cluster of investor obligations are consumer protection. A partial list includes:

> 7. Investors doing business in the ECOWAS region shall when dealing with consumers act in accordance with fair business, marketing and advertising practices and should take all reasonable steps to ensure the safety and quality of the goods or services they provide. They shall in particular, give full and adequate attention to the following key areas: a) Ensure that the goods or services they provide meet all agreed or legally required standards for consumer health and safety, including health warnings and product safety and information labels. b) As appropriate to the goods or services, provide accurate and clear information regarding their content, safe use, maintenance, storage, and disposal sufficient to enable consumers to make informed decisions. c) Provide transparent and effective procedures that address consumer complaints and contribute to fair and timely resolution of consumer disputes without undue cost or burden.[36]

These obligations presumably supplement and enhance broadly applicable tort liabilities under ordinary domestic tort law regimes. To the extent they purport to add more obligation and liability than imposed on nationals, it may be a violation of the nondiscrimination provisions of national treatment or MFN, assuming they can survive the exceptions. Although there is nothing inherently wrong with consumer protection rules, the importation of more obligations from generally applicable laws into an investment treaty points more in the direction of discouragement of foreign investment than encouragement. Its added value in the positive direction is rather unclear beyond serving as evidence of a counterreaction to expansive investor protection jurisprudence that the beneficiary investors of this particular community have nothing to do with.

[35] *Id.* at Art. 32.
[36] *Id.* at Art. 33(7).

The next one relates to/covers corporate governance and responsible business conduct. The obligation is comprehensive. It begins with this sweeping obligation that no state has definitively codified in a binding form: "1. Investors shall comply with all international best practices, regional, and national laws and regulations applicable to corporate governance in the ECOWAS territory in order to promote improved corporate accountability and transparency in the region."[37]

This provision makes obligatory effectively "all international best practices" by providing that "investors shall comply with." Many of the best practices are often advisory and that is why they are called best practices; ECOWIC does, however, make them mandatory vis-à-vis Community investors. This is also more evidence of more cumbersome rules that do not help move the Community's effort of creating a more unified investment regime in the right direction.

Following the corporate responsibility comes the anti-corruption obligation, although it is preceded by elaborate measures to combat bribery, the reason for the inclusion of which in this instrument is not clear,[38] the anti-bribery obligation imposed on the investor is clear and consistent with the United Nations[39] as well as the African Union anti-corruption conventions.[40] It simply states that:

> 1. Investors doing business in ECOWAS territory shall not, prior to the establishment of an investment or there after offer, promise or give any undue pecuniary or any undue advantage to a public official of a Member State or to a member of an official's family, business associate or other person in close proximity to an official or another person or any entity in order that the official acts or refrains from acting in relation to

[37] *Id.* at Art. 34(1). Additional obligations include: "4. In this regard, investors are required to adopt and implement, inter alia, the following provisions: a. ensure equitable treatment of all shareholders, including minority and third party shareholders; b. encourage active cooperation between corporations and stakeholders in creating wealth, jobs and the sustainability of financially sound enterprises; c. ensure that timely and accurate disclosure is made of all materials facts relevant to, inter alia, the financial situation, performance, ownership, and governance of the company, risks related to environmental liabilities, and any other matters in accordance with the relevant regulations and requirements; d. ensure similar disclosure of information relating to human resource policies, such as programmes for human resource development; and e. respect any other requirement agreed to, and adopted, by the Member States pursuant to this Code and the ECOWICP. f. adhere to the financial reporting, disclosure, accounting, and audit practices satisfying the requirements of the International Financial Reporting Standards (IFRS)." *Id.* at Art. 34(4).

[38] *See* ECOWIC, Arts. 36–37, 39–40.

[39] *See* United Nations Convention Against Corruption, entered into force Dec. 15, 2005, available at https://www.unodc.org/documents/brussels/UN_Convention_Against_Corruption.pdf.

[40] *See* African Union Convention on Preventing and Combating Corruption, entered into force on Aug. 5, 2006, available at https://au.int/en/treaties/african-union-convention-preventing-and-combating-corruption. It defines corruption in the following similar way: "(a) the solicitation or acceptance, directly or indirectly, by a public official or any other person, of any goods of monetary value, or other benefit, such as a gift, favour, promise or advantage for himself or herself or for another person or entity, in exchange for any act or omission in the performance of his or her public functions; (b) the offering or granting, directly or indirectly, to a public official or any other person, of any goods of monetary value, or other benefit, such as a gift, favour, promise or advantage for himself or herself or for another person or entity, in exchange for any act or omission in the performance of his or her public functions." *Id.* at Art. IV(1).

> the performance of, or the exercise of, his or her official duties in order to achieve any favour or compromise in relation to the proposed investment.[41]

ECOWIC contains clear and elaborate and appropriate transfer pricing and tax base diminution prevention rules that are not commonly included in investment treaties but are very common and serious problems. The basic rule is succinct:

> Investors and their investments shall conduct their operations in a manner that fully complies with all applicable tax laws and international standards relating to ensuring tax benefits are not reduced through base erosion and profit shifting practices. Investors and their investments shall provide the financial information required by the Member State to ensure compliance with the applicable laws.[42]

This does not, however, address the whole problem because the base erosion and avoidance of taxes occurs through transfer pricing that often fully complies with the applicable tax laws. The drafters knew this and the difficulty of adding substantive rules and opted for reference to existing OECD standards, stating: "(1) Investors and their investments shall ensure that all transactions with related or affiliated parties ('controlled transactions') shall be conducted in accordance with the arm's length principle. (2) The relevant international standard is the Organisation for Economic Cooperation and Development (OECD) 'Transfer Pricing Guidelines for Multinational Persons and Tax Administrations.' "[43]

Although the drafters' effort to add rules on the tax implications of transfer pricing and complex offshore transactions that often end up depriving the host state of tax revenues is commendable, this provision's impact to improve the situation is doubtful as it is mere reference to existing indefinite standards. In any case, consistent with the commentary on the wisdom of the addition of these kinds of obligations, the inclusion of substantive rules on this would also have been equally problematic. The end benefit of this provision appears to be psychological, as the taxation of the types of transactions that this provision refers to depends on each Member state's own domestic tax laws. As such, the fix to this problem must necessarily come from the domestic tax laws. Interestingly, however, the ECOWIC's tax related provision does not address this issue while it attempts to set guidance on the harmonization of double taxation treaties.[44]

[41] ECOWIC, Art. 38(1).

[42] *Id.* at Art. 44.

[43] *Id.* at Art. 41(1–2).

[44] *Id.* at Art. 45 ("(1) This Code shall not affect the rights and obligations of a Member State under Double Taxation Agreements. (2) Member States shall have the right to enter into double tax treaties, provided that whenever a harmonised ECOWAS tax regime is concluded it shall supersede existing double tax arrangements amongst Member States. (3) Member States shall endeavour to conclude regional and international treaties to avoid double taxation and to allow for the exchange of information between the fiscal authorities from the various jurisdictions. (4) Member States shall adequately examine the structure of their respective taxes over the income and profit of taxpayers, including identifying tax havens and examining their taxable basis, rates and fiscal administration through the establishment of a regional body in accordance with the ECOWAS Revised Treaty. (5) In the design and negotiation of Double Tax Agreements, Member States should take special care to maintain the right to collect the tax revenue income earned/sourced within the jurisdiction. (6) Member States shall develop rules and regulations to deter any attempt by a thirdcountry resident or any person or entity to obtain benefits from an income tax treaty for which it was not intended or qualified or to act as a conduit for profits").

Other Provisions

The ECOWIC gets into matters that are not typically considered part of an investment treaty including detailed rules on intellectual property rights, such as folklore,[45] competition rules,[46] and trade related investment measures.[47] The addition of these provisions including those that directly impose substantive obligations on the investor have the potential to create unprecedented problem for dispute settlement. Their interaction with the dispute settlement provision is discussed next.

Procedural Rules and Dispute Settlement

Both the Act and ECOWIC dedicate lengthy provisions to dispute settlement, but neither is a model of clarity relating to state-to-state, investor–state, or state–investor proceedings. The dispute settlement provisions of both the Act and the Code lump all categories of disputes into the same provisions and as such the discussion must proceed likewise. It begins with the 2008 formulation of the main dispute settlement clause in the Act. It is important to take note of the entirety of the provisions of these instruments to appreciate the deep-rooted dilemma and suspicion and the resultant confusion about dispute settlement processes in Africa's international investment law.

Chronologically, the confusion begins with a provision in the Act that attempts to link investor obligation with dispute settlement. It reads in full under the title, Relations of Investor's Liability to Dispute Settlement:

[45] *See* ECOWIC, Art. 49. For example, 49(2) states: "(a) For purposes of this Code, the term 'traditional knowledge' or 'folklore' means the practices, representations, expressions, knowledge, skills—as well as the instruments, objects, artefacts and cultural spaces associated therewith—that communities and groups in Member States recognize as part of their heritage which is transmitted from generation to generation, is constantly recreated by communities and groups in response to their environment, their interaction with nature and their history, and provides them with a sense of identity and continuity. Traditional knowledge or folklore includes but is not limited to—i. oral traditions and expressions; ii. the performing arts; iii. social practices, rituals and festive events; iv. knowledge and practices concerning nature and the universe; and v. traditional craftsmanship. (b) Where traditional knowledge or folklore is sought, used or exploited by investors in a Member State, or is otherwise relevant to their contracts, practices and other operations in such Member State, the investors undertake to protect traditional knowledge under the generally accepted international legal standards and best practices and to adhere to the following minimum standards. i. Local communities in Member States have rights of ownership over their innovations, practices, knowledge and technologies acquired through generations and have a right to collectively benefit from the utilization of such resources. ii. These community rights are to be protected in accordance with norms, practices and customary law found in, and recognized by the local communities in Member States whether such law is written or not. iii. Access by an investor to biological resources and knowledge or technologies of local communities in a Member State is conditioned on the prior informed consent of the local community with rights over the resources. Access carried out without such local consent is invalid. iv. Local communities in Member States may withdraw their consent to access or place restrictions on activities relating to access where such activities are likely to be detrimental to their socio-economic life, or their natural or cultural heritage. v. An investor seeking in the territory of a Member State a patent relating to biological materials or to traditional knowledge or to folklore must provide, as a condition of patent rights, (i) the disclosure of the source and country of the biological resource and traditional knowledge used in the invention; (ii) evidence of prior informed consent through approval of authorities in the source Member State; and (iii) evidence of fair and equitable sharing of benefits with relevant local communities in the source Member State."

[46] ECOWIC, Art. 50.

[47] ECOWIC, Art. 51.

> (1) Where it is established by a court of competent jurisdiction of the host State that an investor has breached Article 13 of this Supplementary Act, the investor shall not be entitled to initiate any dispute settlement process established under this Supplementary Act. A host or home State may raise this as an objection to jurisdiction in any dispute under this Supplementary Act.
>
> (2) Where an investor is alleged by a host Member State or an intervener in a dispute settlement proceeding under this Supplementary Act to have failed to comply with its obligation relating to pre-establishment impact assessment, the tribunal hearing such a dispute shall consider whether this breach, if proven, is materially relevant to the issues before it, and if so, what mitigating or offsetting effects this may have on the merits of a claim or on any damages awarded in the event of such award.
>
> ...
>
> (6) In accordance with the applicable domestic law, a host State or private person or organization, may initiate actions for damages under the domestic law of the host Member State, or the domestic law of the home Member State where such an action relates to the specific conduct of the investor, for damages arising from an alleged breach of the obligations set out in this Supplementary Act. The proceedings in the domestic law Court shall conform to the procedures applicable in the Community Court of Justice.[48]

Each subsection is a seed for considerable procedural confusion in real cases. The first subsection singles out Article 13 of the Act that deals with corruption[49] and turns it into a preliminary jurisdictional objection to "any dispute settlement established under this Supplementary Act." Bear in mind that a court of law of proper jurisdiction, presumably a domestic criminal court applying the anti-corruption law of the concerned state, must first establish that the investor is engaged in corruption. Regardless of this established corruption as a matter of criminal law (under article 30 reproduced in note 1602), the investor then desires to avail itself of the dispute settlement process

[48] Act, Art. 18.

[49] Act, Art. 13 ("ARTICLE 13: ANTI-CORRUPTION (1) Investors and their investments shall prior to the establishment of an investment or afterwards, refrain from involving themselves in corrupt practices as defined in Article 30 of this supplementary Act. (2) Investors and their investments shall not be complicit in any act described in Paragraph (1) of this article, including incitement, aiding and abetting, and conspiracy to commit or authorization of such acts. (3) The acts referred to Paragraph 1 and 2 shall be punishable in conformity with the provisions of Article 30 of this Supplementary Act"). The crossed referenced provision, Art. 30, provides: "ARTICLE 30: OFFENCES AND SANCTIONS (1) Member States shall consider as criminal the following offences and investigate, prosecute and punish the said offences with appropriate sanctions (a) the offering, solicitation or acceptance of an offer, promise or gift of any pecuniary or other nature, whether directly or through intermediaries, to any public official of the host State, for that official or for a third party, in order that the official or third party act or refrain from acting in relation to the performance of official duties to achieve any favour in relation to a proposed investment or any licenses, permits, contracts or other rights in relation to an investment; and (b) any acts constituting any of the acts described in Paragraph (A) including incitement, aiding and abetting, conspiracy to commit or authorization of such acts; shall be made criminal offences in the host Member State and subject to appropriate criminal enforcement and sanctions. (2) All home States shall ensure that any money or other forms of benefits encompassed in Paragraph (1) shall not be recoverable or deductible in any fiscal or tax policies. (3) Home States shall, when possible, provide all available information that might assist a dispute settlement tribunal under this Supplementary Act in determining whether there has been a breach of an anti-corruption obligation." Act, Art. 30.

of the Act. At that point, the host state is permitted to raise the established corruption as a jurisdictional objection. It must presumably say that because a court of law has determined that the investor violated anti-corruption laws, the tribunal or the court, as the case may be, should dismiss the case for want of jurisdiction. The latter proceeding is, therefore, limited to the determination of whether a court of law had in fact determined that the investor violated the host state's anti-corruption laws. Intended or not, this is simply an extraordinary complication in real cases.

The type of dispute settlement process that this jurisdictional objection is meant to preclude is discussed below, but then consider the application of the second subsection on pre-establishment environmental obligations. The tribunal seized of any matter between the investor and the host state must consider the impact of the failure to do pre-establishment environmental assessments on liability and/or damages if the host state raised it as a defense. Except when the dispute is over the environmental obligation itself, it is unclear how and why the issue of environmental obligation makes a part of all conceivable cases. This too is another example of an overzealous rule that adds to the compilation of the dispute settlement processes.

The provision regresses further and ties the Act's dispute settlement with other investor obligation provisions such as corporate governance and hygiene obligations,[50] and culminates with a contradiction in subsection 6 when it categorically grants the domestic courts of the host state primary jurisdiction over any lawsuit against the investor by the host state or any private party for the investor's violations of the Act's provisions on investor obligations. This essentially renders meaningless not only the Act's dispute settlement processes discussed below but also all the subsections that attempt to preclude access to such processes where they apply.

All of this prelude may give the impression that the Act is an attempt to filter appropriate cases for a sound and desirable dispute settlement system that it establishes. But a closer review of the dispute settlement provisions of the Act—even not considering the further complications that the ECOWIC added—suggests that it is not exactly the most cogent. Titled "Dispute Settlement Procedures," following elaborate amicable settlement provisions,[51] it states:

> (6) Any dispute between a host Member State and an Investor, as envisaged under this Article that is not amicably settled through mutual discussions may be submitted to arbitration as follows: (a) a national court; (b) any national machinery for the

[50] Act, Art. 18 ("(3) Where a host Member State or home Member State believes that an investor or its investment has breached Article 13 or has persistently failed to comply with its obligations under Article 14 or 15, and such investor or investment has been notified by the host Member State or home Member State, as appropriate, either the host Member State or the home Member State may initiate proceedings before a tribunal established by this Supplementary Act. (4) Where a persistent failure to comply with Article 14 or 15 is raised by a host Member State defendant or an intervener in a dispute settlement proceeding under this Supplementary Act, the tribunal hearing such a dispute shall consider whether this breach, if proven, is materially relevant to the issues before it, and if so, what mitigating or off-setting effects this may have on the merits of a claim or on any damages award in the event of such award. (5) A host Member State may initiate a counterclaim before any tribunal established pursuant to this Supplementary Act for damages resulting from an alleged breach of the Supplementary Act").

[51] Act, Art. 33(1–5).

settlement of investment disputes; (c) the relevant national court of the Member States.

(7) Where in respect of any dispute envisaged under this Article, there is disagreement as to the method of dispute settlement to be adopted; the dispute shall be referred to the ECOWAS Court of Justice.[52]

This is essentially the dispute settlement privilege that is seemingly guarded under the previous provisions. This provision is not logical. It begins by saying that if amicable resolution fails, presumably both parties have the choice of submitting a claim to one of three overlapping domestic court processes before submitting their disagreement to the Court of Justice for the resolution of their dispute about where to settle their dispute. The Act gives no guidance as to how the Court of Justice may resolve the jurisdictional priority among the "national court," "any national machinery," or "the relevant national court." Apart from the lack of clarity of the differences among these "courts," the task of assigning priority among them by the Court of Justice cannot be anything other than an unprincipled choice of forum for the parties. One might hope that there is some guidance in the Court's own rules that could offer direction, but that does not seem to be the case.

Established in 1991 by the ECOWAS Treaty,[53] the ECOWAS Community Court of Justice[54] has its own Protocol,[55] Supplemental Protocol,[56] Rules of Procedure,[57] and Practice Directions.[58] Article 9 of the Protocol states the Court's competence as follows:

The Court shall ensure the observance of law and of the principles of equity in the interpretation and application of the provisions of the Treaty. 2. The Court shall also be competent to deal with disputes referred to it, in accordance with the provisions of Article 56 of the Treaty, by Member States or the Authority, when such disputes arise between the Member States or between one or more Member States and the Institutions of the Community on the· interpretation or application of the provisions of the Treaty. 3. A Member State may, on behalf of its nationals, institute proceedings against another Member State or Institution of the Community, relating to the interpretation and application of the provisions of the Treaty, after attempts to settle

[52] Act, Art. 33(6–7).

[53] ECOWAS Treaty, Art. 15 ("ARTICLE 15: THE COURT OF JUSTICE, ESTABLISHMENT AND FUNCTIONS 1. There is hereby established a Court of Justice of the Community. 2. The status, composition, powers, procedure and other issues concerning the Court of Justice shall be as set out in a Protocol relating thereto. 3. The Court of Justice shall carry out the functions assigned to it independently of the Member States and the institutions of the Community. 4. Judgments of the Court of Justice shall be binding on the Member States, the Institutions of the Community and on individuals and corporate bodies").

[54] *See* the Court's official website at http://www.courtecowas.org/basic-texts/.

[55] *See* ECOWAS Court of Justice Protocol A/P.1/7/91 at http://www.courtecowas.org/wp-content/uploads/2018/11/Protocol_AP1791_ENG.pdf.

[56] *See* ECOWAS Court of Justice Supplementary Protocol A/SP.1/01/05 at http://www.courtecowas.org/wp-content/uploads/2018/11/Supplementary_Protocol_ASP.10105_ENG.pdf.

[57] *See* ECOWAS Court of Justice Rules of Procedure at http://www.courtecowas.org/wp-content/uploads/2018/11/Rules_of_Procedure_2002_ENG.pdf.

[58] *See* ECOWAS Court of Justice Practice Directions (2012) at http://www.courtecowas.org/wp-content/uploads/2018/11/Instructions_Chief-Registrar_Practice_Directions_ENG.pdf.

the dispute amicably have failed. 4. The Court shall have any powers conferred upon it, specifically by the provisions of this Protocol.[59]

Expanding the jurisdiction of the Court under this provision, the Revised Protocol added, among other powers, the jurisdiction to adjudicate extending to matters referred to it under subsections 7 and 8 of Article 3 of the of the Revised Protocol:

> 7. The Court shall have the powers conferred upon it by the provisions of this Protocol as well as any other powers that may be conferred by subsequent Protocols and Decisions of the Community. 8. The Authority of Heads of State and Government shall have the power to grant the Court the power to adjudicate on any specific dispute that it may refer to the Court other than those specified in this Article.[60]

These catch-all provisions are in addition to some specific jurisdictional grant.[61] By interpretation, therefore, it would appear that the Act's referral to "the dispute," whether that is the dispute about the appropriate dispute settlement mechanism or the actual dispute, gives the Court of Justice jurisdiction under its catch-all jurisdictional grant of the Revised Protocol, which refers to jurisdiction conferred by it by Protocols and Decisions of the Community, because the Act seems to qualify as one such Protocol or Decision of the Community. As such, when the Act says the matter can be referred to the Court as a matter of last resort, it is a jurisdictional grant under the Revised Protocol. It is, however, unclear whether a private investor could refer the matter to the Court.[62]

[59] ECOWAS, Court of Justice Protocol, Art. 9.

[60] ECOWAS, Revised Protocol, Art. 3(6–7).

[61] *See* ECOWAS Revised Protocol, Art. 3. The remaining subsections state: "Article 9 of the Protocol on Community Court of Justice substituted. Article 9 of the Protocol relating to the Community Court of Justice is hereby deleted and substituted by the following new provisions: "Article 9: Jurisdiction of the Court. 1. The Court has competence to adjudicate on any dispute relating to the following: a) The interpretation and application of the Treaty, Conventions and Protocols of the Community; b) The interpretation and application of the regulations, directives, decisions and other subsidiary legal instruments adopted by ECOWAS; c) The legality of regulations, directives, decisions and other legal instruments adopted by ECOWAS d) The failure by Member States to honor their obligations under the Treaty, Conventions and Protocols, regulations, directives, or decisions of ECOWAS; e) The provisions of the Treaty, Conventions and Protocols, regulations, directives or decisions of ECOWAS Member States; f) The Community and its officials; and g) The action for damages against a Community institution or an official of the Community for any action or omission in the exercise of official functions. 2. The Court shall have the power to determine any non-contractual liability of the Community and may order the Community to pay damages or make reparation for official acts or omissions of any Community institution or Community officials in the performance of official duties or functions. 3. Any action by or against a Community Institution or any Member of the Community shall be statute barred after three (3) years from the date when the right of action arose. 4. The Court has jurisdiction to determine case of violation of human rights that occur in any Member State. 5. Pending the establishment of the Arbitration Tribunal provided for under Article 16 of the Treaty, the Court shall have the power to act as arbitrator for the purpose of Article 16 of the Treaty. 6. The Court shall have jurisdiction over any matter provided for in an agreement where the parties provide that the Court shall settle disputes arising from the agreement."

[62] A recent commentary concludes: "From the foregoing survey it can be seen that the ECOWAS Court has—or might have—jurisdiction over a wide variety of possible claims by investors in ECOWAS Member States. There seems little doubt that the Court can adjudicate contractual disputes between foreign investors and their ECOWAS Member host States if their contracts so provide. It seems equally clear that ECOWAS Member States investors in other ECOWAS Member States benefit from the protections in the ECOWAS Supplementary Act on Investments, including the right to bring claims before the ECOWAS Court. It is

That seems to be a reasonable interpretation of the interaction of the various relevant provisions. Regardless, it is unclear why a modern effort meant to clarify and simplify matters employs such convoluted and indirect ways to refer jurisdiction to a standing court as a means of investor–state dispute settlement. As if this does not create enough uncertainty, the ECOWIC enters the foray with dramatic verbosity. Having laid out the state-to-state dispute settlement mechanism fairly clearly,[63] it offers the following options for what it calls "investor–state" and "investor–investor" disputes:

> Article 54: State–Investor or Investor–Investor
>
> (1) Any dispute between a Member State and an investor or between investors may be resolved through the use of consultations, good offices, mediation, conciliation, arbitration or any other agreed dispute resolution mechanism.
>
> (2) Where recourse is made to arbitration, the arbitration may be conducted at any established public or private alternative dispute resolution centres or the arbitration division of the ECOWAS Court of Justice. Member States and investors are encouraged to utilise regional and national alternatives dispute settlement institutions.
>
> (3): Where recourse is made to arbitration, the rules of procedure of the relevant forum shall be applicable, including rules for the submission of claims, selection of arbitrators and conduct of the arbitration.
>
> (4): Except where the investment contract between a Member State and an Investor provides for the use of international mechanisms such as ICSID or UNCITRAL, parties to the investment contract shall exhaust all local remedies including the ECOWAS Court of Justice or national dispute settlement systems, before resorting to the international mechanisms.[64]

Subsections 1 through 3 are all optional and, as such, of no consequence, but subarticle 4 injects an unintelligible twist by deferring to the dispute settlement provisions

less clear whether corporate investors can bring claims against ECOWAS Member States under the Court's human rights jurisdiction but the Court's most recent jurisprudence supports such a conclusion, and it seems uncontentious that individual investors can bring human rights claims. There is an argument that non-ECOWAS Member States investors might enjoy at least some rights under the Supplementary Act on Investments—in particular, the ability to bring claims before the ECOWAS Court alleging expropriation of their investments—but it would take a bold applicant to bring such a claim." Matthew Happold, *Investor-State Dispute Settlement using the ECOWAS Court of Justice: An analysis and some proposals*, ICSID Review (Mar. 2022), available at https://www.bilaterals.org/?investor-state-dispute-settlement-41351.

[63] ECOWIC, Art 53 ("State-State (1) Any dispute between Member States regarding the implementation of this Code shall be resolved through the use of consultations, good offices, mediation, conciliation or any other agreed dispute resolution mechanisms. (2) Where the parties are unable to resolve dispute through the preceding methods, they may proceed to arbitration. (3) Where recourse is made to arbitration, the arbitration may be conducted at any established public or private alternative dispute resolution centres or the arbitration division of the ECOWAS Community Court of Justice. Member States are encouraged to utilise regional and national alternatives dispute settlement institutions. (4) Where the Member States are unable to resolve any dispute regarding the interpretation and application of this Code through any of the preceding methods, they may refer the matter to the ECOWAS Community Court of Justice whose decision shall be final").

[64] ECOWIC, Art. 54.

that may be contained in the investment contract. If there is no agreement for ICSID or UNITRAL or similar arbitration in the investment contract, the parties must first exhaust domestic remedies including, strangely, the ECOWAS Court of Justice before "resorting to the international mechanisms." It is simply not clear what international mechanisms come after all these domestic and international processes have been traversed. This provision does not offer any binding rule on what the mechanism of last resort is in the absence of party agreement. This is additional evidence of continued dilemma and confusion.

The enforcement provision has the potential to fill a very small gap in enforcement rules. It states:

> (1) The final awards or decisions on investment disputes made by arbitration panels and judicial bodies shall be enforceable. To this end, decisions or awards rendered in another Member State shall be enforced as if there were decisions or awards rendered by a judicial body or arbitration panel located in a Member State requested to enforce the award or decision. (2) Decisions of ECOWAS Court of Justice shall be enforced in accordance with its own rules and existing protocols.[65]

The reference to "Decisions and awards rendered in another Member State" is probably to court decisions and arbitral award in situations where the parties voluntarily submit. In that sense, this may operate as a court judgment enforcement and arbitral award enforcement treaty which may overlap with the New York Convention and other regional court judgment enforcement treaties within the Community. It is useful to the extent there is a gap uncovered by all these possibilities. The last part on the enforcement of the ECOWAS Court Decision clarifies the obvious.

The last two provisions have a mixed review: the first adds confusion while the last adds clarity. The confusion in Article 56 on interpretation and application comes from its reintroduction of the Court's adjudicative jurisdiction on matters not only of interpretation but also application, which could bring back original jurisdiction unencumbered by the selection priorities set forth above, albeit permissive. This would mean that any dispute can be presented as a matter of application of the code and brought before the Court as a matter of default in situations where it is clear that the parties cannot agree on a forum. The specific rule is that "any dispute regarding the interpretation and application of this Code shall be referred to the ECOWAS Court of Justice whose decision shall be final."[66] Both the host state and the investor are expressly given access to the Court. To this effect, Article 57 states under the title "Access to the ECOWAS Court of Justice": "For the purposes of instituting or maintaining any action under chapter 16 of this code, access to the ECOWAS Court of Justice is open to Member States, ECOWAS Institutions, corporate bodies, investors and individuals." This is a good clarification of *locus standi* before the court, which includes investors.

[65] ECOWIC, Art. 55.
[66] ECOWIC, Art. 56.

Conclusion

Overall, the ECOWAS system contributes to the development of international investment law by incorporating some established substantive rules with some modification and by adding elaborate, new investor obligation rules. In doing so, it also added more confusion than clarification. The dispute settlement provisions are even more problematic. The long detour did not improve matters. Therefore, ECOWAS's effort of modern adaptation of international investment rules and procedures to Africa's specific circumstances remains a work in progress.

23
The Southern Africa Development Community

The Southern Africa Development Community (SADC) is a community of 16 Southern African countries[1] with its own Protocol on Finance and Investment that entered into force in April 2010. This chapter offers a detailed analysis of this Protocol as it makes up a significant part of Africa's international investment law regimes.

The Southern African Development Community (SADC) was established in 1992 by the SADC Treaty, which replaced its 1980 predecessor, the Southern African Development Co-ordination Conference (SADCC).[2] Signed on August 7, 1992, and first amended on January 1, 2001, and many times thereafter,[3] the SADC Treaty[4] sets forth the objectives and directions of the Community. Although the objectives

[1] *See generally* Southern African Development Community Website at https://www.sadc.int/.

[2] *See* History and Treaty, Southern African Development Community website, at https://www.sadc.int/pages/history-and-treaty. The SADC member states are Angola, Botswana, DR Congo, Lesotho, Madagascar, Malawi, Mauritius, Mozambique, Namibia, Seychelles, South Africa, Swaziland, Tanzania, Zambia, and Zimbabwe. *Id.*

[3] *See id.*

[4] Consolidated Text of the Treaty of the Southern African Development Community, signed Oct. 21, 2015, SADC Website, available at https://www.sadc.int/document/consolidated-text-treaty-southern-african-development-community. *See* SADC Treaty, Art. 5 ("1. The objectives of SADC shall be to: a. promote sustainable and equitable economic growth and socioeconomic development that will ensure poverty alleviation with the ultimate objective of its eradication, enhance the standard and quality of life of the people of Southern Africa and support the socially disadvantaged through regional integration; b. promote common political values, systems and other shared values which are transmitted through institutions which are democratic, legitimate and effective; c. consolidate, defend and maintain democracy, peace, security and stability; d. promote self-sustaining development on the basis of collective self-reliance, and the interdependence of Member States; e. achieve complementarity between national and regional strategies and programmes; f. promote and maximise productive employment and utilisation of resources of the Region; g. achieve sustainable utilisation of natural resources and effective protection of the environment; h. strengthen and consolidate the long standing historical, social and cultural affinities and links among the people of the Region; i. combat HIV/AIDS or other deadly and communicable diseases; j. ensure that poverty eradication is addressed in all SADC activities and programmes; and k. mainstream gender in the process of community building. 2. In order to achieve the objectives set out in paragraph 1 of this Article, SADC shall: a. harmonise political and socio-economic policies and plans of Member States; b. encourage the people of the Region and their institutions to take initiatives to develop economic, social and cultural ties across the Region, and to participate fully in the implementation of the programmes and projects of SADC; c. create appropriate institutions and mechanisms for the mobilisation of requisite resources for the implementation of programmes and operations of SADC and its institutions; d. develop policies aimed at the progressive elimination of obstacles to the free movement of capital and labour, goods and services, and of the people of the Region generally, among Member States; e. promote the development of human resources; f. promote the development, transfer and mastery of technology; g. improve economic management and performance through regional co-operation; h. promote the coordination and harmonisation of the international relations of Member States; i. secure international understanding, co-operation and support, and mobilise the inflow of public and private resources into the Region; and j. develop such other activities as Member States may decide in furtherance of the objectives of this Treaty").

Africa's International Investment Law Regimes. Won L. Kidane, Oxford University Press. © Oxford University Press 2023.
DOI: 10.1093/oso/9780197745571.003.0023

broadly include economic cooperation and harmonization, the Treaty itself contains only one reference to investment, reading:

> AREAS OF CO-OPERATION
>
> 1. Member States shall cooperate in all areas necessary to foster regional development and integration on the basis of balance, equity and mutual benefit.
>
> 2. Member States shall, through appropriate institutions of SADC, coordinate, rationalise and harmonise their overall macro-economic policies and strategies, programmes and projects in the areas of cooperation.
>
> 3. In accordance with the provisions of this Treaty, Member States agree to co-operate in the areas of: a. food security, land and agriculture; b. infrastructure and services; c. trade, industry, finance, *investment* and mining; d. social and human development and special programmes; e. science and technology. f. natural resources and environment; g. social welfare, information and culture; and h. politics, diplomacy, international relations, peace and security. 4. Additional areas of co-operation may be decided upon by the Council.[5]

Predicated on these principles, on August 18, 2006, SADC adopted its Protocol on Finance and Investment ("Protocol" or "SADC Protocol").[6] Although the objectives of the Protocol are very broad,[7] it states its specific investment objectives as: "State Parties

[5] SADC Treaty, Art. 21 (emphasis added).

[6] SADC Protocol on Finance and Investment, available at https://investmentpolicy.unctad.org/international-investment-agreements/treaty-files/2730/download. *See also Financial Sector Liberalisation*, SADC Website, at https://www.sadc.int/pillars/financial-sector-liberalisation (containing information about the process). The official description states: "The need to accelerate growth, investment and employment in the SADC Region through increased cooperation, coordination and management of macroeconomic, monetary and fiscal policies and to establish and sustain macroeconomic stability as a precondition to sustainable economic growth and for the creation of a monetary union in the Region urged SADC Member States to sign the Finance and Investment Protocol in 2006. Through this Protocol Member States acknowledge their collective duty to achieve economic growth and balanced intra-regional development, compatibility among national and regional strategies and programmes, to develop policies aimed at the progressive elimination of obstacles to the to free movement of capital labour, goods and services, and of the residents of the Member States, improve economic management and performance through regional cooperation, and to create appropriate institutions and mechanisms for the implementation of programmes and operations in the Region." *See Protocal on Finance and Investment*, Aug. 18, 2006, at https://www.sadc.int/document/protocol-finance-and-investment-2006.

[7] *See* SADC Protocol, Art. 2 ("1. This Protocol seeks to foster harmonisation of the financial and investment policies of the State Parties in order to make them consistent with objectives of SADC and ensure that any changes to financial and investment policies in one State Party do not necessitate undesirable adjustments in other State Parties. 2. The objective referred to in paragraph 1 shall be achieved through facilitation of regional integration, co-operation and co-ordination within finance and investment sectors with the aim of diversifying and expanding the productive sectors of the economy, and enhancing trade 16 in the Region to achieve sustainable economic development and growth and eradication of poverty by: (a) creating a favourable investment climate within SADC with the aim of promoting and attracting investment in the Region; (b) achieving and maintaining macroeconomic stability and convergence within the Region; (c) co-operating in respect of taxation and related matters within the Region; (d) co-operating and co-ordinating amongst State Parties in collaboration with Central Banks on exchange control policies; (e) establishing principles which will facilitate the creation of a coherent and convergent status in the legal and operational frameworks of Central Banks; (f) establishing a framework for co-operation and co-ordination between (amongst) Central Banks on payment, clearing and settlement systems; (g) co-operating in the area of information technology and communications technology amongst Central Banks; (h) co-operating on bank

shall co-ordinate their investment regimes and cooperate to create a favourable investment climate within the Region as set out in Annex 1."[8] Annex I contains elaborate substantive and procedural investment related rules. These rules are discussed in turn below.

Substantive Investment Law Principles

The principal objective of SADC's the investment law regime is the prescription of substantive rules. This section looks into these rules.

Meaning of Investment and Admission

The 2006 SADAC Protocol was adopted before the innovation rush but introduced unusual modifications of established principles that led the way for what came later in Africa's investment regimes.

Among the provisions that make it appear traditional at first sight is the meaning of investment defined as:

> the purchase, acquisition or establishment of productive and portfolio investment assets, and in particular, though not exclusively, includes: (a) movable and immovable property and any other property rights such as mortgages, liens or pledges; (b) shares, stocks and debentures of companies or interest in the property of such companies; (c) claims to money or to any performance under contract having a financial value, and loans; (d) copyrights, know-how (goodwill) and industrial property rights such as patents for inventions, trade marks, industrial designs and trade names; (e) rights conferred by law or under contract, including licences to search for, cultivate, extract or exploit natural resources: Provided that nothing in this definition shall prevent a State Party from excluding short-term portfolio investments of a speculative nature or any sector sensitive to its development or which would have a negative effect on its economy. A State Party that has invoked this provision shall notify the Secretariat for information purposes within a period of three (3) months.[9]

Many treaties exclude claims to money for purely commercial activity, but the Protocol appears to maintain the pre-innovation era expansive definition of investment.

As is always the case, the admission rules defer decisions to admit or defer to the domestic laws but call for expediency and predictability of the legal

supervision amongst Central Bank (i) co-operating in the activities of DFIs in the Region; (j) co-operating in the area of non-banking financial institutions and services; (k) facilitating the development of capital markets in the Region; (l) co-operating in the area of SADC Stock Exchanges; (m) co-operating with regard to anti-money laundering issues amongst State Parties; and (n) cooperation in respect of a SADC Project Preparation and Development Fund. 2 The objectives set out in paragraph 1, the implementation thereof and the mechanism for such implementation are fully described in the Annexes to this Protocol").

[8] SADC Protocol, Art. 3.

[9] SADC Protocol, Annex I, Definition (investment).

system,[10] including an obligation that "State Parties shall not arbitrarily, and without good reason, amend or otherwise modify to the detriment of investors, the terms, conditions and any benefits specified in the letter of authorisation."[11] This provision starts out as the classic regulatory stabilization rule but limits the stabilization to what is promised in "the letter of authorization." As such, it is a limited stabilization clause. The Protocol does, however, contain an independent and classic regulatory transparency provision.[12]

Investment Protection

The investment protection provisions are also traditional and robust with some significant modification in taxonomy.

Expropriation Comes First

The first investor protection provision is the expropriation provision. Although its place as the lead provision is highly unusual, its substantive textual formulation could not be more classical: It reads under the title "investment protection" in the most familiar classic Hull terms: "Investments shall not be nationalised or expropriated in the territory of any State Party except for a public purpose, under due process of law, on a nondiscriminatory basis and subject to the payment of prompt, adequate and effective compensation."[13] This is an established rule and the drafters of the SADC Protocol saw no particular reason to disturb it.

The Merger of FET and MFN and Reformulation of National Treatment

The Protocol unusually merges FET with MFN and does not directly contain a national treatment rule. It reads under the title "Investors of Third States": "1. Investments and investors shall enjoy fair and equitable treatment in the territory of any State Party. 2. Treatment referred to in paragraph 1 shall be no less favourable than that granted to investors of the third State."[14]

MFN oddly only qualifies FET. Therefore, MFN does nothing more than grant the best FET to all investors of the Community. The function of the MFN provision of the Protocol appears to be limited to providing the best FET to the extent that a third-party benefits from a better formulation of FET. Because this type of situation is highly unlikely, this formulation is quite strange and almost seems like a function of an odd drafting compromise.

In a clear attempt to avoid directly granting national treatment without seeming to reject it expressly, the parties added this unusual provision that preserves the Parties' autonomy to discriminate to achieve what is called "national development objectives":

[10] SADC Protocol, Annex I, Art. 2(1–2).

[11] SADC Protocol, Annex I, Art. 2(3).

[12] SADC Protocol, Annex I, Art. 8 ("State Parties shall promote and establish predictability, confidence, trust and integrity by adhering to and enforcing open and transparent policies, practices, regulations and procedures as they relate to investment").

[13] SADC Protocol, Annex I, Art. 5.

[14] SADC Protocol, Annex I, Art. 6.

> Notwithstanding the provisions of Article 6, State Parties may in accordance with their respective domestic legislation grant preferential treatment to qualifying investments and investors in order to achieve national development objectives. 2. State Parties undertake to eventually harmonize their respective domestic policies and legislation within the spirit of non-discrimination as set out in Article 6. 3. The provisions of Article 3 shall not apply to advantages, concessions or exemptions which may result from a bilateral investment treaty, Free Trade Area, Customs Union, Economic Union, Monetary Union or other multilateral arrangement for economic integration in which a State Party is participating or may participate.[15]

The breadth of this exception is such that it not only trumps National Treatment but also MFN, which in this case equals FET. As such, at the end of the day, all the investor protection provisions, except expropriation, are subject to "national development objectives." This is particularly worrisome because this is not about preference at the point of admission or exclusion, but it is about the treatment of an already admitted investment. As indicated in the previous section, these kinds of broad discretions that the Parties maintain to discriminate for "national development objectives" could potentially swallow the rule of nondiscrimination within an economic community.

Other Provisions

Three other areas covered under the Protocol are also notable. The first relates to environmental protection. This provision is only notable for its nondeparture from the classic "it is inappropriate" formulation:

> State Parties recognise that it is inappropriate to encourage investment by relaxing domestic health, safety or environmental measures and agree not to waive or otherwise derogate from, international treaties they have ratified, or offer to waive or otherwise derogate from, such measures as an encouragement for the establishment, acquisition, expansion or retention in their territories, of an investment.[16]

The next relates to regulatory space. It is also not particularly innovative. It simply states in familiar terms:

> Nothing in this Annex shall be construed as preventing a State Party from exercising its right to regulate in the public interest and to adopt, maintain or enforce any measure that it considers appropriate to ensure that investment activity is undertaken in a manner sensitive to health, safety or environmental concerns.[17]

This is a catch-all regulatory space protection provision that is so broad that it could potentially justify a wide range of restrictive measures at least in the enumerated areas.

The most notable and perhaps most useful provision is the harmonization provision. It states: "State Parties shall pursue harmonisation with the objective of

[15] SADC Protocol, Annex I, Art. 7.
[16] SADC Protocol, Annex I, Art. 13.
[17] SADC Protocol, Annex I, Art. 14.

developing the region into a SADC investment zone, which shall, among others, include the harmonisation of investment regimes including policies, laws and practices in accordance with the best practices within the overall strategy towards regional integration."[18]

This is not only consistent with the SADC Treaties, aspiration of creating an economic community, but also the promotion of the idea of an SADC investment zone. Whether the various exceptions to nondiscrimination rules help this effort is doubtful. There seems to be a serious disconnect between the primary objective of creating one investment zone and the addition of so many regulatory space protection rules in the Protocol. As will be explained further, the more recent instruments did not help clarify this problem, rather aggravating the disconnect in more ways than one.

Finally, the half-heartedness of the opening-up is demonstrated by the capital movements provision which allows movement with one hand and takes it away with the other: "State Parties shall encourage the free movement of capital. 2. Notwithstanding the provisions of paragraph 1, State Parties may regulate capital movements subject to their domestic laws and regulations, when necessitated by economic constraints."[19] It remains an optional opening-up measure. The allowance of such open-ended regulatory measures interacts with the investor protection provisions including the nondiscrimination rules in ways that could only be fleshed out if and when disputes arise challenging the measures as impermissibly discriminatory or confiscatory.

Investor Obligations

Unlike some of the more contemporary African instruments such as COMESA and ECOWAS, the SADC Protocol investor obligation provisions are traditional and modest. The key provision simply states: "Foreign investors shall abide by the laws, regulations, administrative guidelines and policies of the Host State."[20] Each state is thus entitled to prescribe its own rules holding investors to any number of obligations that it deems necessary, presumably subject to the nondiscrimination and expropriation provisions.

Unlike the treaty-based investor obligation, obligations contained in domestic laws require additional jurisdictional consent for dispute settlement purposes. That is to say that a violation of investor obligations assumed under domestic law may only be redressed through domestic processes, unless the investor expresses consent to arbitrate in the investment agreement or elsewhere under domestic law. It is important to note that one of the contributions of the investor obligation provisions in investment treaties is to allow host state counterclaims in ISDS, which is otherwise structurally constrained in traditional investment treaties that grant the investor rights without imposing any reciprocal and redressable treaty obligation on the investor. This goes beyond the mere convenience of consolidation of claims and defenses and may impact the filing of the claims in the first place, at least from a strategic point of view.

[18] SADC Protocol, Annex I, Art. 19.
[19] SADC Protocol, Annex I, Art. 15.
[20] SADC Protocol, Annex I, Art. 10.

Procedural Rules

Two not necessarily coherent procedural provisions of the Protocol address the settlement of disputes between a SADC member host state and a SADC investor. The first one concerns access to domestic courts:

> State Parties shall ensure that investors have the right of access to the courts, judicial and administrative tribunals, and other authorities competent under the laws of the Host State for redress of their grievances in relation to any matter concerning any investment including judicial review of measures relating to expropriation or nationalization and determination of compensation in the event of expropriation or nationalization.[21]

This comes first because the international arbitration provision that comes next rather unartfully enshrines a rule of exhaustion of local remedies in the following terms:

> Disputes between an investor and a State Party concerning an obligation of the latter in relation to an admitted investment of the former, which have not been amicably settled, and after exhausting local remedies shall, after a period of six (6) months from written notification of a claim, be submitted to international arbitration if either party to the dispute so wishes.[22]

Access to international arbitration is thus limited to instances where domestic remedy is exhausted, amicable settlement is attempted, six-month prior notice is given and the time has lapsed. Pursued in earnest, this is a multiyear undertaking to go through domestic administrative tribunals followed by judicial review proceedings. Even after this pre-arbitration process is overcome and not working, the arbitration process is itself not straightforward. Consider what the pertinent provision states:

> Where the dispute is referred to international arbitration, the investor and the State Party concerned in the dispute may agree to refer the dispute either to: (a) The SADC Tribunal; (b) The International Centre for the Settlement of Investment Disputes (having regard to the provisions, where applicable, of the ICSID Convention and the Additional Facility for the Administration of Conciliation, Arbitration and Fact-Finding Proceedings); or (c) An international arbitrator or ad hoc arbitral tribunal to be appointed by a special agreement or established under the Arbitration Rules of the United Nations Commission on International Trade Law.[23]

Domestic remedies having been exhausted, the parties to the dispute are then asked to agree to refer the same matter to arbitration. Not only that; they are also told to agree on one of three alternative options: SADC Tribunal, ICSID, or UNCITRAL. It is unclear why the drafters thought that a party who won all domestic proceedings

[21] SADC Protocol, Annex I, Art. 27.
[22] SADC Protocol, Annex I, Art. 28(1).
[23] SADC Protocol, Annex I, Art. 28(2).

would agree to relitigate or arbitrate the same matter before an international tribunal, but they were sure to include a mandatory selection of UNCITRAL arbitration if the parties fail to agree within three months:

> If after a period of three (3) months from written notification of the claim there is no agreement to one of the above alternative procedures, the parties to the dispute shall be bound to submit the dispute to arbitration under the Arbitration Rules of the United Nations Commission on International Trade Law as then in force. The parties to the dispute may agree in writing to modify these Rules.[24]

Ad hoc arbitration under the UNCITRAL Rules is thus the chosen means of dispute settlement under the SADC Protocol. Access to international arbitration for both the investor and the host state (where it wishes to proceed against the investor's violations of its obligation) is highly encumbered because of the requirements of exhaustion of domestic remedies. As indicated in each of the previous chapters, just like the other African REC investment instruments, the SADC Protocol also treats SADC investors in SADC less favorably than investors of third states especially because the MFN clause in the SADC Protocol equalizes FET only.

Finally, as a practical matter, the SADC Tribunal no longer exists. The Tribunal was set up by the SADC Treaty of 1992 and began its operation in 2005.[25] It was one of few tribunals that gave *locus standi* to individuals. Its supposed strength eventually caused its demise, because the member states decided to suspend it partly because of individual human rights cases involving expropriation and other rights violations claims brought against member states.[26] Its innovations and conceptual struggles remain relevant to the study of this area of law and continues to inform continued reform efforts.

Conclusion

The means of creating a unified investment area with a harmonized and conducive investment environment across member states remains as elusive for SADC members as it does for the RECs reviewed in the previous chapters. The same interactable dilemma lingers. The standards of treatment were modified but were not necessarily

[24] SADC Protocol, Annex I, Art. 28(3).

[25] *See Mandate* and *Suspension*, Southern African Development Community Tribunal, at https://ijrcenter.org/regional-communities/southern-african-development-community-tribunal/.

[26] *Id.* Some of the commonly cited cases include: Mike Campbell (Pvt) LTD and Others v. Zimbabwe, Case No. SADC (T) 2/2007, Main Decision of Nov. 28, 2008 (Case no. 2 of 2007); Barry L.T. Gondo and Others v. Zimbabwe, Case No. SADC (T) 05/2008, Main Decision of Dec. 9, 2010, (Case no. 5 of 2008); Cimexpan v. Tanzania, Case No. SADC (T) 01/2009, Main Decision of June 11, 2010 (Case no. 1 of 2009). *Id.* In 2012, SADC sought to establish a tribunal whose jurisdiction was limited to state-to-state dispute settlement for violations of the provisions of the SADC Treaty. It has not yet attracted the required number of ratifications. The revised Protocol is available at https://ijrcenter.org/wp-content/uploads/2016/11/New-SADC-Tribunal-Protocol-Signed.pdf.

made better. The dispute settlement provision is burdened with exhaustion and unclear escalation steps. The SADC Tribunal that was offered as one of the alternative fora turned out to be infeasible and suspended. In that sense, SADC's effort in improving Africa's international investment regime was as successful as the next REC, if not less.

PART V
AFRICA'S BILATERAL INVESTMENT LAW REGIME

The most significant source of international investment law in Africa, like everywhere else, is the network of Bilateral Investment Treaties (BITs). Globally there are at least 3,803 BITs, of which 2,219 are in effect.[1] About 852 of these BITs have at least one African party.[2] Although this number may seem large, it is only about 5.54% of the number of BITs needed to connect all 54 African countries with other African countries and the rest of the world.[3] In relative terms, with only about 190 Intra-Africa BITs, of which about 130 are not even in effect,[4] BIT connectivity in Africa is minimal. Moreover, Africa is also not moving in the direction of growing those numbers, opting instead for regional investment regimes, which may eventually lead to the realization of the African Economic Community.[5]

This part documents and analyzes the essential features of the Intra-Africa BITs by comparison with Africa's BITs with its economic partners of the West and the East. It is organized geographically as Africa–Western partners (Chapter 24), Africa–Eastern Partners (Chapter 25), and Intra-Africa (Chapter 26), and temporally by decades since the beginning of BIT activity in the 1960s.

[1] *See* UNCTAD International Investments Navigator at https://investmentpolicy.unctad.org/international-investment-agreements.

[2] *See* Erik Denters and Tarasio Gazzini, *The Role of African Regional Organizations in the Promotion and Protection of Foreign Investment*, 18 J. of World Inv. and Trade 449, 452 (2017).

[3] *Id.* at 453.

[4] *See* UNCTAD International Investments Navigator, *supra* note 1647. Arnaud Oulepo has done the computation for Kluwer Arbitration Blog, *see* Arnaud Oulepo, *AfCFTA, the Future Investment Protocol, and the Phasing-Out of Intra-African BITs*, Kluwer Arbitration Blog (Feb. 7, 2021), at http://arbitrationblog.kluwerarbitration.com/2021/02/07/afcfta-the-future-investment-protocol-and-the-phasing-out-of-intra-african-bits/.

[5] *Id.* at 469. *See* also Treaty Establishing the African Community, signed June 3, 1991, entered into force May 12, 1994) at Art. 6, available at https://au.int/en/treaties/treaty-establishing-african-economic-community ("Article 6 Modalities for the establishment of the Community 1. The Community shall be established gradually in six (6) stages of variable duration over a transitional period not exceeding thirty-four (34) years. 2. At each such stage, specific activities shall be assigned and implemented concurrently as follows: (a) First Stage: Strengthening of existing regional economic communities and, within a period not exceeding five (5) years from the date of entry into force of this Treaty, establishing economic communities in regions where they do not exist . . .").

24
Africa's BITs with Its Traditional Partners of the West

The drafters of the 1959 Germany–Pakistan BIT could not have imagined that it would at some future date be chronologically listed as the first of 3,803.[1] The decades that followed saw increased BIT activity primarily involving Germany, Switzerland, France, the Netherlands, and to a lesser extent, the United Kingdom.[2] The earliest African BITs are therefore unsurprisingly with these powers. The first Africa–West BIT was between Togo and Switzerland signed on May 16, 1961.[3] The same year, Switzerland signed a BIT with Tunisia, and Germany signed BITs with Morocco and Liberia.[4]

The 1960s, 1970s, and 1980s saw more BIT activity, with Western Europe dominating the landscape.[5] With few exceptions, most notably the 1980s first-generation China BITs with the Nordic countries and Ghana (1988), the BIT pattern of the initial decades was predominantly Afro–European.[6] It was also almost exclusively North–South.[7] One of the exceptions and perhaps the first Intra-Africa BIT was the 1989 Egypt–Tunisia BIT.[8]

The United States entered the BIT field in 1990 by signing one with Congo.[9] The 1990s and the decades that followed saw BIT activity in almost all directions, but the North–South character remained salient. As will be elaborated further in this chapter and the following, even within the same region or continent, BITs tend to remain wedded to their North–South genetic protectionist character in their occurrence and content,[10] until the recent reversal of trend propelled by the RECs discussed in the previous part and the Pan-African Investment Code discussed last.

[1] See a chronological listing of all known BITs at https://investmentpolicy.unctad.org/international-investment-agreements.

[2] *See id.*

[3] *See id.* The text is not publicly available.

[4] *See id.* French text available for Switzerland- Tunisia, and French, German and Arabic text available for Germany–Morocco, and English text available for German-Liberia.

[5] *See* UNCTAD Chronological Listing of BITs, at https://investmentpolicy.unctad.org/international-investment-agreements.

[6] *See id.* China–Sweden was signed and entered into force on the same day on Mar. 29, 1982. This was China's first BIT, and the beginning of a long era of its own. China–Japan (1988) could also be cited as one of the first Intra-Asia BITs. *See id.*

[7] *See* UNCTAD Chronological Listing, https://investmentpolicy.unctad.org/international-investment-agreements.

[8] *See id.* Text is available in Arabic.

[9] *Id.*

[10] Even within Africa, most of the BITs are between the more advanced economies and the least advanced ones, with Egypt and Mauritius dominating the field.

Africa's International Investment Law Regimes. Won L. Kidane, Oxford University Press.
DOI: 10.1093/oso/9780197745571.003.0024

Africa–West BITs of the 1960s, 1970s, and 1980s

In 1961, Germany signed BITs with three African countries: Togo, Morocco, and Liberia. The same year, Switzerland concluded one with Tunisia.[11] Taken as an example, the Germany–Liberia BIT, although one of the earliest few BITs, contains some of the most fundamental investment protection principles, albeit in a structural order that does not necessarily correspond to the BIT structure that later became more common along the lines of definition of investment: MFN, NT, FSP, FET, Expropriation, state-to-state dispute settlement, and ISDS.

Structurally the same, but with notable textual variation from the first known BIT (Germany–Pakistan),[12] the Germany–Liberia BIT begins with a rule on the admission of investment that defers to each party's domestic laws,[13] which is one of few BIT rules that has survived variation across the board and is faithfully included in almost every BIT to this day, barring ad hoc modifications by collateral instruments such as investment agreements. The provision that contains the admission rules adds a subsection incorporating both National Treatment and MFN in one brush as follows:

> (2) Investments owned by, or under the influence of, nationals or companies of either contracting party shall in the territory of the other contracting party not be treated less favourably by that party than it treats investments of its own nationals or companies or investments of nationals or companies of any third state.[14]

Bifurcating the same principles of National Treatment and MFN into two provisions, the next one offers similar protection in the following terms:

> Neither contracting party shall in its territory subject nationals or companies of the other contracting party, as regards occupational or business matters in connection with investments made by them, conditions less favourable than it imposes on its own nationals or companies or on nationals or companies of any third State.

[11] *See* UNCTAD Chronological Listing, https://investmentpolicy.unctad.org/international-investment-agreements, at Listing No. 3799, 3798, 3797, and 3796.

[12] Treaty between the Federal Republic of Germany and Pakistan for the Promotion and Protection of Investments (Germany–Pakistan BIT), available at https://investmentpolicy.unctad.org/international-investment-agreements/treaty-files/1387/download. Compare, for example, Art. 1 of each BIT. The German-Pakistan taxonomy is as follows: "(1) Each contracting State hereafter called in this Treaty a Party will endeavour to admit in its territory, in accordance with its legislation and rules and regulations framed thereunder the investing of capital by nationals or companies of the other Party and to promote such investments and will give sympathetic consideration to requests for the grant of necessary pemissions. In the case of Pakistan such permissions shall be given with due regard also to their published plans and policies." *See infra* Art. 1 of Germany–Liberia BIT at the following note.

[13] Treaty between the Federal Republic of Germany and Liberia for the Promotion and Protection of Investments (December 12, 1961) (German-Liberia BIT) at Art. 1, available at https://investmentpolicy.unctad.org/international-investment-agreements/treaty-files/1360/download ("(I) Each contracting State, hereinafter referred to in the present Treaty as 'contracting party,' shall in its territory admit the investment, in accordance with its legislation, rules and regulations existing or hereafter to be enacted and promulgated, of capital by nationals or companies of the other contracting party, promote such investments as far as possible, and give sympathetic con· sideration to the Issuance of any relevant permits required").

[14] Germany–Liberia BIT, Art 1(2).

> The same shall apply in respect of the management, use, or enjoyment of such investments.[15]

A combination of these provisions offers National Treatment and MFN in general and some specific terms. Interestingly, however, this BIT contains an additional independent and generic National Treatment provision, which reads: "Either contracting party shall grant national treatment within the framework of the present Treaty in consideration of the fact that national treatment in like manners is also granted by the other contracting party."[16] Because this was the beginning of the BIT era, how the formulation of these nondiscrimination provisions would evolve was at the time unknown.

This BIT does not contain FET, but combines Full Security and Protection and expropriation in one provision. It states in the now familiar FSP formulation in article (3)(1) as "Investments by nationals or companies of either contracting party shall enjoy full protection and security of the law in the territory of the other contracting party."[17] The next subsection of the same provision contains the expropriation provision in the following terms:

> (2) Investments of nationals or companies of either contracting party in the territory of the other contracting party shall not be expropriated except for the public benefit and against just compensation. Such compensation shall represent a fair value of the investment affected; it shall be actually realizable, freely transferable and shall be made without undue delay. Adequate provision shall have been made at or prior to time of the deprivation for the determination and the giving of such compensation. The legality of any such deprivation and the amount of compensation shall be subject to review by due process of law.[18]

Although the Hull Rule of prompt, adequate, and effective compensation was not an unknown concept at the time, this provision uses slightly different terminology to capture the same basic concept by using phrases such as "just compensation" and "fair market value." It adds a procedural due process component for the review of the legality of the expropriation, to see if it was "for the public benefit and against just compensation" or the adequacy of the amount of compensation regardless of the legality of the taking itself. These concepts would later become contentious as seen in the Libyan Oil cases of the 1970s discussed in Chapter 10.

This first Africa–Europe BIT contains a definition of investment that has had an enduring influence on the definition of investment that came in subsequent decades. Inserted in the middle of the text of the Treaty, rather than toward the beginning unlike most modern treaties, the definition of investment in the BIT succinctly captures most types of economic value that the BIT purports to protect. It reads in full:

[15] Germany–Liberia BIT, Art. 2.
[16] Germany–Liberia BIT, Art. 10.
[17] Germany–Liberia BIT, Art. 3(1).
[18] Germany–Liberia BIT, Art 3(2).

(1) The term "investment" shall comprise every kind of asset, and more particularly, though not exclusively all movable and immovable property as well as any other rights in rem, such as chattel real, mortgages, lines, pledges, usufructs and similar rights; b) shares or other kinds of interest in companies: c) titles to money or to any performance having an economic value; d) copyrights, industrial property rights; technical processes, trade-names. and good will; e) concessions under public law. Any alteration of the form in which assets are invested shall not affect their classification as investment.[19]

The dispute settlement provision is unsurprisingly limited to state-to-state disputes, as ISDS had not by then become the hallmark of the international investment law regime. The state-to-state dispute settlement provision unremarkably refers the dispute to ad hoc arbitration in these simple terms: "(2) If a dispute cannot thus be settled, shall upon the request of either contracting party be submitted to an arbitral tribunal."[20] The subsection that follows lays out the details of the formation of the arbitral tribunal in familiar order with the default appointment authority of the chair of the tribunal given to the ICJ president.[21]

The Kenya–Netherlands BIT[22] could be a good sample of the Afro–European BITs of the 1970s, albeit an imperfect indicator of what the other BITs look like. This BIT takes a significantly different approach from the Germany BITs of the 1960s because it focuses more on investment facilitation and encouragement than protection.

Its central principle is FET stated in the following terms: "Each Contracting Party shall ensure fair and equitable treatment to the investments, goods, rights and interests of nationals of the other Contracting Party and shall not impair the management, maintenance, use, enjoyment or disposal thereof by those nationals, by unjustified or discriminatory measures."[23] While this reads like a classic FET provision, it is not

[19] Germany–Liberia BIT, Art. 8(1–2).

[20] Germany–Liberia BIT, Art. 11(2).

[21] Germany–Liberia BIT, Art. 11(3) ("(3) Such arbitral tribunal shall, in each individual case, be constituted as follows: each contracting party shall appoint one member, and these two members, so appointed, shall agree upon a national of a third State as their chairman to be appointed by the Governments of the two contracting parties. Such members shall be appointed within two months, and such chairman within three months from the date on which either contracting party has informed the other contracting party that it wants to submit the dispute to an arbitral tribunal. (4) In the periods specified in paragraph 3 above have not been observed, either contracting party may, in the absence of any other relevant arrangement, invite the President of the International Court of Justice to make the necessary appointments. If the President is a national of either contracting party or if he is otherwise prevented from discharging the said function, the Vice-President should make the necessary appointments. If the Vice President is a national of either contracting party or if he, too, is prevented from discharging the said function, the Member of the International Court of Justice next in seniority who is not a national of either contracting party should make the necessary appointments. (5) The arbitral tribunal shall reach its decisions by a majority of votes. Such decisions shall be binding. Each contracting party shall bear the cost of its own member and of its counsel in the arbitral proceedings; the cost of the chairman and the remaining cost shall be borne in equal parts by both contracting parties. The arbitral tribunal may make a different regulation concerning cost. In all other respects, the arbitral tribunal shall determine its own procedure").

[22] Agreement on Economic Co-operation between the Government of the Kingdom of the Netherlands and the Government of the Republic of Kenya (Kenya–Netherlands BIT), Sep. 11, 1970, available at https://investmentpolicy.unctad.org/international-investment-agreements/treaty-files/1793/download.

[23] Kenya–Netherlands BIT, Art. 7.

sandwiched by the principle of National Treatment, MFN, FSP, and expropriation provisions in the familiar taxonomy and structural pattern.

The BIT does not define the term "investment," but contains a differently worded expropriation provision and another provision that could be considered a limited MFN. The expropriation provision reads:

> Any measures of nationalisation or expropriation, taken by either of the Contracting Parties affecting the investments, goods, rights or interests of their respective nationals in the territory of each other, shall be followed by payment of adequate compensation, transferable to the extent necessary to make it effective, within a reasonable time and in accordance with generally recognised rules of international law.[24]

It resembles the Hull Rule in that it requires adequacy and effectiveness, although it gives the expropriating state a reasonable time frame rather than constraining its authority by the standard of promptness.

The limited MFN provision reads: "1) Where any matter is governed by both the present Agreement and another international agreement binding on both Contracting Parties, nothing in this Agreement shall prevent a national of the one Contracting Party from benefiting by the provisions most favourable to him."[25] Beyond the willful ambiguity in the obligatory nature of the principle because of its "nothing . . . prevents" formulation, operationally, it is limited to benefits that derive from treaties that apply to both parties. Traditionally, MFN clauses equalize benefits across treaties regardless of the mutuality of the application to the present contracting parties. In other words, this particular MFN provision excludes superior benefits that may come from treaties that only one of the contracting parties is a party to. By definition, then, neither Party benefits from any other BITs that the other concludes with better benefits to its investors. Indeed, it is difficult to imagine what other treaties this MFN provision anticipates except perhaps multilateral treaties such as ICSID, the New York Convention, or some cross-regional treaties such as Cotonou Agreement.[26]

More importantly, however, the great majority of the provisions of the Kenya–Netherlands BIT is focused on promotion and cooperation rather than perfection. For example, the more pragmatic and facilitative approach is evident from how the first three provisions are formulated. The first provision is not a definition of terms but instead a statement of cooperation and facilitation: "The Contracting Parties undertake to promote their co-operation in the economic field. The Contracting Parties will cooperate to facilitate the participation of nationals of either Contracting Party in the establishment of productive and commercial activities and the provision of services in the other State."[27] This is followed by more cooperation and facilitation provisions:

[24] Kenya–Netherlands BIT, Art. 9.

[25] Kenya–Netherlands, BIT, Art. 15(1).

[26] *See Cotonou Agreement*, European Commission, at https://home-affairs.ec.europa.eu/pages/glossary/cotonou-agreement_en ("The Partnership Agreement between the members of the African, Caribbean and Pacific (ACP) Group of States of the one part and the European Union and its Member States of the other part, in order to promote and expedite the economic, cultural and social development of the ACP States, with a view to contributing to peace and security and to promoting a stable and democratic political environment").

[27] Kenya–Netherlands BIT, Art. 1.

> To further the achievement of the aims of the present Agreement, each Contracting Party is prepared, within the limits of its legislation, to authorize their respective nationals at their request to deliver capital goods to and carryout public works for governmental and private enterprises in the other State against payment by instalments. Each Contracting Party shall ensure in conformity with its legislation the transfer, when due, of any sums owing to creditors, who are nationals of the other Contracting Party.[28]

The facilitation approach is more express in the following provision:

> The Contracting Parties shall facilitate the intensification of commercial relations between their respective countries. They shall, within the framework of and subject to their national legislation, further the co-operation between the companies, associations, foundations and other organisations of any kind or subsidiary bodies thereof, which are connected with their economic life, and all their nationals engaged in economic activities, in order to develop their national resources.[29]

The following is specific to a sector that the two Parties considered essential in their bilateral relations: "The Contracting Parties agree to promote the development of international shipping services for mutual benefit."[30] This is followed by a broad MFN provision with respect only to tax matters.[31]

Overall, this hybrid facilitation-centric approach was not one that won the day with the great majority of the BITs that came in the following decades opting for a variation of the Germany protection-centric approach. Although the subsequent Dutch BIT models adopted some of the protection-centric approach, a review of the most recent model suggests that the facilitation roots remain evident.[32]

This earlier Dutch BIT contains no ISDS provision, but refers state-to-state dispute to international arbitration with the default appointing authority granted to the president of the ICJ like most of the BITs of the era.[33]

A good example of the 1980s Africa–West BIT is the 1983 Senegal–United States BIT. The US BIT Models do not have significant geographic variability, but are quintessentially North–South in content and occurrence. The BIT Senegal signed with

[28] Kenya–Netherlands BIT, Art. 2.

[29] Kenya–Netherlands BIT, Art. 3.

[30] Kenya–Netherlands BIT, Art. 4.

[31] Kenya–Netherlands BIT, Art 5 ("With respect to the payment of taxes, fees or charges and to the enjoyment of fiscal deductions and exemptions, each Contracting Party shall endeavour to accord in its territory to nationals of the other Contracting Party engaged in any economic activity the same treatment as it accords to nationals of third countries").

[32] *See, e.g.*, the 2019 Dutch BIT Model at https://investmentpolicy.unctad.org/international-investment-agreements/treaty-files/5832/download. The first substantive section (Section II) is on facilitation. Protection comes in Section 3. For example, Art. 3(4) states: "The Contracting Parties strive to strengthen the promotion and facilitation of investments that contribute to sustainable development, including but not limited through regular consultations between investment promotion and facilitation agencies and the exchange of information regarding investment opportunities."

[33] Kenya–Netherlands BIT, Art. 16.

the United States on December 6, 1983,[34] was the first US BIT Model unveiled a year earlier in 1982 for the purpose of ordering investment matters with less developed parts of the world.[35] It later came to be known as the 1984 Model and has been modified every decade since. The most recent is the 2012 BIT Model discussed in the sections below.

The 1983 Senegal–US BIT was a trial run. Although the United States was a latecomer to BIT activity, many of the core international investment law principles have deep roots in the United States as discussed in Chapter 1 of this book, including the origin of the Hull Rule.

The principle of nondiscrimination is front and center. It makes its first appearance in the preambular segment as "agreeing that discrimination on the basis of nationality by either Party against investment in its territory by nationals or companies of the other Party is not consistent with either a stable framework for investment or a maximum effective utilization of economic resources."[36] It packs all the classic nondiscrimination rules in one lengthy provision, which begins with the following broad National Treatment and MFN clause:

> 1. Each Party shall endeavor to maintain a favorable environment for investments in its territory by nationals and companies of the other Party and *shall permit such investments to be established and acquired on terms and conditions that accord treatment no less favorable than the treatment it accords in like situations to investments of its own nationals or companies,* and no less favorable than the treatment it accords in like situations to investments of nationals or companies of any third country.[37]

Although National Treatment and MFN with respect to treatment following admission became common in the decades that followed, the extension of this privilege or protection to admission itself has not and indeed the US BIT Model itself later retracted it in 2004.[38] Even the first US Model BIT permitted sector-based exceptions

34 Treaty Between the United State of America and the Republic of Senegal Concerning The Reciprocal Encouragement and Protection Of Investment, signed Dec. 6, 1983, entered into force Oct. 25, 1990, available at https://investmentpolicy.unctad.org/international-investment-agreements/treaty-files/2249/download.

35 *See* Valerie H. Ruttenberg, *The United States Bilateral Investment Treaty Program*, 19 U. PA. J. INT'L BUS. L. 121, 121–22 (1987) ("'On January 11, 1982, the United States Trade Representative announced the formulation of a prototype Bilateral Investment Treaty (Model BIT).' The BIT program is one aspect of the Reagan Administration's program for improving the climate for investment and capital flows worldwide, especially to the Less Developed Countries (LDCs). 2 The Reagan administration stresses that concluding BITs with developing countries will enhance the attractiveness of these countries to US investors by establishing a common frame of reference and commitment as well as a legal base for dealing with the complex problems that accompany direct private investment in any foreign nation. 'The Reagan administration wants to move away from the position of neutrality on foreign investment announced by President Carter in 1977,' a policy that neither promoted nor discouraged inward or outward investment flows").

36 Senegal–US BIT, Preamble.

37 Senegal–US BIT, Art. II (1) (emphasis added).

38 Compare the above with Article 3 of the 2004 US BIT model, which reads in relevant part: "1. Each Party shall accord to investors of the other Party treatment no less favorable than that it accords, in like circumstances, to its own investors with respect to the establishment, acquisition, expansion, management, conduct, operation, and sale or other disposition of investments in its territory. 2. Each Party shall accord to covered investments treatment no less favorable than that it accords, in like circumstances, to investments in its territory of its own investors with respect to the establishment, acquisition, expansion, management,

to the broad nondiscrimination rules as long as it is notified as part of the Treaty obligation.[39]

Merged into the National Treatment and MFN provisions appears FET in its classic formulation:

> Investment of nationals and companies of either Party shall at all times be accorded fair and equitable treatment and shall enjoy full protection and security in the territory of the other Party. The treatment, protection and security of investment shall be in accordance with applicable national laws, and shall in no case be less than that required by international law.[40]

It adds:

> Neither Party shall in any way impair by arbitrary and discriminatory measures the management, operation, maintenance, use, enjoyment, acquisition, expansion or disposal of investment made by nationals or companies of the other Party. Each Party shall observe any engagement it may have entered into with regard to investment of nationals or companies of the other Party.[41]

Although over the decades that followed the fundamental FET principle remained fairly stable in treaties, interpretive efforts in ISDS caused serious uncertainty regarding its outer limits. As such, the United States clarified is position in the 2004 BIT Model.[42]

conduct, operation, and sale or other disposition of investments." 2004 US BIT Model, available at https://ustr.gov/archive/assets/Trade_Sectors/Investment/Model_BIT/asset_upload_file847_6897.pdf.

[39] *See* Senegal–US BIT, Art II(3) ("3. (a) Notwithstanding the preceding provisions of this Article, each Party reserves the right to maintain limited exceptions to the standard of treatment otherwise required if such exceptions fall within one of the sectors or matters listed in the Annex to this Treaty").

[40] Senegal–US BIT, Art. II(4).

[41] *Id.*

[42] *See* 2004 US BIT Model, Art. 5 ("Article 5: Minimum Standard of Treatment 1. Each Party shall accord to covered investments treatment in accordance with customary international law, including fair and equitable treatment and full protection and security. 2. For greater certainty, paragraph 1 prescribes the customary international law minimum standard of treatment of aliens as the minimum standard of treatment to be afforded to covered investments. The concepts of 'fair and equitable treatment' and 'full protection and security' do not require treatment in addition to or beyond that which is required by that standard, and do not create additional substantive rights. The obligation in paragraph 1 to provide: (a) 'fair and equitable treatment' includes the obligation not to deny justice in criminal, civil, or administrative adjudicatory proceedings in accordance with the principle of due process embodied in the principal legal systems of the world; and (b) 'full protection and security' requires each Party to provide the level of police protection required under customary international law. 3. A determination that there has been a breach of another provision of this Treaty, or of a separate international agreement, does not establish that there has been a breach of this Article. 4. Notwithstanding Article 14 [Non-Conforming Measures](5)(b) [subsidies and grants], each Party shall accord to investors of the other Party, and to covered investments, nondiscriminatory treatment with respect to measures it adopts or maintains relating to losses suffered by investments in its territory owing to armed conflict or civil strife. 5. Notwithstanding paragraph 4, if an investor of a Party, in the situations referred to in paragraph 4, suffers a loss in the territory of the other Party resulting from: (a) requisitioning of its covered investment or part thereof by the latter's forces or authorities; or (b) destruction of its covered investment or part thereof by the latter's forces or authorities, which was not required by the necessity of the situation, the latter Party shall provide the investor restitution, compensation, or both, as appropriate, for such loss. Any compensation shall be prompt, adequate, and effective in accordance with

The one provision that has never gained traction with BITs over the decades is the entry and residence of natural persons. The Senegal–US BIT contained a fairly permissive entry and residence rule albeit constrained by national immigration rules.[43]

Bringing the long history of the Hull Rule to bear, the first US Model BIT concluded with Senegal states the classic expropriation rule in its most elaborate form as follows:

> No investment or any part of an investment of a national or a company of either Party shall be expropriated or nationalized by the other Party or subjected to any other measure or series of measures, direct or indirect, tantamount to expropriation (including the levying of taxation, the compulsory sale of all or part of an investment, or the impairment or deprivation of its management, control or economic value), all such measures hereinafter referred to as "expropriation," unless the expropriation; (a) is done for a public purpose; (b) is accomplished under due process of law; (c) is not discriminatory; (d) does not violate any specific provision on contractual stability or any specific provision on expropriation contained in an investment agreement between the national or company concerned and the Party making the expropriations; and (e) is accompanied by prompt, adequate and effective compensation.[44]

A version of this rule is contained in almost all BITs today. This one is remarkable not only for its clear expression of the Hull Rule of prompt, adequate, and effective compensation, but its addition of elements that may constitute indirect expropriation and

Article 6 [Expropriation and Compensation](2) through (4), mutatis mutandis. 6. Paragraph 4 does not apply to existing measures relating to subsidies or grants that would be inconsistent with Article 3 [National Treatment] but for Article 14 [Non-Conforming Measures](5)(b) [subsidies and grants]").

[43] *See* Senegal–US BIT, Art. II(5) ("5. (a) Nationals of either Party shall be permitted to enter and to remain in the territory of the other Party for the purpose of establishing, developing, directing, administering or advising on the operation of an investment to which they, or a company of the first Party that employs them, have committed or are in the process of committing a substantial amount of capital or other resources. (b) The rights set forth in this paragraph shall be exercised in accordance with the requirements of the laws and regulations of the parties relating to the entry and sojourn of aliens. The provisions of this paragraph shall be subject to the right of either Party to exclude or expel aliens on grounds related to the maintenance of public order, the protection of the public health, safety or morals, or national security").

[44] Senegal–US BIT, Art III. It continues to state: "Compensation shall be equivalent to the fair market value of the expropriated investment. The calculation of such compensation shall not reflect any reduction in such fair market value do to either prior public notice of announcement of the expropriatory action, or the occurrence of the events that constitute or resulted in the expropriatory action. Such compensation shall be paid without delay, shall be effectively realizable, shall bear current interest from the date of the expropriation at a commercially reasonable rate, and shall be freely transferable at the prevailing market rate of exchange on the date of expropriation. 2. If either Party expropriates the investment of any company duly incorporated, constituted or otherwise duly organized in its territory, and if nationals or companies of the other Party, directly or indirectly, own, hold or have other rights with respect to the equity of such company, the Party within whose territory the expropriation occurs shall ensure that such nationals or companies of the other Party receive compensation in accordance with the provisions of the preceding paragraph. 3. Subject to the dispute settlement provisions of any applicable agreement, a national or company of either Party that asserts that all or part of its investment in the territory of the other Party has been expropriated shall have a right to prompt review by the appropriate judicial or administrative authorities of such other Party to determine whether any such expropriation has occurred and, if so, whether such expropriation, and any compensation therefor, conforms to the provisions of the present Treaty." *Id.*

the four factors that may render expropriation lawful: public purpose, due process, nondiscriminatory, and non–breach of contract. Not all of these factors have gained the same level of following, with the stability factor gradually dropping and morphing into what came to be known as the stabilization clause.

The state-to-state dispute settlement is ordinary and clear and gives the default appointment authority to the president of the ICJ[45] like most BITs of the era; however, the ISDS provision suffers from lack of clarity because it was one of the first attempts. It contains escalation clauses, mixes domestic remedies, and culminates in ICSID arbitration.[46] Subsequent US Model BITs have improved and elaborated the ISDS provision.[47]

[45] *See* Senegal–US BIT, Art. VIII.

[46] *See* Senegal–US BIT, Art. VII ("SETTLEMENT OF INVESTMENT DISPUTES BETWEEN ONE PARTY AND A NATIONAL OR COMPANY OF THE OTHER PARTY 1. For purposes of this Article, an investment dispute is defined as a dispute involving the interpretation or application of an investment agreement between a Party and a national or company of the other party; the interpretation or application of any investment authorization granted by the competent authority of a Party to such a national or company; or an alleged breach of any right conferred or created by this Treaty with respect to an investment. 2. In the event of an investment dispute between a Party and a national or company of the other Party with respect to an investment of such national or company in the territory of such Party, the parties to the dispute shall initially seek to resolve the dispute by consultation and negotiation. They may, upon the initiative of either of them and as a part of their consultation and negotiation, agree to rely upon nonbinding, third-party procedures, such as the fact-finding facility available under the Rules of the Additional Facility ("Additional Facility") of the International Centre for the Disputes ("Centre"). If the dispute cannot be resolved through consultation and negotiation, then it shall be submitted for settlement in accordance with the applicable dispute-settlement procedures upon which the parties have previously agreed. In the case of expropriation by either Party, any dispute-settlement procedures specified in an investment agreement between such Party and Such national or company shall remain binding and shall be enforceable in accordance with the terms of the investment agreement and relevant provisions of domestic laws of such Party and treaties and other international agreements regarding enforcement of arbitral awards to which such Party has subscribed. 3. (a) Each Party hereby consents to the submission of any dispute between such Party and a national or company of the other Party to the Centre for settlement by conciliation or binding arbitration if, at any time after six months from the date upon which the dispute arose: (i) the dispute has not, for any reason, been submitted for settlement in accordance with any applicable dispute settlement procedures previously agreed to by the parties to the dispute; and (ii) the national or company concerned has not brought the dispute before the courts of justice or other competent tribunals of the Party that is a party to the dispute. If the national or company concerned consents in writing to the submission of the dispute to the Centre in the circumstances set forth above, either party to the dispute may institute proceedings before the Centre by addressing a request to this effect to the Secretariat of the Centre following the required procedures of Articles 28 and 36 of the Convention on the Settlement of Investment Disputes between States and Nationals of Other States done at Washington March 18, 1965 ("the Convention"). If the parties disagree over whether conciliation or binding arbitration is the more appropriate procedure to be employed, the opinion of the national or company concerned shall prevail. (b) Conciliation or binding arbitration of such disputes shall be done in accordance with the provisions of the Convention and the Regulations and Rules of the Centre. 4. A Party that is party to an investment dispute may not, at any stage of an arbitration or other dispute settlement procedure, raise as a defense the fact that the national or company that is the other party to the dispute has received or will receive, pursuant to an insurance contract, indemnification for all or part of its damages. 5. For the purposes of this Article, a company that is constituted or created by virtue of the law in force in the jurisdiction of one of the Parties but that, before the dispute arose, was owned or controlled by nationals or companies of the other Party, shall be treated as a national or company of such other Party. 6. The provisions of this Article shall not apply to a dispute arising: (a) under the export credit, guarantee or insurance programs of the Export-Import Bank of the United States, or (b) under other official credit, guarantee or insurance arrangements pursuant to which the Parties have agreed to other-means of settling disputes").

[47] *See, e.g.*, 2004 US BIT Model, Arts. 24–30.

Africa–West BITs of the 1990s and 2000s

There was increased BIT activity in the 1990s and more so in the 2000s, and Africa was an active participant. An example of the 1990s Africa–West BIT is the now-terminated Germany–South Africa BIT signed on September 9, 1995, and entered into force on April 10, 1998.[48] It is a modified version of Germany's initial BIT. It contains most of what came to be known as standard investment treaty substantive rules and dispute settlement mechanisms, albeit in not so common order and combination. The FET provision, for example, is combined with investment promotion under Article 2 as follows: "(I) Each Contracting Party shall in its territory promote as far as possible investments by nationals or companies of the other Contracting Party and admit such investment in accordance with its legislation. It shall in any case accord such investment fair and equitable treatment."[49] FET is not a part of the nondiscrimination provision, but a part of the promotion provision. This BIT does also contain a nondiscrimination provision both in the form of national treatment and MFN[50] as well as a nonexpropriation clause, in a fairly standard formulation.[51]

The dispute settlement provision is also standard, referring state-to-state dispute to ad hoc arbitral tribunals, and ISDS to ICSID or ICSID additional facility.[52] Although all of its provisions appear fairly standard, this was one of the many investment treaties that South Africa terminated for fear that the "standard" principles have been and would likely continue to be misinterpreted and misapplied.[53]

BIT activity in the 2000s was highly diverse, to the point that one has to scroll for pages to find an Africa–West BIT. For example, it was not until 2008 that the United States signed its 2004 BIT Model with any African country, and that was with Rwanda. The 2004 Model has made many modifications since the 1983 Senegal–US BIT. The Rwanda-US BIT[54] is modern and contains standard provisions in a more elaborated and more organized manner. Beyond the expansive definition of "investment," it has clear provisions on FET, including a useful interpretive annex for the first time,[55]

[48] Treaty between the Federal Republic of Germany and the Republic of South Africa concerning the Reciprocal Encouragement and Protection of Investments (Germany–South Africa BIT) (1995), available at https://investmentpolicy.unctad.org/international-investment-agreements/treaty-files/1416/download.

[49] *Id.* at Art. 2.

[50] *Id.* at Art. 3(1) ("(I) Neither Contracting Party shall subject investments in its territory owned or controlled by nationals or companies of the other Contracting Pany treatment less favourable than that it accords to investments of its own nationals or companies or to investments of nationals or companies of any third state").

[51] *Id.* at Art. 4(2).

[52] *See id.* at Arts. 10–11.

[53] *See The Protection of Investment Act, 2015*, Republic of S. Afr. Dep't of Trade & Industry (Jan. 23, 2016), http://www.thedti.gov.za/editmedia.jsp?id=3630 [https://perma.cc/ZB3Z-7EH5] ("the introduction of such investment protection legislation is consistent with recent global trends. Countries such as Canada, Australia, India, Brazil and Indonesia have all undertaken reviews of their [BITs] with a view to enacting reforms").

[54] Treaty Between the Government of the United States of America and the Government of the Republic of Rwanda Concerning The Encouragement And Reciprocal Protection Of Investment (Rwanda–US BIT) (2008), available at https://investmentpolicy.unctad.org/international-investment-agreements/treaty-files/2241/download.

[55] Rwanda–US BIT, Art 5 ("Minimum Standard of Treatment 1. Each Party shall accord to covered investments treatment in accordance with customary international law, including fair and equitable treatment and full protection and security. 2. For greater certainty, paragraph 1 prescribes the customary

National Treatment,[56] MFN,[57] and expropriation with an accompanying interpretive annex.[58]

international law minimum standard of treatment of aliens as the minimum standard of treatment to be afforded to covered investments. The concepts of "fair and equitable treatment" and "full protection and security" do not require treatment in addition to or beyond that which is required by that standard, and do not create additional substantive rights. The obligation in paragraph 1 to provide: (a) "fair and equitable treatment" includes the obligation not to deny justice in criminal, civil, or administrative adjudicatory proceedings in accordance with the principle of due process embodied in the principal legal systems of the world; and (b) "full protection and security" requires each Party to provide the level of police protection required under customary international law. 3. A determination that there has been a breach of another provision of this Treaty, or of a separate international agreement, does not establish that there has been a breach of this Article. 4. Notwithstanding Article l4(5)(b), each Party shall accord to investors of the other Party, and to covered investments, non-discriminatory treatment with respect to measures it adopts or maintains relating to losses suffered by investments in its territory owing to armed conflict or civil strife. 5. Notwithstanding paragraph 4, if an investor of a Party, in the situations referred to in paragraph 4, suffers a loss in the territory of the other Party resulting from: (a) requisitioning of its covered investment or part thereof by the latter's forces or authorities; or (b) destruction of its covered investment or part thereof by the latter's forces or authorities, which was not required by the necessity of the situation, the latter Party shall provide the investor restitution, compensation, or both, as appropriate, for such loss. Any compensation shall be prompt, adequate, and effective in accordance with Article 6(2) through (4), mutatis mutandis. 6. Paragraph 4 does not apply to existing measures relating to subsidies or grants that would be inconsistent with Article 3 but for Article 14(5)(b)").

[56] Rwanda–US BIT, Art. 3 ("National Treatment 1. Each Party shall accord to investors of the other Party treatment no less favorable than that it accords, in like circumstances, to its own investors with respect to the establishment, acquisition, expansion, management, conduct, operation, and sale or other disposition of investments in its territory. 2. Each Party shall accord to covered investments treatment no less favorable than that it accords, in like circumstances, to investments in its territory of its own investors with respect to the establishment, acquisition, expansion, management, conduct, operation, and sale or other disposition of investments. 3. The treatment to be accorded by a Party under paragraphs I and 2 means, with respect to a regional level of government, treatment no less favorable than the treatment accorded, in like circumstances, by that regional level of government to natural persons resident in and enterprises constituted under the laws of other regional levels of government of the Party of which it forms a part, and to their respective investments").

[57] Rwanda–US BIT, Art 4 ("Most-Favored-Nation Treatment 1. Each Party shall accord to investors of the other Party treatment no less favorable than that it accords, in like circumstances, to investors of any non-party with respect to the establishment, acquisition, expansion, management, conduct, operation, and sale or other disposition of investments in its territory. 2. Each Party shall accord to covered investments treatment no less favorable than that it accords, in like circumstances, to investments in its territory of investors of any non-Party with respect to the establishment, acquisition, expansion, management, conduct, operation, and sale or other disposition of investments").

[58] Rwanda–US BIT, Art. 6 ("Article 6: Expropriation and Compensation 1. Neither Party may expropriate or nationalize a covered investment either directly or indirectly through measures equivalent to expropriation or nationalization ("expropriation"), except: (a) for a public purpose; (b) in a non-discriminatory manner; (c) on payment of prompt, adequate, and effective compensation; and (d) in accordance with due process of law and Article 5(1) through (3). 2. The compensation referred to in paragraph I(c) shall: (a) be paid without delay; (b) be equivalent to the fair market value of the expropriated investment immediately before the expropriation took place ("the date of expropriation"); (c) not reflect any change in value occurring because the intended expropriation had become known earlier; and (d) be fully realizable and freely transferable. 3. If the fair market value is denominated in a freely usable currency, the compensation referred to in paragraph I (c) shall be no less than the fair market value on the date of expropriation, plus interest at a commercially reasonable rate for that currency, accrued from the date of expropriation until the date of payment. 4. If the fair market value is denominated in a currency that is not freely usable, the compensation referred to in paragraph I (c)—converted into the currency of payment at the market rate of exchange prevailing on the date of payment—shall be no less than: (a) the fair market value on the date of expropriation, converted into a freely usable currency at the market rate of exchange prevailing on that date, plus (b) interest, at a commercially reasonable rate for that freely usable currency, accrued from the date of expropriation until the date of payment. 5. This Article does not apply to the issuance of compulsory licenses granted in relation to intellectual property rights in accordance with the TRIPS Agreement, or to

The 2004 Model also contained provisions on the environment,[59] labor and employment,[60] and transparency and publication requirements.[61] Moreover, both state-to-state and investor state dispute settlement provisions were also included in unusually elaborate terms.[62]

The 2008 Rwanda–US BIT is not only evidence of increased BIT activity, but also evidence of the realization that the previous and relatively brief BITs that contained some of the fundamental investment protection principles such as FET, expropriation, and dispute settlement were problematic. This was not limited to the US BITs, but it was representative of a global effort to address some of the criticism of the ISDS system that applied poorly defined substantive standards. The *Strabag v. Rwanda* case discussed in Part II as arbitrated under this Rwanda US BIT.

Contemporary Africa–West BITs

The most contemporary Africa–West BITs are those concluded in the post-Brexit era designated as such because of Britain's dominance in the treaty field since 2019. The examination of the latest 100 bilateral investment-related activities shows no pattern whatsoever except one notable development: the United Kingdom's post-Brexit robust treaty activity in the form of Trade and Partnership Agreements with states from a wide range of the developmental spectrum, including many African states.[63] Indeed, among the more than 500 BITs signed in the last decade since 2010, Africa–West BITs have only been occasional punctuations. As a matter of fact, excluding the most recent UK Trade and Partnership Agreements, there are no more than 15 Africa–West BITs, with nine of them concluded by Canada and two by Switzerland.[64] Canada signed the same model BIT with Benin and Tanzania in 2013; Cameroon, Nigeria, Senegal, Mali, and Cote d'Ivoire in 2014; and Guinea and Burkina Faso in 2015.[65] Switzerland signed one with Tunisia in 2012 and Egypt in 2010.[66]

These three models—the post-Brexit UK Trade and Partnership Agreement, the Canadian Model signed in 2015 and 2013, and the Swiss Model signed in 2012 and 2010—are profiled in this section in reverse chronological order below.

The post-Brexit UK agreements are mostly trade-related interim partnership agreements with some sporadic investment promotion and protection provisions.

the revocation, limitation, or creation of intellectual property rights, to the extent that such issuance, revocation, limitation, or creation is consistent with the TRIPS Agreement").

[59] Rwanda–US BIT, Art. 12.
[60] Rwanda–US BIT, Art. 13.
[61] Rwanda–US BIT, Art. 11.
[62] Rwanda–US BIT, Arts. 23–30.
[63] *See* latest 100 BITs (2019–2022) on UNCTAD International Investments Navigator at https://investmentpolicy.unctad.org/international-investment-agreements.
[64] *See id.* in reverse chronological order.
[65] *See id.* at No. 258, 263, 353, 369.
[66] *See id.* at No. 375, 489.

For example, the UK–Cameroon Economic Partnership Agreement[67] makes 28 references to investment, but the core protection provision is as simple as the following:

> 1. The UK and Cameroon affirm the need to promote and protect the other Party's investments on their respective territories. 2. In order to encourage UK investment in development projects of special importance to, and promoted by Cameroon, the UK, on the one hand, and Cameroon, on the other, may also conclude agreements relating to specific projects of mutual interest where UK enterprises contribute towards their financing.[68]

Although UNCTAD lists these UK Interim Partnership Agreements as a part of its investment treaties collection, these agreements make no more than frantic reference to investment suggesting that these are just placeholders for future agreements, if any. As to what model the United Kingdom would take, this is not suggested in these interim agreements.[69] Incidentally, unlike these UK Agreements with the African states, the post-Brexit UK–Australia Free Trade Agreement signed in December 2021[70] contains full-fledged investment rules that could be characterized as traditional at its core,[71] indicating the direction that the United Kingdom might be going to replace its interim agreements with its African partners.

Canada's signing of nine BITs with African states within a short period of time between 2013 and 2015 had at the time attracted speculative commentary on the

[67] Interim Agreement establishing an Economic Partnership Agreement between the United Kingdom of Great Britain and Northern Ireland, of the one part and the Republic of Cameroon, of the other part London (March 9, 2021), available at https://investmentpolicy.unctad.org/international-investment-agreements/treaty-files/6343/download.

[68] *Id.* at Annex V, Art. 11.

[69] *See, e.g.*, Interim Trade Partnership Agreement between the United Kingdom of Great Britain and Northern Ireland, of the one part and the Republic of Ghana, of the other part London, March 2, 2021 [Agreement is not in force], available at https://investmentpolicy.unctad.org/international-investment-agreements/treaty-files/6344/download. It makes seven references to investment but makes no suggestion as to what might follow.

[70] UK–Australia Free Trade Agreement (investment sections), available at https://investmentpolicy.unctad.org/international-investment-agreements/treaty-files/6372/download.

[71] *See, e.g.*, *id.* at Art. 13 on Minimum Treatment (FET) ("Minimum Standard of Treatment11 1. Each Party shall accord to covered investments treatment in accordance with applicable customary international law principles, including fair and equitable treatment and full protection and security. 2. For greater certainty, paragraph 1 prescribes the customary international law minimum standard of treatment of aliens as the standard of treatment to be afforded to covered investments. The concepts of "fair and equitable treatment" and "full protection and security" do not require treatment in addition to or beyond that which is required by that standard, and do not create additional substantive rights. The obligation in paragraph 1 to provide: (a) "fair and equitable treatment" includes the obligation not to deny justice in criminal, civil, or administrative adjudicatory proceedings in accordance with the principle of due process embodied in the principal legal systems of the world; and (b) "full protection and security" requires each Party to provide the level of police protection required under customary international law. 3. A determination that there has been a breach of another provision of this Agreement, or of a separate international agreement, does not establish that there has been a breach of this Article. 4. For greater certainty, the mere fact that a Party takes or fails to take an action that may be inconsistent with an investor's expectations does not constitute a breach of this Article, even if there is loss or damage to the covered investment as a result. 5. For greater certainty, the mere fact that a subsidy or grant has not been issued, renewed or maintained, or has been modified or reduced, by a Party, does not constitute a breach of this Article, even if there is loss or damage to the covered investment as a result").

motives,[72] but on the substance and procedure, it was primarily based on Canada's 2004 BIT Model with some post-2010 inclusion of nonmandatory environmental and labor-related standards.[73]

The Canadian BIT model that the African states have signed is one of the principal instruments that moved BITs in a more modern direction by elaborating many of the substantive principles and dispute settlement rules without significantly altering their basic characters. Canada has further modernized its Model BIT, most recently in 2021.[74]

Taking the 2014 Nigeria–Canada BIT[75] as an example, the key substantive investment protection provisions such as National Treatment,[76] MFN,[77] and

[72] *See, e.g.*, Rainbow Willard and Sarah Morreau, *The Canadian Model BIT—A Step in the Right Direction for Canadian Investment in Africa?* (July 18, 2015), at http://arbitrationblog.kluwerarbitration.com/2015/07/18/the-canadian-model-bit-a-step-in-the-right-direction-for-canadian-investment-in-africa/ ("Signing BITs with these African states suggests that Canada's foreign investment in Africa will continue to focus on the mining and energy sectors. For example, Canada is the largest foreign investor in Burkina Faso, resulting primarily from the gold mining industry—gold has been Burkina Faso's primary export since 2008. Canada also has identified mining as a key opportunity for Canadian investors in the Cote d'Ivoire, Mali, and Senegal. Ghana and the Cote d'Ivoire both started to produce oil in 2013, so the petroleum industry in those states is ripe for investment from Canadian oil and gas exploration and production companies").

[73] *See id.* for the suggestion that the CRS and labor provisions were added in 2010.

[74] *See generally* The Government of Canada, *Canada's 2021 Foreign Investment Promotion and Protection Agreement (FIPA) Model*, at https://www.international.gc.ca/trade-commerce/trade-agreements-accords-commerciaux/agr-acc/fipa-apie/index.aspx?lang=eng ("The Government of Canada has updated its model Foreign Investment Promotion and Protection Agreement (FIPA). This new modernized and inclusive model FIPA text will serve as the basis for Canada's future FIPA negotiations, and represents the first comprehensive revision since 2003. The new model benefits from innovations in recent free trade agreements, such as Canada–EU Comprehensive Economic and Trade Agreement (CETA), the Comprehensive and Progressive Trans-Pacific Partnership (CPTPP) and the Canada–US–Mexico Agreement (CUSMA). The model also reflects the Government of Canada's policy to ensure that the benefits of trade and investment are more widely shared, both in Canada and abroad. The development of the new model was informed by public consultations launched in 2018 to gather Canadians' views. A report summarizing the feedback received is available on GAC website. Informed by these broad stakeholder consultations, Canada's new modernized and inclusive model FIPA will: Provide a stable, rules-based investment environment for Canadian businesses investing abroad. Ensure all Canadians, including women, Indigenous peoples and SMEs, are able to benefit from these agreements").

[75] Agreement Between Canada and The Federal Republic of Nigeria For The Promotion And Protection of Investments (Nigeria–Canada BIT), at https://investmentpolicy.unctad.org/international-investment-agreements/treaty-files/3151/download.

[76] *Id.* at Art. 4 ("1. Each Party shall accord to an investor of the other Party treatment no less favourable than that it accords, in like circumstances, to its own investors with respect to the establishment, acquisition, expansion, management, conduct, operation and sale or other disposition of an investment in its territory. 2. Each Party shall accord to a covered investment treatment no less favourable than that it accords, in like circumstances, to investments of its own investors with respect to the establishment, acquisition, expansion, management, conduct, operation and sale or other disposition of an investment in its territory. 3. The treatment accorded by a Party under paragraphs 1 and 2 means, with respect to a sub-national government, treatment accorded, in like circumstances, by that sub-national government to investors, and to investments of investors, of the Party of which it forms a part").

[77] *Id.* at Art. 5 ("Most-Favoured-Nation Treatment 1. Each Party shall accord to an investor of the other Party treatment no less favourable than that it accords, in like circumstances, to investors of a non-Party with respect to the establishment, acquisition, expansion, management, conduct, operation and sale or other disposition of an investment in its territory. 2. Each Party shall accord to a covered investment treatment no less favourable than that it accords, in like circumstances, to investments of investors of a non-Party with respect to the establishment, acquisition, expansion, management, conduct, operation and sale or other disposition of an investment in its territory. 3. For greater certainty, the treatment accorded by a Party under paragraphs 1 and 2 means, with respect to a sub-national government, treatment accorded,

FET[78] are enshrined with reasonable clarity, although this particular model does not attach interpretive text in an annex, a practice that later became common. Expropriation is kept in its classic formulation, but accompanied by an annexed useful interpretive aid.[79] While the ISDS provision is elaborated across several detailed provisions,[80] at the end it has not changed its fundamental ICSID arbitration model, perhaps with the exception of the addition of transparency as a default rule[81] and permission of the submission by third parties of amicus briefs, provided they are not disruptive of the process.[82] Incidentally, the Model that Canada signed with the African states is the same model that it signed with other nations during the same period, including with China in 2012.[83]

The Egypt–Switzerland BIT of 2010[84] offers evidence of some evolution in the investment treaty field since Switzerland's very first effort as one of two first players in the 1960s. Although informed by half a century of treaty activity and jurisprudence in which both Switzerland and Egypt were highly active players (albeit the former as the maker of rules and host to many cases and producer of high-profile arbitrators

in like circumstances, by that sub-national government to investors, and to investments of investors, of a non-Party").

[78] *Id.* at Art. 6 ("Minimum Standard of Treatment 1. Each Party shall accord to a covered investment treatment in accordance with the customary international law minimum standard of treatment of aliens, including fair and equitable treatment and full protection and security. 2. The concepts of "fair and equitable treatment" and "full protection and security" in paragraph 1 do not require treatment in addition to or beyond that which is required by the customary international law minimum standard of treatment of aliens. 3. A breach of another provision of this Agreement, or of a separate international agreement, does not establish that there has been a breach of this Article").

[79] *id.* at Art. 10 ("Expropriation 1. A Party may not nationalize or expropriate a covered investment either directly or indirectly through measures having an effect equivalent to nationalization or expropriation ("expropriation"), except for a public purpose, in accordance with due process of law, in a non-discriminatory manner and on payment of compensation in accordance with paragraphs 2 and 3. For greater certainty, this paragraph shall be interpreted in accordance with Annex B.10")

[80] *Id.* at Arts. 22–37.

[81] *Id.* at Art. 31 ("Public Access to Hearings and Documents 1. A Tribunal award under this Section shall be publicly available, subject to the redaction of confidential information. All other documents submitted to, or issued by, the Tribunal shall be publicly available unless the disputing parties otherwise agree, subject to the redaction of confidential information. 2. Hearings held under this Section shall be open to the public. The Tribunal may hold portions of hearings in camera to the extent necessary to ensure the protection of confidential information. 3. A disputing party may disclose to other persons in connection with the arbitral proceedings such unredacted documents as it considers necessary for the preparation of its case, but it shall ensure that those persons protect the confidential information in those documents").

[82] *Id.* at Art. 32 ("A Tribunal has the authority to consider and accept written submissions from a person or entity that is not a disputing party with a significant interest in the arbitration. The Tribunal shall ensure that a non-disputing party submission does not disrupt the proceedings and does not unduly burden or unfairly prejudice a disputing party").

[83] *See generally* Canada–China BIT, at https://investmentpolicy.unctad.org/international-investment-agreements/treaty-files/3476/download. *See, e.g., id.* at Art. 4 (Minimum Standard of Treatment 1. Each Contracting Party shall accord to covered investments fair and equitable treatment and full protection and security, in accordance with international law. 2. The concepts of "fair and equitable treatment" and "full protection and security" in paragraph 1 do not require treatment in addition to or beyond that which is required by the international law minimum standard of treatment of aliens as evidenced by general State practice accepted as law. 3. A determination that there has been a breach of another provision of this Agreement, or of a separate international agreement, does not establish that there has been a breach of this Article").

[84] Egypt–Switzerland BIT, available at https://investmentpolicy.unctad.org/international-investment-agreements/treaty-files/1113/download.

and the later as a respondent state in a disproportionate number of ISDS cases), these two parties kept the BIT very concise and simple. They kept most of the substantive provisions such as National Treatment, MFN, and FET simple, and merged into one provision, just like the old Swiss BITs did.[85] The expropriation provision is also unremarkable.[86] The Parties have also not made any effort to modify dispute settlement in any significant way, although they added an African Center (the Cairo Regional Center) as one of possible arbitral institutions that the investor may select alongside ICSID or ad hoc arbitration under UNCITRAL Rules.[87]

Conclusion

For the first few decades, BIT activity was almost entirely North–South and overwhelmingly Afro–European. It was unmistakably the reordering of old affairs that had been ordered differently. The failure of the global effort to conclude a multilateral substantive investment treaty that could have complemented the ICSID Convention seems to have increased BIT activity in every direction so much so that the latter decades saw a combination of South–South and North–North, and East–West BITs.

[85] Egypt–Switzerland BIT (2010), Art. 4 ("Protection, treatment (1) Investments and returns of investors of each Contracting Party shall at all times be accorded fair and equitable treatment and shall enjoy protection and security in the territory of the other Contracting Party. Neither Contracting Party shall in any way impair by unreasonable or discriminatory measures the management, maintenance, use, enjoyment, extension or disposal of such investments. (2) Each Contracting Party shall in its territory accord investments and returns of investors of the other Contracting Party treatment not less favourable than that which it accords to investments and returns of its own investors or to investments and returns of investors of any third State, whichever is more favourable to the investor concerned. Each Contracting Party shall in its territory accord investors of the other Contracting Party, as regards the management, maintenance, use, enjoyment or disposal of their investments, treatment not less favourable than that which it accords to its own investors or investors of any third State, whichever is more favourable to the investor concerned. (4) This treatment shall not apply to any advantage accorded to investors of a third State by either Contracting Party based on the membership of that Party in a custom union. common market. free trade zone or a regional arrangement of similar nature or by virtue of an agreement relating to avoidance of double taxation. (5) It is understood that the most favourable treatment referred to in this Article does not encompass mechanisms for the settlement of investment disputes provided for in other international agreements related to investments concluded by the Contracting Party concerned").

[86] *See Id.* at Art. 4 ("Expropriation, compensation Neither of the Contracting Parties shall take measures of expropriation, nationalization or any other measures having the same nature or the same effect against investments of investors of the other Contracting Party, unless the measures are taken in the public interest, on a non-discriminatory basis and under due process of law, and provided that provisions be made for prompt, effective and adequate compensation. Such compensation shall amount to the market value of the investment expropriated immediately before the expropriatory action was taken or became publicly known, whichever is earlier. (2) The amount of compensation shall include interest at a normal commercial rate (3) (4) from the date of dispossession until the date of payment").

[87] *Id.* at Art. 12 ("12(3) (3) If within six months the investment dispute cannot be settled through the procedure of amicable settlement and the investor is not satisfied with the outcome of the domestic administrative procedure, the investor may submit the dispute either to:—the courts of the Contracting Party in whose territory the investment has been made;—the Cairo Regional Centre for International Commercial Arbitration;—an ad hoc-arbitral tribunal which, unless otherwise agreed upon by the disputing parties, shall be established under the arbitration rules of the United Nations Commission on International Trade Law (UNCITRAL); or—the International Centre for Settlement of Investment Disputes (ICSID) provided for by the Convention on the Settlement of Investment Disputes between States and Nationals of other States, opened for signature at Washington, on March 18, 1965").

As time progressed, Afro–European BIT activity slowed down to the point that during the most recent decade there were almost none, with the exception of two Swiss BITs and the UK Interim Free Trade Agreements, with limited and inconsequential investment provisions.

The evolution of the substantive and procedural norms is not insubstantial but not entirely impressive. Some of the more recent BITs define some of the fundamental principles with more clarity but not enough to avoid increasing frustration with the jurisprudence that continued to impact the African states, which explains the slowing of African BIT activity in recent decades.

The Canadian effort to elaborate the substantive principles and procedures of dispute settlement in the BITs that it signed with more than nine African states since 2013 is the most notable development. Chronologically, these Canadian BITs are the most contemporary Africa–West BITs. Although by no means revolutionary, they set forth the substantive principles and dispute settlement rules with more clarity than ever.

25
Africa's BITs with Its Eastern Partners

Although it all began with Germany and Pakistan in 1959, BIT activity remained largely an Afro–European phenomenon throughout the 1960s and 1970s, with the exception of the Republic of Korea's few BITs in the mid-1970s.[1] The 1980s saw modest Asian participation in investment treaty activity with the signing in 1980 of ASEAN-EU treaty,[2] a first-generation Chinese BIT with Sweden in 1982, Japan-Sri Lanka the same year, and the China–Japan BIT in 1988.[3]

Africa–East BITs of the 1990s

There was increased Afro–Asian BIT activity in 1990s, although by no means comparable to the Afro–European levels. With the exception of the 1994 Egypt–Indonesia BIT, many of the 1990s Afro–Asian BITs were with China, including the Chinese BIT with Egypt in 1994; with Morocco in 1995; with Mauritius and Zambia in 1996; with Gabon, Nigeria, Congo, Sudan, and South Africa in 1997; and Ethiopia in 1998.[4] India also signed what appears to be its first set of African BITs with Egypt in 1997 and with Mauritius in 1998, complemented by a comprehensive economic partnership agreement in 2021.[5] Egypt had already signed a BIT with Turkey a year earlier in 1996.[6] There appears to be more Egyptian activity than anyone else's.[7] Indeed, Egypt was one of the major players in treaty activity in all directions during this period, which may incidentally explain the disproportionate number of ISDS cases that it faced over the decades.

One of the earliest Afro–Asian BITs between Egypt and Indonesia signed in 1994.[8] This BIT is brief and contains all the indicia of the older Afro–European BITs with some notable characteristics of its own related to the nondiscrimination provisions such as MFN and FET, but not National Treatment. Indeed, it contains an independent

[1] *See* UNCTAD Chronological Listing of BITs, https://investmentpolicy.unctad.org/international-investment-agreements. Korea signed one with the Netherlands in 1974, Tunisia in 1975, and the United Kingdom in 1976. *Id.*

[2] *Id.* at ASEAN Listing (The Association of Southeast Asian Nations).

[3] *Id.*

[4] *Id.*

[5] *Id. See* Comprehensive Economic Cooperation and Partnership Agreement (CECPA) Between The Republic of Mauritius and The Republic of India, at https://investmentpolicy.unctad.org/international-investment-agreements/treaty-files/6400/download. Although it does not contain elaborate investment related rules, it contains at least 30 references in the context of trade and related matters.

[6] *See* UNCTAD Chronological Listing of BITs, https://investmentpolicy.unctad.org/international-investment-agreements.

[7] *Id.*

[8] Agreement Between the Government of the Republic of Indonesia and the Government of the Arab Republic of Egypt Concerning the Promotion and Protection of Investment (Egypt–Indonesia BIT) (1994), available at https://investmentpolicy.unctad.org/international-investment-agreements/treaty-files/1079/download.

Africa's International Investment Law Regimes. Won L. Kidane, Oxford University Press. © Oxford University Press 2023.
DOI: 10.1093/oso/9780197745571.003.0025

FET provision, and mentions FET in the MFN provision, again in a somewhat unusual way. In that sense, it injects more confusion about FET than offers clarity. It is important to note how this was done for historic background of these principles about which tribunals and treaty drafters continue to struggle.

The first FET provision states: "Investments of either contracting Party shall at all times be accorded fair and equitable treatment and shall enjoy adequate protection and security in the territories of the other Contracting Party."[9]

An independent MFN also contains reference to FET as follows: "Investments of investors of one Contracting Party in the territory of the other Contracting Party and also the returns therefrom shall receive treatment which is fair and equitable and not less favorable than that accorded in respect of the investments of investors of any third State."[10]

It enshrines a standard nonexpropriation provision[11] and refers investor–state disputes to either domestic court, ICSID, or Cairo Regional Arbitration Center, by the investor's choice.[12] The addition of the Cairo Regional Center as one option is a consistent characteristic of the Egyptian BITs even as early as 1994. However, the BIT that Egypt signed with China the same year has entirely different character, because it is the earliest Chinese model BIT that limits international arbitration to the quantum of compensation,[13] although the nondiscrimination and expropriation provisions are defined with better clarity.[14] That is to show that even Egypt, by far the most active and matured BIT participant, did not escape variability based on the preferences of its economic partners, showing that the African parties are always junior partners in this field.

All of the BITs that China signed during this era with the African states mentioned above used the earlier Chinese Model. For example, the Ethiopia–China BIT of 1998 likewise limits international arbitration to the quantum of compensation,[15] a unique Chinse BIT characteristic of the 1990s that China changed subsequently.[16]

[9] Egypt–Indonesia BIT, Art. 2(2).

[10] Egypt–Indonesia BIT, Art. 3(1).

[11] Egypt–Indonesia BIT, Art. 4.

[12] Egypt–Indonesia BIT, Art. 9.

[13] Agreement Between the Government of the Arab Republic of Egypt and the Government of the People's Republic of China Concerning the Encouragement and Reciprocal Protection of Investments (Egypt–China BIT) (1994), Art. 9, available at https://investmentpolicy.unctad.org/international-investment-agreements/treaty-files/730/download.

[14] Egypt–China BIT, Arts. 3–4.

[15] *See* Agreement Between the Government of the Federal Democratic Republic of Ethiopia and the Government of the People's Republic of China Concerning the Encouragement and Reciprocal Protection of Investments (Ethiopia–China BIT) (1998), Art. 9, at https://investmentpolicy.unctad.org/international-investment-agreements/treaty-files/732/download ("3. If a dispute involving the amount of compensation for expropriation can not be settled within six months after resort to negotiations as specified in Paragraph I of this Article, it may be submitted at the request of either party to an ad hoc arbitral tribunal or arbitration under the auspices of the International Center for Settlement of Investment Disputes (ICSID) established by the Convention on the Settlement of Investments Disputes between States and Nationals of Other States opened for signature in Washington on March 18, 1965 once both Contracting Parties become member States thereof. The provisions of this Paragraph shall not apply if the investor concerned has resorted to the procedure specified in the Paragraph 2 of this Article. 4. Such an ad hoc arbitral tribunal shall be constituted for each individual case in the following way: each party to the dispute shall appoint an arbitrator, and these two shall select a national of a third State which has diplomatic relations with the two Contracting Parties as Chairman. The first two arbitrators shall be appointed within two months of the written notice for arbitration by either party to the dispute to the other, and the Chairman be selected within four months. If within the period specified above, the tribunal has not been constituted, either party to the dispute may invite the Secretary General of the International Center for Settlement of Investment Disputes to make the necessary appointments").

[16] For a comprehensive discussion of the Chinese BITs with African states, *see generally* Won L. Kidane and Weidong Zhu, *China–Africa Investment Treaties: Old Rules, New Challenges*, 37 FORDHAM INT'L

Contemporary Africa–East BITs

Afro–Asian treaty activity continued in the 2000s and 2010s with China dominating the field again, although Turkey, India, and Japan also signed a few.[17] Notable examples include China–Kenya (2001), Nigeria–Turkey (2011), Ethiopia–UAE (2016), China–Mauritius (2019), and Morocco–Japan (2020).[18]

The 2001 China–Kenya BIT is China's updated BIT model, which lifted the limitation of the international arbitration to the quantum of compensation that China signed with most of the African states in the 1990s, including with Egypt in 1994 and Ethiopia in 1998. Although the China–Kenya BIT lifted the restrictions of arbitration to quantum of compensation only, it added exhaustion of domestic remedies as a condition.[19] This is also evidence of the incrementality and hesitance of Chinese adoption of international arbitration as a favored means of dispute settlement.

The substantive investment protection provisions of National Treatment, MFN, and FET are incorporated in their classic formulation.[20] Indicative of the Chinese hesitation toward the notion of expropriation from the outset, the expropriation provision does not use the classic Hull Formula and leaves the determination of the legality of the expropriation to the domestic courts.[21] China being the one with the better negotiating power in this relationship, its insistence for domestic court involvement in the determination of legality is a matter of principle lingering from the previous model that limited arbitration to quantum.

The 2011 Nigeria–Turkey BIT is one informed by the controversies that surrounded principles such as FET and directly confront it by linking FET to the minimum standard of treatment under international law similar to efforts made by models such as the 2004 Canadian Model. It reads in relevant part: "Investments of investors made in the territory of the other Contracting Party shall at all times be accorded treatment in accordance with the minimum standard of treatment under international law including fair and equitable treatment and full security and protection in the territory of the other Contracting Party."[22] It offers National Treatment, MFN, and expropriation in fairly standard language,[23] but excludes the application of MFN to dispute settlement provisions countering the highly criticized arbitral decisions that imported ISDS third MFN where it otherwise did not exist.[24]

L. J. 1035 (2014); Won L. Kidane, *China–Africa Bilateral Investment Treaties in Comparative Context*, 49 CORNELL INT'L L. J. 141 (2016).

[17] *See* UNCTAD Chronological Listing of BITs, https://investmentpolicy.unctad.org/international-investment-agreements.

[18] *Id.*

[19] *See* Agreement Between the Government of the People's Republic of China and the Government of the Republic of Kenya on Promotion and Protection of Investments (Kenya–China BIT) (2001), Art. 9, available at https://investmentpolicy.unctad.org/international-investment-agreements/treaty-files/5532/download.

[20] Kenya–China BIT, Art. 3(1–3).

[21] Kenya–China BIT, Art. 4.

[22] Agreement Between the Government of the Republic of Turkey and the Government of the Federal Republic of Nigeria Concerning the Reciprocal Promotion and Protection of Investments (Nigeria–Turkey BIT) (2011), Art. 4, available at https://investmentpolicy.unctad.org/international-investment-agreements/treaty-files/2109/download.

[23] Nigeria–Turkey BIT, Art. 5(1–2), 9.

[24] Nigeria–Turkey BIT, Art. 11(6).

The 2016 Ethiopia–UAE BIT[25] is a modern balancing of the rights of the host states to regulate in the public interest and the protection of the investor's rights, not only because of its maintenance of the core protection principles and modification of the dispute settlement provision, but also its inclusion of some modest realistic investor obligations.

Beginning with the scope of coverage of the BIT, it clarifies that protection attached after the investment is admitted in accordance with the laws of the host state.[26] This has been an area of contention in many ISDS cases.

It then preserves National Treatment and MFN in their classic formulation, although it unartfully bifurcates them into different provisions risking needless repetition.[27] Most importantly, it takes the easy way out to eliminating the confusion surrounding the FET principle: deleting the provision altogether without obvious replacement.[28] In that sense, the core principles are thus National Treatment and

[25] Agreement Between the Government of the Federal Democratic Republic of Ethiopia and the Government of the United Arab Emirates Concerning the Promotion and Reciprocal Protection of Investment (Ethiopia–UAE BIT) (2016), available at https://investmentpolicy.unctad.org/international-investment-agreements/treaty-files/5947/download.

[26] *See* Ethiopia–UAE BIT, Art. 2(1) ("This Agreement applies only to investments once admitted in accordance with domestic laws, regulations and policies of the Contracting Parties").

[27] *See* Ethiopia–UAE BIT, Arts. 3, 4. It first states in Art. 3(3): "3. A Contracting Party shall accord investments of investors of the other Contracting Party protection no less favourable than that which it accords to investments of its own investors or to investments of investors of any third state." It then repeats the same in Art. 4, although it adds specifics: "Each Contracting Party shall in accordance with its laws and regulation, accord to investors and their investments of the other Contracting Party a treatment no less favorable than that which it accords, in like circumstances, to its own investors and to their investments with respect to the management, operation, enjoyment, or disposition of their investments in its territory." It further states the same notion in article 5 (1) as "1. Each Contracting Party shall accord to investors and their investments of the other Contracting Party a treatment no less favorable than that which it accords, in like circumstances, to investors and their investments to any third country with respect to the management, operation, enjoyment, export or disposition of their investments in its territory." The first one merges NT and MFN and omits "like circumstances" but the latter two separate NT and MFN and contain "like circumstances." This formulation leaves room for some confusion if and when these provisions are invoked individually.

[28] The closest to the replacement of the FET principle that this BIT's provisions come is through a combination of the right to regulate, exceptions, and denial of benefits provisions formulated as follows:

Article 18. Right to Regulate

1. In accordance with customary international law and other general principles of international law, the Host State has the right to take regulatory or other measures to ensure that development in its territory is consistent with the goals and principles of sustainable development, and with other social and economic policy objectives.
2. Non-discriminatory measures taken by a Contracting Party to comply with its international obligations under other treaties shall not constitute a breach of this Agreement.

Article 19. General Exceptions

1. Subject to the requirement that such measures are not applied in a manner which would. constitute a means of arbitrary or unjustifiable discrimination between investors or investments were like conditions prevail, nothing in this Agreement shall be construed to oblige a Contracting Party to pay compensation by adopting or enforcing measures designed and applied:
   (a) to protect public morals and safety;
   (b) to protect human, animal or plant life or health; or (c) for the conservation of living or non-living exhaustible natural resources.
2. Nothing in this Agreement shall prevent the Contracting Party from adopting or maintaining reasonable measures for prudential reasons, such as:
   (a) the protection of investors, depositors, financial market participants, policy-holders, policy-claimants, or persons to whom a fiduciary duty is owed by a financial institution;
   (b) the maintenance of the safety, soundness, integrity or financial responsibility of financial institutions; and
   (c) ensuring the integrity and stability of a Contracting Party's financial system.

MFN alongside nonexpropriation, which is maintained in its classic Hull formulation except for the deletion of "effective" from compensation prong of the provision.[29] Investor obligations are softly enshrined toward the end as follows:

1. Investors and investments are subject to the laws and regulations of the Host State.
2. Investors and investments shall strive, to the extent possible, through their management policies and practices, to contribute to the development objectives of the Host State and to the benefit of the local community where the investment is made.
3. An investor shall as far as possible provide such information to the Host State that may be required Concerning the investment in question for purposes of decision-making in relation to that investment or solely for statistical purposes. The Contracting Party shall protect any confidential business information from any disclosure that would prejudice the competitive position of the investor or the investment.[30]

Although the ISDS provision is unnecessarily burdened with permissive and time-bound escalation and alternative avenues, it culminates with the investor's right to

3. Nothing in this Agreement shall apply to non-discriminatory measures of general application taken by any public entity in pursuit of monetary and related credit policies or exchange rate policies. This paragraph shall not affect a Contracting Party's obligations under Article 7 [Transfer of Capital];
4. Nothing in this Agreement shall apply to a Contracting Party's measures that it considers necessary for the fulfilment of its obligations with respect to the maintenance or restoration of international peace or security, or the protection of its national security interests.
5. Nothing in this Agreement requires a Contracting Party to furnish or allow access to any information the disclosure of which it determines to be contrary to its national security interests:

Article 20. Denial of Benefits

1. Each Contracting Party reserves the right to deny the benefits of this Agreement to an investor if the national of a third country owns or controls the investment.
2. If a national of a Contracting Party acquires the nationality of a third state for the sake of the benefit of this Agreement by establishing a legal entity, he shall not be entitled the benefits of this Agreement."

[29] Ethiopia–UAE BIT, Art. 6(1) ("A Contracting Party shall not nationalize or expropriate investments in its territory (a) for the public interest; (b) on a non-discriminatory basis; (c) in accordance with due process of law; and (d) on payment of prompt, and adequate compensation"). The environmental and labor standards are also equally soft. *Id.* at Arts. 12 and 13:

> Article 12 Environmental and labour standards 1. Recognizing the right of each Contracting party to establish its own levels of domestic environmental protection and environmental development policies and priorities, and labour laws and standards, and to adopt or modify such laws, standards and policies, each Contracting Party shall strive to ensure that it provides for high levels of environmental and labour protection and standards and shall strive to continue to improve the same.
>
> Article 13 Corporate Governance Investments shall as far as possible meet national and internationally accepted standards of corporate governance for the sector involved, in particular for transparency and accounting practices.

[30] Ethiopia–UAE BIT, Art 11.

choose ad hoc arbitration under UNCITRAL Rules if all other options breakdown.[31] The Parties have also included a three-year statute of limitation for the investor to initiate an action.[32] Generally, the Ethiopia–UAE BIT appears to be a good, albeit imperfect, modern readaptation of the intricacies of international investment law to modern nonbinary economic relations.

The 2019 China–Mauritius BIT is a thorough revamp of the 1996 China–Mauritius BIT.[33] Informed by developments in the field since the 1990s, this most recent Afro-Asian BIT offers an example of the kinds of update that BITs have gotten more than half a century after their initial introduction.[34]

The Parties have not only carefully redrafted some of the key provisions, but also added explanatory footnotes where needed. It begins with the definition of investment. Note 1, for example, explains not only what is included but also what is not included in the definition of investment in the following terms:

> For greater certainty, some forms of debts, such as bonds, debentures, and long-term notes, are more likely to have the characteristics of an investment while other forms of debts, such as claims to payment that are immediately due and result from the sale of goods or services, are less likely to have such characteristics. Investment does not include claims to money that arise solely from commercial contracts for the sale of goods or services by a national or enterprise in the territory of a Party to a national or enterprise in the territory of the other Party, a bank letter of credit or an extension

[31] Ethiopia–UAE BIT, Art. 15(3):

3. If the dispute cannot be settled within six months after resort to a court or administrative tribunal, either party to the dispute shall be entitled to submit the dispute to the national or international arbitration tribunals. 4. The investor and the Contracting Party concerned in the dispute may agree to refer the dispute either to: a) the International Centre for the Settlement of Investment Disputes having regard to the provisions, where applicable, of the Convention on the Settlement of Investment Disputes between States and Nationals of Other States, opened for signature at Washington DC on 18 March 1965 and the Additional Facility for Administration of Conciliation, Arbitration and Fact-Finding Proceedings b) the Court of Arbitration of the International Chamber of Commerce; or c) an International Arbitrator or Ad Hoc Arbitration Tribunal to be appointed by a special agreement or established under the Arbitration Rules of the United Nations Commission on International Trade Law; or

d) if after a period of three months from written notification of the claim there is no agreement to one of the above alternative procedures listed under sub Article c, the dispute shall at the request in writing of the investor concerned, be submitted to arbitration under the Arbitration Rules of the United Nations Commission on International Trade Law as then in force.

5. The investor has no right to submit the dispute to the international arbitration in accordance with paragraph 4 of this Article, if more than 3 years is passed from the date on which the investor first became aware, or should have known about the origin of the circumstances that caused the dispute
6. The arbitral awards shall be final and binding for both parties to the dispute.
7. Each party to the dispute shall bear the cost of its representation in the arbitral proceedings. The cost of the arbitrators and the remaining costs shall be borne in equal parts by the parties to the dispute.

[32] *See Id.* at Art. (15)(5).

[33] Mauritius–China BIT (2019), available at https://investmentpolicy.unctad.org/international-investment-agreements/treaty-files/6073/download.

[34] *See* Mauritius–China BIT (2019) at Preamble ("For purposes of this Chapter: 1996 Agreement means the Agreement between the Government of the People's Republic of China and the Government of the Republic of Mauritius for the Reciprocal Promotion and Protection of Investments done at Port Louis on 4th May, 1996").

> of credit in connection with a commercial transaction, such as trade financing or any other claims to money that do not involve the kind of interests set out in subparagraphs (a) through (d).[35]

This is obviously a function of arbitral jurisprudence that struggled with the meaning of investment over the decades. Indeed, the actual definition of "investment" is essentially the codification of the *Salini* factors. It states: "Investment means every asset that an investor owns or controls, directly or indirectly, that has the characteristics of an investment, including such characteristics as the commitment of capital or other resources, the expectation of gain or profit, or the assumption of risk."[36]

The same pattern of explanation continues in the other provisions. For example, this BIT also adds explanatory notes for National Treatment and MFN clauses. The NT and MFN provision contains the "like circumstances" phrase that has been a subject of contention in many arbitral cases.[37] The note that follows the NT[38] and MFN provisions reads: "For greater certainty, whether treatment is accorded in 'like circumstances' under Article 8.3 (National Treatment) or Article 8.4 (Most-Favoured-Nation Treatment) depends on the totality of the circumstances, including whether the relevant treatment distinguishes between investors or investments on the basis of legitimate public welfare objectives."[39]

Relatedly, this BIT also corrects the ambiguity surrounding the application of the MFN clause to import dispute settlement provisions into BITs that did not contain them. It reads in relevant part: "4. For greater certainty, the treatment referred to in this Article does not encompass dispute resolution mechanisms or procedures, such as those included in Section B of this Chapter, that are provided for in international investment or trade agreements."[40]

The provision that is commonly considered FET has also gotten a useful upgrade in terms of clarity that could potentially be used by new efforts to codify international investment rules under the AfCFTA and beyond. It reads:

> ARTICLE 8.5: MINIMUM STANDARD OF TREATMENT 1. Each Party shall accord to covered investments fair and equitable treatment and full protection

[35] Mauritius–China BIT, Note 1.

[36] Mauritius–China BIT, Definition of Terms.

[37] One of the most frequently cited cases in this regard is the case of İçkale İnşaat Limited Şirketi v. Turkmenistan, ICSID Case No. ARB/10/24, Award (Mar. 8, 2016). The Tribunal considered the effects of the addition of the "like circumstances" phrase in relation to the "importation" of umbrella clauses via a most favoured-nation clause. *See id.* at ¶ 326.

[38] Mauritius–China, BIT, Art. 8.3 ("1. Each Party shall accord to investors of the other Party treatment no less favourable than that it accords, in like circumstances, to its own investors with respect to the management, conduct, operation, and sale or other disposition of investments in its territory. 2. Each Party shall accord to covered investments treatment no less favourable than that it accords, in like circumstances, to investments in its territory of its own investors with respect to the management, conduct, operation, and sale or other disposition of investments").

[39] Mauritius–China BIT, Art. 3, note 10.

[40] Mauritius–China BIT, Art. 8.4. The remainder of the MFN clause reads:

> 1. Each Party shall accord to investors of the other Party treatment no less favourable than that it accords, in like circumstances, to investors of any non-Party with respect to the management, conduct, operation, and sale or other disposition of investments in its territory.

> and security in accordance with customary international law. 2. For greater certainty, paragraph 1 prescribes the customary international law minimum standard of treatment of aliens as the minimum standard of treatment to be afforded to covered investments. The concepts of "fair and equitable treatment" and "full protection and security" do not require treatment in addition to or beyond that which is required by that standard, and do not create additional substantive rights. The obligation in paragraph 1 to provide: (a) "fair and equitable treatment" includes the obligation not to deny justice in criminal, civil, or administrative adjudicatory proceedings in accordance with due process of law; and (b) "full protection and security" requires each Party to provide the level of police protection required under customary international law. 3. A determination that there has been a breach of another provision of this Agreement, or of a separate international agreement, does not establish that there has been a breach of this Article. 4. For greater certainty, the mere fact that a Party takes or fails to take an action that may be inconsistent with an investor's expectations does not constitute a breach of this Article, even if there is loss or damage to the covered investment as a result. 5. For greater certainty, the mere fact that a subsidy or grant has not been issued, renewed or maintained, or has been modified or reduced, by a Party, does not constitute a breach of this Article, even if there is loss or damage to the covered investment as a result. 6. This Article shall be interpreted in accordance with Chapter 8-Annex-A (Customary International Law).[41]

Not only does this provision elaborate the contours of the principle, but also adds an interpretive annex that has become common in most recent BIT models including the Canadian Model. The Annex is useful. For example, it offers the following guidance to tribunals:

> The Parties confirm their shared understanding that "customary international law" generally and as specifically referenced in Article 8.5 (Minimum Standard of Treatment) results from a general and consistent practice of States that they follow from a sense of legal obligation. With regard to Article 8.5 (Minimum Standard of Treatment), the customary international law minimum standard of treatment of aliens refers to all customary international law principles that protect the economic rights and interests of aliens.[42]

2. Each Party shall accord to covered investments treatment no less favourable than that it accords, in like circumstances, to investments in its territory of investors of any non-Party with respect to the management, conduct, operation, and sale or other disposition of investments.
3. Paragraph 1 and 2 of this Article shall not be construed to oblige any Party to extend to the investors of the other Party or covered investment any treatment, preference or privilege by virtue of any bilateral or multilateral agreement relating to investment in force or signed prior to the date of entry into force of this Agreement.

[41] Mauritius–China BIT, Art. 8.5.
[42] Mauritius–China BIT, Chapter 8, Annex A.

The expropriation provision itself does not contain any particular innovation,[43] but is accompanied by a useful interpretive note under Annex B. Most notably, it includes what has become a common rebuff of the exorbitant "sole effects doctrine":[44] "Except in rare circumstances, non-discriminatory regulatory actions by a Party that are designed and applied to protect legitimate public welfare objectives, such as public moral, public health, safety, and the environment, do not constitute indirect expropriation."[45]

The greatest upgrade that Mauritius and China gave their 1996 BIT in 2019 pertains to the dispute settlement provisions. These new provisions have several defining characteristics that could guide future efforts of refinement of ISDS where the desire to keep it persists.

[43] Mauritius–China BIT, Art. 8.7 ("1. Neither Party may expropriate or nationalize a covered investment either directly or indirectly through measures equivalent to expropriation or nationalization (hereinafter referred to as "expropriation"), except: (a) for a public purpose; (b) in a non-discriminatory manner; (c) on payment of compensation in accordance with this Article; and (d) in accordance with due process of law. 2. The compensation referred to in paragraph 1(c) shall: (a) be paid without delay; (b) be equivalent to the fair market value of the expropriated investment at the time when the expropriation was publicly announced or when the expropriation took place (hereinafter referred to as "the date of expropriation"), whichever is earlier; and (c) be fully realizable and freely transferable"). The subsections that follow describe valuation and two specific rules which are: "5. This Article does not apply to the issuance of compulsory licences granted in relation to intellectual property rights in accordance with the TRIPS Agreement, or to the revocation, limitation, or creation of intellectual property rights, to the extent that such issuance, revocation, limitation, or creation is consistent with the TRIPS Agreement. 6. For greater certainty, the mere fact that a subsidy or grant has not been issued, renewed or maintained, or has been modified or reduced, by a Party, does not constitute an expropriation, even if there is loss or damage to the covered investment as a result." *Id.*

[44] The sole effects doctrine that some tribunals adopted antagonizes the more established and more credible "police powers" doctrine. As Catherine Titi explains: "While the Hull formula focuses on the type of compensation due for an expropriation, the sole effect doctrine relates to the determination of an indirect expropriation, and it is the direct antithesis of the police powers doctrine. According to the sole effect doctrine, the effect of the state measure is the litmus test that allows the tribunal to determine whether an indirect expropriation has taken place. The intent of the state in adopting the measure is irrelevant." Catharine Titi, General Principles of Law and International Investment Arbitration 13 (Andrea Gattini, Attila Tanzi and Filippo Fontanelli eds., 2018) (quoting Saluka Investments BV v. Czech Republic, UNCITRAL, Partial Award (Mar. 17, 2006), at 263–64). The essence of the "police power doctrine" is captured by the Restatement (Third) of the US Foreign Relations Law in the following terms: "A state is not responsible for loss of property or for other economic disadvantage resulting from bona fide general taxation, regulation, forfeiture for crime, or other action of the kind that is commonly accepted as within the police power of states, if it is not discriminatory" (quoted in *id.* at 1). The addition of the explanatory note such as the one contained in the Mauritius–China BIT, which is also contained in the major new BIT Models including the Canadian BIT Model of 2022, is a useful clarification of the original intent surrounding these principles that some arbitral tribunals distorted.

[45] Mauritius–China BIT, Chapter 8, Annex B. The remainder of the interpretive text are also useful:

> The Parties confirm their shared understanding that: 1. An action or a series of actions by a Party cannot constitute an expropriation unless it interferes with a tangible or intangible property right or property interest in an investment. 2. Article 8.7(1) addresses two situations. The first is direct expropriation, where an investment is nationalized or otherwise directly expropriated through formal transfer of title or outright seizure. 3. The second situation addressed by Article 8.7(1) is indirect expropriation, where an action or series of actions by a Party has an effect equivalent to direct expropriation without formal transfer of title or outright seizure. 4. The determination of whether an action or series of actions by a Party, in a specific fact situation, constitutes an indirect expropriation, requires a case-bycase, fact-based inquiry that considers, among other factors: (a) the economic impact of the government action, although the fact that an action or series of actions by a Party has an adverse effect on the economic value of an investment, standing alone, does not establish that an indirect expropriation has occurred; (b) the extent to which the government action interferes with distinct, reasonable investment-backed expectations; and (c) the character and objective of the government action.

Methodologically, the Parties attempted to resolve ambiguity by adding more explanatory text. Given its own subsection and running across 10 provisions, dispute settlement rivals the substantive provisions combined in length.[46]

Beginning with a nonbinding consultation and escalation period of 180 days,[47] it permits the investor to submit its claims of specific categories to arbitral decision-making[48] under the following key operative provision by the investor's choice:

> 3. Provided that 24 months have elapsed since the events giving rise to the claim, a claimant may submit a claim referred to in paragraph 1: (a) under the ICSID Convention and the ICSID Rules of Procedure for Arbitration Proceedings, provided that both the respondent and the non-disputing Party are parties to the ICSID Convention; (b) under the ICSID Additional Facility Rules, provided that either the respondent or the non-disputing Party is a party to the ICSID Convention; (c) under the UNCITRAL Arbitration Rules 27; or (d) if the claimant and respondent agree, to any other arbitration institution or under any other arbitration rules.[49]

Imposing a three-year statute of limitation and more preconditions that are mostly permissive and with questionable importance,[50] it proceeds with the constitution of the tribunal by granting the Secretary General of ICSID the appointing authority.[51]

[46] Mauritius–China BIT, Arts. 8.22–8.33.

[47] *See* Mauritius–China BIT, Art. 8.23.

[48] *See* Mauritius–China BIT, Art. 8.24: "1. In the event that a disputing party considers that an investment dispute cannot be settled by consultations pursuant to Article 8.23 (Consultations) and 180 days have elapsed since the date of the request for consultations: (a) the claimant, on its own behalf, may submit to arbitration under this Section a claim: (i) that the respondent has breached: (A) an obligation under Article 8.3 (National Treatment), Article 8.4 (Most-Favoured Nation Treatment), Article 8.5 (Minimum Standard of Treatment), Article 8.6 (Compensation for Losses), Article 8.7 (Expropriation and Compensation), Article 8.8 (Transfers) and Article 8.10 (Senior Management and Board of Directors); or (B) an investment agreement; and (ii) that the claimant has incurred loss or damage by reason of, or arising out of, that breach." The BIT then repeats the same rule for claims submitted on behalf of enterprises.

[49] Mauritius–China BIT, Art. 8.24(3).

[50] Mauritius–China BIT, Art. 8.26 ("1. No claim may be submitted to arbitration under this Section if more than three years have elapsed from the date on which the claimant first acquired, or should have first acquired, knowledge of the breach alleged under Article 8.24(1) and knowledge that the claimant (for claims brought under Article 8.24(1)(a)) or the enterprise (for claims brought under Article 8.24(1)(b)) has incurred loss or damage.—92—2. No claim may be submitted to arbitration under this Section by national who had the nationality of the Party to the dispute on the date on which the parties consented to submit such dispute to arbitration pursuant to Article 8.24 (Submission of a Claim to Arbitration). 3. No claim may be submitted to arbitration under this Section unless: (a) the claimant consents in writing to arbitration in accordance with the procedures set out in this Section; (b) the claim arises from measures included in the request for consultations submitted by the claimant in accordance with Article 8.23 (Consultations); and (c) the notice of arbitration is accompanied, (i) for claims submitted to arbitration under Article 8.24(1)(a), by the claimant's written waiver, and (ii) for claims submitted to arbitration under Article 8.24(1)(b), by the claimant's and the enterprise's written waivers, of any right to initiate or continue before any administrative tribunal or court under the law of a Party, or other dispute settlement procedures, any proceeding with respect to any measure alleged to constitute a breach referred to in Article 8.24 (Submission of a Claim to Arbitration). 4. Notwithstanding paragraph 3(c)(ii), a waiver from the enterprise shall not be required if the respondent has deprived the claimant of its ownership or control of the enterprise").

[51] Mauritius–China BIT, Art. 8.27 ("1. Unless the disputing parties otherwise agree, the tribunal shall comprise three arbitrators, one arbitrator appointed by each of the disputing parties and the third, who shall be the presiding arbitrator, appointed by agreement of the disputing parties. 2. The Secretary-General shall serve as appointing authority for an arbitration under this Section").

The political importance of this cannot be overemphasized, because it is indicative of a modern day South–South validation of ICSID as the principal player not only by China but also by Mauritius, an African state on the forefront of international arbitral development.

This BIT makes detailed rules on the actual proceedings that are supposed to supplement the chosen arbitral rules whether ICSID or UNCITRAL. Most notably, these rules not only permit the home state to make submissions on the interpretation of the treaty but also allows certain third parties to appear as *amici*.[52] Indeed, in certain limited substantive matters such as financial measures, the BIT anticipates a state-to-state arbitral tribunal to offer interpretation that the ISDS tribunal can then use to adjudicate ISDS matters.[53] Although not totally uncommon, as many other BITs anticipate a state-to-state arbitration to determine the meaning of specific rules, its modern and consolidated appearance in this BIT as one of many prudential measures is a welcome development.[54]

The only reference to domestic remedy is to clarify its optional nature: "Nothing in this Section shall prevent the claimant from resorting to remedies before domestic fora within twenty-four months of the event giving rise to an investment dispute where there has been no amicable settlement of the dispute."[55] The 24-month limitation raises curiosity especially considering the three-year statute of limitation. Other ISDS provisions of the new Mauritius–China BIT are only remarkable for their consistency with broadly accepted principles.

Finally, and most notably, although considered one of the most contemporary China–Africa BITs, Mauritius and China did not venture into the new territory of imposing international obligations on investors beyond their obligations under domestic laws of the respective host states.

The last BIT reviewed under the Afro–Asian category is the Morocco–Japan BIT of 2020.[56] This BIT has many overlapping features with the 2019 Mauritius–China BIT

[52] Mauritius–China BIT, Art. 8.28 ("2. The non-disputing Party may make oral and written submissions to the tribunal regarding the interpretation of this Agreement. 3. After consulting the disputing parties, the tribunal may allow a person or entity that is not a disputing party to file a written amicus curiae submission with the tribunal regarding a matter within the scope of the dispute. Such a submission shall provide the identity of such person or entity (including any controlling entity and any source of substantial financial assistance in either of the two years preceding the submission, e.g. funding around 20% of an entity's overall operations annually), disclose any connection with any disputing party, and identify any person, government or other entity that has provided or will provide any financial or other assistance in preparing the submission. In determining whether to allow such a filing, the tribunal shall consider, among other things, the extent to which: (a) the amicus curiae submission would assist the tribunal in the determination of a factual or legal issue related to the proceeding by bringing a perspective, particular knowledge, or insight that is different from that of the disputing parties; (b) the amicus curiae submission would address a matter within the scope of the dispute; and (c) the amicus curiae has a significant interest in the proceeding").

[53] *See* Mauritius–China BIT, Art. 18.19 ("3. Where an investor submits a claim to arbitration under Section B of this Chapter, and the disputing Party invokes paragraphs 1 and 2 of this Article, the investor–State tribunal established pursuant to Section B of this Chapter may not decide whether and to what extent it is a valid defence to the claim of the investor. It shall seek a report in writing from the Parties on this issue. The investor–State tribunal may not proceed pending receipt of such a report or of a decision of a State-State arbitral tribunal, should such a State-State arbitral tribunal be established").

[54] For other prudential measures, see the whole of Art. 8.19.

[55] Mauritius–China BIT, Art. 8.32.

[56] Agreement Between The Kingdom of Morocco And Japan For The Promotion and Protection of Investment (Morocco–Japan BIT) (2020), available at https://investmentpolicy.unctad.org/international-investment-agreements/treaty-files/5908/download.

reviewed above, which in turn has significant overlapping features with the newest Canadian and the 2012 US BIT Models. The latter have for decades now overtaken the old European models as trendsetters especially since the NAFTA investment chapter and arbitral cases applying them.

The substantive investment protection rules begin with an expansive admission and promotion clause that among other less remarkable subclauses states:

> 8. Each Contracting Party shall, in accordance with its applicable laws and regulations, endeavour to provide, except in cases of emergency or of purely minor nature, a reasonable opportunity for comments by the public before the adoption, amendment or repeal of regulations of general application that affect any matter covered by this Treaty.[57]

It merges National Treatment and MFN into one provision, adds the like circumstances qualification in both, and excepts certain tax matters and subsidies from NT and dispute settlement from MFN all in one provision with subparts.[58] It does, however, contain an independent and somewhat elaborate MFN clause that respects its customary international law origin in the following terms:

1. Each Contracting Party shall in its Territory accord to investments of investors of the other Contracting Party treatment in accordance with customary international law, including fair and equitable treatment and full protection and security.

Note: The Contracting Parties confirm their shared understanding that "customary international law" generally and as specifically referred to in this Article results from a general and consistent practice of States that they follow from a sense of legal obligation. The Contracting Parties also confirm that the customary international law minimum standard of treatment of aliens refers to all customary international law principles that protect the investments of aliens.

2. For greater certainty, a change of the regulation of a Contracting Party does not constitute by itself a violation of paragraph 1.
3. It is understood that:
   (a) "fair and equitable treatment" includes the obligation of the Contracting Parties to guarantee access to the courts of justice and administrative tribunals and not to deny justice in criminal, civil or administrative proceedings in accordance with the principle of due process of law; and
   (b) "full protection and security" requires each Contracting Party to ensure the necessary level of police protection required under customary international law.
4. Neither Contracting Party shall, within its Territory, in any way impair investment activities of investors of the other Contracting Party by unreasonable, arbitrary or discriminatory measures.

[57] Morocco–Japan BIT, Art. 2(8).
[58] Morocco–Japan BIT, Art. 3.

This is a useful and modern version of the FET provision that many contemporary models have adopted. Along with the Mauritius–China BIT, it is also indicative of an African BIT trend toward elaboration of the FET principle rather than the REC model of eliminating the concept altogether.

The expropriation provision in the Morocco–Japan BIT is an embodiment of the Hull Formula, with certain additions that characterize the modern version of the rule contained in many recent models, including the Mauritius–China one. The one notable addition is the domestic review of legality and quantum in the following terms:

> 4. The investors affected by expropriation shall have the right, under the laws and regulations of the Contracting Party that has taken the expropriation, to prompt review, by a judicial authority or administrative tribunals or duly authorised administrative agencies of that Contracting Party, of the legality of the expropriation and the amount of the compensation, in accordance with the principles set out in this Article.[59]

Like these other modern models, this BIT also annexes interpretive guidance.[60] The key part of that is the rejection of the "sole effects doctrine" in the following terms:

> 4. Except in rare circumstances, such as when a measure or a series of measures of a Contracting Party is extremely severe or disproportionate in light of its purpose, non-discriminatory measures of a Contracting Party that are designed and applied to protect legitimate public welfare objectives, such as public health, safety and the environment, do not constitute indirect expropriation.[61]

[59] Morocco–Japan BIT, Art. 9. The remainder of the provision is:

1. Neither Contracting Party shall expropriate or nationalise investments in its Territory of investors of the other Contracting Party or take any measure equivalent to expropriation or nationalisation (hereinafter referred to as "expropriation") except:
   (a) For a public purpose;
   (b) In a non-discriminatory manner;
   (c) Upon payment of prompt, adequate and effective compensation pursuant to paragraphs 2, 3 and 4; and
   (d) In accordance with due process of law.
2. The compensation shall amount to the fair market value of the expropriated investments immediately before the expropriation was publicly announced or the expropriation occurred, whichever is the earlier. The fair market value shall not reflect any change in value occurring because the expropriation had become publicly known earlier.
3. The compensation shall be paid without undue delay and shall include interest at a commercially reasonable rate, taking into account the length of time until the date of payment. It shall be effectively realisable and freely transferrable and shall be freely convertible into freely usable currencies, at the market exchange rate prevailing on the date of expropriation.

...

5. This Article shall not apply to the issuance of compulsory licences granted in relation to intellectual property rights, or to the revocation, limitation or creation of intellectual property rights, to the extent that such issuance, revocation, limitation or creation is consistent with international agreements on intellectual property to which both Contracting Parties are parties.

[60] Morocco–Japan BIT, Annex.

[61] Morocco–Japan BIT, Annex, at (4). The remaining sections state as follows:

Like the Mauritius–China BIT, the Morocco–Japan BIT has also elaborated the dispute settlement provision. The details notwithstanding, in the final analysis it is the usual ICSID or ad hoc UNCITRAL arbitration with a three-year statute of limitation and fork in the road selection rule.[62]

Conclusion

Afro–Asian BIT activity started late but modernized quickly. Unlike the majority of the older Afro–European BITs, a greater number of the Afro–Asian BITs are reactive to the jurisprudential difficulties that the older BITs had to grapple with. Overall, however, Afro–Asia BITs share the same fundamental characteristics with the Afro–European BITs and indeed, it could be concluded that they are essentially wholesale adaptions of them, with a notable exception of the older Chinese model that restricted arbitration to the quantum of compensation before fading to the background as China's economy integrated into the global economy over the last few decades. It must also be mentioned that these Afro–Asian BITs have not yet given rise to many arbitral cases.[63]

1. The Contracting Parties confirm their shared understanding that paragraph 1 of Article 9 is intended to reflect customary international law concerning the obligation of States with respect to expropriation.
2. Paragraph 1 of Article 9 addresses the following two situations:
   (a) The first situation is direct expropriation where investments are nationalised or otherwise directly expropriated through formal transfer of title or outright seizure; and
   (b) The second situation is indirect expropriation where a measure or a series of measures of a Contracting Party has an effect equivalent to direct expropriation without formal transfer of title or outright seizure.
3. The determination of whether a measure or a series of measures of a Contracting Party, in a specific fact situation, constitutes an indirect expropriation requires a case-by-case, fact-based inquiry that considers, among other factors:
   (a) The economic impact of the measure or series of measures, although the fact that such measure or series of such measures has an adverse effect on the economic value of investments, standing alone, does not establish that an indirect expropriation has occurred;
   (b) The extent to which the measure or series of measures interferes with distinct and reasonable expectations arising out of investments; and
   (c) The character of the measure or series of measures, including the duration of such measure, whether such measure is non-discriminatory and whether such measure is disproportionate with regard to the public interest purpose.

[62] Morocco–Japan BIT, Art. 16.

[63] *See, e.g.*, *Chinese Company Sues Ghana US$55 Million For Wrongful Termination of Contract*, The Herald, Feb. 15, 2021, https://perma.cc/YS24-XE23 ("Beijing Everyway Traffic and Lighting Tech Co Ltd, served a notice of arbitration on the government of Ghana on February 10, kicking off an ad hoc arbitration procedure under the China–Ghana bilateral investment treaty. The arbitration is described as one of the first known claims by a mainland Chinese investor against an African country, seeking the colossal US$55 million from Ghana after its contract to develop an intelligent traffic management system for Accra, was cancelled replaced by other Chinese contractors"). *See also* Alison Ross, *Chinese Company Brings Claim Against Ghana*, Global Arbitration Review (Feb. 11, 2021), https://perma.cc/D2UX-7PV9 ("A Beijing-based construction company has brought one of the first known claims by a mainland Chinese investor against an African country, seeking US$55 million from Ghana after its contract to develop an intelligent traffic management system for Accra was cancelled and it was replaced by other Chinese contractors").

26
Intra-Africa BITs

There are approximately 190 known Intra-Africa BITs of which only 20% are in effect.[1] Generationally, they range from the earliest concluded in the 1970s to the most recent, concluded in 2022. This chapter profiles at least one from each generation and shows the congruity and disjuncture with the innovative approaches of the various RECs. Two factors must be noted from the outset, however: that there have only been three known ICSID cases in which any Intra-Africa BITs have ever been invoked,[2] and that the trend in Africa seems inclined toward retiring them with a combination of the use of the different RECs investment-related instruments and adoption of the AfCFTA Investment Protocol,[3] discussed in the final part of this book.

The Earlier Intra-Africa BITs

Chronologically, the Intra-Africa BIT activity largely coincided with the increase in the Afro–Asian BIT activity in the 1990s and 2000s, slowing down thereafter. One of the earliest Intra-Africa BITs is the Egypt–Uganda BIT of 1995.[4] This BIT is structurally and by content basic and is a direct adaptation of the earliest European North–South BITs of the 1980s and 1990s.

The BIT defines terms and its scope of application of the most basic investment protection rules such as National Treatment, MFN, and FET not necessarily separated in those terms. For example, the FET principle contains a National Treatment clause expressly embedded in it. It states in relevant part:

[1] *See* UNCTAD International Investments Navigator at https://investmentpolicy.unctad.org/international-investment-agreements. For the numbers, *see also* Arnaud Oulepo, *AfCFTA, the Future Investment Protocol* (Feb. 7, 2021), Kluwer Arbitration Blog, at http://arbitrationblog.kluwerarbitration.com/2021/02/07/afcfta-the-future-investment-protocol-and-the-phasing-out-of-intra-african-bits/.

[2] *See id.* (citing Oded Besserglik v. Republic of Mozambique, ICSID Case No. ARB(AF)/14/2, Award (Oct. 28, 2019) (South Africa–Mozambique BIT); Courts (Indian Ocean) v Madagascar, ICSID Case No. ARB/13/34 (Mauritius–Madagascar BIT); and LMTE Mauritius v Madagascar, ICSID Case No. ARB/17/28 (Mauritius–Madagascar BIT)).

[3] *See. e.g.*, *id.*, concluding: "What should be the role of the AfCFTA Investment Protocol in the pyramidal structure (domestic, regional, and continental) of investment regulation on the continent? The question will be at the centre of the negotiation of the Protocol. For the sake of harmonisation and predictability, States should consider a phasing-out of intra-African BITs. A majority of them being unratified, and quite a few of them having been invoked in ISDS cases, African States are in much better position than their EU counterparts, should they want to proceed with this option."

[4] Agreement for the Promotion and Protection Of Investments Between the Arab Republic of Egypt and the Republic of Uganda (Egypt–Uganda BIT) (1995), at https://investmentpolicy.unctad.org/international-investment-agreements/treaty-files/1119/download.

Africa's International Investment Law Regimes. Won L. Kidane, Oxford University Press. © Oxford University Press 2023.
DOI: 10.1093/oso/9780197745571.003.0026

2) Investments of investors of each Contracting Party shall at all times be accorded fair and equitable treatment and shall enjoy adequate protection and security in the territory of the other Contracting Party no less than that enjoyed by its nationals. Neither Contracting Party shall in any way impair by unreasonable or discriminatory measures the management, maintenance, use, enjoyment or disposal of investments in its territory of investors of the other Contracting Party.[5]Similarly, this model makes FET an integral part of the MFN clause in ways that have since became uncommon. The formulation, which may now seem somewhat unusual, reads:

1) Investments of investors of one Contracting Party in the territory of the other Contracting Party and also the returns therefrom shall receive treatment which is fair and equitable and not less favourable than that accorded in respect of the investments of investors of any third state. 2) Each Contracting Party shall in its territory accord to investors of the other Contracting Party as regards the management, use, enjoyment or disposal of their investments, treatment which is fair and equitable and not less favourable than that which is accorded to investors of any third state.[6]

Interestingly, it could be observed that although the formulation is slightly different and perhaps better, the Egypt–China BIT signed a year earlier also contains a similar merger of FET and MFN in the following terms:

I. Investments and activities associated with investments of investors of either Contracting Party shall be accorded fair and equitable treatment and shall enjoy protection in the territory of the other Contracting Party. 2. The treatment and protection referred to in Paragraph I of this Article shall not be less favorable than that accorded to investments and activities associated with such investments of investors oca third Stale.[7]

More interestingly, however, the Egyptian BITs with its Western partners do not contain this limitation of NT and MFN to FET. For example, the corresponding provision of the earlier Egyptian BIT with Sweden (1978) simply states:

(1) Neither Contracting Party shall in its territory subject investments completely Owned by nationals' or companies of the other Contracting Party or in which nationals or companies of the other Contracting Party have a substantial interest, to treatment less favourable than it accords to investments of its, own nationals or companies or to, investments of nationals or companies of any third country. (2) Neither Contracting Party shall in its territory subject nationals or companies of the other Contracting Party, as regards their activity, in connection with investments; to

[5] Egypt–Uganda BIT, Art. 2(2).
[6] Egypt–Uganda BIT, Art. 3(1–2).
[7] Egypt–China BIT (1994), Art. 3 (1–2).

treatment less favourable, than it accords to its own nationals or companies or to nationals or companies of any third country.[8]

Likewise, the Egyptian BIT signed with the United States in 1986 keeps the concepts separated: It states in corresponding part:

> 2.(a) Each Party shall accord investments in its territory, and associated activities in connection with these investments of nationals or companies of the other Party, treatment no less favorable than that accorded in like situations to investments of its own nationals and companies or to investments of nationals and companies of any third country, whichever is most favorable. Associated activities in connection with an investment include, but are not limited to...[9]

It is thus not clear whether the merger of these concepts in the Intra-Africa BITs, at least in these BITs, is a conscious limitation of the NT and MFN to FET or an innocuous and sloppy drafting.

Otherwise, the Egypt–Uganda BIT contains a uniquely formulated expropriation provision with some indicia of the Hull rule although not fully acquiescent.[10] The dispute settlement clause offers clear choice to the investor of three alternatives that most of the BITs offer, that is, domestic court, ICSID arbitration or ad hoc arbitration under the UNCITRAL Rules.[11]

The Mauritius–Mozambique BIT signed a few years later (1997)[12] is structurally similar but contains certain characteristics of its own; most notably, it requires a specific written approval under specifically identified domestic laws for the grant of the benefits of the treaty.[13] The inclusion of this precautionary provision that early is interesting because many of the disputes raising the question of whether an investment

[8] Agreement between the Government of Sweden and the Government of the Arab Republic of Egypt on the Mutual Protection of Investments (Egypt–Sweden BIT) (1978), Art. 1 (1–2), available at https://investmentpolicy.unctad.org/international-investment-agreements/treaty-files/1112/download.

[9] Egypt–United States BIT (1986). Art. II(2).

[10] Egypt–Uganda BIT, Art. 5 ("The nationalization, expropriation or any other measure of similar characteristics or effects that may be applied by the authorities of one Contracting Party against the investments in its own territory of investors of the other Contracting Party must be applied exclusively for reasons of public interest pursuant to the law, and shall in no case be discriminatory. The Contracting Party adopting such measures shall pay to the investor or his legal beneficiary adequate indemnity in convertible currency without unjustified delay").

[11] Egypt–Uganda BIT, Art. 8(2).

[12] Investment Promotion and Protection Agreement Between The Republic of Mozambique and The Republic of Mauritius (Mauritius–Mozambique BIT) (1997), available at https://investmentpolicy.unctad.org/international-investment-agreements/treaty-files/1985/download.

[13] Mauritius–Mozambique BIT (1997), Art. 2 (Scope of Application) ("1. This Agreement shall only apply—(a) in respect of the investments in the territory of the Republic of Mauritius, to all investments made by investors of the Republic of Mozambique which are specifically approved in writing by the competent authority designated by the Government of the Republic of Mauritius and upon such conditions, if any, as it shall deem fit. (b) in respect of investments in the territory of the Republic of Mozambique, to all investments made by investors of the Republic of Mauritius which are specifically approved in writing by the competent authority designated by the Government of the Republic of Mozambique in conformity with the law no 4/84, of the 18th of August, 1984, or under the Investment Law no 3/93 of the 24th of June, 1993, or under any other subsequent legislation in force on investments in the Republic of Mozambique").

is admitted to qualify for investment seem to have come later on. In any case, this level of detail, which is helpful, does not appear to be very common.

Focusing on admission further, this BIT expressly links the application of FET to admitted investment in the following terms: "3. Investments approved under Article 2 shall be accorded fair and equitable protection in accordance with this Agreement."[14] Again, this drafting was clearly informed by the issues that arose in connection with what investment is deemed admitted and when protection attaches. This rule obviously minimizes issues relating to when protection attaches by requiring written proof of admission under existing domestic investment laws.

Having taken care to limit FET and other protections to investments admitted under specific conditions, another broader, standalone, and standard FET, NT, and MFN provision overrides all the limitations imposed in the previous articles as follows:

> Investments and returns of investors of either Contracting Party shall at all times be accorded fair and equitable treatment in the territory of the other Contracting Party. Neither Contracting Party shall in any way impair by unreasonable nor discriminatory measures the management, maintenance, use, enjoyment or disposal of investments in its territory by investors of the other Contracting Party. 2. Each Contracting Party shall in its territory accord to investors and to investments and returns of investors of the other Contracting Party treatment not less favourable than that which it accords to investments and returns of investors of any third State.[15]

Although unlike the Egypt–Uganda BIT, this BIT does not limit NT and MFN to FET; it merges all three concepts into one provision and offers broad protection by seemingly overriding the limitations of express admission that the provision above it required. Whether this is a function of unartful drafting or a function of compromise, these kinds of small textual gaps reinforce the impression that South–South adaptations of BITs are halfhearted.

The expropriation provision of the Mauritius–Mozambique BIT is fully Hull-acquiescent.[16] Most interestingly, however, this BIT adopts the earlier Chinese version of the dispute settlement of limiting international arbitration to the quantum of damages, leaving the determination of liability to domestic courts.[17]

[14] Mauritius–Mozambique BIT, Art. 3(3).

[15] Mauritius–Mozambique BIT, Art. 4 (1–2).

[16] Mauritius–Mozambique BIT, Art. 6 (1–2) ("1. Investments of investors of either Contracting Party in the territory of the other Contracting Party shall not be nationalised, expropriated or subjected to measures having effects equivalent to nationalisation or expropriation except for public purposes, under due process of law, on a non-discriminatory basis and against prompt, adequate and effective compensation. Such compensation shall be made without delay, and be effectively realizable. 2. The investor affected by the expropriation shall have a right, under the law of the expropriating Contracting Party to prompt review, by a court of law or other independent and impartial forum of that Contracting Party of the expropriation case. ")

[17] Mauritius–Mozambique BIT, Art 8 (2–3) ("2. If the dispute cannot be settled through negotiations within six months, either party to the dispute shall be entitled to initiate judicial action before the competent court of the Contracting Party accepting the investment. 3. If a dispute involving the amount of compensation resulting from expropriation, nationalisation, or other measures having effect equivalent to nationalisation or expropriation, mentioned in Article 6 cannot be settled within six months after resort to negotiation as specified in paragraph (1) of this Article by the investor concerned, it may be submitted to an international arbitral tribunal established by both parties").

Although these Intra-Africa BITs are almost fully influenced by the European models with limited domestic modifications, it is interesting to see traces of Chinese influence as early as the 1990s.

Intra-Africa BITs of the 2000s

Although there was no systematic and widespread Intra-Africa BIT connectivity effort, there was some increased activity in the 2000s before it slowed down in the 2010s. Notable examples include the Benin–Ghana BIT of 2001[18] and the South Africa–Tunisia BIT of 2002.[19] These are structurally and by content similar to the previous era BITs and contain no particularly significant variations, although they have notably avoided the doctrinal confusion among the various protection principles such as NT, MFN, and FET by clearly delineating each on its own terms, which is a feature of the more modern BITs.

For example, the Benin–Ghana BIT defines the protection in the following standard terms:

> 1. Investments of nationals and companies of each Contracting Party shall at all times be accorded fair and equitable treatment and shall enjoy full and adequate protection and security in the territory of the other Contracting Party. 2. Neither Contracting Party shall, in any way, impair by unreasonable or discriminatory measures, the management, maintenance, use, enjoyment or disposal of investments in its territory of nationals or companies of the other Contracting Party.[20]

This merges the FET provisions with the Full Security and Protection rule, which became virtually inseparable in most modern BITs, and functionally merged in jurisprudence, although the latter came to be associated with the protection of physical property in some cases.

The South Africa–Tunisia BIT's FET provision is identical.[21] The two structure their MFN and National Treatment rules a little bit differently yet the contents are the same. The South Africa–Tunisia BIT merges NT and MFN but dedicates separate subsections for the protection of investments and investors in the following terms:

> (2) Each Contracting Party shall in its territory accord to investments and returns of investors of the other Contracting Party treatment not less favourable than that which it accords to investments and returns of its own investors or to investments and returns of investors of any third State. (3) Each Contracting Party shall in its

[18] Agreement Between the Government of the Republic of Ghana and the Government of the Republic of Benin for the Promotion and Protection of Investments (Benin–Ghana BIT) (2001), available at https://investmentpolicy.unctad.org/international-investment-agreements/treaty-files/442/download.

[19] Agreement Between the Government of the Republic of Ghana and the Government of the Republic of Benin for the Promotion and Protection of Investments (South Africa–Tunisia BIT) (2002), available at https://investmentpolicy.unctad.org/international-investment-agreements/treaty-files/442/download.

[20] Benin–Ghana BIT (2001), Art. 3.

[21] *See* South Africa–Tunisia BIT, Art. 3(1).

> territory according to investors of the other Contracting Party treatment not less favourable than that which it accords to its own investors or to investors of any third State.[22]

The Benin–Ghana corollary does not contain national treatment but otherwise adheres to the more typical formulation of MFN without making a distinction between protections accorded to investments and investors by protecting only investments.[23] Because arbitral tribunals later paid close attention to the most minute variations in text in each treaty considering them intentional variations, it is interesting to observe these types of distinctions and ponder over what differences in the nature and scope of the protection and what outcomes the drafters of each of these BITs intended to pursue. Most notable in these two BITs is their omission of the famous qualifier "same circumstances": a phrase that saved host states that chose to include it great arbitral trouble, as indicated in *İçkale İnşaat Limited Şirketi v. Turkmenistan*.[24]

Although both BITs approximate the Hull Rule in their expropriation provisions, they contain notable textual variation that makes the South Africa–Tunisia BIT more Hull-acquiescent than the Benin–Ghana BIT. The variations are interesting, although the intended difference in outcome is not necessarily ascertainable from the texts alone. Compare South Africa–Tunisia's classic Hull formulation with Benin–Ghana's variation:

> South Africa–Tunisia:
> (1) Investments of investors of either Contracting Party shall not be nationalised, expropriated or subjected to measures having effects equivalent to nationalisation or expropriation (hereinafter referred to as "expropriation") in the territory of the other Contracting Party except for public purposes, under due process of law, on a non-discriminatory basis and against prompt, adequate and effective compensation.[25]
>
> Benin–Ghana:
> 1. Investments of nationals or companies of either Contracting Party shall not be nationalised, expropriated or subjected to measures having effect equivalent to nationalisation or expropriation (hereinafter referred to as "expropriation") in the territory of the other Contracting Party, except where for a public purpose related to its internal needs, a Contracting Party expropriates the investments of nationals or companies of the other Contracting Party, the following conditions shall be complied with: (a) the measures shall be accompanied by provision for the payment of compensation amounting to the full and genuine value of the

[22] South Africa–Tunisia BIT, Art. 3 (2–3).

[23] Benin–Ghana BIT, Art. 4 (1–2) ("1. Neither Contracting Party shall in its territory subject investments or returns of nationals or companies of the other Contracting Party to treatment less favourable than that which it accords to investments or returns of nationals or companies of any third state. 2. Neither Contracting Party shall in its territory subject nationals or companies of the other Contracting Party, as regards their management, maintenance, use, enjoyment or disposal of their investments, to treatment less favourable than that which is accorded to nationals or companies of any third state").

[24] İçkale İnşaat Limited Şirketi v. Turkmenistan, ICSID Case No. ARB/10/24, Award (Mar. 8, 2016), at 326–29.

[25] South Africa–Tunisia BIT, Art. 5(1).

investment expropriated immediately before the expropriation or before the impending expropriation became public knowledge whichever is the earlier. (b) the compensation shall be paid without undue delay. If the compensation is not paid within six months from the date of its determination, it shall after that date attract interest at the normal commercial rate until the date of payment.

Although it adds "internal needs" and does not use the terms "prompt," "adequate," and "effective," it attempts to capture the same notions by using different terms and even fixing time limits. Whether this is a purposeful clarification of lingering doubts that these two parties have had or drafting idiosyncrasies is difficult to determine, but what is real is that tribunals asked to interpret these kinds of variations mostly consider them intentional and attempt to give them their own meaning, which in a way has contributed to the perceived incoherence of the arbitral jurisprudence over the decades.

The Benin–Ghana BIT dispute settlement clause contains many levels of escalation, but effectively ends with UNCITRAL arbitration without limiting the choice to the investor.[26] The South Africa–Tunisia BIT's dispute settlement provision is standard. It gives the investor the choice of domestic court, ICSID arbitration, or UNCITRAL arbitration.[27] Again, whether these differences in formulation are purposeful and functions of the specific bilateral relations, they seek to regulate or simple drafting preferences with no specific goals, tribunals have shown keen interest in all types of textual modifications.

Intra-Africa BITs of the 2010s

Indicative of trend or otherwise, the slowdown in Intra-Africa BIT activity since 2010 is considerable. The notable ones during this period include the Kenya–Mauritius BIT of 2012 revised,[28] and the Morocco–Nigeria BIT of 2016,[29] which contains reliable indicia of Africa's contemporary innovative features. With that exception, it could be observed that many of the fundamental substantive standards and mechanisms of dispute settlement remained fairly stable through the decades. The most contemporary reform efforts commenced in earnest through the RECs and taken to the next level by the Draft Pan African Investment Code (PIAC), which is discussed in detail in the following chapter, have yet to find credible expression in binding treaties.

[26] Benin–Ghana BIT, Art. 9 ("3. If after a period of six months from written notification of the claim there is no agreement to one of the above alternative procedures, the parties to the dispute shall be bound to submit it to arbitration under the arbitration rules of the United Nations Commission on International Trade Law as then in force. The parties to the dispute may agree in writing to modify these rules").

[27] South Africa–Tunisia BIT, Art. 8 (2).

[28] Declaration of Special Arrangements For the Reciprocal Promotion and Protection of Investments (Kenya–Mauritius BIT) (2012), available at https://investmentpolicy.unctad.org/international-investment-agreements/treaty-files/5541/download.

[29] Reciprocal Investment Promotion and Protection Agreement Between The Government of the Kingdom of Morocco And The Government Of The Federal Republic of Nigeria (Morocco–Nigeria BIT) (2016), available at https://investmentpolicy.unctad.org/international-investment-agreements/treaty-files/5409/download.

The 2012 Kenya–Mauritius BIT's protection provisions maintained the most common and enduring formulation of NT, FET, and MFN provisions in these terms:

> (1) Investments and returns of investors of either Contracting Party shall at all times be accorded fair and equitable treatment in the territory of the other Contracting Party. Neither Contracting Party shall in any way impair by unreasonable nor discriminatory measures the management, maintenance, use, enjoyment or disposal of investments in its territory by investors of the other Contracting Party. (2) Each Contracting Party shall accord to investors of the other Contracting Party and to their investments, a treatment no less favourable than the treatment it accords to its own investors and their investments with respect to the acquisition, expansion, operation, management, maintenance, use, enjoyment and sale or other disposal of investments. (3) Each Contracting Party shall in its territory accord to investors and to investments and returns of investors of the other Contracting Party treatment no less favourable than that which it accords to investments and returns of investors of any third State.[30]

Although the actual text of the 2019 revision is not available for review, the China–Mauritius BIT signed the same year (2019), added the "like circumstances" qualifier with a footnote that advises adjudicators of factors they must consider in determining the likeness of the circumstances.[31] The direction that most recent BITs have taken was putting limits to the expansive reading of the classic principles because of the perceived arbitral overreach. This change is also one such example. Similarly, the 2019 revision has also clarified the FET principles by limiting it to the minimum standards of treatment under customary international law and adding useful details that help its determination.[32] The expropriation provision is largely Hull-acquiescent:

> (1) Investments of investors of either Contracting Party in the territory of the other Contracting Party shall not be nationalised, expropriated or subjected to measures having effects equivalent to nationalisation or expropriation except for public purposes, under due process of law, on a non-discriminatory basis and against prompt and full compensation.[33]

The only term missing is "effective." The updated version is more elaborate and contains interpretive annex consistent with the most contemporary BIT Models of Canada as well as the United States.[34]

[30] Kenya–Mauritius BIT, Art. 4 (1–3).

[31] *See* China–Mauritius BIT, Art 8.3 and Note 10 ("For greater certainty, whether treatment is accorded in "like circumstances" under Article 8.3 (National Treatment) or Article 8.4 (Most-Favoured-Nation Treatment) depends on the totality of the circumstances, including whether the relevant treatment distinguishes between investors or investments on the basis of legitimate public welfare objectives").

[32] *See* China–Mauritius BIT (2019), Art. 8.5. Presumably this is one of the updates that the 2019 version of the Kenya–Mauritius BIT contains.

[33] Kenya–Mauritius BIT, Art. 6(1).

[34] The Mauritius–China (2019) BIT adds, for example, Chapter 8, Annex B: "4. The determination of whether an action or series of actions by a Party, in a specific fact situation, constitutes an indirect expropriation, requires a case-bycase, fact-based inquiry that considers, among other factors: (a) the economic

The dispute settlement rules in the Kenya–Mauritius BIT (2012) are consistent with most BITs of the same era, and it culminates with four choices given to the investor: domestic court, ICSID, UNCITRAL, or arbitral institution by agreement of the parties.[35] This provision has gotten serious textual upgrade in Mauritius's 2019 BIT, which included a statute of limitation and lengthy provisions on the constitution of the tribunal and conduct of the proceedings. Ultimately, however, the binding and enforceable rules are more or less the same.[36]

The Nigeria–Morocco BIT of 2016 has been characterized as "the wind of change"[37] for its inclusion of some of the innovative rules designed to bring a better balance between rights and obligations of investors and host states.

Traces of the new balancing approach begin in their expression in the preamble which reads in part:

> REAFFIRMING the right of the State Parties to regulate and to introduce new measures relating to investments in their territories in order to meet national policy I objectives and taking into account any asymmetries with respect to the measures in place, the particular need of developing countries to exercise this right;
>
> SEEKING an overall balance of the rights and obligations among the State Parties, the investors, and the investments under this Agreement.[38]

It contains new provisions such as institutional governance (Article 4) for the purpose of monitoring the implementation of the agreement and amicable resolution of disputes, and exchange of information (Article 5), including changes in the law, taxation, and other requirements. It is only then that the traditional NT, MFN, and FET substantive rules follow in more or less their standard form. NT and MFN contain the "like circumstances" qualifier with useful interpretive note,[39] much like the other BIT models such as the Canadian model. Expropriation is also maintained in its standard

impact of the government action, although the fact that an action or series of actions by a Party has an adverse effect on the economic value of an investment, standing alone, does not establish that an indirect expropriation has occurred; (b) the extent to which the government action interferes with distinct, reasonable investment-backed expectations; and (c) the character and objective of the government action. 5. Except in rare circumstances, non-discriminatory regulatory actions by a Party that are designed and applied to protect legitimate public welfare objectives, such as public moral, public health, safety, and the environment, do not constitute indirect expropriation."

[35] Kenya–Mauritius BIT, Art. 8.

[36] *See* Mauritius–China BIT (2019), Art. 8.24 ("3. Provided that 24 months have elapsed since the events giving rise to the claim, a claimant may submit a claim referred to in paragraph 1: (a) under the ICSID Convention and the ICSID Rules of Procedure for Arbitration Proceedings, provided that both the respondent and the non-disputing Party are parties to the ICSID Convention; (b) under the ICSID Additional Facility Rules, provided that either the respondent or the non-disputing Party is a party to the ICSID Convention; (c) under the UNCITRAL Arbitration Rules 27; or (d) if the claimant and respondent agree, to any other arbitration institution or under any other arbitration rules").

[37] Makane Moise Mbengue and Stefanie Schacherer, *Evolution of International Investment Agreements in Africa: Features and Challenges of Investment Law "Africanization,"* in HANDBOOK OF INTERNATIONAL INVESTMENT LAW AND POLICY 2605 (Julien Chaisse, Leila Choukroune and Sufian Jusoh eds., 2021).

[38] Morocco–Nigeria BIT (2016), Preamble.

[39] Morocco–Nigeria BIT, Art. 6.

Hull-acquiescent formulation.[40] FET is preserved in considerably clarified form as follows:

1. Each Party shall accord to investments treatment in accordance with customary international law, including fair and equitable treatment and full protection and security.
2. For greater certainty, paragraph 1 prescribes the customary international law minimum standard of treatment of aliens as the minimum standard of treatment to be afforded to covered investments. The concepts of "fair and equitable treatment" and "full protection and security" does not require treatment in addition to or beyond that which is required by that standard, and does not create additional substantive rights. The obligation in paragraph 1 to provide:
   (a) "fair and equitable treatment" includes the obligation not to deny justice in criminal, civil or administrative adjudicatory proceedings in accordance with the principle of due process embodied in the principal legal systems o f a Party.
   (b) "full protection and security" requires each Party to provide the level of police protection required under customary international law.[41]

The more novel provisions come later. They include very carefully circumscribed deference to the host state's environmental regulations,[42] requires a pre-establishment environmental and social assessment, and more importantly, it codifies the precautionary principle.[43] It also includes provisions restating the host states and investors obligations under domestic laws with respect to labor, human rights,[44] and anti-corruption.[45]

A set of related but newer provisions also address the investor's postestablishment environmental,[46] human rights,[47] and corporate governance obligations.[48] It also adds a provision reminding the investor that it may be held responsible in

[40] Morocco–Nigeria BIT, Art. 8.

[41] Morocco–Nigeria BIT, Art. 7 (1–2).

[42] Morocco–Nigeria BIT, Art. 13 ("4. Nothing in this Agreement shall be constructed to prevent a Party from I adopting maintaining, or enforcing, in a non-discriminatory manner, any measure otherwise consistent with this Agreement that it considers appropriate to ensure that investment activity in its territory is undertaken in a manner sensitive to environmental and social concerns").

[43] Morocco–Nigeria BIT, Art. 14 ("3. Investors, their investment and host state authorities shall apply the precautionary principle to their environmental impact assessment and to decisions taken in relation to a proposed investment, including any necessary mitigation or alternative approaches of the precautionary principle by investors and investments shall be described in the environmental impact assessment they undertake").

[44] Morocco–Nigeria BIT, Art. 15.

[45] Morocco–Nigeria BIT, Art. 17.

[46] Morocco–Nigeria BIT, Art. 18 ("1. Investments shall, in keeping with good practice requirements relating to the size and nature of the investment, maintain an environmental management system. Companies in areas of resource exploitation and high-risk industrial enterprises shall maintain a current certification to ISO 14001 or an equivalent environmental management standard").

[47] Morocco–Nigeria BIT, Art. 18(2) ("2. Investors and investments shall uphold human rights in the host state").

[48] Morocco–Nigeria BIT, Art. 19 ("1(a) (a) Investments shall meet or exceed national and internationally accepted standards of corporate governance for the sector involved, in particular for transparency and accounting practices").

its home state "for the acts or decisions made in relation to the investment where such acts or decisions lead to significant damage, personal injuries or loss of life in the host state."[49] This presumably requires the Parties to modify the jurisdictional rules of their respective courts to permit the countenance of these types of lawsuits for events that occurred outside the home state's jurisdiction. From a jurisdictional perspective, it is not impossible to do so but it might require tweaking the existing rules to confer general jurisdiction on the courts, although it invites the oldest dilemma of bias against the outsider. In other words, a domestic remedy in the investor's home state may not be the most attractive avenue for redress even for these types of cases.

Related and even longer provisions repeat the right to regulate and corporate responsibility in more elaborate ways, but none of them makes any concrete new rules, as they are either permissive or refer to existing domestic rules or customary international law.[50]

Although the dispute settlement provision begins with an elaborate prevention mechanism,[51] it ends with the standard arbitration rule that grants the investor the choice of ICSID or ad hoc arbitration under the UNCITRAL Rules.[52] A bit unusually, the dispute settlement clause selects the venue[53] of the tribunal and lists the types of government property that the investor may not attach for purposes of execution of the award. Although these properties are the type that are ordinarily protected under domestic sovereign immunities laws or acts,[54] the nonexhaustive formulation of the introductory passage could potentially give rise to controversy. It states in part: "(e) No measures of constraint before or after a final award, such as attachment, garnishment or execution, can be taken against the goods of the Party complained against, in particular."[55]

Finally, and interestingly, although the BIT contains some investor obligations, it does not provide for host state arbitral *locus standi*. It appears that the kind of remedy that the drafters anticipated for the host state is a domestic remedy, whether before its own courts or the courts of the home state.

The Morocco–Nigeria BIT is certainly a postinnovation effort new-generation BIT. It is a credible and careful attempt because not only does it preserve the core principles in their best formulations, it also predicated the investor obligation and related newer rules on existing domestic and customary international rules. In that sense it has avoided some of the doctrinal confusions that some of the recent drafts and models discussed above contain. That said, the greatest accomplishment is one of consolidation of existing rules rather than creating new norms. In any case, this could set a good/more sustainable precedent.

[49] Morocco–Nigeria BIT, Art. 21.
[50] *See* Morocco–Nigeria BIT, Arts. 23–24.
[51] Morocco–Nigeria BIT, Art. 26.
[52] Morocco–Nigeria BIT, Art. 27.
[53] Morocco–Nigeria BIT, Art. 27(2) ("(f) The Tribunal shall interpret its award and give reasons and bases of its decision at the request of either Party. Unless otherwise agreed by the Parties, the venue of arbitration shall be at the seat of the Permanent Court of Arbitration at the Hague (the Netherlands)."
[54] Morocco–Nigeria BIT, Art. 27.
[55] Morocco–Nigeria, BIT, Art. 27(2)(e).

Conclusion

The principally Afro–European Bilateral Investment Treaties that began in the second half of the twentieth century took a detour to Asia before coming back to Africa, connecting a limited number of African states with one another. Their embrace was as hesitant as their delayed occurrence, slow rise, sluggish ratification, gradual dwindling, and apparent halt.

The evidence is now clear that Africa has opted to bypass BIT connectivity by including investment rules in economic blocks step-by-step and eventually ensuring their unification through the attempted Pan African Investment Code (PAIC) or an investment protocol promised to be a part of the AfCFTA. A unified investment code appears to be where the promise now lies. As the modernization of BITs continues, however, the Morocco–Nigeria BIT seems to be the most doctrinally sound embodiment of what Africa's reform efforts want to accomplish.

PART VI
THE FUTURE OF AFRICA'S INTERNATIONAL INVESTMENT LAW REGIMES

Because the regional arrangements share some of the defining characteristics of the fragmentation that bilateral investment treaties by their very nature contain, Africa is attempting to remedy these and related problems of incoherence within itself and across continents by moving beyond bilateralism and regionalism. The principal manifestation of this desire is the recent adoption of the Agreement Establishing the African Continental Free Trade Area (AfCFTA).[1] AfCFTA aims at creating a Free Trade Area and eliminating overlapping regional memberships and parallel, and incongruent obligations, including in investment by adapting an additional Protocol on Investment. The Protocol was adopted as this book was getting ready to go to press. The Protocol builds on the innovative Pan-African Investment Code (PAIC).[2] This part presents a brief exposition of these two instruments (Chapters 27 and 28) and offers a summary of conclusions (Chapter 29).

[1] The Agreement establishing the African Continental Free Trade Area (CFTA) is available at https://au.int/en/treaties/agreement-establishing-african-continental-free-trade-area.

[2] For commentary on the Pan-African Investment Code in light of contemporary developments, *see* Won L. Kidane, *Contemporary Trends in International Investment Law and Africa's Dilemmas in the Pan-African Investment Code*, 50 George Washington Int'l L. Rev. (2018).

27

The Pan-African Investment Code as a Bridge to AfCFTA Investment Protocol

A precursor to the African Continental Free Trade Area (AfCFTA) Investment Protocol, the Pan-African Investment Code (PAIC) was considered an innovative approach that attempted to resolve some of Africa's traditional dilemmas in terms of striking the right balance between investment attraction and protection on the one hand, and the preservation of policy space to the sovereign on the other. This chapter analyzes the approach that PAIC has taken and how the AfCFTA Investment Protocol built on its innovations and corrected some of the excesses.

PAIC was built on preexisting treaties and even sought to replace most over time. Substantively as well as procedurally, it is by no means a complete novelty although the changes that it proposed are not exactly mundane. In particular, it is largely based on such treaties and models as the SADC Model.[1] This chapter critically evaluates PAIC in light of the old rules and institutions and contemporary trends.[2]

Objectives

The objective of PAIC is "to promote, facilitate and protect investments that foster the sustainable development of each Member State, and in particular, the Member State where the investment is located."[3] The emphasis is on the promotion, facilitation, and protection just like any traditional investment treaty; what is unusual is the focus on the nature of this investment, for instance, it has to be one that fosters not just any development, but sustainable development.

The reference to the states' right to regulate for the sake of sustainable development is not the only interesting feature. It also expressly seeks "to achieve an overall balance of the rights and obligations between Member States and the investors under this Code"[4] and recognizes "the crucial role played by women and youth in the development of Africa."[5] Even more interestingly, it includes a matter almost every BIT or

[1] *See* Southern Afr. Dev. Community, SADC Model Bilateral Investment Treaty Template with Commentary, Arts. 20–22 (2012), http://www.iisd.org/itn/wp-content/uploads/2012/10/SADC-Model-BIT-Template-Final.pdf.

[2] A few pages of the discussions in this chapter were previously published by the same author in Kidane, *Contemporary Trends in International Investment Law and Africa's Dilemmas in the Pan-African Investment Code.*

[3] Afr. Union Comm'n, Draft Pan-African Investment Code, Ch. 1, Art. 1 (Dec. 2016), https://au.int/sites/default/files/documents/32844-doc-draft_pan-african_investment_code_december_2016_en.pdf [hereinafter PAIC

[4] *Id.* at Preamble.

[5] *Id.*

Africa's International Investment Law Regimes. Won L. Kidane, Oxford University Press. © Oxford University Press 2023.
DOI: 10.1093/oso/9780197745571.003.0027

RTA expressly wishes to avoid and avoids—the free movement of persons. The PAIC expressly says that "the free movement of people is a fundamental pillar of African integration."[6]

Scope and Structure

The PAIC enshrines the rights and responsibilities of not only the contracting states, but also the investors.[7] Although enshrining investor responsibilities in investment treaties was never a part of the original design of IIL, as indicated in previous chapters, it is becoming increasingly fashionable. The PAIC is part of that trend.

Structurally, the PAIC was designed to replace intra-Africa BITs and any other investment rules in RECs whenever those rules permit their own replacement whether due to the expiry of time or through agreement.[8] In the event of concurrent existence, PAIC provides that the member states "may" provide that PAIC rules supersede.[9] The "may" in the draft is a function perhaps of it being a draft, but the idea is for the member states to make a choice whether they want the Code to override all preexisting intra-Africa investment rules or perhaps permit a reservation. In any case, if the African Union had chosen to adopt the PAIC, it would have become the most dominant, if not the exclusive, intra-Africa investment rule, which would have in turn shaped the African landscape even vis-à-vis the rest of the world. The African Union instead opted for the AfCFTA Protocol discussed in the next chapter.

Substantive Rules

The PAIC contains elaborate standards of treatment, expropriation, and compensation, as well as unique provisions on labor and environment, corporate social responsibility, ethics, and corruption.

Standard of Treatment

The most important rules on the treatment of investment are Most Favored Nation and National Treatment but the principles are stated with some clarity in terms of what is included and what is excluded. It begins with the classic Most Favored Nation formulation: "Each Member State shall accord to investors of another Member State treatment no less favorable than it accords, in like circumstances, to investors of any other Member State or of a third country with respect to the management, conduct,

[6] *Id.*
[7] *Id.* at Art. 2.
[8] *See id.* at Art. 3(1)–(3).
[9] *Id.* at Art. 3(2).

operation, expansion, sale or other disposition of investment."[10] It further defines what constitutes "like circumstances" in some detail,[11] but more importantly, it lists elaborate exceptions to the principle.[12]

The exceptions appear to have the potential to swallow the rule. First, the Code permits each state to have a list of prohibited sectors without imposing any limits.[13] Any member may submit such list at the time of ratification limiting their obligation. Nothing constrains their choice of limiting Most Favored Nation.[14] Second, the exception begins with this broad state power: "Member States may adopt measures that derogate from the Most-Favored-Nation principle."[15] And without linking this broad power to any limitation, the following provision states: "Any regulatory measure taken by a Member State that is designed and applied to protect or enhance legitimate public welfare objectives, such as public health, safety and the environment, does not constitute a breach of the Most-Favored-Nation principle."[16] The next provision adds measures affecting "public morals."[17]

The most interesting aspect of the formulation is not the addition of the exceptions such as "public morals" not commonly seen in other investment treaties, but the totally discretionary nature of what goes into the exceptions list. This is an excellent example of Africa's residual dilemma in this area. African states want to open their markets to each other but still have that fear of the strong stranger taking advantage of them. This might be a demonstration of their zealous guarding of their markets and interests, although the strict guarding appears to be misdirected.

Although the National Treatment provision also maintained its classic formulation,[18] just like Most Favored Nation, it is burdened with broad exceptions. Curiously, however, the exception is stated slightly differently: "Member States may adopt measures that derogate from the National Treatment principle provided such measures are not arbitrary."[19] The Most Favored Nation exception stated above does not contain the arbitrariness limitation. In any case, the states maintain the right to discriminate when it is in the national interest, pertains to national security, health, environment, tax, and government subsidies aimed at national development.[20] Just like Most Favored Nation, the states also have preserved the discretion to attach a list of excluded sectors.[21]

[10] *Id.* at Art. 7(1).
[11] *See id.* at Art. 7(3).
[12] *Id.* at Art. 8.
[13] *See id.* at Art. 18.
[14] *See id.* at Arts. 8(4), 18.
[15] *Id.* at Art. 8(1).
[16] *Id.* at Art. 8(2).
[17] *Id.* at Art. 8(3).
[18] *See id.* at Art. 9(1) ("A Member State shall accord to investors of another Member State treatment no less favorable than it accords, in like circumstances, to its own investors with respect to the management, conduct, operation, and sale or other disposition of investments").
[19] *Id.* at Art. 10(1).
[20] *See id.* at Arts. 10(2)–(8).
[21] *Id.* at Art. 10(5).

Expropriation and Compensation

The expropriation provision does not follow the Hull Rule that many contemporary rules do. The Code states the rule in these terms:

> Investments in Member States shall not be nationalized, expropriated or subjected to measures having effect equivalent to nationalization or expropriation except if the following conditions are met in a cumulative manner:
> (a) a public purpose related to the internal needs of that Member State;
> (b) on a non-discriminatory basis;
> (c) against adequate compensation; and
> (d) under due process of law.[22]

While it adopts the common rule on the timing of the valuation, it omits the Hull principles of promptness and effectiveness of the compensation.[23] This is another example of the less favorable treatment of intra-Africa investment.

Additional Provisions

The PAIC enshrines numerous other rules that are not typically found in existing investment treaties or even in some of the new proposals. Separate chapters are dedicated for development related issues and investor obligations. The development related issues under Chapter 3 comprise performance requirements in Article 17 and lists of scheduled investment sectors in Article 18. Both are detailed and grant enormous discretion to the member states. The discretion includes preferential treatment to local industries and enterprises and remedial measures for historically discriminated groups. The discretion, which essentially qualifies the standards of treatment, including Most Favored Nation and National Treatment, stated in very broad terms:

> 2. Member States may introduce performance requirements to promote domestic investments and local content. Measures covered by this Paragraph include, *inter alia*:
> (a) Measures to grant preferential treatment to any enterprise so qualifying under the domestic law of a Member State in order to achieve national or sub-national regional development goals;
> (b) Measures to support the development of local entrepreneurs;
> (c) Measures to enhance productive capacity, increase employment, increase human resource capacity and training, research and development including of new technologies, technology transfer, innovation and other benefits of investment through the use of specified requirements on investors;

[22] *Id.* at Art. 11(1).
[23] *See id.* at Art. 12.

(d) Measures to address historically based economic disparities suffered by identifiable ethnic or cultural groups due to discriminatory or oppressive measures against such groups prior to the adoption of this Code.[24]

The Scheduled Lists under Article 18 permit member states to exempt any sectors from coverage and primarily from the application of National Treatment. Again, this discretion is unrestricted.[25]

The investor obligation chapter appears to be more elaborate and more intrusive than the traditional and even the contemporary trends. It requires that investments comply with "national and internationally accepted standards of corporate governance,"[26] and among other things must "ensure the equitable treatment of all shareholders, in accordance with national laws."[27] Investors are also required to undertake "socio-political obligations" such as refraining from political interference and showing respect for "socio-cultural values."[28]

The PAIC also contains anti-bribery rules[29] and corporate social responsibility rules, including an obligation to contribute to the achievement of "sustainable development of the host state."[30] There are also elaborate provisions on business ethics and human rights. Most notably, these provisions obligate member states to "support and respect the protection of internationally recognized human rights," and more significantly "ensure equitable sharing of wealth derived from investments."[31]

Finally, in what appears to be a unique addition, the PAIC provides: "Member States may adopt policies on cultural and linguistic diversity in promotion of investments."[32] What is not contained in PAIC is as interesting as what is included. There are two principles of IIL that have been blamed for more than their share of the controversy over the years: fair and equitable treatment and full protection and security. Some African states have been called on to answer charges of violating these principles in ICSID proceedings.[33] The PAIC resolves the interpretive problem by simply omitting them.

The PAIC rewrote some of the most entrenched substantive principles of IIL and added more provisions protective of the states' rights to regulate and shrunk the investor's latitude. Although most of that is consistent with contemporary trends, the PAIC advances the protectionist agenda one step further. The driving force behind this reformulation is a sense of enduring victimization. Ironically, however, the counterreaction selects the least blameworthy for a particularly unfavorable treatment that the AfCFTA Investment Protocol attempted to correct.

24 *Id.* at Art. 17(2).

25 *See id.* at Art. 18(3) ("Any Member State may submit a List of scheduled investment sectors that are excluded from the National Treatment principle where applicable"); *Id.* at Art. 18(4) ("The Lists of scheduled of investment sectors form integral part of this Code and Member States agree to respect them").

26 *Id.* at Art. 19(1).

27 *Id.* at Art. 19(3)(a).

28 *Id.* at Art. 20.

29 *Id.* at Art. 21.

30 *Id.* at Art. 22(3).

31 *Id.* at Art. 24(a), (e).

32 *Id.* at Art. 38.

33 *See* discussion in Part III (discussing the types of cases that African states were involved in and the results).

Investor–State Dispute Settlement

ISDS is perhaps the most controversial aspect of IIL. As a preliminary matter, it is important to note before ISDS is discussed that the Code gives the African Court of Justice the ultimate jurisdiction to adjudicate state-to-state disputes pertaining to the Code. The exact terms are important to see for a meaningful commentary:

> Investor–State
>
> (c) If consultations fail, the dispute may be resolved through arbitration, subject to the applicable laws of the host State and/or the mutual agreement of the disputing parties, and subject to exhaustion of local remedies; and
>
> (d) Where recourse is made to arbitration under Paragraph 3, the arbitration may be conducted at any established African public or African private alternative dispute resolution center. Arbitration shall be governed by the [UNCITRAL] rules.
>
> (2) Once recourse is made to a particular forum of dispute settlement, the forum chosen shall be used to the exclusion of the other. Decisions of this particular forum shall be final.[34]

First of all, this provision, although not entirely clear, appears to require the exhaustion of local remedies under the host state's laws before the investor could resort to arbitration. Second, if arbitration is resorted to (presumably by the investor), it anticipates the use of existing or prospective African institutions. Finally, it also requires that whoever administers the arbitration, the tribunal uses the UNCITRAL Rules, which means that the anticipated African Permanent Court of Arbitration or the African Union Court of Arbitration would not have its own rules of procedure but instead use the UNCTRAL Rules. In any case, as the design of either the African Permanent Court of Arbitration or the African Union Court of Arbitration is not yet complete, the details including the default appointing authority are not clear so far. Nonetheless, it is fair to expect that whether it is the Permanent Court or African Union Court of Arbitration, it would have its own rules of procedure although the UNCITRAL Rules could obviously play a foundational role in the constitutional design. This particular provision has just planted the seed for a Pan-African Court of Arbitration, whether it is called the Permanent Court or the African Union Court.

Another feature of the proposed ISDS system is allowing for host state counterclaims as follows:

> Counterclaims by Member States
>
> 1. Where an investor or its investment is alleged by a Member State party in a dispute settlement proceeding under this Code to have failed to comply with its obligations under this Code or other relevant rules and principles of domestic and international law, the competent body hearing such a dispute shall consider whether this breach, if

[34] PAIC, Art. 42.

> proven, is materially relevant to the issues before it, and if so, what mitigating or offsetting effects this may have on the merits of a claim or on any damages awarded in the event of such award.
>
> 2. A Member State may initiate a counterclaim against the investor before any competent body dealing with a dispute under this Code for damages or other relief resulting from an alleged breach of the Code.[35]

Again, although this provision lacks clarity, the idea is to have the tribunal consider the investor's own possible violations of its obligations under the Code whether for the adjudication of fault (i.e., the merits) or assessment of damages. Relatedly, this provision also gives the host state the right to submit counterclaims and seek setoff or even independent damages in an action that the arbitrator initiates. The technical difficulties of ascertaining investor consent in a treaty between states notwithstanding, this is nothing revolutionary now as it is in line with contemporary trends. Classical IIL evolved as a one-way street largely because traditionally private actors are not considered subjects of international law.[36] But this new trend does not resolve the dilemma completely because the admissibility of counterclaims would still depend on allegations of violations of the Code provisions pertaining to investor obligation such as ethics, environmental, and anti-bribery rules that would have other means of resolution, such as domestic court litigation or contact arbitration. But again, whether the host state could counterclaim on the basis of breach of contract, for example, remains unsettled even in the contemporary drafts. The lack of clarity is not necessarily unintended. States may not necessarily desire an investment tribunal to decide on whatever causes of action that they may have against the investor. They might, for example, prefer to submit their claim to domestic court or even another arbitral tribunal on the basis contract.

In terms of enforcement, because the PAIC does not set up its own enforcement mechanism nor refer to the ICSID enforcement regime, the presumption is that enforcement will take place under the New York Convention. That said, while the preliminary policy choices that the drafters of the Code have made are clear, in its current formulation, the Code's ISDS provisions lack technical clarity. The AfCFTA

[35] *Id.* at Art. 43.

[36] Helene Bubrowski, *Balancing IIA Arbitration Through the Use of Counterclaims*, *in* Improving International Investment Agreements 216 (noting that "as of [2013], IIA fail to impose clear obligations on investors. It remains unresolved whether, in general, private parties can be subject to obligations under international law"). To be sure, the ICSID Convention in Article 46 anticipates that states may submit counterclaims as long as consent is independently established. ICSID Convention, Art. 46. The exact language is the following:

> Except as the parties otherwise agree, the Tribunal shall, if requested by a party, determine any incidental or additional claims or counter-claims arising directly out of the subject-matter of the dispute provided that they are within the scope of the consent of the parties and are otherwise within the jurisdiction of the Centre. *Id.*

But the application of this provision has been a subject of controversy especially as it relates to the manner of expression of consent. Two recent cases have taken opposing views on this issue. *See* Spyridon Roussalis v. Rom., ICSID Case No. ARB/06/1, Award (Dec. 7, 2011) (declining jurisdiction); Goetz v. Burundi, ICSID Case No. ARB/01/2, Sentence (June 21, 2012) (upholding jurisdiction).

Investment Protocol has thus far deferred dispute settlement to a yet to be negotiated Annex. It is expected to correct some of the deficiencies of the PAIC in this regard.

To add to the above issues of lack of clarity, the Code also contains the following independent choice of law rule on top of the previously mentioned choice of law provision: "Any claim or dispute arising from this Code shall be decided in accordance with the provisions of this Code as well any other national, regional or international laws, rules or principles."[37] Article 42(c) appears to give the parties the right to choose the applicable substantive law when it states: "If consultations fail, the dispute may be resolved through arbitration, subject to the applicable laws of the host State and/ or the mutual agreement of the disputing parties."[38] This provision is unclear because "subject to the applicable laws" at first appears to refer to the host state's arbitration law, but closer scrutiny would render that interpretation meaningless because it would mean arbitration is available only to the extent it is mandated or permitted by domestic law. That would effectively reduce the whole ISDS provision to an ad hoc sovereign command because the parties could contract out of it, or the host could preclude it through its domestic law preclude it. To avoid that radical departure, "subject to" could be interpreted to refer to the choice of substantive law.

[37] PAIC, Art. 44.
[38] *Id.* at Art. 42(c).

28
Protocol to the Agreement Establishing the African Continental Free Trade Area on Investment

In February 2023 the Assembly of Heads of State and Government of the Africa Union adopted the long-anticipated Protocol to the African Continental Free Trade Area Agreement (AfCFTA) on Investment ("AfCFTA Investment Protocol" or "AIP") in Addis Ababa.[1] The AIP rests on the foundations laid by the innovative PAIC and regional instruments that predated it.

Indeed, it expressly notes in the Preamble that it is "MINDFUL of best practices incorporated in the Pan African Investment Code, the investment instruments of the Regional Economic Communities, bilateral investment treaties concluded by African States, national investment laws as well as other relevant international investment instruments and agreements."[2] Most importantly, it enshrines the Member States' "[determination] to establish a balanced, coherent, clear, transparent, predictable and mutually advantageous continental framework of principles and rules for investment promotion, facilitation and protection."[3] In that sense, it seeks to correct the overcorrection of the PAIC and regional instruments and strike the right balance between regulatory autonomy and the protection of foreign investment. This chapter assesses how well this most contemporary instrument brings Africa's experience of the last six decades to bear and balances the competing interests.

Relationship with Existing Investment Treaties

Within five to 10 years, the AIP will be the principal source of international investment law governing intra-Africa investment because the Contracting Parties have agreed to replace their bilateral and regional investment treaties within this period.

Article 49 addresses the AIP's relationship with exiting treaties. With respect to BITs, it provides: "1. Existing bilateral investment treaties concluded between the State Parties shall be terminated within five (5) years from the entry into force of this Protocol. Upon termination of existing bilateral investment treaties concluded between the State Parties, their survival clauses shall also be terminated."[4] It anticipates

[1] PROTOCOL TO THE AGREEMENT ESTABLISHING THE AFRICAN CONTINENTAL FREE TRADE AREA ON INVESTMENT (AIP), Preamble. ANNEX ____.
[2] AIP, Preamble.
[3] AIP, Preamble.
[4] AIP, Art. 49.

Africa's International Investment Law Regimes. Won L. Kidane, Oxford University Press. © Oxford University Press 2023.
DOI: 10.1093/oso/9780197745571.003.0028

that all existing BITs between any two states that have ratified AIP will be replaced on the fifth anniversary of the entry into force of AIP, presumably regardless of when each state has ratified the AIP. That presumption is needed because, under Article 48 (2) AIP enters into force: "in accordance with the provisions of Articles 23(2) and 23(4) of the Agreement."[5] Under Article 1 of AIP, "Agreement" refers to the "Agreement Establishing the African Continental Free Trade Area." Article 23(2) says that the Protocol "shall enter into force thirty (30) days after the deposit of the twenty second (22nd) instrument of ratification."[6] For each member, the Protocol comes into effect "on the date of deposit of instrument of ratification or accession."[7]

It is, therefore, possible that any BITs could potentially be replaced as soon as any states parties to the BITs ratify or accede to the AIP as long as five years had lapsed since the AIP came into effect through the ratification of enough number of states. The states that ratify or accede late should recognize that their BITs may be superseded as soon as they ratify the AIP and not necessarily at the time the same pair ratifies. Their ratification could have come at different times as in A ratifying on day one and B on the fifth anniversary. The fifth anniversary would thus have the effect of replacing many intra-Africa BITs.

To clarify a potential confusion about what definition of investment governs after the regime transitions to AIP, Article 49(1) helpfully states: "For the avoidance of doubt, this Protocol shall apply to investments of investors of State Parties that meet the criteria of an investment at the time of the termination of existing bilateral investment treaties concluded between the State Parties."[8] As a matter of fact, the same presumption applies for all substantive and procedural rules. It means that after the BITs are retired, the AIP will be the singular source of law as between those that have ratified it following the five-year grace period.

The AIP strictly prohibits the conclusion of any new BITs as between any Contracting Parties. It is, however, more forgiving to the regional investment agreements. Compare the formulation of the two. The BITs are subject to this mandatory rule in the following terms: "2. State Parties shall not conclude new bilateral investment treaties among themselves after the adoption of this Protocol."[9] On the other hand, the regional agreements are subject to the following best-efforts rule: "3. State Parties shall make best endeavours to review and revise relevant existing regional investment agreements adopted by the Regional Economic Communities to achieve alignment with the Protocol within a period between five (5) to ten (10) years from the entry into force of this Protocol."[10] Because most Intra-African investment is regulated by the regional agreements, AIP's preemptory effect largely remains a matter of regional preference because the obligation that the Contracting Parties have assumed under the AIP vis-à-vis regional investment treaties such as SDAC, COMESA, and ECOWAS is one of best efforts. Because the regional treaties are the sources of the principal confusion, the resolution that AIP offers remains a matter of regional grace.

[5] AIP, Art. 48(2).
[6] AfCFTA, Agreement Art. 23(2).
[7] AfCFTA, Agreement, Art. 23(4).
[8] AIP, Art. 49(1).
[9] AIP, Art. 49(2).
[10] AIP, Art. 49(3).

Owing to its structural limitations, AIP can address investment treaties with third countries only indirectly and that is exactly what it does. It provides that "4. State Parties may take into account the requirements of this Protocol when negotiating international investment agreements and when reviewing existing international investment agreements concluded with Third Parties."[11] As to Third Parties, AIP remains a negotiating set of guidelines.

It does, however, make Africa's position explicit. Whether it will influence Africa's existing and future investment treaties with the East and West will depend on each states individualized negotiation. That said, through the passage of time, some of AIP's explication of existing rules and newly incorporated principles will inevitably continue to crystalize and shape general international law on the protection of foreign investment.

Structure

The text of AIP is divided into eight chapters. Chapter 1 contains general provisions including definition of terms, objectives, and scope of application, admission of investment, and denial of benefits. Chapter 2 covers investment promotion and facilitation. The core of investment protection standards come after facilitation in Chapter 3, giving the appearance that AIP is primarily a facilitation instrument. Many of the more contemporary sustainable development related issues are assembled in Chapter 4 immediately followed by elaborate investor obligations under Chapter 5. Chapter 6 introduces institutional arrangements. Chapter 7 is dedicated to the management and settlement of disputes although it defers the dispute settlement rules to an Annex to be negotiated within a year of the adoption of the AIP. This is indicative of the continued dilemma on ISDS. Chapter 8 concludes with technical final provisions requiring no comments.

Definition, Objectives, and Scope of Application

Like any investment treaty, the most important term that it defines is "investment." It took what could be considered middle-of-the-road approach by limiting the open-endedness in traditional investment treaties by adding such qualifiers as the maintenance of "substantial business in the territory of that Host State."[12] Attempts to codify rules that have emerged out of arbitral jurisprudence over the years including the *Salini* factors and clarify accumulated ambiguities in the jurisprudence. The key codification is: "For greater certainty, the investment must have the following characteristics: commitment of capital or other resources, the expectation of gain or profit, a certain duration, assumption of risk, and a significant contribution to the Host State's sustainable development."[13] To clarify matters further, the definition also contains a negative list.[14]

11 AIP, Art. 49(4).
12 AIP, Art. 1 (Definition of "Investment").
13 AIP, Art. 1 (Definition of "Investment")
14 AIP, Art. 1 (Definition of "investment") ("For greater certainty, investment does not include:

For the purpose of encouraging intra-Africa investment, the AIP aims at striking the right balance between the state's right to regulate and the protection of the investor's rights by "establishing a balanced, predictable and transparent continental legal and institutional framework for investment, taking into account the interests of State Parties, investors and local communities"[15] and "providing a sound legal framework for the prevention, management and settlement of investment disputes."[16]

The scope of application is unremarkable except two points worth highlighting. The first is the exclusion of taxation measures from the scope of coverage in express terms stated as "taxation measures taken in accordance with the applicable laws and regulations of a State Party."[17] If a Contracting State enacts laws that are discriminatory because they violate National Treatment and MFN, the only inquiry permitted under this provision is whether the State acted in accordance with its own laws. The laws could be discriminatory, but their application cannot.

It is a significant carveout. Other contemporary treaties handle this issue differently. For example, the oft-cited 2019 Netherlands Model BIT subjects tax issues to the same MFN and NT rules in the following terms:

> 1. With respect to taxes, fees, charges and to fiscal deductions and exemptions, each Contracting Party shall, regarding the operation, management, maintenance, use, enjoyment and disposal of the investment, accord to investors of the other Contracting Party who are engaged in any economic activity in its territory, treatment not less favorable than that accorded to its own investors or to those of any third State who are in like situations, whichever is more favorable to the investors concerned.[18]

In that sense, it is theoretically possible and indeed likely that just like the PAIC and some of the regional treaties, AIP treats African investors in Africa less favorably than those from third countries because many of the BITs that African states have signed with third world countries subject taxation measures to the nondiscrimination rules. Taxation could be a powerful incentive and disincentive. This AIP rule leaves unlimited discretion in the hands of the Contracting States without leveling the playing field.

The second remarkable exemption seems innocuous but is equally significant: "The Protocol shall not apply to any dispute arising solely from an alleged breach of a contract

debt securities issued by a government or loans to a government or government owned or controlled enterprise;
portfolio investments, that is, investment that does not give the investor the possibility to exercise effective management or influence in the management of the enterprise;
claims to money that arise solely from commercial contracts for the sale of goods or services by a national or enterprise in the territory of a State Party to an enterprise in the territory of another State Party, or the extension of credit in connection with a commercial transaction; or
claims arising from an order or judgment rendered in any judicial, administrative or arbitral proceeding").

[15] AIP, Art. 2(b).
[16] AIP, Art. 2 (c).
[17] AIP, Art. 3(4)(e).
[18] Netherlands 2019 BIT Model, Art. 10(1). Text available at https://arbitrationblog.kluwerarbitration.com/wp-content/uploads/sites/48/2020/05/new-model-Netherlands-BIT.pdf.

between a State Party and an investor."[19] This is designed to disbar the so-called umbrella clause claims. The problem here is a rather technical one and it relates to the definition of investment. AIP defines "investment" to include: "rights under contracts including turnkey, construction, production, management, concession or other contract."[20] If, by definition, rights under contract are considered investment and the only way of enforcing them is through a claim of breach of contract, the AIP takes away what it has given with one hand with the other. If a breach of contract claim is precluded as a remedy, the remedy for a breach of contract claim would not accrue until it rises to the level of other treaty violations such as expropriation and denial of justice discussed in subsequent sections. It is not clear if this was intended or a drafting oversight.

The balancing of the interests does, however, begin in the same chapter under the Denial of Benefits title. There are at least three notable developments under this rubric. First, AIP permits the Contracting Parties to deny the benefits of the Protocol "[if] an investment has no substantial business activity in the territory of the *Home* State."[21] The definition of investment also requires substantiality in the *Host* state.[22] This rule introduces a dual-substantiality requirement. To qualify for protection, investment must pass the substantiality test in both the home and host states. This limits the benefits of the Protocol to enterprises that are already well established in their home state. Not to be denied the benefits of the Protocol, investors of Contracting States who want to start a new substantial business in another Contracting State must first establish a substantial business in their home state and then carry out substantial business activities in the host state.[23]

This denies the benefits of the Protocol to investors who want to start a new substantial business in the host states through new juridical vehicles such as special purpose vehicles (SPVs) because the definition of an investor includes "a legal or juridical person, in accordance with the definition of the legal or juridical person of the Home State in this article, that has made an investment in the territory of the Host State."[24] Under this definition, to be considered an investor, one does not need to have established an investment in the home state. If such person wants to start a new business in the host state, however, the benefits of the AIP could be denied unless such person

[19] AIP, Art. 3(5).

[20] AIP, definition, "Investment" (e).

[21] AIP, Art. 5(a). Emphasis added.

[22] AIP, definition of "investment" (""Investment" means an enterprise or company, as defined in this Article, which is established, acquired or expanded in conformity with the laws and regulations of a Host State by an investor which maintains substantial business in the territory of that Host State. The enterprise or company may possess assets").

[23] AIP defines substantiality as "'Substantial business activity' requires an overall examination of all the circumstances on a case by case basis, by a State Party, of all the circumstances, including, among other factors: i. the nature, size, scope and sector of business, ii. the amount of investment brought into the territory of a State Party, iii. the effect of the investment on the local community, and iv. the length of time the investment has been in operation. Generally, an investment shall be taken to have substantial business activities in the territory of a State Party where it conducts its core and relevant income generating activities, through the employment of a reasonable number of suitably qualified persons and by having a minimum level of expenditure which is proportionate to its level of the relevant activities in the territory of that State Party

For greater certainty, the overall assessment on the case by case basis shall take into account the specific economic and investment policies of the concerned State Party at the time of the admission of the investment").

[24] AIP, Definition, "Investor" (b).

also establishes a substantial business in the home state. It is also unclear whether this was an intended result or a drafting oversight.

Second, the Denial of Benefits provision also permits the Contracting Parties to deny the benefits of AIP for among other things, if "an investor or investment is engaged in activities prejudicial to the essential and national interests of the Host State."[25] This is a broad exception that will have to be determined on a case-by-case basis including presumably through dispute settlement. The effect of this is the suspension of any benefits that the investor would have gotten under AIP. This could potentially take an administrative or even judicial action, which could be disputed by the investor in an ISDS process or may be invoked as a defense by the host state in an action initiated by the investor alleging any violations of its rights under AIP. Because there is no specific definition of national interest and the mechanisms of its determination, it will likely be an additional source of uncertainty and dispute.

Finally, the benefits of the Protocol could also be denied to "an investor or investment [who] has committed a breach of a specific binding obligation under Chapter 5 [investor obligations]."[26] Some of the investor obligations under Chapter 5, for example, include: "Investors and their investments shall carry out their operations in compliance with all relevant domestic laws and regulations, administrative guidelines as well as applicable international law."[27] The violation of any relevant domestic laws or regulations including administrative guidelines by the investor could potentially result in the denial of the benefits of the Protocol. Another example of the breadth of this exclusionary ground is the investors' obligation to comply with business ethics expressed in the following terms: "Investors and their investments shall comply with high standards of business ethics, investment-related human rights and labour standards, and in particular . . . (g) act in accordance with fair business, marketing and advertising practices."[28] These are extremely broad obligations but their violation could result in the denial of benefits of the Protocol. This is yet another demonstration of the precarity of the African investor's tenure in another African state.

The AIP does, however, helpfully outline the mechanics of the application of the denial of benefits provisions by linking it to the dispute settlement provision, which may ameliorate its adverse impact in some ways. It states that "for the avoidance of doubt, the exercise by a Host State of its right to deny benefits to an investor of another State Party and investment of such investor may be subject to review in accordance with Chapter 7 [Dispute Settlement] of this Protocol."[29] If a Contracting State denies an investor the benefits of the Protocol because of any of the substantive grounds of denial, the denying state's compliance with the substantive grounds of denial may be determined through the dispute settlement processes of the Protocol just like any violation of any substantive protection standards. Only this time, the question would be whether the Protocol applies or not. In that sense, the inquiry is analogous to whether there is a covered investment in the first place. Indeed, it is an extension of that inquiry

[25] AIP, Art. 5(1)(c).
[26] AIP, Art. 5(g).
[27] AIP, Art. 32.
[28] AIP, Art. 33(g).
[29] AIP, Art. 5(2).

because, to qualify for protection, an investor must not only prove the existence of a substantial business that meets the definition but should also avoid falling under the grounds of exclusion. Either or both prongs could be a subject or subjects of dispute suitable for resolution under the dispute settlement mechanism set forth in Chapter 7. The link that AIP establishes between the denial of benefit and investor obligations is an additional complication and disfavor which African investors face not faced by investors from third countries.

Investment Promotion and Facilitation

Investment promotion and facilitation is front and center, but the prescriptions are largely discretionary and permissive with two notable exceptions: the provision of information and establishment of a National Focal Point. Both investment promotion and investment facilitation are stated in such terms as "shall endeavour to promote"[30] and "shall, subject to their respective laws and regulations facilitate investments that contribute to sustainable development,"[31] and "may introduce incentives in order to attract."[32]

The only one of two mandatory rules pertains to the establishment of what is called National Focal Point (NFP): "Each Party shall designate a National Focal Point which shall provide support to investors from other state Parties."[33] The purpose of the NFP is to "provide information on the legal, policy and institutional frameworks governing investments."[34] This is linked to the only other mandatory rule, the publication of information: "Each State Party, in accordance with it its capabilities, shall publish and make accessible electronically or through other means, in a reasonable period of time, all relevant laws and regulations which pertain to or affect the operation of this Protocol."[35] In a way, the establishment of the NFP and publication on regulatory and other information is complementary to the obligations assumed under investment protection standards. Standing alone, the promotion and facilitation rules are mostly advisory.

Investment Protection Standards

AIP enshrines the nondiscrimination rules of National Treatment and Most Favored Treatment (MFN) with respectable clarity and proximity to their classic expression. The general rule on National Treatment is stated as: "1. Each State Party shall accord to investors of another State Party and their investments treatment no less favourable than it accords, in like circumstances, to its own investors with respect to the management, conduct, operation, use, expansion and sale or other disposition of their

30 AIP, Art. 6.
31 AIP, Art. 7(1).
32 AIP, Art. 8(1)(a).
33 AIP, Art. 9(1).
34 AIP, Art. 9(2).
35 AIP, Art. 10(1).

investments."[36] The all-important "in like circumstances" qualifier is also properly defined to avoid the kinds of confusion seen in ISDS jurisprudence.[37]

The exceptions do, however, introduce a measure of difficulty that are not common in the principle's ordinary formulation. Three of them are worth highlighting. The first is preferential treatment under national law "in order to achieve national development objectives or address the internal needs of designated disadvantaged persons, groups, or regions."[38] The first prong lacks the specificity that the second prong has. The lack of clarity that could invite misinterpretation pertains to the broad "national development objectives," which could arguably cover any number of matters that could potentially be used as a pretext to deny benefit.

The second exception caries a similar risk of overbreadth, that is, exception pertaining to "sectors or geographical regions that represent strategic importance for the Host State in accordance with its laws and regulations."[39] "Strategic importance," like "national development objectives," gives the host state broad latitude to immunize significant portions of the economy and geographic areas from national treatment. And again, where that occurs, the African investors would be at a great disadvantage compared to third party investors who benefit from treaties that do not contain these newer exceptions. This is particularly so because of the expression provision that states: "For greater clarity, discriminatory measures taken by a State Party to comply with its obligations under other regional or international agreements shall not be construed as a breach of Article 12 [National Treatment]."[40]

MFN appears in its classic formulation and is unburdened with the types of exceptions of National Treatment. It states:

> 1. Each State Party shall accord to investors of another State Party and their investments treatment no less favourable than it accords, in like circumstances, to investors of any other State Party or Third Parties with respect to the management, conduct, operation, use, expansion and sale or other disposition of their investments.[41]

Responding to jurisprudential confusion, it usefully clarifies that "treatment" does not include "dispute settlement procedures."[42]

[36] AIP, Art. 12(1).

[37] AIP, Art. 12(2) ("2. In assessing "in like circumstances" an overall examination is required on a case by-case basis, of all the circumstances of an investment, including, among others:

a. its effects on third persons and the local community;
b. its effects on the local, regional or national environment, the health of the populations, or on the global commons;
c. the sector in which the investor is active;
d. the aim of the measure in question;
e. the regulatory process generally applied in relation to a measure in question; and
f. any other factor directly relating to the investment or investor in relation to the measure in question.

The examination referred to in this Paragraph shall not be limited to or biased towards any one of the factors").

[38] AIP, Art. 13(2).

[39] AIP, Art. 13(3).

[40] AIP, Art. 13(4).

[41] AIP, Art. 14(1).

[42] AIP, Art. 14(3).

The most important departure from the classic investor protection rules comes in the form of elimination of the Fair and Equitable Treatment (FET) rule and its purported replacement with what is titled "Administrative and Judicial Treatment."

> 1. Each State Party shall ensure that, in administrative and judicial matters, investors and investments of another State Party are not subject to treatment which constitutes a fundamental denial of justice in criminal, civil and administrative adjudicative proceedings, an evident denial of due process, a manifest arbitrariness, a discrimination based on gender, race or religious beliefs, or an abusive treatment in administrative and judicial proceedings.[43]

This filters the essential and acceptable elements of FET, but because of lingering uncertainty, the drafters were not satisfied and added the following purported clarification:

> 2. For greater certainty, Paragraph 1 shall not be interpreted as equivalent to fair and equitable treatment. For further certainty, Paragraph 1 includes the minimum standard of treatment under customary international law and does not allow for an interpretation and application of such a standard that would go beyond the elements contained in Paragraph 1.[44]

They took care to say that it is not FET, but it still means "minimum standard of treatment under customary international law." Because many tribunals have equated FET with the minimum standard of treatment under customary international law and because many model BITs, including the Canadian and US Model BITs, have progressively equated FET with minimum standard of treatment, tribunals seized of a matter that requires them to decide the outer limits of Article 17 of AIP will not be spared of the difficulty that other tribunals have faced. They are now told that Article 17 is not FET, but it is "minimum standard of treatment." Subsection (1) of Article 17 would have offered better clarity without subsection (2).

AIP does a better job of expressing the rule on Full Protection and Security by limiting it to "Physical Protection and Security" the only way the standard could have meaningful existence independently of FEF. It states: "1. A State Party shall, subject to its capabilities, accord to investors and their investments physical protection and security no less favourable than that which it accords to the investments of its own investors or to the investments of the investors of any other State Party or Third Party."[45]

In this sense, AIP changes Full Protection and Security (FPS) to Physical Protection and Security (PPS) and mixes it with the nondiscrimination rules of NT and FET and adds a "subject to its capabilities"[46] prong presumably informed by the award in

43 AIP, Art. 17(1).
44 AIP, Art. 17(2).
45 AIP, Art. 18(1).
46 AIP Art. 18(1) para. 2. ("For greater certainty, the expression "subject to its capabilities" refers to the obligation of due diligence that a State Party shall exercise on its territory in accordance with customary international law and does not allow for an interpretation and application of such a standard that would go beyond the elements contained in this Paragraph").

the Zimbabwe cases in which the government's claim of its inability to protect were rejected.[47]

The PPS provision also incorporates the nondiscrimination rules under war and armed conflict related losses and compensation thereof. It does not contain any notable departure except placing this rule under PPS, a relatively new treaty provision.[48]

Overall, it is possible to say that AIP has improved clarity pertaining to what is traditionally the domain of FET by identifying specific and intolerable mistreatments and violations that require a legal remedy such as "a fundamental denial of justice," "evident denial of due process," "a manifest arbitrariness," and "abusive treatment." There is rightfully no reference to the notion of legitimate expectations, which has been a source of serious controversy in the jurisprudence. The drafters of this section of the AIP could not, however, resist the temptation of saying more in subsection 2, which might have added unnecessary confusion.

Expropriation

The expropriation provision begins unremarkably with a restatement of the Hull Rule, but ends with a strange infusion of the FET standard (at least nominally) as:

> 1. State Parties shall not, directly or indirectly, expropriate or nationalise investments in their territory except: a. for a public purpose; b.in accordance with due process pursuant to the procedure established by the laws of the State Party; c. in a non discriminatory manner; and d. against a fair and adequate compensation paid within a reasonable period of time in accordance with Article 21, and taking into account that the assessment of the reasonable period of time shall be made on a case by case basis in accordance with the domestic laws and regulations of the State Party and on a non-discriminatory basis.[49]

The clarity in the first prong is soon taken away by the confusion injected in the second where it refers to another provision for the determination of "fair and equitable compensation," a concept that has its own long and turbulent history but almost never as a part of the compensation prong of the expropriation doctrine. Here it replaces what is traditionally known as the "prompt, adequate and effective" compensation. The latter primarily focuses on the quantum of damages. The AIP approach goes beyond that and focuses on the fairness of the compensatory measure by linking it such substantive inquiries as:

[47] *See, e.g.*, Bernard von Pezold v. Zimbabwe, at ¶ 645.

[48] AIP, Art. 18(2) ("2. Investors of one State Party whose investments in the territory of the other State Party suffer losses as a result of a failure of the Host State to comply with Paragraph 1, owing to war or other armed conflict, revolution, revolt, insurrection or riot in the territory of the Host State shall, as regards restitution, indemnification, compensation or other settlement, be accorded by the Host State treatment no less favourable than that which the Host State accords to investments of its own natural and legal persons or to investments of investors of any other State Party or Third Party").

[49] AIP, Art. 19.

> balance between the public interest and interest of those affected, having regard for all relevant circumstances and taking account of the current and past use of the investment, the history of its acquisition, the fair market value of the investment, the purpose of the expropriation, the extent of previous profit made by the investor through the investment, the previous behaviour of the investor, and the duration of the investment.[50]

This is an entirely different set of considerations than assessing the value of what was taken. This provision turns the compensation prong of expropriation into a whole different substantive liability assessment rather than the determination of quantum. By hybridizing doctrine, the AIP experiment of migrating FET into expropriation does not simplify the most important investor protection rule: it merely sets it up for fresh controversy.

That is not the end of how compensation is assessed; there is more:

> 3. Compensation shall be assessed based on the fair market value of the expropriated investment at the date immediately before the expropriation took place ("date of expropriation") or before the measure became publicly known, whichever is earlier. For greater certainty, the fair and adequate compensation standard also applies in case of unlawful expropriation.
>
> 4. The computation of the fair market value of the expropriated property shall exclude any consequential losses or speculative or windfall profits claimed by the investor.[51]

A tribunal seized of an expropriation matter is offered a complicated template for the assessment of compensation if it finds that an expropriation had occurred. The guidance is not necessarily cogent. It must first determine what is fair and equitable compensation by reference to domestic laws and regulations.[52] It must then balance the equities between the public interest and the interests of those affected by the expropriation.[53] It must then assess the fair market value whether the expropriation is lawful or unlawful.[54] It must then "exclude any consequential losses or speculative or windfall profits claimed by the investor."[55] Applying all of these rules, it should presumably

50 AIP, Art. 21(2).

51 AIP, Art. 19(3)(4).

52 AIP, Art. 21 (1) ("1. Fair and adequate compensation shall be assessed on a case-by-case basis in relation to the fair market value of the expropriated investment, and in a reasonable period of time, in accordance with domestic laws and regulation").

53 AIP, Art. 21(2) ("2. The assessment of fair and adequate compensation shall be based on an equitable balance between the public interest and interest of those affected, having regard for all relevant circumstances and taking account of the current and past use of the investment, the history of its acquisition, the fair market value of the investment, the purpose of the expropriation, the extent of previous profit made by the investor through the investment, the previous behaviour of the investor, and the duration of the investment").

54 AIP, Art. 21(3) ("Compensation shall be assessed based on the fair market value of the expropriated investment at the date immediately before the expropriation took place ("date of expropriation") or before the measure became publicly known, whichever is earlier. For greater certainty, the fair and adequate compensation standard also applies in case of unlawful expropriation").

55 AIP, Art. 21(4) ("4. The computation of the fair market value of the expropriated property shall exclude any consequential losses or speculative or windfall profits claimed by the investor").

assign a number to the loss. While it may have the advantage of a self-contained set of rules for the assessment of damages, the steps in the assessment of damages do not progress in a linear and logical sequence permitting a methodical, step-by-step appraisal. It is a collection of norms in random order the application of which will face significant challenges. It is doubtful that this formulation improves the rule on expropriation. Because expropriation is by far the most advanced doctrine in international investment law, the AIP would have been better off without the additional disturbances.

Sustainable Development Related Issues

Chapter 4 of AIP is exclusively devoted to development related matters. It begins with the right to regulate[56] and covers such areas as environmental and labor standards,[57] climate change,[58] public health,[59] human resources development,[60] and transfer of technology.[61] All of these are formulated like policy guidelines and are as such complementary to the balance of rights and obligations that the Protocol seeks to establish. The Right to Regulate is the most important part of the balance, which crosses over to the investor protection rules. It states in full as follows:

1. In accordance with customary international law and other general principles of international law, each State Party has the right to regulate, including to take measures to ensure that investment in its territory is consistent with the goals and principles of sustainable development, and with other national environmental, health, climate action, social and economic policy objectives and essential security interests.
2. For greater certainty, measures taken by a State Party to comply with its international obligations under other relevant treaties shall not constitute a breach of this Protocol.
3. For avoidance of doubt, the exercise of the right to regulate under Paragraphs 1 and 2 cannot give rise to any claim by an investor for compensation.[62]

Given the overall pro-regulatory space tilt of AIP, the provision on the right to regulate is not as robust as could be expected because it is directly subject to customary international law and general principles of law. If the outer limits of the right to regulate are set by customary international law, it contains no innovation and remains constrained by such rules. It is also doubly surprising that AIP subordinates itself to "other international obligations under other relevant treaties."[63] In express terms, it

[56] AIP, Art. 24.
[57] AIP, Art. 25.
[58] AIP, Art. 26.
[59] AIP, Art. 27.
[60] AIP, Art. 29.
[61] AIP, Art. 30.
[62] AIP, Art. 24 (1–3).
[63] AIP, Art. 24(3).

states that "measures taken by a State Party to comply with its international obligations under other treaties shall not constitute a breach of this Protocol."[64] Because this provision comes under the right to regulate, the expectation is one of preemption rather than compliance. But the latter is what it does. In that sense, the AIP's objective of balancing investment protection with the right to regulate begins with investor protection rights that are essentially akin to the minimum standard of treatment under international law and ends with the right to regulate subject to customary international law. One is left to wonder/one can only speculate whatever else happens somewhere in between.

Investor Obligations

Chapter 5 of AIP is fully dedicated to investor obligations. The great majority of the investor obligations are mere restatements of investor obligations otherwise existing under the host state, home state and international law rules applying to investors. It begins with a catch-all provision that essentially incorporates all domestic and international law obligations as follows: "Investors and their investments shall carry out their operations in compliance with all relevant domestic laws and regulations, administrative guidelines as well as applicable international law."[65] The rest is just an elaboration of this rule in great detail in such areas as business ethics, human rights, labor, standards,[66] environmental protection,[67] respect for indigenous peoples and local communities,[68] anti-corruption,[69] corporate social responsibility,[70] corporate governance,[71] and taxation and transfer pricing.[72]

A few of these obligations are worth highlighting. The first and perhaps most impactful is the rule on environmental studies, which have in the past caused serious problems especially when investor obligations in this regard are not clear in the applicable BITs, domestic laws, and investment contracts. The operative part of the investor's environmental obligations include:

> c. carry out an environmental impact assessment, in accordance with the best international standards and practices and as required by domestic law;
>
> d. apply the precautionary principle to their environmental impact assessment and to decisions taken in relation to a proposed investment, including any necessary mitigating or alternative approaches to the investment, or precluding the investment if necessary; and

[64] AIP, Art. 24(3).
[65] AIP, Art. 32.
[66] AIP, Art. 33.
[67] AIP, Art. 34.
[68] AIP, Art. 35.
[69] AIP, Art. 37.
[70] AIP, Art. 38.
[71] AIP, Art. 39.
[72] AIP, Art. 40.

> e. where their business activities cause or may cause harm to the environment, take steps to mitigate the harm, to restore impacted sites and ensure a clean, healthy and sustainable environment.[73]

This requires pre-establishment environmental studies, codifies the precautionary principle, and requires remedial measures. Although there is reference to domestic laws, the possible deficiencies in this regard in some Contracting States is alleviated through the actual prescription of substantive rule this way. This is perhaps one of the most important contributions of the AIP. This provision also adds that "investors shall not exploit or use natural resources to the detriment of the rights and interests of the Host States and local communities."[74] Although this rule appears to have been written with investors from the more advanced economies operating in the extractive industry in mind, even in intra-Africa investment, the importance of this type of the protection of natural resources and local communities cannot be emphasized enough.

In fact, AIP dedicates an entire provision on matters affecting indigenous peoples and local communities. It is an important development not only because it recognizes their rights to free and informed consent but also their right to participate in the benefits of the investment. This is also an important development that the AIP articulates in some detail.[75]

Finally, the AIP's investor obligation provision tackles the important issue of taxation and transfer pricing. Again, although this was probably drafted with investors from the more advanced economies in mind, even in the intra-Africa context, it is important to ensure that the host states benefit from their natural resources through taxation by avoiding elaborate schemes of transfer pricing that has for long deprived many African states of significant taxation revenues. The operative part of this rule states:

> Investors and their investments . . .
>
> b. conduct their operations in a manner that fully complies with all applicable domestic tax laws and international rules and principles relating to base erosion and profit shifting practices; and c. provide all information required by the Host State to ensure compliance with the applicable laws relating to taxation.

[73] AIP, Art. 34(c–e).

[74] AIP, Art. 34(2).

[75] AIP, Art. 35. ("1. Investors and their investments shall respect the rights and dignity of indigenous peoples and local communities in accordance with relevant domestic laws and regulations, international law, norms and best practices, including the right of indigenous peoples, and local communities where applicable, to free, prior and informed consent and to participate in the benefit of the investment.

For greater certainty, the reference to the right to free, prior and informed consent of indigenous peoples, does not imply any obligation for investors and their investments to conclude agreements with those groups before conducting or operating their investment in the territory of State Parties which do not recognise indigenous peoples, taking into account applicable and relevant domestic laws and regulations.
2. Investors and their investments shall respect legitimate tenure rights to land, water, fisheries, and forests in accordance with relevant laws and regulations. 3. Investors, in accordance with relevant domestic law and regulations, shall submit their environmental and social impact assessments to the competent authorities and make them available and accessible to local communities and indigenous peoples and to any other stakeholder in the territory of the Host State").

> 2. State Parties shall, in accordance with the applicable international legal instruments, cooperate in the detection and prevention of transfer pricing manipulation by investors, including in the provision of information necessary to identify and prevent such practices and providing opportunities for Joint Audits within the framework of mutual administrative assistance in tax matters.[76]

The investors' failure to comply with these rules would have grave consequences which include the denial of the Protocol's benefit as discussed above. There could also be other consequences under domestic laws. The most important benefit that these taxation and transfer pricing rules bring to the host state would be the possible avoidance of liability in cases where the investor complains about expropriation and denial of benefits relating to imposition of taxes and other fees because of offshore transactions representing value in the host state.

The investor obligation provisions of AIP are not as excessive as in some of the contemporary regional instruments. Although most of the provisions repeat the obvious, the textual elaborations add clarity and put the investors on note of their specific obligation in express terms.

Institutional Arrangements

One of the most concrete and consequential steps that the AIP has taken is the establishment of the Pan-African Trade and Investment Agency.[77] The Contracting Parties' seriousness in establishing this Agency is evidenced by their allocation of annual budget for its operation from AfCFTA Secretariate.[78]

The Agency is set up to "assist State Parties, their investment promotion agencies and their private sector through mobilising financial resources, fostering business development and providing technical and other support for the promotion and facilitation of investment in accordance with the provisions of this Protocol."[79] Moreover, the Agency is also tasked with the duty of helping the Contracting States in capacity, stating:

> in the formulation and implementation of investment policies to foster the expansion of intra-African investments, and especially those that increase exports; as well as facilitating coordination, interaction and dialogue between and among national focal points, investment promotion agencies and other relevant stakeholders to enable the sharing of information with respect to trade, export promotion, investment opportunities, peer learning and good practices.[80]

This is a practical way of helping the promotion of intra-Africa investment and perhaps the most important contribution of AIP in advancing intra-Africa investment.

[76] AIP, Art. 40(1)(b–c),(2).
[77] AIP, Art. 42.
[78] AIP, Art. 42(5).
[79] AIP, Art. 42(3).
[80] AIP, Art. 42(4).

Supplementing the above is a provision that requires the AfCFTA Secretariate to coordinate the provision of technical assistance and capacity building in cooperation with Regional Economic Communities.[81] Beyond the actual operational benefits, the creation of these types of institutions would have a far greater role in indirectly harmonizing rules and creating institutional coordination and coherence. Although these institutional provisions are unique additions to an investment treaty, their inclusion is a good step in the right direction especially in the intra-Africa context.

Management and Settlement of Disputes

The adopted AIP defers dispute settlement to an Annex to be negotiated within 12 months of the adoption of the substantive text in February 2023. As of this writing, the Annex on dispute settlement has not been adopted. Because ISDS is a matter of serious contention, the decision to defer is not surprising.

The AIP does, however, contain some indicative provisions on state-to-state dispute settlement, dispute prevention and grievance management,[82] amicable resolution, and escalation.[83] The state-to-state dispute settlement provision is brief and makes reference to Rules of Procedure to be adopted in an Annex form. It states:

> 1. The relevant provisions of the Protocol on the Rules and Procedures on the Settlement of Disputes shall apply to consultations and the settlement of disputes between State Parties relating to the interpretation and application of this Protocol.
>
> 2. For greater certainty, Paragraph 1 incorporates the right for a State Party to submit a claim on behalf of its nationals through the exercise of diplomatic protection and in accordance with customary international law.

Beyond deferring the details of state-to-state dispute settlement to the Annex, the substantive addition is the reference to the inherent right of a state to espouse its citizens' claims under customary international law. The inclusion of this reference at this stage is curious, because it is indicative of the difficulty that the drafters have faced in agreed to proper mechanisms of dispute settlement in this Protocol. For now, the drafters seem to have sought refuge behind customary international law at least in the context of state-to-state dispute settlement.

ISDS is expressly deferred without any parameters except an indication that it should be preceded by attempts of amicable resolution. The relevant provision reads in full:

[81] AIP, Art. 43(2).

[82] AIP, Art. 45 ("State Parties shall, through their designated competent bodies, facilitate the prevention of disputes and management of grievances by: a. receiving complaints or grievances from investors in relation to their investments; b. following-up and undertaking actions for de-escalating potential differences, or disagreements between investors and State Parties; and c. providing effective assistance in resolving difficulties experienced by investors and their investments in such a manner as to avoid disputes").

[83] AIP, Art. 45.

> In the event of a dispute between an investor of a State Party and a Host State relating to an alleged breach of this Protocol, the investor and the Host State shall initially seek to resolve amicably the dispute through consultations, negotiations, conciliation, mediation or other amicable le dispute resolution mechanisms available in the Host State.[84]

AIP does not provide the details of amicable resolution processes, but adds that if such amicable resolution processes fail, the dispute may be escalated to binding resolution under the Rules of Procedures to be adopted. The provisions that defer the binding settlement processes read in full as follows:

> 2. Notwithstanding the outcome of the dispute prevention and grievances management process under Article 45, in the event that an investor of a State Party and the Host State are unable to amicably resolve the dispute in accordance with Paragraph 1 they may seek to resolve such dispute in accordance with the dispute resolution mechanisms to be provided in the Annex referred to in Paragraph 3.
>
> 3. Rules and Procedures governing Dispute Prevention, Management and Resolution of disputes covered by this Protocol shall be set out in an Annex to this Protocol. The Annex shall be negotiated after the adoption of this Protocol by the Assembly of Heads of State and Government of the Africa Union and finalised within 12 months at the latest from the date of adoption of this Protocol. The Annex, upon adoption by the Assembly of Heads of State and Government of the Africa Union shall form an integral part of this Protocol.[85]

Although the state-to-state dispute settlement provision refers to the Rules of Procedure, the provisions that defer the Rules to the Annex seem to only anticipate that the Rules will only be on ISDS. In any case, by adopting the AIP without a proper dispute resolution clause for the enforcement of rights and responsibilities, the adopted AIP text remains tentative.

Conclusion

AIP assumed the difficult task of encouraging intra-Africa investment by balancing the investor's rights with the state's right to regulate. It is informed by more than six decades of intense treaty activity and arbitral jurisprudence. Although it is a significant improvement on all of the previous regional attempts that have overcorrected the perceived inequities and excesses of arbitral jurisprudence, it could not avoid adding its own share of uncertainties through the inclusion of policy-related statements and modification of established rules such as expropriation. This chapter has identified these areas.

84 AIP, Art. 46(1).
85 AIP, Art. 46(2–3).

The most serious deficiency obviously comes from the lack of dispute settlement procedures, without which AIP cannot work. The deferral of both state-to-state and ISDS without any guiding principles is indicative of the difficult of the subject. The choices that will be made in this regard will have significant consequences for the success of AIP and the future of ISDS beyond Africa. The world is watching, and the onus is on Africa to get it right/find its own way.

29
Summary of Conclusions

Across six parts and 28 chapters, this book has provided a detailed appraisal of the sources, contents, and evolution of the substantive principles, norms, rules, and procedures of Africa's international investment law regimes. This chapter offers a summary of the conclusions.

Review of History

When Zimbabwe signed the Bilateral Investment Treaty with the Netherlands in 1996, it may not have suspected that it was inviting external legal scrutiny of its postindependence land reform programs carried out under its Constitution and other constitutionally enacted laws. The BIT was designed to encourage and protect foreign investment. In the words of the *Bernard von Pezold v. Zimbabwe* Tribunal:

> There has been a total failure on the part of the Respondent [Zimbabwe] to divorce the politics of the situation from the underlying necessary duty of the State to protect its citizenry. It is the Respondent's burden to prove that it took the "right" or "correct" decision by doing nothing. The Respondent has submitted that there were no alternative means, except that of appeasement, on the one hand, or "Rhodesian style security" on the other (which would have resulted in bloodshed and loss of life). ... *The Respondent has not demonstrated that it carried out a rigorous process of assessing all possible alternatives, and it failed to take control of the situation by maintaining law and order.*[1]

Without a voluntarily concluded investment treaty, such kind of external legal scrutiny would have been impossible. Although on the facts of this case and the application of the agreed upon legal standards the result is unsurprising, it offers an excellent example of the disconnect between what the African states might have thought they would accomplish by concluding investment treaties and joining ICSID, and what they subsequently found. Over the decades Africa attracted less than 4% of the world's investments,[2] but close to a quarter of the world's investment cases under ICSID. Its reckoning begins with this empirical reality.

[1] Bernard von Pezold v. Zimbabwe, at 645 (emphasis added).

[2] *See, e.g.*, Stephen Morgan, Jarrad Farris, and Michael E. Johnson, *Foreign Direct Investment in Africa: Recent Trends Leading up to the African Continental Free Trade Area (AfCFTA)*, Economic Research Service, U.S. Dep't of Agriculture (Oct. 2022) ("Africa's share of global FDI was low and stagnant over time. African FDI inflows averaged 3 percent of the global total between 2014–18 and 2 percent in terms of total accumulated investment, or inward FDI stock. While Northern and Southern Africa historically have been important sub-regions for FDI inflows, Eastern and Western Africa recently saw increasing FDI"). A summary of the Report is available at https://www.ers.usda.gov/webdocs/publications/

Africa's International Investment Law Regimes. Won L. Kidane, Oxford University Press. © Oxford University Press 2023.
DOI: 10.1093/oso/9780197745571.003.0029

As discussed in Part I, Africa's acceptance of the international investment law framework was celebratory, but its experience over the decades proved rather complicated and did not sustain the initial optimism. Such experience has, however, been a product both of external factors and the African states' own actions and omissions, as detailed in Part II and summarized in the next section.

Africa's ICSID Jurisprudence

The 30 cases included in the qualitative study detailed in Parts II and III paint an extremely complex picture that defies a singular empirical conclusion. They are characterized by remarkable diversity in the claimants, respondents (although Egypt is disproportionately represented), the economic sectors, the types of injuries, the applicable domestic rules, and the nature and level of redress sought.

The result has, however, been incredibly balanced, with the African states prevailing in more than half of the cases, even counting the cases that they lost because of lack of participation or delayed or poor representation in the early decades. To be sure, as detailed in Part II, there were a few cases in which the tribunals chose to push the risk of loss toward the state in an exercise of discretion and without sufficient scrutiny. Otherwise, despite the glaring lack of gender and regional diversity and almost total lack of African representation on the tribunals, a careful examination of these cases reveals no evidence of systemic bias.

Although each tribunal sought to ascertain the rules of decision on an ad hoc basis, there is clear and unmistakable evidence of the gradual formation of a system of justice around certain fundamental principles of law and notions of due process. This is so much the case that in the most recent cases, even the taxonomy of the awards began to echo each other and sound familiar in every respect.

As detailed in Parts II and III, there are some fundamental differences of opinion on some core principles of law and process; however, a very common use of legal authority, for example, is the citation of opposing views as a first step followed by an opinion that renders the resolution of the differences irrelevant for that particular case. Although this approach of legal reasoning is not uncommon in domestic judicial proceedings, it seems to occur more frequently in these ISDS cases. This is almost certainly more of a function of the fluidity of the sources of the legal authority and lack of fear of appellate review and reversal than anything else—notwithstanding the availability of annulment on narrow grounds.

The system formation is, however, more sustained and uniform with respect to process than substance. Unsurprisingly, despite some inherent flexibility, the ICSID Rules have created uniform and consistent procedural norms that almost every tribunal and party follows. The process that ranges from the initial submission of the Request for Arbitration, the constitution of the tribunal, the decision on jurisdiction, disclosure

104996/eib-242_summary.pdf?v=2218.6. Historic numbers are similar. For detailed historic World Bank data, *see* https://data.worldbank.org/indicator/BX.KLT.DINV.WD.GD.ZS?locations=ZG.

and discovery, evidentiary hearings, and the structure of the award is almost identical in almost every case.

Although the African states had a slow and turbulent start, they gradually became full participants in the process with proper representation, which allowed them to share their perspectives and shape the system along the way.

The system is no more incoherent and no less predictable than any legal processes.[3] The African states have experienced no greater difficulty than anyone else. Their participation is no less impactful, if not more so, than any region. No single principle of law has been a source of particular disappointment. Most of the disappointments were essentially derived from the decision-maker's factual determinations and allocations of the risk of loss.

Africa's Regional Treaties

Africa's regional reform efforts are predicated on the assumption that there is something fundamentally wrong with ISDS both as a matter of substance and procedure. This assumption is not limited to Africa, but Africa has taken the reform effort to the next level through regional treaties and other instruments that radically depart from the traditional conceptions of ISDS.

The reform of the substantive rules contained in the adopted regional instruments such as SADC, COMESA, and ECOWAS, while not uniform, attempt to redefine some of the most fundamental rules and add robust investor obligation norms. While these are steps in the right direction, as indicated in respective chapters, some of the changes go beyond what is needed to address the real problem and in fact introduce a new set of uncertainties. An example of this could be the introduction of exceptions to nondiscrimination principles, such as MFN and NT in the regional context. SADC Protocol for example introduces a broad exception based on "national development objectives."[4] The problem is that only investors from the SADC REC are subject to these exceptions.

Indeed, as repeatedly indicated throughout the relevant sections of the book, the most serious problem with the REC instruments is the treatment of their own community investors less favorably than noncommunity investors. In that sense, the reform principles of broader host state rights and more investor obligations targets the wrong investors for less favorable treatment. Because the dissatisfaction with the way the international investment regime has worked comes from Africa's perceived bad experience defending investment claims primarily from Western investors, the

[3] The source of the infamy seems to be the conflicting awards in CME Czech Republic B.V. v. Czech Republic, UNCITRAL, Partial Award (Sep. 13, 2001), 9 ICSID Rep. 121 (2006), and Lauder v. Czech Republic, UNCITRAL, Final Award (Sep. 3, 2001), 9 ICSID Rep. 66 (2006).

[4] *See, e.g.*, SADC Protocol, Annex I, Art. 7 ("1. Notwithstanding the provisions of Article 6, State Parties may in accordance with their respective domestic legislation grant preferential treatment to qualifying investments and investors in order to achieve national development objectives").

remedy implemented in some of the intra-Africa instruments is as misplaced as it is doctrinally doubtful.

As the detailed discussions of the African cases in Parts II and III demonstrate, there is no evidence that any inherent interpretive uncertainty surrounding any particular substantive norm or rule has caused any recurring decisional difficulty. In virtually all cases, the outcome is essentially determined based on the gravity of the state's behavior and the extent of the investor's injury and the tribunal's appreciation of them rather than any choice between competing interpretations of a legal principle, norm, or rule.

Africa's Bilateral Investment Treaties

Africa's BITs are the most important source of Africa's international investment law regimes. They were evaluated in temporal and geographic mix. The earlier African BITs were exclusively with their traditional Western economic partners. These BITs primarily focus on protection. Some of the cases discussed under Parts II and III arose out of these early BITs, especially in the post-2000 era.

Africa's BITs with Eastern economic partners are a more recent phenomenon, with China leading the way since the late 1990s and early 2000s. Although China used its own model, the fundamental substantive principles and mechanisms of dispute resolution remained largely the same, with the exception of the limitation of ISDS to the quantum of compensation in the first-generation Chinese BITs. Unsurprisingly, only one of the 30 published cases covered in this book was an Afro–Asian ICSID case.[5] There are only two more known China–Africa ICSID cases.[6]

The Intra-Africa BITs are an even more recent phenomenon, but at least one ICSID case has arisen out of them. These BITs are substantively and structurally similar to the Afro–European BITs and do not have any unique Intra-Africa characteristics of the type that the regional instruments do. The one ICSID case filed based an Intra-Africa BIT, *Oded Besserglik v. Mozambique* (2019),[7] was dismissed on jurisdictional grounds because the states failed to fulfil the required domestic processes of ratification. The paucity of intra-African disputes is not surprising not only because intra-Africa investment is generally low, but because the BIT connectivity is also relatively low, with only about 60 BITs in effect.[8]

[5] Standard Chartered Bank (Hong Kong) Ltd. v. Tanzania Electric Supply Company Ltd. (Tanesco), ICSID Case No. ARB/10/20, Award (Sep. 12, 2016).

[6] Zhongshan Fucheng Industrial Investment Co. Ltd. v. Federal Republic of Nigeria, Award (Mar. 26, 2021). This case is based on the Nigeria–China BIT of 2001. The investor prevailed. The award is not published but the case information is available at https://investmentpolicy.unctad.org/investment-dispute-settlement/cases/1196/zhongshan-fucheng-v-nigeria.; Beijing Everyway Traffic and Lighting Technology Company Limited v. Republic of Ghana (pending as of Dec. 2022). This case is based on the Ghana–China BIT of 1989. Case information is available at https://investmentpolicy.unctad.org/investment-dispute-settlement/cases/1150/everyway-v-ghana.

[7] Oded Besserglik v. Republic of Mozambique, ICSID Case No. ARB(AF)/14/2, Award (Oct. 28, 2019).

[8] *See* UNCTAD International Investments Navigator at https://investmentpolicy.unctad.org/international-investment-agreements. For the numbers, *see also* Arnaud Oulepo, *AfCFTA, the Future Investment Protocol* (Feb. 7, 2021), Kluwer Arbitration Blog, at http://arbitrationblog.kluwerarbitration.com/2021/02/07/afcfta-the-future-investment-protocol-and-the-phasing-out-of-intra-african-bits/.

Africa's Doubts and the Future of Its International Investment Law Regimes

Africa's international law regimes, like any legal regimes, are characterized by principles, norms, and rules that are applied by selected decision-makers within the crystalizing system of the global investment law regime primarily anchored around ICSID.[9] Africa has been a principal player in the origin and development of the global investment law regime. After more than 60 years of experience, Africa might have felt the deficiencies of the global regime more deeply than any other players. The systemic problems identified by UNCITRAL Group III have affected a range of stakeholders from the least developed to the most advanced, although not equally.

The evaluation in all six parts of this book suggests that the depth of Africa's frustration has two primary sources: the economic reality and the exclusion from decision-making. The most common economic reality that has caused immeasurable dissatisfaction across Africa is best exemplified by a passage from the 2020 *Bay View Group v. Rwanda* award. The Tribunal observed: "Rwanda hoped, no doubt, to attract experienced mining companies. The evidence suggests that it did not succeed. Instead, it attracted entrepreneurs without mining experience attracted by the possibilities of profiting from the acquisition of long-term mining licences in Rwanda. Of these Mr. Marshall was one."[10] It further noted that:

> Mr. Marshall himself remarked that there were no mining companies among the investors. This was certainly the case so far as those behind NRD were concerned. Mr. Marshall described the Zarnacks as *a plumbing company* from Germany and H. C. Starck as minerals processors who had never carried out mining anywhere in the world. In the event, no less than five concessions were granted to the Zarnacks and Mr. Benzinge. NRD was founded to exploit these concessions. The Zarnacks pledged to invest some US$40 million, but did not do so. Instead, they sold NRD to Starck.[11]

Many of the cases discussed in Parts II and III suggest that it is not uncommon for the proverbial plumber to be coming to Africa looking for a mining license that he can later sell. Africa's frustration comes when the plumber who holds a mining license manages to hire good lawyers who could put together a facially colorable treaty claim and drag them through an expensive legal process for years.

The second source of doubt and frustration is the feeling of exclusion from the decision-making process. This is in line with the concerns identified by UNCITRAL Group III.

For the sake of completeness, consider the three important categories of concerns that been identified at the global level.[12] The first category relates to the perceived lack

[9] For the components of regime theory, see JESWALD SALACUSE, THE LAW OF INVESTMENT TREATIES (2010), at 7 (quoting STEPHEN D. KRASNER, *Structural Causes and Regimes Consequences: Regimes as Intervening Variables*, *in* INTERNATIONAL REGIMES 2 (1983), at 2).

[10] *Id.* at 510.

[11] *Id.*

[12] *Report of Working Group III (Investor–State Dispute Settlement Reform)*, United Nations Commission on International Trade Law, U.N. Doc. A/CN.9/964 (2018).

of consistency, coherence, predictability, and correctness of decisions of ISDS tribunals.[13] The second category of concerns relates to arbitrators and decision-makers including their independence and impartiality, lack of diversity, and qualifications. The third category of concerns relates to the level and allocation of costs and duration of the proceedings.[14]

Africa appreciates the first and third categories of concerns more or less equally, but feels the second category more intensely than just about anyone else because of its unacceptably low levels of representation on the ISDS tribunals. Africa's reckoning with each category of concerns is important to consider a little more in connection with the reform efforts that it has undertaken and continues to shape.

The concerns of the inconsistency, incoherence, and accuracy of the jurisprudence, as well as the concerns about costs and duration are overappreciated. The concerns about exclusion from decision-making are grossly underappreciated. Africa's problem is compounded and exceedingly complex. It shares the same concerns about norms and processes but worries more about its de facto exclusion from the decision-making process.

Africa's expressions of doubt and its attempted and proposed reform solutions parallel the concerns expressed under Group III. The first concern relates to the indeterminacy of the substantive standards. Every reform effort in Africa seeks to eliminate the principle of fair and equitable treatment or redefine indirect expropriation. Although there have been cases in which confusion about these standards or disagreement on their outer limits might have affected the outcome of cases globally, in none of the 30 African cases reviewed could a poor, indefensible, or unacceptable decision be fully blamed on confusion around the indeterminacy of any of these standards.

More importantly, these cases suggest that tribunals have no difficulty justifying their preferred outcome in well-reasoned awards no matter what principles they apply. This is not unique to ISDS cases. Many trial court decisions are routinely required to interpret and apply legal principles as broad as the fair and equitable principle. Domestic court structures do, however, attempt to ensure consistency and coherence through appellate review, which serves as a disincentive to creative detours by trial level courts. The most serious disincentive comes from the possibility of appellate review for error of law and clear error of fact, depending on the standard of proof that applies in each jurisdiction.

The textual clarification of broad principles is useful, but the elimination of principles will not eliminate the underlying uncertainty. This is evidenced by some tribunals' use of their own sense of fairness and equity under the expropriation rubric. Principles of fairness and equity cannot be eliminated from legal proceedings by deleting legal text.[15] As such, the effort in clarifying legal text is admirable, but it will

[13] *See, e.g., Working Group III (Investment-State Dispute Settlement Reform): Submission from the Government of South Africa*, United Nations Commission on International Trade Law, U.N. Doc. A/CN.9/WG.III/WP.176 (2019) at 2. Available at https://undocs.org/en/A/CN.9/WG.III/WP.176.

[14] *See id.*

[15] At the theoretical level, the idea of tinkering with the substantive principles comes from the perceived colonial historical origins of these notions. For example, in his recent book, David Schneiderman writes:

> Among the rights granted to investors by investment treaties are those of non-discrimination (national and MFN treatment) and prohibitions against takings (nationalization and

not resolve the problem of inconsistency or incoherence. The source of inconsistent, inaccurate, or even unjust decisions is primarily the decision-making process and the decision-makers, and that is where the solution lies.

Most of the examined awards are well-reasoned and generally endorse outcomes within a reasonable range of possibilities under any system of justice. The great majority of the decisions are unanimous. Unjust and irregular decisions cannot easily garner the support of three jurists, especially when at least one is party appointed. A split in opinion is, however, often indicative of a serious problem. In regular domestic legal proceedings, dissent is often a function of differing legal opinions or ideological preferences. In these ISDS cases, however, differences of opinion on the appreciation of facts seems more common because the tribunals are themselves the fact finders. Differences of opinion on the facts could be indicative of more serious issues of due process. This question becomes even more serious when the dissenting arbitrator is diverse as in *Strabag v. Libya* (2022).

Among the 30 African cases reviewed, there were only four dissenting opinions. All were pro-respondent state opinions, because the respondent state had lost. Three were written by diverse arbitrators. These cases are *Patrick Mitchell v. Congo* (2004), dissent by Mr. Yawovi Agboyibo, a national of Togo; *Waguih Elie v. Egypt* (2009), dissent by Prof Francisco Orrego Vicuna, a national of Chile; *Union Fenosa Gas (UFG) v. Egypt* (2018), dissent by Mr. Mark Alan Clodfelter, a national of the United States of America; and *Strabag SE v. Libya* (2022), dissent by Professor Nassib Ziade, a Lebanese and Chilean national. Although each of the dissenting arbitrators raised matters of law including one that led to annulment in the *Patrick Mitchell* case, the differences of opinion appear to be more on the side of what the final result ought to be rather than what principle of law should govern. Behind these differences of opinion often lurks differing views on the allocation of the risk of loss: that is, who is in the best position to absorb the losses, a question that mostly disfavors the state.

Only about eight of the 88 arbitrators were non-Western. It is remarkable that three of the only four dissenting opinions were written by three of the eight non-Western arbitrators. To be sure, although the African states have won many cases arbitrated by all Western tribunals, it appears that diverse members bring perspectives that could potentially counter deep-rooted and unconscious biases that would remain unchallenged if all three arbitrators come from the same or similar cultures and legal traditions. Although the popular backlash is not necessarily based on concrete evidence of bias or impropriety, some of the African cases suggest that certain evidentiary records

> expropriation or equivalent measures). A 'fair and equitable treatment' standard, pervasive in the modern treaty context, performs functions analogous to a due process clause or one guaranteeing the enforceability of contracts. Each of these standards of protection has their counterpart in the national constitutional systems of capital-exporting states, principally in regard to norms associated with rights to property and to contract. The global promotion of the takings rule in the Fifth and Fourteenth Amendments to the US Constitution, encompassing 'regulatory takings,' is emblematic of efforts to have versions of local law ascend to the plane of the universal. David Schneiderman, International Investment Law's Alibis 77 (Cambridge, 2022).

But this assigns the ownership of notions of justice to those who articulated it in most widely used textual form. It suggests that the underlying notions of justice that got textual expression in the laws and constitutions of the advanced economies did not exist in other systems of justice. The only thing Western about the principle of Fair and Equitable Treatment is the language of its expression.

are reviewed in the lights more favorable to the investor than the state, even in the most recent cases such as the *Bernard von Pezold v. Zimbabwe* (2015) and *Strabag v. Libya* (2020).

The dissenting opinions in all of the African cases have not only contributed to the quality of the jurisprudence in profound ways but also shed light as to how differences of background could improve deliberations and as such the accuracy of the outcome, and more importantly, the legitimacy of the system.

Because Africa's doubt is in large measure rooted in the lack of representation, the resolution rests in the gradual diversification of appointment of arbitrators and encouragement of more robust participation. Although Africa overcame the boycott of the initial decades and participated more actively in recent decades with an appreciable degree of success, the issue of diversity on the tribunals remained stubbornly prevalent. Africa's focus on the modification of substantive rules in intra-Africa instruments and the design of new institutions may be a useful step in the long run but it does not fix the existing issue of lack of representation at the global level.

Africa cannot go back to boycotting a system of justice that it helped create and improve. Africa is where the cornerstone of the most significant development in international investment law was laid. Africa supported ICSID from the very beginning and stayed with it for more than half a century. Although it has had its misgivings, there is no evidence that it has faced systemic and invidious disfavor. The problem is the lack of meaningful representation. Africa is not an island all on itself. A retreat to internal mechanisms will not resolve Africa's dissatisfaction. It must revisit its stance, take ownership of its own legacy in the creation and development of the global investment law regime, continue to play by the rules as it has always done, redouble its efforts, and seek inclusion until it is fully represented in the decision-making processes in each case where its interests are at stake.

Reformers should always be mindful that who decides, and under what checks and balances, is more important than under what rules. As encapsulated by Gary Peller's eloquent note in his famous article "*The Metaphysics of American Law*":[16]

> It is a commonplace that law is "political." Ever since the realists debunked "formalism" in legal reasoning, the received learning has been that legal analysis cannot be neutral and determinate, that general propositions of law cannot decide particular cases. Some policy judgment or value choice necessarily intervenes. It is "transcendental nonsense" to believe that it could be any other way.[17]

[16] Gary Peller, *The Metaphysics of American Law*, 73 CALIF. L. REV. 1151 (1985).

[17] *Id.* at 1151 (referring to Flex Cohen's famous article *Transcendental Nonsense and a Functional Approach*, 35 COLUMBIA L. REV. 809 (1935)).

BIBLIOGRAPHY

14 I.L.M. 265 (1975).

"About the African Union." African Union, https://au.int/en/overview (accessed May 4, 2023).

Afr. Union Comm'n, Draft Pan-African Investment Code (Dec. 2016).

African Union Convention on Preventing and Combating Corruption, entered into force on Aug. 5, 2006. https://au.int/en/treaties/african-union-convention-preventing-and-combating-corruption (accessed May 4, 2023).

Agreement Establishing the Intergovernmental Authority on Development (IGAD). http://treaties.mfa.go.ke/download/231.

Akinkugbe, Olabisi. "Reverse Contributions? African State Parties, ICSID and the Development of International Investment Law." *ICSID Review* 34 (Spring 2019): 434–54.

Arab Maghreb Union Investment Guarantee Agreement, 1990. English text. https://edit.wti.org/document/show/0be1b608-3de3-42b7-b068-94a1013595ce (accessed May 4, 2023).

Article 31(3)(c) of the Vienna Convention on the Law of Treaties, United Nations. *Vienna Convention on the Law of Treaties*, May 23, 1969, Treaty Series, vol. 1155.

Ballantyne, Jack. "Egyptian State Entity Defeats US$3 Billion Claim." GAR News, Feb. 11, 2020. https://www.shearman.com/-/media/files/news/2020/02/gar--20200211--egyptian-state-entity-defeats-us3-billion-claim.pdf?la=en&hash=2F0CB19BE130D78008B3490827FA6D43511ADF28.

Bjorklund, Andrea K. "Can International Investment Law be Restated? Or Is Jurisprudence Constante the El Dorado of Investment Treaty Lawyers?" In 2014–2015 *Yearbook on International Investment Law and Policy*, ed. Lisa E, Sachs, Lise J. Johnson. Oxford: Oxford University Press, 2016.

Bjorklund, A. K., D. Behn, S. Franck, C. Giorgetti, W. Kidane, A. de Nanteuil, & E. Onyema. "The Diversity Deficit in International Investment Arbitration." 21 *Journal of World Investment & Trade* 21 (2020): 410–40.

Black's Law Dictionary, 11th ed. St. Paul, MN: Thomson Reuters, 2019.

Brower, Charles N., & Michael P. Daly. "A Study of Foreign Investment Law in Africa: Opportunity Awaits." In *International Arbitration and the Rule of Law: Contribution and Conformity*, ed. Andrea Menaker, xx–xx. Alphen aan den Rijn: Wolters Kluwer, 2016.

Brownlie, Ian. *Principles of International Law*, 6th ed. 2003.

Bubrowski, Helene. "Balancing IIA Arbitration Through the Use of Counterclaims." In *Improving International Investment Agreements*, ed. Armand De Mestral and Céline Lévesque. Routledge, 2014.

"Canada's 2021 Foreign Investment Promotion and Protection Agreement (FIPA) Model." Government of Canada, https://www.international.gc.ca/trade-commerce/trade-agr

eements-accords-commerciaux/agr-acc/fipa-apie/index.aspx?lang=eng (accessed May 4, 2023).

Cantegreil, Julien. "The Audacity of the Texaco/Calasiatic Award: René-Jean Dupuy and the Internationalization of Foreign Investment Law." *European Journal of International Law* 22 (2011): 441–58.

Caron, David D. "Investor State Arbitration: Strategic and Tactical Perspectives on Legitimacy." *Suffolk Transnational Law Review* 32 (2009).

"Chinese Company Sues Ghana US$55 Million For Wrongful Termination of Contract." *The Herald*, Feb. 15, 2021, https://perma.cc/YS24-XE23.

Cohen, Flex. "Transcendental Nonsense and a Functional Approach." *Columbia Law Review* 35 (1935): 809.

"COMESA Objectives and Priorities." COMESA, https://www.comesa.int/what-is-comesa/ (accessed May 4, 2023).

Convention on the Settlement of Investment Disputes Between States and Nationals of Other States. 17 U.S.T. 1270, 575 U.N.T.S. 159 (Oct. 14, 1966), https://icsid.worldbank.org/sites/default/files/documents/ICSID_Convention.pdf.

Dagbanja, Dominic N. *The Investment Treaty Regime and Public Interest Regulation in Africa*. Oxford: Oxford University Press, 2022.

d'Aspremont, Jean. "International Customary Investment Law: Story of a Paradox." In *International Investment Law: The Sources of Rights and Obligations*, ed. Tracisio Gazzini & Eric De Brabandere. Boston: Martinus Nijhoff Publications, 2012.

Database of ICSID Member States. ICSID, https://icsid.worldbank.org/en/Pages/about/Database-of-Member-States.aspx (accessed May 4, 2023).

Dates of United Nations Membership. United Nations, https://www.un.org/en/about-us/growth-in-un-membership.

Dawson, Frank G., & Ivan L. Head. *International Law, National Tribunals and The Rights of Aliens*. Syracuse:Syracuse University Press, , 1971.

Denters, Erik, & Tarasio Gazzini. "The Role of African Regional Organizations in the Promotion and Protection of Foreign Investment." *Journal of World Investment and Trade* 18 (2017): 449–92.

Dezalay, Yves, & Bryant G. Garth. *Dealing In Virtue: International Commercial Arbitration And The Construction Of A Transnational Legal Order*. Chicago: University of Chicago Press, 1996.

Dolzer, Rudolf, & Christoph Schreuer. *Principles of International Investment Law*, 2nd ed. City: Oxford University Press, 2012.

Douglas, Zachary, Joost Pauwelyn, & Jorge E. Vinuales, eds. *The Foundations of International Investment Law: Bringing Theory Into Practice*. City: Oxford University Press, 2014.

EAC Report of the Committee on Communication, Trade and Investments on the Workshop on Investment Policies and Strategies in EAC The Region. Apr. 23–24, 2015, Kigali–Rwanda. East Africa Legislative Assembly, https://www.eala.org/uploads/Report%20of%20the%20Wrkshp%20On%20Investment%20in%20KGL%20April%202015%20(2)%20-%20Tabled%20on%2018th%20Aug%202015.pdf.

Economic Community of West African States. *The ECOWAS Supplemental Act on Investment*, Jan. 19, 2009. https://investmentpolicy.unctad.org/international-investm

ent-agreements/treaties/treaties-with-investment-provisions/3547/ecowas-supple mentary-act-on-investments.

ECOWAS Common Investment Code (ECOWIC). July 2018. https://nipc.gov.ng/wp-cont ent/uploads/2019/12/ecowiccode.pdf.

ECtHR, *James & Others v. UK*, Judgment, Feb. 21, 1986.

Eisenberg, Theodore, & Geoffrey P. Miller. "The English versus the American Rule on Attorney Fees: An Empirical Study of Public Company Contracts." *Cornell Law Review* 98 (2013).

Federal. Rules. Civil. Procedure. 12(b)(6). https://www.ilnd.uscourts.gov/_assets/_do cuments/_forms/_legal/frcpweb/FRC00013.HTM

Gaillard, Emmanuel. *Legal Theory of International Arbitration*. Lieden: Martinus Nijhoff Publishers, 2010.

Gathii, James Thuo. "A Critical Appraisal of International Legal Tradition of Taslim Olawale Elias." *Leiden Journal of International Law* 21 (2008).

Hand, Learned. "A Personal Confession." In *The Spirit Liberty*, 302–07, 3nd ed., Irving Dillard 1960.

Handbook of the Intergovernmental Authority on Development (IGAD). IGAD, 2020, https://igad.int/wp-content/uploads/2021/07/IGAD-Handbook-2020.pdf.

Happold, Matthew. "Investor–State Dispute Settlement Using the ECOWAS Court of Justice: An Analysis and Some Proposals." *ICSID Review* (Mar. 2022). https://www.bil aterals.org/?investor-state-dispute-settlement-41351.

Harmonization of Remittance Policies in the Intergovernmental Authority on Development (IGAD) Region Inception Report. IGAD and UNCDF, Sep. 2021, https://migrantmo ney.uncdf.org/wp-content/uploads/2021/12/IGAD-Inception-Report-2_upda ted_Pr3-incl-FC.pdf.

Havana Charter for an International Trade Organization. U.N. Conference on Trade & Employment, Final Act and Related Documents, U.N. Doc. E/CONF. 2/78, U.N. Sales No. II.D.4 (1948), https://www.wto.org/english/docs_e/legal_e/havana_e.pdf.

"History and Treaty." Southern African Development Community, https://www.sadc.int/ pages/history-and-treaty (accessed May 4, 2023).

International Court of Justice Statute, Art. 38(1)(b).

International Court of Justice Statute, Art. 59.

ICSID. *History of the Convention: Documents Concerning the Origin and Formulation of the Convention*. https://icsid.worldbank.org/resources/publications/the-history-of-the-icsid-convention, 1968.

"IGAD: Its History and Development." Intergovernmental Authority on Development, https://igad.int/about/ (accessed May 4, 2023).

Investment Agreement for the COMESA Common Investment Area. COMESA, 2007. https://investmentpolicy.unctad.org/international-investment-agreements/treaty-files/3092/download (accessed May 4, 2023).

Kaufmann-Kohler, Gabrielle. "Arbitral Precedent: Dream, Necessity, or Excuse? (The 2006 Freshfields Lecture)." *Arbitration. International* 23 (2007): 357–78.

Kidane, Won L. "The China–Africa Factor in The ICSID Legitimacy Debate." *University of Pennsylvania Journal of International Law* 35 (2014).

Kidane, Won L. "Contemporary International Investment Trends and Africa's Dilemmas in the Draft Pan-African Investment Code." *George Washington International Law Review* 50 (2018).

Kidane, Won L. "Contemporary Trends in International Investment Law and Africa's Dilemmas in the Pan-African Investment Code." *George Washington International Law Review* 50 (2018).

Kidane, Won L. *The Culture of International Arbitration*. City: Oxford University Press, 2017.

Kidane, Won L. "The Culture of Investment Arbitration: An African Perspective." *ICSID Review* 34 (2019): 411–33.

Kidane, Won L. "China–Africa Bilateral Investment Treaties in Comparative Context." *Cornell International Law Journal* 49 (2016).

Kidane, Won L., & Weidong Zhu. "China–Africa Investment Treaties: Old Rules, New Challenges." *Fordham International Law Journal* 37 (2014): 1035–86.

Lauterpacht, Elihu. "Preface." In *The ICSID Convention: A Commentary*, ed. Christoph H. Schreuer. Cambridge: Cambridge University Press, 2001.

Le Bars, Benoit. "The Evolution of Investment Arbitration in Africa." *Global Arbitration Review* (May 11, 2018).

Lemire v. Ukraine, ICSID Case No. ARB/06/18, Award (Mar. 28, 2011).

L. F. H. Neer & Pauline Neer (U.S.A.) v. United Mexican States, 4 R.I.A.A. 60, 62 (1926).

Lipson, Charles. *Standing Guard: Protecting Foreign Capital in The Nineteenth and Twentieth Centuries*. Berkeley: University of California Press, 1985.

Lowenfeld, Andreas F. *International Economic Law*, 2nd ed. City: Oxford University Press, 2008.

Mbengue, Makane Moise, & Stefanie Schacherer. "Evolution of International Investment Agreements in Africa: Features and Challenges of Investment Law 'Africanization.'" In *Handbook of International Investment Law and Policy*, ed. Julien Chaisse, Leila Choukroune and Sufian Jusoh. City: Cambridge University Press, 2021.

"Members of the Commission at the Fifteenth Session (1963)." International Law Commission, https://legal.un.org/ilc/sessions/15/members.shtml (accessed May 4, 2023).

Miles, Kate. *The Origins of International Investment Law: Empire, Environment and The Safeguards of Capital*. City: Cambridge University Press, online publication, October 2013.

Montt, Santiago. *State Liability in Investment Treaty Arbitration: Global Constitutional and Administrative Law in the BIT Generation*. London: Bloomsbury, 2009.

Morgan, Stephen, Jarrad Farris, & Michael E. Johnson. *Foreign Direct Investment in Africa: Recent Trends Leading up to the African Continental Free Trade Area (AfCFTA)*. Washington, DC: Economic Research Service, US Department of Agriculture, Oct. 2022.

Muchlinski, Peter. "Policy Issues." In *The Oxford Handbook of International Investment Law*. ed. Peter Muchlinski, Federico Ortino, Christoph Schreuer. Oxford: Oxford University Press, 2008.

Multilateral Investment Court: Overview of the Reform Proposals and Prospects. Briefing, European Parliament Research Service, Issam Hallak, Jan. 2020. https://www.europarl.europa.eu/RegData/etudes/BRIE/2020/646147/EPRS_BRI(2020)646147_EN.pdf.

Neufeld, H. *The International Protection of Private Creditors from the Treaties of Westphalia To The Congress of Vienna (1648–1815).* Lieden: A.W. Sijthoff, 1971.

Oulepo, Arnaud. "AfCFTA, the Future Investment Protocol, and the Phasing-Out of Intra-African BITs." Kluwer Arbitration blog, Feb. 7, 2021. http://arbitrationblog.kluwerarbitration.com/2021/02/07/afcfta-the-future-investment-protocol-and-the-phasing-out-of-intra-african-bits/.

Parra, Antonio R. "The Participation of African States in The Making of the ICISD Convention." *ICSID Review* 34 (2019): 270–77.

Paulsson, Jan. *Denial of Justice in International Law.* Cambridge University Press, online publication, 2005.

Pauwelyn, Joost. "Rational Design or Accidental Evolution? The Emergence of International Investment Law." In *The Foundations of International Investment Law: Bringing Theory Into Practice,* ed. Zachary Douglas, Joost Pauwelyn, and Jorge E. Vinuales. City: Publisher, 2014.

Peller, Gary. "The Metaphysics of American Law." *California Law Review* 73 (1985).

""Profile: Arab Maghreb Union (AMU)." Institute for Security Studies (ISS), https://issafrica.org/profile-arab-maghreb-union-amu#:~:text=The%20Heads%20of%20State%20of,%2C%20social%2C%20and%20cultural%20areas (accessed May 4, 2023).

"Protocol on Relations Between the African Economic Community and the Regional Economic Communities." World Bank, 1997. https://wits.worldbank.org/GPTAD/PDF/annexes/AEC_protocols.pdf.

"Protocol on the Establishment Of The East African Community Common Market." East African Community. https://www.unhcr.org/4d5259759.pdf (accessed May 4, 2023).

Report of the United Nations Commission on International Trade Law. 77 U.N. GAOR Supp. No. 17, at 46–47, U.N. Doc. A/72/17, 2017. https://undocs.org/en/A/72/17.

Report of Working Group (Investor–State Dispute Settlement Reform. United Nations Commission on International Trade Law, U.N. Doc. A/CN.9/930/Add.1/Rev.1, 2017. https://undocs.org/en/A/CN.9/930/Add.1/Rev.1.

Report of Working Group III (Investor–State Dispute Settlement Reform. United Nations Commission on International Trade Law, U.N. Doc. A/CN.9/935, 2018. https://undocs.org/en/A/CN.9/935.

Report of Working Group III (Investor–State Dispute Settlement Reform). United Nations Commission on International Trade Law, U.N. Doc. A/CN.9/964, 2018. https://undocs.org/en/A/CN.9/964.

Report of Working Group III (Investor–State Dispute Settlement Reform): Note by the Secretariat. United Nations Commission on International Trade Law, U.N. Doc. A/CN.9/WG.III/WP.150, 2018. https://undocs.org/en/A/CN.9/WG.III/WP.150.

Root, Elihu. "The Basis of Protection to Citizens Residing Abroad." *American Journal of International Law* 4 (1910).

Ross, Alison. "Chinese Company Brings Claim Against Ghana." *Global Arbitration Review* (Feb. 11, 2021), https://perma.cc/D2UX-7PV9.

Ruttenberg, Valerie H. "The United States Bilateral Investment Treaty Program." *University of Pennsylvania Journal of International Business Law* 19 (1987).

SADC Protocol on Finance and Investment. SADC. https://investmentpolicy.unctad.org/international-investment-agreements/treaty-files/2730/download.

Salacuse, Jeswald W. "The Emerging Global Regime for Investment." *Harvard International Law Journal* 51 (2010): 427–73.

Salacuse, Jeswald W. *The Law of Investment Treaties*. Oxford: Oxford University Press, 2010.

Schneiderman, David. *Investment Law's Alibis*. Cambridge: Cambridge University Press, 2022.

Sornarajah, Muthucumaraswamy. *The International Law on Foreign Investment*, 3rd ed. City: Cambridge University Press, 2010.

Szasz, Paul C. "The Investment Disputes Convention and Latin America." *Virginia Journal of International Law* 11 (1971): 256–65.

The Protection of Investment Act, 2015. Republic of South Africa Department of Trade & Industry, Jan. 23, 2016. http://www.thedti.gov.za/editmedia.jsp?id=3630 [https://perma.cc/ZB3Z-7EH5].

"The 128 Countries That Had Signed GATT by 1994." World Trade Organization. https://www.wto.org/english/thewto_e/gattemm_e.htm (accessed Dec. 27, 2022).

Titi, Catharine. *General Principles of Law and International Investment Arbitration*. ed. Andrea Gattini, Attila Tanzi, Filippo Fontanelli. City: Publisher, 2018.

Treaty Establishing the Common Market for Eastern and Southern Africa (COMESA). Signed Nov. 5, 1993, entered into force Dec. 8, 1994. https://www.comesa.int/wp-content/uploads/2020/07/Comesa-Treaty.pdf (accessed May 4, 2023).

"UNCTAD Chronological Listing of BITs." UNCTAD. https://investmentpolicy.unctad.org/international-investment-agreements (accessed May 4, 2023).

"UNCTAD Investment Dispute Settlement Navigator (Nigeria)." UNCTAD. https://investmentpolicy.unctad.org/investment-dispute-settlement/country/153/nigeria/respondent, for all Nigerian ISDS cases (accessed May 4, 2023).

"UNCTAD Investment HUB." UNCTAD. https://investmentpolicy.unctad.org/international-investment-agreements/by-country-grouping (accessed May 4, 2023).

United Nations Convention Against Corruption. Entered into force Dec. 15, 2005. United Nations. https://www.unodc.org/documents/brussels/UN_Convention_Against_Corruption.pdf (accessed May 4, 2023).

United Nations Economic Commission for Africa, Investment Policies and Bilateral Investment Treaties in Africa: Implications for Regional Integration, Feb. 2016. https://archive.uneca.org/sites/default/files/PublicationFiles/eng_investment_landscaping_study.pdf (accessed May 4, 2023).

United Nations General Assembly Res. 3281, Dec. 12, 1974. Charter of Economic Rights and Duties of States. https://documents-dds-ny.un.org/doc/RESOLUTION/GEN/NR0/738/83/IMG/NR073883.pdf?OpenElement.

Van Harten, G. *Investment Treaty Arbitration and Public Law*. City: Oxford University Press, 2007.

Von Mehren, Robert, & Nicholas P. Kourides. "International Arbitration between States and Private Parties: The Libyan Nationalization Cases." *American Journal of International Law* 75 (1981).

Waibel, Michael, Kaushal, Asha, Chung Kyo-Hwa, & Balchin, Claire eds. *The Backlash Against Investment Arbitration: Perceptions and Reality*. Kluwer Law International, 2010.

Willard, Rainbow, & Sarah Morreau, "The Canadian Model BIT—A Step in the Right Direction for Canadian Investment in Africa?" Kluwer Arbitration blog, July 18, 2015. http://arbitrationblog.kluwerarbitration.com/2015/07/18/the-canadian-model-bit-a-step-in-the-right-direction-for-canadian-investment-in-africa/.

Working Group III (Investment-State Dispute Settlement Reform): Submission from the Government of South Africa. United Nations Commission on International Trade Law, U.N. Doc. A/CN.9/WG.III/WP.176, 2019. https://undocs.org/en/A/CN.9/WG.III/WP.176.

LIST OF TREATIES

Agreement Establishing the African Continental Free Trade Area (CFTA)
Benin–Ghana BIT (2001)
Canada–China BIT
Community of Sahel–Saharan States Revised Treaty (2013)
Comprehensive Economic Cooperation and Partnership Agreement (CECPA) Between The Republic of Mauritius and The Republic of India (2021)
Cotonou Agreement (2000)
EAC Model Investment Treaty
Egypt–China BIT (1994)
Egypt–Indonesia BIT (1994)
Egypt–Sweden BIT (1974)
Egypt–Switzerland BIT (2010)
Egypt–Uganda BIT (1995)
Ethiopia–China BIT (1998)
Ethiopia–UAE BIT (2016)
Germany–Liberia BIT (1961)
Germany–Pakistan BIT (1961)
Interim Agreement establishing an Economic Partnership Agreement between the United Kingdom of Great Britain and Northern Ireland, of the one part and the Republic of Cameroon, of the other part London (March 9, 2021)
Interim Trade Partnership Agreement between the United Kingdom of Great Britain and Northern Ireland, of the one part and the Republic of Ghana, of the other part London (March 2, 2021)
Kenya–China BIT (2001)
Kenya–Mauritius BIT (2012)
Kenya–Netherlands BIT (1970)
Mauritius–China BIT (2019)
Mauritius–Madagascar BIT (2004)
Mauritius–Mozambique BIT (1997)
Morocco–Japan BIT (2020)
Morocco–Nigeria BIT (2016)
Nigeria–Canada BIT (2014)
Nigeria–Turkey BIT (2011)
Rwanda–US BIT (2008)
SADC Protocol on Finance and Investment (2006)
South Africa–Mozambique BIT (1997)
South Africa–Tunisia BIT (2002)
Southern Afr. Dev. Community, SADC Model Bilateral Investment Treaty Template with Commentary (2012)

Supplementary Act A/SA.3/12/08 Adopting Community Rules on Investment and the Modalities for their Implementation with ECOWAS (entered into force January 9, 2009)
Treaty Establishing the African Economic Community (Abuja Treaty) (signed on June 3, 1991)
Treaty Establishing the Common Market for Eastern and Southern Africa (COMESA) (signed November 5, 1993 and entered into force December 8, 1994)
Treaty Establishing the East African Community (EAC) (signed on November 3, 1999 and entered into force on July 7, 2000)
Treating Establishing the Economic Community of Central African States (CEEAC)
Treaty of the Economic Community of West African States (ECOWAS) (concluded at Lagos on May 28, 1975)
UK–Australia Free Trade Agreement
United States-Senegal BIT (1990)
United States-Zaire BIT (United States-Democratic Republic of Congo BIT) (1986)
Investment Agreement for COMESA Common Investment Area (CCIA)
2004 US BIT Model

List of Cases Included in the Study

Adriano Gardella S.p.A. v. Côte d'Ivoire, ICSID Case No. ARB/74/1, Award, August 29, 1977
AGIP S.p.A. v. People's Republic of the Congo, ICSID Case No. ARB/77/1, Award, November 30, 1979
AHS Niger and Menzies Middle East and Africe S.A. v. Republic of Niger, ICSID Case No. ARB/11/11, Award, July 15, 2013
Antoine Goetz & Consorts et S.A. Affinage des Metaux v. Republique du Burundi, ICSID Case No. ARB/01/2, Award, June 21, 2012
Antoine Lahoud et Leila Lahoud v. Democratic Republic of Congo, ICSID Case No. ARB/10/4, Award, February 7, 2014
Atlantic Triton Company Limited v. People's Revolutionary Republic of Guinea, ICSID Case No. ARB/84/1, Award, April 21, 1986
Bay View Group LLC and The Spalena Company LLC v. Republic of Rwanda, ICSID Case No. ARB/18/21, Award, March 30, 2022
Bernard Henricus Funnekotter and Others v. Republic of Zimbabwe, ICSID Case No. ARB/05/6, Award, April 22, 2009
Bernhard Friedrich And R Diger Von Pezold Elisabeth Regina Maria Gabriele Von Pezold Anna Eleonore Elisabeth Webber (N E Von Pezold), Heinrich Bernd Alexander Josef Von Pezold, Maria Juliane Andrea Christiane Katharina Batthy Ny (N E Von Pezold), Georg Philipp Marcel Johann Lukas Von Pezold, Felix Alard Moritz Hermann Kilian Von Pezold, Johann Friedrich Georg Ludwig Von Pezold Adam Friedrich Carl Leopold Franz Severin Von Pezold v. Republic of Zimbabwe, ICSID Case No. ARB/10/15, Award, July 28, 2015

Biwater Gauff (Tanzania) Ltd. V. United Republic of Tanzania, ICSID Case No. ARB/05/22, Award, July 24, 2008

BP Exploration Company (Libya) Limited v. Government of the Libyan Arab Republic, Merits, October 10, 1973, Award, August 1, 1974, published at 53 ILR 297 (1979).

Buckeye Check Cashing, Inc. v. Cardegna, 546 U.S. 440 (2006)

CDC Group PLC v. Republic of the Seychelles, ICSID Case No. ARB/02/14, Award, December 17, 2003

Champion Trading Company Ameritrade International, Inc. v. Arab Republic of Egypt, ICSID Case No. ARB/02/9, Award, October 27, 2006

Chevron U.S.A., Inc. v. Natural Resources Defense Council, Inc., 468 U.S. 837 (1984).

CMC v. Republic of Mozambique, ICSID Case No. ARB/17/23, Award, October 24, 2019

Compagnie d'Exploitation du Chemin de Fer Transgabonais v. Gabonese Republic, ICSID Case No. ARB/04/5, Award, March 7, 2008

Consortium RFCC v. Kingdom of Morocco, ICSID Case No. ARB/00/6, Award, December 22, 2003

Cortec Mining v. Republic of Kenya, ICSID Case No. ARB/15/29, Award, October 22, 2018

Fiona Trust & Holding Corp v. Privalov, [2007] UKHL 40

Getma International v. The Republic of Guinea, ICSID Case No. ARB/11/29, Award, August 16, 2016

Gustav F W Hamester GmbH & Co KG v. Republic of Ghana, ICSID Case No. ARB/07/24, June 28, 2010

Helnan International Hotels A/S v. Arab Republic of Egypt, ICSID Case No. ARB/05/19, Award, July 3, 2008

Interocean Oil Development Company and Interocean Oil Exploration Company v. Federal Republic of Nigeria, ICSID Case No. ARB/13/20, Award, October 6, 2020

Jan de Nul N.V. & Dredging International N.V. v. Arab Republic of Egypt, ICSID Case No. ARB/04/13, Award, November 6, 2008

Joseph Houben v. Republic of Burundi, ICSID Case No. ARB/13/7, Award, January 12, 2016

Klöckner v. Cameroon, Annulment of ICSID Case No. ARB/81/2, October 21, 1983

L.E.S.I. S.p.A. and ASTALDI S.p.A. v. People's Democratic Republic of Algeria, ICSID Case No. ARB/05/3, Award, November 12, 2008

Liberian Eastern Timber Corporation v. Republic of Liberia, ICSID Case No. ARB/83/2, Award, March 31, 1986

Libyan American Oil Company (LIAMCO) v. The Libyan Arab Republic, Award, April 12, 1977. The award of the arbitral tribunal in the LIAMCO arbitration (April 12, 1977) published at 20 ILM 1 (1981).

Lundin Tunisia B.V. v. Tunisian Republic, ICSID Case No. ARB/12/30, Excerpts of Award made December 22, 2015 made pursuant to Rule 48(4) of the ICSID Arbitration Rules of 2006

Malicorp Limited v. Arab Republic of Egypt, ICSID Case No. ARB/08/18, Award, February 7, 2011

Maritime International Nominees Establishment v. Republic of Guinea, ICSID Case No. ARB/84/4, Award, January 6, 1988

Middle East Cement Shipping and Handling Co. S.A. v. Arab Republic of Egypt, ICSID Case No. ARB/99/6, Award, April 12, 2002

M. Meerapfel Söhne AG v. Central African Republic, ICSID Case No. ARB/07/10, Excerpts of Award dated May 12, 2011 made pursuant to Rule 48(4) of the ICSID Arbitration Rules of 2006

Oded Besserglik v. Republic of Mozambique, ICSID Case No. ARB/14/2, Award, October 20, 2019

Patrick H. Mitchell v. Democratic Republic of the Congo, ICSID Case No. ARB/99/7, Excerpts of Award dated February 9, 2004 made pursuant to Rule 48(4) of the ICSID Arbitration Rules of 1984

Phoenix Action Ltd. v. The Czech Republic, ICSID Case No. ARB/06/5, Award, April 15, 2009

RSM Production Corporation v. Central African Republic, ICSID Case No. ARB/07/2, Excerpt of Award dated July 11, 2011 made pursuant to Rule 48(4) of the ICSID Arbitration Rules of 2006

Salini Costruttori S.p.A. and Italstrade S.p.A. v. Kingdom of Morocco [I], ICSID Case No. ARB/00/4, Decision on Jurisdiction, July 31, 2001

S.A.R.L. Benvenuti & Bonfant v. People's Republic of the Congo, ICSID Case No. ARB/77/2, Award, August 8, 1980

Societe d'Exploitation des Mines d'Or de Sadiola S.A. V. Republic of Mali, ICSID Case No. ARB/01/5, Award, February 25, 2003

Societe d'Investigation de Recherche et d'Exploitation Minière (SIREXM) v. Burkina Faso, ICSID Case No. ARB/97/1, Excerpt of Award dated January 19, 2000

Societe Ouest-Africaine des Bétons Industriels (SOABI) v. Republic of Senegal, ICSID Case No. ARB/82/1, Award, February 25, 1988

Southern Pacific Properties (Middle East) Limited v. Arab Republic of Egypt, ICSID Case No. ARB/84/3, Award, May 20, 1992

Standard Chartered Bank (Hong Kong) Limited v. Tanzania Electric Supply Company Limited (TANESCO), ICSID Case No. ARB/10/20, Award, September 12, 2016

Standard Chartered Bank (Hong Kong) Limited v. United Republic of Tanzania, ICSID Case No. ARB/15/41, Award, October 11, 2019

Strabag SE v. Libya, ICSID Case No. ARB/15/1, Award, June 29, 2020

Tamagot Bumi S.A. and Bumi Mauritania S.A. v. Islamic Republic of Mauritania, ICSID Case No. ARB/14/23, Award, July 27, 2018

Texaco Overseas Petroleum Co. and California Asiatic Oil Company v. Government of the Libyan Arab Republic. The award on the merit (January 19, 1977) is reproduced in 53 ILR (1979) 389

Thomas Gosling, Property Partnerships Development Managers (UK) Limited, Property Partnerships Developments (Mauritius) Ltd, Property Partnerships Holdings (Mauritius) Ltd v. Republic of Mauritius, ICSID Case No. ARB/16/32, Award, February 18, 2020

Togo Electricité and GDF Suez Energie Services v. Republic of Togo, ICSID Case No. ARB/06/07, Award, August 10, 2010

Unión Fenosa Gas, S.A. v. Arab Republic of Egypt, ICSID Case No. ARB/14/4, Award, August 31, 2018

Waguih Elie George Siag and Clorinda Vecchi v. Arab Republic of Egypt, ICSID Case No. ARB/05/15, Award, June 1, 2009

Wena Hotels Limited v. Arab Republic of Egypt, ICSID Case No. ARB/98/4, Award, December 8, 2000

World Duty Free Company Limited v. Republic of Kenya, ICSID Case No. ARB/00/7, Award, October 4, 2006

List of All African ICSID Cases in Chronological Order

ARB/22/17	Comercializadora Mediterránea de Viviendas S.L. v. Kingdom of Morocco (Pending)
ARB/22/1	Louis Claude Norland Suzor and SBEC Systems Limited v. Republic of Senegal (Pending)
ARB/21/62	AGEM Ltd v. Republic of Mali (Concluded)
ARB/21/58	Congo Mining Ltd SARLU and Midus Holdings Limited v. Republic of Congo (Pending)
ARB/21/53	EEPL Holdings v. Republic of Congo (Pending)
ARB/21/50	HeidelbergCement AG and others v. Arab Republic of Egypt (Pending)
ARB/21/47	PETRONAS International Corporation Ltd and Azhan Bin Ali v. Republic of the Sudan (Concluded)
ARB/21/44	Finetis SARL and Finetis Maroc SA v. Kingdom of Morocco (Pending)
ARB/21/38	Menankoto SARL v. Republic of Mali (Concluded)
ARB/21/35	Vicat S.A. v. Arab Republic of Egypt (Concluded)
ARB/21/24	World Natural Resources Ltd v. Republic of Congo (Pending)
ARB/21/21	KGL International for Ports, Warehousing, and Transport K.S.C.C. v. Arab Republic of Egypt (Concluded)
ARB/21/18	AECI Mauritius Ltd v. Burkina Faso (Concluded)
ARB/21/9	Mauritanian Copper Mines S.A. v. Islamic Republic of Mauritania (Pending)
ARB/21/7	Shell Petroleum N.V. and The Shell Petroleum Development Company of Nigeria Limited Federal v. Republic of Nigeria (Concluded)
ARB/21/6	Montero Mining and Exploration Ltd v. United Republic of Tanzania (Pending)
ARB/20/45	Gesenu S.p.A. v. Arab Republic of Egypt (Pending)
ARB/20/41	Eni International B.V., Eni Oil Holdings B.V. and Nigerian Agip Exploration Limited v. Federal Republic of Nigeria (Pending)
ARB/20/40	Qatar National Bank (Q.P.S.C.) v. Republic of South Sudan and Bank of South Sudan (Pending)

ARB/20/38	Nachingwea U.K. Limited (UK), Ntaka Nickel Holdings Limited (UK) and Nachingwea Nickel Limited (Tanzania) v. United Republic of Tanzania (Pending)
ARB/20/25	Winshear Gold Corp. v. United Republic of Tanzania (Pending)
ARB/20/24	Teyliom International and others v. Republic of Benin (Pending)
ARB/20/17	Kansanshi Mining Plc v. Republic of Zambia (Pending)
ARB/20/1	United Agencies Limited SA v. People's Democratic Republic of Algeria (Concluded)
ARB/19/31	Gerald International Limited v. Republic of Sierra Leone (Concluded)
ARB/19/27	CTIP Oil & Gas International Limited v. Arab Republic of Egypt (Pending)
ARB/19/24	AAN Digital Services Holding Company (KSC) v. Democratic Republic of the Congo (Concluded)
ARB/19/17	Richard N. Westbury, Paul D. Hinks and Symbion Power Tanzania Limited v. United Republic of Tanzania (Concluded)
ARB/19/14	Impresa Pizzarotti & C. S.p.A. v. Kingdom of Morocco (Concluded)
ARB/19/8	Ayoub-Farid Michel Saab v. United Republic of Tanzania (Concluded)
ARB/19/7	Petroceltic Holdings Limited and Petroceltic Resources Limited v. Arab Republic of Egypt (Concluded)
ARB/19/3	Energy Utility Corporation Limited KivuWatt Limited v. Rwanda (Concluded)
ARB/19/2	Scholz Holding GmbH v. Kingdom of Morocco (Concluded)
ARB/18/44	SAUR and STEREAU v. People's Democratic Republic of Algeria (Concluded)
ARB/18/36	Société d'Energie et d'Eau du Gabon and Veolia Africa v. Gabonese Republic and Société de Patrimoine du service public de l'eau potable, de l'énergie électrique et de l'assainissement (Concluded)
ARB/18/31	International Holding Project Group and others v. Arab Republic of Egypt (Pending)
ARB/18/29	The Carlyle Group L.P. and others v. Kingdom of Morocco (Concluded)
ARB/18/24	African Petroleum Senegal Limited v. Republic of Senegal (Pending)
ARB/18/22	Tantalum International Ltd. and Emerge Gaming Ltd. v. Arab Republic of Egypt (Concluded)
ARB/18/21	Bay View Group LLC and The Spalena Company LLC v. Republic of Rwanda (Concluded)
ARB/18/16	Togo Terminal v. Republic of Togo (Pending)
ARB/18/11	Société des Parcs d'Alger and Emirates International Investment Company LLC v. People's Democratic Republic of Algeria (Pending)
ARB/18/10	West African Aquaculture Ltd, Kurt Lennart Hansson and Martje Bolt Hansson v. Republic of The Gambia (Pending)
ARB/18/7	Corral Morocco Holdings AB v. Kingdom of Morocco (Pending)

CONC/18/1	Société d'Energie et d'Eau du Gabon v. Gabonese Republic (Concluded)
ARB/17/40	APCL Gambia B.V. v. Republic of The Gambia (Concluded)
ARB/17/39	African Petroleum Gambia Limited and APCL Gambia B.V. v. Republic of The Gambia (Concluded)
ARB/17/38	Petronor E&P Gambia Limited and APCL Gambia B.V. v. Republic of The Gambia (Concluded)
ARB/17/33	EcoDevelopment in Europe AB and EcoEnergy Africa AB v. United Republic of Tanzania (Pending)
ARB/17/31	Future Pipe International B.V.v. Arab Republic of Egypt (Concluded)
ARB/17/28	LTME Mauritius Limited and Madamobil Holdings Mauritius Limited v. Republic of Madagascar (Pending)
ARB/17/23	CMC Muratori Cementisti CMC Di Ravenna SOC. Coop., CMC MuratoriCementisti CMC Di Ravenna SOC. Coop. A.R.L. Maputo Branch and CMC Africa Austral v. LDA Republic of Mozambique (Pending)
ARB/17/18	(DS)2, S.A., Peter de Sutter and Kristof De Sutter v. Republic of Madagascar (Concluded)
ARB/17/1	Ortiz Construccionesy Proyectos S.A. v. People's Democratic Republic of Algeria (Concluded)
ARB/16/37	LP Egypt Holdings I, LLC, Fund III Egypt, LLC and OMLP Egypt Holdings I, LLC v. Arab Republic of Egypt (Concluded)
ARB/16/32	Thomas Gosling and others v. Republic of Mauritius (Concluded)
ARB/16/15	AngloGold Ashanti (Ghana) Limited v. Republic of Ghana (Concluded)
ARB/16/2	Champion Holding Company and others v. Arab Republic of Egypt (Concluded)
ARB/16/1	Al Jazeera Media Network v. Arab Republic of Egypt (Pending)
ARB/15/47	ArcelorMittal S.A. v. Arab Republic of Egypt (Concluded)
ARB/15/46	BSG Resources (Guinea) Limited and BSG Resources (Guinea) SÀRL v. Republic of Guinea (Concluded)
ARB/15/41	Standard Chartered Bank (Hong Kong) Limited v. United Republic of Tanzania (Concluded)
ARB/15/29	Cortec Mining Kenya Limited, Cortec (Pty) Limited and Stirling Capital Limited v. Republic of Kenya (Concluded)
ARB/15/21	Menzies Middle East and Africa S.A. and Aviation Handling Services International Ltd. v. Republic of Senegal (Concluded)
ARB/15/12	PT Ventures, SGPS, S.A. v.Republic of Cabo Verde (Concluded)
ARB/15/11	Total E&P Uganda BV v. Republic of Uganda (Concluded)
ARB/15/7	WalAm Energy LLC v. Republic of Kenya (Concluded)
ARB(AF)/15/1	Strabag SE v. Libya (Concluded)
ARB/14/31	Tariq Bashir and SA Interpétrol v. Burundi Republic of Burundi (Concluded)

ARB/14/23	Tamagot Bumi S.A. and Bumi Mauritania S.A. v. Islamic Republic of Mauritania (Concluded)
ARB/14/22	BSG Resources Limited (in administration), BSG Resources (Guinea) Limited and BSG Resources (Guinea) SÀRL v. Republic of Guinea (Pending)
ARB/14/19	VICAT v. Republic of Senegal (Concluded)
ARB/14/7	African Petroleum Gambia Limited (Block A4) v. Republic of The Gambia (Concluded)
ARB/14/6	African Petroleum Gambia Limited (Block A1) v. Republic of The Gambia (Concluded)
ARB/14/4	Unión Fenosa Gas, S.A. v. Arab Republic of Egypt (Concluded)
ARB(AF)/14/2	Oded Besserglik v. Republic of Mozambique (Concluded)
ARB/14/2	Michael Dagher v. Republic of the Sudan (Concluded)
ARB/13/37	Utsch M.O.V.E.R.S. International GmbH, Erich Utsch Aktiengesellschaft, and Helmut Jungbluth v. Arab Republic of Egypt (Pending)
ARB/13/34	Courts (Indian Ocean) Limited and Courts Madagascar S.A.R.L. v. Republic of Madagascar (Concluded)
ARB/13/29	Cementos La Union S.A. and Aridos Jativa S.L.U v. Arab Republic of Egypt (Pending)
ARB/13/25	Tullow Uganda Operations Pty Ltd and Tullow Uganda Limited v. Republic of Uganda (Concluded)
ARB/13/23	ASA International S.p.A. v. Arab Republic of Egypt (Concluded)
ARB/13/20	Interocean Oil Development Company and Interocean Oil Exploration Company v. Federal Republic of Nigeria (Concluded)
ARB/13/16	Société des Mines de Loulo S.A. v. Republic of Mali (Concluded)
ARB/13/15	Lundin Tunisia B.V. v. Republic of Tunisia (Concluded)
ARB/13/7	Joseph Houben v. Republic of Burundi (Concluded)
ARB/13/5	Ossama Al Sharif v. Arab Republic of Egypt (Concluded)
ARB/13/4	Ossama Al Sharif v. Arab Republic of Egypt (Concluded)
ARB/13/3	Ossama Al Sharif v. Arab Republic of Egypt (Concluded)
ARB/12/36	Société Civile Immobilière de Gaëta v. Republic of Guinea (Concluded)
ARB/12/35	Orascom TMT Investments S.à r.l. v. People's Democratic Republic of Algeria (Concluded)
ARB/12/34	Tullow Uganda Operations PTY LTD v. Republic of Uganda (Concluded)
ARB/12/32	Gelsenwasser AG v. People's Democratic Republic of Algeria (Concluded)
ARB/12/30	Lundin Tunisia B. V. v. Republic of Tunisia (Concluded)
ARB/12/26	Sudapet Company Limited v. Republic of South Sudan (Concluded)
ARB/12/15	Veolia Propreté v. Arab Republic of Egypt (Concluded)
ARB/12/11	Ampal-American Israel Corporation and others v. Arab Republic of Egypt (Concluded)

ARB/12/8	Société Industrielle des Boissons de Guinée v. Republic of Guinea (Concluded)
ARB(AF)/12/2	Grupo Francisco Hernando Contreras v. Republic of Equatorial Guinea (Concluded)
CONC(AF)/12/1	Hess Equatorial Guinea, Inc. and Tullow Equatorial Guinea Limited v. Republic of Equatorial Guinea (Pending)
ARB/11/32	Indorama International Finance Limited v. Arab Republic of Egypt (Concluded)
ARB/11/29	Getma International and others v. Republic of Guinea (Concluded)
ARB/11/16	Hussain Sajwani, Damac Park Avenue for Real Estate Development S.A.E., and Damac Gamsha Bay for Development S.A.E. v. Arab Republic of Egypt (Concluded)
ARB/11/14	Diamond Fields Liberia, Inc. v. Republic of Liberia (Concluded)
ARB/11/11	AHS Niger and Menzies Middle East and Africa S.A. v. Republic of Niger (Concluded)
ARB/11/7	National Gas S.A.E. v. Arab Republic of Egypt (Concluded)
ARB/11/6	Bawabet Al Kuwait Holding Company v. Arab Republic of Egypt (Concluded)
ARB/10/25	Border Timbers Limited, Timber Products International (Private) Limited, and Hangani Development Co. (Private) Limited v. Republic of Zimbabwe (Concluded)
ARB/10/21	International Quantum Resources Limited, Frontier SPRL and Compagnie Minière de Sakania SPRL v. Democratic Republic of the Congo (Concluded)
ARB/10/20	Standard Chartered Bank (Hong Kong) Limited v. Tanzania Electric Supply Company Limited (Tanzania) (Concluded)
ARB/10/15	Bernhard von Pezold and others v. Republic of Zimbabwe (Concluded)
ARB/10/12	Standard Chartered Bank v. United Republic of Tanzania (Pending)
ARB/10/10	Olyana Holdings LLC v. Republic of Rwanda (Concluded)
ARB/10/4	Antoine Abou Lahoud and Leila Bounafeh-Abou Lahoud v. Democratic Republic of the Congo (Concluded)
ARB/09/19	Carnegie Minerals (Gambia) Limited v. Republic of The Gambia (Concluded)
ARB/09/15	H&H Enterprises Investments, Inc. v. Arab Republic of Egypt (Concluded)
ARB/09/14	Mærsk Olie, Algeriet A/S v. People's Democratic Republic of Algeria (Concluded)
ARB/08/20	Millicom International Operations B.V. and Sentel GSM S.A. v. Republic of Senegal (Concluded)
ARB/08/18	Malicorp Limited v. Arab Republic of Egypt (Concluded)
ARB/08/17	Participaciones Inversiones Portuarias SARL v. Gabonese Republic (Concluded)
ARB/07/24	Gustav F W Hamester GmbH & Co KG v. Republic of Ghana (Concluded)

ARB/07/18	Shell Nigeria Ultra Deep Limited v. Federal Republic of Nigeria (Concluded)
ARB/07/10	M. Meerapfel Söhne AG v. Central African Republic (Concluded)
ARB/07/3	Government of the Province of East Kalimantan PT Kaltim Prima Coal and others (Indonesia, Isle of Man and Russia) (Concluded)
ARB/07/2	RSM Production Corporation v. Central African Republic (Concluded)
CONC/07/1	Shareholders of SESAM v. Central African Republic (Concluded)
ARB(AF)/07/1	Piero Foresti, Laura de Carli and others v. Republic of South Africa (Concluded)
ARB/06/12	Scancem International ANS v. Republic of Congo (Concluded)
ARB/06/7	Togo Electricité and GDF-Suez Energie Services v. Republic of Togo (Concluded)
ARB/05/22	Biwater Gauff (Tanzania) Limited v. United Republic of Tanzania (Concluded)
ARB/05/21	African Holding Company of America, Inc. and Société Africaine de Construction au Congo S.A.R.L. v. Democratic Republic of the Congo (Concluded)
ARB/05/19	Helnan International Hotels A/S v. Arab Republic of Egypt (Concluded)
ARB/05/15	Waguih Elie George Siag and Clorinda Vecchi v. Arab Republic of Egypt (Concluded)
ARB/05/6	Bernardus Henricus Funnekotter and others v.Republic of Zimbabwe (Concluded)
ARB/05/3	LESI, S.p.A. and Astaldi, S.p.A. v. People's Democratic Republic of Algeria (Concluded)
CONC/05/1	Togo Electricité v. Republic of Togo (Concluded)
ARB/04/13	Jan de Nul N.V. and Dredging International N.V. v. Arab Republic of Egypt (Concluded)
ARB/04/12	ABCI Investments Limited v. Republic of Tunisia (Pending)
ARB/04/11	Russell Resources International Limited and others v. Democratic Republic of the Congo (Concluded)
ARB/04/5	Compagnie d'Exploitation du Chemin de Fer Transgabonais v. Gabonese Republic (Concluded)
ARB/03/14	Miminco LLC and others v. Democratic Republic of the Congo (Concluded)
ARB/03/11	Joy Mining Machinery Limited v. Arab Republic of Egypt (Concluded)
ARB/03/8	Consortium Groupement L.E.S.I.—DIPENTA v. People's Democratic Republic of Algeria (Concluded)
CONC/03/1	TG World Petroleum Limited v. Republic of Niger (Concluded)
ARB/02/15	Ahmonseto, Inc. and others v. Arab Republic of Egypt (Concluded)
ARB/02/14	CDC Group plc v. Republic of Seychelles (Concluded)
ARB/02/9	Champion Trading Company and Ameritrade International, Inc. v. Arab Republic of Egypt (Concluded)

ARB/01/5	Société d'Exploitation des Mines d'Or de Sadiola S.A. v. Republic of Mali (Concluded)
ARB/01/2	Antoine Goetz and others v. Republic of Burundi (Concluded)
ARB/00/8	Ridgepointe Overseas Developments, Ltd. V. Democratic Republic of the Congo and Générale des Carrières et des Mines (Concluded)
ARB/00/7	World Duty Free Company Limited v. Republic of Kenya (Concluded)
ARB/00/6	Consortium R.F.C.C. v. Kingdom of Morocco (Concluded)
ARB/00/4	Salini Costruttori S.p.A. and Italstrade S.p.A. v. Kingdom of Morocco (Concluded)
ARB/99/7	Patrick Mitchell Democratic v. Republic of the Congo (Concluded)
ARB/99/6	Middle East Cement Shipping and Handling Co. S.A. v. Arab Republic of Egypt (Concluded)
ARB/99/5	Alimenta S.A.v. Republic of The Gambia (Concluded)
ARB/98/8	Tanzania Electric Supply Company Limited v. Independent Power Tanzania Limited (Concluded)
ARB/98/7	Banro American Resources, Inc. and Société Aurifère du Kivu et du Maniema S.A.R.L. v. Democratic Republic of the Congo (Concluded)
ARB/98/4	Wena Hotels Limited v. Arab Republic of Egypt (Concluded)
ARB/98/3	International Trust Company of Liberia v. Republic of Liberia (Concluded)
ARB/97/2	Société Kufpec (Congo) Limited v. Republic of Congo (Concluded)
ARB/97/1	Société d'Investigation de Recherche et d'Exploitation Minière v. Burkina Faso (Concluded)
ARB/95/3	Antoine Goetz and others v. Republic of Burundi (Concluded)
CONC/94/1	SEDITEX Engineering Beratungsgesellschaft für dieTextilindustrie m.b.H. v. Madagascar (Concluded)
ARB/93/1	American Manufacturing & Trading, Inc. v. Democratic Republic of the Congo (Concluded)
ARB/92/1	Vacuum Salt Products Ltd. v. Republic of Ghana (Pending)
ARB/89/1	Manufacturers Hanover Trust Company v. Arab Republic of Egypt and General Authority for Investment and Free Zones (Concluded)
ARB/87/1	Société d'Études de Travaux et de Gestion SETIMEG S.A. v. Gabonese Republic (Concluded)
ARB/86/1	Ghaith R. Pharaon v. Republic of Tunisia (Concluded)
ARB/84/4	Maritime International Nominees Establishment v. Republic of Guinea (Concluded)
ARB/84/3	Southern Pacific Properties (Middle East) Limited v. Arab Republic of Egypt (Concluded)
ARB/84/1	Atlantic Triton Company Limited v. People's Revolutionary Republic of Guinea (Concluded)
ARB/83/2	Liberian Eastern Timber Corporation v. Republic of Liberia (Concluded)

CONC/82/1	SEDITEX Engineering Beratungsgesellschaft für die Textilindustrie m.b.H. Democratic Republic of Madagascar (Concluded)
ARB/82/1	Société Ouest Africaine des Bétons Industriels v. Republic of Senegal (Concluded)
ARB/78/1	Guadalupe Gas Products Corporation v. Nigeria (Concluded)
ARB/77/2	S.A.R.L. Benvenuti & Bonfant v. People's Republic of the Congo (Concluded)
ARB/77/1	AGIP S.p.A. v. People's Republic of the Congo (Concluded)
ARB/72/1	Holiday Inns S.A. and others v. Morocco (Concluded)

LIST OF ANNEXES

ANNEX I

SDAC PROTOCOL ON FINANCE AND INVESTMENT

PREAMBLE

WE, the Heads of State or Government of: The Republic of Angola

The Republic of Botswana
The Democratic Republic of the Congo
The Kingdom of Lesotho
The Republic of Madagascar
The Republic of Malawi
The Republic of Mauritius
The Republic of Mozambique
The Republic of Namibia
The Republic of South Africa
The Kingdom of Swaziland
The United Republic of Tanzania
The Republic of Zambia
The Republic of Zimbabwe

HAVING regard to Article 21 of the Treaty which enjoins Member States to cooperate in all areas necessary to foster regional development and integration;

NOTING Article 22 of the Treaty which calls for the conclusion of protocols as may be necessary in each area of co- operation and which shall spell out the objectives and scope of, and the institutional mechanisms for, co- operation and integration;

FURTHER noting that the RISDP map and targets for enhancing socio-economic development and deeper regional integration;

CONSCIOUS of their collective duty to achieve economic growth and balanced intra regional development, compatibility among national and regional strategies and programs, to develop policies aimed at the progressive elimination of obstacles to the free movement of capital and labor, goods and services, and of the residents of the Member States, improve economic management and performance through regional cooperation, and to create appropriate institutions and mechanisms for the implementation of programs and operations in the Region;

CONVINCED of the need to accelerate growth, investment and employment in the SADC Region through increased co-operation, coordination and management of macroeconomic, monetary and fiscal policies and to establish and sustain macroeconomic stability as a precondition to sustainable economic growth and for the creation of a monetary union in the Region;

RECOGNISING the increasing importance of the development and strengthening of financial and capital markets, and the role played by investment and the private sector in productive capacity and increased economic growth and sustainable development;

RECOGNISING the importance of the link between investment and trade, and the need for greater regional cooperation to enhance the attractiveness of the Region as an investment destination;

MINDFUL of the different levels of economic development of Member States and of the need to share equitably in the benefits of regional integration;

HEREBY AGREE as follows:

CHAPTER ONE DEFINITIONS AND OBJECTIVES

ARTICLE 1

DEFINITIONS

1. In this Protocol, terms and expressions defined in Article 1 of the Treaty shall bear the same meaning unless the context otherwise requires.
2. In this Protocol, unless the context otherwise requires:

"Annex" means an Annex to this Protocol; "BIS" means the Bank for International Settlements; "capital market" means a market where capital funds, debt or equities and any other financial instrument are traded

"CCBG" means the Committee of Central Bank Governors in SADC;

"Central Bank" means, in relation to a State Party, the central bank of that State Party;

"Committee of Ministers" means the Committee of Ministers responsible for Finance andfor policy development and policy making Investment" for finance and investment matters, or such similar body as the Council may establish;

"Committee of Senior Officials" means the technical advisory body to the Treasury Committee of Ministers for Finance and Investment consisting of Heads of Treasuries;

"DFIs" means, in relation to a State Party, those financial institutions which are designated, or classified, as "Development Finance Institutions" by that State Party;

"financial markets" means markets for the exchange of capital and credit in the economy;

"Protocol" means this SADC Protocol on Finance and Investment including its annexes;

"RISDP" means the Regional Indicative Strategic Development Plan.

"State Party" means a Member State that has ratified or acceded to this Protocol; and

ARTICLE 2

OBJECTIVES

1. This Protocol seeks to foster harmonization of the financial and investment policies of the State Parties in order to make them consistent with objectives of SADC and ensure that any changes to financial and investment policies in one State Party do not necessitate undesirable adjustments in other State Parties.
2. The objective referred to in paragraph 1 shall be achieved through facilitation of regional integration, co-operation and co-ordination within finance and investment sectors with the aim of diversifying and expanding the productive sectors of the economy, and enhancing trade in the Region to achieve sustainable economic development and growth and eradication of poverty by:
   (a) creating a favorable investment climate within SADC with the aim of promoting and attracting investment in the Region;
   (b) achieving and maintaining macroeconomic stability and convergence within the Region;
   (c) co-operating in respect of taxation and related matters within the Region;
   (d) co-operating and coordinating amongst State Parties in collaboration with Central Banks on exchange control policies;
   (e) establishing principles which will facilitate the creation of a coherent and convergent status in the legal and operational frameworks of Central Banks;
   (f) establishing a framework for co-operation and co-ordination between (amongst) Central Banks on payment, clearing and settlement systems;
   (g) co-operating in the area of information technology and communications technology amongst Central Banks;
   (h) co-operating on bank supervision amongst Central Banks;
   (i) co-operating in the activities of DFIs in the Region;
   (j) co-operating in the area of non-banking financial institutions and services;
   (k) facilitating the development of capital markets in the Region;
   (l) co-operating in the area of SADC Stock Exchanges;
   (m) co-operating with regard to anti-money laundering issues amongst State Parties; and
   (n) cooperation in respect of a SADC Project Preparation and Development Fund.

2 The objectives set out in paragraph 1, the implementation thereof and the mechanism for such implementation are fully described in the Annexes to this Protocol.

CHAPTER TWO

CO-OPERATION ON INVESTMENT

ARTICLE 3

CO-OPERATION ON INVESTMENT

State Parties shall co-ordinate their investment regimes and cooperate to create a favorable investment climate within the Region as set out in Annex 1.

CHAPTER THREE

MACROECONOMIC CONVERGENCE

ARTICLE 4

MACROECONOMIC CONVERGENCE

State Parties shall converge on stability-orientated economic policies and shall co-operate as set out in Annex 2.

CHAPTER FOUR

CO-OPERATION IN TAXATION AND RELATED MATTERS

ARTICLE 5

CO-OPERATION IN TAXATION AND RELATED MATTERS

State Parties shall co-operate in taxation matters and co-ordinate their tax regimes within the Region as set out in Annex 3.

CHAPTER FIVE

CO-OPERATION AMONG CENTRAL BANKS

ARTICLE 6

CO-OPERATION AND CO-ORDINATION ON EXCHANGE CONTROLS

State Parties shall co-operate and co-ordinate their exchange control policies as set out in Annex 4.

ARTICLE 7

THE LEGAL AND OPERATIONAL FRAMEWORKS

State Parties shall harmonize the legal and operational frameworks of their respective Central Banks as set out in Annex 5.

ARTICLE 8

PAYMENTS, CLEARING AND SETTLEMENT SYSTEMS

State Parties shall ensure co-operation amongst their respective Central Banks in relation to payments, clearing and settlement systems as set out in Annex 6.

ARTICLE 9

CO-OPERATION IN THE AREA OF INFORMATION AND COMMUNICATION TECHNOLOGY

State Parties shall ensure co-ordination and co-operation amongst their respective Central Banks in relation to operations in the area of information and communication technology as set out in Annex 7.

ARTICLE 10

CO-OPERATION BETWEEN BANKING SUPERVISORS

State Parties shall facilitate co-operation between (amongst) regional banking supervisors and the harmonization of banking supervisory standards and practices as set out in Annex 8.

CHAPTER SIX
NETWORK OF DFIs

ARTICLE 11

FACILITATION OF ACTIVITIES OF DFIs

In order to increase effectively cross border flows of finance for projects, State Parties agree to establish a Development Finance Institutions Network and to facilitate the activities of their respective Development Finance Institutions and to ensure co-operation between these Development Finance Institutions as set out in Annex 9.

CHAPTER SEVEN

CO-OPERATION IN REGIONAL CAPITAL AND FINANCIAL MARKETS

ARTICLE 12

REGULATION AND SUPERVISION OF NON-BANKING FINANCIAL SERVICES

State Parties shall harmonize the regulation of non-banking financial institutions and shall facilitate co-operation between the respective regulators and supervisors of such institutions as set out in Annex 10.

ARTICLE 13

DEVELOPMENT OF CAPITAL AND FINANCIAL MARKETS

State Parties shall co-operate in developing and strengthening national capital and financial markets with the intention of creating a regional capital and financial market as set out in Annexes 10 and 11.

ARTICLE 14

CO-OPERATION AMONG MEMBER STOCK EXCHANGES

State Parties shall facilitate co-operation between their respective stock exchanges as set out in Annex 11.

CHAPTER EIGHT

ANTI-MONEY LAUNDERING

ARTICLE 15

CO-OPERATION WITH REGARD TO ANTI- MONEY LAUNDERING

State Parties shall co-operate with regard to anti-money laundering.

CHAPTER NINE

PROJECT PREPARATION AND DEVELOPMENT FUND

ARTICLE 16

DEVELOPMENT OF A SADC PROJECT PREPARATION AND DEVELOPMENT FUND

State Parties agree to establish a Project Preparation and Development Fund to finance the preparation and development of projects by way of providing technical assistance towards project identification, project selection and feasibility studies and to participate in the financing of selected projects.

CHAPTER TEN

INSTITUTIONAL AND ADMINISTRATIVE ARRANGEMENTS

ARTICLE 17

ESTABLISHMENT OF INSTITUTIONS

The following institutions are to be established in accordance with Articles 9, 10 and 11 of the SADC Treaty:

(a) the Committee of Ministers for Finance and Investment;
(b) the Committee of Central Bank Governors in SADC; and
(c) the Peer Review Panel.

ARTICLE 18

THE COMMITTEE OF MINISTERS FOR FINANCE AND INVESTMENT

The Committee of Ministers for Finance and Investment shall consist of the Ministers responsible for finance and for investment of each State Party and it shall meet at least once a year.

ARTICLE 19

THE COMMITTEE OF CENTRAL BANK GOVERNORS IN SADC

1. The CCBG shall consist of the Governor of the Central Bank of each State Party.
2. The CCBG shall meet at least once a year and will report to the Committee of Ministers for Finance and Investment.

ARTICLE 20

PEER REVIEW PANEL

1. The Peer Review Panel shall consist of:
   (a) the Committee of Ministers for Finance and Investment; and
   (b) Central Bank Governors from each of the State Parties.
2. The Peer Review Panel shall meet once a year to effect the provisions of macroeconomic monitoring and surveillance as provided for in Article 7 of Annex 2.

ARTICLE 21

INSTITUTIONAL MECHANISMS

1. The institutional mechanisms for implementation of this Protocol shall comprise the Integrated Committee of Ministers, the Committee of Ministers for Finance and Investment, the CCBG, the Peer Review Panel and the Secretariat.
2. The Committee of Ministers for Finance and Investment shall create such committees, sub-committees or institutions as it deems necessary for purposes of the effective implementation of this Protocol.

ARTICLE 22

FUNCTIONS AND RESPONSIBILITIES

1. The functions and responsibilities of the Integrated Committee of Ministers are as set out in Article 12 of the SADC Treaty.
2. The Committee of Ministers for Finance and Investment shall oversee the implementation of this Protocol.
3. The CCBG shall be responsible for the implementation of those aspects that are specifically allocated to it:
   (a) by the Committee of Ministers for Finance and Investment; and
   (b) in the various Annexes of this Protocol.
4. The Secretariat shall ensure close collaboration with;
   (a) State Parties; and
   (b) all relevant institutions on finance, investment and other related matter the Region.

CHAPTER ELEVEN

FINAL PROVISIONS

ARTICLE 23

ANNEXES

1. State parties may develop and adopt annexes for the implementation of this Protocol.
2. An Annex shall form an integral part of this Protocol.
3. The adoption of annexes under this Article shall be done in accordance with Article 26.

ARTICLE 24

SETTLEMENT OF DISPUTES

1. State Parties shall use their best endeavors, through co-operation and consultation, to achieve consensus in the interpretation, application and implementation of this Protocol.
2. Where State Parties are unable to achieve consensus in the interpretation, application and implementation of any Article of this Protocol, as contemplated in paragraph 1, and:
   (a) the Annex relating to such Article contains provisions which deal with disputes or differences arising in relation to such Article, such provisions shall be applied in respect of the dispute or difference relating to such Article;
   (b) the Annex relating to such Article does not contain provisions which deal with disputes or differences arising in relation to such Article, the State Parties which are parties to the dispute or difference relating to such Article will use their best endeavors to settle such dispute or difference through negotiations in good faith.
3. State Parties agree that if, in relation to a dispute or difference contemplated in paragraph 2 (b) the State Parties which are parties to such dispute or difference are unable to settle such dispute or difference through negotiation within three months from the time the disputes or differences arose, such dispute or difference shall be referred to the Tribunal for adjudication.

ARTICLE 25

GENERAL UNDERTAKING

1. State Parties shall take such appropriate measures as are necessary to ensure that their respective obligations arising from this Protocol are fulfilled.
2. State Parties shall co-operate with each other in addressing any impediments that may arise as a result of any action, or lack of action, by any State Party on

issues having a material bearing on those finance and investment matters which are not covered in this Protocol.

ARTICLE 26

AMENDMENTS

1. Any State Party may propose amendments to this Protocol.
2. Proposals for amendments to this Protocol shall be made to the Executive Secretary who shall duly notify all Member States of the proposed amendments at least thirty (30) days in advance of consideration of the amendments by the States Parties. Such notice may be waived by the Member States.
3. Amendments to this Protocol shall be adopted by a decision of three quarters of all the State Parties and shall become effective thirty (30) days after such adoption.

ARTICLE 27

SIGNATURE

This Protocol shall be signed by the duly authorized representatives of the Member States.

ARTICLE 28

RATIFICATION

This Protocol shall be subject to ratification by the signatory States in accordance with their constitutional procedures.

ARTICLE 29

ENTRY INTO FORCE

This Protocol shall enter into force thirty (30) days after the deposit of instruments of ratification by at least two-thirds of all of the Member States.

ARTICLE 30

ACCESSION

This Protocol shall remain open for accession by any Member State.

ARTICLE 31

WITHDRAWAL

1. Any State Party may withdraw from this Protocol upon the expiration of twelve (12) months from the date of giving written notice to the Executive Secretary to that effect.
2. Any State Party that has withdrawn pursuant to paragraph 1 of this Article shall cease to enjoy all rights and benefits under this Protocol upon the withdrawal becoming effective.
3. Any State Party that has withdrawn pursuant to paragraph 1 of this Article shall remain bound by the obligations under this Protocol for a period of twelve (12) months from the date of giving notice.

ARTICLE 32

DEPOSITARY

1. This original text of this Protocol, all instruments of ratification and all instruments of accession shall be deposited with the Executive Secretary, who shall transmit certified copies thereof to all Member States.
2. The Executive Secretary shall notify the Member States of the dates on which instruments of ratification and instruments of accession have been deposited under paragraph 1.
3. The Executive Secretary shall register this Protocol with the Secretariat of the United Nations, the Commission of the African Union and such other organizations as the Council may determine.

IN WITNESS WHEREOF, WE, the Heads of State or Government, have signed this Protocol.

DONE at....................................on...........day of................ 2006 in three (3) original texts in the English, French and Portuguese languages, all texts being equally authentic.

Republic of Angola	Republic of Botswana
Democratic Republic of Congo	Kingdom of Lesotho
Republic of Madagascar	Republic of Malawi
Republic of Mauritius	Republic of Mozambique
Republic of Namibia	Republic of South Africa
Kingdom of Swaziland United	Republic of Tanzania
Republic of Zambia	Republic of Zimbabwe

Annex 1

CO-OPERATION ON INVESTMENT

PREAMBLE

The High Contracting Parties:

COMMITTED to achieving the broad objectives of the SADC as set out in the

Treaty and specifically to achieving economic growth and sustainable development through regional integration and working through IPAs in the Region;

RECOGNISING the increasing importance of the role played by investment to advance productive capacity and increase economic growth and sustainable development and the importance of the link between investment and trade;

CONCERNED with the low levels of investment into the SADC, even though a number of measures have been taken to improve the investment environment;

AIMING to create new employment opportunities and improve living standards in our territories;

ACKNOWLEDGING that there is a need for greater regional cooperation among IPAs in **the Region** in order to enhance the attractiveness of the Region as an investment destination;

CONSCIOUS that without effective policies on investment protection and promotion, the Region will continue to be marginalized in terms of investment inflows and sustainable economic development; and

WISHING to be guided by the ideals, objectives and spirit of the Protocol in the facilitation and stimulation of investment flows and technology transfer and innovation into the Region

HEREBY AGREE as follows:

ARTICLE 1

DEFINITIONS

1. In this Annex, terms and expressions defined in Article 1 of the Protocol shall bear the same meaning unless the context otherwise requires.
2. In this Annex, unless the context otherwise requires:

"bond" means a debt instrument in terms of which the issuer thereof is obliged to re-pay, to the bondholder on a specified maturity date, the principal amount of a loan (and, ordinarily, interest thereon) made by the bondholder to the issuer;

"company"	means any entity constituted or organized under the applicable laws of any State, whether or not for profit, and whether privately or governmentally owned or controlled, and includes a corporation, trust, partnership, sole proprietorship, branch, joint venture, association, or other such organization;
"Host Government"	means the government of the State Party in whose territory an investment is made or located;
"Host State"	means the State Party in whose territory an investment is made or located;
"ICSID Convention"	means the Convention on the Settlement of Investment Disputes between States and Nationals of Other States, done at Washington, March 18, 1965;
"investment"	means the purchase, acquisition or establishment of productive and portfolio investment assets, and in particular, though not exclusively, includes: (a) movable and immovable property and any other property rights such as mortgages, liens or pledges; (b) shares, stocks and debentures of companies or interest in the property of such companies; (c) claims to money or to any performance under contract having a financial value, and loans; (d) copyrights, know-how (goodwill) and industrial property rights such as patents for inventions, trade marks, industrial designs and trade names; (e) rights conferred by law or under contract, including licenses to search for, cultivate, extract or exploit natural resources: Provided that nothing in this definition shall prevent a State Party from excluding short-term portfolio investments of a speculative nature or any sector sensitive to its development or which would have a negative effect on its economy. A State Party that has invoked this provision shall notify the Secretariat for information purposes within a period of three (3) months;
"IPAs"	means the investment promotion agencies of State Parties that: (a) actively promote and facilitate investments; (b) proactively identify business opportunities for investments; (c) encourage expansion of existing investments; (d) develop a favorable investment image of their countries; (e) make recommendations for improvements of their countries as investment destinations;

(f) keep track of all investors entering and leaving the country for the purpose of analysis in terms of investment performance; or

(g) play the role of advising investors upon request on the availability, choice or sustainability of partners in joint venture projects.

2. Nothing in this definition prevents a State Party from excluding short-term portfolio investments of a speculative nature or any sector sensitive to its development or which would have a negative effect on its economy. State Parties who have invoked this clause shall notify the SADC Secretariat for information purposes within a period of three (3) months.

"investor" means a person that has been admitted to make or has made an investment;

"least-developed" means, for purposes of Article 19 of this Annex, those countries State Parties classified as such by the United Nations;

"MIGA" means the Multilateral Investment Guarantee Agency;

"MIGA Convention" means the Convention Establishing the Multilateral Investment Guarantee Agency

"New York Convention" means the United Nations Convention on the Recognition and Enforcement of Foreign Arbitral Awards; "person" means a natural person or a company;

"PPP" means Public Private Partnership;

"returns" means the amounts yielded by an investment and in particular, though not exclusively, includes profits, interest, capital gains, dividends, royalties and fees;

"SMME" means Small Micro and Medium Enterprises, as defined by each State Party in its relevant legislation as qualifying for such status;

"State entity" means, any agency, department or instrumentality of the Government of a State Party and any corporation, juristic person, institution, undertaking or entity which is directly or indirectly owned or controlled by that State Party, which are engaged in activities of a commercial nature;

"territory" means, in relation to a State Party, the total land area of that State Party and, in relation to a coastal State Party, includes, in addition, the territorial sea and any maritime area situated beyond the territorial sea of that coastal State Party which has been, or might in the future be, designated under the national law of that coastal State Party,

	in accordance with international law, as an area within which that coastal State Party may exercise rights with regard to the sea-bed, subsoil and natural resources;
"third State"	means any state that is not a State Party; and
"UNCITRAL Arbitration"	means the arbitration rules of the United Nations Commission on International Trade Law. Rules"

ARTICLE 2

PROMOTION AND ADMISSION OF INVESTMENTS

1. Each State Party shall promote investments in its territory, and admit such investments in accordance with its laws and regulations.
2. The Host State shall facilitate and create favorable conditions to attract investments in its territory through suitable administrative measures and in particular in the matter of expeditious clearance of authorizations in accordance with its laws and regulations.
3. For the purposes of creating a predictable investment climate, State Parties shall not arbitrarily, and without good reason, amend or otherwise modify to the detriment of investors, the terms, conditions and any benefits specified in the letter of authorization.

ARTICLE 3

PROMOTION OF LOCAL AND REGIONAL ENTREPRENEURS

1. State Parties shall support the development of local and regional entrepreneurs and enhance regional productive capacity within the Region through, inter alia:
   (a) skills development and enhancement programs;
   (b) SMME development;
   (c) appropriate investments into supporting infrastructure; and
   (d) other supply-side measures and policies necessary to enhance global competitiveness.
2. In providing support described in paragraph 1 of this Article, State Parties may place emphasis on industries that provide up-stream and down-stream linkages and have a favorable effect on attracting foreign direct investment and generating increased employment.

ARTICLE 4

PUBLIC PRIVATE PARTNERSHIPS

State Parties shall co-operate on policies and other related issues that will encourage and facilitate the use of PPPs to ensure development in the Region.

ARTICLE 5

INVESTMENT PROTECTION

Investments shall not be nationalized or expropriated in the territory of any State Party except for a public purpose, under due process of law, on a non- discriminatory basis and subject to the payment of prompt, adequate and effective compensation.

ARTICLE 6

INVESTORS OF THE THIRD STATE

1. Investments and investors shall enjoy fair and equitable treatment in the territory of any State Party.
2. Treatment referred to in paragraph 1 shall be no less favorable than that granted to investors of the third State.

ARTICLE 7

GENERAL EXCEPTIONS

1. Notwithstanding the provisions of Article 6, State Parties may in accordance with their respective domestic legislation grant preferential treatment to qualifying investments and investors in order to achieve national development objectives.
2. State Parties undertake to eventually harmonize their respective domestic policies and legislation within the spirit of non-discrimination as set out in Article 6.
3. The provisions of Article 3 shall not apply to advantages, concessions or exemptions which may result from a bilateral investment treaty, Free Trade Area, Customs Union, Economic Union, Monetary Union or other multilateral arrangement for economic integration in which a State Party is participating or may participate.

ARTICLE 8

TRANSPARENCY

State Parties shall promote and establish predictability, confidence, trust and integrity by adhering to and enforcing open and transparent policies, practices, regulations and procedures as they relate to investment.

ARTICLE 9

REPATRIATION OF INVESTMENT AND RETURNS

Each State Party shall ensure that investors are allowed facilities in relation to repatriation of investments and returns in accordance with the rules and regulations stipulated by the Host State.

ARTICLE 10

CORPORATE RESPONSIBILITY

Foreign investors shall abide by the laws, regulations, administrative guidelines and policies of the Host State.

ARTICLE 11

SOURCING OF REQUISITE SKILLS

State Parties shall, subject to their national laws and regulations, permit investors to engage key personnel and other necessary human resources of their choice, regardless of nationality under the following circumstances:

(a) where the skills do not exist in the Host State and the Region;
(b) where State Parties are satisfied that the sourcing of such skills will be in compliance with regional policies; and where such sourcing would enhance the development of local capacity through skills transfer.

ARTICLE 12

OPTIMAL USE OF NATURAL RESOURCES

State Parties shall promote the use of their natural resources in a sustainable and an environmentally friendly manner.

ARTICLE 13

ENVIRONMENTAL MEASURES

State Parties recognize that it is inappropriate to encourage investment by relaxing domestic health, safety or environmental measures and agree not to waive or otherwise derogate from, international treaties they have ratified, or offer to waive or otherwise derogate from, such measures as an encouragement for the establishment, acquisition, expansion or retention in their territories, of an investment.

ARTICLE 14

RIGHT TO REGULATE

Nothing in this Annex shall be construed as preventing a State Party from exercising its right to regulate in the public interest and to adopt, maintain or enforce any measure that it considers appropriate to ensure that investment activity is undertaken in a manner sensitive to health, safety or environmental concerns.

ARTICLE 15

CAPITAL MOVEMENTS

1. State Parties shall encourage the free movement of capital.
2. Notwithstanding the provisions of paragraph 1, State Parties may regulate capital movements subject to their domestic laws and regulations, when necessitated by economic constraints.
3. State Parties that introduce new regulations in the circumstances described in paragraph 2 shall notify the Secretariat for information purposes within a period of three (3) months of introducing such regulations.

ARTICLE 16

COMPETITION POLICY

State Parties undertake through co-operation to advance a competition policy in the Region.

ARTICLE 17

INTRA-REGIONAL AND EXTRA-REGIONAL AGREEMENTS FOR THE AVOIDANCE OF DOUBLE TAXATION

1. With a view to encouraging the movement of capital within the Region, particularly to the least-developed countries, State Parties undertake, in line with their undertakings as set out in Annex 3, to conclude between themselves agreements for the avoidance of double taxation.
2. State Parties agree, in line with their undertakings as set out in the Annex 3, to approach their negotiations for agreements for the avoidance of double taxation with countries outside the region on the basis of mutually agreed principles.

ARTICLE 18

TRADE, INVESTMENT AND INDUSTRIAL POLICY

In recognizing the importance of the link between trade and investment, State Parties agree to pursue trade openness and intra-regional industrial policies and to reduce barriers to intra-regional trade in pursuance of the principles of the SADC Protocol on Trade and any other relevant SADC instruments.

ARTICLE 19

HARMONISATION OF POLICIES AND LAWS

State Parties shall pursue harmonization with the objective of developing the region into a SADC investment zone, which shall, among others, include the harmonization of investment regimes including policies, laws and practices in accordance with the best practices within the overall strategy towards regional integration.

ARTICLE 20

CONDITIONS FAVOURING LEAST DEVELOPED COUNTRIES

1. State Parties shall establish conditions favoring the participation of least-developed countries of SADC in the economic integration process, based on the principles of non-reciprocity and mutual benefit.
2. For the purpose of ensuring that least-developed countries of SADC receive effective preferential treatment, State Parties shall investigate the establishment of market openings as well as the setting up of programs and other specific forms of cooperation including in relation to derogations in respect of investment incentives.

ARTICLE 21

ADHERENCE TO INTERNATIONAL CONVENTIONS AND PRACTICES

State Parties may consider acceding to multilateral agreements on investment designed to promote or protect investments, such as:

(a) the ICSID Convention of 1965; (b) the MIGA Convention, 1985; and (c) the New York Convention, 1958.

ARTICLE 22

REGIONAL COOPERATION ON INVESTMENT

State Parties shall through their relevant institutions promote regional cooperation in the area of investment, including PPPs, to ensure development in the Region;

ARTICLE 23

INVESTMENT PROMOTION AGENCIES

State Parties shall ensure that their IPAs:

(a) carry out their investment promotion activities, in line with their national and regional development priorities;
(b) advise the Government of that State Party, the private sector and other stakeholders in the formulation and review of policies and procedures that affect investment and trade; and
(c) increase awareness of their investment incentives, opportunities, legislation, practices, major events affecting investments and other relevant activities through regular exchange of information.

ARTICLE 24

THE ROLE OF THE SECRETARIAT

The Secretariat shall ensure close collaboration with State Parties and all relevant institutions on investment and other related matters in the Region.

ARTICLE 25

RELATIONSHIP WITH OTHER ORGANISATIONS

State Parties shall pursue and promote policies that will increase cooperation with other regional and international organizations on issues relating to investment.

ARTICLE 26

BILATERAL INVESTMENT TREATIES

State Parties may conclude bilateral investment treaties with third States.

ARTICLE 27

ACCESS TO COURTS AND TRIBUNALS

State Parties shall ensure that investors have the right of access to the courts, judicial and administrative tribunals, and other authorities competent under the laws of the Host State for redress of their grievances in relation to any matter concerning any investment including judicial review of measures relating to expropriation or nationalization and determination of compensation in the event of expropriation or nationalization

ARTICLE 28

SETTLEMENT OF INVESTMENT DISPUTES

1. Disputes between an investor and a State Party concerning an obligation of the latter in relation to an admitted investment of the former, which have not been amicably settled, and after exhausting local remedies shall, after a period of six (6) months from written notification of a claim, be submitted to international arbitration if either party to the dispute so wishes.
2. Where the dispute is referred to international arbitration, the investor and the State Party concerned in the dispute may agree to refer the dispute either to:
   (a) The SADC Tribunal;
   (b) The International Centre for the Settlement of Investment Disputes (having regard to the provisions, where applicable, of the ICSID Convention and the Additional Facility for the Administration of Conciliation, Arbitration and Fact-Finding Proceedings); or
   (c) An international arbitrator or ad hoc arbitral tribunal to be appointed by a special agreement or established under the Arbitration Rules of the United Nations Commission on International Trade Law.
3. If after a period of three (3) months from written notification of the claim there is no agreement to one of the above alternative procedures, the parties to the dispute shall be bound to submit the dispute to arbitration under the Arbitration Rules of the United Nations Commission on International Trade Law as then in force. The parties to the dispute may agree in writing to modify these Rules.
4. The provisions of this Article shall not apply to a dispute, which arose before entry into force of this Annex.

Annex II

INVESTMENT AGREEMENT FOR THE COMESA COMMON INVESTMENT AREA

PREAMBLE

The Governments of Burundi, Comoros, Democratic Republic of Congo, Djibouti, Egypt, Eritrea, Kingdom of eSwatini, Ethiopia, Kenya, Libya, Madagascar, Malawi, Mauritius, Rwanda, Seychelles, Sudan, Swaziland, Uganda, Zambia and Zimbabwe, Member States of the Common Market for Eastern and Southern Africa (COMESA);

REAFFIRMING the importance of having sustainable economic growth and development in all Member States and the region, including through joint efforts in liberalizing and promoting intra-COMESA trade and investment flows;

RECALLING the decision of the Third COMESA Summit of the Authority held on 29 June 1998 in Kinshasa, Democratic Republic of Congo, to establish the COMESA Common Investment Area (hereinafter referred to as "CCIA"), in order to enhance COMESA's attractiveness and competitiveness for promoting foreign direct and cross border investments;

RECALLING the establishment of the COMESA Free Trade Area (FTA) on

31st October 2000 and recognizing that direct investment is an important source of finance for sustaining the pace of economic, industrial, infrastructure and technology development; hence, the need to attract higher and sustainable level of direct investment flows in COMESA;

RECALLING that the Member States have agreed under paragraph 1 of Article 159 of the Treaty Establishing COMESA to encourage and facilitate private investment flows into COMESA;

RECOGNISING that particular pressures on the balance of payments of a Member State in the process of economic development or economic transition may necessitate the use of restrictions to ensure, *inter alia*, the maintenance of a level of financial reserves adequate for the implementation of its program of economic development or economic transition;

UNDERSTANDING that this Agreement is designed to recognize the right of Member States to regulate and to introduce new measures relating to investments in their territories in order to meet national public policy objectives;

DETERMINED to realize the vision of COMESA to establish a competitive COMESA Common Investment Area through a more liberal and transparent investment environment; and

BEARING IN MIND that the measures agreed upon shall contribute towards the realization of the Common Market and the achievement of sustainable development in the region.

HAVE AGREED AS FOLLOWS:

PART ONE PRELIMINARY PROVISIONS

ARTICLE 1

Definitions

In this Agreement, unless context otherwise requires:

"**Agreement**" means the Investment Agreement for the COMESA Common

Investment Area;

"**CCIA**" means the area that covers the whole of the territories of Member

States of COMESA as defined by their respective legislation;

"**CCIA Committee**" means the Committee referred to under Article 7 of this

Agreement;

"**COMESA**" means the Common Market for Eastern and Southern Africa established under Article 1 of the COMESA Treaty;

"**COMESA investor**" means:

(i) a natural person of a Member State; or
(ii) a juridical person of a Member State,

making an investment in another Member State, in accordance with the laws and regulations of the Member State in which the investment is made.

For purposes of the definition of COMESA investor:

(i) "**Natural person**" means a person having citizenship of a Member State in accordance with its applicable laws and regulations; and

(ii) "**Juridical person**" means any legal entity duly constituted or otherwise organized under the applicable laws and regulations of a Member State provided that a juridical person owned or controlled by foreign nationals shall not qualify as a COMESA investor unless it maintains substantial business activity in the Member State in which it is duly constituted or organized;

"**COMESA Treaty**" means the Treaty establishing the Common Market for Eastern and Southern Africa;

"**Council**" means the Council of Ministers of COMESA as established under Article 7 of the COMESA Treaty;

"economic activities" means all economic activities of the economy, including services, where investment, as defined in this Article, is taking place;

"enterprise or company" means any entity duly constituted or otherwise incorporated under the applicable laws and regulations of a Member State provided that it maintains substantial business activity in the Member State in which it is located;

"freely convertible currency" means a convertible currency as classified by the International Monetary Fund or any currency that is widely traded in regional or international foreign exchange markets;

"home state" means, a State from where the COMESA investor originates;

"host state" means the Member State where the investment is located;

"investment" means an enterprise or a company, which is established, acquired or expanded by an investor, including through the constitution, maintenance or acquisition of shares, debentures or other ownership instruments of such an enterprise, provided that the enterprise or company is established or acquired in accordance with the laws of the Member State. In order to qualify as an investment under this Agreement the investment must have the following characteristics: the substantial business activity, commitment of capital or other resources, the expectation of gain or profit, the assumption of risk, and significance for the host State's development but does not include;

(a) debt securities issued by a government or loans to a government;
(b) portfolio investments;
(c) claims to money that arise solely from commercial contracts for the sale of goods or services by a national or enterprise in the territory of a Member State to an enterprise in the territory of another Member State, a bank letter of credit or an extension of credit in connection with a commercial transaction, such as trade financing;
(d) investments of a speculative nature, such as futures, swaps, forwards and derivatives;

"LIBOR" means London Interbank Offered Rate;

"measures" means any legal, administrative, judicial or policy decision that is taken by a Member State, directly relating to and affecting an investment in its territory, after this Agreement has come into effect;

"Member State" means a Member State of COMESA that has ratified or acceded to this Agreement;

"returns" mean the amount yielded by an investment and in particular, though not exclusively, includes dividends, profit, interest, capital gains or other equivalent charges, royalties and other payments deriving from licenses, franchises, concessions and other similar rights; and

"**Substantial business activity**" requires an overall examination, on a case- by-case basis, of all the circumstances, including, inter alia:

(a) the amount of investment brought into the country;
(b) the number of jobs created;
(c) its effect on the local community; and
(d) the length of time the business has been in operation.

PART TWO GENERAL PROVISIONS

ARTICLE 2
Objective

The parties to this agreement hereby designate the COMESA region as a common investment area with the following objectives:

(a) promote investments that support sustainable development in Member States;
(b) encourage the gradual elimination of investment restrictions and conditions, which may impede investment flows and the operation of investment projects in COMESA and promote a more transparent investment environment;
(c) provide COMESA investors, in the conduct of their business, with an overall balance of rights and obligations between investors and Member States, in accordance with this Agreement;
(d) strengthen and increase the competitiveness of COMESA's economic activities; and
(e) promote COMESA as an attractive investment area.

ARTICLE 3
Coverage

1. This Agreement shall only apply to investments of COMESA investors that have been registered by relevant authority of the host State as listed in Schedule IV, and in accordance with the relevant procedures of the host state.
2. Subject to paragraph 1 of this Article, this Agreement shall cover investments of COMESA investors made in the territory of Member States in accordance with their laws and regulations prior to or after entry into force of this Agreement.
3. This Agreement shall not be applicable to claims arising out of any measures, which occurred or were taken prior to entry into force of the Agreement.

ARTICLE 4
Transparency

1. Each Member State shall make available to the CCIA Committee relevant measures, which pertain to, or affect, the operation of this Agreement. This shall also apply to international agreements pertaining to or affecting investment to which a Member State is also a signatory.
2. Each Member State shall publish relevant measures, which pertain to, or affect, the operation of this Agreement.
3. Each Member State shall, within 30 days of the enactment or the introduction of any new measure or any changes in existing measures, which affect investments or its commitments under this Agreement, inform the CCIA Committee and the general public.
4. Nothing in this Agreement shall require any Member State to provide confidential information, the disclosure of which would impede law enforcement, or otherwise be contrary to the public interest, or which would prejudice legitimate commercial interests of particular enterprises, public or private.

ARTICLE 5
General Obligations

To realize the objectives referred to in Article 2, the Member States shall:

(a) undertake appropriate actions to promote transparency and consistency in the application and interpretation of their investment laws, regulations and administrative procedures;
(b) strengthen the process of facilitation, promotion and liberalization which would contribute continuously and significantly to achieving the objective of a more liberal and transparent investment environment;
(c) take appropriate actions to enhance the attractiveness of their investment environment for direct investment flows;
(d) promote, maintain and encourage competition to enhance economic efficiency in investment and consumer protection;
(e) prohibit any anti-competitive investment conduct that prevents, restricts or distorts competition at the national and regional levels;
(f) not waive or otherwise derogate from or offer to waive or otherwise derogate from measures concerning labour, public health, safety or the environment as an encouragement for the establishment, expansion or retention of investments;
(g) develop national policies to guide investors in developing human capacity of the labor force. Such policy may include incentives to encourage employers to invest in training, capacity building and knowledge transfer;
(h) develop national policies that pay particular attention to special needs of youth, women, persons with disabilities and other vulnerable groups;

(i) take measures to protect the health, safety and economic interests of consumers and their right to information, education and to organize themselves in order to safeguard their interests; and
(j) take such reasonable actions as may be available to them to ensure observance of the provisions of this Agreement by the regional and local government authorities within their territories.

ARTICLE 6
International Multilateral Agreements

Member States are encouraged, where appropriate, to endeavor to accede to the following multilateral agreements designed to promote, facilitate and protect investment:

(a) the New York Convention on the Recognition and Enforcement of Foreign Arbitral Awards;
(b) the International Convention on Settlement of Investment Disputes between States and Nationals of other States;
(c) the Convention Establishing the Multilateral Investment Guarantee Agency;
(d) the Agreement Establishing the African Trade Insurance Agency; and
(e) any other multilateral agreement designed to promote or protect investment.

ARTICLE 7
Institutional Arrangements

1. The following COMESA Organs shall be responsible for administering this Agreement:
   (a) Ministers responsible for investment of each Member State, or cabinet representatives, which for the purposes of this Agreement, shall be known as the COMESA Common Investment Area Committee ("CCIA Committee"); and
   (b) the Technical Committee on Investment composed of senior officials from Ministries responsible for investment and Chief Executives of Investment Promotion Agencies as may be designated by each Member State, which for the purposes of this Agreement, shall be known as the Technical Committee on Investment (TCI).
2. The CCIA Committee shall be responsible for:
   (a) overall supervision of the implementation of this Agreement;
   (b) making decisions or issuing directions that may require to be made under this Agreement;
   (c) recommending to the Council any review of this Agreement when necessary;

(d) making recommendations to the Council on any policy issues that need to be made to enhance the objectives of this Agreement. For example the development of common minimum standards relating to investment in areas such as:
   (i) environmental impact and social impact assessments;
   (ii) labor standards;
   (iii) respect for human rights;
   (iv) conduct in conflict zones;
   (v) corruption; and
   (vi) subsidies and incentives; and

(e) conducting a review of the effectiveness of this Agreement and its implementation in the light of its objectives four years after its entry into force and every four years thereafter.

3. The Technical Committee shall be responsible for:
   (a) advising on the technical aspects of the Agreement;
   (b) submitting its reports and recommendations to the CCIA Committee, either on its own initiative or upon the request of the CCIA Committee, concerning the implementation of the provisions of this Agreement;
   (c) preparation and development of action plans for the implementation of this Agreement; and
   (d) carrying out such other functions as are assigned to it by or under this Agreement.
4. The COMESA Secretariat shall provide secretarial services to the institutions described in paragraph 1 of this Article.
5. The head of the COMESA Regional Investment Agency or his/her representative shall participate in all the meetings of the organs described under paragraph 1 as an ex-officio member.
6. Subject to this Agreement and any directions given by Council, the CCIA Committee and the TCI shall meet as often as necessary for the proper discharge of their functions and shall determine their own Rules of Procedure.

ARTICLE 8
Implementing Programs and Action Plans

1. Member States shall, for purpose of the implementation of the obligations under this Agreement, undertake the joint development and implementation of the following programs:
   (a) co-operation and facilitation program as specified in Schedule I annexed hereto;
   (b) promotion and awareness program as specified in Schedule II annexed hereto;

2. Member States shall submit action plans for the implementation of programs mentioned in paragraph 1 to the CCIA Committee within a year of ratifying or acceding to this Agreement.
3. The Action Plans shall be reviewed by the CCIA Committee every two years to ensure that the objectives of this Agreement are achieved.

Article 9
Liberalization Program

1. The parties shall adopt a liberalization program, whereby they shall:

(a) unilaterally reduce and eliminate restrictive investment measures and review their investment regimes regularly towards further liberalization. In this context, Member States may undertake actions to liberalize, among others:
 (i) rules, regulations and policies relating to investment;
 (ii) rules on licensing conditions;
 (iii) rules relating to access to domestic finance; and
 (iv) rules to facilitate payment, receipts and repatriation of profits by investors;

(b) undertake individual action plans to:
 (i) open up all industries for investment to COMESA investors in accordance with the provisions of this Agreement; and
 (ii) extend national treatment to all COMESA investors in accordance with the provisions of this Agreement; and

(c) pro mote free flow of capital, skilled labor, professionals and technology among COMESA Member States.

2. The liberalization program under paragraph 1 shall be implemented in a manner to be determined by the parties.

ARTICLE 10
Relation to Dispute Settlement

No recourse to dispute settlement shall be initiated for any matter relating to Part Two of this Agreement.

PART THREE

STANDARD OF TREATMENT OF INVESTORS AND INVESTMENTS

ARTICLE 11

Admission

Each Member State shall promote, encourage and facilitate investments in its territory, and admit such investments in accordance with its laws and regulations.

ARTICLE 12

Encouragement and support of investments

Member States may introduce incentives in order to attract investments. Such incentives may include:

(a) financial incentives in the forms of investment insurance, grants or loans at concessionary rates;
(b) fiscal incentives such as tax holidays, pioneer status and reduced tax rates;
(c) subsidized infrastructure or services, market preferences;
(d) development-oriented incentives, to encourage preferential markets schemes and specific investors within the region;
(e) incentives for technical assistance or technology transfer requirements; or
(f) investment guarantees.

ARTICLE 13

Support to domestic investors

Notwithstanding any other provision of this Agreement, Member States may support the development of local and regional industries that provide, *inter alia*, up-stream and down-stream linkages and have a favourable effect on attracting investments and generating increased employment in Member States. The support covered by this paragraph include:

(a) measures to grant preferential treatment to any qualifying enterprise under the domestic law of a Member State in order to achieve national or regional development goals;
(b) measures to support the development of local entrepreneurs;
(c) measures to enhance productive capacity, increase employment, increase human resource capacity, research and development including, new technology,

technology transfer, innovation and other benefits of investment through the use of specified requirements on investors; or

(d) measures to address historically based economic disparities suffered by identifiable ethnic or cultural groups due to discriminatory or oppressive measures against such groups.

ARTICLE 14

Fair judicial and administrative treatment

1. Member States shall ensure that investments of investors of another Member State are not subjected to measures that constitute:
   (a) denial of justice in criminal, civil or administrative proceedings;
   (b) un-remedied and egregious violations of due process;
   (c) targeted discrimination on manifestly unjustified grounds, such as gender, race or religious belief; or
   (d) manifestly abusive treatment, such as coercion, duress and harassment.
2. A determination that there has been a breach of another provision of this Agreement, or of a separate international agreement, does not establish that there has been a breach of this Article.

ARTICLE 15

Transfer of Assets

1. Taking account of the need to facilitate, promote and enhance the movement of capital in the CCIA, Member States shall accord to COMESA investors the right to freely and without any inordinate delay, and according to their laws and regulations:
   (a) repatriate investment returns;
   (b) repatriate funds for repayment of loans;
   (c) repatriate proceeds from compensation upon expropriation, the liquidation or sale of the whole or part of the investment including an appreciation or increase of the value of the investment capital;
   (d) transfer payments for maintaining or developing the investment project, such as funds for acquiring raw or auxiliary materials, semi-finished products as well as replacing capital assets; and
   (e) remit the unspent earnings of expatriate staff of the investment project.
2. Notwithstanding provision in paragraph 1, a Member State may delay or prevent a transfer in a non-discriminatory manner and in good faith application of its laws relating to:
   (a) fulfilment of tax obligations to the host state;

(b) bankruptcy, insolvency, or the protection of the rights of creditors;
(c) issuing, trading or dealing in securities, futures, options or derivatives;
(d) criminal or penal offences and the recovery of the proceeds of crime;
(e) financial reporting or record keeping of transactions when necessary to assist law enforcement or financial regulatory authorities;
(f) ensuring compliance with orders or judgments in judicial or administrative proceedings;
(g) social security, public retirement or compulsory savings schemes; (h) severance entitlements of employees; or
(i) the formalities required to register and satisfy the central bank and other relevant authority of a host state.

ARTICLE 16

Movement of Labor

Taking account of the need to facilitate labor resources, in the CCIA and subject to the laws in force in the host state, Member States shall accord to investors the right to hire technically qualified persons, necessary for investment from any Member State. Such persons shall have the right to enter and receive the necessary authorizations to reside in the Member State. However, COMESA investors shall accord a priority to workers who possess the same qualifications or expertise and are available in the host Member State or any other Member State.

ARTICLE 17

National Treatment

1. Subject to Article 19, each Member State shall accord to COMESA investors and their investments treatment no less favorable than the treatment it accords, in like circumstance, to its own investors and to their investments with respect to the management, operation and disposition of investments in its territory.
2. For greater certainty, references to 'like circumstances' in paragraph 1 of this Article requires an overall examination on a case by case basis of all the circumstances of an investment including, inter alia:
   (a) its effects on third persons and the local community;
   (b) its effects on the local, regional or national environment, including the cumulative effects of all investments within a jurisdiction on the environment;
   (c) the sector the investor is in;
   (d) the aim of the measure concerned;
   (e) the regulatory process generally applied in relation to the measure concerned; or

(f) other factors directly relating to the investment or investor in relation to the measure concerned,

and the examination shall not be limited to or be biased towards any one factor.

ARTICLE 18

Most Favored Nation Treatment

1. Subject to the exceptions provided for under paragraph 3 of this Article, each Member State shall accord to COMESA investors and their investments treatment no less favorable than that it accords, in like circumstances, to investors and their investments from any third country with respect to the management, operation and disposition of investments in its territory. This paragraph shall not apply to investment agreements entered into by Member States with non-Member States prior to the entry into force of this Agreement.
2. For greater certainty, references to 'like circumstances' in paragraph 1 of this Article requires an overall examination on a case by case basis of all the circumstances of an investment including, inter alia:
   (a) its effects on third persons and the local community;
   (b) its effects on the local, regional or national environment, including the cumulative effects of all investments within a jurisdiction on the environment;
   (c) the sector the investor is in;
   (d) the aim of the measure concerned;
   (e) the regulatory process generally applied in relation to the measure concerned; or
   (f) other factors directly relating to the investment or investor in relation to the measure concerned,

   and the examination shall not be limited to or be biased towards any one factor.
3. Nothing in paragraph 1 of this Article shall oblige a Member State to extend to COMESA investors the benefits of any treatment, preference or privilege resulting from:
   (a) any customs union, free trade area, common market or monetary union, or any similar international convention or other forms of regional preferential arrangements, present or future, of which any of the Member States is or may become a party;
   (b) any matter, including international agreements, pertaining wholly or mainly to taxation;
   (c) any other international agreements, or chapters of international agreements, pertaining to the promotion or protection of investment; or
   (d) any dispute settlement procedures in any other treaty.

ARTICLE 19

Specific Exceptions

1. Articles 17 and 18 shall not apply to:
   (a) any measures existing at the date of entry into force of this Agreement maintained by each Member State under its laws and regulations or any amendment or modification to such measures, provided that the amendment or modification does
   not decrease the conformity of the measure as it existed immediately before the amendment or modification;
   (b) privileges available within the Member State's economy made for the exclusive benefit of its own nationals within the framework of its national development programs;
   (c) subsidies, incentives under Article 12 or grants provided by a government or a state enterprise, including government-supported loans, guaranties and insurance; or
   (d) taxation measures aimed at ensuring the effective collection of taxes, except where this results in arbitrary discrimination.
2. Notwithstanding any other provision of this Agreement, a Member State may take measures necessary to address historically based economic disparities suffered by identifiable ethnic or cultural groups due to discriminatory or oppressive measures against such groups prior to the signing of this Agreement.
3. The implementation of these exceptions shall not entitle any investor or investment to compensation for any competitive disadvantages he may suffer.
4. For greater certainty, non-discriminatory measures taken by a Member State to comply with its international obligations under other treaties shall not constitute a breach of this Agreement.

ARTICLE 20

Expropriation

1. Member States shall not nationalize or expropriate investments in their territory or adopt any other measures tantamount to expropriation of investments except:
   (a) in the public interest; and
   (b) in accordance with due process of law.
2. Where expropriation has been carried out, prompt and adequate compensation shall be paid.
3. Adequate compensation shall normally be assessed in relation to the fair market value of the expropriated investment immediately before the expropriation took place ("date of expropriation") and shall not reflect any change

in value occurring because the intended expropriation had become known earlier. However, where appropriate, the assessment of fair and adequate compensation shall be based on an equitable balance between the public interest and interest of those affected, having regard for all relevant circumstances and taking account of the current and past use of the property, the history of its acquisition, the fair market value of the investment, the purpose of the expropriation, the extent of previous profit made by the foreign investor through the investment, and the duration of the investment. Compensation may be adjusted to reflect the aggravating conduct by a COMESA investor or such conduct that does not seek to mitigate damages.

4. If payment is made in a currency of the host or home state, compensation shall include simple interest at the 6-month average U.S. dollar LIBOR rate from the date of expropriation until the date of actual payment.
5. If a Member State elects to pay in a currency other than a host or home state currency, the amount paid on the date of payment, if converted into a host or home state currency at the market rate of exchange prevailing on that date, shall be no less than if the amount of compensation owed on the date of expropriation had been converted into that host or home state currency at the market rate of exchange prevailing on that date, and simple interest had accrued at the 6-month average U.S. dollar LIBOR rate from the date of expropriation until the date of payment.
6. On payment, compensation shall be freely transferable. Awards that are significantly burdensome on a host state may be paid yearly over a period agreed by the Parties, subject to interest at the rate established by agreement of the disputants or by a tribunal. Where the Parties do not agree on a specific period, the matter shall be referred to a competent tribunal to determine the period within which the award shall be paid.
7. This Article shall not apply to the issuance of compulsory licences granted in relation to intellectual property rights, or to the revocation, limitation or creation of intellectual property rights, to the extent that such issuance, revocation, limitation or creation is consistent with applicable international agreements on intellectual property.
8. A measure of general application shall not be considered an expropriation of a debt security or loan covered by this Agreement solely on the ground that the measure imposes costs on the debtor that cause it to default on the debt.
8. Bona fide regulatory measures taken by a Member State or awards by judicial bodies of a Member State that are designed and applied to protect or enhance legitimate public welfare objectives, such as public health, safety and the environment, shall not constitute an expropriation or measures tantamount to expropriation under this Article.
9. The investor affected by the expropriation shall have a right under the law of the Member State making the expropriation, to a review by a juridical or other independent authority of that Member State, of his/its case and the valuation of his/its investment in accordance with the principles set out in paragraphs (1) to (8) of this Article. The Member State making the expropriation shall ensure that such a review is carried out promptly.

10. The Parties confirm their shared understanding that:
    (a) expropriation may be direct or indirect:
        (i) direct expropriation occurs when an investment is nationalized or otherwise directly expropriated through formal transfer of title or outright seizure; and
        (ii) indirect expropriation occurs if a measure or series of measures of a Party has an effect equivalent to direct expropriation, in that it substantially or permanently deprives the investor of the fundamental attributes of property in its investment, including the right to use, enjoy and dispose of its investment, without formal transfer of title or outright seizure; and
    (b) the determination of whether a measure or a series of measures have an effect equivalent to expropriation requires a case-by-case, fact-based inquiry, that takes into consideration:
        (i) the economic impact of the measure or series of measures, although the sole fact that a measure or series of measures of a Party has an adverse effect on the economic value of an investment does not establish that an indirect expropriation has occurred;
        (ii) the duration of the measure or series of measures of a Party;
        (iii) the character of the measure or series of measures, notably their object, context and intent; and
        (iv) whether a measure by a Party breaches the Party's prior binding written commitment to the investor whether by contract, license or other legal document.

ARTICLE 21

Compensation for Losses

1. COMESA investors whose investments in the territory of the Member States suffer losses owing to war or other armed conflict, revolution, a state of national emergency, revolt, insurrection or riot shall be accorded treatment, as regards restitution, indemnification, compensation or other settlement, not less favorable than that which Member States accord to their own investors or to investors of any third State. Resulting payments shall be freely transferable at the exchange rate applicable on the date of transfer pursuant to the exchange regulations in force.
2. Without derogating from the provisions of paragraph (1) of this Article, any investor who, in any of the situations referred to in that paragraph, suffers losses in a Member State resulting from:
    (a) requisitioning of their property by the forces or authorities of the Member States, acting under and within the scope of the legal provisions relating to their competences, duties and command structures; or
    (b) destruction of their property by the forces or authorities of the Member States, which was not caused in combat action or was not required by the necessity of the situation or observance of any legal requirement;

(c) shall be accorded restitution, or adequate compensation not less favourable than that which the Member States accord to their own investors or to investors of any third State.

3. For the purposes of this Article, state of emergency excludes natural disaster.

ARTICLE 22

General Exceptions

1. Subject to the requirement that such measures are not applied in a manner which would constitute a means of arbitrary or unjustifiable discrimination between investors where like conditions prevail, or a disguised restriction on investment flows, nothing in this Agreement shall be construed to prevent the adoption or enforcement by any Member State of measures designed and applied to protect or enhance legitimate public welfare objectives such as:
   (a) national security and public morals;
   (b) human, animal or plant life or health;
   (c) environment; or
   (d) public health and safety.
2. Nothing in this Agreement shall be construed to:
   (a) preclude a Member State from applying measures that it considers necessary for the fulfilment of its obligations under the United Nations Charter with respect to the maintenance or restoration of international peace or security;
   (b) preclude a Member State from applying measures that it considers necessary for the protection of its own national security interests; or
   (c) require a Member State to furnish or allow access to any information the disclosure of which it determines to be contrary to its essential security interests.
3. A Member State reserves the right to deny an investor the benefits of this Agreement, and to grant special and differential treatment to any investor and investment in such cases, where the investor is engaged in activities inimical to the economic and security interest of the Member State.

ARTICLE 23

Taxation

1. This Agreement shall not apply to taxation measures except as provided for in paragraph 3 of this Article.
2. Member States, with a view to encouraging cross-border investments, may conclude between themselves double taxation avoidance agreements.

3. Noting in this Article prevent an investor from claiming that a taxation measure by a Member State is tantamount to an expropriation of investment that contravenes Article 20.
4. Where an investor makes a claim under paragraph 3, that investor shall refer the matter to the Secretary General who shall use his good offices with a view to assisting the Member State and the investor to reach to an amicable solution.
5. Where, within 6 months of a referral under paragraph 4, no amicable solution has been reached, the investor may refer the matter to arbitration in the manner provided for under this Agreement.

ARTICLE 24

Measures to Safeguard Balance of Payments

1. In the event of serious balance of payment and external financial difficulties or threat thereof, a Member State may adopt or maintain restrictions on investments on which it has undertaken commitments provided for in Articles 15, 17, 19 and 20, including on payments or transfers for transactions related to such commitments.
2. Where measures to safeguard balance of payments are taken pursuant to this Article, notice of such measures shall be given to the CCIA Committee within 14 days from the date such measures are taken.
3. The measures referred to in paragraph 1 shall:
   (a) not discriminate among Member States;
   (b) be consistent with Article VIII of the Agreement of the International Monetary Fund;
   (c) avoid unnecessary damage to the commercial, economic and financial interests of any other Member State;
   (d) not exceed those necessary to deal with the circumstances described in paragraph 1; and
   (e) be temporary and be phased out progressively as the situation specified in paragraph 1 improves.
4. A Member State adopting the balance of payment measures shall commence consultations with Member States through the CCIA Committee within 90 days from the date of notification in order to review the balance of payment measures adopted by it.
5. The CCIA Committee shall determine the rules applicable to the procedures under this Article.

PART FOUR

INVESTOR AND INVESTMENT OBLIGATIONS

ARTICLE 25

Compliance with domestic laws

COMESA investors and their investments shall comply with all applicable domestic laws and measures of the host state.

ARTICLE 26

Framework for corporate governance

1. COMESA Investors and their investments shall meet or exceed national and internationally accepted standards of corporate governance for the sector involved, in particular for transparency and accounting practices. In this regard, Member States, public bodies and companies are encouraged to improve the legal, institutional and regulatory framework for corporate governance that result from the separation of ownership and control and any other issues relevant to a company's decision -making process, such as environmental or ethical concerns, as set forth in this Agreement.
2. COMESA Investors and their investments shall ensure that all transactions with related or affiliated companies shall be arm's length transactions at fair market price. Investors and their investments shall not undertake any transfer pricing practices between themselves or any other related or affiliated companies.
3. COMESA Investors and their investments shall, in accordance with domestic laws and regulations:
   (a) ensure the equitable treatment of all shareholders, in accordance with national laws;
   (b) encourage active co-operation between corporations and stakeholders in creating wealth, jobs and the sustainability of financially sound enterprises;
   (c) ensure that timely and accurate disclosure is made on all material matters regarding a corporation, including the financial situation, performance, ownership, and governance of the company, risks related to environmental liabilities, and any other matters in accordance with the relevant regulations and requirements; and
   (d) provide information relating to human resource policies, such as programs for human resource development.

ARTICLE 27

Socio-political obligations

1. COMESA Investors and their investments shall adhere to socio- political obligations including, but not exclusively, the following:
   (a) respect for national sovereignty and observance of domestic laws, regulations and administrative practices;
   (b) respect for socio-cultural values;
   (c) non-interference with internal political affairs; and
   (d) non-interference with intergovernmental relations.
2. COMESA Investors and their investments shall refrain from influencing the appointment of persons to public office or finance political parties.
3. COMESA Investors and their investments shall refrain from all acts that may be prejudicial to public order, morals or to the public interest. The investor shall also to refrain from exercising restrictive practices and from trying to achieve gains through unlawful means.

ARTICLE 28

Bribery and Corruption

1. COMESA Investors and their investments shall not offer, promise or give any undue pecuniary or other advantage, whether directly or through intermediaries, to a public official of a Member State, or to an official's relative or business associate or other person in close proximity to an official, for that official or for a third party, in order that the official or third party act or refrain from acting in relation to the performance of official duties, in order to achieve any favor in relation to a proposed investment or any other rights in relation to an investment.
2. COMESA Investors and their investments shall also not be complicit in any act described in paragraph 1 of this Article, including through incitement, aiding and abetting or conspiracy to commit or authorize such acts.
3. Member States shall adopt such legislative and other measures as may be necessary to establish jurisdiction and enforce laws and procedures against any criminal offence committed in whole or in part in their territory by a national, or a COMESA investor and investment or its agent, or by any other person acting in relation to an investment in a Member State.
4. A breach of this article by a COMESA investor or its investment is deemed to constitute a breach of the domestic law of the Host State concerning the establishment and operation of an investment.

ARTICLE 29

Business Ethics and Human Rights

1. COMESA investors and their investments shall observe the United Nations Guiding Principles on Business and Human Rights with modifications necessary for local circumstances.
2. COMESA investors and investments shall among others:
   (a) support and respect the protection of internationally proclaimed human rights;
   (b) ensure that they are not complicit in human rights abuses;
   (c) uphold the freedom of association and the effective recognition of the right to collective bargaining;
   (d) eliminate all forms of forced and compulsory labor, including the effective abolition of child labor; and
   (e) eliminate discrimination in respect of employment and occupation.

Where it is necessary to prioritize actions to address actual and potential adverse human rights impacts, COMESA investors should first seek to prevent and mitigate those that are most severe or where delayed response would make them irremediable.

ARTICLE 30

Corporate Social Responsibility

1. In pursuit of their economic objectives, COMESA investors and their investments shall proceed in ways that do not conflict with the social and economic development of host countries. Investors shall be sensitive to changes in the social and economic goals of the host countries.
2. Investors and their investments should act in accordance with fair business, marketing and advertising practices when dealing with consumers and should ensure the safety and quality of goods and services they provide.

ARTICLE 31

Environmental Protection and Social Impact Assessment

1. COMESA Investors and their investments shall, in performing their activities, protect the environment and where such activity causes damages to the environment; take reasonable steps to restore it as far as possible, and to ensure fair compensation is paid to those impacted by the environmental damages.
2. COMESA Investors or their investments shall comply with environmental and social assessment screening criteria and assessment processes applicable to their

proposed investments prior to their establishment, as required by the laws of the host state for such an investment.

3. The impact assessments required under paragraph 2 shall include assessments of the impacts on the human rights of the persons in the areas potentially impacted by the investment.
4. COMESA Investors or their investments shall make the environmental and social impact assessments:
   (a) public; and
   (b) accessible to the local communities, or other areas with potentially affected interests, in an effective and sufficiently timely manner so as to allow comments to be made to the investor, investment and/or government prior to the completion of the host state processes for establishing an investment.
5. COMESA Investors, their investments and the host state authorities shall apply the precautionary principle to their environmental impact assessment and to decisions taken in relation to a proposed investment, including any necessary mitigating or alternative approaches to the investment, or precluding the investment if necessary. The application of the precautionary principle by investors and investments shall be described in the environmental impact assessment.

ARTICLE 32

Environmental Management and Improvement

1. COMESA investments shall, in keeping with good practice requirements relating to the size and nature of the investment, and as required under the domestic laws, maintain an environmental management system consistent with recognized international environmental management standards and good business practice standards.
2. Emergency response and decommissioning plans shall be included, and regularly reviewed and updated in the environmental management system process, and made accessible to the host state and the public.
3. A closure fund to ensure that resources are available to implement the decommissioning plan shall be established and maintained by the Investor or its Investment in accordance with good industry practice for such funds.
4. Environmental management plans shall include provision for the continued improvement of environmental management technologies and practices over the life of the Investment. Such improvements shall be consistent with applicable laws, but shall strive to exceed legally applicable standards and always maintain high levels of environmental performance consistent with best industry practice.

ARTICLE 33

Implications of breach of investors' obligations

Without prejudice to other rights and remedies of a host state or its population, a host state may initiate a proceeding against a COMESA investor or its investment in the courts of the host state for breaches of its obligations under this Agreement. By specific written agreement, the disputing parties may submit the dispute to an arbitral tribunal in accordance with Article 36.

PART FIVE

DISPUTE SETTLEMENT

ARTICLE 34

Negotiation and Mediation

1. In the event that a dispute arises from the interpretation or application of this Agreement between Member States, or between a Member State and a COMESA investor, the party wishing to raise the dispute shall issue a notice of intention to initiate a claim under the dispute resolution process provided for under Articles 35 or 36 under this Agreement to the other potential disputing party ("notice of intention").
2. For the purposes of this Agreement, there shall be the minimum of a six-month cooling-off period between the date of a notice of intention under this Agreement ("the cooling-off period"), and the date a party may formally initiate a dispute under Articles 35 or 36.
3. The parties shall seek to resolve potential disputes through amicable means, both prior to and during the cooling-off period.
4. Where amicable means fail, the disputing parties shall seek the assistance of a mediator to resolve disputes during the cooling-off period required under this Agreement between the notice of intention and the initiation of dispute settlement proceedings under Articles 35 or 36. The potential disputants shall use a mediator from the list established by the COMESA Secretariat for this purpose, or another one of their joint choosing. Recourse to mediation does not alter the minimum cooling-off period.
5. If no mediator is chosen by the disputing parties prior to three months before the expiration of the cooling-off period, the President of the COMESA Court of Justice or his/her designate shall appoint a mediator from the COMESA Secretariat's list who is not a national of the Member State of the COMESA investor or the Member State(s) party to the dispute. The appointment shall be binding on the disputing parties.
6. If the parties accept a mediation ruling, the ruling shall immediately be implemented thereafter.

ARTICLE 35

Settlement of Disputes between Member States

1. Any dispute between Member States as to the interpretation or application of this Agreement not satisfactorily settled through amicable means in the cooling-off period may be referred for decision to the COMESA Court of Justice sitting as a court of arbitration, in accordance with Article 28(b) of the COMESA Treaty.
2. The decision under paragraphs 1 shall be final and binding.

ARTICLE 36

Investor–State Disputes

1. In the event that a dispute between a COMESA investor and a Member State has not been resolved, pursuant to Article 34, a COMESA investor may, subject to the exhaustion of local remedies in the host state, submit a claim to the COMESA Court of Justice under Article 26 (1) of the Treaty.
2. Paragraph 1 shall apply unless the disputing parties, by specific written agreement, submit the dispute to the following arbitral fora:
   (a) an African international arbitration institution; or
   (b) under any other arbitration institution or under any other arbitration rules, as both parties to the dispute agree.
3. A COMESA investor or its investment may submit a claim to arbitration pursuant to this Agreement, provided that the COMESA investor or investment, as appropriate:
   (a) has first submitted a claim before the domestic courts of the Host State for the purpose of pursuing local remedies, after the exhaustion of any administrative remedies, relating to the measure underlying the claim under this Agreement, and a resolution has not been reached within a reasonable period of time from its submission to a local court of the host state; or
   (b) demonstrates on a motion to permit arbitration that there are no reasonably available legal remedies capable of providing effective remedies for the dispute concerning the underlying measure, or the legal remedies provide no reasonable possibility of such remedies in a reasonable period of time.
4. No claim shall be submitted to arbitration if more than three (3) years have elapsed from the date on which the COMESA investor or its investment first acquired, or should have first acquired, knowledge of the breach and knowledge that the COMESA investor or its investment has incurred loss or damage.
5. If the COMESA investor elects to submit a claim at one of the fora set out in paragraph 1 of this Article, that election shall be definitive and the investor may not thereafter submit a claim relating to the same subject matter or underlying measure to other fora.

6. Each Member State consents to the submission of a claim to arbitration under this Agreement in accordance with its provisions. Each COMESA investor or its investment, by virtue of establishing or continuing to operate or own an investment subject to this Agreement, consents to the terms of the submission of a claim to dispute resolution under this Agreement.
7. A Member State against whom a claim is brought by a COMESA investor or its investment under this Article, may assert as a defense, counterclaim, right of set off or other similar claim, that the COMESA investor or its investment bringing the claim has not fulfilled its obligations under this Agreement, including the obligations to comply with all applicable domestic measures or that it has not taken all reasonable steps to mitigate possible damages.

ARTICLE 37

Enforceability of Final Awards and Other Decisions

Enforceability of final awards and other decisions shall be governed by the rules of civil procedure in force in the Member State in which execution is to take place.

PART SIX FINAL PROVISIONS

ARTICLE 38

Other Agreements

1. This Agreement or any action taken under it shall not affect the rights and obligations of the Member States under existing agreements to which they are party.
2. Nothing in this Agreement shall affect the rights of the Member States to enter into other agreements not contrary to the principles, objectives and terms of this Agreement.
3. In the event of inconsistency between this Agreement and such other agreements between Member States mentioned in paragraph 2 of this Article, this Agreement shall prevail to the extent of the inconsistency, and in so far as it is more favorable to the investor.

ARTICLE 39

Amendments

Any amendments to this Agreement shall be adopted by the Council and shall enter into force when ratified by two thirds of the Member States that have ratified or acceded to the Agreement.

ARTICLE 40

Supplementary Arrangements

Annexes and any other arrangements arising under this Agreement shall form an integral part of this Agreement.

ARTICLE 41

Adoption of Regulations

The Council may on the recommendation of the CCIA Committee adopt additional regulations to this Agreement, which shall come into force in accordance with the provisions of Article 43 of this Agreement.

ARTICLE 42

Entry into Force

1. This Agreement shall enter into force when signed and ratified by at least two thirds Member States.
2. This Agreement shall enter into force in relation to an acceding Member State on the date its instrument of accession shall be deposited.

ARTICLE 43

Accession

Any Member State that has not ratified this Agreement on the date of its entry into force may accede to this Agreement.

ARTICLE 44

Depository

This Agreement and all instruments of ratification or accession shall be deposited with the Secretary General who shall transmit certified true copies of this Agreement to all the Member States.

ARTICLE 45

Withdrawal

1. This Agreement shall remain in force unless terminated by consensus of Member States.
2. A Member State may withdraw from this Agreement by written notification to the Secretary General who shall immediately inform all the Member States. The Agreement shall expire for that Member State one year after the date of such notification, provided that the rights of COMESA investors where an investment is substantially in the process of being established or has been established shall survive for a period of five years from such withdrawal.

IN WITNESS WHEREOF, the undersigned being duly authorized by their respective Governments, have signed this Investment Agreement for the COMESA Common Investment Area.

DONE at .... this .... day of...... ... .2018, in the English, French and Arabic languages, all three texts being authentic.

The President of the Republic of Burundi

The President of the Union of the Comoros

The President of the Democratic Republic of Congo

The President of the Republic of Djibouti

The President of the Arab Republic of Egypt

The President of the State of Eritrea

His Majesty the King of the Kingdom of Swatini

The President of the Federal Democratic Republic of Ethiopia

The President of the Republic of Kenya

The President of the State of Libya

The President of the Republic of Madagascar

The President of the Republic of Malawi

The Prime Minister of the Republic of Mauritius

The President of the Republic of Rwanda

The President of the Republic of Seychelles

The President of the Republic of Sudan

The President of the Republic of Uganda

The President of the Republic of Zambia

The President of the Republic of Zimbabwe

SCHEDULE I

CO-OPERATION AND FACILITATION PROGRAMME

In respect of the Co-operation and Facilitation Program, Member States shall take:

(a) individual initiative to:
   (i) increase transparency of Member State's investment rules, regulations, policies and procedures through the publication of Such information on a regular basis and making such information widely available;
   (ii) simplify and expedite procedures for applications and approvals of investment projects at all levels; and
   (iii) expand the number of bilateral Double Taxation Avoidance Agreements among COMESA Member States;

(b) collective initiative to:
  (i) establish a Database for COMESA Supporting Industries and COMESA Technology Suppliers;
  (ii) establish a COMESA database to enhance the flow of COMESA investment data and information on investment opportunities in COMESA:
  (iii) promote public-private sector linkages through regular dialogues with the COMESA business community and other international organizations to identify investment impediments within and outside COMESA and propose ways to improve the COMESA investment environment;
  (iv) identify target areas for technical co-operation, e.g. development of human resources, infrastructure, supporting industries, small and medium-sized enterprises, information technology, industrial technology, R & D and co-ordinate efforts within COMESA and other international organizations involved in technical co-operation;
  (v) review and where possible improve the Investment Agreement for the COMESA Common Investment Area; and
  (vi) examine the possibility of a COMESA Double Taxation Agreement.

SCHEDULE II

PROMOTION AND AWARENESS PROGRAMME

In respect of the Promotion and Awareness program, Member States shall:
(a) organize joint investment promotion activities e.g. seminars, workshops, inbound familiarization tours for investors from capital exporting countries, joint promotion of specific projects with active business sector participation;
(b) conduct regular consultation among investment agencies of COMESA on investment promotion matters;
(c) organize investment-related training programs for officials of investment agencies of COMESA;
(d) exchange lists of promoted sectors/industries where member States could encourage investments from other member States and initiate promotional activities; and
(e) examine possible ways by which the investment agencies of Member States can support the promotion efforts of other member States.

SCHEDULE III

List of national authority contact points for Member States for the purposes of registering an investment under Article 3.

ANNEX III

ECOWAS Supplementary Act on Investments

THE HIGH CONTRACTING PARTIES

MINDFUL of Articles 7, 8 and 9 of the ECOWAS Treaty as amended establishing the Authority of Heads of State and Government and defining its composition and functions;

MINDFUL of Article 3 of the ECOWAS Treaty stipulating the areas in which the Community should focus its activities in order to achieve its aims and objectives;

RECOGNIZING that the development of a more vibrant and dynamic private sector helps to create job opportunities, promote technology transfer, support long term economic growth and contributes effectively to the fight against poverty;

ANXIOUS to promote and consolidate within ECOWAS, an environment conducive to the development of the activities of the private sector and to make the latter a genuine engine of economic growth;

NOTING that national investment codes in force in Member States offer investors different incentives and protection measures;

CONVINCED of the need to establish within the ECOWAS region, reliable, transparent, stable and predictable conditions for investments;

DESIROUS of adopting common regional rules on investments and defining the modalities for their implementation, in order to achieve the afore-mentioned objectives;

HAVING CONSIDERED the opinion of the ECOWAS Parliament;

ON THE RECOMMENDATION of the sixty first ordinary session of the Council of Ministers, held in Ouagadougou from 27 29 November 2008.

AGREE AS FOLLOWS:

Chapter I. General Provisions

Article 1. Definitions

(a) "company" means any corporate entity constituted or organized under the applicable law of any ECOWAS Member State, whether or not for profit, and whether privately or govemmentally owned or controlled;
(b) "national" means a person who is a citizen of any Member State of ECOWAS;
(c) "investment" means
   i) a company;
   ii) shares, stock and other forms of equity participation in a company, and bonds, debentures and other forms of debt interests in a company;

iii) contractual rights, such as under turnkey, construction or management contracts, production or revenue-sharing contracts, concessions or other similar contracts;
iv) tangible property, including real property; and intangible property, including rights, such as leases, mortgages; liens and pledges on real property;
v) rights conferred pursuant to law, such as licenses and permits provided that:
   - Such investments are not in the nature of portfolio investments which shall not be covered by this Supplementary Act;
   - There is a significant physical presence of the investment in the host State;
   - The investment in the host State is made in accordance with the laws of that host State;
   - The investment is part or all of a business or commercial operation; and
   - The investment is made by an investor as defined herein.

(d) "investor" is any individual or company of any Member State of ECOWAS or a company that has invested or is making an investment in the territory of a Member State;
(e) "measures" includes any legal, administrative, legislative, judicial or policy decision that is taken by the host State, directly relating to and affecting an investment in the territory of the host State, but does not include measures in draft form;
(f) Member State, means a State of ECOWAS
(g) "home State" means a Member State of ECOWAS from where the investment or the investor comes;
(h) "host State" is the ECOWAS Member state where the investment is located;
(i) "ECOWAS" means the Economic Community of West African States whose creation was reiterated by Article 2 of the Revised Treaty.
(J) "Third Country" is any other State which is not a member of ECOWAS
(k) "ILO" means the International Labor Organization

Article 2. Adoption of the Regional Instrument
The Community Rules on investment as defined in this Supplementary Act are hereby adopted.

Article 3. Objective
The objective of the Community Rules on investment is to promote Investment that supports sustainable development of the region.

Article 4. Scope of Coverage
(1) This Supplementary Act applies to all investments by an investor, whether the investment is made before or after the entry into force of this Supplementary Act.
(2) This Supplementary Act applies to any measure adopted or maintained by a Member State, after the entry into force of this Supplementary Act by a governmental authority of the host State.

(3) This Supplementary Act does not create retroactive obligations or responsibilities for investors. However investors who are not in compliance with on going obligations and responsibilities shall seek to comply with them within twenty four (24) months of the entry into force of this Supplementary Act.

Chapter II. Standards of Treatment to Member States' Investors

Article 5. National Treatment

(1) Each Member State shall accord to investors of another Member State treatment no less favorable than that, which it accords, in like circumstances to any other investor operating in its territory, with respect to the management, conduct, operation, expansion and sale or other disposition of investments.
(2) Each Member State shall accord to investments of investors from another Member State treatment no less favorable than that which it accords, in like circumstances, to investments of its own investors with respect to the, managements, conduct, operation, expansion and sale or other disposition of investments.
(3) The treatment accorded by a Member State under Paragraphs (1) and (2) means, with respect to a local authority, treatment no less favourable than that which it accords, in like circumstances, to investors within the Community.
(4) The concept of "in like circumstances" requires an overall examination, on a case by-case basis, of all the circumstances of an investment, including notably:
a) its effects on third persons and the local community;
b) its effects on the local, regional or national environment, the health of the populations, or on the global commons;
c) the sector in which the investor is active;
d) the aim of the measure in question;
e) the regulatory process generally applied in relation to a measure in question; and
f) other factors directly relating to the investment or investor in relation to the measure in question.

Article 6. Most-favored-nation Treatment

(1) This Article applies to:
a) all measures of a Member State covered by this Supplementary Act, and
b) all the substantive provisions of other international agreements on investment that enters into force after this Supplementary Act has entered into force.
(2) Each Member State shall accord to investors of another Member State treatment no less favorable than that it accords in like circumstances, to investors of any other state within the Community with respect to the management, conduct, operation, expansion, sale or other disposition of investments.
(3) Each Member State shall accord to investments made by investors of another Member State treatment no less favorable than that it accords in like circumstances, to investments made by investors of any other Member State of the

Community or of a third party with respect to the management, conduct, operation, expansion, sale or other disposition of investments.

(4) Each Member State shall accord to investors of another Member State and to investments made by investors from other Member States, the better of the treatment required by this Article, and the national treatment obligation.

(5) Paragraphs (2) to (4) above do not oblige a State within the Community to extend to the investors of another Member State the benefit of any treatment, preference or privilege contained in:

i) any existing or future customs union, free trade area, common market agreement or any international arrangement relating to the current or future environment to which the investor's home State is not a Party, or

ii) any international agreement or arrangement relating wholly or mainly to taxation or any domestic legislation relating wholly or mainly to taxation.

Article 7. Minimum Regional Standards

(1) Each Member State shall accord to investors from a Member State or their investments, treatment in accordance with customary international law, including fair and equitable treatment and reasonable protection and security under the domestic law. This obligation shall be understood to be consistent with the obligation of ECOWAS Member States.

(2) Paragraph (1) prescribes the customary usage of international law minimum standard of treatment of aliens as the minimum standard of treatment to be accorded to investments. The concepts of "fair and equitable treatment" and "full protection and security" are included within this standard, and do not create additional substantive rights.

(3) Each Member State shall accord to investors and their investments non-discriminatory treatment with respect to measures it adopts or maintains relating to losses suffered by investments in its territory owing to armed conflict or civil strife.

(4) Notwithstanding Paragraph (3) , if an investor of a State, in the situations referred to in that Paragraph, suffers a loss in the territory of another Member State resulting from:

i) requisitioning of its investment or part thereof by the latter's forces or authorities; or

ii) destruction of its investment or part thereof by the latter's forces or authorities, which was not required by the necessity of the situation, the host State within the Community shall provide the investor restitution or compensation, which in either case shall be prompt, adequate and effective; and with respect to compensation, shall be in readily convertible form.

Article 8. Expropriation

(1) No Member State may directly or indirectly nationalize or expropriate an investment in its territory ("expropriation"), except:

a) for a public purpose;

b) on a non discriminatory basis;
c) in accordance with due process of law; and
d) on payment of compensation in accordance with Paragraphs (2) to (6).

(2) Appropriate compensation shall normally be equivalent to the fair market value of the expropriated investment immediately before the expropriation took place ("date of expropriation"), and shall not reflect any change in value occurring because the intended expropriation had become known earlier. Valuation criteria shall include going concern value, asset value including declared tax value of tangible property, and other criteria, as appropriate, to determine fair market value;

(3) Compensation shall be paid without delay and be fully realizable;

(4) Payment should be made in a convertible currency and compensation shall include interest at a commercially reasonable rate for that currency from the date of expropriation until the date of actual payment.

(5) On payment, compensation shall be freely transferable. Awards that are significantly burdensome on a host State may be paid yearly over a period of three (3) years or such other period as may be agreed by the Member States, subject to interest at the rate established by mutual consent.

(6) This Article does not apply to the issuance of compulsory licenses granted in relation to intellectual property rights, or to the revocation, limitation or creation of intellectual property rights, to the extent that such issuance, revocation, limitation or creation is consistent with applicable international agreements on intellectual property.

(7) A non-discriminatory measure of general application shall not be considered an expropriation of a debt security or loan covered by this Supplementary Act solely on the ground that the measure imposes costs on the debtor that cause it to default on the debt.

Article 9. Senior Management and Boards of Directors

(1) No Member State may require that an investor appoint to senior management positions individuals of any particular nationality.

(2) No Member State may require that some members of the board of directors or any committee thereof, of an investment, be of a particular nationality, or resident in the territory of that State, provided that the requirement does not materially impair the ability of the investor to exercise control over its investment.

(3) Subject to generally applicable rules of entry, no Member State may unduly restrict or prevent the cross-border movement of staff engaged in respect of investments from another Member State.

Article 10. Transfers of Assets

(1) Each Member State shall permit all transfers relating to an investment to be made freely and without delay. Such transfers include:

a) profits, dividends, interest, capital gains, royalty payments, management fees, technical assistance and other fees, returns, physical assets and other amounts derived from the investment;
b) proceeds from the sale of all or any part of the investment or from the partial or complete liquidation of the investment;
c) payments made under a contract entered into by the investor or its investment, including payments made pursuant to a loan agreement;
d) payments made pursuant to Article 8 of this Supplementary Act; and
e) payments arising under any dispute settlement process.

(2) Each Member State shall permit transfers to be made in a freely convertible currency at the market rate of exchange prevailing on the date of transfer with respect to spot transactions in the currency to be transferred.

(3) Notwithstanding Paragraphs (1) and (2) , a host State within the Community may prevent a transfer through the equitable, non-discriminatory and good faith application of its laws relating to:
a) bankruptcy, insolvency or the protection of the rights of creditors;
b) issuing, trading or dealing in securities;
c) criminal or penal offences;
d) transfers of currency or other monetary instruments; or
e) ensuring the satisfaction of judgments in adjudicatory proceedings

(4) Notwithstanding Paragraph (2) , a host State may restrict transfers or returns in circumstances where it could otherwise restrict such transfers under this Supplementary Act.

Chapter III. Obligations and Duties of Investors and Investments

Article 11. General Obligations

(1) Investors and Investments are subject to the laws and regulations of the host State

(2) Investors and investments must comply with the host State measures prescribing the formalities of establishing an investment, and accept host State jurisdiction with respect to the investment.

(3) Investors shall strive through their management policies and practices, to contribute to the development objectives of the host States and the local levels of government where the investment is located.

(4) An investor shall provide such information to a potential host State Party to this Supplementary Act, as that Party may require,

Concerning the investment in question for purposes of decisionmaking in relation to that investment or solely for statistical purposes. The host State shall protect any confidential business information from any disclosure that would prejudice the competitive position of the investor or the investment. Nothing in this Paragraph, shall be construed to prevent any Member State of the Community from otherwise obtaining or disclosing information in connection with the equitable and good faith application of its domestic law.

Article 12. Pre-establishment Impact Assessment

(1) Investors and Investments shall conduct an environmental and social impact assessment of the potential investment. Investors or the investments shall comply with environmental assessment screening criteria and assessment processes applicable to their proposed investments prior to their establishment, as required by the laws of the host Member State for such an investment or the laws of the home State for such an investment. The investor shall comply with the minimum standards on environmental and socio-cultural impact assessment and screening that the Member States shall adopt at the first meeting of the Parties, to the extent that these are applicable to the investment in question.

(2) Investors or the investments shall make the environmental and social impact assessments accessible in the local community and to affected interests in the host State where the investment is intended to be made prior to the completion of the host State measures prescribing the formalities for establishing such investment.

(3) Investors, their investments and host State authorities shall apply the precautionary principle to their environmental and social impact assessment. The application of the precautionary principle by investors and investments shall be described in the environmental and social impact assessment they undertake.

Article 13. Anti-corruption

(1) Investors and their investments shall prior to the establishment of an investment or afterwards, refrain from involving themselves in corrupt practices as defined in Article 30 of this supplementary Act.

(2) Investors and their investments shall not be complicit in any act described in Paragraph (1) of this article, including incitement, aiding and abetting, and conspiracy to commit or authorization of such acts.

(3) The acts referred to Paragraph 1 and 2 shall be punishable in conformity with the provisions of Article 30 of this Supplementary Act.

Article 14. Post-establishment Obligations

(1) Investors or investments shall, in keeping with best practice requirements relating to their activities the size of their investments, strive to comply with on hygiene, security, health and social welfare rules in force in the host country.

(2) Investors shall uphold human rights in the workplace and the community in which they are located. Investors shall not undertake or cause to be undertaken, acts that breach such human rights. Investors shall not manage or operate the investments in a manner that circumvents human rights obligations, labour standards as well as regional environmental and social obligations, to which the host State and/or home State are Parties

(3) Investors shall not by complicity with, or in assistance with others, including public authorities, violate human rights in times of peace or during socio-political upheavals.

(4) Investors and investments shall act in accordance with fundamental labor standards as stipulated in the ILO Declaration on Fundamental Principles and Rights of Work, 1998.

Article 15. Corporate Governance and Practices

In accordance with the size and nature of an investment,

(1) Investments shall comply with and maintain national and internationally accepted standards of corporate governance for the sector involved, in particular for transparency and accounting practices.
(2) Investors and relevant public authorities of the host State(s) shall make available to the public, any investment contract or agreement with the host State govemment(s), subject to the law governing the release of confidential business information.
(3) Investors shall, where appropriate, establish and maintain with the local community, liaison processes in accordance with regionally accepted standards.
(4) Where relevant regionally accepted standards of the type described in this Article are not available or have been developed without the participation of member countries, the Community shall establish such standards.

Article 16. Corporate Social Responsibility

(1) In addition to the obligation to comply with:
    - All applicable laws and regulations of the host Member State;
    - And the obligations in this Supplementary Act and in accordance with;
    - The size, capacities and nature of an investment, and taking into account;
    - The development plans and priorities of the host State;
    - The Millennium Development Goals and;
    - The indicative list of corporate social responsibilities agreed by the Member States.
(2) Where standards of corporate social responsibility increase, investors should endeavor to apply and achieve the higher level standards.

Article 17. Investor Liability

Investors shall be subject to civil actions for liability in the judicial process of their host State for acts or decisions made in relation to the investment where such acts or decisions lead to significant damage, personal injuries or loss of life in the host State.

Article 18. Relation of Investor's Liability to Dispute Settlement

(1) Where it is established by a court of competent jurisdiction of the host State that an investor has breached Article 13 of this Supplementary Act, the investor shall not be entitled to initiate any dispute settlement process established under this Supplementary Act. A host or home State may raise this as an objection to jurisdiction in any dispute under this Supplementary Act.
(2) Where an investor is alleged by a host Member State or an intervener in a dispute settlement proceeding under this Supplementary Act to have failed to

comply with its obligation relating to preestablishment impact assessment, the tribunal hearing such a dispute shall consider whether this breach, if proven, is materially relevant to the issues before it, and if so, what mitigating or offsetting effects this may have on the merits of a claim or on any damages awarded in the event of such award.

(3) Where a host Member State or home Member State believes that an investor or its investment has breached Article 13 or has persistently failed to comply with its obligations under Article 14 or 15, and such investor or investment has been notified by the host Member State or home Member State, as appropriate, either the host Member State or the home Member State may initiate proceedings before a tribunal established by this Supplementary Act.

(4) Where a persistent failure to comply with Article 14 or 15 is raised by a host Member State defendant or an intervener in a dispute settlement proceeding under this Supplementary Act, the tribunal hearing such a dispute shall consider whether this breach, if proven, is materially relevant to the issues before it, and if so, what mitigating or off-setting effects this may have on the merits of a claim or on any damages award in the event of such award.

(5) A host Member State may initiate a counterclaim before any tribunal established pursuant to this Supplementary Act for damages resulting from an alleged breach of the Supplementary Act.

(6) In accordance with the applicable domestic law, a host State or private person or organization, may initiate actions for damages under the domestic law of the host Member State, or the domestic law of the home Member State where such an action relates to the specific conduct of the investor, for damages arising from an alleged breach of the obligations set out in this Supplementary Act. The proceedings in the domestic law Court shall conform to the procedures applicable in the Community Court of Justice.

Chapter IV
Host State Obligations

Article 19
Procedural Fairness

In accordance with the requirements of Article 7

(1) Host Member States shall ensure that their administrative, legislative and judicial processes do not operate in a manner that is arbitrary or that does not deny administrative and procedural fairness to investors and their investments. Investors or investments shall be notified in a timely fashion of administrative or judicial proceedings and changes thereof directly relating to them, unless such notice is contrary to domestic law on an exceptional basis.

(2) Hosts Member States shall act in a manner that does not create a denial of justice in judicial and administrative proceedings.
(3) Administrative decision-making processes shall include the right of administrative appeal of decisions, commensurate with the level of development of the host Member State. Judicial review of administrative decisions should also be available through domestic or regional judicial review processes.
(4) Notwithstanding the differences in administrative, legislative and judicial systems, Member States shall strive to improve the transparency, efficiency, independence and accountability of their legislative, regulatory, administrative and judicial processes, and shall provide review or appeal procedures to ensure that they operate in accordance with applicable domestic laws.
(5) Judicial and administrative review processes shall be open to the public and documents shall be accessible by the public unless prohibited in accordance with domestic and regional laws. Decisions of such bodies shall however be available to the public.

Article 20
Maintenance of Environmental and other Standards

Member States recognize that it is inappropriate to encourage investment by relaxing domestic labor, public health, safety or environmental measures and thus shall not waive or otherwise derogate from, or offer to waive or otherwise derogate from, such measures as an encouragement for the establishment, acquisition, expansion or retention in their territories, of an investment.

Article 21

Minimum Standards for Environmental, Labor and Human Rights Protection

(1) Each Member State shall ensure that its laws and regulations provide for appropriate levels of environmental protection and shall strive to continue to improve those laws and regulations.
(2) Each Member State shall ensure that its laws and regulations provide for high levels of labor and human rights protection appropriate to existing regional and international treaties that it enters into, and shall strive to continue to improve these laws and regulations.
(3) All Member States shall have a domestic social, health and environmental impact assessment laws that meet the minimum standards adopted by the Community on these matters.
(4) All Member States shall ensure that their domestic laws and policies are consistent with the ILO Declaration on Fundamental Principles and Rights of Work, 1998.

(5) All Member States shall ensure that their laws, policies and actions are consistent with the international human rights agreements to Which they are a Party and at a minimum, with the list of human rights obligations and agreements already adopted.

Article 22
Publication of Information

Host Member States shall make available to the public any investment contracts or agreements with an investor involved in the investment authorization process, subject to the release of confidential business information.

Article 23
Incentives

Potential host Member States should avoid competition for the attraction of investment or investments through incentives or other means that distort regional competition for investments. To this effect, Member States shall initiate negotiations to harmonise the adequate incentive schemes aimed at implementing sensitization and mobilization activities.

Chapter V

Host State Rights

Article 24
Performance Requirements

(1) Member States recognize their obligations regarding trade-related investment measures established in other international agreements to which they are a Party.
(2) Subject to Paragraph (1) , host States may impose performance requirements to promote domestic development benefits from investments. Measures adopted prior to the completion of the host State measures prescribing the formalities for establishing an investment shall be deemed to be in compliance with this Supplementary Act. If such measures are taken after the completion of the host State measures prescribing the formalities for establishing an investment, they shall be subject to the provisions of this Supplementary Act.

(3) Measures covered by this Article may include requirements:
a) to export a given level or percentage of goods or services;
b) to achieve a given level or percentage of domestic content;
c) to purchase, use or accord a preference to goods produced or services provided in its territory;
d) to purchase goods or services from persons in its territory;
e) to relate the volume or value of imports to the volume or value of exports or to the amount of foreign exchange flows associated with such investment;
f) to restrict sales of goods or services in its territory that such investment produces by relating such sales to the volume or value of its exports or foreign exchange earnings; and
g) similar measures intended to promote domestic development.

Article 25
Implementation of Community Rules on Investment Promotion and Facilitation of Investment

(1) The Community shall create regional structures for the implementation of the Community Investment Rules Member States in the area of the promotion and the facilitation of investments.
(2) Member States shall establish or maintain appropriate National structures for the same purpose.
(3) The Member States shall take appropriate steps to facilitate Diaspora investment into the region.
(4) Member States shall adopt relevant regional initiatives to promote investments in the region including investment guarantee mechanisms, integration of capital and other measures.

Article 26
Access to Investor Information

(1) Host States have the right to seek information from a potential investor or its home State about its corporate governance history and its practices as an investor, including in its home State.
(2) Host States shall protect confidential business information they receive in this regard.
(3) Host States may make the information provided available to the public in the community where the investment may be located, subject to the protection of confidential business information and to other applicable domestic laws.

Chapter VI
Home State Rights and Obligations

Article 27
Assistance and Facilitation for Cross-border Investment

(1) Home States may facilitate cross border investment to other States in the Community in line with ECOWAS Treaty. However such assistance shall be consistent with the development goals and priorities of the receiving States of such investment and must not violate the commitments of Members States to the Community. Such assistance may include:
  a) capacity building with respect to host State agencies and programs on investment promotion and facilitation;
  b) insurance programs based on commercial principles;
  c) technology transfer; and
  d) periodic trade missions, support for joint business councils and other cooperative activities to promote sustainable investments.

(2) Home States shall inform host States of the form and extent of available assistance as appropriate for the type and size of different investments.

Article 28
Information

(1) Home States shall, on request and in a timely manner, provide to a potential host State such information as is requested and available for the purposes of the host State to meet its obligations and perform its duties in relation to an investor or investment under this Supplementary Act and the host State's domestic law. Home States shall protect confidential business information in this regard.

(2) Home States shall, on request, and in a timely manner, provide information relevant to the home State standards that might apply under like circumstances to the investment proposed by its investor, including but not limited to the home State's environmental and social public health impact assessment process.

Article 29
Investor Liability In Home State

Home States shall ensure that their legal systems and rules allow for, or do not prevent or unduly restrict, the bringing of court actions on their merits before domestic courts relating to the civil liability of investors for damages resulting from alleged acts or decisions made by investors in relation to their investments in the territory of other Member States. The host State laws on liability shall apply to such proceedings.

Article 30
Offences and Sanctions

(1) Member States shall consider as criminal the following offences and investigate, prosecute and punish the said offences with appropriate sanctions
   (a) the offering, solicitation or acceptance of an offer, promise or gift of any pecuniary or other nature, whether directly or through intermediaries, to any public official of the host State, for that official or for a third party, in order that the official or third party act or refrain from acting in relation to the performance of official duties to achieve any favor Annexin relation to a proposed investment or any licenses, permits, contracts or other rights in relation to an investment; and
   (b) any acts constituting any of the acts described in Paragraph (A) including incitement, aiding and abetting, conspiracy to commit or authorization of such acts; shall be made criminal offences in the host Member State and subject to appropriate criminal enforcement and sanctions.

(2) All home States shall ensure that any money or other forms of benefits encompassed in Paragraph (1) shall not be recoverable or deductible in any fiscal or tax policies.

(3) Home States shall, when possible, provide all available information that might assist a dispute settlement tribunal under this Supplementary Act in determining whether there has been a breach of an anti-corruption obligation.

Chapter VII
Relation to other Agreements

Article 31
Relation to other Investment Agreements and Obligations

(1) All investment agreements entered into by Member States prior to entry into force of this Supplementary Act, shall to the extent that the provisions of such Agreements are inconsistent with the provisions of this Supplementary Act, renegotiate those agreements within a transition period of twenty-four (24) months to make them consistent with the present Community Investment Supplementary Act.

(2) Member States shall ensure that all future investment agreements to which they may become Party are fully consistent with this Supplementary Act on Investment; particularly with the balance of rights and obligations it establishes, and the principal features of the dispute settlement system. Member States may be called upon to assess compliance with these obligations.

Article 32
Relation to other International Agreements

(1) Member States shall ensure that the provisions of other international trade agreements to which they are a party are consistent with the provisions of this Supplementary Act. Member States shall collaborate to ensure the effective application of the provisions of this Act within the international trade agreements.
(2) In the event of any dispute arising on this issue, the Member States shall seek to resolve such dispute within the framework of this Supplementary Act as a first step.

Chapter VIII
Dispute Settlement

Article 33
Dispute Settlement Procedures

(1) In the event of a dispute between Member States, or between a Member State and an investor, or between an investor and a host State, the party wishing to raise the dispute shall issue a notice of intention to initiate arbitration to the other potential disputing Party or Parties using a dispute settlement procedure prescribed below.
(2) There shall be a minimum period of six months between the date of a notice of intention to initiate a dispute settlement process under this Supplementary Act, and the date a Party or investor as the case may be, may formally initiate a dispute. During this period, Member States make efforts to reach an amicable settlement of possible disputes. The use of good offices, conciliation, mediation or any other agreed dispute resolution process may also be applied.
(3) Where mediation is adopted as the dispute resolution process, the disputants shall use an approved mediator for this purpose.
(4) If no mediator is chosen by the disputing parties prior to three months before the expiration of the amicable settlement period, a mediator who is not a national of one of the State parties to the dispute shall be appointed. The conditions for the appointment of the said mediator shall be set out in the relevant regulation.

(5) Member States may also establish national mediation centers to facilitate the resolution of disputes between Parties and investors or investments, taking into account regional rules, customs and traditions on investment. Mediators officially appointed to such centers shall be incorporated into the Agency's list through the national mediation centers.

(6) Any dispute between a host Member State and an Investor, as envisaged under this Article that is not amicably settled through mutual discussions may be submitted to arbitration as follows:
 (a) a national court;
 (b) any national machinery for the settlement of investment disputes;
 (c) the relevant national court of the Member States.

(7) Where in respect of any dispute envisaged under this Article, there is disagreement as to the method of dispute settlement to be adopted; the dispute shall be referred to the ECOWAS Court of Justice.

Article 34
Transparency of the Dispute Settlement Procedures

(1) All documents relating to a notice of intention to arbitrate, the settlement of any dispute, the initiation of a panel or appeal, or the pleadings, evidence and decisions in them shall be available only to the parties to the disputes.

(2) Procedural and substantive oral hearings shall be open to the public also.

Article 35
Enforceability of Final Awards/decisions

(1) The Final Awards/Decisions on Investment disputes made by mediations, arbitrations and judicial bodies shall be enforceable

(2) Member States parties to the Supplementary Act shall abide by the decisions of mediation, arbitration and judicial bodies on investment disputes. Notwithstanding this provision, disputant parties may seek redress from competent jurisdictions.

Article 36
Governing Law In Disputes

When a claim is submitted to a panel or an appeal tribunal, it shall be decided in accordance with this Supplementary Act, and subsidiarily, any other national, Community, and international law/rules agreed upon by the parties.

Chapter IX. General Exceptions

Article 37.
National Security

Nothing in this Supplementary Act shall be construed:

a. to require a Member State to furnish or allow access to any information the disclosure of which it determines to be contrary to its essential security interest; or
b. to preclude a Member State from applying measures that it considers necessary for the fulfillment of its obligations under the United Nations Charter with respect to the maintenance or restoration of international peace or security, or the protection of its own essential security interests.

Article 38
General Reservations and Exceptions

(1) The provisions of this Supplementary Act, except Article 8, do not apply to any law or other measure of a host State the purpose of which is to promote the achievement of equality in its territory, or designed to protect or advance persons, or categories of persons, disadvantaged by long-term historic discrimination in its territory, provided that such law or other measure is compatible with the requirements of Article 19.

(2) State Parties may take such measures as are necessary to avoid or abate a balance of payments emergency. Such measures shall be kept in force for as short a time as possible to address the emergency situation. Such measures shall not be subject to this Supplementary Act.

Chapter X
Final Provisions

Article 39
Regional Co-operation

Member States may conclude co-operation agreements on matters covered by this Supplementary Act, as well as on the development of regional capacities in this field.

Article 40

Amendment and Revision

(1) Any Member State, the Council of Ministers, the ECOWAS Parliament and the ECOWAS Commission may submit proposals for the amendment or revision of this Supplementary Act.
(2) Proposals not emanating from the ECOWAS Commission shall be submitted to it. The Commission shall forward all proposals for amendment and revision to the Member States not later than thirty (30) days after their receipt. Upon expiration of the thirty (30) days notice given to Member States, the Authority of Heads of State and Government shall examine the proposals for amendment or revision of the Supplementary Act.
(3) The amendments or revisions shall be adopted by the Authority of Heads of State and Government in accordance with the provisions of Article 9 of the ECOWAS Treaty. The adopted amendments and revisions shall enter into force upon their publication in the Official Journal of the Community.

Article 41

Publication

This Supplementary Act shall be published by the ECOWAS Commission in the Official Journal of the Community within Thirty (30) days of its signature by the Chairperson of the Council of Ministers. It shall also be published by each Member State in its National Gazette within thirty (30) days after notification by the Commission.

Article 42

Entry Into Force

1. This Supplementary Act shall enter into force upon its publication. Consequently, signatory Member States and the Institutions of ECOWAS undertake to commence the implementation of its provisions on its entry into force,
2. This Supplementary Act is annexed to the ECOWAS Treaty of which it is an integral part.

Article 43

Depository Authority

This Supplementary Act shall be deposited with the Commission which shall transmit certified true copies thereof to all Member States and shall register it with the African Union, the United Nations and such other organizations as Council may determine.

IN WITNESS WHEREOF, WE, THE HEADS OF STATE AND GOVERNMENT OF THE ECONOMIC COMMUNITY OF WEST AFRICAN STATES, HAVE SIGNED THIS SUPPLEMENTARY ACT

DONE AT ABUJA THIS 19 DAY OF DECEMBER 2008

IN SINGLE ORIGINAL IN THE ENGLISH, FRENCH AND PORTUGUESE LANGUAGES, ALL THREE (3) TEXTS BEING EQUALLY AUTHENTIC

ANNEX IV

ECOWAS Common Investment Code

(ECOWIC)

JULY 2018

DRAFT ECOWAS COMMON INVESTMENT CODE

PREAMBLE

THE HIGH CONTRACTING PARTIES

MINDFUL of Articles 7, 8 and 9 of the Revised ECOWAS Treaty establishing the Authority of Heads of State and Government and defining its composition and functions;

MINDFUL of Article 3 of the Revised ECOWAS Treaty stipulating the areas in which the

Community should focus its activities in order to achieve its aims and objectives;

MINDFUL of the Supplementary Act A/SA.3/12/08 Adopting Community Rules On

Investment and the Modalities for their Implementation within ECOWAS;

RECOGNIZING that the development of a more vibrant and dynamic private sector can help to create job opportunities, promote technology transfer, support long-term economic growth and contributes effectively to the fight against poverty;

ANXIOUS to promote and consolidate within ECOWAS an environment conducive to the development of the activities of the private sector and to make the latter a genuine engine of economic growth;

DESIRING to promote further the trade and investment existing between and amongst the Member States;

RECOGNIZING the importance of fostering a conducive and predictable environment for international trade and investment;

RECOGNIZING the vision, aims and objectives of the ECOWAS Investment Policy

TAKING into account membership of some of the Member States in other international organizations such the World Trade Organization (WTO) and noting that this Code is without prejudice to the rights and obligations of the Member States where applicable, under such agreements, understandings, and other instruments relating thereto or concluded under the auspices of the WTO;

RECOGNIZING the potential benefits to each Party resulting from increased international trade and investment;

RECOGNIZING the essential role that both domestic and foreign private investment when accompanied by appropriate environmental and labor policies, can play in the sustainable development of the Parties, including in reducing poverty, increasing productive capacity, furthering growth, creating jobs, expanding trade, improving technology and transfer of technology, furthering human rights and human development and enhancing economic development;

SEEKING to promote, encourage and increase investment opportunities that enhance sustainable development goals within the territories of the Parties;

UNDERSTANDING sustainable development requires the fulfilment of the economic, social and environmental pillars that are embedded within the concept;

FURTHER RECOGNISING the right of each Member State to establish its own level of domestic environmental protection and its own sustainable development policies and priorities;

DESIRING to encourage and facilitate private sector and business contacts between and amongst the Parties;

NOTING that national investment codes in force in Member States offer investors different incentives and protection measures;

CONVINCED of the need to establish within the ECOWAS region, reliable, transparent, harmonised and predictable conditions for investments;

DESIROUS of adopting common regional rules on investments and defining the modalities for its implementation, in order to achieve the afore-mentioned objectives;

TAKING into account the need to eliminate non-tariff barriers in order to facilitate greater access of investors to the markets of the Parties and the mutual benefits thereof;

CONSIDERING that it would be in the respective interests of the Parties to establish a mechanism between the Parties for encouraging the liberalization of trade and investment between and amongst them, including through the appropriate regional bodies and mechanisms;

DESIRING to ensure that trade and environmental policies are mutually supportive in furtherance of sustainable development;

AFTER THE OPINION of the ECOWAS Parliament;

ON THE RECOMMENDATION of the....Session of the Council of Ministers, held in..............................from..................to...................;

TO THIS END, THE PARTIES AGREE AS FOLLOWS:

CHAPTER 1. GENERAL PROVISIONS

Article 1: Definitions

Under this Code:

(a) "**Annex Scheduled List**" means schedules of excluded sectors or any other list approved by Member States from time to time
(b) "**Commission**" means the executive body of the Economic Community of West African States;
(c) "**Community**" means the Economic Community of West African States;
(d) "**Community citizen or citizens**" means any national(s) of Member States who satisfy the conditions stipulated in the Protocol defining Community citizenship;
(e) "**Enterprise or company**" means any entity duly constituted or otherwise incorporated under the applicable laws and regulations of any ECOWAS Member State, provided it maintains substantial business activity in the Member State in which it is located, whether privately or governmentally owned or controlled;
(f) "**Home State**" means a Member State of ECOWAS from where the investment or the investor originates;
(g) "**Host State**" is the ECOWAS Member state where the investment is located and/or undertake.
(h) "**Investment**" means an enterprise or a company as defined in paragraph (e), which is established, acquired, or expanded by an investor, having business or commercial operations or other interests such as:
   i. a company or an enterprise;
   ii. shares, stocks or other forms of equity participation in a company or an enterprise, and bonds, debentures and other forms of debt interests in a company or an enterprise;
   iii. contractual rights such as turnkey, construction, management contracts, production or revenue-sharing contracts, concessions or other similar contracts;
   iv. tangible property, including real property; and intangible property, including rights such as leases, mortgages, liens and pledges or such other securities;
   v. similar assets or rights conferred pursuant to law of a Member State provided that
      - such investments are not in the nature of portfolio investments which shall not be covered by this Code;
      - there is a significant physical presence of the investment in the host State;
      - the investment in the host State is made in accordance with the laws of that host State;
      - the investment is part or all of a business or commercial operation; and the investment is made by an investor as defined in this Code.

For greater certainty, investment does not include:

(i) Debt securities issued by a government or loans to a government;
(ii) Portfolio investments;
(iii) Claims to money that arise solely from commercial contracts for the sale of goods or services by a national or enterprise in the territory of a Member State to an enterprise in the territory of another Member State, or the extension of credit in connection with a commercial transaction, or any other claims to money that do not involve the kind of interests set out in Subparagraphs (i) through (v) above;
(iv) Investments of a speculative nature;
(v) Investments in any sector sensitive to its development or which would have an adverse impact on its economy;
(vi) Commercial activities.

In order to qualify as an investment under this Code, the investment must have the following characteristics: substantial business activity according to Paragraph e, commitment of capital or other resources, the expectation of gain or profit, the assumption of risk, and a significant contribution to the host State's economic development. Substantial business activity requires overall examination, on a case by case basis, of all the circumstances, including, inter alia: the amount of investment to be brought into the host state; the number of jobs to be created; its effect on the local community; the length of time the business has been in operation

(i) **"Investor"** is any individual, company or enterprise legally originating from any Member State of ECOWAS or an individual, company or enterprise from a third country that has made an investment in a Member State;
(j) **"Labor legislation"** means legislation, or provisions thereof, that are directly related to the following internationally recognized labor rights:
  (i) the right of association;
  (ii) the right to organize and bargain collectively;
  (iii) prohibition on the use of any form of forced or compulsory labor;
  (iv) minimum age for the employment of children;
  (v) acceptable conditions of work with respect to minimum wages, hours of work, and occupational safety and health;
(k) **"Measures"** means any legal, administrative, legislative, judicial or policy decision that is taken by the host State, directly relating to and affecting an investment in the host State;
(l) **"Member State (s)"** means any Member State or Member States of ECOWAS as defined in Article 2, Paragraph 2, of the Revised ECOWAS Treaty;
(m) **"National"** means a person who is a citizen of any Member State of ECOWAS;
(n) **"Portfolio investment"** refers to any investment where the investor owns less than 10% of shares in a company, either made through a stock exchange or otherwise, does not give the portfolio investor the possibility to exercise effective management or influence on the management of the investment;
(o) **"Public official(s)"** means any person who has been selected, appointed or elected and who performs public functions on a permanent or temporary basis. This includes persons who, at the national, regional or local level holds

a legislative, administrative, judicial or military office, or who, performing a public function, is an employee of a Government or of a public or governmental authority or agency or who otherwise performs a public activity or function in the name of the State or in the service of the State, at any level of its hierarchy;

(p) **State contracts** are contracts entered into between a Member State or the State's agents and the investor or investors conferring contractual rights pursuant to the definition of an investment under this Code;

(q) **"Third Country"** is any country which is not a member of ECOWAS

Article 2: Objectives

1) The objective of this code is to establish in the ECOWAS territory, transparent, harmonized and predictable legal and institutional framework that applies to investment and to any investment-related measures designed to implement the ECOWAS Investment Policy.
2) To this end, this code seeks to:
   a) promote, facilitate, and protect investment that foster sustainable development of the region and in particular, the Member State in which the investment is located
   b) promote the adoption of common regional rules on investments and define the modalities for their implementation, in order to achieve the aforementioned objective;
   c) improve investment and trade relations with and within the region and between the region and foreign investors, conducive to regional stability and sustainable development;
   d) enhance the role of both domestic and foreign direct investments in reducing poverty, increasing productive capacity, furthering growth, creating jobs, expanding trade, improving technology and transfer of technology, furthering human rights and human development, enhancing economic development; among others;

Article 3: Scope and Application

(1) This Code applies to the rights and obligations of Member States and investors.
(2) This Code applies to any measure adopted or maintained by a Member State, after the entry into force of this Code.
(3) This Code does not create retroactive obligations for Member States and investors.

CHAPTER 2: STANDARDS OF TREATMENT TO INVESTORS

Article 4: Admission and Establishment

(1) Each Member State shall in admitting an investment into its territory follow the parameters of the investment policy in force at the time the investment is made and in accordance with its national laws and regulations.

(2) Each Member State shall accord investors full rights of entry and establishment to all natural and legal persons engaged in cross-border business, based on the principle of national treatment with the aim of promoting free flows of investment within the region and in accordance with the West Africa Common Industrial Policy.

Article 5: Regulation of Investment

The admission and regulation of investment in any Member State shall be subject to the following conditions:

(a) Investments shall be subject to the laws and regulations of the Host State;

(b) The benefits of this Code shall apply to any investment by the investor in any Member State which is duly approved by the competent authority in accordance with the laws and regulations of the host State(s);

(c) Once a Member State admits an investment it shall provide in accordance with its laws and regulations all necessary permits related to such investment.

Article 6: National Treatment

1) A Member State shall accord to investors of another Member State treatment no less favorable than that, which it accords, in like circumstances, to its own investors with respect to the management, conduct, operation, expansion and sale or other dispositions of investments.

2) A Member State shall accord to investments from another Member State treatment no less favorable than that which it accords, in like circumstances, to investments of its own investors with respect to the management, conduct, operation, expansion and sale or other dispositions of investments.

3) For purposes of this Code, the concept of "in like circumstances" requires an overall examination, on a case by-case basis, of all the circumstances of an investment, including:

(a) its effects on the local community;
(b) its effects on the local, regional or national environment, the health of the populations, or on the global commons;
(c) the sector in which the investor is active;
(d) the aim of the measure in question;
(e) the regulatory process generally applied in relation to a measure in question; and
(f) other factors directly relating to the investment or investor in relation to the measure in question.

Article 7: -Exceptions to National Treatment

1. Member States may adopt measures that derogate from the National Treatment principle provided such measures are not arbitrary and subject to the conditions set out in this Article.
2. Any regulatory measure taken by a Member State that is designed and applied to protect or enhance legitimate public welfare objectives, such as national interests, public health, safety and the environment, does not constitute a breach of the National Treatment principle.
3. Member States may, in accordance with their respective domestic legislation, grant preferential treatment to qualifying investments and investors in order to achieve national development objectives.
4. A Member State reserves the right to deny an investor the benefits of this Code where:
   (a) The investor does not have substantial business activities in the Member State; or
   (b) The investor is engaged in activities inimical to the economic interest of Member States.
5. A Member State may deny national treatment if advantages available within the Member State's economy are made for the exclusive benefit of its own nationals within the framework of its national development programs or its List of scheduled investment sectors where applicable.
6. The National Treatment principle shall not apply:
   (a) to subsidies or grants provided to a government or a State enterprise, including government-supported loans, guarantees and insurance; or
   (b) to taxation measures aimed at ensuring the effective collection of taxes, except where this results in arbitrary discrimination.
7. In accordance with national laws and regulations, Member States may accord more favorable treatment to address the internal needs of designated disadvantaged persons, groups or regions.
8. The implementation of these exceptions shall not entitle any investor to compensation for any competitive disadvantages they may suffer.

Article 8: Most-Favored-Nation Treatment

(1) Each Member State shall accord to investors of another Member State treatment no less favorable than that it accords, in like circumstances, to investors of any other Member State with respect to the management, conduct, operation, expansion, sale or other disposition of investment.
(2) Each Member State shall accord to investments made by investors of another Member State treatment no less favorable than that it accords, in like circumstances, to investments made by investors of any other Member State with respect to the management, conduct, operation, expansion, sale or other disposition of investments.
(3) Paragraphs (1) to (2) above do not oblige a Member State to extend to the investors of a third country the benefit of any treatment, preference or privilege contained in:
   (a) The existing or future customs union, free trade area, common market agreements, or any international agreement to which the investor's home State is not a Party, or
   (b) Any international agreement or domestic legislation relating wholly or mainly to taxation.
(4) For greater certainty, the "treatment" referred to in Paragraphs 1 to 3, does not include dispute settlement procedures provided for in other treaties. Substantive obligations in other treaties do not in themselves constitute "treatment," and thus cannot give rise to a breach of this Article.

Article 9: Exceptions

(1) General Exceptions

Subject to the requirement that such measures are not applied in a manner that would constitute a means of arbitrary or unjustifiable discrimination between Member States or their investors in like circumstances, nothing in this Code shall be construed to prevent the adoption or enforcement by any Member State of measures taken in good faith and designed and applied:
(a) to protect public morals or to maintain public order;
(b) to protect human, animal, or plant life or health;
(c) to secure compliance with the national laws or regulations which are not inconsistent with this Code, including those relating to:
   (i) for the prevention of deceptive and fraudulent practices to deal with the effects of a default on a contract;
   (ii) to the protection of the privacy of individuals in relation to the processing and dissemination of personal data and the protection of confidentiality of individual records and accounts; or
   (iii) for safety reasons;

(d) to ensure the equitable or effective imposition or collection of direct taxes in respect of investors of another Member State and their investments;
(e) to protect national treasures of artistic, historic, or archaeological value;(f) for the conservation of exhaustible natural resources if such measures are made effective in conjunction with restrictions on domestic production or consumption.
(g) to promote the achievement of equality in its territory, land planning, or designed to protect or advance categories of disadvantaged persons.
(h) to preserve and promote cultural and linguistic diversity.
(i) to preserve and protect the biodiversity and the rights of local communities, in conformity with the relevant multilateral instruments.

(2) Security Exceptions

Nothing in this Code shall be construed to:

(a) require any Member State to furnish any information, the disclosure of which it considers contrary to its essential security interests; or
(b) prevent any Member State from taking any action which it considers necessary for the protection of its essential security interests, including, but not limited, to:
  (i) action relating to fissionable and fusionable materials or the materials from which they derived;
  (ii) action relating to the traffic in arms, ammunition, and implements of war and to such traffic in other goods and materials as is carried on directly or indirectly for the purpose of supplying a military establishment;
  (iii) action taken in time of war or other emergency in domestic or international relations;
  (iv) action taken so as to protect critical public infrastructure, including communication, power, and water infrastructure, from deliberate attempts intended to disable or degrade such infrastructure; or
(c) prevent any Member State from taking any action pursuant to its obligations under the United Nations Charter for the maintenance of international peace and security.

(3) Subject-Specific Exceptions

(a) A Member State may, in exceptional financial, economic or industrial circumstances, adopt any exceptional measure in the sectors or with respect to the matters specified in its Annex of schedules of excluded sectors or any other list as maybe approved by Member States from time to time, provided that such are consistent with the provisions of this Code.
(b) Nothing in this Code shall be construed to prevent a Member State from adopting or maintaining measures that restrict transfers when the Member state experiences serious balance of payments difficulties.
(c) Restrictions imposed on transfers related to trade in goods, shall not substantially impede those transfers from being made in a freely usable currency at a market rate of exchange and may not take the form of tariff surcharges or similar measures.

(d) An interested Member State shall prior to the entry into force of the exceptional measure:
   (i) endeavor to notify the other Member State of the elements of the exceptional measure as set out;
   (ii) provide, upon request by that other Member State, particulars of the exceptional measure to that other Member State;
   (iii) allow that other Member State reasonable time to make comments in writing;
   (iv) hold, upon request by that other Member State, consultations in good faith with
   that other Member State with a view to achieving mutual satisfaction; and
   (v) take an appropriate action based upon the written comments made pursuant to subparagraph (iii) of this paragraph or the results of the consultations held accordingly.

(4) **Financial and Prudential Measures**
   (i) A Member State may take reasonable measures for prudential reasons to:
      (a) protect investors, depositors, financial market participants, policyholders, policy claimants, or persons to whom a fiduciary duty is owed by a financial institution;
      (b) maintain the safety, soundness, integrity or financial responsibility of financial institutions;
      (c) ensure the integrity and stability of a Member State's financial systems; and
      (d) enhance Balance of Payments situations.
   (ii) Nothing in this Code shall apply to non-discriminatory measures of general application taken by any public entity in pursuit of monetary and related credit policies or exchange rate policies.

(5) **Mutual Recognition**
   (a) A Member State may by agreement or arrangement, recognize a certificate, qualification, diploma or experience from another Member State or third country, in any area of service delivery.
   (b) An existing agreement or arrangement for the recognition of certificates, qualifications, diplomas or experiences, between two or more member States or a third country, shall not extend to another Member State.
   (c) A non–contracting party to an existing agreement or arrangement, for the recognition of certificates, qualification or experience, may accede to such existing agreement or arrangement for the mutual recognition of certificates, qualifications, diplomas or experience within the Community.
   (d) Nothing in 9 (a) to (c) above shall prevent member states from taking concrete steps towards the harmonization of standards for the recognition of certificates, qualifications, diplomas and experience in the Community, in accordance with the objectives of this Code.
   (e) Member States shall not apply discriminatory measures in the application of standards for the recognition of certificates, qualification, diplomas or experience from other Member States

Article 10: Treatment in Case of Armed Conflict or Civil Strife

Investors who suffer within the territory of a Member State damage in relation to their investments owing to the outbreak of hostilities or a state of national emergency such as revolt, insurrection or riot, shall be accorded treatment no less favourable than that accorded to investors of such Member State or to investors of any third country in like circumstances, as regards to any measure to be taken by the concerned Member State including restitution, compensation or other valuable consideration.

Article 11: Expropriation and Compensation

1. No Member State shall expropriate or nationalize an investment in its national territory, except:
   (a) for a public purpose;
   (b) on payment of prompt, adequate and effective compensation; and
   (c) in accordance with due process of law.
2. Compensation shall:
   (a) be paid without delay;
   (b) be equivalent to the fair market value of the expropriated investment immediately before the expropriation took place (the date of expropriation);
   (c) not reflect any change in value occurring because the intended expropriation had become known earlier; and
   (d) be fully realizable and freely transferable.
3. Compensation awards that are significantly burdensome on a Member State may be paid under periodic instalments as agreed by the Parties, subject to simple interest at the rate agreed by the parties or through mediation and or judicial process
4. If the fair market value is denominated in a freely usable currency, the compensation paid shall be no less than the fair market value on the date of expropriation, plus simple interest at a commercially reasonable rate for that currency, accrued from the date of expropriation until the date of payment.
5. If the fair market value is denominated in a currency that is not freely usable, the compensation paid, converted into the currency of payment at the market rate of exchange prevailing on the date of payment, shall be no less than:
   (a) the fair market value on the date of expropriation, converted into a freely usable currency at the market rate of exchange prevailing on that date; plus
   (b) interest, at a commercially reasonable rate for that freely usable currency, accrued from the date of expropriation until the date of payment.
6. Where appropriate, the assessment of fair and adequate compensation shall be based on an equitable balance between the public interest and interest of those affected, having regard for all relevant circumstances and taking account of: the current and past use of the property, the history of its acquisition, the fair market

value of the investment, the purpose of the expropriation, the extent of previous profit made by the foreign investor through the investment, and the duration of the investment.

7. This Article shall not apply to the issuance of compulsory licenses granted in relation to intellectual property rights in accordance with the relevant international agreements on intellectual property, or to the revocation, limitation, or creation of intellectual property rights to the extent that the issuance, revocation, limitation, or creation is consistent with the relevant international agreements on intellectual property.
8. For greater certainty, a Member State's decision not to issue, renew, or maintain a subsidy or grant, or its decision to modify or reduce a subsidy or grant:
   (a) in the absence of any specific commitment under law or contract to issue, renew, or maintain that subsidy or grant; or
   (b) in accordance with any terms or conditions attached to the issuance, renewal, modification, reduction, and maintenance of that subsidy or grant, standing alone, does not constitute an expropriation.

Article 12: Transfer of Funds

(1) Types of Transfers Covered

Member States shall permit all transfers relating to an investment to be made freely and without delay. Such transfers may include:

(a) profits, capital gains, dividends, royalties, interest and other current income accruing from an investment;
(b) the proceeds of the total or partial liquidation of an investment;
(c) repayments made pursuant to a loan agreement in connection with an investment;
(d) license fees in relation to investment;
(e) payments in respect of technical assistance, technical service and management fees;
(f) payments in connection with contracting projects;
(g) earnings of nationals of a Member State who work in connection with an investment in the territory of the other Member State;
(h) compensation, restitution, indemnification or other settlement pursuant to the investments.

(2) **Capital Importation**

(a) Investment funds may be imported into the Community through any licensed financial institution in a Member State who shall issue a certificate of capital importation to the investor within the time prescribed in national laws.
(b) The certificate of capital importation shall be registered with the appropriate regulatory authority for financial institutions in the Member State.

(3) **Nature of the Obligations**
   (a) Each Member State shall permit transfers to be made in a convertible currency at the market rate of exchange prevailing on the date of transfer.
   (b) Unless otherwise agreed by the investor, transfers shall be made in any convertible currency at the rate of exchange applicable on the date of transfer pursuant to the exchange regulations in force.

(4) **Exceptions**
   (a) Capital can only be transferred two years after the investment entered the territory of a Member State unless its national legislation provides for a more favorable treatment.
   (b) Proceeds of the investment can only be transferred one year after the investment entered the territory of a Member State.
   (c) Notwithstanding paragraphs 1, 2 and 3, a Member State may prevent or delay a transfer through the equitable, non-discriminatory, and good faith application of its national laws relating to:
      (i) bankruptcy, insolvency, or the protection of the rights of creditors;
      (ii) issuing, trading, or dealing in securities, futures, options, or derivatives;
      (iii) criminal or penal offences;
      (iv) financial reporting or record keeping of transfers when necessary to assist law enforcement or financial regulatory authorities; or
      (v) ensuring compliance with orders or judgments in judicial or administrative proceedings.
   (d) A Member State may adopt or maintain measures not conforming with its obligations relating to cross-border capital transactions:
      (i) in the event of serious balance-of-payments and external financial difficulties or threat thereof; or
      (ii) in cases where, in exceptional circumstances, movements of capital cause or threaten to cause serious difficulties for macroeconomic management, in particular, monetary and exchange rate policies.
   (e) Measures referred to in paragraph (d) above shall:
      (i) not exceed those necessary to deal with the circumstances set out above;
      (ii) be temporary and be eliminated as soon as conditions permit;
      (iii) be as approved by the ECOWAS Common Investment Market Council (ECIM Council), and
      (iv) be promptly notified to the affected Member State.

Article 13: Denial of Benefits

1. A Member State may deny the benefits of this Code to an investor of another Member State that is an enterprise of such Member State and to the investments of such investor in the event that investors of a non-Member State own or control such enterprise, provided that the denying Member State adopts or maintains

measures with respect to the non-Member State that prohibit transactions with such enterprise, or that otherwise would be violated or circumvented if the benefits of this Code were accorded to that enterprise or to its investments.

2. A Member State may deny the benefits of this Code to an investor of another Member State that is an enterprise of such Member State and to investments of such investors if investors of a non-Member State own or control the enterprise and the enterprise has no substantial business activities in the territory of the Member State under whose law it is constituted or otherwise organized.

Article 14: Subrogation

If a Member State, or any agency, institution, statutory body or corporation designated by the Member State, makes a payment to an investor of the Member State under a guarantee, a contract of insurance or other form of indemnity that it has entered into with respect to an investment, the other Member State in whose territory the investment was made shall recognize the subrogation or transfer of any rights the investor would have possessed under this Code with respect to the investment but for the subrogation, and the investor shall be precluded from pursuing these rights to the extent of the subrogation.

Article 15: Transparency

(1) Governmental Information

(a) A Member State shall endeavor to ensure that its laws, policies, regulations, procedures, administrative rulings and judicial decisions of general application, as well as international agreements after their entry into force, which may affect investments in its territory, including among others, exchange regimes and those of fiscal nature, are promptly published, or otherwise made publicly available. Such information shall be regularly updated and published at least annually.

(b) A Member State shall provide to the other Member State aggregated information on foreign investment and investment opportunities in its territory with respect to origin, economic activities benefited, investment modalities and other information which may be available.

(c) Upon request of an investor, a Member State shall provide information to enable investors to fully assess the legal status of investment assets.

(d) A Member State shall designate a contact point or points to facilitate communications between the Member States on any matter covered by this Code.

(2) Corporate Information

Member States have the right to seek information from a potential investor or its home state about its corporate governance history and its practices as an investor in its home state or in a third country. Member States oblige themselves to protect confidential business information they receive in this regard.

(3) Exchange of Information

(a) A Member State shall upon request by another Member State, promptly respond to specific questions and provide that other Member State with information on matters set out above.

(b) The provisions of paragraph (a) of this Article shall not be construed so as to oblige a Member State to disclose confidential information, the disclosure of which would impede law enforcement or otherwise be contrary to the public interest, or which would prejudice privacy or legitimate commercial interests.

(4) Duty to Disclose Investment Information

(a) As and when prescribed by the ECIM Council, investors shall make available to the public in the Member State where they are operating information relating to payments made to the Member State's public authorities, including taxes, royalties, surcharges, fees and all other payments relating to the investment contract or agreement.

(b) Information related to any investment contract or agreement involved in the investment authorization process shall also be made available to the public, subject to the protection of confidential business information.

(5) **Answering Requests for Information**

An investor shall provide such information to a Member State concerning the investment in question for purposes of decision-making in relation to that investment or solely for statistical purposes.

(6) **Notification Requirements**

a) An investor or a Host State may request a review of an investment agreement on terms that are mutually agreed by parties;

b) An investor shall comply with such audit as may be requested by a Host State in order to ascertain compliance with the terms of the investment agreement;

c) An investor shall not, without prior consultation with the Host State, fix or alter the prices of products or services in sectors identified by that Member State to be critical to economic and social development.

(7) **Confidentiality**

(a) Member States shall protect any confidential business information from any disclosure that would prejudice the investor or the investment.

(b) Nothing in paragraph (a) above shall be construed to prevent a Member State from otherwise obtaining or disclosing information in connection with the equitable and good faith application of its relevant domestic laws and regulations.

(c) Nothing in this Code requires any Member State to provide confidential information, the disclosure of which would impede law enforcement, or otherwise be contrary to the public and policy interest, or which would prejudice legitimate economic interests of particular enterprises, public or private.

(8) Enforcement
 (a) Member States recognize that it is inappropriate to encourage investment by relaxing domestic measures and regulations of investments on the protection and enforcement of rights and duties pertaining to the investments as well as on the prevention of their abuse.
 (b) No Member State should waive or derogate from, or offer to waive or otherwise derogate from investment measures as an encouragement for the establishment, acquisition, expansion or retention in its territory of an investment.
 (c) If a Member State considers that another Member State has derogated from investment measures in violation of paragraph (a) and (b) above, it may report the matter to ECIM Council. The ECIM Council shall take appropriate measures as necessary to address the issue.

CHAPTER 3: STATE CONTRACTS

Article 16: Nature, Negotiation and Renegotiation

1. Member States and investors shall negotiate and implement State contracts in good faith. In such contracts, especially long-term ones, review or renegotiation clauses should normally be included.
2. In the absence of such clauses and where there has been a fundamental change of the circumstances on which the contract or agreement was based, transnational corporations, acting in good faith, should co-operate with Member States for the review or renegotiation of such contract or agreement
3. Review or renegotiation of such contracts or agreements should be subject to the laws of the Member State(s) and international legal principles.

CHAPTER 4: HOST COUNTRY OPERATIONAL MEASURES

Article 17: Coverage and Duration

1) Member States may introduce measures to promote domestic investments and local content. Measures covered by this Paragraph include, inter alia:
 (a) measures to grant preferential treatment to any enterprises qualifying under the domestic law of a Member State in order to achieve national, sub-national or regional development goals;
 (b) measures to support the development of local entrepreneurs;
 (c) measures to enhance productive capacity, increase employment, increase human resource capacity and training, research and development including of

new technologies, technology and skills transfer, innovation and other benefits of investment through the use of specified requirements on investors;

(d) measures to address historically based economic disparities suffered by identifiable ethnic or cultural groups due to discriminatory or oppressive measures against such groups prior to the adoption of this Protocol. (2) With a view to ensuring that these instruments may be maintained by Member States till such time that their developmental needs demand, there will be a transition period to provide Member States the necessary flexibility to implement development policies intended to address, among others, social, regional, economic, and technological concerns that may help reduce the disparities they face.

(3) Member States shall within 5 years of the coming into force of this Investment Code define objective criteria on the basis of which a phase-out period can be considered and approved by the ECIM Council according to their development needs.

Article 18: Contact Point

(1) Each Member State shall establish a National Authority or designate one of its departments or agencies as a contact point for purposes of the implementation of this Code. The functions of the focal point shall include:

a) liaising with the ECIM Council;

b) facilitating regular communication and coordination between Member States concerning issues arising under the Code, including requesting or transmitting information from or to another Member State;

c) providing a contact for assistance in investment promotion and facilitation;

d) maintaining statistics about inward and outward investment of the Member State;

a) handling enquiries in relation to the conduct of investments or investors of a Member State;

b) investigating and seeking to resolve concerns or conflicts raised by individuals or civil society groups in relation to the conduct of investors or investments concerning their obligations under this Code or the additional responsibilities set out in this Code;

c) reporting on any matters dealt with under Paragraph f; and

d) any other functions the Member State incorporates into its work.

(2) The focal point shall operate in a visible, accessible, transparent and accountable manner. It shall receive and consider information, statements of concern or other information from government officials, nongovernmental groups or individuals from the Member State in which it is established, or from any other Member State or third country.

CHAPTER 5: INCENTIVES

Article 19: Nature and Character of incentives

(1) Member States may introduce incentives in accordance with ECOWAS Investment
Policy (ECOWIP) to attract investments. Such incentives may include:
  a) financial incentives in the forms of investment insurance, grants or loans at concessionary rates;
  b) fiscal incentives such as tax holidays, pioneer status and reduced tax rates;
  c) subsidized infrastructure or services, market preferences;
  d) development-oriented incentives, to encourage preferential markets schemes and specific investors within the region;
  e) incentives for technical assistance, or technology transfer;
  f) Investment guarantees.

(2) Member States shall harmonize incentives for investments which are of strategic interest to the region. Member States undertake to harmonize incentives in accordance with standards to be prescribed from time to time by ECIM Council. In prescribing harmonization of incentive, ECIM Council shall give due consideration to the peculiarities of the investments concerned and, without prejudice to the generality of the foregoing, may provide for the following:
  a) national incentives to investment designed to promote sustainable, export-led industrial and service-oriented development;
  b) investment facilitation through the removal of bureaucratic impediments; and
  c) non-discrimination in the granting of incentives among Community nationals

(3) For the purpose of such harmonization, Member States shall exchange information concerning all incentives related to investments that they provide to their domestic investors.

(4) Member States shall notify the ECIM Council and other Member State of their incentives in order to enable ECIM Council and other Member States to evaluate their economic effects and to understand the operation of the notified measures and programs.

Article 20: Non-Discrimination

(1) The rights and obligations under Articles 6 &7 (National Treatment and Most Favored Nation Treatment principles) do not apply to subsidies or grants provided to a government or a State enterprise, including government-supported loans, guarantees and insurance.

(2) Exceptions and exemptions from the most-favored nation and from the national treatment obligations within the context of incentives shall apply only if Member States make due commitments in this respect in their Annexes schedules of excluded sectors.
(3) The rights and obligations under Articles 6 & 7 (National Treatment and Most Favored Nation Treatment principles) do not apply with regard to taxation measures aimed at ensuring the effective collection of taxes, except where this results in arbitrary discrimination duly noted and reported by the investor.

CHAPTER 6: ENVIRONMENT AND SUSTAINABLE DEVELOPMENT

Article 21: General Protection of the Environment

1. The Member States re-affirm their commitment to promote within the ECOWAS territory mutually supportive environmental-related investment policies, encourage high levels of environmental protection, facilitate the effective enforcement of national environmental laws, and enhance the capacities of the Member States to address environmental-related investment issues through regional co-operation.
2. For the purpose of this section, "environmental legislation" means any legislation of Member States, or provision thereof, the primary purpose of which is the protection of the environment, or the prevention of harm to human, animal, or plant life or health, including but not limited to legislation related to the:
   (i) prevention, abatement or control of the release, discharge, or emission of pollutants or environmental contaminants;
   (ii) control of environmentally hazardous or toxic chemicals, substances, materials and wastes, and the dissemination of information related thereto;
   (iii) protection or conservation of wild flora or fauna, including endangered species,

   their habitat, and specially protected natural areas in the Member State's territory; implementation of any relevant and subsequent agreements on environment.
3. The Member States further recognize that it is unlawful under this Code to encourage investment by relaxing national health, safety, or environmental measures. Accordingly, no Member State shall waive or otherwise derogate from, or offer to waive or otherwise derogate from, such measures as an encouragement for the establishment, acquisition, expansion, or retention of an investment in its national territory.
4. If a Member State considers that another Member State has offered an encouragement referred to in paragraphs 3, the Member State may request consultations with the other Member State, and the two Member States shall consult with a view to avoiding any such encouragement. In the event that the Member

States are unable to resolve their differences under this paragraph through bilateral consultations, either Member State shall submit the matter to the ECOWAS Common Investment Market Council for the resolution thereof.

Article 22: Member States Obligations

1. The Member States recognize the importance of mutually supportive investment, trade, and environmental policies and practices to improve national and regional environmental protection in the furtherance of sustainable, inclusive, and collective economic development.
2. The Member States further recognize the sovereign right of each Member State to establish its own levels of national environmental protection and its own national environmental priorities, and to establish, adopt, or modify its environmental laws and policies accordingly.
3. Each Member State shall strive to ensure that its national environmental laws and policies provide for, and encourage, high levels of environmental protection and to continue to improve its respective levels of environmental protection.
4. Without prejudice to paragraph 2, the Member States understand that it is unlawful to encourage investment or trade in their jurisdictions by reducing the protection afforded in their respective environmental laws. A Member State shall not waive or otherwise derogate from, or offer to waive or otherwise derogate from, its national environmental laws in a manner that reduces the protection afforded in those laws in order to encourage cross-border investment or trade between and amongst the Member States in the ECOWAS territory.
5. In furtherance of paragraph 4, no Member State shall fail to enforce its national environmental laws through a sustained or recurring course of action or inaction in a manner affecting investment or trade in the ECOWAS territory after the date of entry into legal force and effect of this Code for that Member State.
6. The Member States recognize that each Member State retains the right to exercise discretion and to make decisions regarding: (a) national investigatory, prosecutorial, regulatory, and compliance matters; and (b) the allocation of national environmental enforcement resources with respect to other national environmental objectives determined to have higher priorities. The Member States further recognize that, with respect to the enforcement of national environmental laws, a Member State is in compliance with paragraph 5 if a course of action or inaction reflects a reasonable exercise of administrative discretion, or results from a *bona fide* decision regarding the allocation of its national resources in accordance with its national priorities for the enforcement of its national environmental laws.
7. For greater clarity, nothing in this Section shall be construed to empower the administrative authorities of any Member State to undertake any environmental law enforcement activities in the national territory of another Member State.

Article 23: Multilateral Environmental Agreements

1. The Member States recognize that multilateral environmental agreements to which they are a party play a strategic role, globally, regionally, and nationally, in protecting the natural environment, and that their respective implementation of these agreements is critical to achieving the environmental objectives of these agreements. Each Member State affirms its commitment to implement in its national territory the multilateral environmental agreements to which it is a party.
2. The Member States emphasize the need to enhance the mutual supportiveness amongst investment, trade, and environmental policies and laws through dialogue between the Member States on such issues of mutual interest, particularly with respect to the negotiation and integrated implementation of the relevant multilateral investment, trade, and environmental agreements.

Article 24: Procedural Matters

1. Each Member State shall promote public awareness of its national environmental policies and laws, including enforcement and compliance procedures, by ensuring that relevant information is made available to the general public.
2. Each Member State shall ensure that an interested person residing or established in its national territory may request that the competent national environmental authorities of that Member State investigate alleged violations of its national environmental laws, and that the competent national authorities accord those requests due consideration in accordance with all applicable national laws of the Member State.
3. Each Member State shall ensure that judicial, quasi-judicial, or administrative proceedings for the enforcement of its national environmental laws are available under its law, and that those proceedings are not only fair, equitable, and transparent, but also comply with due process of law. Any hearings in such administrative proceedings shall, in accordance with its applicable national laws, be open to the public, except when the administration of justice otherwise requires.
4. Each Member State shall ensure that persons with a recognized interest under its law in a particular matter have appropriate access to the administrative proceedings referred to in paragraph 3.
5. Each Member State shall provide appropriate sanctions or remedies for any violations of its national environmental laws for the effective enforcement thereof. Such sanctions or remedies may include a right to bring an action directly against the violator to seek damages or injunctive relief, or a right to seek governmental action.
6. Each Member State shall ensure that it takes appropriate account of all relevant factors in the establishment of the sanctions or remedies referred to in paragraph 5. Those factors may include the nature and gravity of the violation, damage to the natural environment, and any economic benefit that the violator derived from the violation.

Article 25: Opportunities for Public Participation

1. Each Member State shall seek to accommodate requests for information regarding the implementation of this Section through its national environmental authorities.
2. Each Member State shall make use of existing, or establish new, consultative mechanisms, such as national advisory committees, to seek views on matters related to the implementation of this Section. These mechanisms may include persons with relevant experience, as appropriate, including experience in business, natural resource conservation and management, or other environmental matters.

Article 26: Regional Cooperation Frameworks

1. The Member States recognize the strategic importance of regional co-operation as a facilitative mechanism to implement this Section, to enhance its benefits, and to strengthen the joint and individual capacities of the Member States to protect the natural environment and to promote sustainable, inclusive, and collective economic development in the ECOWAS territory.
2. Taking into consideration their respective national priorities and circumstances and available resources, the Member States shall cooperate to address matters of joint or common interest among them that are related to the implementation of this Section, especially in cases in which mutual benefits from regional co-operation is anticipated. Such co-operation may be carried out on a bilateral or plurilateral basis between and amongst the Member States and, subject to consensus by the participating Member States, may include non-governmental bodies or organizations and non-Member States.
3. Each Member State shall designate the national administrative authority or authorities responsible for any regional co-operation in respect of the implementation of this Section to serve as its national contact point on matters that relate to regional co-operation and co-ordination activities. Each Member State shall notify the other Member States in writing, within ninety (90) days of the date of entry into legal force and effect of this Code for that Member State, of its national contact point.
4. Upon notifying the other Member States of its national contact point, or at any time thereafter through the contact points, a Member State may:
   (a) share its priorities for co-operation with the other Member States, including the objectives of that co-operation;
   (b) propose co-operation activities related to the implementation of this Section to another Member State or Member States;
   (c) report to the ECOWAS Common Market Council all relevant issues raised during the regional co-operation undertaken under this Article;
   (d) assist the ECOWAS Common Market Council to formulate regional environmental proposals that are consistent with the ECOWICPF, and that

take into consideration the different levels of economic development, capacity, and financial resources of the Member States; and

(e) act as a channel for communication with the general public in its respective national territory.

5. When appropriate, the Member States shall seek to complement and use their existing co-operation mechanisms and take into account the relevant work of regional and international organizations.
6. In furtherance of the preceding paragraphs of this Article, regional co-operation may be carried out through various mechanisms, including dialogue, workshops, seminars, conferences, collaborative programs and projects, technical assistance and support to facilitate co-operative training, the sharing of internationally-recognized environmental policies, practices, and procedures, and the exchange of experts.
7. In developing co-operative activities and programs, a Member State shall, if relevant, identify performance measures and indicators to assist in examining and evaluating the efficiency, effectiveness, and progress of specific co-operative activities and programs and share those measures and indicators, as well as the outcome of any evaluation during or following the completion of any co-operative activity or program, with the other Member States.
8. Each Member State shall promote public participation in the development and implementation of all regional co-operative activities, as appropriate, under this Article.

Article 27: Investor Environmental Obligations

1. Investors doing business in the ECOWAS territory shall comply with the following environmental obligations under this Code to:
   (a) carry out their business activities in strict conformity with the applicable national environmental laws, regulations, and administrative practices of the Member States and other multilateral agreements applicable to their investments;
   (b) undertake pre-investment environmental and social impact assessments of their proposed business activities and investments with respect to the natural environment and the local population in the relevant jurisdiction;
   (c) apply the precautionary principle to their environmental and social impact assessments and to decisions taken in relation to a proposed investment, including any necessary mitigating or alternative approaches to such investment;
   (d) make the investor environmental and social impact assessments available to the general public and accessible to the affected local communities and to any other affected interests in the Member State of the proposed investment;
   (e) perform the restoration, using appropriate technologies, for any damage caused to the natural environment and to pay adequate compensation to all affected interested persons;

(f) provide to the competent national environmental authorities, in respect of the products, processes, and services of the investor's enterprises, all relevant environmental information, together with measures and costs necessary to avoid and mitigate against any potentially harmful effects; and
(g) implement in the Member States standards of operation with regard to hazardous waste generation and disposal that are equivalent to, or no less stringent than, those in their home country of origin for investments carried out by investors of other Member States, or investors of non-Member States.

2. To ensure compliance with the obligations set out in paragraph 1, each Member State shall encourage investors operating within its national territory, without prejudice to Article 34 (Responsible Business Conduct) of this Code, to adopt as part of their responsible business conduct policies, internationally-recognized environmental standards and guidelines that have been endorsed or are supported by that Member State.

Article 28: Voluntary Mechanisms to Enhance Environmental Performance

1. The Member States recognize that flexible and voluntary mechanisms, such as voluntary auditing and reporting, market-based incentives, voluntary sharing of achievement and maintenance of high levels of environmental protection and complement national regulatory measures. The Member States also recognize that those mechanisms should be designed in a manner that maximizes their environmental benefits and avoids the creation of unnecessary barriers to investment or trade.
2. In accordance with its national policies, laws, and regulations, and to the extent that it considers appropriate, each Member State shall encourage:
   (a) the use of flexible and voluntary mechanisms to protect natural resources and the environment in its national territory; and
   (b) its relevant environmental authorities, business organizations, non- governmental organizations, and other interested persons involved in the development of criteria used to evaluate environmental performance, with respect to these voluntary mechanisms, to continue to develop and improve such criteria.
3. In cases in which private sector entities or non-governmental organizations develop voluntary mechanisms for the promotion of products based on their environmental qualities, each Member State shall encourage those entities and organizations to develop voluntary mechanisms that, among other things:
   (a) are truthful, are not misleading, and that take into account all relevant scientific and technical information;
   (b) if applicable and available, are based on relevant international standards, recommendations, or guidelines;
   (c) promote competition and innovation; and
   (d) do not treat a product less favorably on the basis of its country of origin.

Article 29: Transfer of Environmentally Sound Management Practices

1. Member States and Investors shall recognize environmental management as among the highest corporate priorities and as a key determinant to sustainable development. Accordingly, investors shall take the following amongst other necessary measures:
   i) increase the efficiency of resource utilization, including increasing recycling and reducing waste discharge and especially by providing adequate knowledge and assistance;
   codes of conduct promoting best environmental practices, by providing adequate and timely information regarding the potential health aspects of all their activities and shall also provide the relevant expertise for the enterprise and support public information and community awareness programs;
   iii) adopt global policies on sustainable development and arrange for environmentally sound technologies to be available to affiliates of parent companies in Member States on fair terms and, where appropriate, the use of environmental auditing;
   iv) establish partnership schemes with small and medium-sized enterprises to help facilitate the exchange of experience in managerial skills, market development and technological know-how;
   v) increase both domestic and global research and development of environmentally sound technologies and environmental management systems;
   vi) ensure responsible and ethical management of products and processes from the point of view of environmental aspects;
   vii) adopt and implement, wherever they operate, policies and standards of operation with reference to hazardous waste generation and disposal that are equivalent to or no less stringent than those in their country of origin, including siting decisions, impact on local communities resources and foreseeable environmental and environmentally related health risks of products as well as from the generation, transport and disposal of waste; and
   viii) prepare contingency plans for the prevention and mitigation of environmental damages.

CHAPTER 7: HUMAN CAPITAL

Article 30: Labor and Employment Standards

(1) Member States recognize that it is inappropriate to encourage investment by relaxing domestic labor legislation. Accordingly, each Member State shall

ensure that it does not waive or derogate from such legislation as an encouragement for the establishment, maintenance or expansion of an investment in its territory.

(2) Member States shall ensure that national laws and regulations provide for high levels of labor and human rights protection appropriate to its economic and social situation provided that the key principles of the Common Investment Code are not sacrificed in the process.

(3) Member States shall in consultation with investors design employment schemes in accordance with existing ECOWAS Social Security and Labor/Employment Policy, in particular to:

i. conform to government policies designed to extend equality of opportunity and treatment, including on wages, benefits and conditions of work;
ii. observe freely negotiated obligations concerning employment stability and social security in conjunction with the trade unions or other representatives of employees;
iii. not discriminate on the basis of race, color, sex, religion, language, social, national and ethnic origin or political or other opinion;
iv. maintain the highest standards of health, risks and safety in the workplace;
v. apply the relevant and or to establish industrial dispute resolution mechanisms that provide due process and appropriate procedure to employers and workers, in conformity with domestic laws and policies;
vi. not use child labor and to support efforts for the elimination of all forms of child labor including forced or compulsory labor within the Community;
vii. make every effort to mitigate to the greatest possible extent every adverse effect of any purported investments changes on employees and the economy in the Member State.

In this regard, investors shall take the following steps:

i. consult with host country authorities and national employers' and workers' organizations in order to keep manpower plans in harmony with national social development policies, making optimal use of labor available locally and within the Community to provide substantial employment or reduce unemployment;
ii. give priority to the employment and promotion of host country nationals;
iii. use technologies which generate employment; and
iv. Promote, within relevant regulatory regimes and provisions in Member States, employment in the Community by entering into supply contracts with local enterprises and by prioritizing the use and the processing of local raw materials.

(4) Investors shall take into considerations issues submitted by Member States and related to the empowerment of local communities, and adopt measures aimed at facilitating the location of investments in low income or economically depressed areas.

CHAPTER 8: DEVELOPMENT OBJECTIVES AND SOCIAL RESPONSIBILITY

Article 31: Development Obligations

(1) Member States shall, in accordance with the general principles of international law, have the right to pursue their own development objectives and priorities.

(2) Member States recognize their obligations regarding trade-related investment measures established in other international agreements to which they are a Party.

(3) Investors doing business in the ECOWAS territory shall in pursuit of their economic objectives, proceed in ways that do not conflict with the social and economic

development of host countries in particular, they shall be sensitive to changes in the social and economic goals of their hosts. Accordingly, there should be no conflict between the obligations of the parties in the investment agreement and the sovereign right of countries to pursue other key policy objectives.

(4) Member States may impose performance requirements to promote domestic development benefits from investments. Measures adopted prior to the completion of the host state measures prescribing the formalities for establishing an investment shall be deemed to be in compliance with this Code. If such measures are taken after the completion of the host state measures prescribing the formalities for establishing an investment, they shall be subject to the provisions of this Code.

(5) Measures to promote domestic development covered by this Article include requirements to:

a) transfer technology, a production process or other proprietary knowledge to a national or company in the Member State's territory, pursuant to relevant rules and processes duly agreed;

b) carry out a particular type, level or percentage of research and development in the Member State's territory;

c) appoint as executives, managers or members of boards of directors, individuals of any nationality;

d) train or employ local workers in positions where shortages have been demonstrated, except through due authorization; and

(6) Member States shall enforce any existing universal service policy or legislation in a transparent and non-discriminatory manner and shall ensure that the application of such universal service policy or legislation is not more burdensome than necessary for the kind of universal service that it prescribed or required.

(7) Member States shall take account of the following criteria, among others, in the assessment of a proposed investment:

(a) importance of the investment;

(b) participation in the implementation of the economic and social plans;

(c) creation of employment and vocational training;

(d) use of appropriate technologies and equipment;

(e) priority of use of local raw materials and in general, local products;

(f) registered office established in a Member State and;
(g) environmental and social impact assessment report.

Article 32: Socio-Political Obligations

(1) Investors conducting business in the ECOWAS territory shall adhere to the following principles including but not limited to:
a respect for national sovereignty and observance of domestic laws, regulations and administrative practices;
b) respect for socio-cultural objectives and values;
c) non-interference in internal political affairs; and e) non-interference in intergovernmental relations;
(2) Investors shall not influence the appointment of persons to public office or finance political parties or organizations;
(3) The investor shall be bound by the laws and regulations in force in the host state and shall refrain from all acts that may disturb public order or morals or that may be prejudicial to the public interest. The investor is also to refrain from exercising restrictive practices and from trying to achieve gains through unlawful means.

Article 33: Consumer Protection

1. The Member States recognize the importance of consumer protection policy and its enforcement for the purposes of creating efficient and competitive markets and enhancing consumer welfare in the ECOWAS territory.
2. For the purposes of this Article, fraudulent and deceptive commercial activities refer to those fraudulent and deceptive commercial practices that cause actual harm to consumers, or that pose an imminent threat of such harm if not prevented, for example:
   (a) a practice of making misrepresentations of material fact, including implied factual misrepresentations, that cause significant detriment to the economic interests of misled consumers;
   (b) a practice of failing to deliver products or provide services to consumers after the consumers are charged; or
   (c) a practice of charging or debiting consumers' financial, telephone, or other accounts, without any authorization.
3. Each Member State shall adopt or maintain consumer protection laws or other laws or regulations that proscribe fraudulent and deceptive commercial activities. Such laws and regulations shall be compatible and consistent with the ECOWAS Supplementary Act on Competition.
4. The Member States recognize that fraudulent and deceptive commercial activities increasingly transcend national borders, and that cooperation and

coordination between the Member States is desirable to address these activities effectively.

5. In accordance with paragraph 4, the Member States shall promote, as appropriate, cooperation and coordination on matters of mutual interest related to fraudulent and deceptive commercial activities, including in the enforcement of their national consumer protection laws in accordance with the ECOWAS Supplementary Act on Competition.
6. The Member States shall endeavor to cooperate on the matters set out in this Article under the auspices of the ECOWAS Regional Investment Competition Authority through coordination between the regional authority and the competent national public bodies or officials responsible for national consumer protection policies, laws, and enforcement as determined by each Member State.
7. Investors doing business in the ECOWAS region shall when dealing with consumers act in accordance with fair business, marketing and advertising practices and should take all reasonable steps to ensure the safety and quality of the goods or services they provide. They shall in particular, give full and adequate attention to the following key areas:
   a) Ensure that the goods or services they provide meet all agreed or legally required standards for consumer health and safety, including health warnings and product safety and information labels.
   b) As appropriate to the goods or services, provide accurate and clear information regarding their content, safe use, maintenance, storage, and disposal sufficient to enable consumers to make informed decisions.
   c) Provide transparent and effective procedures that address consumer complaints and contribute to fair and timely resolution of consumer disputes without undue cost or burden.
   d) Not make representations or omissions, nor engage in any other practices, that are deceptive, misleading, fraudulent, or unfair.
   e) Respect consumer privacy and provide protection for personal data.
   f) Co-operate fully and in a transparent manner with public authorities in the prevention or removal of serious threats to public health and safety deriving from the consumption or use of their products.

Article 34: Corporate Governance and Responsible Business Conduct

1. Investors shall comply with all international best practices, regional, and national laws and regulations applicable to corporate governance in the ECOWAS territory in order to promote improved corporate accountability and transparency in the region.
2. Investors conducting business in the ECOWAS territory shall endeavor to promote and engage in corporate social responsibility in accordance with international best practices, taking into account the peculiar development plans

and priorities of Member State and in particular the needs of for the local communities.

3. The Member States shall adopt or maintain, as the case may be, national legal and regulatory frameworks applicable to corporate governance in accordance with the internationally-recognized standards referred to in this Code.
4. In this regard, investors are required to adopt and implement, inter alia, the following provisions:
   a. ensure equitable treatment of all shareholders, including minority and third party shareholders;
   b. encourage active cooperation between corporations and stakeholders in creating wealth, jobs and the sustainability of financially sound enterprises;
   c. ensure that timely and accurate disclosure is made of all materials facts relevant to, inter alia, the financial situation, performance, ownership, and governance of the company, risks related to environmental liabilities, and any other matters in accordance with the relevant regulations and requirements;
   d. ensure similar disclosure of information relating to human resource policies, such as programs for human resource development; and
   e. respect any other requirement agreed to, and adopted, by the Member States pursuant to this Code and the ECOWICPF.
   f. adhere to the financial reporting, disclosure, accounting, and audit practices satisfying the requirements of the International Financial Reporting Standards (IFRS);

CHAPTER 9: CORRUPTION AND UNETHICAL PRACTICES

Article 35: General

1. Member States affirm their resolve to eliminate bribery, fraud, and corruption in respect of international investment and trade in the ECOWAS territory.
2. The scope of this Section is limited to measures to eliminate bribery, fraud, and corruption with regard to any matter covered by this Code.
3. Member States recognize that the description of offences adopted or maintained in accordance with this Section, and of the applicable legal defenses or legal principles controlling the lawfulness of conduct, is expressly reserved to the national laws of each Member State, and that those offences shall be prosecuted and punished in accordance with such national laws.
4. Each Member State shall ratify or accede to the United Nations Convention against Corruption, done at New York on October 31, 2003 (UNCAC), within one hundred and eighty (180) days after the entry into legal force and effect of this Code for that Member State. For those Member States that have already ratified the UNCAC, such Member States shall continue to maintain their membership status thereto in conformity with this Code.

Article 36: Measures to Combat Corruption

1. Each Member State shall adopt or maintain legislative and other measures as may be necessary to establish as criminal offences under its national laws certain conduct, acts, or omissions that, when committed intentionally by any person subject to its jurisdiction, can affect cross-border international investment or trade, including:
   (a) the promise, offering, or giving to a public official, directly or indirectly, of a gift, favor or an undue advantage for the official or another person or entity in order that the official act or refrain from acting in relation to the performance of, or the exercise of, his or her official duties;
   (b) the solicitation or acceptance by a public official, directly or indirectly, of a gift, favor or an undue advantage for the official or another person or entity in order that the official acts or refrains from acting in relation to the performance of, or the exercise of, his or her official duties;
   (c) the promise, offering, or giving to a foreign public official or an official of a public international organization, directly or indirectly, of an undue advantage for the official or another person or entity in order that such official acts or refrains from acting in relation to the performance of, or the exercise of, his or her official duties in order to obtain or retain business or other undue advantage in relation to the conduct of international business;
   (d) any promise or declaration by any person that he can exercise some influence on decisions or actions of persons occupying positions in the public or private sector, whether the influence had been exercised or not and whether or not the supposed influence had the desired result;
   (e) the diversion by a public official of any assets whether moveable or immovable, deeds or securities of a State in his possession either for his own benefit or for the benefit of another person; and
   (f) the aiding or abetting or conspiracy in the commission of any of the offences described in subparagraphs (a) through (e).
2. Each Member State shall make the commission of an offence described in Article 37 paragraphs a to e liable to sanctions, in accordance with its national laws, that take into account the gravity of that offence.
3. Each Member State shall adopt or maintain national measures as may be necessary, consistent with its legal principles, to establish the liability of juridical persons for offences described in Article 37, paragraphs a to e, whether or not the offence is committed in whole or part in its territory or the offender is one of its nationals, or an investor or its agent, or any other person acting in relation to an investment in a Member State. In furtherance of this provision, each Member State shall ensure that juridical persons held liable for offences described in paragraph 1 or 5 are subject to effective, proportionate, and dissuasive criminal or non-criminal sanctions, which can include monetary sanctions, seizure and forfeiting of assets and other proceeds of such crime.

4. No Member State shall allow a person subject to its jurisdiction to deduct from any tax liability expenses incurred in connection with the commission of an offence described in Article 37 paragraphs a to e.
5. In order to prevent fraud and corruption, each Member State shall adopt or maintain national measures as may be necessary, in accordance with its national laws and regulations, regarding the maintenance of books and records, financial statement disclosures, and accounting and auditing standards to prohibit the following acts carried out for the purpose of committing any of the offences described in Article 37 paragraphs (a-e):
   (a) the establishment of off-the-books accounts;
   (b) the making of off-the-books or inadequately identified transactions;
   (c) the recording of false expenditures;
   (d) the book entry of liabilities with incorrect classifications;
   (e) the use of false documents; and
   (f) the intentional destruction of bookkeeping documents before the time limit established by applicable national law.
6. Each Member State shall consider adopting or maintaining national measures to protect against any unjustified or retaliatory treatment any person who, in good faith and on reasonable grounds, reports to the competent national authorities any facts concerning any offences described in Article 37, paragraphs a to e.

Article 37: Promoting Integrity Amongst Public Officials

1. To regulate and effectively control fraud and corruption in matters that affect cross- border investment and trade, each Member State shall promote, among other attributes, integrity, honesty, and responsibility among its public officials. In furtherance of this goal, each Member State shall endeavor, in accordance with the fundamental principles of its national legal system, to adopt or maintain:
   (a) national measures to provide adequate procedures for the selection and training of individuals for public positions considered particularly susceptible to fraud and corruption, and the rotation, if appropriate, of such individuals to other public positions;
   (b) national measures to promote transparency in the behavior of public officials in the exercise of their public functions;
   (c) effective and transparent national policies and procedures to identify and manage actual or potential conflicts of interest of public officials;
   (d) national measures that require senior and other appropriate public officials to make declarations to the competent national authorities regarding, among other potential conflicts, their outside activities, employment, investments, assets, and

   substantial gifts or benefits from which a conflict of interest may result with respect to their functions as public officials; and

(e) national measures to encourage the reporting by public officials of any acts of fraud or corruption to the competent national authorities in cases in which such officials, in the discharge of their public functions, become aware of any such acts as committed by any other public official or by any other person subject to its jurisdiction.

2. Each Member State shall endeavor to adopt or maintain national codes or standards of conduct to encourage the correct, honorable, and proper performance of public functions, as well as national measures providing for disciplinary or other measures, if warranted, against public officials who violate such codes or standards.
3. Each Member State, to the extent consistent with the fundamental principles of its national legal system, shall consider establishing procedures through which a public official accused of an offence described in Article 37may, where appropriate, be removed, suspended, or reassigned by the competent national authority, provided that the principle of the presumption of innocence is respected in all cases in accordance with the national laws of a Member State.
4. Each Member State shall, in accordance with the fundamental principles of its national legal system and without prejudice to the independence of its judicial courts, adopt or maintain national measures to strengthen public official integrity and to prevent opportunities for fraud and corruption among members of the judiciary in matters that affect international investment or trade in the ECOWAS territory. Such measures may include any rules governing the conduct of the members of the judiciary of any Member State.

Article 38: Obligations of Investors

1. Investors doing business in ECOWAS territory shall not, prior to the establishment of an investment or there after offer, promise or give any undue pecuniary or any undue advantage to a public official of a Member State or to a member of an official's family, business associate or other person in close proximity to an official or another person or any entity in order that the official acts or refrains from acting in relation to the performance of, or the exercise of, his or her official duties in order to achieve any favor or compromise in relation to the proposed investment.
2. The investors shall cooperate with Member States in eliminating corruption in public governance and shall accordingly, not encourage, incite, aid, abet or conspire with any official or another person or any entity to commit or authorise the commission of acts described in Article 37 above.

Article 39: Regional Co-operation

1. The Member States recognize the importance of co-operation and coordination among States to eliminate bribery, fraud, and corruption in respect of

international investment and trade in the ECOWAS territory. In recognition of this principle, each Member State shall:

(a) cooperate in the area of investment-related crime of bribery, fraud, and corruption by exchanging information on such crimes in accordance with the ECOWIPCPF;
(b) cooperate, as appropriate, on issues of cross-border enforcement, including through notification, consultation and exchange of information.
(c) cooperate, as appropriate, on issue of mutual legal assistance and other law enforcement cooperative measures necessary to facilitate the investigation, prosecution and extradition of offenders for any act of corruption and other offences created pursuant to this Code in their national laws.
(d) ensure that investigation and prosecution for acts of corruption shall not be influenced by consideration of national economic interest, the potential effect upon relations with a Member State or a third country or the identity of the natural or legal person involved; and
(e) promote transparency in banking practices and transactions within its national jurisdictions and ensure that bank secrecy does not impede or hinder criminal investigations or other legal proceeding relating to fraud, bribery, corruption or related illicit practices in business practices and transactions

3. The offences created pursuant to the provisions of this Code shall be considered as crimes leading to extradition under existing ECOWAS Convention on Extradition or any other existing treaties on extradition between Member States or with other countries. Where such offences are not mentioned in existing treaties, Member States shall ensure that they are included.

Article 10: Trans-National Bribery

(1) Member States shall adopt such legislative and other measures as may be necessary to establish jurisdiction over a criminal offence established in accordance with Chapter 9 of this Code where:
  (a) the offence is committed in whole or in part in its territory;
  (b) the offender is one of its nationals, or an investor or its agent,or any other person acting in relation to an investment in a Member State;
(2) Member States shall pursue effective enforcement of existing laws prohibiting corruption in international commercial transactions, to encourage the adoption of laws for those purposes where they do not exist, and to call upon private and public corporations, including investors and trans-national corporations and individuals within their jurisdiction engaged in international commercial transactions to promote the objectives set out in this Chapter.
(3) Member States shall deny, the tax deductibility of bribes paid by any private or public corporation or individual of a State to any public official or elected representative of another country and, to that end, to examine their respective modalities for achieving these objectives.

(4) Member States shall ensure that bank secrecy provisions do not impede or hinder criminal investigations or other legal proceedings relating to corruption, bribery or related illicit practices in business practices and transactions.
(5) Member States legislation on corruption shall prohibit and punish corruption by measures which include:
   i. deprivation of liberty for natural persons
   ii. payment of fines or monetary sanction for non natural legal persons
   iii. seizure and forfeiture of assets and other proceeds of crime.
(6) The offences created pursuant to the provisions of this Code shall be considered as crimes leading to extradition under existing ECOWAS Convention on Extradition or any other existing treaties on extradition between Member States or with other countries. If the offences are not mentioned in existing extradition treaties, Member States shall ensure that they are included.
(7) Member States undertake to assist each other with mutual legal assistance and other law enforcement cooperation measures necessary to facilitate the investigation and prosecution of acts of corruption and other offences created pursuant to this Code in national laws
(8) Member States may impose additional civil or administrative sanctions upon a person subject to prosecution for act of corruption
(9) Investigation and prosecution for acts of corruption shall not be influenced by considerations of national economic interest, the potential effect upon relations with a Member State or a third country or the identity of the natural or legal persons involved.

CHAPTER 10: TRANSFER PRICING

Article 41: Obligation to Comply with International Transfer Pricing Standards

(1) Investors and their investments shall ensure that all transactions with related or affiliated parties ("controlled transactions") shall be conducted in accordance with the arm's length principle.
(2) The relevant international standard is the Organization for Economic Cooperation and Development (OECD) "Transfer Pricing Guidelines for Multinational Persons and Tax Administrations."
(3) Where there is any inconsistency between Member States domestic transfer pricing regulations and OECD Guidelines, the regulations shall prevail.

Article 42: Investor Obligations to Provide Transfer Pricing Documentation

(1) Investors must have in place contemporaneous transfer pricing documentation that verifies that the conditions in its controlled transactions for the relevant tax year are consistent with the arm's length principle.

(2) Transfer pricing documentation shall include, but is not limited to:
a) an overview of the investor's business operations,
b) a description of the corporate organizational structure of the group,
c) general written description of the investor's business,
d) a description of controlled transactions (amounts, connected persons, copies of material intercompany agreements).

(3) The obligation of the investor to provide this documentation is established without prejudice to the power of the Member State to request additional information that in the course of audit procedures it deems necessary to carry out its functions.

Article 43: Member State Obligations to Cooperate on Transfer Pricing Issues

(1) To avoid any further harmful fiscal competition within the Community, Member States shall ensure that their national laws are compatible with international standards on transfer pricing.

(2) Furthermore, Member States shall cooperate in the detection and prevention of transfer pricing manipulation by investors, including in the provision of information necessary to identify and prevent such practices, and opportunities for joint tax audit.

Article 44: Investor Obligations Not to Engage in Base Erosion and Profit Shifting

Investors and their investments shall conduct their operations in a manner that fully complies with all applicable tax laws and international standards relating to ensuring tax benefits are not reduced through base erosion and profit shifting practices. Investors and their investments shall provide the financial information required by the Member State to ensure compliance with the applicable laws.

CHAPTER 11: TAXATION

Article 45: Jurisdiction to Tax

(1) This Code shall not affect the rights and obligations of a Member State under Double Taxation Agreements.

(2) Member States shall have the right to enter into double tax treaties, provided that whenever a harmonized ECOWAS tax regime is concluded it shall supersede existing double tax arrangements amongst Member States.

(3) Member States shall endeavor to conclude regional and international treaties to avoid double taxation and to allow for the exchange of information between the fiscal authorities from the various jurisdictions.

(4) Member States shall adequately examine the structure of their respective taxes over the income and profit of taxpayers, including identifying tax havens and examining their taxable basis, rates and fiscal administration through the establishment of a regional body in accordance with the ECOWAS Revised Treaty.
(5) In the design and negotiation of Double Tax Agreements, Member States should take special care to maintain the right to collect the tax revenue income earned/sourced within the jurisdiction.
(6) Member States shall develop rules and regulations to deter any attempt by a third- country resident or any person or entity to obtain benefits from an income tax treaty for which it was not intended or qualified or to act as a conduit for profits.
(7) Member States are encouraged to put in place measures for transparency, streamlining, due process and good governance in their fiscal legislations and regulations, in particular, to financial reporting, disclosure, accounting, and audit practices satisfying the requirements of the International Financial Reporting Standards (IFRS).

CHAPTER 12 HOME STATE MEASURES

Article 46: Home State Operational Measures

(1) **Definition**

Home country measures are measures that are used to promote the flow of investments within the community.

(2) **Member States Obligations**

Member States undertake to adopt a harmonized ECOWAS Investment incentives regime to promote the flows of investments by Community citizens across the region and from third countries

(3) **Home State incentives**
  (a) A Home State shall refrain from frustrating the effects of development relief granted by Host Country in respect of new investment. Third country governments are encouraged to support investment flows to the region by facilitating such flows through incentives and other measures.
  (b) Home Country shall not obstruct flows of investment from its territory to Member States and is encouraged to adopt appropriate measures to facilitate such flows, including taxation agreements, investment guarantees, technical assistance, and the provision of information.

(4) **Cooperation on Information Sharing**
  (a) Member States undertake to cooperate and to share information on the operations of investors from their territories and to implement the outcome of judicial or administrative decision made by host state with regards to the operations of investors in host state.

(b) Member states shall, on request, and in a timely manner, provide to a requesting member state such information as is requested and available for the purposes of the Member State to meet its obligations and perform its duties in relation to an investor. Home states shall protect confidential business information in this regard.

(c) Third country governments are encouraged to cooperate with Member States in the sharing of information on the operations of investors from their territories.

CHAPTER 13: TECHNOLOGY TRANSFER

Article 47: Promotion of Technology Transfer

(1) Member States can provide incentives in their territories for the purpose of promoting and encouraging the transfer of appropriate technology in their territory.

(2) Investors shall ensure that the technology being transferred complies with the science, technology and innovation policies and plans of the Member States in which they operate, and is appropriate and will contribute to the development of local and national innovative capacity.

(3) Investors shall adopt, where practicable in the course of their business activities, practices that permit the transfer and rapid diffusion of technologies and know-how, with due regard to the protection of intellectual property rights, on reasonable terms and conditions and in a manner that contributes to the long term development prospects of the host country.

(4) In order to facilitate the implementation of these provisions, Member States and investors shall provide, on request and on mutually agreed terms and conditions, technical and financial cooperation in favor of requesting Party.

(5) Member States undertake to cooperate and facilitate the international transfer of technology by various measures such as:

a) getting access to available information regarding description, location and, as far as possible, approximate cost of technology,

a) establishing or strengthening of technology transfer centers;

b) providing training for research, engineering, design and other personnel engaged in the development of national technologies or in the adaptation and use of technologies transferred;

c) providing assistance in the development and administration of laws and regulations with a view to facilitating the transfer of technology;

d) granting credits on terms more favorable than the usual commercial terms for financing the acquisition of capital and intermediate goods in the context of approved development projects involving transfer of technology transaction;

e) assisting in the development of technological capabilities of the companies and their personnel.

Article 48: Technology Diffusion

(1) Investors shall diffuse technology and upgrades as well as improvements thereof through various mechanisms such as the demonstration and competition effects, the movement of labor from foreign affiliates to local firms and through the creation of linkages between foreign and local companies and their customers.
(2) Investors are encouraged to establish linkages with local firms, industries and institutions towards assisting the development of local technological capabilities.

Article 49: Treatment of Intellectual Property Rights

(1) **Scope and Coverage**
   (a) For purposes of this Code, intellectual property covers copyright and related rights; industrial property rights; plant breeders rights; rights to traditional knowledge, folklore and genetic resources; and other rights and flexibilities recognized under the TRIPS Agreement, the Convention on Biological Diversity and the International Agreement on Plant Genetic Resources.
   (b) Member States affirm their existing rights and obligations under the Trade Related Intellectual Property Services (TRIPS) Agreement and intellectual property agreements concluded or administered under the auspices of the World Intellectual Property Organization (WIPO) and the World Trade Organization (WTO) to which they are a party.
   (c) Each Member State shall make available to right holders civil judicial procedures concerning the enforcement of intellectual property rights.
(2) **Traditional Knowledge and Folklore**
   (a) For purposes of this Code, the term "traditional knowledge" or "folklore" means the practices, representations, expressions, knowledge, skills—as well as the instruments, objects, artefacts and cultural spaces associated therewith—that communities and groups in Member States recognize as part of their heritage which is transmitted from generation to generation, is constantly recreated by communities and groups in response to their environment, their interaction with nature and their history, and provides them with a sense of identity and continuity. Traditional knowledge or folklore includes but is not limited to -
      i. oral traditions and expressions;
      ii. the performing arts;
      iii. social practices, rituals and festive events;
      iv. knowledge and practices concerning nature and the universe; and
      v. traditional craftsmanship.
   (b) Where traditional knowledge or folklore is sought, used or exploited by investors in a Member State, or is otherwise relevant to their contracts,

practices and other operations in such Member State, the investors undertake to protect traditional knowledge under the generally accepted international legal standards and best practices and to adhere to the following minimum standards.

i. Local communities in Member States have rights of ownership over their innovations, practices, knowledge and technologies acquired through generations and have a right to collectively benefit from the utilization of such resources.
ii. These community rights are to be protected in accordance with norms, practices and customary law found in, and recognized by the local communities in Member States whether such law is written or not.
iii. Access by an investor to biological resources and knowledge or technologies of local communities in a Member State is conditioned on the prior informed consent of the local community with rights over the resources. Access carried out without such local consent is invalid.
iv. Local communities in Member States may withdraw their consent to access or place restrictions on activities relating to access where such activities are likely to be detrimental to their socio-economic life, or their natural or cultural heritage.
v. An investor seeking in the territory of a Member State a patent relating to biological materials or to traditional knowledge or to folklore must provide, as a condition of patent rights, (i) the disclosure of the source and country of the biological resource and traditional knowledge used in the invention; (ii) evidence of prior informed consent through approval of authorities in the source Member State; and (iii) evidence of fair and equitable sharing of benefits with relevant local communities in the source Member State.

(3) **Registration of Intellectual Property Rights**
The registration of intellectual property rights, including the protection of traditional knowledge by a regional Intellectual Property Rights Registration Agency shall be recognized by Member States without a further requirement of registration of those rights.

CHAPTER 14: COMPETITION

Article 50: Restrictive Business Practices

(1) The following shall be prohibited as incompatible with the ECOWAS Common Market: all agreements between enterprises, decisions by associations of enterprises and concerted practices which may affect trade between ECOWAS Member States and the object or effect of which are or may be the prevention, restriction, distortion or elimination of competition within the Common Market, and in Particular those which:

(a) directly or indirectly fix purchase or selling prices, terms of sale, or any other, trading conditions;
(b) limit or control production, markets, technical development, or investment; (c) share markets, customers, or sources of supply;
(d) apply dissimilar conditions to equivalent transactions with other trading parties; thereby placing them at a competitive disadvantage; or
(e) make the conclusion of contracts subject to acceptance by the other parties of supplementary obligations which, by their nature or according to commercial usage, have no connection with the subject of such contracts.

(2) Any agreement or decision prohibited under the sub-paragraph 1 of this Article shall be automatically void and of no legal effect in any Member State of the ECOWAS Community
(3) Member States also undertake to prevent the abuse of intellectual property rights such as resort to practices which unreasonably restrain, adversely affect or set barriers to trade in intellectual property rights or intangible goods including the transfer of technology.
(4) **Harmonization Measures**

In order to facilitate the implementation of this chapter of this Code, Member States undertake to implement the provisions of the ECOWAS Supplementary Acts on Competition rules and the establishment of Competition Authority.

CHAPTER 15: TRADE-RELATED INVESTMENT MEASURES

Article 51: Trade Related Investment Measures

(1) Member States shall adopt investment related trade measures to enhance regional economic integration in accordance with the provisions of Article 31.
(2) **Sectorally-Managed Trade Arrangements**
Due attention shall be paid to the relevant regional and multilateral instruments, with a view to fulfilling development priority needs of Member States.
(3) **Regional Trade Agreements**
Nothing in this Article shall be construed so as to oblige a Member State to extend to investments or investors of a Third Country advantages resulting from any existing or future association or participation in a free trade area, customs union, common market, economic and monetary union or any other similar institution of economic integration or to extend to investments or investors of third countries deductions, fiscal exemptions or any other similar advantages resulting from double taxation agreements or any other agreement regarding tax matters negotiated by Member States among themselves or with any other third country.

(4) **Export Promotion Devices**
Member States are encouraged to design a framework to harmonize the functions and operations of export processing zones (EPZ) in order to attract investment and to prevent abuse of the scheme. In this regard, the operational guidelines for EPZs shall be included in the ECOWAS Investment Policy.

(5) **Establishment of Special Economic Zones in the ECOWAS Territory**

1. The Member States may establish any class or kind of special economic zones anywhere in their national territories in conformity with the ECOWICPF, this Code, and the national laws of the Member States.
2. In furtherance of paragraph 1, the Member States shall endeavor, to the extent practicable, to adhere to the internationally-recognized standards as set out in the ECOWICPF when adopting their national legal, regulatory, and institutional frameworks.

Article 52: Regional Investment Promotion

(1) Member States are encouraged to establish by national legislation investment promotion agencies to facilitate the inflows of investment to their territories. The independence of such agency shall be guaranteed by law.

(2) National Investment Promotion Agencies shall cooperate towards the implementation of this Code by harmonizing practices and policies especially investment incentives. In this regard, ECOWAS Commission shall establish a Regional Investment Promotion Agency on a Public Private Partnership basis.

CHAPTER 16: DISPUTE SETTLEMENT MECHANISMS

Article 53: State-State

(1) Any dispute between Member States regarding the implementation of this Code shall be resolved through the use of consultations, good offices, mediation, conciliation or any other agreed dispute resolution mechanisms.

(2) Where the parties are unable to resolve dispute through the preceding methods, they may proceed to arbitration.

(3) Where recourse is made to arbitration, the arbitration may be conducted at any established public or private alternative dispute resolution centers or the arbitration division of the ECOWAS Community Court of Justice. Member States are encouraged to utilize regional and national alternatives dispute settlement institutions.

(4) Where the Member States are unable to resolve any dispute regarding the interpretation and application of this Code through any of the preceding methods, they may refer the matter to the ECOWAS Community Court of Justice whose decision shall be final.

Article 54: State–Investor or Investor–Investor

(1) Any dispute between a Member State and an investor or between investors may be resolved through the use of consultations, good offices, mediation, conciliation, arbitration or any other agreed dispute resolution mechanism.
(2) Where recourse is made to arbitration, the arbitration may be conducted at any established public or private alternative dispute resolution centers or the arbitration division of the ECOWAS Court of Justice. Member States and investors are encouraged to utilize regional and national alternatives dispute settlement institutions.
(3) Where recourse is made to arbitration, the rules of procedure of the relevant forum shall be applicable, including rules for the submission of claims, selection of arbitrators and conduct of the arbitration.
(4) Except where the investment contract between a Member State and an Investor provides for the use of international mechanisms such as ICSID or UNCITRAL, parties to the investment contract shall exhaust all local remedies including the ECOWAS Court of Justice or national dispute settlement systems, before resorting to the international mechanisms.

Article 55: Enforceability of Final Awards

(1) The final awards or decisions on investment disputes made by arbitration panels and judicial bodies shall be enforceable. To this end, decisions or awards rendered in another Member State shall be enforced as if there were decisions or awards rendered by a judicial body or arbitration panel located in a Member State requested to enforce the award or decision.
(2) Decisions of ECOWAS Court of Justice shall be enforced in accordance with its own rules and existing protocols.

Article 56: Interpretation and Application

Any dispute regarding the interpretation and application of this Code shall be referred to the ECOWAS Court of Justice whose decision shall be final.

Article 57: Access to the ECOWAS Court of Justice

For the purposes of instituting or maintaining any action under chapter 16 of this code, access to the ECOWAS Court of Justice is open to Member States, ECOWAS Institutions, corporate bodies, investors and individuals.

CHAPTER 17 REGIONAL MONITORING STRUCTURE

Article 58: Implementation

(1) Member States shall adopt such appropriate measures that are necessary to ensure that any obligation arising from this Codeis fulfilled.
(2) Member States shall co-operate in addressing any impediment that may arise as a result of any action, or lack thereof, by any Member State on issues having a material bearing on the implementation of this Code.
(3) Member States shall publish all relevant measures which pertain to or affect the implementation of this Code.
(4) Member States should respond promptly to all requests by any other Member State and or by the Commission for specific information on any of its measures covered under this Code.

Article 59: Monitoring Structure

(1) For the purpose of administration, implementation and monitoring of the provisions of this Code, the Community shall in accordance with Article 25 of the ECOWAS Supplementary Act on Investment Rules, establish the necessary regional structure.
(2) The ECOWAS Common Investment Market Council shall identify and establish the relevant mechanisms to assist Member States to implement the provisions of this Code.
(3) The ECOWAS Commission shall act as the Depository for the Lists of scheduled investment sectors of Member States in accordance with the relevant obligations under this Code.
(4) The ECOWAS Commission shall regularly update and publish the Lists of scheduled investment sectors to Member States and investors

CHAPTER 18: MISCELLANEOUS MATTERS

Article 60: Observer Status

Representatives of investors within the Community may be allowed observer status at meetings of ECOWAS institutions in accordance with the existing rules and regulations.

Article 61: Amendments and Revisions

(1) Any Community Institution may submit proposals for the amendment or revision of this Community Investment Code.

(2) Proposals for amendment or revision shall be submitted to the Commission. The Commission shall forward such proposals to Member States not later than thirty (30) days after receipt. Upon expiration of the thirty (30) days the Authority of Heads of State and Government shall examine the proposal and if approved shall be adopted by the Authority of Heads of State and Government in accordance with the provisions of Article 9 of the ECOWAS Treaty.

Article 62: Entry into Force and Publication

This Code shall be published by the ECOWAS Commission in the Official Journal of the Economic Community of West African States within thirty (30) days of its signature by the Chairman of the Council of Ministers. It shall also be published by each Member State in its National Gazette within thirty (30) days after notification by the Commission.

Article 63: Transitional Provision

In order to ensure the participation of all Member States in the implementation of this Code, there will be a transition period of 5 years, to provide Member States the necessary flexibility to address developmental needs and other economic concerns that they face in the normal and smooth implementation of this Code.

Article 64: Relationship with other investment agreements

(1) Where there are differences or inconsistencies in the provisions of this code and other legal instruments under the ECOWAS Treaty, the provisions of this code shall prevail to the extent of the differences and inconsistencies.
(2) Member States shall ensure that all future investment agreements to which they may become Party are fully consistent with the code.
(3) In the case of a conflict between this Code and any intra- African BIT, investment chapter under any intra-African trade agreement, or regional investment arrangements, this Code shall prevail.

Article 65: Language of Publication

(1) This Code shall be published in the official languages of the Community, namely: English, French and Portuguese.
(2) The authentic texts of this Code are in English, French and Portuguese.

ANNEX V

African Union Commission

Economic Affairs Department

Draft Pan-African Investment Code
Draft, December 2016

Preamble

The Member States,

RECALLING the Abuja Treaty establishing the African Economic Community and the adoption of Agenda 2063 by the African Union Heads of State and Government;

RECOGNIZING the need for a comprehensive guiding instrument on investment for all

African Union Member States;

RECOGNIZING the growing importance of trade and investments for the growth and development of Africa;

AFFIRMING the desire of Member States to promote an attractive investment climate and expand trade and investments for long-term development;

CONSIDERING the African Union objectives stated in the Constitutive Act aimed at fast- tracking the political and socio-economic integration of the continent;

RECOGNIZING that the vision for regional integration and development is to strengthen the regional market, create wealth in Africa, and enhance competitiveness through increased production, trade and investment flows in African countries;

MINDFUL of the increasing importance of the development and strengthening of financial and capital markets, and the role played by investment and the private sector in productive capacity, increased economic growth and sustainable development;

DESIRING to promote within Member States an environment conducive to the development of a more vibrant and dynamic private sector that facilitates job creation, promotes technology transfer, supports long-term economic growth and contributes effectively to the fight against poverty;

RECOGNIZING that investment and trade based activities represent one of the major avenues for illicit financial flows from Member States and that corrupt practices underpin these outflows, and *AFFIRMING* their desire to promote corruption free investment and trade regimes and improved laws and regulations that promote transparency and accountability in governance;

RECOGNIZING their right to regulate all the aspects relating to investments within their territories with a view to meeting national policy objectives and to promoting sustainable development objectives;

SEEKING to achieve an overall balance of the rights and obligations between Member States and the investors under this Code;

MINDFUL of the crucial role played by women and youth in the development of Africa;

RECALLING that the free movement of people is a fundamental pillar of African integration;

RECOGNIZING the role played by the New Economic Partnership for African Development (NEPAD)and the complementary existing regional and international initiatives relating to a transformational economic agenda for Africa;

DESIROUS of the need to ensure national and continental coherence in investment policymaking;

TAKING into account the various regional arrangements on investment across the continent;

TAKING into account the Sustainable Development Goals (SDGs) and the Investment Policy Framework for Sustainable Development of the United Nations Conference on Trade and Development (UNCTAD);

TAKING into account obligations of some of the Member States under relevant international instruments;

DETERMINED therefore to use the Pan-African Investment Code (hereinafter, the Code) as a guiding instrument

THE MEMBER STATES HAVE AGREED AS FOLLOWS:

CHAPTER 1

GENERAL PROVISIONS

Article 1

Objective

The objective of this Code is to promote, facilitate and protect investments that foster the sustainable development of each Member State, and in particular, the Member State where the investment is located.

Article2

Scope

1. This Code shall apply as a guiding instrument to Member States as well as investors and their investments in the territory of Member States as defined by this Code.
2. This Code defines the rights and obligations of Member States as well as investors, and principles prescribed therein.

Article 3

Relationship With Other Investment Agreements

1. This Code does not affect rights and obligations of Member States deriving from any existing investment agreement.
2. Notwithstanding Paragraph 1, Member States may agree that this Code could be reviewed to become a binding instrument and to replace the intra-African bilateral investment treaties (BITs) or investment chapters in intra-African trade agreements after a period of time determined by the Member States or after the termination period as set in the existing BITs and investment chapters in the trade agreements.
3. Member States and Regional Economic Communities (RECs) shall take into account as far as possible the provisions of this Code when entering into any new agreement with a third country in order to avoid any conflict between their present or future obligations under this Code and their obligations in other agreements.

Article 4

Definitions
In this Code, unless the context otherwise requires:

1. "enterprise or company" means any entity duly constituted or otherwise incorporated, under the applicable laws and regulations of a Member State provided that it maintains substantial business activity in the Member State in which it is located. Substantial business activity requires an overall examination, on a case-by-case basis, of all the circumstances, including, inter alia: (i) the amount of investment to be brought into the host State, (ii) the number of jobs to be created, (iii) its effect on the local community, and (iv) the length of time the business has been in operation;

2. "home State" means a Member State from where the investment or the investor originates;
3. "host State" is the Member State where the investment is located;
4. "investment" means an enterprise or a company, as defined under Paragraph 1, which is established, acquired or expanded by an investor, including through the constitution, maintenance or acquisition of shares, debentures or other ownership instruments of such an enterprise, provided that the enterprise or company is established or acquired in accordance with the laws of the host State; An enterprise or company may possess assets such as:
   a. shares, stocks, debentures and other equity instruments of the enterprise or another enterprise;
   b. a debt security of another enterprise;
   c. loans to an enterprise;
   d. movable or immovable property and other property rights such as mortgages, liens or pledges;
   e. claims to money or to any performance under contract having a financial value;
   f. copyrights, know-how, goodwill and industrial property rights such as patents, trademarks, industrial designs and trade names, to the extent they are recognized under the law of the host State.

   For greater certainty, investment does not include:
   i. debt securities issued by a government or loans to a government;
   ii. portfolio investments;
   iii. claims to money that arise solely from commercial contracts for the sale of goods or services by a national or enterprise in the territory of a Member State to an enterprise in the territory of another Member State, or the extension of credit in connection with a commercial transaction, or any other claims to money that do not involve the kind of interests set out in subparagraphs (a) through (f) above;
   iv. investments of a speculative nature;
   v. investments in any sector sensitive to its development or which would have an adverse impact on its economy;
   vi. commercial activities.

   In order to qualify as an investment under this Code, the investment must have the following characteristics: the substantial business activity according to Paragraph 1, commitment of capital or other resources, the expectation of gain or profit, the assumption of risk, and a significant contribution to the host State's economic development.

   For avoidance of doubt, establishment, acquisition and expansion under this Code only apply to the post-establishment phase.
5. "investor" means any national, company or enterprise of a Member State or a national, company or enterprise from any other country that has invested or has made investments in a Member State;
6. "list of scheduled investment sectors" means schedules of excluded sectors of Member

States or any other list submitted by Member States where applicable;
7. "Member State" means a Member State as defined in the Constitutive Act of the African Union;
8. "measures" include any legal, administrative, legislative, judicial or policy decision that is taken by the host State, relating to and affecting an investment in the host State;
9. "national" means a natural person who is a citizen of any Member State;
10. "portfolio investment" refers to any investment where the investor owns less than 10% of shares in a company or through stock exchange, or otherwise does not give the portfolio investor the possibility to exercise effective management or influence on the management of the investment;
11. "public official" means any persons appointed or elected who performs public functions on a permanent or temporary basis. This includes persons who work for an organ of the State or an organ of the central Government or an organ of a territorial unit of the State at the national, regional or local levels;
12. "State contract" means a contract entered into between Government of a Member State or a territorial unit, on one hand, and an investor on the other hand;
13. "third country" means a State which is not a Member of the African Union.

CHAPTER 2

STANDARDS OF TREATMENT OF INVESTORS AND INVESTMENTS

Article 5

Admission and Establishment

1. Each Member State shall promote, encourage and facilitate investments in its territory, and admit such investments in accordance with its laws and regulations.
2. Each Member State shall accord investors rights of entry and establishment, in accordance with its laws and regulations with the aim of promoting free flows of investment within the region.

Article 6

Encouragement and Support of Investments

1. Member States may introduce incentives in order to attract investments. Such incentives may include *inter alia*:
   a. financial incentives in the forms of investment insurance, grants or loans at concessionary rates;

b. fiscal incentives such as tax holidays, pioneer status and reduced tax rates;
c. subsidized infrastructure or services, market preferences;
d. development-oriented incentives, to encourage preferential markets schemes and specific investors within the region;
e. incentives for technical assistance, technology transfer requirements; and
f. investment guarantees.

2. Member States may harmonize incentives for investments that are of strategic interest to the Member States or as prescribed by relevant African Union bodies. Member States may harmonize incentives in accordance with standards to be prescribed from time to time by relevant African Union bodies.

Article 7

Most-Favored-Nation Treatment

1. Each Member State shall accord to investors of another Member State treatment no less favorable than it accords, in like circumstances, to investors of any other Member State or of a third country with respect to the management, conduct, operation, expansion, sale or other disposition of investment.
2. Each Member State shall accord to investments made by investors of another Member State treatment no less favorable than it accords, in like circumstances, to investments made by investors of any other Member State or of a third country with respect to the management, conduct, operation, expansion, sale or other disposition of investments.
3. The concept of "in like circumstances" requires an overall examination, on a case by-case basis, of all the circumstances of an investment, including, among others:
   a. its effects on third persons and the local community;
   b. its effects on the local, regional or national environment, the health of the populations, or on the global commons;
   c. the sector in which the investor is active;
   d. the aim of the measure in question;
   e. the regulatory process generally applied in relation to a measure in question;
   f. company size; and
   g. other factors directly relating to the investment or investor in relation to the measure in question.

   The examination referred to in this Paragraph shall not be limited to or be biased towards any one factor.
4. For greater certainty, the "treatment," referred to in Paragraphs 1 and 2, does not include dispute settlement procedures provided for in other treaties. Substantive obligations in other treaties, do not in themselves constitute "treatment," and thus cannot give rise to a breach of this Article.

Article 8

Exceptions to Most-Favored-Nation Treatment

1. Member States may adopt measures that derogate from the Most-Favored-Nation principle.
2. Any regulatory measure taken by a Member State that is designed and applied to protect or enhance legitimate public welfare objectives, such as public health, safety and the environment, does not constitute a breach of the Most-Favored-Nation principle.
3. The measures taken by reason of national security, public interest, public health or public morals are not considered as a "less favorable treatment," in the meaning of Article 7.
4. The Most-Favored-Nation principle shall not apply to sectors excluded in a Member State's List of scheduled investment sectors.
5. The Most-Favored-Nation principle does not oblige a Member State to extend to the investors of another Member State or of a third country the benefit of any treatment, preference or privilege contained in:
   a. the existing or future free trade area, customs union, common market agreement or any international arrangement to which the investor's home State is not a Party, or
   b. any international agreement or domestic legislation relating wholly or mainly to taxation.

Article 9

National Treatment

1. A Member State shall accord to investors of another Member State treatment no less favorable than it accords, in like circumstances, to its own investors with respect to the management, conduct, operation, and sale or other disposition of investments.
2. A Member State shall accord to investments from another Member State treatment no less favorable than it accords, in like circumstances, to investments of its own investors with respect to the management, conduct, operation, and sale or other disposition of investments.
3. The concept of "in like circumstances" requires an overall examination, on a case by-case basis, of all the circumstances of an investment, including, among others:
   a. its effects on third persons and the local community;
   b. its effects on the local, regional or national environment, the health of the populations, or on the global commons;
   c. the sector in which the investor is active;
   d. the aim of the measure in question;

e. the regulatory process generally applied in relation to a measure in question;
f. company size; and
g. other factors directly relating to the investment or investor in relation to the measure in question.

The examination referred to in this Paragraph shall not be limited to or be biased towards any one of the factors.

Article 10

Exceptions to National Treatment

1. Member States may adopt measures that derogate from the National Treatment principle provided such measures are not arbitrary.
2. Any regulatory measure taken by a Member State that is designed and applied to protect or enhance legitimate public welfare objectives, such as national interests, public health, safety and the environment, does not constitute a breach of the National Treatment principle.
3. Member States may, in accordance with their respective domestic legislation, grant
   preferential treatment to qualifying investments and investors in order to achieve national development objectives.
4. A Member State reserves the right to deny an investor the benefits of this Code, and to grant special and differential treatment to any investor and investment in such cases, though not limited to instances where:
   a. the investor does not have substantial business activities in the Member State; or
   b. the investor is engaged in activities inimical to the economic interest of Member
   States.
5. A Member State may deny national treatment if advantages available within the Member State's economy are made for the exclusive benefit of its own nationals within the framework of its national development programs or its List of scheduled investment sectors where applicable.
6. The National Treatment principle does not apply:
   a. to subsidies or grants provided to a government or a State enterprise, including government-supported loans, guarantees and insurance; or
   b. to taxation measures aimed at ensuring the effective collection of taxes, except where this results in arbitrary discrimination.
7. In accordance with national laws and regulations, Member States may accord more favorable treatment to address the internal needs of designated disadvantaged persons, groups or regions.
8. The implementation of these exceptions shall not entitle any investor to compensation for any competitive disadvantages they may suffer.

Article 11

Expropriation and Compensation

1. Investments in Member States shall not be nationalized, expropriated or subjected to measures having effect equivalent to nationalization or expropriation except if the following conditions are met in a cumulative manner:
   a. a public purpose related to the internal needs of that Member State;
   b. on a non-discriminatory basis;
   c. against adequate compensation; and d. under due process of law.
2. The investor affected shall have the right, under the laws of the Member State expropriating, to prompt review, by a judicial or other independent authority of that Member State, of its case and of the valuation of its investment in accordance with the procedure established by the laws of the Member State.
3. A non-discriminatory measure of a Member State that is designed and applied to protect or enhance legitimate public welfare objectives, such as public health, safety and the environment, does not constitute an indirect expropriation under this Code.
4. This Article shall not apply to the issuance of compulsory licenses granted in relation to intellectual property rights, or to the creation, limitation or revocation of intellectual property rights, to the extent that such issuance, revocation, limitation or creation is consistent with applicable international agreements on intellectual property.

Article 12

Determination of the Value of Compensation

1. Adequate compensation shall normally be assessed in relation to the fair market value of the expropriated investment immediately before the date of expropriation and shall not reflect any change in value occurring because the intended expropriation had become known earlier. In no event shall the valuation date be moved to any future date. The computation of the fair market value of the property shall exclude any consequential or exemplary losses or speculative or windfall profits claimed by the investor, including those relating to moral damages or loss of goodwill.
2. Where appropriate, the assessment of adequate compensation shall be based on an equitable balance between the public interest and interest of the investor affected, having regard to all relevant circumstances and taking into account the current and past use of the property, the history of its acquisition, the extent of previous profit made by the foreign investor through the investment, and the duration of the investment.

3. If the compensation is not paid within six months from the date of its determination, it shall after that date attract simple interests at the normal commercial rate where applicable at the national level of the host State.
4. Any payment shall be made in a freely convertible currency.

Article 13

War and Civil Disturbance

Investors who suffer within the territory of a Member State damage in relation to their investments owing to the outbreak of hostilities or a state of national emergency such as, revolt, insurrection or riot, shall be accorded treatment no less favorable than that accorded to investors of such a Member State or to investors of any third country, as regards to any measure to be taken by the concerned Member State including restitution, compensation or other valuable consideration.

Article 14

General Exceptions

1. This Code shall not prevent any Member State from adopting or enforcing measures relating to the protection of human, animal or plant life or health, or to the maintenance of international peace and security, or to the protection of its national security interests, subject to the requirement that these measures are not applied in a manner which would constitute a means of arbitrary or unjustifiable discrimination between investors in like circumstances or a disguised restriction on investment flows.
2. Member States shall not be required to change nor relax their appropriate level of protection of human, animal or plant life or health in pursuit or attraction of investments.
3. Any interested Member State may request information on the reasons for the measures taken under Paragraph 1. The Member State taking such measures shall respond to the request for information within three months.

Article 15

Transfer of Funds

Member States shall, subject to national laws, permit all transfers relating to an investment to be made freely and without delay. Such transfers may include:

a. profits, capital gains, dividends, royalties, interests and other current income accruing from an investment;
b. the proceeds of the total or partial liquidation of an investment;
c. repayments made pursuant to a loan agreement in connection with an investment;
d. license fees in relation to investment;
e. payments in respect of technical assistance, technical service and management fees;
f. payments in connection with contracting projects;
g. earnings of nationals of a Member State who work in connection with an investment in the territory of the other Member State; and
h. compensation, restitution, indemnification or other settlement pursuant to the investments.

Article 16

Exceptions to the Transfer of Funds

1. A Member State shall apply restrictions on international transfers of funds and payments for current transactions relating to investments made in its territory in accordance with its taxation as well as financial laws and regulations.
2. Exceptions to the transfer of funds are permitted under the following conditions:
   a. capital can only be transferred after a period of five years after full operation of the investment in a Member State unless its national legislation provides for more favorable treatment; or
   b. proceeds of the investment can be transferred one year after the investment entered the territory of a Member State unless its national legislation provides for more favorable treatment.
3. A Member State may prevent a transfer in a non-discriminatory manner and in accordance with its laws relating to:
   a. bankruptcy, insolvency or other legal proceedings to protect the rights of creditors;
   b. criminal or administrative violations; or
   c. ensuring the satisfaction of judgments in adjudicatory proceedings.
4. A Member State may adopt or maintain measures not conforming with its obligations relating to cross-border capital transactions:
   a. in the event of serious balance-of-payments and external financial difficulties or threat thereof; or
   b. in cases where, in exceptional circumstances, movements of capital cause or threaten to cause serious difficulties for macroeconomic management, in particular, monetary and exchange rate policies.
5. Measures under paragraph 4 shall be made public, be temporary and be eliminated as soon as conditions permit.

DEVELOPMENT RELATED ISSUES

Article 17

Performance Requirements

1. Member States may support the development of local, regional and continental industries that provide, *inter alia,* up-stream and down-stream linkages and have a favorable impact on attracting investments and generating increased employment in Member States.
2. Member States may introduce performance requirements to promote domestic investments and local content. Measures covered by this Paragraph include, *inter alia*:
    a. measures to grant preferential treatment to any enterprise so qualifying under the domestic law of a Member State in order to achieve national or sub-national regional development goals;
    b. measures to support the development of local entrepreneurs;
    c. measures to enhance productive capacity, increase employment, increase human resource capacity and training, research and development including of new technologies, technology transfer, innovation and other benefits of investment through the use of specified requirements on investors; and
    d. measures to address historically based economic disparities suffered by identifiable ethnic or cultural groups due to discriminatory or oppressive measures against such groups prior to the adoption of this Code.

Article 18

Lists of Scheduled Investment Sectors

1. The process of harmonizing the investment regimes among Member States takes place with due respect for national policy objectives and the level of development of individual Members States. There shall be appropriate flexibility for Member States to prescribe their national List of scheduled investment sectors open for liberalization, in line with their development situation.
2. Any Member State may also, within its List of scheduled investment sectors, use further classification into subsectors and/or decide segments of sectors to better inform on the scope of its commitments under this Code.
3. Any Member State may submit a List of scheduled investment sectors that are excluded from the National Treatment principle where applicable.
4. The Lists of scheduled investment sectors form integral part of this Code; and Member States agree to respect them.

INVESTORS OBLIGATIONS

Article 19

Framework for Corporate Governance

1. Investments shall meet national and internationally accepted standards of corporate governance for the sector involved, in particular for transparency and accounting practices.
2. In this regard, Member States, public bodies and companies are encouraged to improve the legal, institutional and regulatory framework for corporate governance and any other issues such as environmental or ethical concerns.
3. Investors shall:
   a. ensure the equitable treatment of all shareholders, in accordance with national laws;
   b. encourage active co-operation between corporations and stakeholders in creating wealth, jobs and the sustainability of financially sound enterprises;
   c. ensure that timely and accurate disclosure is made on all material matters regarding a corporation, including the financial situation, performance, ownership, and governance of the company, risks related to environmental liabilities, and any other matters in accordance with the relevant regulations and requirements; and
   d. provide information relating to human resource policies, such as program s for human resource development.

Article 20

Socio-political Obligations

1. Investors shall adhere to socio-political obligations including, but not exclusively, the following:
   a. respect for national sovereignty and observance of domestic laws, regulations and administrative practices;
   b. respect for socio-cultural values;
   c. non-interference in internal political affairs;
   d. non-interference in intergovernmental relations; and e. respect for labor rights.
2. Investors shall not influence the appointment of persons to public office or finance political parties.
3. Investors shall refrain from exercising restrictive practices and from trying to achieve gains through unlawful means.

Article 21

Bribery

1. Investors shall not offer, promise or give any unlawful or undue pecuniary or other advantage or present, whether directly or through intermediaries, to a public official of a Member State, or to a member of an official's family or business associate or other person in order that the official or other person act or refrain from acting in relation to the performance of official duties.
2. Investors shall also not aid or abet a conspiracy to commit or authorize acts of bribery.

Article 22

Corporate Social Responsibility

1. Investors shall abide by the laws, regulations, administrative guidelines and policies of the host State.
2. Investors shall, in pursuit of their economic objectives, ensure that they do not conflict with the social and economic development objectives of host States and shall be sensitive to such objectives.
3. Investors shall contribute to the economic, social and environmental progress with a view to achieving sustainable development of the host State.

Article 23

Obligations as to the use of Natural Resources

1. Investors shall not exploit or use local natural resources to the detriment of the rights and interests of the host State.
2. Investors shall respect rights of local populations, and avoid land grabbing practices vis-à-vis local communities.

Article 24

Business Ethics and Human rights

The following principles should govern compliance by investors with business ethics and human rights:

a. support and respect the protection of internationally recognized human rights;

b. ensure that they are not complicit in human rights abuses;
c. eliminate all forms of forced and compulsory labor, including the effective abolition of child labor;
d. eliminate discrimination in respect of employment and occupation; and e. ensure equitable sharing of wealth derived from investments.

CHAPTER 5

INVESTMENT RELATED ISSUES

Article 25

Intellectual Property Rights and Traditional Knowledge

1. Each Member State shall ensure the enforcement of intellectual property rights within its territory and in accordance with the rights and obligations under the Trade Related Aspects of Intellectual Property Rights (TRIPS) agreement and other relevant international instruments.
2. Member States may provide exceptions to the exclusive rights conferred by an intellectual property right, and allow for its use without the authorization of the right holder, including use by the government or third parties authorized by the government.
3. Member States and investors shall, in accordance with generally accepted international legal standards and best practices, protect traditional knowledge systems and expressions of culture as well as genetic resources that are sought, used or exploited by investors, or are otherwise relevant to their contracts, practices and other operations in such Member States.
4. Member States shall provide, within national laws, principles for the patenting of biological materials or of traditional knowledge systems and expressions of culture for the protection of local communities in such Member States.

Article 26

State Contracts

1. State contracts should be negotiated and implemented, subject to national laws and regulations, in a mutually supportive manner with due respect to and taking into consideration the legitimate development objectives of Member States as set out in their investment policies, while giving due consideration to the rights and interests of investors.
2. Member States may set thresholds in the amount of tenders and procurements, as well as sectors and subsectors limited to the exclusive benefit of local

suppliers, especially the small and medium size enterprises, provided that such measures are not applied in such a manner as to nullify or impair the benefits accruing to any Member State under this Code.

Article 27

Public Private Partnership

Member States may cooperate on policies and other related issues that encourage and facilitate the use of Public Private Partnership to ensure development in Member States.

Article 28

Competition Law and Policy

Member States shall:

a. promote, maintain and encourage competition to enhance economic efficiency in investment at the national and regional levels;
b. prohibit any anti-competitive investment conduct that prevents, restricts or distorts competition at the national and regional levels;
c. adopt and implement clear and transparent rules on competition to increase the ability of the regional economy to attract investment and to maximize the benefits of such investment.

Article 29

Transfer of Technology

1. Member States shall put in place policies for the purpose of promoting and encouraging the transfer and acquisition of appropriate technology.
2. Investors are encouraged to adopt in the course of their business activities, practices that permit the transfer and rapid diffusion of technologies and know -how, with due regard to the protection of intellectual property rights, on reasonable terms and conditions and in a manner that contributes to the research and development goals of the host State.
3. Member States undertake to cooperate and facilitate the international transfer of technology by various measures such as:
   a. getting access to available information regarding description, location and, as far as possible, approximate cost of technology;
   b. establishing or strengthening of technology transfer centers;

c. providing training for research, engineering, design and other personnel engaged in the development of national technologies or in the adaptation and use of technologies transferred;
d. providing assistance in the development and administration of laws and regulations with a view to facilitating the transfer of technology;
e. granting credits on preferential terms for financing the acquisition of capital and intermediate goods in the context of approved development projects involving transfer of technology transaction; and
f. assisting in the development of technological capabilities of the companies and their personnel.

Article 30

Environment and Technologies

1. Member States and investors should take all practicable steps to promote, facilitate, and finance, as appropriate, the transfer of, or access to, environmentally sound technologies and know-how, based on the relevant international instruments, without prejudice to their rights and obligations, where applicable, under these texts. The access and transfer of those technologies by the investors shall take place under fair and most favorable terms, including on concessional and/or preferential terms where mutually agreed, based on international and local standards for the transfer of environmentally sound technologies.
2. Investors are encouraged to provide adequate financial resources, including for the transfer of technology, needed for implementing measures to assist the Member States that are particularly vulnerable to the adverse effects of climate change in meeting costs of adaptation to, or mitigation of those adverse effects.

Article 31

Banking Law and Policy

In order to facilitate investment flows, Member States are encouraged to establish a framework for co-operation and co-ordination between National Central Banks on banking regulatory and supervisory matters with the view to:

a. promoting the identification, measurement and management of banking risks, including systemic risks;
b. integrating the payment systems; and
c. sharing information regarding depositor protection, anti-money laundering compliance, co-operation in cyber tracking and criminality, and combating the financing of terrorism.

Article 32

Foreign Exchange Controls

1. Investors shall have free access to foreign exchange subject to the applicable laws, regulations and monetary policies in Member States.
2. Each Member State shall permit transfers to be made in a convertible currency at the market rate of exchange prevailing on the date of transfer.
3. Unless otherwise agreed by the investor, transfers shall be made in any convertible
   currency at the rate of exchange applicable on the date of transfer pursuant to the exchange regulations in force.

Article 33

Prudential Measures

In the event of serious balance-of-payments and external financial difficulties or threat thereof, a Member State may adopt or maintain restrictions on investments under the provisions of this Code. These measures shall be temporary and be phased out progressively as there are changes in the initial circumstances surrounding the use of the measures.

Article 34

Labor Issues

1. Member States shall not encourage investment by relaxing domestic labor legislation. Accordingly, each Member State shall ensure that it does not waive or derogate from such legislation as an encouragement for the establishment, maintenance or expansion of an investment in its territory.
2. In this regard, investors may:
   a. consult with the host State authorities and national employers' and workers' organizations in order to keep manpower plans in harmony with national social development policies, making optimal use of labor available locally and within the sub region to provide substantial employment or reduce unemployment;
   b. ensure the employment and promotion of the host State nationals;
   c. use technologies that specifically generate employment; and
   d. promote employment in the Member States by entering into supply contracts with local enterprises and by prioritizing, to the full extent possible, the use and processing of local raw materials.

3. Investors shall comply with international conventions and existing labor policies and, in particular, not use child labor and shall support efforts for the elimination of all sort of child labor, including forced or compulsory labor within Member States.

Article 35

Foreign Workers and Visa Requirements

1. Member States may facilitate the granting of visas and permits to foreign workers, employees and consultants as designated by the investor in order to assist in the management of the enterprise or company and provide services to the investor in accordance with applicable national laws and regulations. Each such foreign worker, employee and consultant shall not be exempted from income taxes and social security obligations as per the conditions set forth in the national laws and procedures, if applicable,
   in Member States.
2. In relation to the management and operation of the investment in the host State, investors and business community members may enjoy the benefit of fast-track visa applications and smooth process in the issuance of such visas.

Article 36

Human Resources Development

1. Member States may develop national policies to guide investors in developing human capacity of the labor force. Such policies may include incentives to encourage employers to invest in training, capacity building and knowledge transfer.
2. Member States should develop national policies that pay particular attention to the special needs for youth, women and other vulnerable groups.
3. Member States should develop policies for the mutual recognition for certificates and diplomas.

Article 37

Environment

1. Member States shall ensure that their laws and regulations provide for environmental protection.

2. In this regard, Member States shall not encourage investment by relaxing or waiving compliance with domestic environmental legislation. If a Member State considers that another Member State has encouraged such relaxation or non-compliance, it may request consultations with the other Member State and the two Member States shall consult with a view to avoiding any such encouragement.
3. Investors shall, in performing their activities, protect the environment and where such activities cause damages to the environment, take reasonable steps to restore it as far as possible.
4. Member States and investors shall carry out Environmental Impact Assessment (EIA) in relation to investments.

Article 38

Cultural Diversity

Member States may adopt policies on cultural and linguistic diversity in promotion of investments.

Article 39

Taxation

1. This Code shall not affect the rights and obligations of a Member State under Double Taxation Agreements.
2. Member States are encouraged to put in place measures for transparency, streamlining due process and good governance in their fiscal legislations and regulations.
3. Member States, with a view to encouraging the movement of investment, may conclude between themselves Double Tax Avoidance Agreements.
4. Regional Economic Communities may establish a comprehensive network of Double Tax Avoidance Agreements.

Article 40

Consumer Protection

1. Member States and investors shall take measures to protect the health, safety and economic interests of consumers and their right to information, education and to organize themselves in order to safeguard their interests.

2. Investors should act in accordance with fair business, marketing and advertising practices when dealing with consumers and should ensure the safety and quality of the goods and services they provide.

CHAPTER 6

DISPUTE SETTLEMENT

Article 41

State-State

Member States are encouraged to resolve any disputes regarding the interpretation and application of this Code initially through consultations, negotiations or mediation.

1. Where Member States agree to arbitration, the arbitration shall be conducted at any established African public or African alternative dispute resolution center.
2. Where Member States are unable to resolve any dispute regarding the interpretation and application of this Code, through any of the methods under Paragraph 1 of this Article, within six months, any of the disputing Member State may refer the matter to the African Court of Justice whose decision shall be final and binding.

Article 42

Investor–State

1. Member States may, in line with their domestic policies, agree to utilize the Investor– State dispute settlement mechanism. In the event that the Investor–State dispute settlement mechanism is agreed upon, the process below shall apply;
   a. Disputes arising between investors and Members States under the specific agreements that govern their relations shall be resolved under those agreements;
   b. In the event of an investment dispute between an investor and a Member State pursuant to this Code, the investor and the Member State should initially seek to resolve the dispute within six months at the latest, through consultations and negotiations, which may include the use of non-binding third-party mediation or other mechanisms;
   c. If consultations fail, the dispute may be resolved through arbitration, subject to the applicable laws of the host State and/or the mutual agreement of the disputing parties, and subject to exhaustion of local remedies; and
   d. Where recourse is made to arbitration under Paragraph 3, the arbitration may be conducted at any established African public or African

private alternative dispute resolution center. Arbitration shall be governed by the United Nations Commission on International Trade Law (UNCITRAL) rules.

2. Once recourse is made to a particular forum of dispute settlement, the forum chosen shall be used to the exclusion of the other. Decisions of this particular forum shall be final.

Article 43

Counterclaims by Member States

1. Where an investor or its investment is alleged by a Member State party in a dispute settlement proceeding under this Code to have failed to comply with its obligations under this Code or other relevant rules and principles of domestic and international law, the competent body hearing such a dispute shall consider whether this breach, if proven, is materially relevant to the issues before it, and if so, what mitigating or off-setting effects this may have on the merits of a claim or on any damages awarded in the event of such award.
2. A Member State may initiate a counterclaim against the investor before any competent body dealing with a dispute under this Code for damages or other relief resulting from an alleged breach of the Code.

Article 44

Applicable Law in Disputes

Any claim or dispute arising from this Code shall be decided in accordance with the provisions of this Code as well as any other national, regional or international laws, rules or principles.

CHAPTER 7

PROCEDURAL ISSUES AND INSTITUTIONAL ARRANGEMENTS

Article 45

Application

1. Member States shall endeavor to adopt appropriate measures to apply the rules contained in this Code.

2. Member States shall co-operate with each other in addressing any impediment to the application of the rules contained in this Code.
3. Member States shall publish all relevant measures of general application, which pertain to, or affect the application of the rules contained in this Code.
4. Member States are encouraged to respond promptly to all requests by other Member States for specific information on measures related to investments under this Code.
5. In order to ensure the participation of all Member States in the implementation of this Code, there will be a transition period to provide Member States the necessary flexibility to address developmental needs and other economic concerns that they face to reduce disparities in the effect of implementation of this Code.

Article 46

Co-operation and Technical Assistance

Member States may, in order to facilitate the implementation of this Code, co-operate to provide technical assistance.

Article 47

Role of the African Union Commission and the Regional Economic Communities

1. The African Union Commission and the Regional Economic Communities shall co- operate on investment and other related matters.
2. The African Union Commission and the Regional Economic Communities shall design and develop programs to assist Member States, in the promotion and facilitation of investment.

Article 48

Non-retroactivity

This Code does not create retroactive obligations or responsibilities for Member States or investors.

Article 49

Amendments and Revisions

1. Member States may submit proposals for the amendment or revision of this Code.
2. Any such amendment or revision shall be governed by the internal rules and procedures of the African Union Commission.

Article 50

Implementation Structure

The African Union Commission shall identify and establish the relevant mechanisms for the purpose of assisting Member States in the adoption of the rules contained in this Code within their national legislation and international investment agreements.

Article 51

Adoption and Publication

1. This Code shall come into effect upon adoption by the Assembly of Heads of State and Government of the African Union.
2. This Code shall be published by the African Union Commission, in accordance with its relevant internal rules and procedures.
3. This Code shall be published in the African Union official languages: Arabic, English, French and Portuguese.

Article 52

Authentic Text

1. The original text of this Code is English.
2. This Code is drawn up in four (4) texts in the Arabic, English, French and Portuguese languages, all four (4) being equally authentic.

Annex VI

AFRICAN UNION

الاتحاد الأفريقي

UNION AFRICAINE

UNIÃO AFRICANA

Addis Ababa, ETHIOPIA P.O. Box 3243 Telephone: +251-115-517 700 Fax : +251-115517844

website: www.au.int

Seventh Extraordinary Session of the Specialized Technical Committee on
Justice and Legal Affairs (Experts Meeting)
16–21 **January 2023**
Accra, Ghana

STC/Legal/Exp
Original: English

PROTOCOL TO THE AGREEMENT ESTABLISHING THE AFRICAN CONTINENTAL FREE TRADE AREA ON INVESTMENT

Draft

Accra, GHANA
January 2023

Preamble

We, Member States of the African Union,

RECALLING Decision Ext/Assembly/AU/Dec.1(X) of the Assembly of Heads of State and Government during its 10th Extraordinary Session held in Kigali, Rwanda, on 21 March 2018 adopting the Agreement Establishing the African Continental Free Trade Area;

DESIRING to strengthen the bonds of friendship and cooperation between African nations;

REAFFIRMING the African Union's vision for Agenda 2063 of an integrated, prosperous, and peaceful Africa driven by its own citizens and representing a dynamic force in the international arena;

PURSUANT to the objectives and principles of the Agreement Establishing the African Continental Free Trade Area signed at Kigali, Rwanda on 21 March 2018;

TAKING INTO ACCOUNT Article 7 of the Agreement Establishing the African Continental Free Trade Area which requires State Parties to enter into Phase II negotiations in respect of, among other areas, investment;

MINDFUL of best practices incorporated in the Pan-African Investment Code, the investment instruments of the Regional Economic Communities, bilateral investment treaties concluded by African States, national investment laws as well as other relevant international investment instruments and agreements;

DETERMINED to establish a balanced, coherent, clear, transparent, predictable and mutually- advantageous continental framework of principles and rules for investment promotion, facilitation and protection;

MINDFUL of the different levels of development of the State Parties and the challenges they may face in the adoption and implementation of this Protocol and other related investment policies;

RECALLING the 2030 Agenda for Sustainable Development, as contained in Resolution A/RES/70/1 of the United Nations General Assembly, and in particular the 17 Sustainable Development Goals;

TAKING INTO ACCOUNT the Investment Policy Framework for Sustainable Development of the United Nations Conference on Trade and Development (UNCTAD) and other relevant UNCTAD instruments that support new generation investment policies for inclusive growth and sustainable development;

COGNISANT of the increasing importance of trade and investment for the inclusive growth and industrial development of Africa, and the role played by the private sector in expanding productive capacity, creating jobs, facilitating transfer of technology as well as building regional, continental and global value chains;

RECOGNISING the significant contribution investment can make to the sustainable development of the State Parties, including the reduction of poverty, and the furtherance of investment-related human rights and human development while understanding that sustainable development requires the fulfilment of its economic, social and environmental pillars;

MINDFUL of the necessity of retaining, and expanding intra-African investment to increase economic resilience, and enable diversification in furtherance of achieving sustainable development in Africa;

DESIRING to establish within State Parties an overall attractive investment climate conducive to the development of a more vibrant and dynamic private sector that encourages mutually beneficial partnerships;

SEEKING to create a framework for investment cooperation and facilitation and for the prevention of investment disputes;

AFFIRMING the desire to promote accountability, good governance and responsible business conduct in a fair, transparent and predictable investment environment;

SEEKING to achieve an overall balance of the rights and obligations between State Parties and investors under this Protocol;

REAFFIRMING the inherent right of State Parties to regulate in their territories and to introduce measures in order to achieve their national public policy objectives, promote sustainable development objectives and protect legitimate public welfare objectives, such as public health, national security, the environment, the conservation of living and non-living exhaustible natural resources, labour standards, the integrity and stability of the financial system and public morals;

RECOGNISING the importance of encouraging investment activities that benefit economically disadvantaged areas, small and medium-sized enterprises, local communities, indigenous peoples, and underrepresented groups, including women and youth;

DESIRING to increase the share of African countries in global flows of foreign direct investment and to benefit from it in accordance with the objectives set out in this Protocol;

TAKING INTO ACCOUNT the relevant obligations of State Parties under international law and international agreements to which they are parties;

HAVE AGREED AS FOLLOWS:

CHAPTER 1

GENERAL PROVISIONS

Article 1
Definitions

For the purpose of this Protocol:

"AfCFTA" means the African Continental Free Trade Area;

"AfCFTA Secretariat" means the Secretariat of the African Continental Free Trade Area as established under Article 13 of the Agreement;

"Agreement" means the Agreement Establishing the African Continental Free Trade Area;

"Enterprise or company" means any legal or juridical person duly constituted or otherwise incorporated and operated under the applicable laws and regulations of a State Party;

"Freely Convertible Currency" means a convertible currency as classified by the International Monetary Fund or any currency that is widely traded in international foreign exchange market;

"Home State" means, in relation to:

a. a natural person, the State Party of nationality or citizenship of the investor in accordance with the laws and regulations of that State Party;
b. a legal or juridical person, the State Party of incorporation or registration of the investor in accordance with the laws and regulations of that State Party, and where that legal or juridical person maintains its statutory seat together with substantial business;

"Host State" means the State Party where the investment is made, undertaken or located;

"Investment" means an enterprise or company, as defined in this Article, which is established, acquired or expanded in conformity with the laws and regulations of a Host State by an investor which maintains substantial business in the territory of that Host State. The enterprise or company may possess assets, such as:

a. shares, stocks, or any other form of participation of the enterprise/company or another enterprise/company;
b. movable and immovable property including mortgages, liens, pledges, and any other similar rights as defined in conformity with the laws and regulations of the State Party in whose territory the property is situated;
c. intellectual property rights such as copyrights, patents, trademarks, industrial designs, trade names, know-how and goodwill to the extent they are acquired, maintained and protected under the law of the Host State;
d. rights conferred by the law of the Host State or under contract, including licences to cultivate, or to extract or exploit natural resources; or
e. rights under contracts including turnkey, construction, production, management, concession or other contract;

For greater certainty, the investment must have the following characteristics: commitment of capital or other resources, the expectation of gain or profit, a certain duration, assumption of risk, and a significant contribution to the Host State's sustainable development;

For avoidance of doubt, establishment, acquisition and expansion under this Protocol only apply to the post-establishment phase;

For further avoidance of doubt, only investment that meet the criteria under the present Article qualify as eligible investments under this Protocol; For greater certainty, investment does not include:

a. debt securities issued by a government or loans to a government or government- owned or controlled enterprise;
b. portfolio investments, that is, investment that does not give the investor the possibility to exercise effective management or influence in the management of the enterprise;
c. claims to money that arise solely from commercial contracts for the sale of goods or services by a national or enterprise in the territory of a State Party to an enterprise in the territory of another State Party, or the extension of credit in connection with a commercial transaction; or
d. claims arising from an order or judgment rendered in any judicial, administrative or arbitral proceeding;

"Investment-related human rights" mean human rights directly related to investment activity, including in particular environmental, health and core labour rights";

"Investor" means:

a. a natural person, who is a national of a State Party in accordance with its laws and regulations, who has made an investment in the territory of another State Party. For greater certainty, a natural person who holds dual nationality shall be deemed to be exclusively a national of the country of her or his effective nationality or where she/he ordinarily or permanently resides;
b. a legal or juridical person, in accordance with the definition of the legal or juridical person of the Home State in this article, that has made an investment in the territory of the Host State;

"Measures" include any regulatory, administrative, legislative, judicial or policy decision that is taken by the Host State, relating to or affecting an investment in the Host State;

"Protocol" means the Protocol to the Agreement Establishing the AfCFTA on Investment;

"State Party" means a Member State that has ratified or acceded to the Protocol and for which the Protocol is in force;

"Substantial business activity" requires an overall examination of all the circumstances on a case-by-case basis, by a State Party, of all the circumstances, including, among other factors: (i) the nature, size, scope and sector of business, (ii) the amount of investment brought into the territory of a State Party, (iii) the effect of the investment on the local community and (iv) the length of time the investment has been in operation;

Generally, an investment shall be taken to have substantial business activities in the territory of a State Party where it conducts its core and relevant income generating activities, through the employment of a reasonable number of suitably qualified persons and by having a minimum level of expenditure which is proportionate to its level of the relevant activities in the territory of that State Party;

For greater certainty, the overall assessment on the case-by-case basis shall take into account the specific economic and investment policies of the concerned State Party at the time of the admission of the investment;

"Sustainable Development" embodies, in accordance with relevant United Nations documents and resolutions, the three interdependent and mutually reinforcing pillars that are economic development, social development and environmental protection;

"Third Party" means a State that is not a party to this Protocol;

Article 2
Objectives

The objectives of this Protocol are as follows:

a. encouraging intra-African investment flows and opportunities and promoting, facilitating, retaining, protecting and expanding investments that foster sustainable development of State Parties;
b. establishing a balanced, predictable and transparent continental legal and institutional framework for investment, taking into account the interests of State Parties, investors and local communities;
c. providing a sound legal framework for the prevention, management and settlement of investment disputes;
d. encouraging the acquisition and transfer of appropriate and relevant technology in Africa; and
e. promoting, enhancing and consolidating coordinated positions and cooperation on matters related to investment promotion, facilitation and protection within the continent.

Article 3
Scope of Application

1. This Protocol sets out the rights and obligations for State Parties, investors and investments.
2. This Protocol shall apply to:
   a. all investments of investors of State Parties made after the entry into force of this Protocol; and
   b. all investments of investors of State Parties made prior to the entry into force of this Protocol provided that they meet the criteria of an investment under Article 1 of this

Protocol and that they are still present on the territory of the Host State at the time of the entry into force of this Protocol.

3. The obligations of a State Party under this Protocol shall apply to measures adopted or maintained by:
   a. its central, regional or local governments and administrations; and
   b. non-governmental bodies when exercising powers delegated by central, regional or local governments or authorities.

For greater certainty, in the implementation of its obligations and commitments defined under this Protocol, each State Party shall take reasonable steps to ensure that regional and local governments and authorities and relevant non-governmental bodies within its territory comply with them.

4. This Protocol shall not apply to:
   a. any investment dispute that arose or any claim that was settled before the entry into force of the Protocol;
   b. government procurement;
   c. subsidies or grants provided by a State Party, including government-supported loans, guarantees and insurance under national development programmes;
   d. investments made with capital or assets of illegal origin in accordance with the applicable laws and regulations of a State Party;
   e. taxation measures taken in accordance with the applicable laws and regulations of a State Party;
   f. any special advantages accorded in the Host State by finance institutions for the purpose of development assistance or the development of small and medium businesses or new industries;
   g. operations of public debt and state enterprise debt restructuring taken by one of the State Parties; and
   h. real estate or other property other than acquired for the purpose of economic benefit or other business purposes.
5. This Protocol shall not apply to any dispute arising solely from an alleged breach of a contract between a State Party and an investor.
6. For greater certainty, and subject to the applicable international law, references to "indigenous people", "local communities" and "underrepresented groups" in this Protocol do not apply on the territory of State Parties which do not recognise those groups under their domestic laws and regulations.

Article 4
Admission of Investment

Each State Party shall admit investments in accordance with its domestic laws and regulations.

Article 5
Denial of Benefits

1. A State Party may at any time deny an investor of another State Party and the investment of such investor the benefits of this Protocol if:
   a. an investment has no substantial business activity in the territory of the Home State;
   b. an investment has been established or restructured with the primary purpose of gaining access to the dispute settlement mechanism under this Protocol;

c. an investor or investment is engaged in activities prejudicial to the essential and national interests of the Host State;
d. an investment is owned or controlled, directly or indirectly, by natural or juridical persons of a Third Party with which the denying Party does not maintain a diplomatic relationship or toward which it prohibits transactions;
e. an investment is owned or controlled, directly or indirectly, by natural or legal persons of the denying Host State;
f. an investment is owned or controlled, directly or indirectly, by natural or juridical persons of a non-State Party that has no substantial business in the territory of a State Party; or
g. an investor or investment has committed a breach of a specific binding obligation under Chapter 5 of this Protocol.

2. For the avoidance of doubt, the exercise by a Host State of its right to deny benefits to an investor of another State Party and investment of such investor may be subject of review in accordance with Chapter 7 of this Protocol.

CHAPTER 2

INVESTMENT PROMOTION AND FACILITATION

Article 6
Investment Promotion

The State Parties shall endeavour to promote and increase awareness of Africa as the preferred investment destination including by:

a. encouraging investments among the State Parties;
b. organising joint investment promotion activities between or among State Parties;
c. promoting business matching events, partnerships, and joint ventures between companies in Africa;
d. organising and supporting the organisation of various continental or international conferences and seminars on investment opportunities and on investment laws, regulations, and policies;
e. coordinating with the Pan-African Trade and Investment Agency and Regional Economic Communities to undertake investment promotion activities;
f. conducting information exchanges on other issues of mutual concern relating to investment promotion; or
g. promoting investments that contribute to gender equality, the empowerment of women, youth and people with disabilities.

Article 7
Investment Facilitation

1. State Parties shall, subject to their respective laws and regulations, facilitate investments that contribute to sustainable development.
2. State Parties shall, subject to their respective laws and regulations, facilitate the granting of visas and permits to foreign workers, employees and consultants as designated by the investor.

3. State Parties are encouraged to streamline investment administration procedures and requirements, establish mechanisms for business entry facilitation including setting up One Stop Shops, aftercare services and digitalisation of business facilitation procedures.
4. State Parties are encouraged to establish a framework for cooperation and coordination between relevant and competent national regulatory authorities with a view to facilitating investment flows.
5. State Parties may cooperate on policies and other related issues that encourage and facilitate the use of "special purpose vehicles" to increase the participation of the private sector in development programmes of State Parties.
6. State Parties are encouraged to cooperate in the provision of aftercare services for cross border investments to encourage retention and expansion of investment in the continent.

Article 8
Incentives for Sustainable Investments

1. State Parties may introduce incentives in order to attract, retain and expand investments that foster sustainable development of State Parties. Such incentives may include among others:
   a. financial and fiscal incentives, such as investment insurance, grants or loans at concessionary rates;
   b. subsidised infrastructure or services, and market preferences;
   c. development-oriented incentives to encourage preferential markets schemes and specific investments in Africa especially in the sectors related to attaining sustainable development;
   d. incentives for technology, technical assistance, technology transfer, and research and development;
   e. investment guarantees;
   f. incentives for low-carbon investments; or
   g. incentives to encourage investors' responsible business conduct.
2. State Parties may harmonise incentive policies for investments that are of strategic interest to such State Parties with the assistance of the AfCFTA Secretariat.

Article 9
National Focal Points

1. Each State Party shall designate a National Focal Point which shall provide support to investors from other State Parties.
2. State Parties shall, through their National Focal Points, provide relevant information on the legal, policy and institutional frameworks governing investments, including among others:
   a. regulatory matters and procedures, administrative practices and legislation on the establishment of companies and joint ventures or other investment-related public policies;
   b. requirements and procedures, fees, taxes and charges, financial and fiscal incentives, technical standards, construction permits, capital transfers, procedures for appealing or reviewing decisions on applications for authorisation and indicative timeframes for processing applications; and
   c. investment-related government programmes and incentives.
3. Each State Party shall ensure that its National Focal Point cooperates and liaises with other National Focal Points in order to carry out their functions under this Article.

Article 10
Publication of Information

1. Each State Party, in accordance with its capabilities, shall publish and make accessible electronically or through other means, in a reasonable period of time, all relevant laws and regulations which pertain to or affect the operation of this Protocol. International and regional agreements pertaining to or affecting bilateral, regional or international investment to which a State Party is a signatory shall also be published.
2. State Parties shall provide adequate information on relevant national laws and policies to enable investors carry out their operations in compliance with such laws and policies.
3. Each State Party shall respond within a period not exceeding six (6) months to all formal requests by any other State Party for specific information on any of its laws, regulations, measures, international and regional agreements pertaining to this Protocol. State Parties to the extent practicable shall also respond to any question from any other State Party relating to any measure that might substantially affect the operation of this Protocol.

Article 11
Non-Disclosure of Confidential Information

Nothing in this Protocol shall require any State Party to disclose confidential information and data, the disclosure of which would impede law enforcement, prejudice legitimate commercial and strategic interests of particular enterprises or institutions whether public or private or would otherwise be contrary to the public or essential security interests.

CHAPTER 3

INVESTMENT PROTECTION STANDARDS

Article 12
National Treatment

1. Each State Party shall accord to investors of another State Party and their investments treatment no less favourable than it accords, in like circumstances, to its own investors with respect to the management, conduct, operation, use, expansion and sale or other disposition of their investments.
2. In assessing "in like circumstances" an overall examination is required on a case by-case basis, of all the circumstances of an investment, including, among others:
   a. its effects on third persons and the local community;
   b. its effects on the local, regional or national environment, the health of the populations, or on the global commons;
   c. the sector in which the investor is active;
   d. the aim of the measure in question;
   e. the regulatory process generally applied in relation to a measure in question; and
   f. any other factor directly relating to the investment or investor in relation to the measure in question.

The examination referred to in this Paragraph shall not be limited to or biased towards any one of the factors.

Article 13
Exceptions to National Treatment

1. Measures taken by a State Party that are designed and applied to protect or enhance legitimate public policy objectives such as, but not limited to, public morals, public health, prevention of diseases and pests in animals or plants, climate action, essential security interests, safety and the protection of environment shall not be construed as a breach of Article 12.
2. Preferential treatment granted by State Parties to national investments and investors, in accordance with domestic laws and regulations, in order to achieve national development objectives or address the internal needs of designated disadvantaged persons, groups, or regions shall not be construed as a breach of Article 12.
3. Each State Party reserves the right to adopt or maintain certain exceptions to the standard of national treatment provided by Article 12 to investments made by investors of another State Party in its territory if those exceptions fall within one of the sectors or geographical regions that represent strategic importance for the Host State in accordance with its laws and regulations.
4. For greater certainty, discriminatory measures taken by a State Party to comply with its obligations under other regional or international agreements shall not be construed as a breach of Article 12.

Article 14
Most-Favoured Nation Treatment

1. Each State Party shall accord to investors of another State Party and their investments treatment no less favourable than it accords, in like circumstances, to investors of any other State Party or Third Parties with respect to the management, conduct, operation, use, expansion and sale or other disposition of their investments.
2. The provisions of Article 12, Paragraph 2 of this Protocol on assessing "in like circumstances" shall apply *mutatis mutandis* to this Article.
3. For greater certainty, the "treatment" referred to in Paragraphs 1 and 2 does not include dispute settlement procedures, including, but not limited to, those related to admissibility and jurisdiction, provided for in other treaties. Substantive obligations in other investment treaties, do not in themselves constitute "treatment", and cannot give rise to a breach of this Article.

Article 15
Exceptions to Most-Favoured Nation Treatment

1. Measures taken by a State Party that are designed and applied to protect or enhance legitimate public policy objectives, such as, but not limited to, public morals, public health, prevention of diseases and pests in animals or plants, climate action, essential security interests, safety and the protection of environment, shall not be construed as a breach of Article 14.
2. Nothing in Article 14 shall oblige a State Party to extend to the investors and their investments the benefit of any treatment, preference or privilege contained in:
   a. any existing or future free trade area, customs union, common market agreement or any similar international agreements or arrangements to which the investor's Home State is not a Party; or
   b. any existing or future international agreement or domestic legislation relating wholly or mainly to taxation.

Article 16

Interpretation of Non-Discrimination

Articles 12, 13, 14 and 15 shall govern the definition, scope, application and interpretation of all references to non-discrimination or non-discriminatory measures under this Protocol.

Article 17

Administrative and Judicial Treatment

1. Each State Party shall ensure that, in administrative and judicial matters, investors and investments of another State Party are not subject to treatment which constitutes a fundamental denial of justice in criminal, civil and administrative adjudicative proceedings, an evident denial of due process, a manifest arbitrariness, a discrimination based on gender, race or religious beliefs, or an abusive treatment in administrative and judicial proceedings.
2. For greater certainty, Paragraph 1 shall not be interpreted as equivalent to fair and equitable treatment. For further certainty, Paragraph 1 includes the minimum standard of treatment under customary international law and does not allow for an interpretation and application of such a standard that would go beyond the elements contained in Paragraph 1.

Article 18

Physical Protection and Security

1. A State Party shall, subject to its capabilities, accord to investors and their investments physical protection and security no less favourable than that which it accords to the investments of its own investors or to the investments of the investors of any other State Party or Third Party.

For greater certainty, the expression "subject to its capabilities" refers to the obligation of due diligence that a State Party shall exercise on its territory in accordance with customary international law and does not allow for an interpretation and application of such a standard that would go beyond the elements contained in this Paragraph.

2. Investors of one State Party whose investments in the territory of the other State Party suffer losses as a result of a failure of the Host State to comply with Paragraph 1, owing to war or other armed conflict, revolution, revolt, insurrection or riot in the territory of the Host State shall, as regards restitution, indemnification, compensation or other settlement, be accorded by the Host State treatment no less favourable than that which the Host State accords to investments of its own natural and legal persons or to investments of investors of any other State Party or Third Party.

Article 19

Expropriation

1. State Parties shall not, directly or indirectly, expropriate or nationalise investments in their territory except:
   a. for a public purpose;
   b. in accordance with due process pursuant to the procedure established by the laws of the State Party;
   c. in a non-discriminatory manner; and

d. against a fair and adequate compensation paid within a reasonable period of time in accordance with Article 21, and taking into account that the assessment of the reasonable period of time shall be made on a case-by-case basis in accordance with the domestic laws and regulations of the State Party and on a non- discriminatory basis.

2. For the purposes of this Protocol:
   a. direct expropriation occurs when an investment is nationalised or expropriated directly, through a formal transfer of ownership or outright seizure;
   b. indirect expropriation results from a measure or a series of measures having an equivalent effect of direct expropriation without formal transfer of title or outright seizure. The sole fact that a measure or a series of measures has an adverse effect on the economic value of an investment does not establish that an indirect expropriation has occurred; and
   c. the determination of whether a measure or a series of measures have an effect equivalent to expropriation requires a case-by-case, fact-based inquiry, that takes into consideration among others:
      i. the duration of the measure or series of measures of a State Party; and
      ii. the character of the measure or series of measures, notably their object, context and intent.

Article 20
Exceptions to Expropriation

1. Nothing in Article 19 shall prevent the issuance of compulsory licences granted in relation to intellectual property rights, or to the revocation, limitation, or creation of intellectual property rights, in accordance with international obligations and other relevant Protocols under the Agreement, where applicable.
2. Non-discriminatory regulatory actions by a State Party designed to protect legitimate public policy objectives, such as public morals, public health, prevention of diseases and pests in animals or plants, climate action, essential security interests, safety and the protection of the environment, labour rights or to comply with other international obligations, shall not constitute indirect expropriation.

Article 21
Compensation for Expropriation

1. Fair and adequate compensation shall be assessed on a case-by-case basis in relation to the fair market value of the expropriated investment, and in a reasonable period of time, in accordance with domestic laws and regulation.
2. The assessment of fair and adequate compensation shall be based on an equitable balance between the public interest and interest of those affected, having regard for all relevant circumstances and taking account of the current and past use of the investment, the history of its acquisition, the fair market value of the investment, the purpose of the expropriation, the extent of previous profit made by the investor through the investment, the previous behaviour of the investor, and the duration of the investment.
3. Compensation shall be assessed based on the fair market value of the expropriated investment at the date immediately before the expropriation took place ("date of expropriation") or before the measure became publicly known, whichever is earlier. For greater certainty, the fair and adequate compensation standard also applies in case of unlawful expropriation.

4. The computation of the fair market value of the expropriated property shall exclude any consequential losses or speculative or windfall profits claimed by the investor.
5. Any payment of compensation according to this Article shall be made in a freely convertible currency. Payment shall include simple interest at the applicable commercial rate in the Host State from the date of expropriation until the date of actual payment. On payment, compensation shall be freely transferable.

Article 22
Transfer of Funds

1. State Parties shall, in accordance with national laws and regulations, permit all transfers relating to an investment to be made freely and without delay in and out of the territory after payment of the respective taxes and duties, such transfers may include:
   a. initial capital and additional amounts to maintain or increase investment;
   b. profits, capital gains, dividends, royalties, interests and other current income accruing from an investment;
   c. the proceeds from sale of all or any part of or from total or partial liquidation of a covered investment;
   d. repayments made pursuant to a loan agreement in direct connection with an investment;
   e. license fees in relation to investment;
   f. payments in respect of technical services and management fees;
   g. payments in connection with contracting projects;
   h. earnings, such as wages and salaries, of staff who work in connection with an investment; or
   i. payments arising under the dispute settlement mechanism of this Protocol or any compensation paid in relation to an investment.
2. The Host State, subject to the choice of the investor, shall allow transfers to be made in the currency of the host economy, or in a freely convertible currency recognised by the International Monetary Fund (IMF), at the market rate of exchange prevailing on the date of the transfer, in accordance with the laws and regulations of the Host State.

Article 23
Exceptions to Transfer of Funds

1. A State Party may apply non-discriminatory restrictions on transfers of funds relating to investments made in its territory in accordance with its domestic laws and regulations where applicable and in particular, relating to:
   a. fulfilment of tax obligations to the Host State;
   b. bankruptcy, insolvency, or the protection of the rights of creditors;
   c. issuing, trading or dealing in securities, futures, options or derivatives;
   d. criminal or penal offences and the recovery of the proceeds of crime;
   e. financial reporting or record keeping of transactions when necessary to assist law enforcement or financial regulatory authorities;
   f. ensuring compliance with orders or judgments in judicial or administrative proceedings;
   g. social security, public retirement or compulsory savings schemes;
   h. severance entitlements of employees; or
   i. anti-money laundering and financing of terrorism.

2. A State Party may adopt or maintain non-discriminatory measures not conforming with its obligations relating to the free transfer of funds:
   a. in the event or threat of serious balance-of-payments deficits or external financial difficulties; or
   b. in exceptional circumstances where movements of capital cause or threaten to cause serious economic or financial difficulties in the State Party concerned.
3. Subject to the reservations of each State Party, nothing in Article 22 shall affect the rights and obligations of a State Party that is a member of the IMF under the IMF Articles of Agreement, including the right to apply a safeguard measure at the request of the IMF.
4. The State Party applying a safeguard measure contemplated in Paragraphs 1 and 2 shall promptly notify the AfCFTA Secretariat and provide a schedule for its removal within a reasonable period of time. For greater certainty, these safeguard measures shall:
   a. avoid unnecessary damage to the economic and financial interests of investors and other State Parties;
   b. be proportionate in the circumstances; and
   c. be temporary and phased out progressively as the situation necessitating the safeguard measure improves.

CHAPTER 4

SUSTAINABLE DEVELOPMENT-RELATED ISSUES

Article 24
Right to Regulate

1. In accordance with customary international law and other general principles of international law, each State Party has the right to regulate, including to take measures to ensure that investment in its territory is consistent with the goals and principles of sustainable development, and with other national environmental, health, climate action, social and economic policy objectives and essential security interests.
2. For greater certainty, measures taken by a State Party to comply with its international obligations under other relevant treaties shall not constitute a breach of this Protocol.
3. For avoidance of doubt, the exercise of the right to regulate under Paragraphs 1 and 2 cannot give rise to any claim by an investor for compensation.

Article 25
Minimum Standards on the Environment, Labour and Consumer Protection

1. State Parties shall ensure environmental, labour, and consumer protection, taking into account domestic policies, international best standards and relevant international agreements to which they are parties, and shall continue to improve their standards within their domestic laws and regulations.
2. State Parties shall not encourage investment by relaxing or waiving domestic standards, or compliance with environment, labour and consumer protection laws and international minimum standards.

Article 26
Investment and Climate Change

In accordance with their domestic climate change policies, the principle of Common but Differentiated Responsibilities, and relevant international climate change instruments, each State Party shall:

a. promote and facilitate investments that support actions to mitigate greenhouse gas emissions and measures to adapt to the negative impacts of climate change;
b. promote and facilitate investments that support initiatives conducive to the financing of regional climate mitigation and adaptation programmes;
c. promote and facilitate investment of relevance for a fair and just transition in sectors such as renewable energy, low-carbon technologies, and by adopting policy frameworks conducive to transfer and deployment of climate-friendly technologies and goods and services, taking into account socio-economic constraints, in particular those related to the transition of the workforce;
d. promote, facilitate and encourage new investment regimes, such as low or zero carbon Special Economic Zones;
e. encourage investments that mitigate climate change impacts on exhaustible natural resources such as fresh water and biological diversity; and
f. cooperate with the other State Parties on investment-related aspects of climate change policies and measures.

Article 27
Investment, Public Health and Pandemics

1. Each State Party has the right to determine its public health policies and priorities, to establish its own levels of domestic public health protection, and to adopt or modify its relevant laws and measures in the context of epidemics, pandemics and other public health emergencies in accordance with its international commitments.
2. Each State Party shall, in accordance with national laws and regulations, promote and facilitate investments in the public health sector and the subsectors and related industries, including medical equipment, pharmaceuticals especially for chronic diseases, vaccines and Intensive Care Units requirements.
3. State Parties shall cooperate to identify relevant investment policies and measures to address epidemics, pandemics and other public health emergencies in accordance with the decisions and declarations of the African Union.

Article 28
Pursuit of Development Goals

Pursuant to the objectives set out in this Protocol, State Parties may introduce measures to promote domestic development including local content, taking into account Articles 12, 13, 14 and 15. Measures covered under this Article include among others:

a. granting of preferential treatment to any enterprise or company qualifying under the domestic law of a State Party in order to achieve national, sub-regional, or regional development goals;
b. supporting the development of local entrepreneurs and to establish linkages with local firms, supply chains, industries and institutions with a view to strengthening local capabilities;

c. enhancing productive and trade capacity, generating employment, wealth creation, developing human resource capacity and training, research and development;
d. appointing, where appropriate, as executives, managers or members of board of directors, nationals from the State Party where the investment is made;
e. promoting transfer of technology, skills and know-how, innovation and other benefits, a production process or other proprietary knowledge; or
f. addressing economic and development disparities suffered by identifiable ethnic or cultural groups, including historically marginalised groups or geographical regions and localities.

Article 29
Human Resources Development

1. State Parties shall develop national policies to guide investors in developing human capacity of the labour force, including for mid-level and managerial positions. Such policies may include incentives to encourage employers to invest in training, capacity building and knowledge transfer.
2. In developing such policies, State Parties shall pay particular attention to the needs of youth, women, persons with disabilities and vulnerable groups.
3. State Parties are encouraged to develop and enforce mutual recognition agreements on human resource development in collaboration with the AfCFTA Secretariat, in particular on qualification and experience leading to certificates and diplomas.

Article 30
Transfer of Technology

State Parties, in accordance with their domestic laws and regulation and their respective capabilities, shall facilitate the intra-regional and international transfer of technology by various measures, such as:

a. accessing available information regarding description, location and, as far as possible, approximate cost of technology;
b. establishing or strengthening of technology transfer centres;
c. providing training for research, engineering, design and other personnel engaged in the development of national technologies or in the adaptation and use of technologies transferred;
d. providing assistance in the development and implementation of laws and regulations with a view to facilitating the transfer of technology;
e. encouraging the granting credits on preferential terms for financing the acquisition of capital and intermediate goods in the context of approved development projects involving transfer of technology transaction;
f. assisting in the development of technological capabilities of the companies and their personnel;
g. encouraging investors to adopt in the course of their business activities, practices that permit the transfer and rapid diffusion of technologies and know-how, with due regard to the protection of intellectual property rights, on reasonable terms and conditions; and
h. fostering conditions that encourage investors to undertake research and development in a manner that contributes to the national development goals of the Host State.

CHAPTER 5

INVESTOR OBLIGATIONS

Article 31

Relation to State Party Obligations

1. Notwithstanding the investor obligations set out in this Chapter, the provisions in this Chapter are without prejudice to the obligations of the State Parties to promote and enforce, among others:
   a. laws and policies to protect investment-related human rights, labour rights and the environment;
   b. anti-corruption, anti-money laundering, anti-terrorism financing and anti-bribery measures; or
   c. laws and policies to protect the rights of indigenous peoples and local communities.
2. State Parties shall ensure that investors and their investments comply with their domestic law and regulations and international law.

Article 32

Compliance with National and International Law

Investors and their investments shall carry out their operations in compliance with all relevant domestic laws and regulations, administrative guidelines as well as applicable international law.

Article 33

Business Ethics, Human Rights and Labour Standards

Investors and their investments shall comply with high standards of business ethics, investment-related human rights and labour standards, and in particular shall:

a. support and respect the protection of internationally recognised human rights;
b. ensure that they are not complicit in human rights abuses;
c. comply with the International Labour Organisation (ILO) standards, including the ILO Declaration on Fundamental Principles and Rights at Work, and domestic labour legislations;
d. not use child labour or forced and compulsory labour;
e. eliminate discrimination in respect of employment and occupation;
f. refrain from discriminatory or disciplinary action against employees who submit reports to the company's board or to the competent public authorities about practices that violate domestic laws, this Protocol, or other standards of corporate governance to which the company is subject; and
g. act in accordance with fair business, marketing and advertising practices when dealing with consumers and must ensure the safety and quality of goods and services they provide.

Article 34

Environmental Protection

1. Investors and their investments shall, in carrying out their business activities, respect and protect the environment, and, in particular shall:
   a. respect the right to a clean, healthy and sustainable environment, as reflected in Article 24 of the African Charter of Human and Peoples' Rights, and the Resolution of the

United Nations General Assembly A/RES/76/300 ("The human right to a clean, healthy and sustainable environment");

b. comply with the principles of prevention and precaution when conducting their business activities to anticipate and prevent any risk of significant harm to the environment;
c. carry out an environmental impact assessment, in accordance with the best international standards and practices and as required by domestic law;
d. apply the precautionary principle to their environmental impact assessment and to decisions taken in relation to a proposed investment, including any necessary mitigating or alternative approaches to the investment, or precluding the investment if necessary; and
e. where their business activities cause or may cause harm to the environment, take steps to mitigate the harm, to restore impacted sites and ensure a clean, healthy and sustainable environment.

2. Investors shall not exploit or use natural resources to the detriment of the rights and interests of the Host State and local communities.

Article 35
Indigenous Peoples and Local Communities

1. Investors and their investments shall respect the rights and dignity of indigenous peoples and local communities in accordance with relevant domestic laws and regulations, international law, norms and best practices, including the right of indigenous peoples, and local communities where applicable, to free, prior and informed consent and to participate in the benefit of the investment.

For greater certainty, the reference to the right to free, prior and informed consent of indigenous peoples, does not imply any obligation for investors and their investments to conclude agreements with those groups before conducting or operating their investment in the territory of State Parties which do not recognise indigenous peoples, taking into account applicable and relevant domestic laws and regulations.

2. Investors and their investments shall respect legitimate tenure rights to land, water, fisheries, and forests in accordance with relevant laws and regulations.
3. Investors, in accordance with relevant domestic law and regulations, shall submit their environmental and social impact assessments to the competent authorities and make them available and accessible to local communities and indigenous peoples and to any other stakeholder in the territory of the Host State.

Article 36
Socio-Political Obligations

Investors shall refrain from any interference in the internal affairs of State Parties and in their intergovernmental relations, in particular to influence the appointment of persons to public office, finance political parties or undermine the political stability or security of the Host State or to influence public opinion in a manner contrary to this Article.

Article 37
Anti-Corruption

1. Investors and their investments shall not offer, promise or give any unlawful or undue pecuniary or other advantage or present, whether directly or through intermediaries, to a public official of a State Party, or to a member of an official's family or business associate

or other person in order to obtain a favour or that the official or other person act or refrain from acting in relation to the performance of official duties.

2. Investors shall cooperate with State Parties in preventing and eliminating corruption in public governance and shall not encourage, incite, aid, abet or conspire with any official or another person or any entity to commit or authorise the commission of an act of corruption, taking into account applicable and relevant domestic laws and regulations, the African Union Convention on Preventing and Combatting Corruption, the United Nations Convention against Corruption and other applicable international legal instruments.
3. Notwithstanding relevant international obligations of State Parties regarding anti-corruption, a breach of this Article by an investor is deemed to constitute a breach of the domestic laws and regulations of the Host State concerning the establishment and operation of an investment.

Article 38
Corporate Social Responsibility

1. Investors and their investments shall endeavour to achieve the highest possible level of contribution to the sustainable development of the Host State and the local community, through the adoption of a high degree of socially responsible practices, in accordance with the principles and standards set out in Paragraph 2 of this Article.
2. Investors and their investments shall endeavour to:
   a. stimulate economic, social and environmental progress, aiming at achieving sustainable development;
   b. encourage the strengthening of local capacities through close cooperation with the local community;
   c. encourage the development of human capital, especially by creating employment opportunities and facilitating access of workers to professional training;
   d. promote gender equality and inclusiveness in their activities;
   e. refrain from seeking exemptions that are not established in the legislation of the Host State, relating to environment, health, security, work or financial incentives, or other issues;
   f. develop and apply effective self-regulatory practices and management systems that foster a relationship of mutual trust between the companies and the community in which the operations are conducted;
   g. promote the knowledge of workers about corporate policies, through appropriate dissemination of these policies, including programmes for professional training;
   h. encourage, whenever possible the business associates, including service providers and sub-contractors, to apply the principles of corporate social responsibility provided for in this Article; and
   i. foster the benefit sharing arising from an investment with the local communities concerned based on mutually agreed terms to facilitate access to an adequate standard of living.
3. State Parties undertake to encourage investors operating within their territories or subject to their jurisdiction to incorporate into their internal policies internationally recognised standards, guidelines and principles of corporate social responsibility including those set out in Paragraph 2 of this Article.

Article 39
Corporate Governance

1. Investors and their investments shall meet national, regional and internationally accepted standards of corporate governance, in particular in respect of transparency and accounting practices.

2. Investors and their investments shall, in accordance with domestic laws and regulations:
   a. ensure the equitable treatment of all shareholders;
   b. encourage active cooperation with their stakeholders to create wealth, jobs, and sustainable financial management;
   c. make timely and accurate disclosure on all material matters regarding an enterprise or company, including the financial situation, performance, ownership, and governance of the enterprise or company, risks related to environmental liabilities, and any other matters relating to the enterprise and company in accordance with the relevant and applicable regulations and requirements; and
   d. comply with national policies on human resource development and to the extent possible invest in training, capacity building, and knowledge transfer through programmes for human resource development.
3. State Parties are encouraged to improve their regulatory and institutional framework for corporate governance in support of the requirements of this Article.
4. State Parties shall put in place measures enhancing transparency in financial reporting, disclosure, accounting, and audit practices in support of the requirements of this Article, in accordance with domestic laws, regulations and applicable international standards and obligations.

Article 40
Taxation and Transfer Pricing

1. Investors and their investments shall:
   a. ensure that all transactions with related or affiliated companies are arm's length transactions at fair market price in accordance with the domestic regulations of the Host State and relevant international best practices;
   b. conduct their operations in a manner that fully complies with all applicable domestic tax laws and international rules and principles relating to base erosion and profit shifting practices; and
   c. provide all information required by the Host State to ensure compliance with the applicable laws relating to taxation.
2. State Parties shall, in accordance with the applicable international legal instruments, cooperate in the detection and prevention of transfer pricing manipulation by investors, including in the provision of information necessary to identify and prevent such practices and providing opportunities for Joint Audits within the framework of mutual administrative assistance in tax matters.

CHAPTER 6

INSTITUTIONAL ARRANGEMENTS

Article 41
Committee on Investment

1. The Committee on Investment, as established in accordance with Article 11 of the Agreement ("the Committee"), shall carry out such functions as assigned to it by the Council of Ministers to facilitate the implementation of this Protocol and further its objectives.

2. The Committee may establish such sub-committees and working groups as it considers necessary for the effective discharge of its functions with the approval of the Council of Ministers.

Article 42

Establishment of the Pan-African Trade and Investment Agency

1. The Assembly of Heads of State and Government of the African Union hereby establishes the Pan-African Trade and Investment Agency ("the Agency") as a technical institution of the AfCFTA Secretariat.
2. The Council of Ministers shall recommend to the Assembly of Heads of State and Government of the African Union, the adoption of the appropriate governance and administrative structures, functions of the Agency, as well as, rules and procedures for the administration and operation of the Agency, including determination of the seat of the Agency that shall be elaborated in an Annex. Upon adoption by the Assembly of Heads of State and Government of the African Union, the Annex shall form an integral part of this Protocol.
3. The Agency shall assist State Parties, their investment promotion agencies and their private sector through mobilising financial resources, fostering business development and providing technical and other support for the promotion and facilitation of investment in accordance with the provisions of this Protocol.
4. The Agency shall also assist State Parties in building their capacity in the formulation and implementation of investment policies to foster the expansion of intra-African investments, and especially those that increase exports; as well as facilitating coordination, interaction and dialogue between and among national focal points, investment promotion agencies and other relevant stakeholders to enable the sharing of information with respect to trade, export promotion, investment opportunities, peer learning and good practices.
5. The resources of the Agency's budget shall be derived from the annual budget of the AfCFTA Secretariat. Other sources of budget may be recommended by the Council of Ministers, for the consideration of the Executive Council of the African Union including:
   a. fees collected by the Agency in the course of its operations;
   b. any grants, donations, bequests or other contributions made to the Agency; and
   c. all other payments due to the Agency in respect of any matter incidental to its functions.
6. The AfCFTA Secretariat shall undertake the functions of the Agency, on an interim basis, until its operationalisation.

Article 43

Technical Assistance, Capacity Building and Cooperation

1. State Parties shall support the provision of technical assistance, capacity building and cooperation to promote and facilitate investment under this Protocol.
2. To further the implementation of these provisions, the AfCFTA Secretariat working with the Agency upon its operationalisation, State Parties, Regional Economic Communities and partners shall coordinate the provision of technical assistance and undertake activities to enhance capacity building.

CHAPTER 7

MANAGEMENT AND SETTLEMENT OF DISPUTES

Article 44
State-State Dispute Settlement

1. The relevant provisions of the Protocol on the Rules and Procedures on the Settlement of Disputes shall apply to consultations and the settlement of disputes between State Parties relating to the interpretation and application of this Protocol.
2. For greater certainty, Paragraph 1 incorporates the right for a State Party to submit a claim on behalf of its nationals through the exercise of diplomatic protection and in accordance with customary international law.

Article 45
Dispute Prevention and Grievance Management

State Parties shall, through their designated competent bodies, facilitate the prevention of disputes and management of grievances by:

a. receiving complaints or grievances from investors in relation to their investments;
b. following-up and undertaking actions for de-escalating potential differences, or disagreements between investors and State Parties; and
c. providing effective assistance in resolving difficulties experienced by investors and their investments in such a manner as to avoid disputes.

Article 46
Dispute Resolution

1. In the event of a dispute between an investor of a State Party and a Host State relating to an alleged breach of this Protocol, the investor and the Host State shall initially seek to resolve amicably the dispute through consultations, negotiations, conciliation, mediation or other amicable dispute resolution mechanisms available in the Host State.
2. Notwithstanding the outcome of the dispute prevention and grievances management process under Article 45, in the event that an investor of a State Party and the Host State are unable to amicably resolve the dispute in accordance with Paragraph 1, they may seek to resolve such dispute in accordance with the dispute resolution mechanisms to be provided in the Annex referred to in Paragraph 3.
3. Rules and Procedures governing Dispute Prevention, Management and Resolution of disputes covered by this Protocol, shall be set out in an Annex to this Protocol. The Annex shall be negotiated after the adoption of this Protocol by the Assembly of Heads of State and Government of the Africa Union, and finalised within 12 months at the latest from the date of adoption of this Protocol. The Annex, upon adoption by the Assembly of Heads of State and Government of the Africa Union, shall form an integral part of this Protocol.

Article 47
Investor Liability

1. Investors and their investments shall, where applicable and in accordance with domestic laws and regulations, be subject to civil actions for liability in the judicial process of their

Home State for the acts, decisions or omissions made in the Host State in relation to the investment where such acts, decisions or omissions lead to damage, personal injuries or loss of life in the Host State.

2. State Parties shall develop rules and procedures that allow for, or do not prevent or unduly restrict, the bringing of court actions relating to the civil liability of investors in the territory of their Home States, taking into account rules governing conflict of laws and the recognition and enforcement of foreign judgments.
3. For greater certainty, this Article does not exclude the possibility to bring civil actions against investors and their investments before the domestic courts of the Host State.

CHAPTER 8

FINAL PROVISIONS

Article 48
Entry into Force

1. This Protocol shall be open for signature, ratification and accession by the State Parties to the Agreement, in accordance with their respective constitutional procedures.
2. This Protocol shall enter into force in accordance with the provisions of Articles 23(2) and 23(4) of the Agreement.

Article 49
Relationship with other International Investment Agreements

1. Existing bilateral investment treaties concluded between the State Parties shall be terminated within five (5) years from the entry into force of this Protocol. Upon termination of existing bilateral investment treaties concluded between the State Parties, their survival clauses shall also be terminated.

For the avoidance of doubt, this Protocol shall apply to investments of investors of State Parties that meet the criteria of an investment at the time of the termination of existing bilateral investment treaties concluded between the State Parties.

2. State Parties shall not conclude new bilateral investment treaties among themselves after the adoption of this Protocol.
3. State Parties shall make best endeavours to review and revise relevant existing regional investment agreements adopted by the Regional Economic Communities to achieve alignment with the Protocol within a period between five (5) to ten (10) years from the entry into force of this Protocol.
4. State Parties may take into account the requirements of this Protocol when negotiating international investment agreements and when reviewing existing international investment agreements concluded with Third Parties.

Article 50

Relationship between the Protocol on Investment and other Protocols of the AfCFTA

Upon its adoption, this Protocol, as an integral part of the Agreement, shall not modify rights and obligations under other Protocols of the Agreement. In case of conflict between this Protocol and other Protocols of the Agreement in relation to matters specifically governed by the other Protocols, the provisions of the latter shall prevail to the extent of the conflict.

Article 51

Notification

1. For the purposes of this Protocol, each State Party shall inform the AfCFTA Secretariat of the identity of its National Focal Point.
2. Each State Party shall notify the AfCFTA Secretariat of any international and regional agreements pertaining to or affecting investment with other State Parties and Third Parties to which they are signatory prior to or after the entry into force of this Protocol.
3. Each State Party shall notify the AfCFTA Secretariat, as soon as possible and at least annually, of the introduction of any new, or any amendments to existing laws or regulations or any measure which pertain to this Protocol.
4. State Parties shall inform the AfCFTA Secretariat of the complaints or grievance mechanisms available to investors in their territory.
5. The AfCFTA Secretariat shall promptly circulate the information received under this Article with the State Parties.

Article 52

Application

1. Each State Party shall apply appropriate measures to bring effect to the rules and procedures set out in the provisions of this Protocol. State Parties shall cooperate with each other in complying with the provisions of this Protocol.
2. State Parties shall, within a period of five (5) years from the entry into force of this Protocol, bring their national laws, regulations and policies into alignment with this Protocol.

Article 53

Amendments

Amendments to this Protocol shall be in accordance with Article 29 of the Agreement.

Article 54

Authentic Texts

This Protocol is drawn up in five (5) original texts in the Arabic, English, French, Portuguese and Spanish languages, all of which are equally authentic.

INDEX

For the benefit of digital users, indexed terms that span two pages (e.g., 52–53) may, on occasion, appear on only one of those pages.

Figures are indicated by *f* following the page number